# Handbook of Research on Innovations in Technology and Marketing for the Connected Consumer

Sumesh Singh Dadwal
*Northumbia University, London, UK*

A volume in the Advances in Marketing, Customer Relationship Management, and E-Services (AMCRMES) Book Series

IGI Global
DISSEMINATOR OF KNOWLEDGE

Published in the United States of America by
IGI Global
Business Science Reference (an imprint of IGI Global)
701 E. Chocolate Avenue
Hershey PA, USA 17033
Tel: 717-533-8845
Fax: 717-533-8661
E-mail: cust@igi-global.com
Web site: http://www.igi-global.com



Library of Congress Cataloging-in-Publication Data

Names: Dadwal, Sumesh, 1973- editor.
Title: Handbook of research on innovations in technology and marketing for the connected consumer / Sumesh Singh Dadwal, editor.
Description: Hershey, PA : Business Science Reference, 2020.
Identifiers: LCCN 2019016868| ISBN 9781799801313 (hardcover) | ISBN 9781799801337 (ebook)
Subjects: LCSH: Information technology--Economic aspects. | Internet marketing.
Classification: LCC HC79.I55 I5625 2020 | DDC 658.8/72--dc23 LC record available at https://lccn.loc.gov/2019016868

This book is published in the IGI Global book series Advances in Marketing, Customer Relationship Management, and E-Services (AMCRMES) (ISSN: 2327-5502; eISSN: 2327-5529)

British Cataloguing in Publication Data
A Cataloguing in Publication record for this book is available from the British Library.

All work contributed to this book is new, previously-unpublished material. The views expressed in this book are those of the authors, but not necessarily of the publisher.

For electronic access to this publication, please contact: eresources@igi-global.com.

# Advances in Marketing, Customer Relationship Management, and E-Services (AMCRMES) Book Series

Eldon Y. Li
National Chengchi University, Taiwan & California Polytechnic State University, USA

ISSN:2327-5502
EISSN:2327-5529

## Mission

Business processes, services, and communications are important factors in the management of good customer relationship, which is the foundation of any well organized business. Technology continues to play a vital role in the organization and automation of business processes for marketing, sales, and customer service. These features aid in the attraction of new clients and maintaining existing relationships.

**The Advances in Marketing, Customer Relationship Management, and E-Services (AMCRMES) Book Series** addresses success factors for customer relationship management, marketing, and electronic services and its performance outcomes. This collection of reference source covers aspects of consumer behavior and marketing business strategies aiming towards researchers, scholars, and practitioners in the fields of marketing management.

## Coverage

- Customer Relationship Management
- Legal Considerations in E-Marketing
- Database marketing
- Telemarketing
- Relationship Marketing
- CRM and customer trust
- Ethical Considerations in E-Marketing
- Customer Retention
- Text Mining and Marketing
- Electronic Services

IGI Global is currently accepting manuscripts for publication within this series. To submit a proposal for a volume in this series, please contact our Acquisition Editors at Acquisitions@igi-global.com or visit: http://www.igi-global.com/publish/.

The Advances in Marketing, Customer Relationship Management, and E-Services (AMCRMES) Book Series (ISSN 2327-5502) is published by IGI Global, 701 E. Chocolate Avenue, Hershey, PA 17033-1240, USA, www.igi-global.com. This series is composed of titles available for purchase individually; each title is edited to be contextually exclusive from any other title within the series. For pricing and ordering information please visit http://www.igi-global.com/book-series/advances-marketing-customer-relationship-management/37150. Postmaster: Send all address changes to above address. 

# Titles in this Series

For a list of additional titles in this series, please visit:
*https://www.igi-global.com/book-series/advances-marketing-customer-relationship-management/37150*

***Digital Marketing Strategies for Tourism, Hospitality, and Airline Industries***
José Duarte Santos (Instituto Superior Politécnico Gaya, Portugal) and Óscar Lima Silva (Instituto Superior Politécnico Gaya, Portugal)
Business Science Reference • © 2020 • 267pp • H/C (ISBN: 9781522597834) • US $225.00 (our price)

***Exploring the Power of Electronic Word-of-Mouth in the Services Industry***
Sandra Maria Correia Loureiro (Instituto Universitário de Lisboa, Portugal) and Hans Ruediger Kaufmann (University of Applied Management Studies, Germany)
Business Science Reference • © 2020 • 463pp • H/C (ISBN: 9781522585756) • US $265.00 (our price)

***Green Marketing as a Positive Driver Toward Business Sustainability***
Vannie Naidoo (University of KwaZulu-Natal, South Africa) and Rahul Verma (Department of Training and Technical Education, India)
Business Science Reference • © 2020 • 356pp • H/C (ISBN: 9781522595588) • US $225.00 (our price)

***Strategies and Tools for Managing Connected Consumers***
Ree C. Ho (Taylor's University, Malaysia)
Business Science Reference • © 2020 • 365pp • H/C (ISBN: 9781522596974) • US $275.00 (our price)

***Handbook of Research on Narrative Advertising***
Recep Yilmaz (Ondokuz Mayıs University, Turkey)
Business Science Reference • © 2019 • 400pp • H/C (ISBN: 9781522597902) • US $285.00 (our price)

***Breaking Down Language and Cultural Barriers Through Contemporary Global Marketing Strategies***
Mehdi Khosrow-Pour, D.B.A. (Information Resources Management Association, USA)
Business Science Reference • © 2019 • 339pp • H/C (ISBN: 9781522569800) • US $235.00 (our price)

***Myth in Modern Media Management and Marketing***
Jan Kreft (Jagiellonian University, Poland) Sylwia Kuczamer-Kłopotowska (University of Gdańsk, Poland) and Anna Kalinowska-Żeleźnik (University of Gdańsk, Poland)
Business Science Reference • © 2019 • 317pp • H/C (ISBN: 9781522591009) • US $215.00 (our price)

IGI Global
DISSEMINATOR OF KNOWLEDGE

701 East Chocolate Avenue, Hershey, PA 17033, USA
Tel: 717-533-8845 x100 • Fax: 717-533-8661
E-Mail: cust@igi-global.com • www.igi-global.com

# Editorial Advisory Board



# List of Reviewers

# List of Contributors

# Table of Contents

# Detailed Table of Contents

The way by which the communication is done depends upon the purpose of the communication. The complex technology driven environment is affected by a syndrome called post-truth. Post-truth scenario is marred with a situation where there are spread of lies, rumors, propaganda, and deceit. Human perception is distorted by the spread of lies and fake news. We struggle hard to decide whether any communication which we read, or listen to, or share is true or untrue. The strategic advancements aspired by any company are based more or less on the marketing tactics of the product or service. Many strategies of the organisations are based on the communicative interactions of the corporate world with the consumers. The era of post-truth is based on emotions, opinions, and distorted facts. False advertising tactics are hitting the emotions and sentiments of the public at large. Many social media players in the move to curb the menace of false news, misinformation, and false advertisements have opted for a voluntary code of ethics.This chapter analyses the marketing communication in the era of post-truth.



Over recent years, technology has rapidly advanced and is accelerating the emergence to Industry 4.0, particularly due to the connectivity abundance, volume increase of smart devices, and a growing interconnectivity between humans and technology. Within the last two years, 90% of the data in the world today was generated and in the next few years the volume of IoT interactions is said to reach approximately 4800 per day, which equates to a human interaction every 18 seconds. This correlates well with research undertaken regarding how consumers are exchanging information through smart devices and behavioural changes due to the technology adoption. The Generation Y and Z demand for smart devices, consumer behaviour online, and almost immediate data experiences is seeing fast consumption and data exchange without any preconceived concerns of trust, privacy, security, data profiling, or how data is used without their knowledge by third parties. This chapter will also analyse technology innovations to better protect identity data and processing of data through blockchain technology.



The chapter is putting forward the idea that internal marketing is a tool of which there are many to embed a culture to combat cybersecurity threats. This conceptual paper is suggesting that cybersecurity threats are multi-facet and although internal marketing is a major contributing factor in reducing the threats, other factors are in play. The shape of the organisation (i.e., bureaucratic or organic) has an important bearing on the implementation of a marketing-oriented culture, including that of internal marketing and, thus, the success of a cybersecurity-conscious organisational culture. Another significant factor in creating a cybersecurity-conscious organisational culture is the management willingness to empower and employees and their willingness to accept the responsibility to make decisions and be accountable, which requires acceptance of the authority.

Innovation in technology is advancing by the day. As a latest and useful technology, augmented reality (AR) is drawing and getting attention from every sectors such as marketing, engagement, and user experience. Augment reality (AR) has become a recent trend for modern marketing. Marketers nowadays invest money and time in creation of new digital marketing platform for connected consumers. In this chapter, the researcher aims to discuss the impact of augmented reality advertisement on changing customer attitude towards brands. The purpose of this chapter is to discuss the impact of AR advertising on customer engagement and enhance user experience. Furthermore, this research has pinpointed the impact of augmented reality advertisement on cognitive, affective, and behavioural engagement.



The value of the clothing industry in the UK was estimated at £57.7 billion in 2017 and is forecasted to experiment a slow growth of 3.8% reaching £68.69 billion in 2022. Currently, blogging has become one of the most common ways to communicate as well as share information. Fashion blogging has grown considerably over the years and is one of the major topic areas covered by bloggers. This phenomenon is composed of young women displaying their fashion outfits and styles, as well as their interests in fashion. Fashion blogging started around 2000 with the desire of young women to have a distinct place to share their passion and interest for fashion as well as expressing their thoughts on fashion trend with others.



This chapter provides a theoretical analysis on the role of digital marketing, social media, and digital marketing tools and techniques (DMTT) in developing customer-based brand equity (CBBE). The chapter discuses different types of digital marketing tools and techniques. The review has found that the consumer's behavioural engagement with brands via social media has a positive effect on customer-based brand equity. Digital media has a positive effect on buyer's intentions because it creates a strong connection between customers and business. Web 2.0-based technologies let users create and collaborate and exchange information and values. This has further led to consumers participating in the process of production of goods and services, as co-creators. Customer engagement, co-creating, and sharing of information via online platforms enhances customer relationship and brand equity.



This chapter explores education as a business. It considers the various functional factors of education within a knowledge economy and the importance, in order to maintain competitive advantage, of knowledge management. It also considers more specifically technological innovation within this sector and the implications to marketing. Within the management of knowledge, the chapter analyses the higher education institutions producing knowledge, the staff who deliver this knowledge, and the students who purchase and engage in this knowledge. The chapter therefore also explores student enrolment, retention and outcomes, staff development, and product innovation.



Technology is playing a pivotal role in shaping the operations and marketing and events industry. The modern event manager has understood that the event success or failure may depend on the technology used or the lack of it. An event is a set of activities with specific purpose goals and needs of the attendees. An event can be defined as an organised occasion, it provides some lived experience and meaning. The technology has the potential to be used at each stage of the consumers' experience of events. The chapter has taken a resource-based view and analysed how technology can be a tool for operations and service innovation and ultimately a strategics for creating core competencies and core capabilities. This chapter explores how technology can be used in the management event, technology in the value delivery network of events, and marketing of events. Various new technologies like block-chain technology, augment relativity, RFID, social media, digital promotional tactics are discussed.



Tourism businesses have become virtual organisations linked to information technology available for innovation in marketing as well as using other platforms in the social media environment such as Facebook, Instagram, etc. This use of social media is creating innovation, as the tourists are becoming co-designers, co-producers, co-marketers, and co-consumers of tourism experiences. The branding strategies methods, tools, and process are changing since the adoption of digital technology in marketing and branding. The organisations are able to reach their tourism appeal through multisensory information that touches the five senses in a more effective way. The use of liquid branding and audio branding to introduce, enhance, and develop various audio and visual elements of the brand is a new trend in branding. Therefore, as brick and mortar or virtual organisations, the destination marketing organisation should innovate their marketing efforts and should respond to change within a dynamic business environment.



The Himalayas are one of the trendy tourist attractions that actually developed a special interest tourism type: Himalayan tourism. A considerable number of research studies have so far covered Himalayan tourism from numerous perspectives. However, innovative technology-supported marketing for sustainable tourism in the Himalayas in practice has limited knowledge. The aim of this research is to outline aspects of innovative technology adoption for sustainable tourism marketing in the Himalayas. From the Nepal part of the Himalayas context, this conceptual research outlines the features of innovative technology

# Foreword

Information is one of the highly valued assets of our modern era and with the fast-growing development of cloud-based architecture, smart technology such as Internet of Things (IoT) and many other new developments of Artificial Intelligence (AI) and Machine Learning (ML) has caused a large increase in data volumes and more complexities in how to handle them. This book could not be more timely and aim to highlight the business reform and engagement with the emerging digital revolution of Industry 4.0.

Over recent years the interfaces between humans and technology have been growing due to technology advancement, the connectivity abundance and vast volume of smart devices to a point that within the last two years 90 percent of the data in the world today was generated. This, as a result, has created enormous amount of research to be undertaken to understand how consumers of technology are exchanging information through various forms of technology and how behaviours in the way strategic business planning may change due to the adoption and use.

The contemporary strategic management leaders are required to understand and be aware of their way of navigating through the emerging digital features and behaviours in the application of data and they require to give consideration to the potential for misuse of sensitive data by third parties, and more acute considerations of the human/machine interface.

This book through the instructive guidance for readers interested in tackling these huge, contemporary problems. The deals with the transformative power of smart technologies, the role of social media as a marketing enabler, analysis trust and privacy from Y and Z generation to supply chain in the digital era and the Role of advertising in shaping consumption choices.

This book will provide learners, practitioners, and policymakers alike with an outstanding reference guide for the multi-faceted issues that they will be faced to deal with in the years to come.

I hope you enjoy the read and ready for any challenges.

*Bruno Mascitelli*
*Swinburne University of Technology, Australia*
*23 August 2019*

# Preface

The motivation to edit this book was to provide comprehensive, practical and contemporary researches in the areas of technology-enabled marketing to the connected consumers. This book is a result of findings a gap in the current literature of business and technology post the era of innovations and technology embeddedness in all of the fields of the business.

The new technologies are changing the ways the organisations and business are managed. The technological are bringing new opportunities and challenges. Some organisation is proactive to embed technologies in their new business models, however, there is much other organisation which is quite passive in adopting and adapting technologies for their purposes. The use of technologies is becoming a source of core competencies, core capabilities and sustainable competitive advantages for the organisations.

While working as a consultant, an academic, and a researcher, the editor of this book noticed the enlarging gap between traditional ways of marketing, traditional business models and modern methods of digital marketing and new technology-enabled business models. Many of the currently available textbooks are written for the old world and has not fully taken care of the new globalised world of technologies made of modern Ubers, AirBnbs, Smarthomes, Amazons, YouTubes, Social networking websites, etc., wherein the previously known consumers have taken the new roles of prosumers.

New applications of technologies including social media, big data, Augmented reality, virtual reality, a community of consumers are the uptrends in the marketing. This has happened due to connected consumers, who are using a range of devices like smartphones, iPods, laptops, glasses, VR equipment, and watches - to access the content. In such a scenario a marketing department needs to provide an integrated marketing campaign across these different devices and become proficient in making use of technology in marketing.

The business environmental changes, globalisations and spread of technologies have brought new strategic challenges to the managers. Marketing managers have turned to Information Technology (IT) to cope with the ongoing challenge. Unlike conventional forms of mass media marketing, the internet is unique in its capacity to broaden the scope of the business models. The book has covered technical applications in different stages of the value chain; in business operations, in supply chain and in marketing and consumer behaviour areas. The book explores the uses and implications of integrating information technology with SCM and marketing capabilities.

Information communication technologies are shrinking the global village and also bringing in the new issues of digital data, safety and security management. Whereas most of the contemporary books in the field of business or marketing have not very well covered the issues of online securities, cybersecurity, and associated technologies such as Blockchain, Internet of things (IoT), Augmented Reality Marketing (ARM). Hence, this book has paid special attention to the use of new technology and on the concerns of safety security, and threats of ransomware, etc by covering some chapters in these areas. The book has covered utilities of various new technologies such as Smart Technologies, Artificial Intelligence (AI), Social Media networks (SMN), Gamification, Sharing economy Technologies, Cyborgs, Blockchain, big data analytics, Digital platforms, Augmented Reality Marketing (ARM), in the field of marketing, and business management.

Marketing is context-dependent and when a contextual element (IT) changes, it can have a significant impact on the nature and scope of the discipline. The marketing strategy has remained the same for generations, but with the arrival of IT, the domain of marketing is changing fast. Technology-enabled marketing, commonly referred to as Digital or e-Marketing, encompasses a broad set of interaction-enabling technologies that are frequently used in business-to-business (B2B) markets, Business to consumers(B2C). markets, customer relationship management (CRM) software, Digital platforms, e-commerce websites, and so on. Information Technology is viewed as a collective term for a wide range of software, hardware, telecommunications, and information management techniques, applications. IT technologies create new ways to configure businesses, organise companies, serve customers, and has profound effects on the structure, strategy and competitive dynamics of and business models of the industries. Many of the managerial and operational changes in this area involve the liaising of marketing department with the IT and Supply chain management (SCM) department.

As new and different technologies emerge, the potential benefits in a business or marketing campaign might not be immediately apparent and might eventually evolve in profoundly different directions. New applications of technologies including social media, big data, Augmented reality, the community of consumers are the uptrends in the marketing. This has happened due to connected consumers, who are using a range of devices like smartphones, iPods, laptops, glasses, VR equipment, and watches - to access the content. In such a scenario the marketing department needs to provide an integrated marketing campaign across these different devices and become proficient in making use of technology in the marketing. The technological innovations also lead to questions about their adoptions and also issues. The book also addresses the adoption of innovation and technology and related factors.

The use of ICT in business has also raised issues related to cybersecurity etc. The book has developed some chapters exclusively for cybersecurity, ransomwares and associated preventive actions.

With the advent of web2.0, the spread of social media and the growth of mobile phones and related technologies, the consumers are very much connected to each other as well to the organisations. Under this new era of digital disruptions and that of connected consumers, the business models in general and marketing strategies in particular needs innovation. The organisation and managers are looking for inventive methods of marketing their products, services or ideas more effectively in this highly competitive click away environment. Mangers are looking for the solutions and also the associated. In this new online world of information overload, this book is an endeavour to bring together a concise and one place solution in form of a range of technology enabled strategic marketing options for marketing and business decision-maker.

This book has used the expertise of the authors who have undertaken contemporary research into areas of technology-enabled business and marketing. The book covers the principles, tools, and practices of Technology empowered marketing and digital marketing. The book systematically develops the fundamentals of Technology empowered marketing and digital marketing and thus a unique book that comprehensibly covers models, practices and all major aspects in the field. The new themes like big data, Augmented reality, a community of consumers, etc, where there is least available research have been also explored in this book.

## AUDIENCE

This book is written from the perspective of learners, practitioners, educationist, researchers, and policymakers of organisations in a range of industries and national economies. Managers and policymakers need to understand the processes behind developing integrated technology-enabled business models and marketing programme. This book will be a useful handbook for students, marketers, managers, brand teams, researchers, educationists, technologists, Applications developers, and IT technologist to understand and apply the principles and the practices of Technology empowered marketing and digital marketing in the developed as well as in less developed countries. The book also has covered applications in a range of industries; gamification, data analytics, transportation, education, tourism, events management, education, marketing and branding, etc.

## KEY FEATURES OF THE BOOK

Pedagogically this book has scholarship blended with contemporary applications, examples and managerial orientation. Several real examples and cases have been used to illustrate the points. The chapters are theory-driven and special care is taken to underpin the concepts and their interrelations using the grand theories. To understand the chapter and its aim more quietly each chapter has a very crispy abstract, keywords and also the chapter has given the definitions of the key terms used.

## ORGANISATION OF THIS BOOK

This book also has taken an approach of integrating various functional areas of management using technology. The book has explored areas of technology at various levels of management, starting with the business model level, supply chain management, at the Marketing level and at Industry level application of technology. The book not only discusses the technology in marketing in general but has also considered a number specific industries such as tourism, events, transportation, shared economy, financial and education industry, small and medium enterprise, to illustrate the utility of technology in marketing for connected consumers.

This book is organised into 21 chapters. A brief description of the chapter is given in the next sections.

### Chapter 1: Transformative Power of Smart Technologies Enabled by Advances in AI – Changing Landscape for Digital Marketing

This chapter covers the fundamentals and applications of Artificial intelligence in digital marketing and Swarm marketing. As the information age is maturing, it is entering a new era of the 4th industrial revolution where internet's reach is coupled with the smart technologies powered by AI, cloud-based scalable infrastructure, sensor infusion harvesting ever greater amount of data. The internet has transformed the landscape in the field of marketing and consumer behaviour in the last two decades, enabling unprecedented reach to the consumers for marketers, inducing low costs in general, providing opportunities to analyse interactions and facilitating the development of novel strategies in digital marketing. The chapter argues that the consumers' demands and preferences have never been more sophisticated, as they are in this era. The author has argued that the digital marketing field will go through a period of tremendous changes, in which pre-established norms and practices will no longer serve the purpose of attracting and engaging consumers. The unique features of this chapter are that the chapter has analysed new approaches to reach the readers. In this light, the chapter has discussed 'A thought experiment' using a 'Persona' for the effectiveness of existing digital marketing models. The chapter has also introduced and explored the concept of 'Swarm marketing' using AI. This chapter will be of great importance to digital marketers using AI and chatbots etc.

## Chapter 2: Reshaping Business Organizations Through Gamification

The new generation of consumers loves to play online games. This chapter is making use of current habits and future trends of Gamification of marketing. Gamification is the application of game-design elements, mechanism, and principles in non-game contexts, typically as an online marketing technique to encourage engagement with a product or service, improve organizational productivity, crowdsourcing, learning, and employee recruitment. The significance of this chapter can also be understood from the fact that the global gamification market was valued at USD 2.17 billion in 2017 and is expected to reach USD 19.39 billion by 2023, at a CAGR of 44.06% over the forecast period (2018-2023). The consumers are adopting Smartphones and for the new ' handheld generations' the fun and gamification go hand in hand. Thus the growth of smartphone and smart devices have attributed to the growth of a vast base of gamification market. This growth is also supplemented by the increasing recognition of gamification systems as a method to architecture human behaviour to induce innovation, productivity, or engagement. This chapter has contributed towards analysis on the role of gamification in reshaping business organizations with reference to select cases on gamification used by corporates for promotion, active customer & employee engagement, and brand loyalty. Naturally, this chapter is very useful for tech-savvy marketers, technologist to entail gamification in the marketing and thus engaging customers for mutually beneficial transactions.

## Chapter 3: Social Media Use as an Enabler of Marketing Evolution in Knowledge-Intensive SMEs

The technological adoptions are not only significant for larger business but also for small and medium enterprises (SMEs). This chapter is unique as, the chapter identifies the operating and dynamic capabilities interactions that are supported by social media use in small and medium-sized enterprises (SMEs), specifically knowledge-intensive business services (KIBS). The focus on social media market intelligence accumulation and assimilation as an operating capability which enables dynamic marketing capability development in the SME marketing context. The chapter complements the prevalent focus of the literature on SME adoption and use of social media, as well as literature on how dynamic capabilities alter operating capability. The authors have also discussed a case study of a KIBS SME operating in South East England. The chapter has also used empirical data, which was collected via semi-structured interviews with key actors and social media data and data were thematically analysed. The chapter has concluded with empirical findings that the company develops absorptive capacity at the operating level by absorbing intelligence through social media use, and this learning is captured and transformed at the marketing planning level as a dynamic capability, reconfiguring future marketing operational capabilities. The chapter will be very useful for SME managers and policymakers in order to enhance productivity and dynamic capabilities of the organizations.

## Chapter 4: Technology and Sharing Economy-Based Business Models for Marketing to Connected Consumers

This chapter has a unique contribution to a social economy based on new business models, such as Uber, Airbnb, etc. The sharing economy provides a huge potential of creating millions of jobs by leveraging the business sector and providing a new way to producers and consumers to meet each other's needs. The new technological innovations are changing the ways business are being operated. Sharing economy based new business models (SEBMs) using technology have many benefits at national organizational, community and individual levels. To maintain and enhance the use of technology-enabled sharing economy-based models (SEBMs), it is paramount to understand these SEBMs models and the behaviour of the market, particularly on how to influence the market's attitude towards using SEBMs. This book chapter analyses the new sharing economy based and technologically enabled business models and their antecedents. Thus this chapter will be a very important contribution for understanding the concepts of business models, social economy, and for developing technology-based business models for a new generation of connected consumers.

## Chapter 5: Post-Truth and Marketing Communication in the Technological Age

The spread of social media has also led to issues of truths, lies and fake news, etc. This chapter explores the concept of post-truth marketing, with a focus on communication ways and the impacts of communication on the believably of the information. The complex technology-driven environment is affected by a syndrome called post-truth. The post-truth scenario is marred with a situation where there are spread of lies, rumours, propagandas, and deceit. Consumer perceptions can be influenced or distorted by the spread of information (lies and fake news) in a particular way. It is difficult for the users of information, whether any communication which we read or listen or share is true or untrue. The strategic advancements aspired by any company are based more or less on the marketing tactics of the product or service. Many strategies of the organisations are based on the communicative interactions of the corporate world with the consumers. The era of post-truth is based on emotions, opinions and distorted facts. False advertising tactics are hitting the emotions and sentiments of the public at large. Many social media players in the move to curb the menace of false news, misinformation, and false advertisements have opted a voluntary code of ethics. This chapter analyses the marketing communication in the era of post-truth. This chapter may be very usefull for the publicity, public relations, and propaganda management department of an organisation.

## Chapter 6: Millennials vs. Cyborgs and Blockchain Role in Trust and Privacy

The lifecycle of the traditional web of the internet is under challenge due to the introduction of a new way of Blockchain technology. Over recent years, technology has rapidly advanced and is accelerating the emergence to Industry 4.0, particularly due to the connectivity abundance, a volume increase of smart devices and growing interconnectivity between humans and technology. A huge amount of data is being generated for an instant, within the last two years, 90% of the data in the world today was generated. Sooner, the volume of IoT interactions is said to reach approximately 4800 per day, which equates to a human interaction every 18 seconds. This huge data brings its challenges and opportunities. Also, the private data also raises concerns about privacy and security via traditional web-based internet.

Thus Blockchain- an online register of transactions and communication is seen as a potential solution in many areas. The generation Y and Z demand for smart devices, consumer behaviour online and almost immediate data experiences are seeing fast consumption and data exchange without any preconceived concerns of trust, privacy, security, data profiling or how data is used without their knowledge by third parties. This chapter has analysed technology innovations to better protect identity data, data security, and processing of data through blockchain technology. This chapter will be very usefull for policymakers, managers, and other stakeholders, in understanding the theocentric of Blockchain technology and its applications in various sectors.

## Chapter 7: Internal Marketing Cybersecurity-Conscious Culture

The adoption of Technology, eCommerce, cyber-attacks, data stealing, and online presences etc have led to concerns related to cybersecurity. This chapter' contribution is that the chapter puts forward the idea that internal marketing is a tool of which there are many to embed a culture to combat cybersecurity threats. This conceptual chapter is suggesting that cybersecurity threats are multi-facet and although internal marketing is a major contributing factor in reducing the threats, other factors are in play. The shape of the organisation i.e. bureaucratic or organic all have an important bearing on the implementation of a marketing-oriented culture, including that of internal marketing and thus the success of a cybersecurity conscious organisational culture. Another, significant factor in creating a cybersecurity conscious organisational culture is the management willingness to empower and employees and their willingness to accept the responsibility to make decisions and be accountable, which requires acceptance of the authority. The chapter will be interesting to read by policymakers, marketers, employees, etc.

## Chapter 8: Cyber Threat Ransomware and Marketing to Networked Consumers

Modern cybercrimes have exponentially grown over the last decade. This chapter explores the new generation of Malwares- Ransomwares as big cybersecurity concern. Marketing is a process of creating capturing and exchanging 'value' for the mutual benefits of marketers, customers, intermediaries, and other stakeholders. Such a transaction requires trust as it might be facing a range of online Cyber risks. Modern cybercrimes have exponentially grown over the last decade. Ransomware is one of the types of malware which is the result of a sophisticated attempt to compromise the modern computer systems. The businesses, governments and large corporations are investing heavily to combat this cyber threat against their critical infrastructure. New technological shift help to improve marketing and business productivity and keep the company's global competitiveness in an overflowing competitive market. However, the businesses and the systems involved need security measures to protect integrity and availability which will help avoid any malfunctioning to their operations due to the cyber-attacks. There have been several cyber-attack incidents on several businesses such as healthcare, pharmaceutical, water cleaning, and energy sector. The authors argue that new technological shift of investing in critical infrastructure will help improves business productivity and keeps the company's global competitiveness in an overflowing competitive market. However, the businesses and the systems involved need security measures to protect integrity and availability which will help avoid any malfunctioning to their operations due to the cyber-attacks. There have been several cyber-attack incidents on several businesses such as healthcare, pharmaceutical, water cleaning, and energy sector, recently. So this chapter offers a remedy and proactive strategies for policymakers, managers, consumers, vendors, and other stakeholders.

## Chapter 9: Impact of Supply Chain Digitalization on a Connected Global Market

The success of marketing is driven by value addition due to the supply chain. This chapter focuses on the impact of supply chain digitalisation on a connected global market. The first section of the chapter has focused on the dynamic consumer requirements and preferences. The second section of the chapter has appraised the segmentation and mapping of digital technologies. The third section has examined the contemporary application of digital technologies including big data, blockchains, artificial intelligence, machine learning, and data analytics. The final section analyses the rules and regulations for the contemporary framework for the governance of digital technologies. So this chapter is unique to bring in the thought of integrating marketing function with supply chain and then also contributes to the literature by linking the application of a range of new technology for enhancing values to the consumers.

## Chapter 10: Integrating Big Data Analytics Into Retail Services Marketing Management – The Case of a Large Shopping Centre in London, UK

The retail service is the final touchpoint with the consumers. A lot of data is generated at the retailing end of customer services. This chapter explores the extent to which the recent trends in digitalization of marketing and related services are leading to a massive amount of consumers' information (big data) and its implication. The chapter also suggests possible strategic solutions and recommendations. The chapter has analysed an as of a large shopping centre in London (UK) as a meaningful example, to explore that how retailers might exploit big data analytics such as sentiment and image analytics to get useful consumers' insights to be successfully integrated into marketing strategies. The chapter has also critically discussed the implications for scholars and practitioners and proposes a future research agenda in areas of big data.

## Chapter 11: Supply Chain Collaboration and Technology-Enabled Marketing

The concept of inter-functional coordination to create superior customer value has long been the main goal of marketing. This chapter explores an integrated approach to supply chain management, supply chain integration, and technology-enabled marketing. The chapter analyses how the technologies in supply chain management (SCM) that can be used for improved marketing. The chapter critically discussed the chemistry between marketing and supply chain management. The concept of movement of materials and information is quite interrelated. Effective SCM needs firms to create and establish close long-term close relationships that base the strategic partnership between the trading partners in the chain. Thus the chapter highlighted the importance of supply chain collaboration for technology-enabled marketing. The marketing mix is explored using the technologies and supply network collaboration perspectives. This study also extended the relational view theory in the context of relationship orientation to form collaborative relationships in the supply chain. This study suggested that the organisation could harness the synergy through integrating marketing strategies and supply chain collaboration. Understanding the needs for integration between Marketing and SCM to survive and thrive in this ever-changing competition business environment is one of the key contributions this study can offer. Hence, it is recommended for the mangers to integrate technology-enabled marketing and form a collaborative relationship between the partners in the chain to sustain competitive advantage.

## Chapter 12: Characteristics of Millennials and Technology Adoption in the Digital Age

This chapter explores the attitude and behaviour of Millennials towards Digital platforms. As business is intending to use technologies in business operation, it is paramount to understand user's and consumers intentions to use technologies for emergency or other purposes. However, some studies indicate that the currently availed consumer behaviour models are incomplete or are not able to address the needs of a new generation of consumers – the millenniums. In 2016, there were around 1.8 billion Millennials worldwide (out of 7.4 billion people), and the estimation indicates that by 2020 around half of the world's workforce will be of Millennials and a buying power of $1000.0 billions by 2020. Millennial or Generation Y is much talked about Generation among business circles at the moment and considering their ways of thinking, behaving and preferences organisations are altering their practices as they are the active workforce at the moment. In this chapter, authors have explored various aspects of Millennials life, preferences, practices and attitude including their behaviour towards technology, corporate social responsibility, cultural variations. education, buying patterns and technology, technological devices and social/digital platforms. Millennial consumers' behaviours are affected many personal factors; such as gender identity, income level, education, geography, political affiliations, and religion and non-personal factors, such as organisational effort, brand, technological factors, social pressures, and so on the chapter will be of much use for targeting technology-enabled marketing to this new generation of Millennial.

## Chapter 13: The Role of Digital Advertising in Shaping Ideals and Consumption Choices in the Digital Era – Effectiveness of Digital Advertisements

This chapter discusses the role of advertisements in shaping the choices of consumers in the era of digital technologies. Consumption choices refer to the journey where consumers make decisions based on the problem-solving attributes of the products and services. The choices are often influenced by combinations. Advertising is one of the most dominant elements of a communication mix. Digital Advertising is one of the most dominant elements of a communication mix often debate the extent of cultural interference on advertising design and delivery to the target audiences. Consumption choices refer to the journey where consumers make decisions based on the problem-solving attributes of the products and services . The choices are conditioned with the reality shaped around us and social processes that impose ideal, self-identity, self-concept, ideal self, gender identities, and consumer cultures via visual digital designs and celebrities portrayals. Organisations aim to build digital advertisement strategies and create awareness of certain goods and services, but at the same time, the advertisement plays a significant role in generating new needs, new identities for consumers and new role expectations Digital technologies enables marketers to predict consumption behaviour and measure the consumers responses on key metrics of advertisements effectiveness. The advertisement plays a significant role with the aim of generating new needs for consumers, and therefore advertising creates meanings around those needs as a choice justification at the early stages of the consumption journey. Digital transformation enables marketers to predict consumer behaviour. The ideological system of meanings is translated to consumers through the identities and lifestyle ideals portrayed in media and advertisements. The chapter will be usefull for a number of stakeholders including consumers, ad agencies, policymakers, etc.

## Chapter 14: The Impact of Augmented Reality Advertisement on Customer Engagement in the Era of Connected Consumers

This chapter analyses the Concept of Augmented Reality (AR). As a latest and useful technology Augmented Reality (AR) is drawing and getting attention from marketing, customer engagement, and user experience, etc. Augment reality (AR) has become a recent trend for modern marketing. Marketers nowadays are investing money and time in the creation of a new digital marketing platform for the connected consumer. With information overload, business managers are seeking new and innovative ways to reach and engage their targeted consumers. The augmented reality marketing and augmented reality marketing are some of the fields, where marketers are putting their positive hopes. In this chapter, the researcher has exp0lored the concept of Augment reality and has discussed the impact of augmented reality advertisement (ARA) on customer attitude towards brands. The chapter has also analyzed the impact of AR advertising on customer engagement and enhance user experience too. Furthermore, this research has pinpointed the impact of augmented reality advertisement on cognitive, affective and behavioural engagement. The chapter will be an important contribution to the literature of digital advertisement and augmented reality advertisements.

## Chapter 15: The Effect of Blogging on Fashion Consumption

Web2.0 technology has empowered people and communities to express themselves. This chapter analyses the concept of blogging and its impacts on the consumption of fashion products. The sector of fashion consumption is a significant area to study, as the value of the clothing industry in the UK is currently estimated at £57.7 billion in 2017 and is forecasted to experiment a slow growth of 3.8% reaching £68.69 billion in 2022. Currently, blogging has become one of the most common ways to communicate as well as share information. The author states that Fashion blogging has grown considerably over the years and is fashion is one of the major topic areas covered by bloggers. This phenomenon is composed of young women displaying their fashion outfits and styles, as well as their interests in fashion. Fashion blogging started around 2000 with the desire of young women to have a distinct place to share their passion and interest in fashion as well as expressing their thoughts on fashion trend with others. The chapter is usefull to the organisation to make use of blogging and community of consumers as tools for better consumer engagement with the brands.

## Chapter 16: Using Social Media and Digital Marketing Tools and Techniques for Developing Brand Equity with Connected Consumers

The branding is a topic of interest to all organization, consumers, and marketers. The brands command value for each stakeholder. The advancements in technology have brought a phenomenal increase in usage of social media through platforms like smartphones, tablets, smartwatches, smart TV, etc to share, co-create, discuss, and modify user-generated content. This chapter has assessed the role of social media and digital marketing in branding. A thorough literature review has resulted in a conceptual model that relates the digital marketing & social media with consumer-based brand equity (CBBE). The theoretical model explains the relationship between social media and digital marketing in creating brand awareness and impact on purchasing decision of users/customers. Consumers who are sensitively attached to the brand have a stronger urge for purchase intention through social media. The literature review revealed that there was a significant impact of social media on consumer behavioural outcomes.

## Chapter 17: Digital Trends in Education Operations and Marketing

The education sector has been one of the pioneer sectors to adopt technology in its operations. This chapter explores the use of technology in education as a business. It considers the various functional factors of education within a knowledge economy and the importance, in order to maintain competitive advantage, of knowledge management. The chapter has also considered technological innovation within this sector and the implications for the marketing of education. Within the management of knowledge, the chapter has analysed the Higher Education Institutions producing knowledge, the staff who deliver this knowledge and the students who purchase and engage in this knowledge. The chapter has also explored the areas of student enrolment, retention and outcomes, staff development and product innovation using innovative technologies. Thus the chapter is unique in its own sense as it has explored the use of technology in education, not only in operations but also in marketing to students (consumers).

## Chapter 18: Innovative Trends in Technology for Marketing of Events

The events industry is one of the significant industry contributing to national culture, consumption of new demand and national income. Technology is playing a pivotal role in shaping the marketing and events industry. This chapter explores the use of technology in the value delivery network of event industry. The modern event managers have understood that an event's success or failure may depend on the use of appropriate technology. An event is a set of activities with specific purpose goals and needs of the attendees An event can be defined as an organized occasion, it provides some 'lived experience & meaning'. The authors have argued that technology has the potential to be used at each stage of the consumers' experience of the events. This chapter explores how technology can be used in event management and marketing of the events. The chapter has explored the use of new technologies like Drone streaming, Augmented reality, Blockchain technology, Artificial intelligence, and digital promotional, etc. This chapter has contributed to theoretical and empirical fields of technology in the events management and marketing sector, in order to engage attendees and create immersing long-lasting liv in experiences for the vent attendees. Thus the chapter will be very useful for managers of the organisation working in events management.

## Chapter 19: Marketing Innovation in Tourism

This chapter has discussed the use of technology for service innovation in the tourism sector. Tourism contributes to the national economy. Hence this chapter will be usefull for not only for executives but also for the policymakers. The internet and associated technologies have transformed the landscape in the field of marketing and consumer behaviour in the last two decades, enabling unprecedented reach to the consumers for marketers, inducing low costs in general, providing opportunities to analyse interactions and facilitating the development of novel strategies in digital marketing. As the information age is maturing, it is entering a new era of the 4th industrial revolution (industry 4.0) where internet's reach is coupled with the smart technologies powered by artificial intelligence (AI), cloud-based scalable infrastructure, sensor infusion harvesting ever greater amount of data. The authors have argued that as the consumer demands and preferences are ever more sophisticated, hence the field of digital marketing will go through a period of tremendous change, where established norms and practices will no longer serve the purpose of attracting and engaging consumers. Thus this is paramount for the organisation in the tourism sector to adopt innovations and innovative technologies.

## Chapter 20: Technology-Supported Marketing for Sustainable Tourism in the Himalayas

The technology has supported the organisation to create sustainable products and services as well in the delivery of suitable products or services. The chapter has analysed the use of technology for suitable tourism in the Himalayan mountains. The Himalayas Mountains is one of the trendy tourist attractions that actually developed a special interest tourism type: 'the Himalayan Tourism'. A considerable number of research studies have so far covered the Himalayan Tourism from numerous perspectives. However, innovative technology-supported marketing for sustainable tourism in the Himalayas Mountains in practice has limited knowledge. The chapter covers the aspects of innovative technology adoption for sustainable tourism marketing in the Himalayas Mountains. From the Nepal part of the Himalayas Mountains context, this conceptual research outlines the features of innovative technology adoption from Roger's theoretical understanding and incorporates relevant debates and arguments. This research advocate for adopting innovative technologies to ensure and support sustainability concerns in the Himalayas Mountains. This research concludes that the adoption of innovative technology for tourism marketing in this part of the world can support sustainable practices in tourism. Sustainable development is one of the global agenda for policymakers, consumers, societies and organisational managers. Hence this chapter is an important contribution in this line where adoption of technology has been argued as a strategy for sustainable tourism.

## Chapter 21: Digitalisation of Global FinTech Industry

This chapter analyses the digital trends in the financial sector. Since the introduction of ATMs in the 1950s, digital Trends in Global Financial Marketing has become central to the success of businesses across the globe. The authors have argued that mere adaptation of digital media to comply with trends does not guarantee success and a lot of success relies on successful digital campaigns, the extent to which digitalization is being adopted and executed in the light of demographics of the target market. The digitalisation of Global Financial technology and Marketing is central to the success of many banking organisations across the globe. Digital disruption a change that occurs when new emerging digital technologies and business models affect the value proposition of existing goods and services for low end demanding customers or for new market customers. Digital Banking or online or virtual banking is leading to the digitization of all the traditional banking activities, products, process or services. It is needless to state that mere adaptation of digital media to comply with trends does not guarantee success The digital trends in the banking industry has seen banks focusing on digitalizing core processes, increasing awareness, financial inclusions and undertake sustainable practices, Fintech i.e Financial technology is competing with traditional financial methods in the delivery of financial services. And reaching the unbanked segment of society, particularly in developing countries. There is a strong need to understand drivers and trends in the FinTech industry. The banking industry is profoundly focusing on branchless banking as it views it as a way to address the unbanked segment of society, particularly in developing countries where the mobile wallet is aimed at targets. The technology and innovation adoptions have huge impact FinTech sector. thus this chapter will be interesting reading for the mangers, educations, and policymakers.

## CONCLUSION

This book is unique in its own sense as the book has taken an integrated approach to the marketing, and supply chain, online business models, new business model using technologies. The book has contributed to literature research in the areas of new business models, digital marketing & consumer behaviour, Digital Advertisements & Branding, post-truth marketing, cybersecurity, social economy, use of new technologies like Augmented reality marketing (ARM), Artificial intelligence (AI) big data, social media, Blockchain, Gamification and Internet of Things (IoT), etc. in the global world of connected consumers and a new generation of millenniums. The book has chapters devoted to sectors like Events marketing, Financial sectors, Supply chain, tourism, sustainable tourism, and education sector. So this book is a fundamental and theory-driven and this book also illustrated practical applications of innovations and technologies in marketing to the connected consumers in a number of industries.

# Acknowledgment

It is my pleasure to thank numerous individuals, who have directly or indirectly supported me on this book project.

Many thanks to almighty God for always being with me in his/her infinite forms & non-forms, in my thoughts and also giving me this awareness to meditate on Him.

I would like to thank all contributing authors, who have very diligently and patiently given their valuable time to write, and revise their work a number of times, so as to produce a well-researched and insightful high-quality piece of work.

Thanks to all of the Editorial board team members, and all of the reviewers (many of the authors have also acted as reviewers); for reading other authors' works and providing very constructive feedback. Your support has made it possible to deliver a high-quality output that fits with the purpose of the book and in line with the needs of the target audiences.

I would also like to thank my network of excellent academicians and individuals, whose invaluable advice and continues support was very motivating to continue to work on this project as per the schedule.

My mother and father deserve a special mention, a million thanks to both for cultivating educational, ethical, hardworking and so many more values in me. I am also very sad that my mother will not be able to see the final version of this book, as she left this world at the start of the year 2019. This book is my tribute to my loving mother, whom I will always miss for her love, guidance, simplicity, patience, and infinite support.

Special thanks to my siblings for their continues encouragement. They have been often calling me a 'Lion'. That has always been and will be ever motivating.

This project took a lot of my time, the time which was the right of my wife- *Sony* and our son-*Yash* and our daughter *Shanaya*. Thank you very much my dears, for providing me the unconditional support and bearing my lesser involvement in the family during the process of editing this book. I owe you a lot, for your love and your chirpings around, always.

Last but not the least, I want to convey my thanks to IGI publishing and their team for their continued support and shaping this project into a final unique piece of work.

Thanks to the readers, as your needs of knowing more have been the driving force for this whole project.

Enjoy reading.

Regards,

*Sumesh S. Dadwal*
*Northumbia University, London, UK*

# Chapter 1
# Transformative Power of Smart Technologies Enabled by Advances in AI:
## Changing Landscape for Digital Marketing

**Anwar ul Haq**
*Northumbria University, London, UK*

**Asim Majeed**
*QA Higher Education, UK*

**George D. Magoulas**
https://orcid.org/0000-0003-1884-0772
*Birkbeck College, University of London, UK*

**Arshad Jamal**
*Northumbria University, London, UK*

## ABSTRACT

*The internet has transformed the landscape in the field of marketing and consumer behaviour in the last two decades, enabling unprecedented reach to the consumers for marketers, inducing low costs in general, providing opportunities to analyse interactions and facilitating the development of novel strategies in digital marketing. As the information age is maturing, it is entering a new era of the fourth industrial revolution where internet's reach is coupled with the smart technologies powered by AI, cloud-based scalable infrastructure, sensor infusion harvesting an ever greater amount of data. The consumer demands and preferences are ever more sophisticated. In this context, the digital marketing field will go through a period of tremendous change, where established norms and practices will no longer serve the purpose of attracting and engaging consumers. A thought experiment is discussed using a persona for the effectiveness of existing digital marketing models. Further, a concept of swarm marketing using AI has been also discussed.*

DOI: 10.4018/978-1-7998-0131-3.ch001

## DIGITAL MARKETING: BRIEF INTRODUCTION

According to Merriam-Webster ("Marketing I Definition of Marketing by Merriam-Webster," 2019), marketing is defined as, "the process or technique of promoting, selling, and distributing a product or service" and Encyclopaedia Britannica (Grayson, Kotler, & Hibbard, 2019), defines it as, "the sum of activities involved in directing the flow of goods and services from producers to consumers". There is an interesting notion of emphasis in both definitions, pointing the reader to "process" or "sum of activities", referring to enablers, structures, and mediums used in specific ways to bridge the gap between the point of production of goods and services and delivery to consumers. In the context of managing digital marketing interactions, Chaffey & Ellis-Chadwick (Chaffey & Ellis-Chadwick, 2019) coin the term of '5Ds': Digital Devices, Digital Platforms, Digital Media, Digital Data, Digital Technology – differentiating the digital marketing from the general marketing terminology. Digital Devices are referred to smartphones, computers, smart watches, digital assistants e.g. Apple Siri and range of other devices such as cloud-based sensors and internet of things – e.g. Amazon Alexa controlled toaster or ambient lighting and music system in the living room. Digital Platforms include the customer interaction captured currently mostly through browser and apps, for example when consumers use online services, either in-house built or provided by service providers e.g. Google, Facebook, Salesforce, Apple, Microsoft, and Amazon. Digital Media referred to communication channels e.g. email, search engines, and social networks. Digital Data is increasingly becoming important, the data businesses collect when interacting with consumers, clients, potential customers, and other related stakeholders to build user profiles and develop insights, increasingly coming under legal and social scrutiny. Digital Technology refers to marketing technology used to create interactive experience cohesively. Chaffey & Ellis-Chawick (ibid.) define digital marketing as, "Achieving marketing objectives through applying digital media, data, and technology". The businesses have been using Email Lists, Telemarketing, Digital Television, Online Chats, Informational websites, AdWords, Searches and Social Media for digital marketing for several years and in some cases over the last few decades (Tiago & Verı́ssimo, 2014). The adoption and application of these technologies have matured, and techniques and processes are well understood from a marketing perspective. For example, the shift from the *push*-based marketing strategies, traditionally relied on broadcast media to passive listeners or viewers to *pull*-based marketing strategies where consumers *pull* information beneficial to them (Court, Elzinga, Mulder, & Vetvik, 2009), in some cases become brand ambassadors and create a cluster of digital communities around products and services, they are passionate about - the digital marketing at its best. However, the shift from passive consumption of content to active participation in generating the content and, increasingly co-creating the content, influencing development and growth of products and services and the ways marketed and delivered have opened new opportunities and challenges. To understand how businesses, leverage and potentially could enhance the customer interactions and experience, the technological and digital trends are discussed in the next section leading to developments in artificial intelligence and implications for digital marketing.

## INDUSTRIAL REVOLUTION AND DIGITAL TRENDS

The technological revolution is on the brink of today's life and will fundamentally alter the work we do and the way we live. The predictive transformation would be like anything which humankind would have never experienced due to its complexity, scope, and scale. The mystery of how it would unfold the future still remains a mystery but one thing is clear that the response to it would be comprehensive and integrated. All the stakeholders of the global polity would be involved in it from civil society to academia and from the public sector to the private sector (Pee et al., 2010).

The First Industrial Revolution used water and steam power to mechanize production (Schwab, 2017). The Second used electric power to create mass production (Schwab, 2017). The Third used electronics and information technology to automate production (Schwab, 2017). Now a Fourth Industrial Revolution is building on the Third, the digital revolution that has been occurring since the middle of the last century (Schwab, 2017). It is characterized by a fusion of technologies that is blurring the lines between the physical, digital, and biological spheres. For example, Uber, the world's largest taxi company, owns no vehicles. Facebook, the world's most popular media owner, creates no content. Alibaba, the most valuable retailer, has no inventory. And Airbnb, the world's largest accommodation provider, owns no real estate. Something interesting is happening.

The speed of current technological breakthroughs has no historical precedent (Bock et al., 2015). When compared with previous industrial revolutions, the Fourth is evolving at an exponential rather than a linear pace (Frolov et al., 2017). Moreover, it is disrupting almost every industry in every country. And the breadth and depth of these changes herald the transformation of entire systems of production, management, and governance (Yao et al., 2015).

The possibilities of billions of people connected by mobile devices, with unprecedented processing power, storage capacity, and access to knowledge, are unlimited (Palos et al., 2016). And these possibilities will be multiplied by emerging technology breakthroughs in fields such as artificial intelligence, robotics, the Internet of Things, autonomous vehicles, 3-D printing, nanotechnology, biotechnology, materials science, energy storage, and quantum computing. Artificial intelligence (AI) is the simulation of human intelligence processes (Input information, learning, knowledge, making meaning, reasoning, conclusions, self-reflection, and self-correction, etc) by machines, especially computer systems and the similar electro-mechanical agents.. Already, artificial intelligence is all around us, from self-driving cars and drones to virtual assistants and software that translate or invest. Impressive progress has been made in AI in recent years, driven by exponential increases in computing power and by the availability of vast amounts of data, from software used to discover new drugs to algorithms used to predict our cultural interests (Salanova et al., 2013). The concept of Mobile Crowd Sensing also perpetuates on how digital fabrication technologies, meanwhile, are interacting with the biological world on a daily basis. Engineers, designers, and architects are combining computational design, additive manufacturing, materials engineering, and synthetic biology to pioneer a symbiosis between microorganisms, our bodies, the products we consume, and even the buildings we inhabit (Wsi, 2013). For example, the heating system could be controlled remotely, the out-of-date products in the fridge could be detected, the correct medication would be dispensed by the pillbox at the correct time or otherwise, an alert could be broadcasted throughout every connected device. These apps can update the weather forecast, inform about pollutants in the indoor air and sensor fusion to enable intelligent environment will help the communities in general and on a wider range.

## Challenges and Opportunities

Like the revolutions that preceded it, the Fourth Industrial Revolution has the potential to raise global income levels and improve the quality of life for populations around the world (Salanova et al., 2013). To date, those who have gained the most from it have been consumers able to afford and access the digital world; technology has made possible new products and services that increase the efficiency and pleasure of our personal lives (Seybert, 2012). Ordering a cab, booking a flight, buying a product, making a payment, listening to music, watching a film, or playing a game any of these can now be done remotely (Salanova et al., 2013). For example, Uber takes all payments online, eBay helps to buy and sell products online and also make online transactions only.

In the future, technological innovation will also lead to a supply-side miracle, with long-term gains in efficiency and productivity. Transportation and communication costs will drop, logistics and global supply chains will become more effective, and the cost of trade will diminish, all of which will open new markets and drive economic growth.

At the same time, the revolution could yield greater inequality, particularly in its potential to disrupt labour markets. As automation substitutes for labour across the entire economy, the net displacement of workers by machines might exacerbate the gap between returns to capital and returns to labour (Steelman, 2014). On the other hand, it is also possible that the displacement of workers by technology will, in the aggregate, result in a net increase in safe and rewarding jobs.

In addition, to be a key economic concern, inequality represents the greatest societal concern associated with the Fourth Industrial Revolution. The largest beneficiaries of innovation tend to be the providers of intellectual and physical capital the innovators, shareholders, and investors which explains the rising gap in wealth between those dependent on capital versus labour (Wang, 2016). Technology is, therefore, one of the main reasons why incomes have stagnated, or even decreased, for a majority of the population in high-income countries: the demand for highly skilled workers has increased while the demand for workers with less education and lower skills has decreased. This is witnessed in Malaysia since there is a huge demand risen for qualified and educated people. The result is a job market with a strong demand at the high and low ends, but a hollowing out of the middle.

This helps explain why so many workers are disillusioned and fearful that their own real incomes and those of their children will continue to stagnate. It also helps explain why middle classes around the world are increasingly experiencing a pervasive sense of dissatisfaction and unfairness (Wang, 2016). A winner-takes-all economy that offers only limited access to the middle class is a recipe for democratic malaise and dereliction.

Discontent can also be fuelled by the pervasiveness of digital technologies and the dynamics of information sharing typified by social media. More than 30 percent of the global population now uses social media platforms to connect, learn, and share information (Weinberg & Pehlivan, 2011). In an ideal world, these interactions would provide an opportunity for cross-cultural understanding and cohesion. However, they can also create and propagate unrealistic expectations as to what constitutes success for an individual or a group, as well as offer opportunities for extreme ideas and ideologies to spread. Digital communities could respond to this kind of situations and to implement this, the communities have to organise their presence and respond quickly before the message spreads out.

## The Impact on Business

An underlying theme is that the acceleration of innovation and the velocity of disruption are hard to comprehend or anticipate and that these drivers constitute a source of constant surprise, even for the best connected and most well informed. Indeed, across all industries, there is clear evidence that the technologies that underpin the Fourth Industrial Revolution are having a major impact on businesses (Thaichon & Quach, 2016).

On the supply side, many industries are seeing the introduction of new technologies that create entirely new ways of serving existing needs and significantly disrupt existing industry value chains. Disruption is also flowing from agile, innovative competitors who, thanks to access to global digital platforms for research, development, marketing, sales, and distribution, can oust well-established incumbents faster than ever by improving the quality, speed, or price at which value is delivered (Mathews et al., 2016).

Major shifts on the demand side are also occurring, as growing transparency, consumer engagement, and new patterns of consumer behaviour force companies to adapt the way they design, market, and deliver products and services.

A key trend is the development of technology-enabled platforms that combine both demand and supply to disrupt existing industry structures, such as those we see within the "sharing" or "on-demand" economy. These technology platforms rendered easy to use by the smartphone, convene people, assets, and data thus creating entirely new ways of consuming goods and services in the process (Wsi, 2013). In addition, they lower the barriers for businesses and individuals to create wealth, altering the personal and professional environments of workers (Steelman, 2014). These new platform businesses are rapidly multiplying into many new services, ranging from laundry to shopping, from chores to parking, from massages to travel.

On the whole, there are four main effects that the Fourth Industrial Revolution has on business on customer expectations, on product enhancement, on collaborative innovation, and on organizational forms (Seybert, 2012). Whether consumers or businesses, customers are increasingly at the epicentre of the economy, which is all about improving how customers are served. Physical products and services, moreover, can now be enhanced with digital capabilities that increase their value. New technologies make assets more durable and resilient, while data and analytics are transforming how they are maintained (Pee, 2010). A world of customer experiences, data-based services, and asset performance through analytics, meanwhile, requires new forms of collaboration, particularly given the speed at which innovation and disruption are taking place. And the emergence of global platforms and other new business models, finally, means that talent, culture, and organizational forms will have to be rethought.

Overall, the inexorable shift from simple digitization (the Third Industrial Revolution) to innovation based on combinations of technologies (the Fourth Industrial Revolution) is forcing companies to re-examine the way they do business. The bottom line, however, is the same: business leaders and senior executives need to understand their changing environment, challenge the assumptions of their operating teams, and relentlessly and continuously innovate.

Neither technology nor the disruption that comes with it is an exogenous force over which humans have no control. All of us are responsible for guiding its evolution, in the decisions we make on a daily basis as citizens, consumers, and investors. We should thus grasp the opportunity and power we have to shape the Fourth Industrial Revolution and direct it toward a future that reflects our common objectives and values.

To do this, however, it is to develop a comprehensive and globally shared view of how technology is affecting our lives and reshaping our economic, social, cultural, and human environments. There has never been a time of greater promise, or one of greater potential peril. Today's decision-makers, however, are too often trapped in traditional, linear thinking, or too absorbed by the multiple crises demanding their attention, to think strategically about the forces of disruption and innovation shaping our future.

In the end, it all comes down to people and values. There is a need to shape a future that works for all of us by putting people first and empowering them. In its most pessimistic, dehumanized form, the Fourth Industrial Revolution may indeed have the potential to "robotize" humanity and thus to deprive us of our heart and soul. But as a complement to the best parts of human nature creativity, empathy, stewardship it can also lift humanity into a new collective and moral consciousness based on a shared sense of destiny. It is incumbent on us all to make sure the latter prevails.

## DIGITAL MARKETING (DM), HISTORY AND EVOLUTION

Advertising, as a marketing tool, is the art of persuading others. It bundles communication, the study of behaviour and psychology, design, spatial understanding, storytelling, the calling and attracting, action to make deals and measurement of the initiatives, has the potential to change societal behaviours at large. Customer Behavior is the process by which an individual search, select, purchase & use products or services and respond to the utilities of the products or services (Peter & Olson, 2010). The consumers are influenced via marketing efforts i.e. marketing mix (Product, Price, Place Promotion) in general and via advertisements in particular. Any advertisement form of mass communication using a range of medias to make consumers aware about a product or services and also influence their attitude and behavior towards the product or service (Peter & Olson, 2010).

A milestone in the development of modern advertising was the advent of the printing press in 14 and 15th centuries. The cost of printing books and other materials reduced dramatically compared to earlier times, where written artifacts were produced mainly by manual processes. The printing press enabled larger sections of the population to have access to written books, for example, manuscript books in Europe could be counted to few thousands before the invention of printing, in only 50 years by 1500, about 9,000,000 books were printed (Encyclopædia Britannica, 2019). In the 17th century, adverts started to appear in newspapers, laying the foundations of modern-day advertisement (Ryan & Jones, 2005, Chapter 1). The 18th and 19th centuries saw increasing use of mail ordering advertisement, pioneered by Pryce Jones (Newtown Drenewydd, 2019), that leveraged the developing network of the infrastructure of the postal system (Royal Mail, 2019). Another major trigger for disruption in the advertising space was the arrival of radio broadcasting in the early 20th century that offered a completely new channel to reach out to potential customers and clients (BT, 2019). The advent of television marks an important step in the evolution of electronic broadcasting, now it is the part and parcel of modern-day living. Nearly, 3.572 billion people watched the 2018 FIFA world cup in 2018, accounting for almost half of the global population (FIFA, 2019). The internet was created to protect the US and western Europe's communication infrastructure in the event of nuclear war with USSR. The ARPA project linked the mainframes of the government agencies, military installation, and universities around the country, laying the foundation of the modern-day Internet (Kleinrock, 2010). The internet triggered the era of digital marketing and advertisement, giving unprecedented power and choice to the consumers; no longer the marketing content passively consumed but the active participation and co-creation of content through sharing experience is the hallmark of the modern-day digital marketing landscape.

The internet has broadened the reach and scope of marketing. Unlike traditional mass media marketing, it overcomes the geographical and time zone boundaries in a cost-effective manner offering the potential of targeting very specific niche marketing segments, enhancing the effectiveness of the message manifold.

However, new opportunities throw new challenges for companies. For example, the unprecedented reach to the prospective clients and customers comes with the tremendous amount of data generation and accumulation of the data through interactions with the users using digital communication tools over the internet.

The modern tools range from the RSS feeds to full-spectrum interaction through the Social Media channels such as Facebook, YouTube, Twitter, Instagram, LinkedIn, Meetup, Digital Television Interactive Services to Email-based marketing. The plethora of tools could cause confusion, and information and choice overload (Lee, Son, & Kim, 2016). In this context, it is important to understand modern techniques to smartly use digital communication mediums for the marketing purpose in order to reap maximum benefit through initiatives and campaigns.

Developments in the field of AI also promise to assist in the field of digital marketing, especially addressing issues such as information overload and smart data handling for marketing purposes. In the next section, the evolution of AI and relevance to digital marketing is explored.

## ARTIFICIAL INTELLIGENCE (AI) AND Digital Marketing (DM)

The tech sector is developing at a dizzying pace, whether it is a new generation of mobile phones, blockchain technology, and digital currencies, smart speakers, online translators, augmented reality, online shopping, gaming devices, App stores, they are all changing the way we live, work and operate in the society.

Whilst progress in technology is rapid, however, the utility, deployment, and implications can be difficult for users and organisations to grasp (Chris Yapp, 2018). For instance, if a driverless car is about to hit two pedestrians, due to an accident, which one, the algorithm running the car, will choose to save; what if, the algorithm is biased to safe younger people against older people – what the law say about this? One of the issues presented by the unprecedented development in the technology is that the societal structures and legal frameworks seemed to be in perpetual catching up game.

For businesses, the problem is more acute. If the businesses are not careful in adopting the right technologies at the right time generating new capabilities and competencies to remain competitive in the increasingly tough market, they might find themselves stagnate or out of the market completely. A typical example is many high street brands closing down (BHS, HMV, Toys 'R' Us) in recent years due to pressures from online shopping and the dominant position of eCommerce players like Amazon (CRR, 2019).

As already mentioned that AI is Artificial Intelligence is the simulation of human intelligence processes (Input information, learning, knowledge, making meaning, reasoning, conclusions, self-reflection, and self-correction, etc) by machines, especially computer systems and the similar electro-mechanical agents. The AI has huge potential to be used in the field of marketing, where some routine and non-routine decision are made. It is important for the business to understand the changing nature of markets, consumer behaviour, technological implications, and their own capacity to function competitively. The reaching out to the potential customers and clients in a meaningful way, maximising the window of opportunity, whilst interacting with the users on the digital platforms, to showcase the services and products on offer and build relationship to add value, and meet their needs could hold the key to remain competitive and successful as a business in the current market. Development in Artificial Intelligence could be leveraged to fulfill this goal. However, many businesses still don't fully grasp how new developments in AI could be utilised, or worse, how this may impact their own business. In the next section key developments in the field of AI will be discussed before looking at potential applications in the field of digital marketing to reach out to potential customer and clients more effectively.

The concept of Intelligent machine dates to the 18th century, for example, TURK chess-playing the machine, although we will look at a relatively modern perspective. The major turning point in the development of the AI was in the 60s with the advent of Knowledge-Based Expert Systems. In comparison to earlier efforts that focused on solving logical inference and algebraic theorem proving through AI-based systems (Buchanan, 2005), an expert system is a knowledge-intensive system which mimics tasks or operations performed by a human expert, e.g. diagnosing a fault in a vehicle, assisting in the medical diagnosis of a disease. An expert system functions in many ways as a human expert does, such as asking many questions and reasoning heuristically through defined rules, reaching conclusion and making judgments. The expert systems are narrow in reference to their domain of expertise, functions, and services they provide unlike a human expert, who normally has a breadth of knowledge and range of experiences and understanding of fundamental principles (Hayes-roth, 1984). The applications of Expert systems range from financial planning, blood disorder diagnosis, waste management control, plant process control, Chip design, power transmission protection, business game to agriculture planning (Liao, 2005).

Another notable development in the evolution of AI was the development of Neural Network-based approaches. This is particularly important as it provides the foundation of modern machine learning-based approaches in the field of AI, discussed in a later section. A neural network is a model which emulates biological neural network. The natural state of a biological neuron is resting. The neuron will receive the signals in the form of electro-chemical pulses from dendrites of other neurons. The dendrites are fibre like tissues attached to the cell body of neuron with a nucleus at the centre. The pulse stimulates the cell body of the neuron, which is received from the dendrite of other neuron cells, connected through the cells own dendrite and reached to the body of the cell via Axon, connecting cell body and dendrite. There are various types of neuron specialising in various tasks e.g. sensory neurons (capturing sensory input such as light), motor neurons (related to muscle movement) and other neurons dealing with reasoning and so on. The neuron is a simple structure but billions of them connected in complex connections, acting together in a complex way, making the human brain the most complex and amazing biological machine in the known universe. A simplified form of this concept is applied in artificial neural networks, which comprise of layers of neurons-essentially an artificial neuron is a unit that processes certain data, receiving a number of input signals, some of which are more influential than others. It adds the input signals and the sum is compared with a threshold value, if an aggregate is more than the threshold the neuron is fired depending on the threshold values assigned (Kevin, 2012). In this way, an artificial neuron behaves similarly to a biological neuron. The above depiction is a very simple view of the artificial neuron; there are a number of different weights and functions are applied to it to standardise the output and make it more efficient and effective for the task assigned. In an artificial neural network paths through layers of neurons, stacked together, are established, and data passing through firing neurons create pathways which potentially lead to the output neuron that represents the correct outcome, e.g. identifying the correct numeral from an image of poorly written numerical digits, or identification of pattern in a medical scan leading to correct diagnosis of a disease.

In 1997 Deep Blue beat Gary Kasparov, a world champion, in the epic battle of a Chess game. This was a watershed moment in the field of artificial intelligence. The game of chess considered to be the ultimate test of human uniqueness and superiority in the 80s by people. This claim was laid to rest by Deep Blue, shocking not only the common people but also Gary who was visibly frustrated on the occasion, beaten by the machine (IBM, 2019b). The algorithm for the Deep Blue was still based on more efficient Heuristics (rules governing program behaviour and decisions) than the previous generations (Stanford CS221, 2013).

The IBM embarked on a different set of challenges, with developing an intelligent machine to play Jeopardy. The Jeopardy is a television show based game, played through a general knowledge quiz competition, where participants are presented with the clues to the answers and they must form responses in the form correct question (Corea Nana, 2011). The IBM developed the machine and named it Watson, with capabilities to process and reason in natural language and didn't rely solely on pre-processing of the massive amount of information made available to it months before the game, as was the case with Deep Blue. Machine learning played a key role in the development of the new generation of the intelligent machine.

The IBM's Watson played Jeopardy against two best standing winners of the game with the prize money worth 5 million US dollars between them, Ken Jennings and Brad Rutter. Watson won the game with $77,147, against $21,600 and $24,000, won by Rutter and Jennings respectively (IBM Research, 2013). Watson's algorithms were based on the deep learning concept, layering algorithms to create an artificial neural network, constantly learning, checking if the decisions were correct, constantly improving on results, learning through existing experience. The algorithms can handle unstructured data, e.g. pictures, videos, natural language text, and audio, which makes it a very powerful tool to be used in more natural settings and scenarios where human life and work. For instance, Watson can deconstruct the sentences and explore the relations between various components within the sentence such as sentiments, emotions, keywords used and narratives. This is particularly useful in the digital marketing and design field to capture the sentiments of the users to improve on marketing campaigns or design of the product and services.

Digital marketing is conducted through the utilisation of tools such as User Search, Email Marketing, Paid Search, Blog Post, Video creation, online pay per click advertising. Digital marketing is not so different from conventional marketing as it conveys the value of a product or service to the costumers but through digital channels.

Content generation is the core fuelling channel of digital marketing. It is based on human expertise of the application domain, identification of customers and clients needs, and of their patterns of behaviours, and is generally assisted by analytical tools, which help developing insights over the long term to fill the digital channels with effective and meaningful content, generating business value. In the near future, content generation is expected to increasingly rely on AI, based on the advancements in natural language processing and machine learning. Digital marketing content could be created in partnership with human experts and machines, generatively, creating hundreds of models within hours against weeks and months, enabling comparison and analytical processing to decide on a highly attune service for customers and clients, fulfilling their needs more richly.

For instance, OpenAi is a non-profit organisation whose mission is to democratise artificial intelligence. The project GPT-2 was launched in Feb 2019 with the aim to generate text on a variety of topics with seed words. The cut-down version is available to the public (Figure. 1), which is less coherent. This was due to the fear of misuse of the application. Nevertheless, this application shows the potential of AI-generated content. To demonstrate, the words "artificial intelligence and job losses" were input to the app and the corresponding text was generated as follows:

*Artificial intelligence and job losses—from an initial 15,000 to just 5,000 jobs over the past seven years—may not seem like a big deal. Yet it is.*

*The rise of the robots and the rise of automation—from manufacturing jobs to office jobs to retail jobs to assembly line jobs to construction jobs and more—make this phenomenon look small.*

*Figure 1. Application of language model GPT-2*

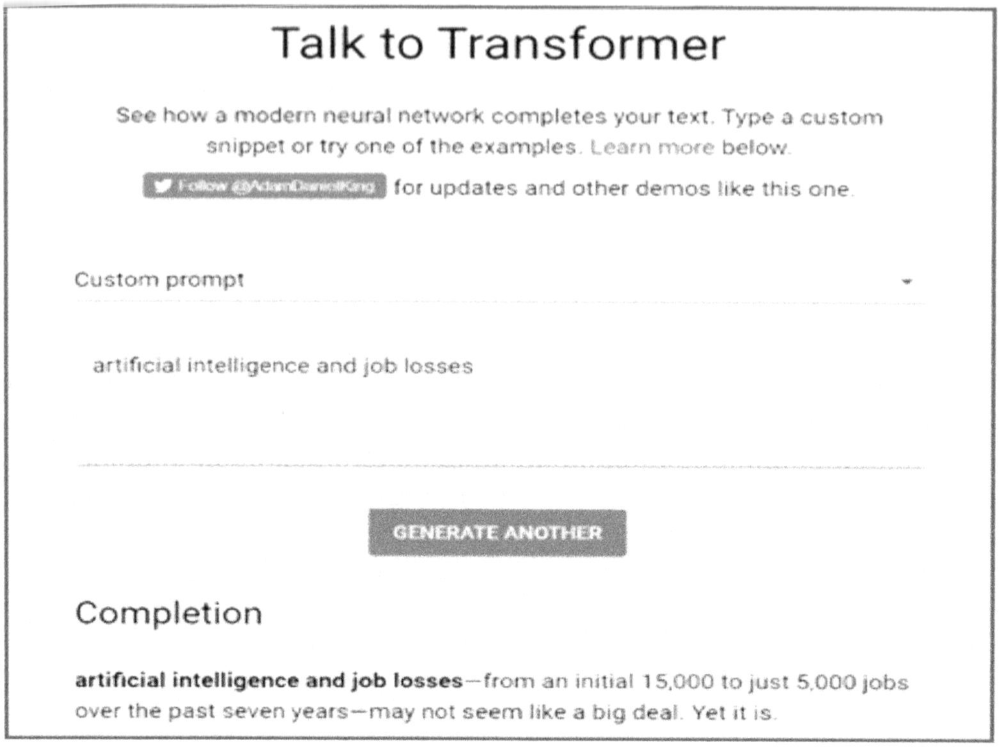


*The reason for that, according to MIT professor, and writer and co-founder of MIT's MIT Digital Labs Robert Scoble, is that, by focusing on an artificial intelligence system's capacity to perform in a given task or to improve itself in a given task, we have taken on a role of overseer of that artificial intelligence system. And we are doing a hell of a job of it.*

*The robot problem as Scoble sees it begins with our ability—over the past six years or so—to take on more and more tasks that are far beyond our control. As Scoble explains:*

*As machines have become more efficient, we've gone from taking on a specific task only to taking on it all the time. This process.*

The generative AI technologies will have a serious impact on the individuals and society, with serious ethical issues being raised, for example, what if, the same technology is used to generate fake news or biased viewpoints against certain individuals. The humans are heavily influenced by the number of people around them of viewpoints of others, a typical example is the influence of reviews when buying products on platforms such as Amazon. A full discussion on the ethical and security dimension of AI based technologies is beyond the scope of this chapter. However, there is a growing body of literature available and the marketeers, managers and decision-makers should be aware of the advances in this domain and legal developments impacting the businesses and individuals.

Digital marketing is at the cusp of a new era where a connected world would not only involve interaction with people, it will involve also interaction with devices and sensors, increasing the canvas to develop deep insights, providing opportunities to provide better services, adaptable to customer needs of present and future. The predictive power of such systems and approaches will increase manifold.

For example, most of the major players in the automotive industry are reinventing themselves, calling themselves 'mobility service' companies, such as Ford Car company. The Ford pioneered the assembly line production 100 years ago, in Dearborn, Michigan. The Ford company, today, leveraging technologies such as AI and machine learning in next-generation connected car solutions to driverless vehicles. Implications of AI in digital marketing is elaborated using a thougth experiment in the next section.

## THOUGHT EXPERIMENT

A 'thought experiment' is a hypothetical tool facilitating Conceptual Analysis, using visualization techniques, investigating imaginative scenarios based on a theoretical framework, inventions, innovations, and technological developments (Weir, 2011). A 'thought experiment' is run using the Persona below to explore how the advancements in AI could impact the prospective customer of Ford motor company (see Figure 2. A persona is a set of characteristics or profiling of target segment of customers, which include various aspect of customer's characteristics, needs, motivations and environment etc and those characteristics are perceived, identified, presented and targeted by an organisation for effective marketing (SmartInsights, 2019).

*Figure 2. The persona of a car user and potential customer of new vehicle*

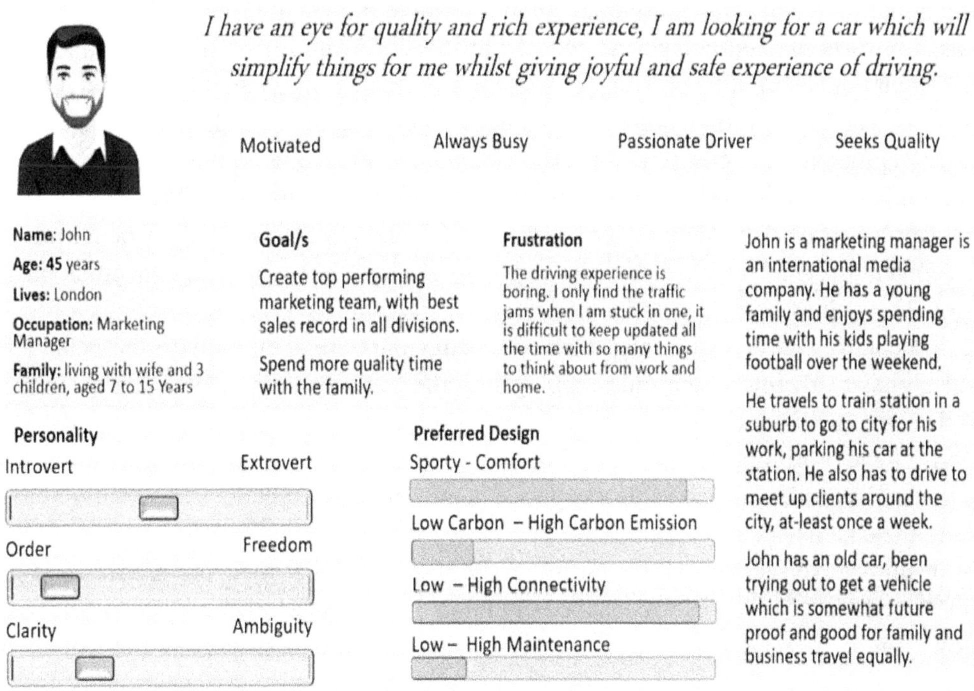

First, some of the current developments and capabilities of the Ford car company are discussed. The Ford company has introduced 'All Wheel Intelligent drive system', which can switch between various drive and torque modes for the wheels, enabling exceptional handling on varying terrain such as wet, dry or icy conditions. Ford vehicles are increasingly equipping with AI enabled technologies, interacting directly with the driver, learning driving styles of the driver, preferences on infotainment, seat positioning, monitoring acceleration and braking to improve fuel efficiency. Ford SYNC system enables users to effortlessly access the smartphone features through voice controls, touch screen and steering-wheel-mounted controls, including access to vehicle's entertainment system. The vehicles come with the self-parking feature, including cross-traffic alert to alert the driver for incoming traffic, which potentially could be missed due to the blind spot, e.g. when getting the vehicle out of the parking bay on to the main road.

The next generation of technology features involves more cellular and wireless technology integration, communicating with other vehicles directly, roadside infrastructure, traffic sign, services in the vicinity. The vehicle will see hear and understand the environment it is operating in and making AI enable decisions in conditions like bad weather, blind road intersections, heavy traffic route, fuel efficiency, refuel planning, real-time route planning, and diagnostics through various sensors embedded in the vehicle. The AI would enable the company to do the supply chain and resource management more effectively, for example, it will be able to predict the number of cars coming to a particular service station with a specific problem and the inventory will be adequately sourced to fulfill the demand during specific days or week. The AI will have a profound impact on marketing operations and backbone platforms e.g. digital analytics, dashboards, marketing automation, content generation and enhancing CRM system, data management, and API and integration handling of services.

## Swarm Marketing

An offshoot of Artificial intelligence is Swam intelligence –'Collective Wisdom'. The idea has come from small animals like ants, who individually can do simple things, however, collectively they can do complex tasks. Swarm marketing is an AI-enabled process of using inputs from a number of sources, generating insights and facilitating profiling of persona and create a digital marketing strategy to enhance marketing effort. Thus, the swarm marketing is a process of making use of collective wisdom of a number of sources for segmenting the customers' profile or creating a persona on one side and then using AI for social and other marketing efforts to change the behavior of the customer. The AI tools can collect data from a number of personal and sensor sources, and such data can be used for better profiling, i.e. to create a segment of 'One'. Further, AI tools can be used to reach the targeted consumer via a number of organisional as well as social networks.

In such a scenario where customer interactions, behaviours are coupled with the behaviour of the vehicle and digital marketing is not only tapping into the traditional channels such as emails, social media but the canvas is increased to sensor infused system, connected and control through the cloud. The user and vehicle profiling will generate a huge amount of data and opportunities to understand what environment user live and work and vehicles operate in, presenting tremendous opportunities to enhance the service to the customers.

This is an immersive scenario where customers will demand that their preferences and needs are readily understood and acted upon. This is the beginning of 'Swarm Marketing' era as presented in the model below (figure. 3), which depicts the transitions from traditional marketing to Swarm Marketing

*Figure 3. Tech -marketing interaction model*

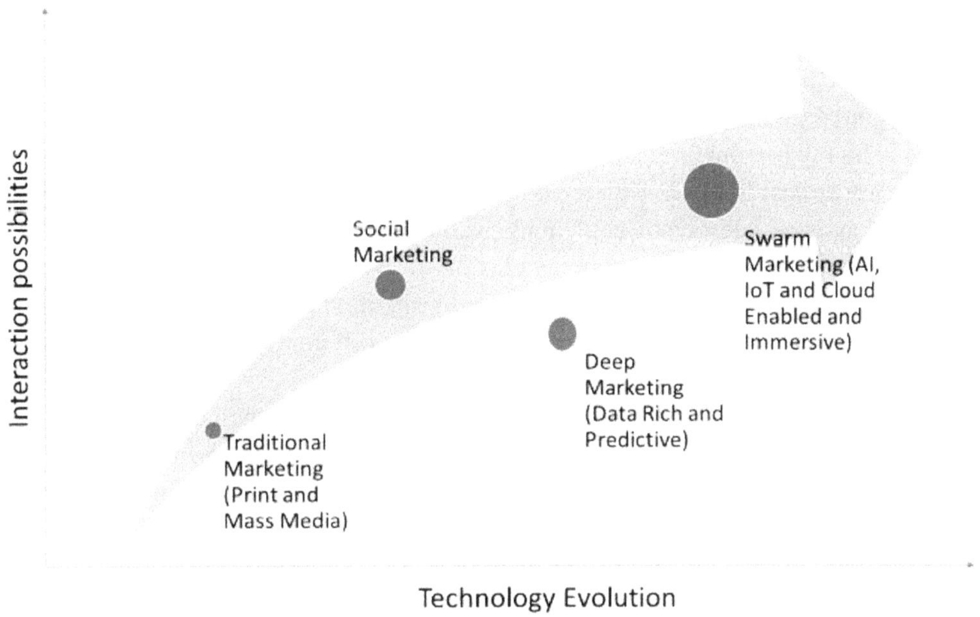


fuelled by technological advancement particularly AI-enabled technologies and increase in the canvas of interaction possibilities.

The advances in deep neural networks, text to speech algorithms, persuasive voice generation, back up by sentiment analysis are opening new venues for many sectors including digital marketing. For example, IBM has developed a system to debate with human experts, named Project Debater, (IBM, 2019a). This technology has tremendous implications for various sectors and particularly for digital marketing.

The Debater integrates three components, data-driven speech writing, ability to understand spontaneous human speech to build rebuttal arguments and model differing perspectives of the arguments based on existing debates on the topic (IBM, 2019). It incorporates techniques such as text segmentation, stance identification for the arguments, deep understanding of human languages and contextual scenarios, detecting evidence for the claims and counterclaims in the speech, filtering the strongest claims, and generating themes to create the base of the narratives and setting the motion in the debate. It uses a technique of knowledge graph, (Levy, Bogin, Gretz, Aharonov, & Slonim, 2018), to explore grey areas and general human dilemmas related to the debated topic, based on deep neural network and argumentative content search engine to facilitate the arguments, tone, and sentiments for the debate. It was believed this sort of technology is not possible because the debater has to deal with so many different parameters, contexts and need to have deep knowledge of the subject in a meaningful way and assess opponent's stances. The presentation has to take into account the behavioural and psychological aspects of the debate and the audience mood and reactions, using sentiments as a cue for the rebuttal. The advances in the text to speech and voice-based interaction and searches hold tremendous potential in the field of digital marketing. For example, most of the eCommerce users are familiar with Amazon and the power of product reviews and ratings in purchasing decisions. Coupling of new advancement in voice and content generation technologies could multiply the impact on new leads and materialisation of sales. The companies also need to take measures to safeguard the customers from fake product reviews and fabricated accounts of customer experiences, AI could assist in this domain to identify the patterns of such accounts.

The whole concept of customer worldview and customer journey needs to look at from new angles. For example, for the Persona (John) given in figure 2, Artificial Intelligence can help to find out the pain and touch points faced by him in a much deeper level, driven by the data and profiles available. This could lead to highly personalised and customised service leveraging the maximum from the touch points, e.g. when a customer interacts with the brand through website, email or physically attending the showroom. The AI assisted salesperson could understand the requirements of the customer much more comprehensively, equipped with the scenario and history of the individual but also through the knowledgebase of thousands of interaction cases logged previously of other customers, identifying beneficial patterns and behaviours among customers from the similar (or different) backgrounds, generating offers and services which result in deep customer satisfaction.

The preferences and choices of existing customers will be captured, including driving patterns, services used and interaction within the vicinity, interaction with the environment, communication with the other vehicles and identification of clusters of family, friends, community, influencers – all will be taking into account to generate highly bespoke service and marketing interaction model for John.

In a not too distant future, John will be able to drive an autonomous vehicle. Increasingly, John will use other services such as sharing a car with other members of the community, actually, the car will earn him money while John is working in the office. The car will know John's routines and commitments intrinsically and will be available for the service for John exactly when needed. Based on the technological advancements such as IBM debater, the car will speak to John as an intelligent entity, suggesting alternative routes in a similar manner a friend sitting in the car will do. The car will plan the grocery shopping for John, while he is enjoying time with his family. The Ford is experimenting with autonomous delivery robots and other companies such as Amazon are experimenting with the delivery pods (CNN Business, 2019). The car will be able to interact with these autonomous agents and seamlessly provide service to John in travel, planning, supermarket trips, suggestions on the possibility of dinner with a friend and sharing thoughts on a book that John as recently read. The interaction possibilities will be endless and continuous, hence in this brave new world, the digital marketing needs to reinvent itself and understand the canvas it will be operating in if the companies and organisations want to remain competitive and relevant.

## CONCLUSION

Artificial neural networks and deep learning have evolved in the last few years as effective machine learning tools to equip software used for decision making in marketing. These methods are able to learn from data and identify hidden relationships or associations between different types of data, such as geodemographic data, and generalise to deal with new situations when predicting demand or customer expectations. These features can be eminently suitable for decision making in marketing by effectively aiding market segmentation tasks, improving the accuracy of forecasting demand or performance metrics while reducing costs and uncertainty. For example, identify key patterns in customer groups and consumers purchasing behaviour, combine these patterns with socio-economic characteristics, and use this insight to streamline marketing efforts, or monitor and analyse the performance of campaigns. Lastly, these methods offer a promising alternative to statistical models, which are traditionally used, when decision making is informed by incomplete, noisy or sparse data. Customer profiling, personalised advertisements, and recommendations are some of the applications of these methods in this area.

Machine learning and AI methods, in general, have also found important marketing applications analysing social networks, user-generated content and social behaviour online. Methods for analysis and simulation of social networks help to understand consumer behaviour and perform opinion mining and sentiment analysis. In this context, a variety of methods have been used from K-nearest neighbour algorithms, K-means clustering and naive Bayes classifiers to Random Forests (a machine learning method that creates an ensemble of decision trees), convolutional neural networks and recurrent networks, enabling transformational changes.

As AI technologies and machine learning are incorporated into many marketing applications, they impact their usability and user expectations and introduce additional ethical considerations. Trust to AI decisions depends on users' expectation that applications are useful, behave consistently and perfectly, and provide explanations about their decisions, which is not always the case with data-driven AI and machine learning methods. To this end, it is important to increase users understanding of how AI tools operate, their potential imperfections, and in which situations they are likely to work. Users should also be able to intervene, set decision thresholds, and in general interact with AI and control AI tools' behaviour in a way that meets their own perceptions of accuracy of systems that incorporate AI capabilities and machine learning.

The digital marketers should observe the technological developments acutely, tapping into the opportunities presented through new channels and mediums to interact and engage with the customers and users. The infusion of sensors, cloud-based controls, and communications and artificial intelligence-enabled capabilities is changing and will further change the way we live and work in society. The old tried and tested methods and techniques will get obsolete or irrelevant, so it is very important to understand the changing technological landscape and implications, facilitating in devising new techniques, approaches and strategies to remain relevant and prosper in the business.

## REFERENCES

BT. (2019). *The history of radio in the UK*. BT.

Buchanan, B. (2005). A (Very) Brief History of Artificial Intelligence. *AI Magazine*, *26*(4), 53–60.

CNN Business. (2019). *Ford's delivery robot walks like a human*. CNN.

Chaffey, D., & Ellis-Chadwick, F. (2019). Introduction – how has digital marketing transformed marketing? In *Digital Marketing* (7th ed.). Pearson.

Chris Yapp. (2018). *The Road Ahead: Navigation AI's Pitfalls*. Oxford University Press; doi:10.1093/itnow/bwy008

Corea Nana. (2011). *How to Play Jeopardy*. YouTube.

Court, D., Elzinga, D., Mulder, S., & Vetvik, O. J. (2009). *The consumer decision journey*. McKinsey.

CRR. (2019). Who's Gone Bust to end-March 2019. Centre for Retail Research.

Encyclopædia Britannica. (2019). *History of Publishing*. Author.

FIFA. (2019). *2018 FIFA World Cup Russia™ - News - More than half the world watched record-breaking 2018 World Cup*. FIFA.com.

Grayson, K. A., Kotler, P., & Hibbard, J. D. (2019). *Marketing | business*. Retrieved from Britannica.com

Hayes-roth, F. (1984). Expert Systems. *Computer*, *17*(10), 263–273. doi:10.1109/MC.1984.1658976

IBM. (2019a). *How it works - Project Debater*. IBM Research AI.

IBM. (2019b). *IBM100 - Deep Blue*. IBM.

IBM Research, . (2013). *Watson and the Jeopardy! Challenge*. YouTube.

Kevin, W. (2012). *Artificial Intelligence: The Basics*. Routledge.

Kleinrock, L. (2010). An early history of the internet. *IEEE Communications Magazine*, *48*(8), 26–36. doi:10.1109/MCOM.2010.5534584

Lee, A. R., Son, S. M., & Kim, K. K. (2016). Information and communication technology overload and social networking service fatigue: A stress perspective. *Computers in Human Behavior*, *55*, 51–61. doi:10.1016/j.chb.2015.08.011

Levy, R., Bogin, B., Gretz, S., Aharonov, R., & Slonim, N. (2018). *Towards an argumentative content search engine using weak supervision*. Academic Press.

Liao, S. H. (2005). Expert system methodologies and applications-a decade review from 1995 to 2004. *Expert Systems with Applications*, *28*(1), 93–103. doi:10.1016/j.eswa.2004.08.003

Marketing. (2019). Definition of Marketing by Merriam-Webster.

Newtown Drenewydd. (2019). *A Brief History of Newtown - Part 2*. Author.

Peter, J. P., & Olson, J. C. (2010). *Consumer behaviour & marketing startegy*. Retrieved from https://www.academia.edu/6078770/CONSUMER_BEHAVIOR_and_MARKETING_STRATEGY_CONSUMER_BEHAVIOR_and_MARKETING_STRATEGY

Royal Mail. (2019). *Our story*. Author.

Ryan, D., & Jones, C. (2005). *Developing Strong Listening and Communication Skills*. doi:10.1017/CBO9781107415324.004

SmartInsights. (2019). *Marketing personas*. Retrieved July 17, 2019, from https://www.smartinsights.com/persuasion-marketing/marketing-personas/

Stanford CS221. (2013). *Deep Blue*. Stanford.

Tiago, M. T. P. M. B., & Veríssimo, J. M. C. (2014). Digital marketing and social media: Why bother? *Business Horizons*, *57*(6), 703–708. doi:10.1016/j.bushor.2014.07.002

Weir, A. (2011). Formalism in the philosophy of mathematics. Stanford Encyclopedia of Philosophy.

Wsi. (2013). *Digital Minds: 12 Things Every Business Needs to Know about Digital Marketing*. Victoria: Friesen Press.

Yao, X., Phang, C. W., & Ling, H. (2015). Understanding the influences of trend and fatigue in individuals' SNS switching intention. *48th Hawaii international conference on system science.*

## KEY TERMS AND DEFINITIONS

**Advertisement:** A paid form of mass communication using a range of medias to make consumers aware about a product or services and also influence their attitude and behavior towards the product or service.

**Artificial Intelligence:** Is the simulation of human intelligence processes (input information, learning, knowledge, making meaning, reasoning, conclusions, self-reflection, and self-correction, etc.) by machines, especially computer systems and the similar electro-mechanical agents.

**Customer Behavior:** A process by which an individual search, select, purchase, and use products or services and respond to the utilities of the products or services.

**Digital Marketing:** A process of achieving marketing objectives through applying digital media, data, and technology; such as using email lists, telemarketing, digital television, online chats, informational websites, AdWords, searches, and social media, etc.

**Persona:** A persona is a set of characteristics or profiling of target segment of customers, which include various aspect of customer's characteristics, needs, motivations and environment etc and those characteristics are perceived, identified, presented and targeted by an organisation for effective marketing.

**Swarm Marketing:** Is an AI-enabled process of using inputs from number of sources, generating insights and facilitating profiling of persona and create digital marketing strategy to enhance marketing effort.

**Thought Experiment:** A thought experiment is a hypothetical tool facilitating conceptual analysis, using visualization techniques, investigating imaginative scenarios based on a theoretical framework, inventions, innovations, and technological developments.

# Chapter 2
# Reshaping Business Organizations Through Gamification

**Sukhvinder Singh**
*Maharaja Agrasen Institute of Technology, GGS Indrapratha University, India*

**Vandana Gupta**
*Amity University, Noida, India*

## ABSTRACT

*Gamification is the application of game-design elements, mechanisms, and principles in non-game contexts, typically as an online marketing technique to encourage engagement with a product or service, improve organizational productivity, crowdsourcing, learning, and employee recruitment. The global gamification market was valued at USD 2.17 billion in 2017, and is expected to reach USD 19.39 billion by 2023, at a CAGR of 44.06% over the forecast period (2018-2023). The growth of smartphone and smart devices have attributed towards the growth of a vast base of gamification market. This growth is also supplemented by the increasing recognition of gamification systems as a method to architecture human behavior to induce innovation, productivity, or engagement. This chapter explains the role of gamification in reshaping business organizations with reference to select cases on gamification used by corporates for promotion, active customer and employee engagement, and brand loyalty.*

## INTRODUCTION

Information and Communication Technologies (ICT) applications have been developed to support users towards consumption (Huber & Hilty, 2014). Gamification refers to the process of applying elements of game playing to content marketing technique by making it appealing.

"The use of game-thinking and game mechanics to engage users and solve problems." (Zichermann & Cunningham, 2011)."The use of game elements and game design techniques in non-game contexts." (Werbach & Hunter, 2012).

DOI: 10.4018/978-1-7998-0131-3.ch002

Thus, Gamification is a technology-driven process of enhancing services quality with motivational affordances in order to invoke graceful psychological experiences as games that further behavioral outcomes (Hamari, Koivisto, & Sarsa, 2014). Gamification is better as a next-generation method for marketing and customer engagement tool.

Gamification incorporates both fun and elements of competition to the organizational marketing strategies. The idea behind Gamification is to make an emotional connection with the audience and lead a longer relationship. Gamification is about taking the essence of games—fun, play, transparency, design and challenge—and applying it to real-world objectives. Gamification is an emerging trend and an increasing number of corporates are applying this technique to gain a competitive edge and actively engage their customers.

The global gamification market was valued at USD 2.17 billion in 2017 and is expected to reach USD 19.39 billion by 2023, at a CAGR of 44.06% over the forecast period (2018-2023). The use of gamification systems has also extended beyond their traditional scope of marketing, as now they are extensively used in advance applications like crowdsourcing. Enterprise gamification systems are expected to witness substantial growth during the forecast period. Organizations have shown a heavy inclination towards collaborative systems, which do not create a competitive environment, as they are widely considered counterproductive. However, the increasing awareness and functionality of these systems are expected to result in greater attention and research from academics and industry experts, leading to the improvement and evolution of technology.

## LITERATURE REVIEW

The term Gamification was initially coined by Nick Pelling in 2002. Gamification is essentially the implementation of game design techniques and elements into non-game contexts and activities (Deterding, Dixon, Khaled, & Nacke, 2011; Zichermann & Cunningham, 2011).

'Gamification', has become today's latest business buzzword and is rapidly gaining attention. However, the concept of using gamified elements to drive engagement, interest, and learning, dates back to almost a century ago. In one of the first evidence of gamification, Kellogg's cereals, in 1910, offered its first "premium," Moving-Pictures book, free with every two boxes, to increase sales.

In 1959, a garment factory in Chicago introduced a daily ritual game in which workers steal a banana to stave off boredom and monotony. Games are believed to elevate satisfaction and productivity, inspiring research into this field. In the 1980s, professors at the Massachusetts Institute of Technology began considering the possibility of using gamified elements in the field of education.

In 2011, Volkswagen divulged a gamified campaign of crowdsourcing in China, where consumers were invited to design vehicles and rate other entries, online, results being tracked on leaderboards. (McCormick, 2013). Zickermann (2010) explored that the educational games industry has released various attractive and successful games. He also said that very few games in the past have been proved to be successful. McGonigal (2011) supported the Zickermann's statements and further explained that educational games or game-based learning is short-lived and thus do not meet the needs of today's customer. He also argued that educational games are not making significant and long term association with the customers.

The Gamification technique has worked its way into various industries. The purpose of converting gamification into competitive games fulfills multiple training needs. (Millet, 2017).

Gamification specifically in application development, also known as "app" development, can be utilized to add game and videogame elements to everyday tools that are used by the masses; having a powerful impact on the user. Gamification has been used to increase user engagement, improve knowledge and learning, and enhance overall learning experiences (Shchimmoeller, Mauzy, Meredith, & Austin, 2017).

Mood and Specht (1954) argues that "a virtue of gaming that is sometimes overlooked by those seeking grander goals it's unparalleled advantages in training and various educational programs. A game can easily be made interesting enough to overlook the dull part or facts." Some people perceive the gamification is related to the basic word-game, which literally meant for play, non-productivity, entertainment and is not at all linked with learning or education. Whereas on the other side, the gamification basic concept originates for students, customers, and learners. Gee (2007) also stated that the games on learning principles are strongly discovered by using cognitive science- that science which studies the brain and identifies the development of various goals and learning on the basis of requirement.

However, the gamification concept is supported through various evidence-based research that identifies the use of various theories and principles during its implementation which verifies that the concept is not only related to play.

Simoes et. Al (2013) explained the working of gamification in the game-based learning approach. He elaborated that gamification increases the involvement and engagement of customers. Gamification in today's scenario is a continuous and ongoing process that yields the most engaging game parts or components and thus increases the level of engagement and motivation among learners. Folmar (2015) also identified that game-based learning is long term as compared to engagement, which is considered to be as short-lived. But when Gamification is clubbed with engagement, it is bringing out the best outcome. This combination brings out positive results and helps in increasing customer involvement and perception. Seaborn and Fells (2015) reviewed the literature and found that there is a connection between gamification, motivation, and engagement.in similar lines, Challco et al. (2015) stated that gamification is helping in the learning of a customer individually because of gaining points and winning awards associated with it. On the same time, the aspect of gamification is identified socially through collaboration and competition.

## Drivers To Use Gamification

It is important to understand the factors that drive users to use games or gamification. The motivations to use gamification may be due to 'different needs and desires: extrinsic motive (tangible intangible rewards) and intrinsic motives (status, achievements, self-expression, and competition) and so on (Ruti, Dafni, Shimon, & Tomer, 2018). Various motivations like; involving imagination, playfulness, flow, fun, emotions, creativity, and cognitive skills of the individual, etc. have been cited as the cause of usage of games (Ruti, Dafni, Shimon, & Tomer, 2018). The users like to use the gamification, due to first impression of the game (on usefulness, ease of using, game-based mechanics, aesthetics, and game thinking to engage people, motivate action, promote learning, and solve problems); gamification elements and associated achievements (Points, levels, badges, trophies, ranking, leadboards, scoreboards or virtual goods); and other motivational factors) .

Games use the 'fun', that affect emotions and have the ability to involve users more deeply, thus games motivate users towards the specific course of action (Huber & Hilty, 2014). That is the reason, that many times such gamification related technologies are known as persuasive technologies as they motivate or persuade users to immerse in the playful way in gamifications and; thus change their attitude and behavior. This is in line of Theory of Reasons Action (TRA) and Theory of planned behavior (TPB). Theory of reasoned action (TRA) postulates that intention to use is determined by the attitude towards the product/technology/behavior and subjective norms (Fischbein & Janzen, 1975). The Theory of Planned Behavior (TPB) postulates that in addition to attitude, and social norms, the other factors namely perceived control and self-efficacy also have an important role in adoption new technology or product (Ajzen 1985). TRA and TPB postulate that behavior intentions are determined by the attitude towards the behavior, social norms and perceived behavior control.

Garm & Slinger, (2014) had used Unified Theory of Acceptance and Use of Technology (UTAUT) model (Venkatesh et al. 2003) and come up with the six factors; Performance Expectancy, Effort Expectancy, Social Influence, Facilitating Conditions and Behavioral Intention as main drivers of actual using of as a possible explanation of adoption of gamification by users.

According to Gee (2005), the users adopt games because they feel more satisfied in a gamification environment and thus highlights the social effects and elements of relatedness. It is also identified that when players are engaged in a gamified environment, they fulfill the virtual challenges resulting in fun and play. These factors may be related to intrinsic motivation and are being fulfilled by individuals without any prior conditioning. (Francisco-Aparicio, Gutierrez-Vela, Isla-Martes & Sanches, (2013). Developing this further, Robson et al. (2015) proposed a model framework that the gamification relies on three principles of dynamics, mechanics, and emotions. The research has shown that playing games releases 'Dopamine- a neurotransmitter, involved in attestation, learning, reinforcement of behavior, and activation of the pleasure'- a state of flow (Huber & Hilty, 2014). The flow is a state of being fully involved and absorbed in the process and such a stage is usually lying between feelings of boredom on one side and anxiety on the other side of it. (Hamari, Koivisto, & & Sarsa, 2014). This indicates that Games in marketing can increase consumer involvement in the process and, hence more engagement with the product and services. The TRA and TPB that highlights the importance of usefulness, relevance, ease of use and self-efficacy as a precursor of change in behavior(Fischbein & Ajzen, 1975). The learning theories postulate that consumers can be made to learn to change their behavior. In games, as the people are working together and possibly they learn from each other with social interactions, So,; it is worthwhile to apply theory of social learning-' new patterns of behavior can be acquired through direct experience or by observing the behavior of others' (Hamari, Koivisto, & & Sarsa, 2014).

The Organisations have tried using Gamification in various salutations, For example, ' Toyota' eco-friendly drive technology' shows a drive the mileage that one has covered since the last fill-up of the tank, and this attribute has been used by drivers to play to run maximum miles per gallon (Hamari, Koivisto, & & Sarsa, 2014)

Thus, another way to look at this change in behaviour can be that the process of gamification brings in motivational affordance, that leads to psychological expenses (motivation, attitude, novelty, and enjoyment) and, ultimately it leads to behavior outcomes (using or buying products, services or technologies, etc.) (Hamari, Koivisto, & Sarsa, 2014). The motivational affordance means being motivated by the sense of achievements and rewards in the form of gaining points, achievements, badges, levels, rewards, positive feedback, higher challenges, progress and so on. Nan, Zeng et al (2014) identified literature of gamification in education. Their research looked at some of the elements used to gamify education like points, levels, leaderboards, storylines, progress bars, prizes, rewards, and feedback. Ryan and Deci (2000) gave some evidence to prove the intrinsic and extrinsic factors of motivation related to the concept. Similarly, Dicheva et al (2015) also identified some of the design elements used by gamification in education and getting visible status, freedom to fail, goals and challenges, rapid feedback, personalization, etc. In some of the elements, the challenges and competitions are created which looked for social engagements. They also stated that this type of process and game elements are used in almost every field of study like science, technology, information, computer technology, engineering, etc.

Researchers also justified that playing video games in gamification improves the cognitive abilities, emotions, motivation and social benefits. Granic et al (2014). Gee (2007) identifies various learning principle which is a part of the gamification process. Some of these are semiotics domains, critical learning, meta-level thinking, self-knowledge, achievement learning, etc.

## CATEGORIES OF GAMIFICATION

As per Dixon, (2011), depending on the nature and characteristics of the players, the games can be; classified as; Achievement oriented games (Advancement, Mechanics, Competition); Social oriented games (Socialising, Relationship, Teamwork) and; Flow & Immersion oriented Games (Discovery, Role-playing, Customization, Escapism and flow). Citing studies of Kallio et all, Dixon, (2011) stated that that a game might be targeted at Social Mentalities (Gaming with Kids, Gaming with Mates, Gaming for Company); Casual Mentalities (Killing Time, Filling Gaps, Relaxing) and for Committed Mentalities (Having Fun, Entertainment, Immersion). Depending upon the purpose and target audience of the game, Werbach & Hunter (2012) created a three types classification system for gamification as given below:

**Internal Gamification:** The use of "gamification to improve productivity within the organization in order to foster innovation, enhance camaraderie, or otherwise derive positive business results through their own employees" (Werbach & Hunter, 2012, Ch. 1). In other words, this is using gamification to improve internal business processes and reduce costs. This category can be is seen similar to social-oriented or mentally games.

**External Gamification:** The use of gamification involving customers as a "way to improve the relationships between businesses and customers, producing increased engagement, identification with the product, stronger loyalty, and ultimately higher revenues" (Werbach & Hunter, 2012, Ch. 1). In other words, this is using gamification to improve customer relations and customer engagement. Such games can include social as well as achievement-oriented games. For example, In order to improve the quality and quantity of reviews Amazon.com started the 'Amazon's Top Reviewers' program, which rewards customers for good quality reviews. 'By simply clicking 'yes' or 'no' next to a review, customers tell Amazon if a review has been helpful for them. The number of reviews a customer has written and the perceived quality translates into points, which are shown on the reviewer's profile page. To increase the competitive element, there's also a leader board which ranks the reviewers publicly' (Dixon, 2011).

**Behavior-Change Gamification:** This "seeks to form beneficial new habits among a population. That can involve anything from encouraging people to make better health choices…to redesigning the classroom to make kids learn more while actually enjoying school" (Werbach & Hunter, 2012, Ch. 1). In other words, this is using gamification to increase productivity and motivate people. These kinds of games can be also seen as t Flow & Immersion or committed mentality games. For example, Heineken Star player has been developed to engage the viewers of the Heineken sponsored Champions League (soccer) games more with the brand (Boer, ND).

## PROCESS OF GAMIFICATION

A game has game elements, game thinking in a non-game environment and is used to target behaviour and engagement (Dixon, 2011). As with most of the marketing efforts, effective Gamification needs a plan: It's important to think about the business goals, the target audience, and the target behaviour. As aims of the gamification Instead of immediately starting to implement Points, Badges and Leader boards, effective Gamification is benefited by a well-designed Gamified system.

Therefore, Professor Kevin Werbach of Pennsylvania University has created the Gamification Design Framework. This framework helps marketers and other professionals to step by step design a Gamified system that encourages certain behaviour and stimulates engagement. Starting with the business goals, every aspect of a Gamified system is covered to finally decide which game elements should be applied in the system. The figure 1, shows the Process of Gamification.

The 6 steps in the gamification design framework are:

1. **Define Business Objectives:** Gamification must benefit the organisation. The ultimate goal of gamification must be defined.
2. **Delineate Target Behaviour:** Gamification must define what behavior is expected of its players and how they should be rewarded.
3. **Describe the Players:** Gamification must consider the target audience and who should be playing in the system.
4. **Devise the Activity Loops:** These make sure the players keep playing and are engaged in the system.
5. **Don't Forget the Fun:** Gamification must add an element of fun and competition.
6. **Deploy the Appropriate Tools:** Gamification must deploy appropriate tool necessary to design the system.

### Elements of Game Mechanism

Gamification has several use cases for successful application in the social media marketing of many corporates. It has now become an innovative way to engage and motivate customers using game mechanics. Several organizations have started creating social loyalty programs to improve their brand image. In order to achieve this, they are leveraging gamification behavior platform to structure such strategies. The typical architecture of any gamification initiative is essentially based on the following game mechanism –

1. **Rewards & Incentives**: To stay competitive, organizations prefer to run reward campaigns to offer discounts, promotions, and incentives to their employees, customers, and partners through Loyalty programs. Organizations design rewards structure that encourages desired behaviors in the employee-facing environment.
2. Badges-Badges or medals are awarded when an individual completes a task. This gives the user instant gratification. Badges act as a form of a digital identity. It serves as a source of one's accomplishment.
3. **Leaderboards**: Leaderboards are external motivational tools. It is an emerging practice in forward-looking organizations to assign Leaderboards in different areas of domain expertise across business

*Figure 1. Process of gamification*

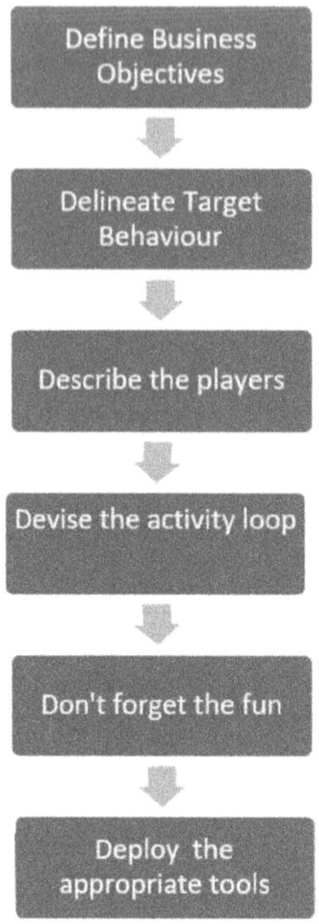


functions. People normally like to validate if they are performing well as per expectations or not. Leaderboard helps people to know where they stand relative to their colleagues or peers thereby inculcating a spirit of competition.

4. **Point System and Score**s: Users are given points whenever they accomplish something the system is trying to encourage them to do. Points keep score, provide immediate feedback, create a sense of progression and provide valuable data for the game designers. Points come in many different forms like experience points, redeemable points, Skill, karma and Reputation, etc. The criteria for awarding points broadly depend on following key attributes such as the speed of response, frequency of participation, quality of participation and learning outcomes.
5. **Levels (Status)**: Levels are a further indication of a user's progress within a game, and generally have one of two meanings. The first meaning indicates a user's status and mastery of a system (e.g. a "level 5" user is two levels higher than a "level 3" user).
6. **Level (Progress)-** The second meaning of levels indicates a user's position within a system. For example, a gamified system may have ten levels or areas that a user has to progress through, and a user on level five is only halfway through.
7. **Challenges & Quests**-Challenges are "puzzles or tasks that require effort to solve". They "give players direction for what to do within the world of the gamified experience". Usually, challenges and quests build on top of point-based systems and are focused on motivating users to accomplish even more difficult tasks.

8. **Competition**- Competition is something that can describe a situation where success can be measured in terms of outcome. Competition may take one or other form of a parameter such as speed, accuracy, creativity, strategic tactics, Knowledge and time. Competitions allow users to compete with one another, with a clear winner and loser.
9. **The cooperation-t**he opposite of competition, these allow users to work together and collaborate to accomplish certain tasks
10. **Narrative**- Narrative is a "consistent, ongoing storyline". In gamification, the narrative is perhaps one of the most overlooked aspects of games, which is problematic as videogame narrative is often one of the most powerful tools to engage users to complete a game.

## APPLICATION OF GAMIFICATION IN ORGANISATIONS

As mentioned in the previous sections that the usage of gamification is influenced by various intrinsic and extrinsic motivations, Performance Expectancy, self-efficacy, Social Influence, Facilitating Conditions and Behavioral Intention, and by various elements of the game, etc. The ramifications further result in a state of flow, immersions, absorptions and playfulness and enjoyment. Thus, the use of gamification results in a range of benefits to organizations.

### Benefits of Gamification

1. Gamification helps in building brand awareness. It helps to attract potential customers. By engaging the potential customer to follow, share or like a game /brand on social media
2. Gamification appeals to Millennial and Generation Z- Millennial and Generation Z like to connect digitally to the world. They are the generation who like to read, think critically and challenged. They are almost immune to the traditional form of advertising.
3. Gamification helps in the engaging customer. Gamification is an apt tool to influence user behavior, action, and purchase decision.
4. Gamification helps to gather relevant data and potential leads. For example, after engaging a customer in-game customer details can be seen in a non-intrusive way.
5. Gamification helps in creating a satisfying experience for customers. Offering customers rewards for winning contests, quizzes or comments keeps them coming back for more and builds loyalty.

The games and gamification have the potential to be used for a number of business areas. (Dixon, 2011) states that a game can be used in Marketing & promotions, HRM &Employee teamwork or Productivity, public policy and behavior changes, education & training and customer loyalty programs and so on.

### Games for Promotion

The purpose of the promotion is 'to inform present or potential consumers about the benefits of the product and inducing a consumer to either start buying or continue to buy the company product or service'(Kotler &Keller, 2006). There is a range of promotional mix elements such as; advertisements, sales promotion, Personal selling, and public relations, etc. that can be used to integrate the overall communication campaign. Gamification is an additional way to influence and engage consumers. The utilitarian (usefulness, ease of use) and hedonic (enjoyment, playfulness) factors are the main drivers of promoting users' involvement in gamification applications, At the beginning, the game mechanics should provide extrinsic rewards for like discounts, freebies, etc.; as the game progresses and the desired behaviour becomes more and more frequent, the rewards should be intrinsic and focus on special titles, social recognition, etc. (Adina, Valentin, Aurelian, Mihaela, & Rozalia, 2015). The next section describes some examples of Gamification in the promotion.

## Case of Prezi as Gamification:'Prezi Ambassador Program

As an alternative Microsoft PowerPoint, Prezi hosts its services online and offers a range of services in presentations such as zooming, turning, one big picture and so on. In order to attract to younger demographic pollution and the students (and potential users), the Prezi has started the 'Prezi Ambassador Program'. Globally, the students can apply for a voluntary Prezi Ambassador for their campuses. (Dixon, 2011) The selection criteria require the student to write a Prezi presentation plan to promote Prezi at the students' and run workshops for other students. All these activities will earn the participant Prezi status, some points, and merchandise (game elements). Further, the participants compete for bigger prizes such as a trip to the Prezi offices in San Francisco and Budapest. This increase brand buzz, customer engagement, fun, challenges and ultimately brand recall and loyalty.

## Case of M&M's Eye-Spy Pretzel

M&M'S one of the most loved brands among all ages is to a gamification classic(see figure 2) . In the year 2013, they launched an incredibly successful game as a part of its *'M&M's pretzel marketing campaign'*. This game was based on the eye-spy logic. It was inexpensive and simple, and yet became an instant hit among the audience of M&M's. The concept was that the users were basically presented with a large graphic design of M&M's candy, with one small pretzel hidden among them. The task

*Figure 2. M & M's EyeSpy Pretzel*

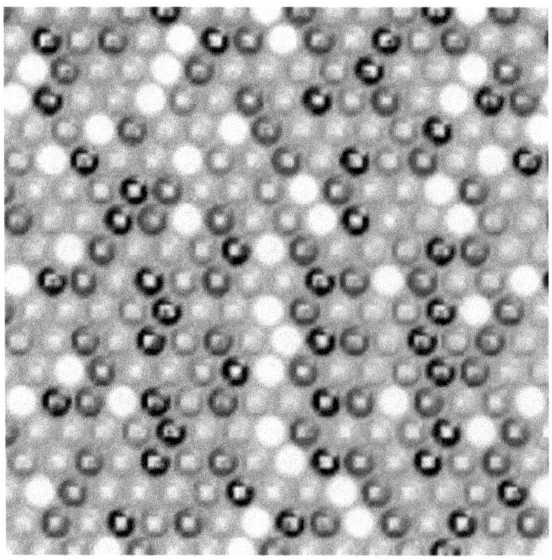

was to simply find the hidden pretzel. Though this game was a minuscule part of a massive marketing campaign, it offered a new fun way to engage with the company's new product and effectively helped to spread the word about it all over social media.

## Case of Nike: Nike+ Fuelband

One of the renowned company Nike uses personalized fitness tracking Nike+ and Fuel band accessories that allows Nike to connect with their customers and also gather valuable information about them. The personal data that Nike collects of their customers is a useful way of enhancing their targeted content marketing campaigns. Nike+ Fuelband gives its users some incentives for using the athletic tracking devices to compete against others while running and working out (see figure 3) . Some of the features of this device are that the NikeFuel app can be linked to social media, which enables its users to share and compare accomplishments. Badges are awarded for the same which influences buyers to use this.

## The Samsung Nation

To motivate its users to get more interactive and learn more from each other, Samsung had introduced another tech function that enabled its users to watch clips and discuss issues (see figure 4). In return, the most active users got badges through levels of progress.

## Games in HRM and Employee Team Work or Productivity

Human Resource Management (HRM 'is designing management systems to ensure that human talent is used effectively and efficiently to accomplish organizational goals' (Robert & John, 2008). Thus, it requires creating and maintain an environment in which employees increase their human capital (skills

*Figure 3. Nike fuel band*

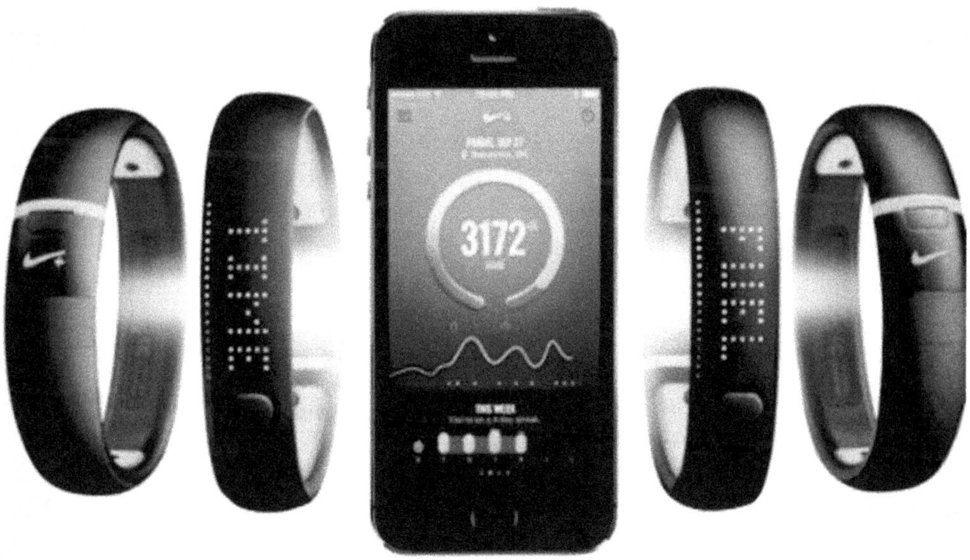

*Figure 4. Samsung nation*

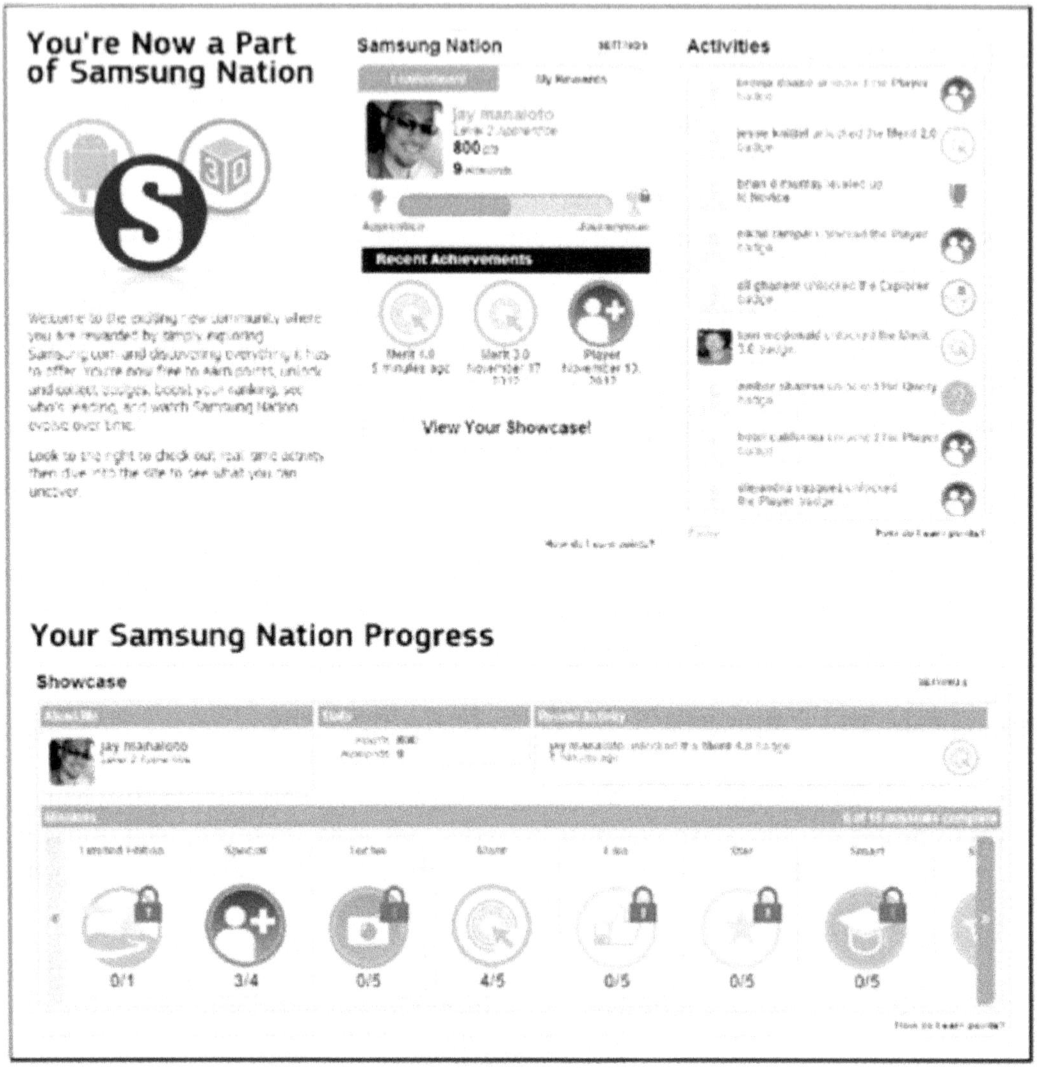


and competence) remain engaged, motivated and productive and become a core competency of an organisation. 'productivity is a measure of the quantity and quality of work done, considering the cost of the resources used' (Robert & John, 2008). The higher product has a range of antecedents including, employee engagement, motivation, team work, etc. Use of gamification has advantages to improve the competencies of employees and such gamification serve a range of benefits, as given below:

## Boredom to Interesting

Gamification enables to tweak processes and approaches by adding an element of fun in them, this makes the entire system interesting and removes the redundancy from it. Gamification in the workplace, market research and interacting with customers makes the process enjoyable and entertaining which improves the results and attitudes of employees and customers.

## Self-Motivated Employees

Employers that integrate gamification in the work experience will have a competitive advantage when it comes to attracting and retaining talent. Corporate reputations built by delivering creative ways to keep talented employees engaged goes a long way in attracting talented workers and sustaining employee satisfaction. When the organization puts a program in place for its employees, it keeps the employees motivated and builds a sense of belongingness within the organizations. 61% of surveyed CEOs, CFOs, and other senior executives say they take daily game breaks at work.

## Continuous and Instant Feedback

In today's always connected world, our attention spans have reduced. Everyone has grown used to ready access to information and real-time feedback. Gamification leverages this information derived through continuous and instant feedback and uses it to reinforce desired behavior. This loop of feedback enables valuable customer opinions to be obtained during launch cycles.

## Productivity and Return on Investment

Organizations are becoming more focused on business objectives, gamification helps in making the workplace more engaging and productive It changes the principles of engagement and inspires employees to change behaviors as a result. This shows a positive impact on productivity because the game like program brings in the sense of competition and achievement, which motivates employees to perform and excel at each level. The games can be customized according to business objectives, in order to reap most benefits from it.

## Case of Bunchball: Nitro for Salesforce

Bunchball, has developed a game like App Nitro for Salesforce, that uses cloud-based platforms to improve the efficiency of various organizational process; such as Sales management, CRM, inventory management, teamwork and HRM services (Dixon, 2011). The game lets' managers provide ' game points' to reward some specific behaviours of their subordinates; while the subordinates compete for game elements like trophies, badges, and status. The manager can give game points for specific expected behaviours (e.g., provide customer profiles, support with cold calls, Sharing specific information), which will actuary support a sales subordinate make a better sale.

## Games For Public Policy And Behavior Changes

The public policy includes the principles that guide the administration and governments for the public good. One of the public policy issues is sustainability. Sustainable development implies meeting the needs of the present generation without compromising the ability of future generation to serve their needs too (Ali& Frew, 2014). In other words, a sustainable or eco-friendly destination will balance the requirements of environment, economic and socio-cultural aspects.

## Sustainability

Gamification is a very viable and unique organizational strategy, games can be replayed multiple times, without incurring additional costs to the companies. It is a powerful tool for sustainability, as it combines fun with the process of business objectives, and makes the system more enjoyable, social and rewarding. Many organizations are applying gamification to protect our environment, as it empowers everyone to participate in the movement and have fun in the process.

The next section discusses some examples of Games related to public policy or behaviour change.

## Case of Foodzy: As Calorific Intake

Foodzy is an Amsterdam start up that helps people finding the perfect using A gamification App (Dixon, 2011). Everything a participant eats is noted as calorific intake. The participates can set goals for healthy living, compare and compete with friends and earn badges for healthy – and sometimes unhealthy – behaviour. Also, the app can be connected to hardware like the Fitbit – to measure movements and caries burnet, etc.

## Case of Volkswagen: 'Piano Stairs'

'The fun theory' was used by Volkswagen to enter their consumers were asked to come up with ideas to encourage positive behaviour by making it more fun. In one case, the people were asked to design fun games to encourage other people to take the stairs instead of the escalator. The outcome was a design where the stairs look and sound like a piano. Every touch of stair results in a different note. When the piano stairs where build, a lot of people changed their behaviour and took to the stairs (Dixon, 2011).

**Another Example is Volkswagen's** Speed Camera Lottery. When a participant passes the camera and keeps to the speed limit, he or she enters the lottery to win a cash prize. The prize is paid from the fines to the people that don't keep to the speed limit (Dixon, 2011).

## Games to Enhance Customer Loyalty

Gamification is making its mark in nearly every form of business, and this is being accelerated as data is available at real time. Organizations need actionable insights faster than ever before to stay competitive, reduce risks, meet customer expectations, and capitalize on time-sensitive opportunities. Consumer behavior can be tracked in real-time, analyzed and applied to plan strategies. In today's dynamic environment, all the users are accessible on a real-time basis and they demand information and updates on a real-time basis, this shows the changing business scenario and one which can be matched by gamification optimally.

A lot of companies use loyalty programs already. For example, Tesco club card, or Sainsbury Nectar and Amazon' Prime membership.

## A Case of GetGlue to Encourages Loyalty

A Game is designed by GetGlue to encourages loyalty for TV-series and films. Users that watch certain TV-series often or have watched a lot of series in the same genre can earn badges (Dixon, 2011).

## A Case of Starbucks Loyalty Programs

Gamification technique is introduced by Starbucks with the help of their loyalty programs. Starbucks rewards help to increase customer involvement and encourages repeat sales (see figure 5). The reward members from Starbucks keep on receiving various incentives like food and drinks free of charge. The customers also get certain points or stars with every purchase they make with Starbucks, which can later be redeemed for certain products or items. Free beverages on the birthdays and refills are other different rewards which are given to customers to increase their stars. More purchases help the customers to attain god status to get the best of offers. With this, the company gives the customers a sense of belongingness and achievement with the concept of customer loyalty. It is well intimated to them that if they are loyal, rewards will be reinforced with every purchase and transaction.

## Gamification in Education and Training And engagement

Learning is 'a holistic and circular process, which includes experiencing, reflecting, thinking, and acting accordingly (Kolb & Kolb, 20010). An experiencing of enjoyable and competitiveness in learning can enhance the learners' engagement in the process due to the feelings of pleasure, and to the stimulation to reflect (Kolb & Kolb, 2010). Thus, Including gamification elements in the learning process can benefit the learner's experience.Educational institutions use Web 2, based Learning Management Systems to manage the learning process and offer a variety of electronic courses with learning resources and activities. Such a platform is suitable for gamification.

*Figure 5. Starbuck rewards*

### A Case of Codecademy Applies Gamification

For example, Codecademy applies Gamification to teach people to code. On this free online platform, everyone can learn the basics of JavaScript, HTML5, and PHP (Dixon, 2011). By completing assignments and challenges, the player can earn points and badges.

### A Case of Domino's: 'Pizza Mogul'

Famous Food joint and an early mobile-adopter Domino's launched its latest play to yet again dominate the fast food pizza market – by a social gamification initiative dubbed '*Pizza Mogul*' (see figure 6). Pizza Mogul by Domino's is a responsive website and a mobile app that gives its consumers an opportunity to design their own pie, identity, and branding, and then share with their networks on social media and also earn a part of the revenue generated by its sales if that pizza turns out to be popular. The idea of this latest concept is to appeal the entrepreneurs as well as social media savvy pizza fanatics, giving them the freedom to use the Domino's like a pizza marketplace platform and create something that with influence a good image of the brand.

## GAMIFICATION ACROSS INDUSTRIES

Organizations across all industries are turning to gamification to encourage, incentivize and reward stakeholders to engage and implement the new business system, processes, and applications.

*Figure 6. Domino's pizza mogul*

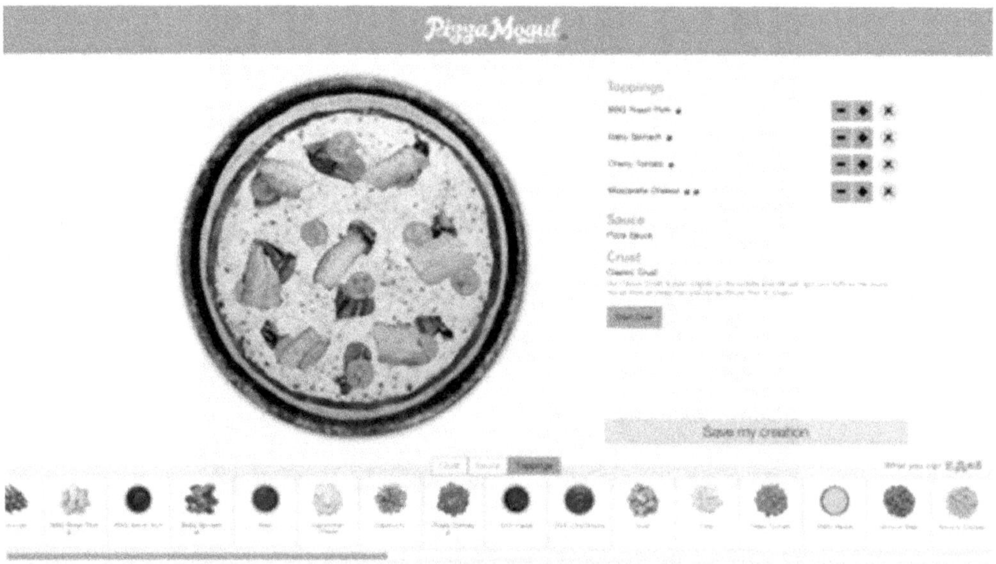

*Table 1. Games used in travel and hospitality industry*

| Game | Benefits | Game elements/ Features | Social Features |
|---|---|---|---|
| Gigya | Customer engagement Marketing campaign | Economy/Marketplace Levels & missions Profiles Ranks & badges | Activity feed Likes & comments Live chat Ratings & reviews Share plugin Social login |
| Badgeville | Customer engagement Marketing campaign | Competition Feedback Levels & missions Profiles Ranks & badges | Activity feed Ratings & reviews Social media log |
| Bamboo | Customer engagement Marketing campaign | Competition | Activity feed Social login |

Source: adapted from (Adina, Valentin, Aurelian, Mihaela, & Rozalia, 2015)

## Travel And Hospitality Industry

The buyers of gamification services in the tourism industry are hotel chains, restaurants, tour operators, local institutions, Destination marketing organisations, and NGOs.

Some of the Games used in Travel and hospitality industry cited by (Adina, Valentin, Aurelian, Mihaela, & Rozalia, 2015) are given below in Table 1:

## Automobile Industry

Ford Motor Company in Canada included gamification to its learning portals to assist the sales team that must have exhaustive information on new car models & features, financing plans and upgraded technologies every year. This resulted in 100% increased actions per user within 5 weeks and improved sales and customer satisfaction.

Volkswagen introduced gamification by crowdsourcing ideas for its product line and achieved 33 million webpage hits and 119,000 ideas through its People's Car Project which allowed people to design their "perfect car".

## Telecom Industry

CaLLogix wellness program reduced attrition by 50% and absenteeism by 80% while cutting insurance premium increase and improving overall company performance. The company saved $380,000 per year.

Verizon implemented personalized gamification as a result of which users spend over 30% more time on-site with social login games versus a regular site login.

## Banking, Financial Services, and Insurance Industry

Extraco Bank used gamification to educate their customers about the benefits and services the bank has to offer, their game had around 4,250 visitors and raised customer acquisition by 700%.

Australia's Commonwealth Bank developed Investorville, a real estate-investing game that improved the real estate knowledge of potential home buyers. The game featured an online simulator allowing players to experiment in real estate and investing without risking their equity. The most beneficial part of the game was that users can, in the true sense, try the property before they actually buy. The game generated about 600 loans within 1 year of launch.

### E-Commerce Industry

E-commerce site NextJump has taken corporate wellness program to the next level with gamification, where they encourage and incentivize employees to work out at the gym and are made to compete against peers and earn the chance of winning $1,000 each week.

### Entertainment Industry

MTV My Chart allows users to create their video chart based on various game dynamics and obtained 500,000 votes and 150,000 videos viewed within 3 months.

Much Music executed a social loyalty program, rewarding users with tangible gifts such as concert tickets and led to weekly activity increase by 59%.

## CONCLUSION

In today dynamic business environment where time and span of attention is limited, Gamification provides the opportunity to engage and build a relationship with the majority of customers in the company. Gamification as a concept has shown tremendous growth in achieving various social business initiatives in the corporates. Gamification has introduced a new way of thinking by aligning game objectives with the desired outcome in the corporates. Social business strategies are based more on high-end customer engagement and connections where consumer behavior patterns are highly dynamic Most of the global organizations have recognized the need to build customer communities that would encourage innovation, assess customer feedback and align product and services as per their requirement and demand. Gamification platforms are becoming key drivers to recognize customers who have performed key behaviors and motivate them to actively engage in these communities.

Gamification is a valuable resource organization can use today. Today most of the corporates are adopting the latest nexus of technologies such as mobile, cloud, business analytics, and artificial intelligence for their customers, investors, supplier, partners, employees, and expert. However, more and more organizations are adopting gamification. Gamification framework will play an important role to offer design for customer's efficient and fast gamification deployment.

## REFERENCES

Adina, L. N., Valentin, T., Aurelian, S., Mihaela, F. T., & Rozalia, V. R. (2015). Exploring Gamification Techniques and Applications for Sustainable Tourism. *Sustainability*, 11160–11189.

Ajzen, I. (1985). From intention to actions: A theory of planned behavior. In J. Kuhl & J. Bechmann (Eds.), *Action Control: From Cognitions to Behavior* (pp. 11–39). New York: Springer-Verlag. doi:10.1007/978-3-642-69746-3_2

Ajzen, I. (1991). The theory of planned behavior. *Organizational Behavior and Human Decision Processes*, *50*(2), 179–211. doi:10.1016/0749-5978(91)90020-T

Ajzen, I., & Madden, T. J. (1986). Prediction of goal-directed behavior: Attitudes, intentions, and perceived behavioral control. *Journal of Experimental Social Psychology*, *22*(5), 453–474. doi:10.1016/0022-1031(86)90045-4

Ali, A., & Frew, A. J. (2014). Technology innovation and applications in Sustainable destination development. *Information Technology & Tourism, 14*(4), 265-290.

Beltrán, J., Sánchez, H., & Rico, M. (2016). Increase motivation in learning Java Programming Fundamentals using Gamified Moodle: CaseL Central University of Ecuador. *2016 11th Iberian Conference on Information Systems and Technologies (CISTI)*, 1-4. 10.1109/CISTI.2016.7521419

Boer, P. (2013). *Introduction to Gamification in Docent Online Marketing*. Academic Press.

Boer, P. V. (n.d.). *Introduction to Gamification*. Retrieved 07 10, 2019, from CD University: https://cdu.edu.au/olt/ltresources/downloads/whitepaper-introductiontogamification-130726103056-phpapp02.pdf

Bogost, I. (2011, August 8). Gamification is Bullshit. *Ian Bogost*. Retrieved January 8, 2019, from http://www.bogost.com/blog/gamification_is_bullshit.shtml

Bradley, A. J., & McDonald M. P. (2011). *The Social Organization*. Harvard Business Review Press.

Burke, B. (2012). *Gamification 2020: What Is the Future of Gamification*. Gartner, Inc.

Challco, C. G., Moreira, A. D., Bittencourt, I., Mizoguchi, R., & Isotani, S. (2015). Personalization of Gamification in Collaborative Learning Contexts using Ontologies. *IEEE Latin America Transactions, 13*(6). 10.1109/TLA.2015.7164227

Charles, D., Charles, T., McNeill, M., Bustard, D., & Black, M. (2011). Game-based feedback for educational multi-user virtual environments. *British Journal of Educational Technology*, *42*(4), 638–654. doi:10.1111/j.1467-8535.2010.01068.x

Deloitte. (2012). *Tech Trends 2012: Elevate IT for digital business*. Author.

Deloitte. (2013). *Tech Trends 2013: elements of postdigital*. Author.

Deterding, S., Dixon, D., Khaled, R., & Nacke, L. (2011). From game design elements to gamefulness: Defining "gamification." In A. Lugmayr, H. Franssila, C. Safran, & I. Hammouda (Eds.), *Proceedings of the 15th International Academic MindTrek Conference* (pp. 9–15). New York, NY: ACM. 10.1145/2181037.2181040

Dicheva, D., Dichev, C., Agre, G., & Angelova, G. (2015). Gamification in education: A systematic mapping study. *Education Technology & Society*, *18*(3), 1–10.

Dixon, D. (2011). *Player Types and Gamification*. CHI, Vancouver, BC, Canada. Retrieved 07 10, 2019, from http://gamification-research.org/wp-content/uploads/2011/04/11-Dixon.pdf

Folmar, D. (2015). *Game it up: Using gamification to incentivize your library*. Rowman & Littlefield.

Francisco-Aparicio, A., Guti'errez-Vela, F., Isla-Montes, J., & Sanches, J. (2013). Gamification: Analysis and application. In V. Penichet (Ed.), *New trends in Interaction, Virtual Reality and Modeling, Human Computer Interaction Series* (pp. 113–126). London: Springer-Verlag.

Garm, L., & Slinger, J. (2014). Gamification in Consumer Marketing - Future or Fallacy? *Procedia - Social and Behavioral Sciences*, 194 – 202. Retrieved 07 10, 2019, from https://core.ac.uk/download/pdf/82546276.pdf

Gee, J. P. (2005). The new literacy studies: From'socially situated'to the work. Situated Literacies. *Reading and Writing in Context*, *2*, 177–194.

Gee, J. P. (2007). *What video games have to teach us about learning and literacy* (Rev. Ed.). New York, NY: Palgrave Macmillan.

Granic, I., Lobel, A., & Engels, R. C. M. E. (2014). The benefits of playing video games. *The American Psychologist*, *69*(1), 66–78. doi:10.1037/a0034857 PMID:24295515

Hamari, J., Koivisto, J., & Sarsa, H. (2014). Does Gamification Work? A Literature Review of Empirical Studies on Gamification. *Proceedings of the 47th Hawaii International Conference*. Retrieved 07 10, 2019, from https://www.researchgate.net/profile/Michael_Armstrong6/post/What_empirical_evidence_is_there_for_various_gamification_techniques/attachment/59d61dcb79197b8077979ce0/AS:273513875738624@1442222197132/download/2014-hamari_et_al-does_gamification_work.pdf

Huber, M. Z., & Hilty, L. M. (2014). Gamification and Sustainable Consumption: Overcoming the Limitations of Persuasive Technologies. In *ICT Innovations for Sustainability. Advances in Intelligent Systems and Computing*. Springer. Retrieved 07 10, 2019, from https://www.ifi.uzh.ch/rerg/people/kolpondinos/2014_Huber_Hilty_Gamification_and_Sustainable_Consumption_AAM.pdf

Hung, A. (2017). A Critique and Defense of Gamification. *Journal of Interactive Online Learning Volume, 15*(1).

Kolb, A. Y., & Kolb, D. A. (2010). Learning to play, playing to learn: A case study of a ludic learning space. *Journal of Organizational Change Management*, *23*(1), 26–50. doi:10.1108/09534811011017199

McGonigal, J. (2011). *Reality is Broken: Why games make us better and how they can change the world.* New York: Penguins Press.

Mood, A. M., & Specht, R. D. (1954). *Gaming as a technique of analysis*. Alexandria, VA: Department of Defense.

Nah, F. F.-H., Zeng, Q., Telaprolu, R., Ayyappa, A. P., & Eschenbrenner, B. (2014). Gamification of Education: A review of literature. In F. F.-H. Nah (Ed.), *HCI in Business* (pp. 401–409). Heraklion, Greece: Springer.

Palmer, Lunceford, & Patton. (n.d.). *The Engagement Economy - How gamification is reshaping businesses*. Deloitte Review Report. Retrieved from http://www.deloitte.com/ view/en_US/us/Insights/Browse-by-Content-Type/deloitte-review/c7cee86d96498310 VgnVCM1000001956f00aRCRD.htm

Phillips, C. (2014, July 9). *Domino's Unveils Social Gamification Initiative 'Pizza Mogul'*. Retrieved January 7th, 2019, from Power Retail.com: http://www.powerretail.com.au/technology/dominos-unveils-pizza-mogul/

Robert, L. M., & John, H. J. (2008). *Human Resource Managment* (Vol. 12). Mason, OH: Thomson South-Western. Retrieved 07 10, 2019, from https://core.ac.uk/download/pdf/33797590.pdf

Robson, K., Plangger, K., Kietzman, J. H., Mccarthy, L., & Pitt, L. (2015). Is it all a game? Understanding the principles of gamification. *Business Horizons*, *58*(4), 411–420. doi:10.1016/j.bushor.2015.03.006

Ruti, G., Dafni, B. A., Shimon, E., & Tomer, C. (2018). The effects of gamification elements in e-learning platforms. *Research, Organization, and Applied Innovation, 6*(2), 37-53. Retrieved 7 10, 2019, from http://www.iiakm.org/ojakm/articles/2018/volume6_2/OJAKM_Volume6_2pp37-53.pdf

Ryan, R. M., & Deci, E. L. (2000). Intrinsic and extrinsic motivations: Classic definitions and new directions. *Contemporary Educational Psychology*, *25*(1), 54–67. doi:10.1006/ceps.1999.1020 PMID:10620381

Schimmoeller, M. (2017). Strategies For Success. Academic Press.

Schwandt, F. (2018, February 25). *Mobile Application Revenue*. Retrieved from http://www.statista.com

Seaborn, K., & Fels, D. I. (2015). Gamification in theory and action: A survey. *International Journal of Human-Computer Studies*, *74*, 14–31. doi:10.1016/j.ijhcs.2014.09.006

Simões, J., Redondo, R. D., & Vilas, A. F. (2013). A social gamification framework for a K-6 learning platform. *Computers in Human Behavior*, *29*(2), 345–353. doi:10.1016/j.chb.2012.06.007

Stafford, C., & Mearns, M.A. (2009). What happens when organisations embrace social networking? Knowledge sharing at a multinational business solutions corporation. *South African Journal of Information Management, 11*(4).

Starbucks. (2013). *My Starbucks Rewards. Starbucks Coffee Company*. Retrieved January 7, 2019, from http://www.starbucks.ca/card/rewards

Volkswagen. (2009). Rolighetsteorin. *YouTube*. Retrieved January 7th, 2019, from http://www.youtube.com/user/Rolighetsteorin

Werbach, K., & Hunter, D. (2012). *For the Win: How Game Thinking Can Revolutionize Your Business*. Wharton Digital Press.

Zichermann, G. (2011). *Gamification - The New Loyalty*. Retrieved from http://vimeo.com/25714530

Zichermann, G., & Cunningham, C. (2011). *Gamification by Design: Implementing Game Mechanics in Web and Mobile Apps*. O'Reilly Media.

Zichermann, G., & Linder, J. (2013). *The Gamification Revolution: How Leaders Leverage Game Mechanics to Crush the Competition* (1st ed.). McGraw-Hill.

Zichermann. (n.d.). *The Six Rules of Gamification*. Retrieved from http://www.gamification.co/2011/11/29/the-sixrules-of-gamification

Zickermann, G. (2010, October 26). *Fun is the future: Mastering gamification*. San Francisco, CA: Google Tech Talk. Retrieved from https://www.youtube.com/watch?v=6O1gNVeaE4g

## KEY TERMS AND DEFINITIONS

**External Gamification:** The use of gamification involving customers as a "way to improve the relationships between businesses and customers, producing increased engagement, identification with the product, stronger loyalty, and ultimately higher revenues.

**Gamification:** The use of game-thinking and game mechanics to engage users and solve problems, it involves the use of game elements and game design techniques in non-game contexts. The motivations to use gamification may include extrinsic motives (tangible intangible rewards), intrinsic motives (status, achievements, self-expression, and competition) and so on.

**Human Resource Management (HRM):** Is designing management systems to ensure that human talent is used effectively and efficiently to accomplish organizational goals.

**Internal Gamification:** The use of "gamification to improve productivity within the organization in order to foster innovation, enhance camaraderie, or otherwise derive positive business results through their own employees.

**Learning:** Is a holistic and circular process, which includes experiencing, reflecting, thinking, and acting accordingly.

# Chapter 3
# Social Media Use as an Enabler of Marketing Evolution in Knowledge-Intensive SMEs

**Iva Atanassova**
*University of Essex Online, UK & Kaplan International, UK*

**Lillian Clark**
*QA Higher Education, UK*

## ABSTRACT

*This chapter identifies the operating and dynamic capabilities interactions that are supported by social media use in small and medium-sized enterprises (SMEs), specifically knowledge-intensive business services (KIBS). The focus on social media market intelligence accumulation and assimilation as an operating capability which enables dynamic marketing capability development in the SME marketing context, complements the prevalent focus in the literature on SME adoption and use of social media, as well as literature on how dynamic capabilities alter operating capability. The chapter presents a case study of a KIBS SME operating in South East England. Data was collected via semi-structured interviews with key actors and social media data, and thematically analysed. The findings suggest that the company develops absorptive capacity at the operating level by absorbing intelligence through social media use, and this learning is captured and transformed at the marketing planning level as a dynamic capability, reconfiguring future marketing operational capabilities.*

## INTRODUCTION

In an increasingly turbulent and knowledge-based economy, companies face a growing need for real-time market knowledge. Market knowledge and the ability to generate it are at the core of organisational competitiveness (Soto-Acosta, Popa, Palacios-Marques, 2017; Spender, 1996). Experiential learning is considered one of the most significant concepts for analysing the SMEs' ability to develop new understanding for problem-solving, opportunity identification (Covin and Slevin, 1989; O'Driscoll et al.,

DOI: 10.4018/978-1-7998-0131-3.ch003

2000; Paniagua and Sapena, 2014), and engagement in strategic renewal processes (Cope, 2005; Cope and Watts, 2000).

Although the SME literature is shifting from a static trait-based interpretation of the entrepreneur toward the entrepreneur as a permanent learner (Cope, 2005; Franco and Haase, 2009; Secundo et al., 2017) who is continuously engaged in entrepreneurial learning process, from a theoretical perspective many aspects of SME 'learning by doing' marketing approaches remain poorly understood (Cope, 2005).

Both academics and practitioners agree that social media has the potential to enhance organisational knowledge-sharing capabilities (Nguyen et al., 2015; Razmerita and Kirchner, 2011) and improve tacit knowledge accumulation and transfer (Lam et al., 2016; Panahi et al., 2012). To date, however, there is a lack of precise specification or empirical evidence for the exact processes and mechanisms of learning (Kim et al., 2013; Sun and Anderson, 2010; Zhang et al., 2006). Even less is known regarding social media's contribution to SME 'learning by doing' ad-hoc marketing practices (Durkin et al., 2013; Paniagua and Sapena, 2014).

These experiential learning processes are particularly important for high-tech firms, services, creative industries, academic and research spin-offs, as these companies generally play a critical role as knowledge providers. The expansion of the KIBS depends on development and management of new knowledge (Kim et al., 2013; Rae and Carswell, 2001). Due to the rapid changes in such industries, KIBS usually absorb information and favour exploration, experiential practices and iterative routines (Cope and Watts, 2000; Yli-Renko et al., 2001) in order to learn faster than the competition rather than to outplay them (Snyman and Kruger, 2004).

This book chapter describes a case study of an established KIBS SME and uses the MIATSM model of Atanassova and Clark (2015) to explore the marketing evolution triggered through their daily social media use. The MIATSM model draws on the dynamic capability (DC) and absorptive capacity construct (Teece et al., 1997; Cohen & Levinthal, 1990, Zahra & George 2002, Todorova & Durisin, 2007). The MIATSM recognises and conceptualises the organisational internal learning processes and impacting conditions of continuous market-based learning through the use of social media market intelligence as a source of organisational marketing capabilities and evolution. The data, collected through semi-structured interviews, observation, informal discussions, and social media data, allowed the researchers to understand processes that capture learning at the operating and dynamic capability levels, and transform this learning to marketing evolution. The marketing evolution is a process and stages through which the marketing concepts, philosophies, mechanisms, tools & techniques, and orientations of marketing are changing and has changed over the period of the history of marketing (Atanassova and Clark, 2015).

By developing and applying the MIATSM model of how social media contributes to firm evolution, the authors argue that the social media market intelligence is a strategic asset, the daily use of social media is an important operating capability within SMEs, and the corresponding DC is marketing strategy and operations planning and development.

## SME LEARNING AND MARKETING DEVELOPMENT

The organisational learning is a process of continually acquiring, developing and sharing knowledge skills and practices to enhance organisational effectiveness s(Catherine et aa, 2012). SMEs execute bottom-up, interactive approaches, without long-time planning of their marketing practices (Stokes and Nelson, 2013). High-performing SMEs "live" continuously with the market, by innovating their customer orientation through the development and maintenance of meaningful relationships with key customers (Lam, Sleep, Henning-Thurau, et al, 2018; Shaw, 2006). The SME's unique organisational settings facilitate shorter lines of communication, better internal information dissemination and experimental learning through interactions and relationships (Carson and Gilmore, 2000; Olavarrieta and Friedmann, 2008; Raju et al., 2011).

Market intelligence related to current and future customer needs enables superior organisational performance through a greater understanding of those needs (Kim et al., 2013; Kohli and Jaworski, 1990). The role of the entrepreneur to sense and exploit such opportunities and to encourage the development of 'deeper and wider' learning is confirmed as pivotal in SME marketing literature (Blackburn et al., 2013; Resnick, Cheng, Simpson, & Lourenço, 2016; Wiklund and Shepherd, 2003).

The SME's ability to mobilise resources and capabilities and align them dynamically with emerging environmental opportunities is vital to survival and creating competitive advantage (Kim et al., 2013; Liao et al., 2009). Continuous learning processes allow SMEs to develop and grow through constantly accessing vital and inexpensive environmental information (Franco and Haase, 2009; O'Donnell, 2014).

## SME SOCIAL MEDIA USE

Social media is the collective of web 2,0 based online communications channels through which communities can create contents, input, interact, share and collaborate information, co-create knowledge or contents, etc (Nguyen et al., 2015; Coyle, Smith, and Platt 2012). Social media platforms are eminently suitable for the types of personal networking and relationship building approaches practiced by SMEs. Social media is inexpensive, does not require advanced technical knowledge, and is easy to implement (Zeiller and Schauer, 2011). Social media can empower SMEs to overcome restrictions of their limited partnerships and geographic location by linking them with otherwise disconnected groups in a cost-effective way (Barnes et al., 2012; Harrigan 2015). Social media enables interaction, relationships, and mutual trust by giving companies opportunities to observe, listen and share (Nguyen et al., 2015; Coyle, Smith, and Platt 2012). SME social media use has been studied in the following context (see Table 1):

Studies have demonstrated various benefits of social media use for SMEs, such as fostering user engagement, participation, dialogue, engagement with core customers and building communities (Barnes et al., 2012; Clark, Black, and Judson 2017; Harrigan et al., 2012), knowledge reuse, collective innovation and personalization (Nguyen et al., 2015; Kim, Lee, & Lee, 2011; Bharati et al., 2015). Social media enables connection, co-creation, collaboration, crowd sourcing, and speeds up decision-making and value-creation (Nguyen et al., 2015). In addition, social media use is favourable for the development of proactive and collaborative cultures and mutual trust (Choudhury and Harrigan, 2014; Gnizy et al., 2014). Moreover, the knowledge accumulated through the use of social media is a strategic resource (Bharati et al., 2015; Lam et al., 2016; Kim, & Choi, 2019) and the organisational ability of market-sensing and customer-linking are critical influencers of firm performance (Trainor et al., 2013, 2014).

Although social media provides a platform for experience sharing, knowledge accumulation, and organizational learning (Nguyen et al., 2015), SMEs may not be realising the enhanced capabilities resulting from social media use (Barnes et al., 2012; Durkin et al., 2013; McCann and Barlow, 2015). In fact, the actual "utilization" of learning may take place long after the experience itself (Cope, 2005; Liao et al., 2003; O'Dwyer, 2009). Therefore, this book chapter explores the learning processes taking

*Table 1. Studies on Social Media*

| Studies of SME Social Media Use | Reference |
|---|---|
| Adoption of social media | Durkin et al., 2013; Meske and Stieglitz, 2013; Wu, 2013; Zeiller and Schauer, 2011 |
| Business operations | Seltsikas and Brown, 2006 |
| Internationalisation | Gnizy et al., 2014; Moini and Tesar, 2005 |
| Innovation | Hamburg and Brien, 2014; Mount, 2014; Lam, Yeung, & Cheng, 2016 |
| Customer relationships and communication | Durkin et al., 2014; Trainor et al., 2014; Guha, Harrigan, and Soutar, 2018 |
| Branding | Kim et al., 2011; Laroche et al., 2013; Nguyen et al., 2015 |
| Marketing, engagement, and managing brand communities | Berger and Thomas, 2014; Gilmore et al., 2007; Harris and Rae, 2009; Ramos-Rodriguez et al., 2011; Li and Du, 2011; Rui et al., 2010; Trusov et al., 2009; Lipsman et al., 2012; McCarthy et al., 2014; Michaelidou et al., 2011 |
| SME Knowledge management and sharing for value creation | Bharati et al., 2014, 2015; Gnizy et al., 2014; Hamburg, 2014; Hamburg and Brien, 2014 ; Hamburg, 2012; Panahi et al., 2012; Razmerita and Kirchner, 2011; Sawyer et al., 2014; Wong and Aspinwall, 2005; Zhang et al., 2015; Soto-Acosta, Popa, Palacios-Marques, 2017; Kim, J., & Choi, H., 2019 |
| Team collaboration | Cardon and Marshall, 2014; Zeiller and Schauer, 2011 |
| Marketing intelligence for CRM | Choudhury and Harrigan, 2014; Harrigan, 2013; Harrigan et al., 2009, 2011, 2012, 2015; Harrigan and Miles, 2014; Sethna et al., 2013; Trainor et al., 2014; Cheng, C., & Shiu, E., 2018 |
| Social media for internal collaboration | Huang et al., 2015 |
| Social Media performance measurement | Angel and Sexsmith, 2011; Berger & Thomas, 2014; Divol et al., 2012; Hoffman and Fodor, 2010; McCann and Barlow, 2015; Murdough, 2009; Stockdale et al., 2012 |
| Social media analytics for decision making | Bekmamedova and Shanks, 2014; Erevelles et al., 2016 |

(source: Authors)

place in an established (over 15 years old) KIBS SME, as it is considered more likely to have experienced the enhanced capabilities and strategic benefits of social media use.

Despite the growing importance of learning processes as a way of SME development and growth, previous research in organisational social media use has mainly focused on organisational outbound social media practices and on users' behaviour and little is known, particularly in relation to the impact of social media in SME marketing (Barger, Peltier, and Schultz 2016; Hodis et al., 2015; Lam et al., 2016; Guha, Harrigan, and Soutar, 2018. It is crucial to understand how managers are able to integrate the insight developed through social media use in their marketing decision-making (Chen et al., 2012).

## THE MIATSM MODEL

This chapter argues for market intelligence derived from social media as a strategic asset and a source of continuous learning processes development for marketing improvement in SMEs. In order to develop this argument, a suitable model is needed to study these processes - the MIATSM model.

The MIATSM model (Atanassova and Clark, 2015) is based on Dynamic Capability (DCs) theoretical lens. Dynamic capability theories that concentrate on growth by explaining change are incorporated in this model to understand SME experiential and idiosyncratic learning processes, and how these learning processes unfold and result in enhanced competencies (Franco and Haase, 2009; Zhang et al.,

2006). SMEs are naturally predisposed to develop and exhibit DCs and it is very important to understand the dynamics of their learning practices development, management and application as sources of high-quality, high-wage employment, innovative marketing practices and wealth creation (Freel, 2006; Whalen et al., 2016).

Knowledge and continuous organisational learning are considered core resources in the creation of DC, and are known in DC literature as "absorptive capacity" (Teece et al., 1997). These learning processes are fueled by context specific real-time market information, and as a result enable the organisational evolution through competencies and/or routines of acquiring, distributing, interpreting and storing external knowledge (Eisenhardt and Martin, 2000; Wang and Ahmed, 2007; Zahra and George, 2002). Moreover, of crucial importance is the ability to learn from mistakes and unlearn and destroy rigid routines in order to prevent strategic paralysis (Slater and Narver, 1995).

A key factor for competitive advantage is resources and capabilities heterogeneity, also known as VRIN (valuable, rare, inimitable, non-substitutable), and their imperfect distribution (Caloghirou et al., 2004). In the context of this research social media market intelligence is considered a strategic VRIN resource.

There are two types of organisational capabilities: operating and dynamic. Operating capabilities are routines, oriented toward fulfilment of day-to-day activities, such as: marketing operations, product development, social media use. Dynamic capabilities alter operating capabilities, known as evolutionary fitness. They are future-oriented, and are difficult to imitate organisational knowledge, skills and processes: strategic marketing planning, decision-making, product development (Day, 1994; Makadok, 2001; Winter, 2003).

In the context of this research, organisational operating capabilities depend on how well a firm coordinates the operating capabilities of information acquisition and sense-making through activities such as daily interactions on social media, while the dynamic capability determines how this learning is put into practice by changing the operating capabilities of online and offline marketing. The success of DC development is measured through changes in operating capability (Eisenhardt and Martin, 2000; Winter, 2003; Zahra et al., 2006).

Moreover, the MIATSM model recognises that '[o]rganizational learning is stimulated both by environmental changes and internal factors in a complex and iterative manner' (Dodgson, 1993, p. 387) and synthesises impacting internal and external factors in explaining the processes and their outcomes (Zhang et al., 2006). There is a need for a coherent, integrated framework to incorporate elements of the OL system, which comprises the 'continually evolving knowledge stored in individuals, groups, and the organization and constitutes the fundamental infrastructure that supports a firm's strategy formulation and implementation processes' (Vera and Crossan, 2003: 123). And for understanding the particular processes of entrepreneurial learning But the same cannot be said about empirical research on entrepreneurship, where a process orientation has been conspicuously absent.

As shown in Figure 1 Modified MIATSM Model, the key conditions that enable interactive learning processes are the exogenous conditions, where the company usually does not have control but instead have to sense and react to:

- Market dynamism,
- Triggers (if exogenous),

and the endogenous conditions, on which company has greater control and influence:

- Trigger (if endogenous),
- Background / prior knowledge,
- Resources (physical),
- Actors,
- Structure & systems,
- Internal culture.

These factors and conditions have been synthesized from both DC literature (Ambrosini and Bowman, 2009; Cohen and Levinthal, 1990; Todorova and Durisin, 2007; Zahra and George, 2002) and entrepreneurial marketing literature (Hill and McGowan, 1996). The latter factors and conditions have been investigated at the operating capability level of daily social media use, in order to achieve an in-depth understanding of the first two learning processes. The factors have been removed from the exploitation stage of the research (see MIATSM model, Atanassova & Clark, 2015, p.171), when the exact changes in the marketing operations are to be considered.

The MIATSM model guides this study as it brings together the three processes of interest - the process used to absorb market intelligence, the process of making sense of that learning, and lastly how that sense-making is exploited in terms of reconfiguration of marketing operating capabilities - and the impacting factors identified through the extensive literature review, to provide an in-depth understanding development of this under-researched area.

## RESEARCH DESIGN

Case studies and qualitative research methods have been recommended as appropriate to study SME learning processes (Secundo et al., 2017), decision-making processes within small firms (Curran and Blackburn, 2001; Gilmore and Carson, 1996; O'Dwyer et al., 2009) and also SME marketing practices (Harrigan & Miles, 2014). In this book chapter, a single case study is described to demonstrate how a

*Figure 1: Modified MIATSM Model of the processes of market intelligence accumulation through social media use and its assimilation and application in SME marketing activities*

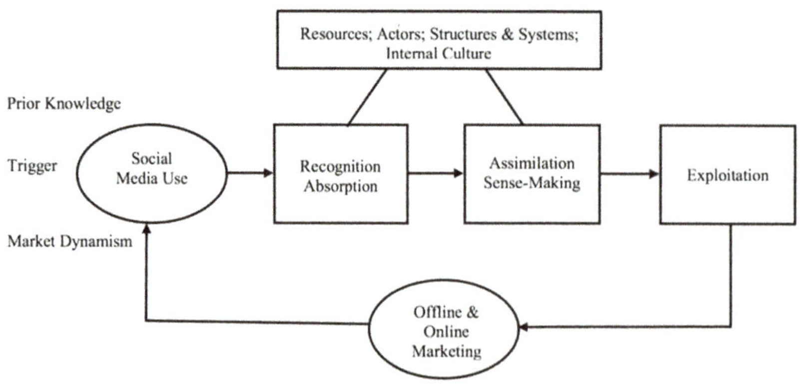

knowledge-intensive SME uses social media to develop new understanding and learning processes and subsequent marketing evolution.

The MSM model and the case study design enable identification of the processes and the impacting organisational components (Yin, 2003). It also provides an opportunity to observe how such processes unfold among organizational actors and how changes in external and internal organisational context (synthesized constructs) influence the processes of interest. As a result, the research design helps in explaining the results observed and how differences in the motivations and abilities of organizational actors, resources dedicated, structure and systems and internal culture contributed to those results.

## Data Analysis

The researchers built their understanding of how learning processes at exploration and exploitation level unfold through the MIATSM model, identifying patterns in Company A's marketing choices that were a result of social media use. The interview data were triangulated with social media data extracted from company social media accounts to illustrate examples and/or uncover discrepancies between what was said during the interview and actual practice. The data collected for Company A was coded under key constructs of the MIATSM model and thematically analysed through Nvivo11. The analysis examined each construct of the model separately - absorptive capacity on operating and dynamic capability levels and the contributing context - and then how the three routines developed over time and enabled marketing evolution.

## Development of the Case Study

Company A is one of the fastest-growing and leading digital agencies in the South East of England. Company A has its own platform that collects and integrates data from a multitude of sources across all digital initiatives. The company has 49 employees and has over a decade of experience.

Data was collected through interviews with the company's Head of Marketing (HoM) and the Services Director (SD), and triangulated with social media data, work environment observation and informal discussions with employees. Both participants worked for more than three years at Company A and have an in-depth understanding of the business.

In order to draw conclusions about how social media intelligence empowers the interactions between operating and dynamic capabilities and how the latter affects organisational marketing evolution, the analysis consisted of four phases:

1. The organisational background was developed using MIATSM model (MIATSM model's factors) in order to better understand the context, market dynamism, triggers for social media use, and prior knowledge.
2. An understanding of how absorptive capacity processes took place at the operating capability level through the daily use of social media was developed by focusing on knowledge recognition and absorption and the enabling/hampering conditions.
3. Following on from the above, assimilation and sense-making processes were explored by again considering the enabling/hampering conditions, and the transfer of the learning to a higher-order dynamic level.

4. Lastly, the exploitation of the developed learning is studied, in terms of changed marketing routines, followed by an exploration of how it affected as a result organisational subsequent choices for corporate re-branding / unlearning, seen as a dynamic capability.

## PRESENTATION AND DISCUSSION OF FINDINGS

### Background / Prior History

Information about the first condition facilitating the researched learning processes as part of the conceptual model was collected in the first stage of the research by understanding Company A's internal context. The concept of path / prior knowledge recognises that history matters and that the opportunities are "closed in" to previous activities (Cohen and Levinthal, 1990; Teece et al., 1997). It is critical to understand how Company A's prior learning enables individuals with a sense of direction and belonging, and helps keep the organisational focus clear and enables them to search, identify and acquire the external knowledge befitting organisational objectives (Kim et al., 2013).

Company A is one of the leading agencies in the South of England and this is reflected in their numerous industry awards and recognitions. They acknowledge, however, that the competition is very intense, and according to the HoM:

*we are the only search agency, or the only digital agency, to offer this level of data insight at this stage right now, I mean the industry is catching up and they're hot on our heels...*

The participants explained that they have to constantly evolve, and were able to identify early market signals indicating the need for automation of their data mining processes, developing their own data mining platform which gave them a competitive edge. To understand the strategic position and purpose of the organisation, the participants were asked to articulate the organisational mission and values. Both the HoM and the SD explained their mission and organisational philosophy around being open, creative and transparent, aimed at learning and educating both employees and audiences.

#### Marketing Strategy

Company A pursues an aggressive goal to expand market share and develop their branch office. To achieve this, they set up specific marketing objectives around brand awareness and reaching new audiences. The company constantly iterates their organisational actions and tactics to fit the environment and their marketing plan is under continual revision. The company has a six-month plan, a one-year plan and a five and ten-year plan and a series of campaign-based tactical plans. The HoM reviews campaigns performance every Friday, and adjust tactics and actions accordingly by meeting with the marketing team every Monday.

*HoM: ...things move so quick that if we just stop what we were going to do twelve months ago we'd be losing now.*

## Social Media Adoption Triggers / Exogenous Shocks

The second and third facilitating conditions - trigger of social media use and market dynamism - were also explored as part of the first stage of the interview.

Changes in technologies and a dynamic marketplace have been pointed out as drivers of change in Company A's business practices and triggers of social media use. The company started as a search engine optimisation (SEO) agency, however their portfolio has evolved constantly. As trends and technologies developed, such as content marketing and social media, the company leadership quickly identified early signals and continually added services/products to their portfolio and adopted organisational expertise and practices to stay ahead of the competition.

*SD: ...Google do updates all the time and we just have to make sure that we're aware of them...*

Particularly in relation to Social Media use, the HoM explains:

*...I think that social media has massively opened up the doors for that fact that Twitter feeds come up now in result pages so they're sharing their information so it's just making sure that you see that as an opportunity that we seized quite early on...*

## Social Media Use on a Daily Basis

Company A sees social media as an important component of their digital communication mix. The company has active accounts in numerous social media sites however, they mainly use Facebook and Twitter.

The content produced is customer-centred with clear focus on educating the readers. Their company blog is called a "learning blog"; and its focus is on creating content that provides value and enhances their customers' business. They create immersive experiences, through the use of data, technology and storytelling.

Examples of blog topics:

*Getting your landing page design right can make all the difference to your conversions....*

*What's actually involved in driving those 12,734 clicks a client achieved in the past month? ...*

*Real people's opinions and soundbites add colour, personality, and credibility to an article. To enrich your content, here are ten interviewing tips.*

*You've no doubt heard of UX >> Check out the benefits it can have for your business.*

## Sources of Market Intelligence

Both participants agreed that they are aiming to be constantly open and receptive to signals indicating changes in their market place. Amongst the other social media platforms, the HoM highlighted specialised industry blogs as crucial sources of information, particularly for spotting new opportunities and trends in changes in customer behaviour and technology.

The participants pointed out the key role of their own data platform in supplying market intelligence that is regularly monitored such as: who's checking their profiles, who's engaging with their social media, who their key influences are, what their activities are.

The three learning processes and impacting conditions have been synthesized in Tables 2-4, which shows the interlinking role of the market intelligence supplied by social media at the operating and dynamic capability level.

The market intelligence gathered has an impact at both levels but for different purposes. A discussion of the main findings at each learning process level and affecting conditions follows.

## Absorptive Capacity as an Operating Capability – Recognition, and Absorption (Exploration)

### Internal Culture, Structure and Systems

The participants claimed a high sense of purpose, integrity, and motivation. Their organisational culture has been described by both participants as receptive and innovative. The MIATSM model highlighted Company A's internal culture as a particularly important key enabler of the recognition and absorption process. Particularly, their collaborative learning and shared values are important antecedents and facilitators of the processes of market knowledge absorption.

*Everything we do is about improvement, is being the best that we can be, so... There's a sales guy in the sales team who used to deliver PPC, he said to me the other day he used to deliver PPC at his old job and now he sells it, he said he's learned more since he came here to sell it than he knew before when he was delivering it...So the people who just learn new stuff all the time and there's nobody who comes here who doesn't say they've learned so much since they've joined, and it's just constant...*

### Actors: Everybody is Encouraged to Spot Intelligence

Company A constantly invests in developing their people competencies and skills. They have a staff development 'package', and provide a wide variety of half-day classes to develop their employees' skills and encourage them to develop a second area of specialism.

*HoM: We do have a very much, without sounding too cheesy, what with the [Company A] there's a huge investment from the management team into the staff, we run a massive training programme, everyone's involved in everything, like we have the transparencies summer parties, that kind of thing, so there is a kind of helping each other out kind of feel to everything...*

Company A organises internal social media competitions to vary the content and incentivise employees to contribute to organisational social media presence and in their networks, and thus become brand ambassadors. For example, the company recently held a "Twitter takeover" in which every employee was encouraged to take over the Twitter account for two days to see who they would reach.

*Table 2. Absorptive capacity process "Recognition & Absorption" taking place at operating and dynamic capabilities level in Company A*

| Absorptive Capacity Processes | Operating Capability | Conditions Impacting | | | | Dynamic Capability |
|---|---|---|---|---|---|---|
| | | Internal Culture | Structure & Systems | Actors | Resources | |
| Recognition & Absorption | Daily Use of Social Media; Outside-in activity of Recognition, Creation & Acquiring of Relevant Information; **Sources of Information:** Combination of Social Media platforms, Marketing blogs, Own software, Apps to aggregate news; | Perceive social media as a knowledge source; informal, open culture; embrace experimentation; sharing, motivational (competitions, fun), sense of purpose, facilitative leadership / endogenous entrepreneurship; owner involved in social media use; trial and error approach to social media; Incentives to use/manage/contribute to company social media: team buildings, conferences, games room; constant investment of resources to create content and update / engage; | Clearly defined and communicated mission, strategic goal, objectives; Focus on scanning and detecting early signals "every piece of information is of interest to us" | Could be anyone in the company depending on a specialism, mainly the marketing team; | Budgets to develop and educate staff; Budgets for Advertising on Social Media; own software; | Incoming market intelligence from the operating level; learning at the operating level; prior knowledge / experience; Head of Marketing, Head of Social Media, Services Director, CEO |

(source: Authors)

*Table 3. Absorptive capacity process "Assimilation & Sense-Making" taking place at operating and dynamic capabilities level at Company A*

| Absorptive Capacity Processes | Operating Capability | Conditions Impacting | | | | Dynamic Capability |
|---|---|---|---|---|---|---|
| | | Internal Culture | Structure & Systems | Actors | Resources | |
| Assimilation & Sense-Making | Sense-Making of incoming information in the context of marketing; Transfer to Relevant Actors, Departments & Storage & Using the Market Intelligence Acquired to refine Marketing/Branding; to inform strategic decisions on the base of the understanding developed; | Mission is interwoven in sense-making; clear purpose, objectives; | Regular cross and interdepartmental meetings (weekly, monthly) Informal lunches etc.; constant revisions of strategy; Internal blog & CRM database for knowledge storage and management; open space office, use social media for collaboration on projects, sharing and saving; internal blog, skype, e-mail; social tagging; **Performance Measurement/Technical Fitness:** KPI software, CRM database, own software; | The Social Media Director, Head of Marketing, Services Director, CEO & any employee in the company; constant investment to develop employees' skills: external and internal training; teach each other; | KPI software to evaluate, internal blog, own software, CRM database; | Sense-making process of determination whether knowledge from operating capability level should lead to changes, iterations or unlearning / complete ceasing of a particular marketing activity & Higher-order process of using the knowledge to take a decision about the current and future marketing, CRM, corporate brand in the interest of firm evolution; |

(source: Authors)

*Table 4. Absorptive capacity process "Exploitation" taking place at operating and dynamic capabilities level at Company A*

| Absorptive Capacity Processes | Operating Capability | Conditions Impacting | | | | Dynamic Capability |
|---|---|---|---|---|---|---|
| | | Internal Culture | Structure & Systems | Actors | Resources | |
| Exploitation | Implementation of the New Corporate Brand; Delivery of the refined marketing activity to the audience (new website, blog posts, other social networking activities to promote / educate people about their brand evolution); | Inside out activity; Changes implementation by relevant actors | | | | Adaptive Capability; Implementing the strategic decision / choice at an operating level. Implications for corporate brand presentation on social media, offline marketing materials, social media; storytelling capability development; product and service development; Source expertise, ideas, skills; Development of multiple VRIN resources: clear differentiation, concise brand image; internally: dialogue, speed, transparency & externally: awareness, loyalty, motivation, relationships, engagement |

(source: Authors)

*SD: I wrote a haiku poem for every member of staff to describe them and posted it as a series of haikus, but that was fun…when the initiatives and things like that are fun nobody really says no I'm not going to do this...*

Moreover, it is seen as a privilege by employees to contribute content and engage with organisational social media accounts, and this is emphasized as a meaningful activity.

*HoM: it's quite a thing to be part of the A team, you know I've been picked to be in the A team and I get chosen to do that, so it's making sure that people feel kind of proud of the brand I suppose really.*

The MIATSM model highlights the company management as vital for the processes of exploration. The leadership exhibits ability to translate business goals into customers and employee-friendly initiatives that are welcomed and enjoyed by everyone.

In a blog post, one of the company employees pointed out:

*A culture that recognises the importance of growth, respect and trust plays a central role in making [Company A] a great place to work.*

In another blog post, an employee adds:

*Our CEO [name] and the team of directors have worked hard to craft a culture that nurtures talent, encourages positivity and makes being at work both fun and rewarding.*

## Facilitative Leadership

The owner-manager has been described by both participants as the biggest proponent of social media and the driver of the collaborative-learning culture, always reading and sharing on social media. The owner-manager drives the organisational mission and vision and strategic direction, leading the interactive learning processes.

*SD: It does come from [the owner-manager] I guess because people see that behaviour as a good thing and [the owner-manager] encourages it in others...*

## Bad Reviews are Seen as an Opportunity

Furthermore, the participants consider bad reviews as opportunities to turn bad reviews into a positive customer experience.

*HoM: ... because everybody knows that no-one's perfect or what have you, I actually think there's huge opportunity with negative reviews so just think you've got to play to your strengths really.*

Participants are not afraid of making mistakes, avoid blaming and solve problems by experimentation. To them, the real problem is when bad reviews are ignored and left unanswered, which reflect negatively on the company's image by creating a social media "storm".

*HoM: ...so it's all about sharing and learning and yes it's helped relationships, and some people are averse to change so... you have to keep evolving and keep changing stuff, and some people regard that as a negative...*

The participants conclude that employees should be stimulated and given the opportunity to experiment with social media, listen, understand, and engage with the people, skills that the HoM points out are incredibly difficult to teach. As skills of secondary importance, the participants ranked conventional marketing planning knowledge.

## Assimilation and Sense-Making (Transformation)

The second process in the MIATSM model is the process of assimilation and sense-making. For this stage of the research, data was collected on how the learning at an operating level is transferred to a higher order strategic level and exploited in terms of translation to actual decisions in relation to marketing strategy/practice changes.

This process of learning transfer and storing is acknowledged as very challenging to organisations from an OL point of view, as individual tacit knowledge is the most difficult type of knowledge to acquire, convert and store, (Pawlowsky, 2001; Senge, 1990; Zhang et al., 2006).

## Internal Culture, Structure and Systems

The HoM explained that everyone has input into someone else's job and provides an example from cross-departmental meetings where one of the accountants often gives valuable advice and helps to market employees spot solutions.

*...you're letting somebody else look at you and see it from another angle and going well here's an idea. Our accounts [name]...sometimes come up with some nice gems in our meetings, [they] go well have you tried this? Cos [they] sit quite outside of it and we all go oh, good idea, why did not we think of that?*

This collaboration, creativity, and integrity are reflected also in their open space office layout, which supports sharing and collaboration.

*HoM: I think we're all happy to learn, we're an industry that's moving really, really fast and we're all dead chuffed to be part of that industry and I think that kind of feeds through, you know the whole transparency and the trust and you know...*

Through a process of gradual sharing and assimilation of ideas and knowledge, they constantly and evolve.

*HoM: There's a lot of osmosis going on round here.*

## Actors

Once again, the process of assimilation and sense-making is seen as a shared responsibility:

*SD: I share information regarding tools or things I've found that I think everyone should read, the MD shares a lot of stuff, a lot of members of staff do the like tip sessions for each other...the social media guys might stand up and do a little ten minute tips session on how to get more out of Twitter.*

The company mission is interwoven in everything they do and staff is constantly searching, sharing, learning and teaching each other.

*HoM: we have like an internal mission and vision that works about innovation and it's something that's kind of fed through everything that we try and do so we're always trying to, it's not about I'm in it for me, I'm in it for us so we try very much to not fight against each other, we're all on the same side so if I can help you then absolutely I will, ...so I think that it's a cultural thing rather than a particular...basically we're teaching each other about things we're discovering which is really important.*

## Integration and Storage of New and Old Knowledge

SMEs face particular challenges in knowledge codification and retention stage, as their knowledge is stored mainly in employees' and owner's heads (Wong and Aspinwall, 2004). Company A, however, uses an internal blog for storing important information. The employees use this blog as a repository for research, policies, statistics, internal articles, and blog articles for future use. Additionally, they have a CRM database where all information about clients and prospects is stored.

## Exploitation

Lastly, the exact dynamic capabilities performed by the company and the resulting changes triggered in their marketing operating activities are identified. The developed absorptive capacity makes it possible for the company to identify how and where to absorb, assimilate and exploit new knowledge within the social media community. Company A's frequent interactions with external and internal audiences lead them to become proactive and optimistic about the prospects identified. This, in turn, leads to an emphasis on new knowledge and technologies as drivers of development.

*HoM: Yeah we're constantly evolving, I mean Google has a philosophy that it will create something and it will get it out onto the marketplace and then improve it as the market started to use it, I think our approach is the same thing, just get it going and just constantly tweak it and make it better as you go along...*

### Relationships, Engagement, Learning (VRIN resources)

Company A reported multiple VRIN resources that were developed through their daily interactions and social media learning. The main VRIN resources developed are relationships, trust, and engagement, both externally and internally.

### Unlearning and Learning from Mistakes as a Dynamic Capability

Company A recently consolidated their three sub-brands in response to signals indicating brand inconsistency. They identified that the numerous interactions taking place under different brands were confusing and fragmented both for their employees and their clients, and claimed social media helped them to understand, realise and take actions to solve this issue. By consolidating sub-brands and launching a new website, they were able to transform this fragmented image into a consistent brand image and achieve differentiation, building a clearly communicated competitive advantage and integrated customer experience.

*HoM: ...we've got members of staff who say they work for one brand and members of staff who say they work for another, that means on Linkedin you've got all three different brands, on Twitter you've got people posting as [brand name] and [brand name], and it means you're actually fragmenting your ability to push the marketplace and to talk to people with one voice, so we decided to consolidate under one brand again which was a big decision for us last year, and we did that with the new site in February, and that was a response to just circumstance really, it just proved to be too difficult, and we've still retained our important message of having specialists deliver the service but now we can say those specialists work for the same brand and it just makes it feel like a bigger agency, and I think that was a necessary change...*

The advantages of the re-branding were highly valued.

*HoM: ...it's very, very clear who our type of audience is, how we're going after them, how we can service them, our key differentiators, got one message, it's incredibly strong, whereas before it was like oh [Name of First Company], yeah that's not our strap line, our key thing is momentum but [Name of Another Brand] were all about content-driven research but [Name of the Third Brand] were all about, can't even remember what [Name of Third Brand] was now, and then we had [Name of Parent Brand] as well, and it was all disjointed and mish mash so yeah, it's a huge relief for clients as well so yeah.*

Moreover, Company A cut the costs involved in supporting three sub-brands. Their new master brand strategy provided benefits for the company which lies mainly in minimising the business challenges and opportunities they face in today's fragmented media landscape. Their marketing communications were iterated to reflect and promote the new brand image, for example, paid targeted advertising was introduced to support building the organic following of their new web site.

*HoM: We learnt that we weren't doing ourselves any favours so we changed it.*

In an internal blog post from 2015, the owner-manager of the company referred to the consolidation of brands as " the next step in our evolution".

## SOLUTIONS AND RECOMMENDATIONS

This study suggests that the operating capability of daily social media use and dynamic capabilities of marketing activity planning have complementary roles in facilitating SME marketing evolution. These findings also highlight the SME context and leadership as crucially important for absorptive capacity development on the operating and dynamic capability level, as defined from an absorptive capacity perspective (Van den Bosch, Van Wijk & Volberda, 2003) and a DCs perspective (Eisenhardt & Martin, 2000; Ambrosini & Bowman, 2009). Organisational context is also pointed out as highly important in the SME literature due to its variety in the SME context (Carson, Gilmore, & Rocks, 2004; Resnick et al., 2016).

Company A demonstrates a combination of processes, infrastructure and culture to gather, transform, and exploit knowledge from social media, relevant to future marketing actions. The company built their skills base and developed the ability to rapidly identify opportunities and areas of improvement on the basis of ad hoc learning through social media, leading to almost constant extension and diversification of organisational marketing operating capabilities. Directed by their visionary leadership, the company achieved alignment of their overall corporate strategic purpose and mission and their digital initiatives by nurturing an agile culture, and having the right organisational factors/conditions (internal culture, structure and systems, actors, resources) in place, which emerged as dramatically important for the learning processes development. This adaptive culture and operational effectiveness were established as more important than the long-term marketing strategy.

## FUTURE RESEARCH DIRECTIONS

The researchers are aware of the limitation of the single case study research strategy in terms of generalizability (Denzin, 1997). Despite these limitations, the research has uncovered several valuable theoretical and practical contributions.

Through the MIATSM model linkage between daily social media use, market intelligence accumulation and KIBS SME marketing evolution is established. This research makes an original contribution by presenting a theoretical model and empirical evidence of how daily social media use is an important operating capability and a source of continuous learning for KIBS SME marketing evolution through dynamic capabilities development.

Practical implications of this research are in highlighting the importance of establishing mechanisms to exploit social media as a knowledge source, enabling learning and marketing evolution. It is recommended that SME OMs should approach social media with an open mind, in order to generate informational advantages. SMEs that have failed to benefit from the use of social media as a knowledge source for marketing development are encouraged to use the proposed framework to identify weak areas associated with their social media use for development of marketing activities. They should carefully assess which of the proposed impeding factors are inhibiting the particular absorptive capacity process development.

Future research needs to explore the suitability of the MIATSM model to uncover the learning processes taking place in SMEs of different kinds, size, and age and in larger samples. It is suggested that the MIATSM model could provide valuable insight to larger businesses as well, as they are often limited in transformational activities and evolution due to their hierarchical organisational structure, bureaucracy and rigid routines (Argyris, 1986).

## CONCLUSION

Although research confirms that companies must utilize customer insights obtained from social media to continuously redefine their marketing activities (Erevelles et al., 2016; Nguyen et al., 2015; Story, O'Malley, & Hart, 2011) what has been lacking is precise specification of the exact processes, contributing context, and empirical evidence of 'learning by doing' processes taking place in SME marketing context as a result of their social media.

Through the lens of the MIATSM model (Atanassova and Clark, 2015), it is clear that social media market intelligence is a strategic asset that penetrates all areas of the studied KIBS SME and enables real-time learning and market evolution. Consistent with the MIATSM model and dynamic capability theory, the marketing planning process in this study was shown to transform developed learning into corporate re-branding. This transformation underscores the implications of social media use at the firm level (Hodis et al., 2015; Lam et al., 2016) and the entrepreneurial 'learning by doing' processes taking place in the KIBS SME (Cope, 2005; Secundo et al., 2017).

## REFERENCES

Ambrosini, V., & Bowman, C. (2009). What are dynamic capabilities and are they a useful construct in strategic management? *International Journal of Management Reviews*, *11*(1), 29–49. doi:10.1111/j.1468-2370.2008.00251.x

Atanassova, I., & Clark, L. (2015). Social media practices in SME marketing activities: A theoretical framework and research agenda. *Journal of Customer Behaviour*, *14*(2), 163–183. doi:10.1362/14753 9215X14373846805824

Barger, V., Peltier, J. W., & Schultz, D. E. (2016). Social Media and Consumer Engagement: A Review and Research Agenda. *Journal of Research in Interactive Marketing*, *10*(4), 268–287. doi:10.1108/JRIM-06-2016-0065

Barnes, D., Clear, F., Dyerson, R., Harindranath, G., Harris, L., & Rae, A. (2012). Web 2.0 and micro-businesses: An exploratory investigation. *Journal of Small Business and Enterprise Development*, *19*(4), 687–711. doi:10.1108/14626001211277479

Bharati, P., Zhang, W., & Chaudhury, A. (2015). Better Knowledge with Social Media? Exploring the Roles of Social Capital and Organizational Knowledge Management. *Journal of Knowledge Management*, *19*(3), 456–476. doi:10.1108/JKM-11-2014-0467

Blackburn, R. A., Hart, M., & Wainwright, T. (2013). Small business performance: Business, strategy and owner-manager characteristics. *Journal of Small Business and Enterprise Development*, *20*(1), 8–27. doi:10.1108/14626001311298394

Caloghirou, Y., Protogerou, A., Spanos, Y., & Papagiannakis, L. (2004). Industry-Versus Firm-specific Effects on Performance: Contrasting SMEs and Large-sized Firms. *European Management Journal*, *22*(2), 231–243. doi:10.1016/j.emj.2004.01.017

Carson, D., & Gilmore, A. (2000). Marketing at the Interface: Not 'What' but 'How'. *Journal of Marketing Theory and Practice*, *8*(2), 1–7. doi:10.1080/10696679.2000.11501863

Chen, H., Chiang, R., & Storey, V. (2012). Business intelligence and analytics: From big data to big impact. *Management Information Systems Quarterly*, *36*(4), 1165–1188. doi:10.2307/41703503

Cheng, C. C., & Shiu, E. C. (2018). How to enhance SMEs' customer involvement using social media: The role of social CRM. *International Small Business Journal*, *36*, 1–21. doi:10.1177/0266242618774831

Choudhury, M. M., & Harrigan, P. (2014). CRM to social CRM: The integration of new technologies into customer relationship management. *Journal of Strategic Marketing, Taylor & Francis*, *22*(2), 149–176. doi:10.1080/0965254X.2013.876069

Chui, M., Miller, A., & Roberts, R. (2009, February). *Six ways to make Web 2.0 work. The McKinsey Quarterly*.

Clark, M., Black, H. G., & Judson, K. (2017). Brand Community Integration and Satisfaction with Social Media Sites: A Comparative Study. *Journal of Research in Interactive Marketing*, *11*(1), 39–55. doi:10.1108/JRIM-07-2015-0047

Cohen, W., & Levinthal, D. (1990). Absorptive Capacity : A New Perspective on Learning and Innovation. *Administrative Science Quarterly*, *35*(1), 128–152. doi:10.2307/2393553

Cope, J. (2005). Toward a Dynamic Learning Perspective of Entrepreneurship. *Entrepreneurship Theory and Practice*, *29*(4), 373–397. doi:10.1111/j.1540-6520.2005.00090.x

Cope, J., & Watts, G. (2000). Learning by doing: An exploration of experience, critical incidents and reflection in entrepreneurial learning. *International Journal of Entrepreneurial Behaviour & Research*, *6*(3), 104–124. doi:10.1108/13552550010346208

Covin, J. G., & Slevin, D. (1989). Strategic management of small firms in hostile and benign environments. *Strategic Management Journal*, *10*(1), 75–87. doi:10.1002mj.4250100107

Coyle, J. R., Smith, T., & Platt, G. (2012). I'm Here to Help. *Journal of Research in Interactive Marketing*, *6*(1), 27–41. doi:10.1108/17505931211241350

Cuervo, A. (2005). Individual and environmental determinants of entrepreneurship. *The International Entrepreneurship and Management Journal*, *1*(3), 293–311. doi:10.100711365-005-2591-7

Curran, J., & Blackburn, R. (2001). *Researching the Small Enterprise*. London: SAGE Publications. doi:10.4135/9781849209847

Day, G. (1994). *The capabilities of market-driven organizations. The Journal of Marketing*, 58, 37–52.

Denzin, N. K. (1997). Interpretive ethnography: Ethnographic practices for the 21st century. *Sage (Atlanta, Ga.)*.

Dodgson, M. (1993). Organizational Learning—A Review of Some Literatures. *Organization Studies*, *14*(3), 375–394. doi:10.1177/017084069301400303

Durkin, M., McGowan, P., & McKeown, N. (2013). Exploring social media adoption in small to medium-sized enterprises in Ireland. *Journal of Small Business and Enterprise Development*, *20*(4), 716–734. doi:10.1108/JSBED-08-2012-0094

Eisenhardt, K. M., & Martin, J. (2000). Dynamic capabilities: What are they? *Strategic Management Journal*, *21*(10–11), 1105–1121. doi:10.1002/1097-0266(200010/11)21:10/11<1105::AID-SMJ133>3.0.CO;2-E

Franco, M., & Haase, H. (2009). Entrepreneurship: An organisational learning approach. *Journal of Small Business and Enterprise Development*, *16*(4), 628–641. doi:10.1108/14626000911000965

Gilmore, A., & Carson, D. (1996). "Integrative" qualitative methods in a services context. *Marketing Intelligence & Planning*, *14*(6), 21–26. doi:10.1108/02634509610131126

Gnizy, I., Baker, W. E., & Grinstein, A. (2014). Proactive learning culture: A dynamic capability and key success factor for SMEs entering foreign markets. *International Marketing Review*, *31*(5), 477–505. doi:10.1108/IMR-10-2013-0246

Guha, S., Harrigan, P., & Soutar, G. (2018). Linking social media to customer relationship management (CRM): A qualitative study on SMEs. *Journal of Small Business and Entrepreneurship*, *30*(3), 193–214. doi:10.1080/08276331.2017.1399628

Harrigan, P., Ramsey, E., & Ibbotson, P. (2011). Critical factors underpinning the e-CRM activities of SMEs. *Journal of Marketing Management*, *27*(5-6), 503–529. doi:10.1080/0267257X.2010.495284

Harrigan, P., Ramsey, E., & Ibbotson, P. (2012). Exploring and explaining SME marketing: Investigating e-CRM using a mixed methods approach. *Journal of Strategic Marketing*, *20*(2), 127–163. doi:10.1080/0965254X.2011.606911

Harrigan, P., Soutar, G., Choudhury, M. M., & Lowe, M. (2015). Modelling CRM in the social media age. *Australasian Marketing Journal*, *23*(1), 27–37. doi:10.1016/j.ausmj.2014.11.001

Harrison, R. T., & Leitch, C. M. (2005). Entrepreneurial learning: Researching the interface between learning and the entrepreneurial context. *Entrepreneurship Theory and Practice*, *29*(4), 351–372. doi:10.1111/j.1540-6520.2005.00089.x

Hill, J., & McGowan, P. (1996). Marketing development through networking: A competency based approach for small firm entrepreneurs. *Small Business and Enterprise Development*, *3*(3), 148–156. doi:10.1002/(SICI)1099-1662(199611)3:3<148::AID-SBE64>3.0.CO;2-C

Hodis, M. A., Sriramachandramurthy, R., & Sashittal, H. C. (2015). Interact with me on my terms: A four segment Facebook engagement framework for marketers. *Journal of Marketing Management*, *31*(11–12), 1255–1284. doi:10.1080/0267257X.2015.1012535

Kim, J., & Choi, H. (2019). Value co-creation through social media: A case study of a start-up company. *Journal of Business Economics and Management*, *20*(1), 1–19. doi:10.3846/jbem.2019.6262

Kim, Y., Akbar, H., Tzokas, N., & Al-Dajani, H. (2014). Systems thinking and absorptive capacity in high-tech small and medium-sized enterprises from South Korea. *International Small Business Journal*, *32*(8), 876–896. doi:10.1177/0266242613483632

Kohli, A., & Jaworski, B. (1990). Market Orientation: The Construct, Research Propositions, and Managerial Implications. *Journal of Marketing*, *54*(2), 1–18. doi:10.1177/002224299005400201

Lam, H. K. S., Yeung, A. C. L., & Cheng, T. C. E. (2016). The impact of firms' social media initiatives on operational efficiency and innovativeness. *Journal of Operations Management*, *47–48*(1), 28–43. doi:10.1016/j.jom.2016.06.001

Lam, S. K., Sleep, S., Hennig-Thurau, T., Sridhar, S., & Saboo, A. R. (2017). Leveraging frontline employees' small data and firm-level big data in frontline management: An absorptive capacity perspective. *Journal of Service Research, Vol.*, *20*(1), 12–28. doi:10.1177/1094670516679271

Liao, J., Kickul, J. R., & Ma, H. (2009). Organizational Dynamic Capability and Innovation: An Empirical Examination of Internet Firms. *Journal of Small Business Management*, *47*(3), 263–286. doi:10.1111/j.1540-627X.2009.00271.x

Makadok, R. (2001). Toward a Synthesis of the Resource - Based and Dynamic - Capability Views of Rent Creation. *Strategic Management Journal*, *22*(5), 387–401. doi:10.1002mj.158

McCann, M., & Barlow, A. (2015). Use and measurement of social media for SMEs. *Journal of Small Business and Enterprise Development*, *22*(2), 273–287. doi:10.1108/JSBED-08-2012-0096

Nguyen, B., Yu, X., Melewar, T. C., & Chen, J. (2015). Brand innovation and social media: Knowledge acquisition from social media, market orientation, and the moderating role of social media strategic capability. *Industrial Marketing Management*, *51*, 11–25. doi:10.1016/j.indmarman.2015.04.017

O'Donnell, A. (2014). The Contribution of Networking to Small Firm Marketing. *Journal of Small Business Management*, *52*(1), 164–187. doi:10.1111/jsbm.12038

O'Driscoll, A., Carson, D., & Gilmore, A. (2000). Developing marketing competence and managing in networks: A strategic perspective. *Journal of Strategic Marketing*, *8*(2), 183–196. doi:10.1080/096525400346240

O'Dwyer, M., Gilmore, A., & Carson, D. (2009). Innovative marketing in SMEs. *European Journal of Marketing*, *43*(1/2), 46–61. doi:10.1108/03090560910923238

Olavarrieta, S., & Friedmann, R. (2008). Market orientation, knowledge-related resources and firm performance. *Journal of Business Research*, *61*(6), 623–630. doi:10.1016/j.jbusres.2007.06.037

Panahi, S., Watson, J., & Partridge, H. (2012). Social media and tacit knowledge sharing: developing a conceptual model. World Academy of Science, Engineering and Technology (WASET), 1095–1102.

Paniagua, J., & Sapena, J. (2014). Business performance and social media: Love or hate? *Business Horizons*, *57*(6), 719–728. doi:10.1016/j.bushor.2014.07.005

Pawlowsky, P. (2001). The Treatment of Organizational Learning in Management Science. In M. Dierkes, A. Berthoin Antal, J. Child, & I. Nonaka (Eds.), *Handbook of Organizational Learning & Knowledge* (pp. 61–88). Oxford, UK: Oxford University Press.

Rae, D., & Carswell, M. (2001). Towards a conceptual understanding of entrepreneurial learning. *Journal of Small Business and Enterprise Development*, *8*(2), 150–158. doi:10.1108/EUM0000000006816

Raju, P. S., Lonial, S. C., & Crum, M. D. (2011). Market orientation in the context of SMEs: A conceptual framework. *Journal of Business Research*, *64*(12), 1320–1326. doi:10.1016/j.jbusres.2010.12.002

Razmerita, L., & Kirchner, K. (2011). How wikis can be used to manage knowledge in SMEs: A case study. *Business Information Review*, *28*(3), 175–178. doi:10.1177/0266382111420354

Resnick, S. M., Cheng, R., Simpson, M., & Lourenço, F. (2016). Marketing in SMEs: A "4Ps" self-branding model. *International Journal of Entrepreneurial Behaviour & Research*, *22*(1), 155–174. doi:10.1108/IJEBR-07-2014-0139

Secundo, G., Schiuma, G., & Passiante, G. (2017). Entrepreneurial learning dynamics in knowledge-intensive enterprises. *International Journal of Entrepreneurial Behaviour & Research*, *23*(3), 366–380. doi:10.1108/IJEBR-01-2017-0020

Senge, P. (1990). *The Fifth Discipline*. London: Random House.

Shaw, E. (2006). Small Firm Networking: An Insight into Contents and Motivating Factors. *International Small Business Journal*, *24*(1), 5–29. doi:10.1177/0266242606059777

Slater, S. F., & Narver, J. C. (1995). The Positive Effect of a Market Orientation. *Journal of Business Research*, *48*(1), 69–73. doi:10.1016/S0148-2963(98)00077-0

Snyman, R., & Kruger, C. J. (2004). The interdependency between strategic management and strategic knowledge management. *Journal of Knowledge Management*, *8*(1), 5–19. doi:10.1108/13673270410523871

Soto-Acosta, P., Popa, S., & Palacios-Marqués, D. (2017). Social web knowledge sharing and innovation performance in knowledge-intensive manufacturing SMEs. *The Journal of Technology Transfer*, *42*(2), 425–440. doi:10.100710961-016-9498-z

Spender, J. C. (1996). Making Knowledge the Basis of A Dynamic Theory of the Firm. *Strategic Management Journal*, *17*(S2), 45–62. doi:10.1002mj.4250171106

Stokes, D., & Nelson, C. (2013). Word of Mouth to Word of Mouse: Social Media and the Entrepreneur. In Z. Sethna, R. Jones, & P. Harrigan (Eds.), *Entrepreneurial Marketing: Global Perspectives*. Bingley, UK: Emerald Group Publishing Limited.

Story, V., O'Malley, L., & Hart, S. (2011). Roles, role performance, and radical innovation competencies. *Industrial Marketing Management*, *40*(6), 952–966. doi:10.1016/j.indmarman.2011.06.025

Sun, P., & Anderson, M. (2010). An examination of the relationship between absorptive capacity and organisational learning. *International Journal of Management Reviews*, *12*(2), 130–150. doi:10.1111/j.1468-2370.2008.00256.x

Teece, D. J., Pisano, G., & Shuen, A. (1997). Dynamic Capabilities and Strategic Management. *Strategic Management Journal*, *18*(7), 509–533. doi:10.1002/(SICI)1097-0266(199708)18:7<509::AID-SMJ882>3.0.CO;2-Z

Todorova, G., & Durisin, B. (2007). Absorptive Capacity: Valuing a Reconceptualization. *Academy of Management Review*, *32*(3), 774–786. doi:10.5465/amr.2007.25275513

Trainor, K. J., Andzulis, J., Rapp, A., & Agnihotri, R. (2014). Social media technology usage and customer relationship performance: A capabilities-based examination of social CRM. *Journal of Business Research*, *67*(6), 1201–1208. doi:10.1016/j.jbusres.2013.05.002

Van den Bosch, F., Van Wijk, R., & Volberda, H. W. (2003). Absorptive capacity: antecedents, models and outcomes. In M. Easterby-Smith & M. A. Lyles (Eds.), *The Blackwell Handbook of Organizational Learning and Knowledge Management*. Oxford, UK: Blackwell.

Walters, P. G. P. (2008). Adding value in global B2B supply chains: Strategic directions and the role of the Internet as a driver of competitive advantage. *Industrial Marketing Management*, *37*(1), 59–68. doi:10.1016/j.indmarman.2007.06.010

Wang, C. L., & Ahmed, P. K. (2007). Dynamic capabilities: A review and research agenda. *International Journal of Management Reviews*, *9*(1), 31–51. doi:10.1111/j.1468-2370.2007.00201.x

Whalen, P., Uslay, C., Pascal, V. J., Omura, G., McAuley, A., Kasouf, C. J., ... Deacon, J. (2016). Anatomy of competitive advantage: Towards a contingency theory of entrepreneurial marketing. *Journal of Strategic Marketing*, *24*(1), 5–19. doi:10.1080/0965254X.2015.1035036

Wiklund, J., & Shepherd, D. (2003). Knowledge-based resources, entrepreneurial orientation, and the performance of small and medium-sized businesses. *Strategic Management Journal*, *24*(13), 1307–1314. doi:10.1002mj.360

Winter, S. G. (2003). Understanding dynamic capabilities. *Strategic Management Journal*, *24*(10), 991–995. doi:10.1002mj.318

Wong, K., & Aspinwall, E. (2004). Characterizing knowledge management in the small business environment. *Journal of Knowledge Management*, *8*(3), 44–61. doi:10.1108/13673270410541033

Yin, R. (2003). Designing Case Studies. Case Study Research: Design and Methods, 19–56.

Yli-Renko, H., Autio, E., & Sapienza, H. J. (2001). Social capital, knowledge acquisition, and knowledge exploitation in young technology-based firms. *Strategic Management Journal*, *22*(6–7), 587–613. doi:10.1002mj.183

Zahra, S., & George, G. (2002). Absorptive Capacity: A Review, Reconceptualization, and Extension. *Academy of Management Review*, *27*(2), 185–203. doi:10.5465/amr.2002.6587995

Zahra, S., Sapienza, H., & Davidsson, P. (2006). Entrepreneurship and dynamic capabilities: A review, model and research agenda. *Journal of Management Studies*, *43*(4), 917–955. doi:10.1111/j.1467-6486.2006.00616.x

Zeiller, M., & Schauer, B. (2011). Adoption, motivation and success factors of social media for team collaboration in SMEs. In *Proceedings of the 11th International Conference on Knowledge Management and Knowledge Technologies - i-KNOW '11*. ACM Press. 10.1145/2024288.2024294

Zhang, M., Macpherson, A., & Jones, O. (2006). Conceptualizing the Learning Process in SMEs: Improving Innovation through External Orientation. *International Small Business Journal*, *24*(3), 299–323. doi:10.1177/0266242606063434

## KEY TERMS AND DEFINITIONS

**Dynamic Capabilities:** Dynamic capabilities are evolutionary, future-oriented, and difficult to imitate organizational core strengths, embedded knowledge, skills and processes for continuous evolutional fitness of an organisation with its changing environment.

**Marketing Evolution:** The marketing evolution is a process and stages through which the marketing concepts, philosophies, mechanisms, tools and techniques, and orientations of marketing are changing and has changed over the period of the history of marketing.

**MIATSM Model:** The Market Intelligence Accumulation Through Social Media is a model of the processes of market intelligence accumulation through social media use and its assimilation and application in marketing activities.

**SME Learning:** A SME organisational learning process of continually acquiring, developing and sharing knowledge skills and practices to enhance the organisational effectiveness of an SME.

**Social Media:** Social media is the collective of web 2,0 based online communications channels through which communities can create contents, input, interact, share and collaborate information, co-create knowledge or contents, etc.

# Chapter 4
# Technology and Sharing Economy-Based Business Models for Marketing to Connected Consumers

**Sumesh Singh Dadwal**
*Northumbria University, London, UK*

**Arshad Jamal**
*QA Higher Education, UK & Northumbria University, London, UK*

**Tim Harris**
*QA Higher Education, UK*

**Guy Brown**
*Northumbria University, Newcastle, UK*

**Siti Raudhah**
*Northumbria University, London, UK*

## ABSTRACT

*The new technological innovations are changing the ways businesses are being operated. The sharing economy-based new business models (SEBMs) using technology have many benefits at national, organisational, community, and individual levels. The sharing economy provides a huge potential of creating millions of jobs by leveraging the business sector and providing a new way to producers and consumers to meet each other's needs. To maintain and enhance the use of technology-enabled sharing economy-based models (SEBMs), it is paramount to understand these SEBMs models and the behavior of the market, particularly on how to influence the market's attitude towards using SEBMs. This chapter analyses the new sharing economy-based and technologically-enabled business models and their antecedents.*

DOI: 10.4018/978-1-7998-0131-3.ch004

## INTRODUCTION

The tremendous growth in information and communication technology (ICT) during the last two decades has left a huge effect on our socio-cultural ways and living. The businesses have understood the significance of the use of technology and the importance of understating of consumers' reaction and intentions to technological changes. The organisations are using disruptive innovations in ICT in almost all functional areas of the management. The adoption of technology is leading to paradigm shifts in the value chain, value networks and business models of the companies. Despite many kinds of business models, the business models based on sharing economy or called here as Shared Economy Business Models (SEBMs) have shown huge potential and opportunities. The term sharing economy is also known as collaborative consumption, peer economy, and collaborative economy (Botsman, 2013; Belk, 2014). The sharing economy is an 'economic activity of giving or taking the rights' of ownership, usage, enjoyment of products, services or ideas by people.

The sharing economy is viewed as an evolving phenomenon in national economies, which is driven by the growth of information and communication technology. The social economy drove business models are changing consumer awareness, social commerce and web-sharing communities (Botsman and Rogers, 2010).

The sharing economy is 'the peer-to-peer-based activity of obtaining, giving or sharing the access to goods and services, and the economy is coordinated through community-based online service' (Hamari, Sjöklint, and Ukkonen, 2015). Sharing economy is an economic activity of sharing the underutilized assets, resources, or services directly from individuals; either free or for a fee (Botsman 2015).

Since the start of the 21st century, the sharing economy has been developing rapidly all over the world and even has grown at a faster rate than some of the social media platforms such as Facebook, Yahoo, and Google combined (WEF, 2016). This economic model is changing the consumption patterns all over the world. The multinational companies such as Airbnb and Uber, are the forerunners of these technology-enabled innovative business models (PWC, 2015). According to PWC (2015), five key sectors; ride-sharing, travel, staffing, finance, music, and video streaming have tremendous potential to raise global revenues via shared economy based business models (SEBMs). The rise of sharing economy based on e-commerce systems have simplified the sharing of products or services for new companies like Blablacar, Uber, and Couchsurfing, etc (Galbreth, Ghosh, and Shor; 2012). The growth in the smartphone has further allowed easy connection between suppliers and buyers via communications as well as location sharing technologies. For an instant, in case of 'ride-sharing services' such as Uber or Blablacar it is much easier for a customer (who needs a ride to a particular place) to connect with a car driver who can drive the customer to that place (Cramer and Krueger, 2016).

The 'rides sharing industry' is one of the pioneers of sharing economy based business models (SEBMs). As per Statisca (2019), the global revenue of 'ride-sharing industry' is US$156,176m and it will grow at 10.2% to reach US$230,085m by 2023. In terms of growth of revenue, the top countries are; USA (US$49,848Ml), China (US$35,801Ml), India (US$29,333Ml), Indonesia (US$5,325Ml) and the UK (US$2,834m). Globally the number of rides sharing users have increased from 577.4 million (2017) to 824.9 million in 2019. The number is expected to reach 1,109.05 million by the year 2023 (Statista 2019). The global user penetrations rate is expected to rise from 8% (2017) to 14.5% of the population by 2023. Singapore is at the top position with 32% user penetration, followed by China (20.4%), USA (20.2%), UK (16%), and Ireland (15%) (Statsta, 2019).

During 2006-2012, there were economic crises that have caused negative impacts around the world. The 'ride-sharing economy' is creating a million jobs along, letting people help each other by sharing underused assets and involving people in sustainable behavior (Prothero et al., 2011).

With technological progress, the use of technology is changing the way people live their lives, the way they work, and the way they interact. Thus, the technological environment is effecting other external business environmental drivers such as Political, social, economic, legal and ecological factors. The innovations and transformation in technology have caused many positive and adverse effects. One of its negative effects has been the increase in economic inequality between developed and developing countries. This inequality has given rise to searching for new economic models, such as frugal innovations & technology and sharing economies. The sharing economy has enabled people to sharing tangible and intangible assets or resources through the online or digital platforms. Thus, the sharing economy is contributing to matching the supply with demand. The sharing economy is expected to cause a major impact on the society, hence a study is significant to the policymakers as well as practitioners. The sharing economy is predicted to become the biggest part of the global economy. In 2013, the sharing economy started to gain popularity world over. However, there is still a lack of research related to technologically enabled sharing economy models and corresponding consumer behavior (Tussyadiah, 2016).

Also, a sharing economy is driven by a responsibility to share, help other people, thus it may involve a sustainable behavior (Prothero et al.,2011). A chapter on 'sharing economy based business models' and understanding of user or consumers behavior towards such business models will be useful for the industry and the government.

This chapter aims to examine the impact of technology, the rise of sharing economy, business models based sharing economy and drivers for shared economy business models (SEBMs). The paper also explores the drivers that encourage consumers to adopt sharing economy business models.

## LITERATURE REVIEW AND THEORETICAL DEVELOPMENT

### Business Model

A business model is a collection of an internal and external decision imposed by an organization on its employees for the process of production and exchange of values with its customers, in order to create and sustain competitive advantage (Casadesus-Masanell & Heilbron, 2015). The dynamic capabilities approach identifies a set of opportunities to capture the value that persist despite changing external environment. Thus, a business model has an internal constitution of an organisation (value chain and value delivery network) and an external alignment of the organisation (with the dynamic market environment, suppliers, customers, distributors, etc) in order to create and capture the value (Casadesus-Masanell & Heilbron, 2015). A business model is driven from a business strategy and the business model 'depicts the content, structure, and governance of transactions designed so as to create value through the exploitation of business opportunities in a novel way' (Amit & Zott, 2001, cited in Casadesus-Masanell & Heilbron, 2015).

A business model is a core logic of an organisation to create and capture value within the value network. As shown in Table 1 (see table: 1), a business model includes a set of Activities (strategic choices, the value network, creating value and capturing value), Pillars (Product/need, Customer/market segments, Technology/functions/infrastructure management, customer interfaces, and Financial aspects); Elements

(Core capabilities, Value Configuration, Revenue Streams, Cost structure, Value proposition, Customer Segments, Distribution & Communication Channels, partnerships, Customer relationship,) and A range of Actions (who, what, when, why, how and how much) (Olofsson & Farr, 2006).

As shown in figure -1 (see Figure 1), a business model sits between business strategy and business's operational processes; hence it is related to business strategy; however, it differs from business strategy. Whereas a business model is a way of capturing value, the strategy is a long term position of differentiating and creating valuc (Olofsson & Farr, 2006). A business model is the architecture of revenue streams and cost/profits associated with an organisations, which is used to create, deliver and exchange values (Teece, 2010).

Thus, in a technology-enabled environment, a business model helps firms to structure their internal constituents inbound, operations, R&D, marketing, distributions, services, and customer transactions) as well as external alignment with the suppliers, customers, distributors and other external stakeholders.

In the age of ICT, the organisation such as Amazon, eBay, Uber, Airbnb, etc have found new ways of creating, capturing and exchange values with their customers. One can easily relate this understanding of business model to apply to say ' share riding services' organisations such as Uber: it is about Uber's process of creating and capturing value, its internal constituents of IT-based systems, apps, back-end support, and external alignment with its suppliers (car drivers) and customers that determines the transactions efficiency and revenue streams at Uber technologies.

*Figure 1. Relations of the Business model with business strategy and operations, Adapted from (DaSilva & Trkman, 2014)*

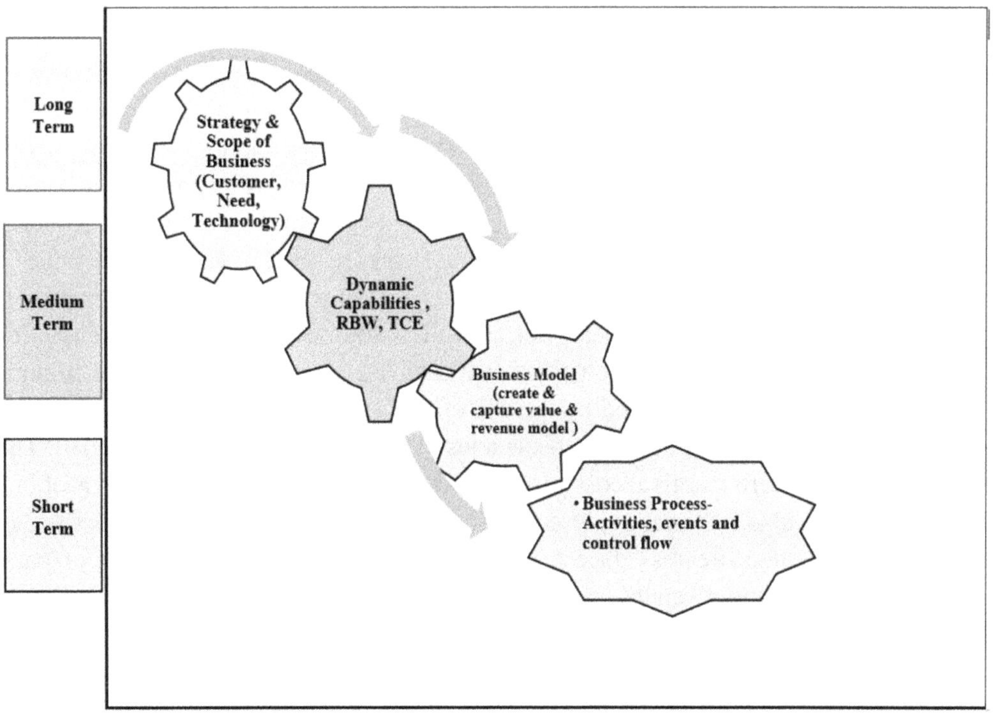

*Table 1. Components of business models: Adapted from Olofsson & Farr, 2006*

| Strategy | Value network | Crete value | Capture Value |
|---|---|---|---|
| Competencies and capabilities | Supplier negotiations and relationship management | Resources / Assets (owned/ outsources) | Cost |
| Branding/ differentiating | R&D and internal operations / product service flows (owned/ outsources) | Processes/ activities (owned/ outsources) | Financial aspects |
| Cost/revenue streams (lean/ fat / diversified) | Marketing | | Profit |
| Output strategy | Services | | |
| Target customers segments | Distributors and agents | | |
| Value preposition (low/ high/ different) | Customer relationship management (owned/ transactional / partners) | | |
| | IT systems | | |

Similarly, the business models at Ryanair or Walmart or Amazon.com are based on high power incentive structure to the managers; which ensures that employees are highly passionate to work for organisation's effective internal constituents and an external aligned with suppliers, customers, etc.

In the era of ICT, a business model is a new way of doing business as a result of disruptive innovations. The resource-based view (RBW) of the organisation and theories of transactions costs economics (TCE) or transaction efficiency are seen as the basis of success of any new business model (Amit & Zott, 2001 in DaSilva & Trkman, 2014). The RBW views organisations as a bundle of unique resources and capabilities, whereas TCE argues for transactional efficiencies in terms of time, costs and hassles in exchanges or transactions of values. Thus business models are seen as internal competencies of the companies and their abilities to decrease the transactions costs. For example, Ikea furniture's' business model is based on its internal competencies for design skills, supplier relations, sourcing networks, IT systems and cultural factors that lead to decrease transactions costs and, thus improving overall values for Ikea's customers. Similarly, Ryanair's business model is a combination of internal resources competencies (e.g., non-unionized workforce, standard-plane fleet) and the IT systems, which the company uses to undertake transactions efficiently (e.g., online ticket bookings). The technology-enabled business models can be both sources of core competencies as well as sources of minimising transactions costs and dis-intermediations. Thus reorganization of internal business operations and external alignment with stakeholders could be efficiently achieved by the use of ICT, and which in turn becomes the basis of core competencies (RBW) and transactional efficiencies (TCE) (DaSilva & Trkman, 2014). The digital transactions can achieve a zero marginal cost after a breakeven point. The reorganisations of businesses using e-business models also let firms capture the wastes or externalities or by product services thus can create additional revenue streams. For example, mobile phone service providing companies have developed a range of streams of revenues from peripheral services such as selling accessories & related products, tunes, music, etc. Ryanair's revenue model includes revenue streams from customers ticketing fares, and by charging for a large number of miscellaneous charges and fees, in-flight food, merchandise and third-party advertising on seats and lockers; a car-hire partnership with Hertz; travel insurance, transfer services; and a mobile-phone roaming service etc (DaSilva & Trkman, 2014). Similarly, Amazon.com an original online book store saw its potential revenue stream and, so gradually entered into electronic (Kindle book reader) and ultimately became as one of the largest online store or platform. Again the business model is driven by core capabilities, dynamic capabilities and abilities to undertake more transactions with its value networks efficiently. Similarly, Uber technologies have diversified from Uber car to Uber food and more related delivery and transportations services.

Graphically a business model is a set of subsystems, actors and activities with the interactive relationship, tractions, and exchange of values among them. For example in traditional brick and mortar retail system is based on more direct transactions (both the flow of products and payments) between the supermarket (retailer) and consumers or suppliers (see Figure 2). On the other hand, in the case of E-commerce based retailer, the transactions and relationships quite different (see Figure 3). In a case of the online retailer, products flow from suppliers to the customers via intermediaries (product delivery services) and payments flow by online banking systems. Figure 2 and Figure 3 (see Figure 2 and Figure 3) show a graphical illustration of two different kinds of business models.

*Figure 2. Traditional brick and mortar retail system*

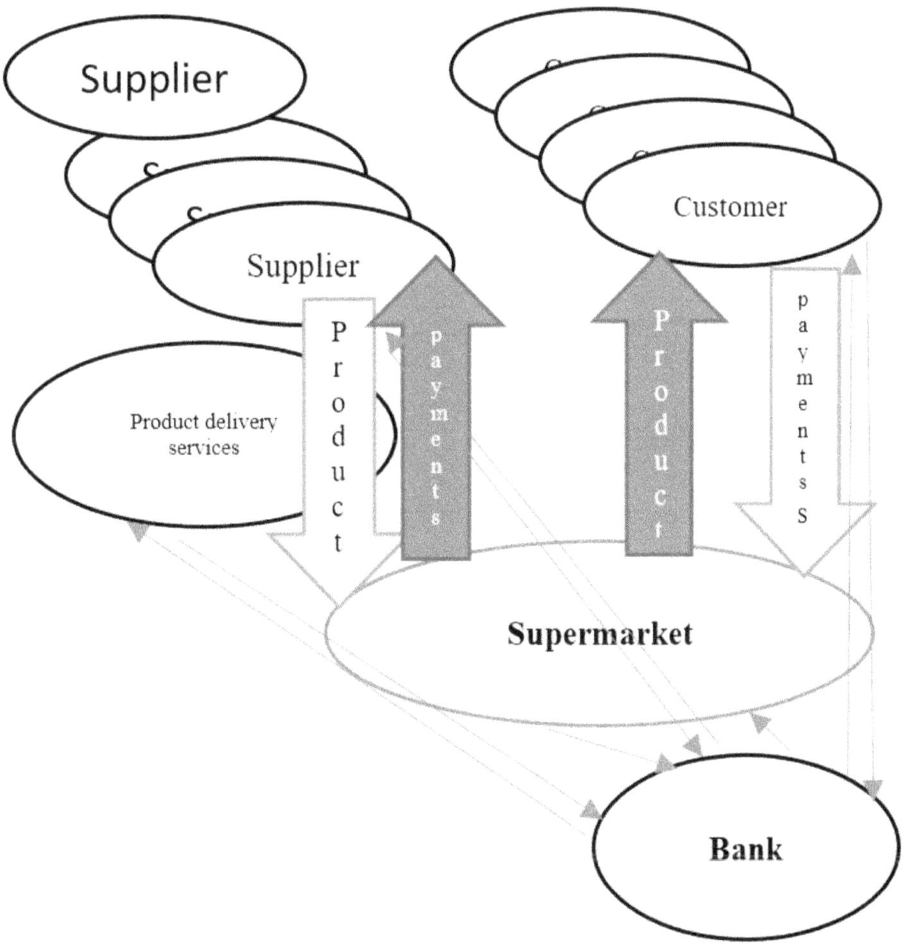

Figure 3. New E-platform based SBEMs retail system

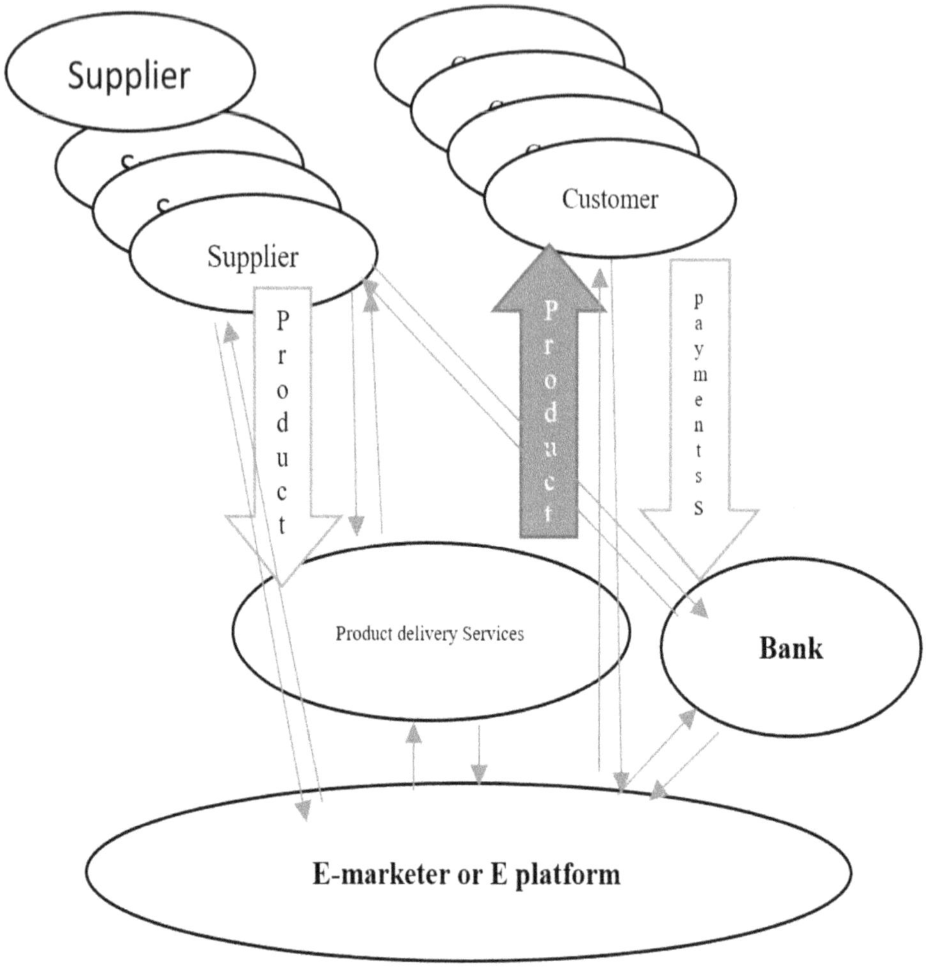


## The Sharing Economy: Basic Concepts

One of the oldest human behaviors is sharing. Sharing is intertwined inevitably with the evolution of human growth, which is intrinsic and intuitive. The term sharing economy or 'Collaborative Consumption' engages individual and groups in the new kind of collaborative economic activities (Felson and Spaeth,1978). The definitions of the concept of sharing economy are evolving with the evolution and development of the business models of sharing economy. This concept has been called under different names such as 'gig economy' and 'peer to peer economy (Buda & Lehota, 2017). In a sharing economy, 'users share their unused capacities' or untapped resources (e.g. Unused capacities, tangible assets, services, money, information, ideas, knowledge) with each other on an 'On-demand basis' (immediately when the need arises). The business models of sharing economy, require mutual trust, a sense of giving & sharing, and a motivation for personal & community-based interactions (Buda & Lehota, 2017).In an article, Belk (2014) has cited a range of researchers; who have used a range of terms to describe this concept as 'act of sharing' (Belk, 2014), *'prosumption'* (Kotler, 1986; Toffler, 1980), 'consumer participation' (Fitzsimmons, 1985), 'product-service systems' (Mont, 2002), 'online volunteering' (Postigo, 2003), 'co-creation' (Prahalad & Ramaswamy, 2004), 'co-production' (Humphreys & Grayson, 2008), 'collaborative consumption' (Botsman & Rogers, 2010), 'the mesh'(Gansky, 2010), 'commercial sharing systems' (Lamberton & Rose, 2012), 'access based consumption' (Bardhi & Eckhardt, 2012), and sharing i.e. 'mothering and the pooling and allocation of household resources' so on.

Clearly, the concept of business models of sharing economy has been evolving. As the methods of production, exchange, and consumption of values have changed over the period, the meaning of the sharing economy model has also changed. A business model is a way of making money by managing the value chain and exchange of the 'values. Also, such a business model indicates the process of internal constitutions of resources and external alignment of an organisation (Ibid.).

The sharing economy is based on the 'sharing paradigm' and 'sharing turn', which means borrowing or lending goods or services from others instead of buying it (Belk, 2014),. The organizations have adopted new ways of reconstructing their internal operations and core competencies and they have well-aligned themselves with external stakeholders, suppliers, customers, and communities. For example, Airbnb, use a business model that has replaced traditional ways of renting homes or the traditional way of booking hotels. The Airbnb platform has allowed the suppliers to reconstitute their offering & increase their reach using an Airbnb platform at much lower transactions costs.

Collaborative Consumption models focus on minimising idleness or excess capacity of goods by enhancing access to information from suppliers of goods to the parties interested in those goods. Thus in a sharing economy the consumers grant temporary access to the underused physical assets to each other The activity of the sharing economy is usually based on mutual trust and through an Information Technology platform.

## The Concept of Business Model in A Shared Economy

Due to the dynamic growth of the sharing economy, the concept and its meaning are evolving over time. The sharing economy also implies collaborative consumption, gig economy, access economy, and platform economy (Botsman and Rogers, 2011). Thus. a sharing economy is based on sharing the underutilised resources as collaborative consumptions. On similarl lines, the peer economy is a marketplace for individuals to share assets with some mutual trust. On the other hand, De Grave (2014) argues that the sharing economy is a part of the collaborative economy and is a process of sharing of the distributed production and consumption of open-source knowledge.

As mentioned earlier, a business model is a process of creating, capturing and exchanging values by making use of RBW, dynamic capabilities and TCE theories (Ibid.). The sharing economy allows consumers to access and use the resources completely without having to own or purchase them. The models of sharing economy use 'shared knowledge of communities' for developing dynamic capabilities, the organisation's core competencies and ICT platforms so as to minimise transactions costs of exchange of values. Belk (2014) argues that sharing economy-based business model is a temporary arrangement for online sharing, peer-to-peer sharing, and online facilitated sharing. Botsman (2013), argues that each of the terminologies such as sharing economy, collaborative consumption, and peer economy have different definitions but have a common underlying spirit of 'sharing' of the underused goods/services for monetary or non-monetary purposes. A sharing or collaborative economy model is based on the concept of collaborative consumption. This model is somewhat related to traditional systems of bartering, renting, sharing, gigging, trading, and swapping goods/service but through technology and peer communities (Hamari et al. 2013, Botsman and Rogers (2010).

*Thus a Sharing Economy business model (SEBM) may be defined as a strategic process that an organisation uses to create and capture customer values by making use of innovation, technologies, online sharing, peer-to-peer sharing, or collaborative consumption in order to reconstitute organisational internal core competencies, external alignment, & dynamic capabilities and thus achieving sustainable competitive advantages.*

A business model of collaborative consumption is based on the distributed networks of connected consumers and communities (as opposed to centralised institutions) and such a distributed systems determine how we produce, consume, and learn (Bostman, 2013). The sharing economy is based on the 'sharing paradigm' (Belk, 2014), and 'sharing turn', which means borrowing or lending goods or services from others instead of buying it. Clearly. the business models of organisations such as Uber, Airbnb, etc. are such that they do not own resources or assets (cars, homes), but the originations only provide platforms for reach and transaction and exchange of values between suppliers and the consumers. Also, in Medical equipment industry, the renting out of the equipment has become possible because of shared economy-based models.

Graphical differences between traditional and shared economy business models are illustrated in Figures 4 and Figure 5 (see Figure 4 and Figure 5). It can be seen from the Figures 4 and Figure 5 (see Figure 4 and Figure 5) that instead of owning the assets, the innovative organisations in 'ride-sharing industry' are using the supplier's assets (cars). Also, the information model platform is used to manage a flow of information and revenue streams, the platform links suppliers (independent car owners) with the customers (travellers). The flow of payments & revenues takes place via transactions among customers, organisation, banks, etc at much higher efficiency and speed. The analogous model can be also pictured considered for Airbnb industry.

Thus a sharing economy business model entails sharing or renting of product or services using digital platform and with some financial or non-financial costs (Botsman, 2013).

The various ICT technologies-based platforms have supported opportunities for personal interaction and community experience with sustainability. The agility of such systems has let the demands match with the supplies more efficiently at dynamic but low prices.

## Technology as a Driver of Sharing Economy

The internet and mobile technologies have provided new opportunities and methods for people to connect, produce, communicate and share ideas, knowledge and other tangible or intangibles resources, goods, and services. Digital technologies; which include electronic tools, systems, devices and resources to generate, store or process data are important developments, which are aiding in connecting consumers, suppliers and communities (Government state Victoria, 2018). Digital technologies such as social media, online games, multimedia, and mobile smartphones and associated technologies are the most vital factors which have influenced the rise and growth of the sharing economy and challenging the traditional market behavior (Kaplan and Haenlein, 2010). Social media is also called 'participatory media' because it facilitates amateur audiences to create and share content (Schradie, 2011). Due to expansions of information technologies the sharing economy and its associated technological platforms have expanded.

*Figure 4. Traditional taxi services business model*

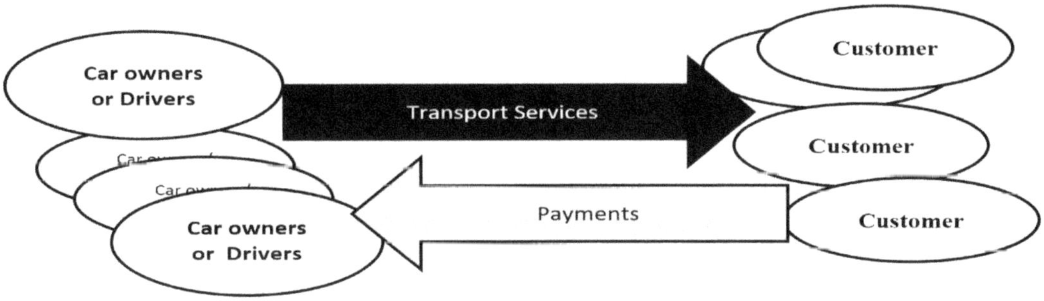


*Figure 5. A new business model of taxi services and ride sharing SBEM*

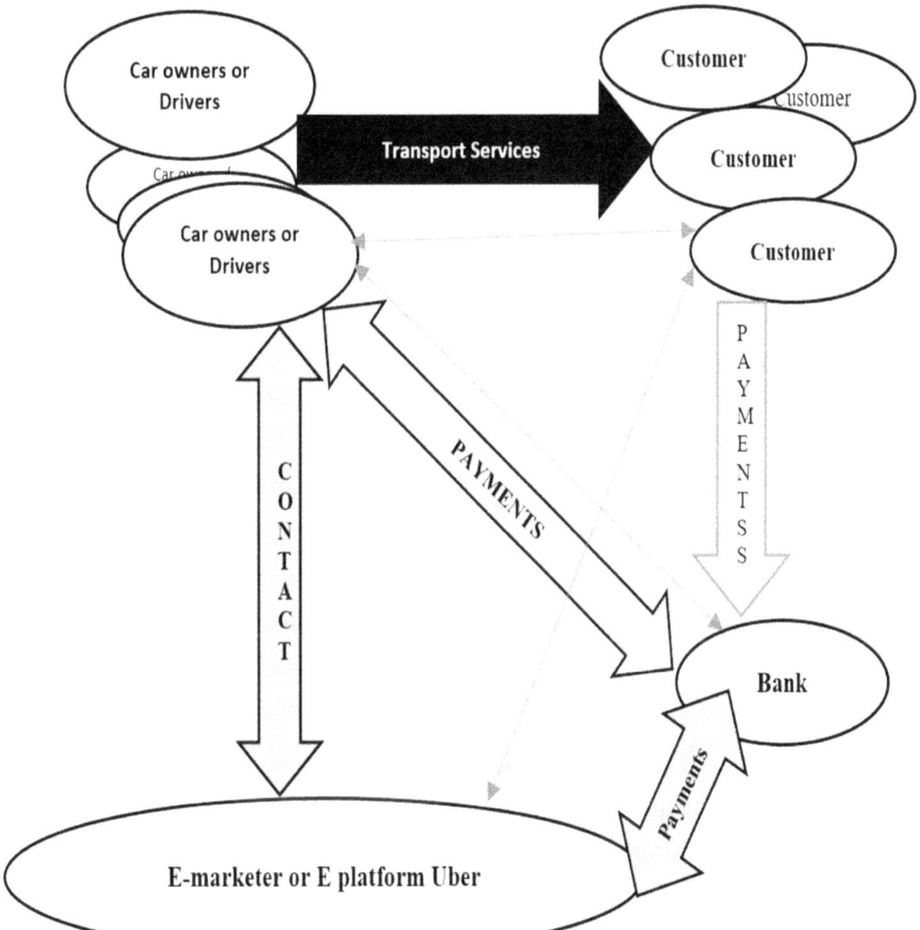

This, in turn, has encouraged in further sharing and collaboration of products and information by the users (Kaplan and Haenlein, 2010). These online platforms depend on social dynamics for real sharing and collaboration.

The actual 'sharing' is influenced by a range of factors such as; lower transaction costs, opportunities for mutual trust among larger communities, low entry and exit barriers, economies of scale in sharing, just in time demand-supply match, abundance of low cost ICT technologies, the social dynamics of enjoyment and self-marketing by a community (Lin and Lu, 2011 cited in Botsman & Rogers, 2011).

Since the sharing economy business models (SEBMs) are associated with the participation of individuals, thus the models rely on the interconnection of a large number of people among each other via online platforms. There is a range of different examples of the sharing economy-based models and platforms which are helping in balancing the supply and demand of resources or ideas efficiently and rapidly at lower prices. For example, YouTube, Wikipedia, and Instagram are platforms to share audio-visual and written contents at zero financial cost to the users. Similarly, PirateBay is a platform for peer-to-peer file sharing. Kiva is a platform for peer-to-peer financing in microloans and 'Kickstarter' is a platform for crowdfunding services. The sharing economy models create opportunities for perfect competition, as there are a large number of suppliers, who exchange similar products or ideas and they can easily entre or exit from a market sector (Buda & Lehota, 2017). The connected consumers are naturally attracted to such a perfect market structure due to the fact that the consumers are the determiners of the low prices. Further, the research has shown many other consumer motivations to join the sharing economy. Consumers' motivations to go for 'sharing economy business models' include; better price, transactional efficiencies, flexible system, immediate reaction/response, easy and transparent use, fairness, reliability, credibility, trendiness, personal experience, cashless settlement, traceability, and sustainability (Buda & Lehota, 2017). Growth of the number of people using sharing economy typically is supported by an increasing number of internet users, who are open to novelties, frequently use applications, and regularly use online payment systems for purchases (Buda & Lehota, 2017)

## INDUSTRIES WITH SHARED ECONOMY BUSINESS MODELS [SEBMs]

Much before the industrial revolution and coming of MNCs, the idea of sharing economy was existing in the medieval period or even before as a bartering system at a village level. The notion of sharing economy is that parties can share and exchange value from an under-utilized skill or goods or services or asset or idea, or other tangible or intangible resources; through a shared marketplace, or collaborative platform, or coworking or, crowdsourcing or cobranding or peer-to-peer application (Miller, 2019). The growth of 'SEBMs' is evidenced from the facts that venture capitalists have pumped in more than $23 billion into the various industries which are intending to use 'sharing economy-based models' since 2010 (Miller, 2019). Further, the market capitalisation of the companies (e.g. Airbnb-$31 Billion, Uber $72 Billion) with 'sharing economy models' is huge and around 20-30% workforce of EU and USA is working in the shared economy-based industries (Miller, 2019). A sharing economy not only creates a new market, but it also helps in the methods the consumers can access and exchange their underused assets. The sharing economy has become a new industry in itself and is often discussed in the popular current press (Economist, 2013).

So wherever there are opportunists for exchange of values (goods or services or asset or idea, or other tangible or intangible resources) through a shared marketplace (collaborative consumption, or coworking or crowdsourcing or cobranding or peer-to-peer sharing); there is a scope to apply a sharing, economy-based model. Hence, it can be inferred that almost all of the economic activities in the primary, secondary or tertiary sector can and will be affected by the sharing economy-based models. The future educational industry, banking industry, transportation industry, playing and entertainment industry, renting & housing industries and so on will be quite different.

According to Miller (2016), most of the business in the sharing economy are basically duplicating the services that already exist. For examples, industries in the sharing economy include; ride-sharing, shared-house or properties, shared workspaces, crowdfunding, social lending, and sharing clothing trades, etc. Those products or services were already offered previously but via a different business model. The traditional business model separates some big suppliers from a larger number of individual buyers. However, under the sharing economy, the number of suppliers has expanded. In the era of new business models, the roles of buyers and suppliers are becoming reversible and interchangeable. The producer at one instant can be a consumer at the other time. People have moved from being Consumers to Prosumers with far more influence than ever before. When people produce for use or exchange, production and consumption are united in the same person. So the distinctions between producers and consumers are diminishing. Such that some authors have started the term' '*Pro-summers*' (producers + Consumers), to represent the players in such a connected market of role-reversible producers and consumers (Toffler, 1980; Kotler, 1986). Toffler (1980) had argued that in the post-industrial age number of the pure consumer will decline and will give rise to prosumers, who will produce many of their own goods and services for self-consumptions. Such '*Prosumption*' activities can increase, if the undertaking of such activities promises a high-cost saving, require minimal skill, consume little time and effort, and yield high personal satisfaction (Kotler, 1986). Modern computers have permitted consumers to participate more in designing the products they want. For example, General Motors' Saturn project V4 had visualized car buyers entering a showroom, sitting down at a computer terminal and responding to questions about what they want in the way of the car's colour, engine, seat material, radio, and so on! The contemporary examples of *presumption*-based models include social network sites such as Facebook, LinkedIn, Twitter, Instagram, or video sharing platforms such as YouTube, online e-commerce companies like eBay, Amazon, etc, and other services in a range of industries from the taxi, housing, hotel, and other industries. In all of those examples, the same person acts as a producer at one time and acts as a consumer at other times. These examples of industries in the sharing economy have many similarities but are also dissimilar in some respects.

The sharing economy encompasses a triangular relationship of an intermediary that connects a service provider to a user. So it is as if, one parry creates a playground/platform on which others (buyers and suppliers) meet, interact and exchanges goods, resources and services of values with each other. So for example, Uber Technologies has created a platform for suppliers (car owners) and buyers (transportation customers). Similarly, YouTube, Facebook, LinkedIn, Instagram, eBay, Alibaba, doctor-on-demand, TaskRabbit, etc have created platforms for buyer and sellers to connect, share and exchange information, goods, services, ideas or resources, etc. This way it is also becoming difficult to classify the platform creator as belonging to a specific industry. For example, Uber offers transportation or ride-sharing services but is classified as a technology company. A study shows that the sharing economy will increase from$14 billion in 2014 to $335 billion by 2025. (Keir, 2018). The main industries which have already adopted the 'Shared economy-based business model' are given in the next section (see Table 2).

## Consumer Goods and Retailing Industry

The pioneer industry to adopt ICT and shared economy-based modes is the consumer goods selling retailing industry. In 2019, with high market capitalisation, companies such as eBay ($34.68 Billion,2019), Etsy($9.4 Billion), Rent the Runway ($1.0 Billion),Alibaba ($512 Billion) etc (MacroTrends, 2019) have revolutionised the retailing and consumer goods and its retailing industry (see Table 2) . The new retailing industry offers better affordability, convenience, and efficiency and those have become strong drivers of consumer goods purchasing decision.

*Table 2. Industries with shared economy business models*

| Company | Sector | Industry | Market Cap or East value (in the $, year June 2019) | Sales (in the $, year June 2019) |
|---|---|---|---|---|
| Uber Technologies | Computer and Technology | internet Services: transportation and food ordering services | $73.807B | $11.270B |
| eBay | Retail/ Wholesale | Internet Commerce | $34.687B | $10.746B |
| Alibaba | Retail/ Wholesale | Internet Commerce | $512.000B | $56.152B |
| Etsy | Computer and Technology | Online and offline marketplaces retailing. The company's product includes art, home and living, mobile accessories, jewelry, wedding, and other | $7.617B | $0.604B |
| Lyft | Computer and Technology | Internet Commerce- a transportation platform that connects passengers with drivers | $17.259B | $2.157B |
| Didi Chuxing | | Internet Commerce- a transportation platform that connects passengers with drivers | $51.600 B | $5.614B |
| FIVERR INTL | Professional services/ Retail/ Wholesale | Internet Commerce- an online marketplace for selling goods and services-logo, poster and brochure designing, content marketing and translation services. | $0.845B | $0.075B |
| Upwork | Computer and Technology | Internet Services / Professional services/: recruitment services. The Company offers jobs in categories such as website developers, virtual assistants, sales and marketing experts, accountants and consultants: | $1.694B | $0.253B |
| TaskRabbit: | | a marketplace that matches freelance labour with local demand, allowing consumers to find immediate help with everyday tasks, including cleaning, moving, delivery and handyman work | $0.0504B | $0.253B |
| Teladoc, Inc. | Medical | Medical Services and Healthcare to share medical equipment telemedicine and doctors with other healthcare facilities telehealth services via mobile devices, internet, video | $4.889B | $0.418B |
| American Well | | Medical Services and Healthcare: let hospitals to share medical equipment telemedicine and doctors with other healthcare facilities | $0.441B | $0.250B |
| Doctor on Demand | | Healthcare: let hospitals to share medical equipment and doctors with other healthcare facilities | $0.160B | NA |

*continues on following page*

*Table 2. Continued*

| Company | Sector | Industry | Market Cap or East value (in the $, year June 2019) | Sales (in the $, year June 2019) |
|---|---|---|---|---|
| Cohealo | | Healthcare: let hospitals to share medical equipment and doctors with other healthcare facilities | $0.012B | $0.0036B |
| Airbnb | Renting, Hospitality, housing, and Hotel Industry | Renting, Hospitality, housing, and Hotel Industry | $38.0B | $3.800B |
| Couchsurfing | Renting, Hospitality, housing, and the Hotel Industry | Renting, Hospitality, housing, and the Hotel Industry | | |
| Neighbor | housing and Self-Storage | housing and Self-Storage | | |
| Rover | Professional services | Professional services Dog care - pet owners to get connected with sitters | | |
| JustPark | Renting Parking space | parking space-sharing companies | | |
| Lending Club | Banking, financing, and crowdfunding | Banking, financing, and crowdfunding: easy loan and lending | | |
| Poshmark | Clothing and personal accessory sharing industry. | Clothing and personal accessory sharing industry. - online peer-to-peer clothing marketplace | | |
| SitterCity | Professional services | Professional services online caregiving community is an easy way for parents and sitters to get connected | | |
| Kickstarter | Banking, financing, and crowdfunding | Banking, financing, and crowdfunding: easy loan and lending . | $2.000B | |
| Lemonade | Insurance | Insurance: insurance as a shared asset | | |

Sources: (Forbes, 2019, Miller, 2019; MacroTrends, 2019)

## Transportation and Supply Chain Industry

The transportation and supply chain industry has very well adopted shared economy models (see Table 2). The ride-sharing services or 'Transportation Network Companies' such as Uber, Ola, Lyft, My Taxi, etc. requires digital platforms and apps to offer the rides for the passengers by the drivers (Statista, 2018). Through the online platforms, the passengers can request a ride to their preferred destination and then their needs will be matched with the driver, who is heading in the same direction. The range of the ride-sharing services has also expanded to 'Carpooling' platform such as BlaBlaCar (Statista, 2018). The successful ride-sharing companies such as Uber, Grab, Kuadi, Ola(India) and Easy Weixing (China) has left an impact in the transportation sector.

By utilizing an efficient mobile application and network of vetted drivers, various transportation industry companies such as Uber ($73 Billion), Didi Chuxing ($52 Billion), Lyft ($17.25 Billion-A ride-sharing service for people to find rides from "regular" people), Postmates, RVshare etc has captured the industry (see Table 2) (MacroTrends, 2019). These companies already satisfy consumers' transportation needs and product/service delivery services more efficiently at better prices, time and flexibility. Traditionally, core providers, such as truck leasing companies used dedicate assets to carry planned loads at pre-negotiated rates. However, by utilising a shared platform the third party logistic (3PL) market has become more effective in matching the excess capacity with the demand. Google-backed RelayRides enables people to borrow cars from neighbours. Getaround lets people borrow cars from others (Forbes, 2019) ForestCar, offers car owners free airport parking in exchange for renting out their vehicles (Keir, 2018).

Ride sharing platform is not only impacting the ride-sharing segments but also public transit, automotive industry and the choices of people's shopping, working, and socializing destinations. The ride-sharing services have also helped in minimizing the parking difficulties and even helped to reduce the stress of travel timing etc. Ride-sharing companies such as Uber, Grab, Ola, Easy Weixing BangJek, TransJek, Wheel Line, Blue-Jek, and Ojeks Syar'i are penetrating the whole world market including USA, United Kingdom, Mexico, France, Spain, Belgium, Canada, Australia, Taiwan, Russia, India, South Korea, Philippine, and Indonesia (Dharmasaputra, 2015).

## Professional, Services and Personal Products Renting Industries

This kind of services requires special knowledge, skills, experience, certifications, or training such as copywriters, accountants, or plumbers, etc. The companies like Fiverr, Upwork (hire people to do job), Zaarly (market their services, from home repair to mobile repair), TaskRabbit (hire people to do job) Rover (Dog care), DogVacay (Dog care), SitterCity, Fon (share home Wi-Fi network in exchange from each other), and Gumtree etc are pioneer in this area (see Table 2). In India and Dubai, RentSher lets household consumers rent their household goods: baby carriages and party supplies, such as tents and speaker systems (Wallenstein & Urvesh, 2017). Availability of abundant local labour lets RentSher send teams into the field to photograph and prepare a list of goods on behalf of owners and transport the goods to renters (Wallenstein & Urvesh, 2017).

## Healthcare Industry

The inefficiency of traditional healthcare-based Systems is giving rise to SEBMs in the healthcare sector (see Table 2). The total healthcare industry is expected to generate annual revenues of $8.7 trillion by 2020 (Miller, 2019). There is sprout in venture capitalist investment into digital and shared economy-based models in healthcare. The equipment and skills of healthcare professionals have non-synchronous demand. This means that at times most of the capacities are underutilised or over utilised. To match the demand and supply in a better way, a shared economy-based model is a better solution. That's why some companies such as American Well, CrowdMed, Doctor on Demand and Cohealo, etc are already expanding their wings in this sector (Miller, 2019).

## Renting, Hospitality and Storage Industries

The renting and hospitality industry are also not untouched from shared economy business models. The higher costs of renting and storage has led to the creation of sharing platforms by entrepreneurs in this sector. The companies like Airbnb, Neighbor, Couchsurfing, JustPark have innovated the housing, hotel or space renting owning services already.

## Banking, Financial and Crowd Funding Industries

To undertake any being or business transactions, people need money. The traditional banking system has put some barriers for potentials customers to get loans or funds. In responses to that, a range of companies is meeting the financial and banking needs of their clients using SEBMs (see Table 2). A range of crowdfunding and credit offering companies are growing world over. For example; Kickstarter, Lending Club ($1.0 Billion, is a network to get cold hard cash), etc. The Global crowdfunding industry potential is expected to reach $80 billion by 2025 from $16 billion in 2014 (Jeune, 2016).

## Insurance Industry

In response to crowd sharing and collaborative use and sharing of assets, the insurance industry is facing challenges to decide about the ownership of the rented products and then insuring an asset that is used by a number of clients as a shared product or asset. Thus, the insurance companies are working out the options to cover a wide range of peer-to-peer transactions. The companies like Lemonade, a US property and casualty InsurTechhas started offering insurance as a shared asset; such an insurance policy allows premiums to be paid by networks of communities of the users (Keir, 2018).

## Clothing and Personal Accessory Sharing Industry

Online peer-to-peer clothing marketplace is a new field under sharing economy. For example, companies like Poshmark, etc provide an online peer-to-peer clothing marketplace by letting people buy or sell their clothing.

## Entertainment and Music Industry

The entertainment and music industry was one of the pioneer industries to use the sharing economy, business models. Spotify is a very well know company in the music industry. However, if we extend our logic a bit we will start seeing companies like YouTube etc are also in a big way based on shared economy. Consumers are renting music via streaming services such as Spotify and Apple Music (Wallenstein & Urvesh, 2017). Other companies in this industry are BitTorrent protocol sites such as; The Pirate Bay, Grokster, iTunes, Rhapsody, Pandora, and Spotify that offer downloads or streaming music, films and television programs (Belk, 2014).

### Trust Building Industry

As the basis of the sharing economy relies on peer to peer interactions, communication, technology usage, and trust. Hence, a new kind of organisations is appearing, whose whole job is to create and enhance trust between the players of the sharing economy. People are already familiar with companies like Trustpilot, TripAdvisor, etc. Another organisation named Deeply provides a reputation and social verification platform that supports online communities and sharing economy businesses to increase trust between their users (Keir, 2018). Even social media networks such as Facebook, Twitter, Instagram, etc are used for enhancing trust.

### Social Networking Platforms Industry

These platforms offer opportunities to users to supply and receive information, communications and other time pass entertaining activities and ideas, etc. Photo sharing sites like Flickr and social media sites like Facebook and Twitter as well as interest-sharing sites like Pinterest are important examples of Social networking platforms.

### Miscellaneous Industries

The new kind of offerings and industries are emerging. For example Boatbound (leisure boat rental), PeerBy (neighborhood exchange of household items), and Trump (rooms rented out as office space) (Wallenstein & Urvesh, 2017). Even the energy industry has started using sharing economy-based models. For example wind farm in Denmark, is partly funded by the residents. Similarly the community solar projects by solar share companies such as American Mosaic in the USA and Canadian Solar Share Canada (PWC, 2015).

## CLASSIFICATION OF SEBMs

A business model is an art of how one plans to exchange and monetise his or her idea, knowledge, resources, goods, or services or so on (Ovans, 2015).In simple term, a business model is 'how one plans to make money or exchange values. The term has become popular with the expansion of dot.com boom, where a business model for companies meant how to attract a large number of people to websites and the advertise and sell products to the crowds (Ovans, 2015). Peter Drucker stated that a business model is an action or process based on a set of business environment-related and consumer-related assumptions about what a company is paid for! (Ovans, 2015). A business model is based on a competitive business strategy or game plan. A business model is a description of how a business runs its operations, however, a competitive strategy explains how an organisation creates a competitive advantage over its rivals. Thus a business model explains how an enterprise works using various functions in its value chain Who are its customers? what customers value? and how managers can exchange value at profit using a range of activities such as value chain, value proposition, customer relationships, channels, customer segments, cost structures, and revenue streams, etc ? (Ovans, 2015) . A new business model is the result of disruptive innovation. The life of business models ends when any incremental improvement in the model ads very little value to the stakeholders.

To distinguish the sharing economy from other economic business models, Frenken et al. (2015) have argued to consider four elements. First, the activities in a sharing economy are hosted as online services, which are easy to access via digital devices real-time on platforms that can match the local demand. Second, all sharing economy schemes provide a lot of options for the consumers at reduced the cost. Third, such models are based on trust and social interaction. Finally, the sharing economy aims to build an emotional relationship and is designed for a customised user journey.

## Typology of SEBMs of Sharing Economy

Based on a buyer-supplier exchange, a business model can be Customer to Customer (C2C), Business to Customer (B2C) and Business to Business (B2B) (see Table 3). A business model of sharing economy was first initiated from the Consumer to Consumer (C2C). In C2C model the private individuals contact each other and share their tangible assets, spare devices, or knowledge using some online platforms. The example of the companies which are using C2C type sharing economy services includes; AirBnB, Uber, BlaBlacar, and ZipCar in the service sector. Similarly, Wikipedia and Facebook are other examples of digital platforms for sharing knowledge or information.

The second exchange-based business model is Business to Consumer (B2C). In the B2C model, the company acts as a supplier that operates the digital platform and provides products or services by replacing the individual owners (Frick et al., 2013).

The Third Model is Business to Business (B2B), where one business organisation transacts with other business organisation.

## Consumer to Consumer (C2C) Business Model

This model results from the collaboration between ‘equal partners’, as the providers and users of services are brought together through by a third company using IT platforms (PWC, 2015) . Consumers contact each other through a digital platform and share their spare devices, knowledge or tangible assets or skills or services. Such services are provided for instance by Uber, Airbnb or BlaBlaCar, Skillshare, Wikipedia or even Facebook (see Table 3) In all of the cases, consumers play on a playground/platform that is designed, developed and maintained by the business’ organisations for profit (Buda & Lehota, 2017).

## Business to Consumer (B2C) Model

In a B2C model, the supplier of the goods or services and the operator of the intermediation channel are one and the same company and the receivers are the customers (PWC, 2015). The examples include Daimler (car2Go) and BMW (DriveNow); the MOL Bubi (community bicycle scheme) etc.

## Business to Business (B2B) Model

The players are business organisations and the platform also belongs to some other company. Such a B2B business model not only provides a playground/platform, but it also provides the products and services as suppliers. E.g. companies Mol Bubi, ZipCar, Car2Go, ReachNow owned by BMW car, Netflix, Spotify etc work on this model (Buda & Lehota, 2017).

*Table 3. Typology of Shared economy-based models as per buyer and suppliers transactions*

| Good / Services | Expected growth Revenue CAGR (2013 – 2025) | C2C or P2P (user, platform & provider) | B2C (provider with platform and user) | B2B |
|---|---|---|---|---|
| Transportation/ Car renting/ Sharing/ delivery | +23% | Blablacar<br>Turo | Zipcar, Uber, Lyft | |
| Accommodation/ Hotel, office or space sharing renting, Parking | +31% | Airbnb/,<br>Onefinestay,<br>HomeAway,<br>Sharemystorage<br>Couchsurfing, HomeExchange,<br>KAPTÁR, JustPark | Wework | Regus<br>Workspade or other Leasing companies |
| Payments/money transfers | +15% | Currencyfair,<br>Transferwise | | Visa |
| Retailing | +8% | Ebay, Amazon | Ebay, Amazon | |
| Bike renting / sharing | +10% | MOL Bubi | JC Decaux, CitiBike, Barclays | |
| equipment | +5% | Miutcánk.hu. | Getable | |
| Luxury or hand made good resale and rental | +10% | Etsy | The Real, Real Rent the Runaway | |
| Video games , music and books | +17% | Gloss, Netflix,<br>PirateBay, Gamefly, Kickstarter. | GameFly, Netflix,<br>Rukkola.hu (books) | |
| Apparel and accessories | +15% | Swap.com, Rent the Runaway, Gwynnie Bee, Rehashclothes. com. Le Tote, Buymyheels.com | | |
| Staffing/ Recruiting | +37% | | Skillsshare, Linkedin, Lynda, | |
| 'Freelancer'and professional services | +20% | Yummber (cooking) | Sitters.co.uk | |
| Education and skills | +15% | Home advisor, Linkedin, Taskrabbit, Skillsesh, Upwork, Freelancer,<br>Skillshare | Chegg | |
| Finance, Crowdfunding and lending | +63% | LendingClub,<br>Lendico, Lufax,<br>Prosper, Jimubox,<br>Lendinvest | Crowdcube,<br>Fundingcircle | |
| Insurance | +15% | Inspeerme, heyguevara,<br>friendsurance,<br>inshared | | |
| Miscellaneous | +10-20% | WattPad (media).<br>Stubhub (Entertainment),<br>Myways (delivery/logistics),<br>Szatyorbolt (picking delivery) | | |

Sources adapted from (Jeune, 2016 and PWC, 2015)

## Types of Business Models Based on the Resources shared

As per Botsman and Rogers, (2011), there are there three systems or business models based on the types of resources shared. (see Table 4) The three systems or business models are Redistribution Markets, Product Service Systems, and Collaborative Lifestyles (Botsman and Rogers, 2011).

### Redistribution Markets Type SEBMs

'Redistribution Markets' based SEBMs motivate people to reuse or re-sell the unused or underutilised products instead of destroying them. This redistribution markets-based business model helps in decreasing wastage of` unused resources For example organisations such as; eBay, Gmarket, Auction, etc pursue this kind of business models (see Table:4).

### Product Service Systems SEBMs

A 'Product Service Systems business models ' help in sharing of services owned by a corporation. This system interrupts the traditional industries to use private ownership's model, there's no need for the consumer to pay for the products or their maintenance, insurance, or repair fee. E.g. Uber, BlaBlaCar, ZipCar, GreenCar, Grab, Linux, Dropbox, Amazon, Saleforce.com, etc have this kind of business models (see table 5).

### Collaborative Lifestyles SEBMs

The last type of business model is a 'Collaborative Lifestyles' based model, which requires a great amount of trust since the focus of the exchange is more on peer to peer interaction rather than an exchange of tangible product (Botsman and Rogers, 2011). 'Collaborative Lifestyles business models' are expanding around the world because of the growth of the internet and many consumer motivations. Instead of trading, sharing, or swapping physical goods (such as cars and bikes, homes, parking lots, experiences, skills, and money), the consumers are exchanging their intangible or tangible assets based on their

*Table 4. Categories of shared economy business models by resources shared*

| Overview | Sharing Resources | Examples |
|---|---|---|
| Product Service Systems business models | Sharing car, motorcycle, and bicycle. | Uber, BlaBlaCar, ZipCar, GreenCar, and Grab. |
| | Open Source Software (OSS), cloud computing service, or Software as a service (SaaS). | Linux, Dropbox, Amazon, Saleforce.com, Naver cloud, and etc. |
| Redistributions Markets business models | Exchanging or redistributing the products in open marketplaces. | eBay, Gmarket, Auction, etc. |
| Collaborative Lifestyles business models | Sharing houses, spare rooms, renting, and other idle capacities such as working spaces, parking lots, experiences, and money. | Airbnb, TaskRabbit, Kickstarter, Kozaza, Zopa, Albachunkuk, Quirky, and etc. |

Source: (Jaehun, 2017)

similar interests (Kathan, Matzler, and Veider, 2016; Miller, 2016). For instants organisation such as Airbnb, TaskRabbit, Kickstarter, Kozaza, Zopa, Albachunkuk, Quirky, etc. have adopted 'Collaborative Lifestyles business models' (see Table 4).

## EMPIRICAL STUDIES REGARDING THE PARTICIPATION AND USAGE OF SEBMs

The sharing economy-based business models (SEBMs) and new industries are emerging due to decreasing transaction costs, a spurt of smartphones, internet connectivity, organisational economics, Innovations, cloud storage facilities and a number of consumer motivations. The external factors have improved search efficiency for the consumers for getting their desired goods or services (Wallenstein & Urvesh, 2017). Further, the boom of technology also means faster logistics and delivery of physical products. Thus, the transactions have become more efficient and hassle-free for the participants. The consumer motivations for participation in the sharing economy include; personal factors, economic factors, socio-demographic factors and a range of other motivational factors (Hellwig, 2015, Van de Glind 2013).

The previous researchers have analysed a range of 'Supplier side' and 'Demand-side factors' that effects participants' intention to participate in shared economy-based business models (Hamari et al. 2015, Van de Glind (2013). The next section discusses a model of intention to use 'shared economy business models' (see Figure -6).

### Supply Side Drivers of 'Sharing Economy Based Models'

#### Matchmaking and Internet of Things Factors

The internet of things will let equipments communicate with each other and with their users in real-time. Thus, it means the more spare capacity of the equipments can be released and that can be matched with demand with dynamic pricing in real-time. This will further engage people and organisations in sharing economy-based models.

#### Logistics Technology Factor

The development in the technofixes related to drones, self-driving cars, and delivery robots etc will further aid in faster movement of physical goods and assets at less effort and lesser costs; thus making more availability of shareable goods at much better ease and lower transaction costs (Wallenstein & Urvesh, 2017).

#### Blockchain and Smart Contracts Factors

The Blockchain and Smart Contracts technologies are already creating its ripple in banking and Crypto-currency industry. A blockchain (a sort of distributed ledger) will help document the assets' provenance, usage history, and identity in a more secure, trustworthy and contract implementable ways. Hence the technology will lead to enhancement of trust- A important factor needed for shared economy. Thus, the application of shared economy models has further potential to boom.

*Figure 6. Demand-side and supply-side factors for adoption of shared economy models*

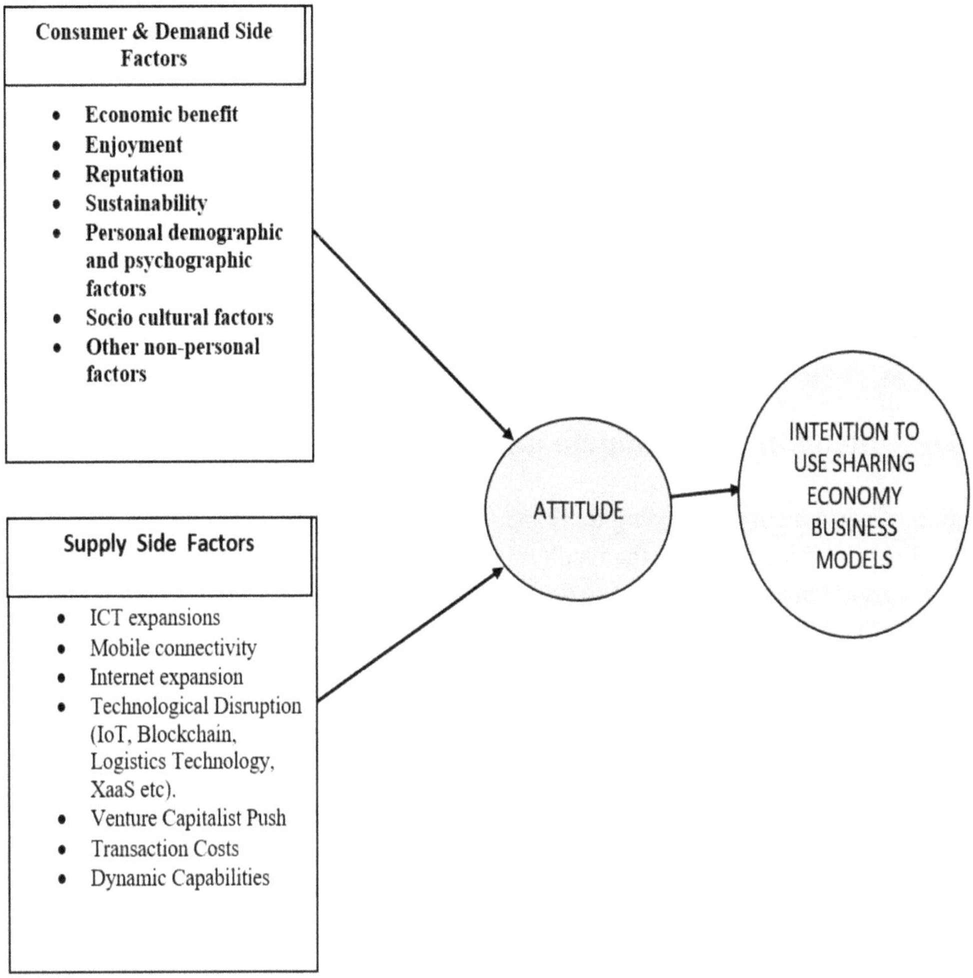


## Venture Capitalist Interest Factor

In the B2C market, the business models on shared workspaces, storage and delivery, and logistics (a category that includes pet sitting and parking spaces) are attracting more venture capitalist. For example, organizations such as; WeWork and Vrumi have received nearly $2 billion in investments and similarly; Vehicle sharing, car rentals, and bicycle rentals business models have received $810 million from venture capitalists (Wallenstein & Urvesh, 2017). Similarly, in the B2B market, companies such as; YardClub -a construction-equipment rental business has received $150 million capital (Wallenstein & Urvesh, 2017). Between 2009 to 2015 around $23 billion has been invested in sharing economy and the total market capitalisation of sharing economy had reached $219 billion in 2015 (Jeune, 2016).

### XaaS Business Models Factors

Consumers buy products or services for some benefits or services from them. Hence, everything is becoming an intangible service. Even the tangible products we buy or rent, offer us a service. Consumers are renting music via streaming services such as; Spotify and iTunes or Apple Music etc. The Cloud technology is allowing 'softwares as services' (SAS), thus letting the organisations and consumers access software, storage, and other resources as a service (Wallenstein & Urvesh, 2017). Similarly, any tangible assets like clothes, boats, cars, medical equipment, etc may be less costly to rent & share than to completely buy or own them. This is another driver for 'Shared economy business models'.

## CONSUMERS AND DEMAND-SIDE FACTORS OF SEBMs

### Consumers' Intention to Participate in the Sharing Economy

The definition of participation according to Verba, Schlozman, and Brady (1995) is 'an activity that is directly or indirectly intended or has the result of affecting government action'. Consumers should be able to operate digital platforms in order to be able to participate in the sharing economy. A study by Hamari et al. (2015) showed that the economic, sustainability, and convenience are the main drivers that motivated the user to participate in the sharing economy. Nielsen (2014) found that people are willing to share their underutilized assets drives the sharing economy. Nielsen (2014) also found that people intend to share Electronic devices (28%), intellectual property (25%), power tools (23%), Bicycle (22%), Clothing (22%), and household items (21.5%).

Hamari (2015) found a strong relationship between behavioural intention and consumers motivations such as; sustainability, enjoyment, reputation, and economic benefits, attitude. Kim, Lee, and Choi (2014) found that geographical regional factors and choice of destinations (commercial centric, station, and bus spheres) influenced the frequency of car sharing. The researchers had found a relationship between motivation, perceived security, attitude, and loyalty toward Airbnb. Kim, Lee, and Choi (2014) found that the younger generation has a higher intention to use ride-sharing as compared to the older generation. According to a study by PWC (2017), 53% of the users of the sharing economy are under 40 or young millennials.

Thus, there is a range of reasons for participants' preferences for the sharing economy. The personal reasons for 'non-reciprocal share' (open sharing or demand share) and ' benefit seeking to share'. The personal reasons might include functional reasons such as the need for survival or being altruistic, courtesy, or kindness to others. The reciprocal sharing or ' benefit seeking to share' is driven by other reason such as; for-profit, mutual returns, temporary borrowing, or reciprocal returns or bartering, lending, trading, renting, etc (Belk, 2014). Nielsen (2014), found that millennials are willing to pay more for sustainable products or services. Millennials and young adults have grown up in a period of rapid technological change and so are very comfortable and have positive intentions to use technology and seems to value good experiences over materialistic things (Keir, 2018). Communication, trust, reputation, and technology usage are the basis of participation in shared economy-based business models.

The next sections discusses some of the consumers' motivation sin details.

## ECONOMIC BENEFITS AND SEBMs

When the users are participating in sharing, they trade or substitutes the ownership of assets they need with some lower-cost options. There are two types of motivational factors (intrinsic and extrinsic) and thus potential future rewards such as economic benefits (Hars and Ou, 2001). According to self-determination theory, there are two factors of motivations; intrinsic and extrinsic motivations (Deci and Ryan, 1985). The intrinsic motivations are the enjoyment associated with the given activity. The extrinsic factors include reputation and monetary gains. Lindenberg (2001) suggested that intrinsic motivations are distinguished into two; the first one is the value resulting from acting properly and adapting to norms and the second one is resulting from the activity itself. The intention to use is not only affected by their motives to enjoy an activity but also their level of association with other people (Lakhani and Wolf, 2005); Nov et al., 2010). As the association with others can affect the way consumers would reflect upon the activity due to the social norm and personal reputation. The intrinsic motivation is the social value and extrinsic motivation factors include; time savings, cost savings, and convenience (Block et al. (2005 and Hamari et al. 2015). The saving economic resourced the main motivation to participate in sharing (Luchs et al. (2011).

### Customer Enjoyment and SEBMs

One of the important personal motivation to use shared economy models is the need of enjoyment The intrinsic need of enjoyment, flow and proficiency are the main motivations for participation on the sharing economy (Lakhani and Wolf, 2005; Nov 2007; Roberts et al., 2006; Wasko and Faraj, 2000). This is in line with the Technology Adoption Model (TAM) and related factors of self-efficacy, social norms and perceived usefulness of the activities. The enjoyment is also the main reasons for using social networking services, along with the effectiveness and opportunities to connect with a number of peers (Lin and Lu, 2011). Most of the social networking platforms such as Facebook or Instagram or YouTube have adopted features of 'likeness' to represent enjoyment (Hamari and Koivisto, 2015).

### Reputation and SEBMs

Self-esteem or Ego need is an important driver of peoples' behaviour. Need for 'Reputation' controls the participation in the sharing economy activities and also other online collaboration activities such as open-source projects or information sharing (Lakhani and Wolf, 2005; Nov et al., 2010, Wasko and Faraj, 2005). According to Wasko and Faraj (2005), the contribution towards sharing knowledge via electronic networks is caused by the individual's perception that such sharing will develop a personal reputation among peers and communities. The motivation for sharing in open source project or online collaboration come from the reputation that one gains among compatible people (Parameswaran and Whinston, 2007). In the sharing information platform such as Wikipedia, the reputation and commitment to the community are the vital aspects (Anthony, Smith, and Williamson, 2009). Thus, the probability to collaborate in online sharing platforms is driven by the need for building self-reputation and self-marketing (Hars and Ou, 2001).

### Sustainability and SEBMs

The sharing economy has roots in sharing and altruism. Thus, eco-friendly consumption and environmentally sustainable are important motives that expected by participants from the participation in the sharing economy (Prothero et al., 2011; Sacks, 2011). These intrinsic motivations are mostly related to norms and ideology (Prothero et al., 2011; Sacks, 2011). The sharing economy platforms are used to maximize the consumption of social, environmental, and economic values to fulfill the needs of today's generation as well that of the future generations (Phipps, Ozanne, Luchs et al., 2011). For some people participation in peer production and open-source (Wikipedia) or software development is driven by selfless motives such as honesty and freedom of information (Nov et al, 2010). Therefore, sustainability that related to norms is one of the intrinsic motivational factors to participate in shared Economy business models.

### Consumer's Attitude and SEBMs

According to Ajzen (1991), one of the key factors of people's behaviour is their attitude. Motivation is a precursor of the attitude towards sharing (Bucher et al. (2016). Therefore, the attitude towards sharing economy and technology would have a strong effect on the intention to participate in the sharing. The easy and useful technology that can facilitate the sharing economy will enhance participants to use sharing economy activities. The attitude can also be influenced by social pressures and social norms in a shared economy environment (Goldstein, Cialdini, and Griskevicius (2008).

In conclusion, there are various supply-side and demand-side factors that influence participants (supplier, intermediates and consumers) to participate in the sharing economy based business models.

## CHALLENGES AND ISSUE RELATED TO SEBMs

Though the shared economy models are showing great future, however, a few challenges to the sharing economy models should also be needed to be considered. As the new business models have some disruptive effects on the existing players of the related industry, so there is often a backlash on sharing economy. For instant, Uber faces backlash from taxi rental companies and governments and other stakeholders, whose interests are negatively affected by expansions of ride-sharing services. On same lines, Airbnb is facing backlash from the hotel and renting industry and related lobbies. The traditional business and their employees are arguing that they are losing jobs, profits, and business to these new shared economy-based models. Further, as the sharing economy is more about sharing assets (cars, equipment, technologies, skills, etc.), so the fundamental ways of insuring those tangible assets by the insurance industry is going to change, resulting in disruption in insurance industry and insurance costs to the participants Now the assets are shared by many people, so a one to one individual insurance of such 'shared assets' is difficult to implement. Kerr (2018) has pointed out that, "the world of one person being insured for one thing for a long period of time is fundamentally dying. There are also many regulatory problems related to taxation & grey economy, user's security & protection, health & safety, financial frauds, data protection, contractual laws, competition regulation, consumer protection, etc that needs to be addressed to unshackle shared economy-based business models (PWC, 2015).

## CONCLUSION

The word 'Sharing Economy' is a new way of social and business etiquettes and behaviours of the people. Thus there is increasing interest in the 'shared economy-based business models' (seems). The advancements information and communication technologies (ICT) and their utilities have further given a push to shared economy-based business models. Sharing economy allows the members of society to share certain assets or services that they owned but have been underutilized. The sharing economy has a number of benefits for the national economies such as; creating new jobs, efficient usage of national resources, leveraging the business sector and sustainable production. To create a sustainable competitive advantage, the organizations are adopting innovative social economy-based business models. A business model is the sum total of ways to create and capture values by creating new revenue streams. The organisations use shared economy-based business models, due to the strategic needs of developing core competencies (resource-based theory), to attain minimum transactions costs (Transaction cost economy) and ultimately attain dynamic capabilities. The business models help organisations in constituting their internal competencies and align their actions with external stakeholders.

The various types of Customer To Customer (C2C), Business To Bushisms (B2B, Business To Customers(B2C), Redistribution Markets, Product Service Systems, and Collaborative Lifestyles have come into existence under the umbrella of shared economy business models (SEBMs). The Shared economy business models (SEBM) have been adopted across many industries such as Consumer Goods and Retailing Industry; Transportation and Supply Chain Industry; Professional, Services and Personal Products Renting Industries ; Healthcare Industry; Renting, Hospitality and Storage Industries; Banking, Financial and Crowd Funding Industries; insurance Industry ;Clothing and Personal Accessory Sharing Industry; Entertainment and Music Industry; Trust building Industry ;Social Networking Platforms Industry and other Miscellaneous Industries .

The literature review has evidenced that various supplier side and demand-side factors drive the participants to participate in SEBMs. Considering the huge potential of the sharing economy based business models, it is for sure that this trend will stay for long. Further, the advancements in technology, usage of artificial intelligence, big data and data analytics are enabling the business to use technology in SEBM and in their business operation or marketing areas. As the users are giving more importance to experiences over ownership of the assets, the movement of sharing economy will further grow in the future. Thus, it is advisable to companies to adapt and adopt their business models to this new trend and wave of sharing economy-based models.

## REFERENCES

Ajzen, I. (1991). The theory of planned behaviour. *Organizational Behavior and Human Decision Processes*, *50*(2), 179–211. doi:10.1016/0749-5978(91)90020-T

Anthony, D., Smith, S. W., & Williamson, T. (2009). Reputation and reliability in collective goods the case of the online encyclopaedia Wikipedia. *Rationality and Society*, *21*(3), 283–306. doi:10.1177/1043463109336804

B'enabou, R., & Tirole, J. (2003). Intrinsic and extrinsic motivation. *The Review of Economic Studies*, *70*(3), 489–52. doi:10.1111/1467-937X.00253

Belk, R. (2001). You are what you can access; Sharing and collaborative consumption online. *Journal of Business Research, 67*(8), 1595–1600. doi:10.1016/j.jbusres.2013.10.001

Belk, R. (2014). You are what you can access: Sharing and collaborative consumption online. *Journal of Business Research, 67*, 1595–1600. Retrieved from https://collaborativeeconomy.com/wp/wp-content/uploads/2015/05/Belk-R.2014.-You-are-what-you-can-access-Sharing-and-collaborative-consumption-online.Journal-of-Business-Research.pdf

Bock, G. W., Zmud, Kim, & Lee. (2005). Behavioral intention formation in knowledge sharing: Examining the roles of extrinsic motivators,Social-psychological forces, and organizational. *Management Information Systems Quarterly, 29*(1), 87–111. doi:10.2307/25148669

Bocker, L., & Meelen, T. (2017). *Sharing for people, planet or profit? Analysing motivations for intended sharing economy participation*. Working Paper Series: Innovation Studies Utrecht.

Botsman, R. (2013). *The Sharing Economy Lack a Shared Definition: Giving Meaning to the Terms.* Retrieved Sept 5, 2018, from Fast Company: https://www.fastcompany.com/3022028/the-sharing-economy-lacks-a-shared-definition

Botsman, R. (2015). *Defining the Sharing Economy: What Is Collaborative Consumption – And What Isn't?* Retrieved from http://www.fastcoexist.com/3046119/

Botsman, R., & Rogers, R. (2010). Beyond Zipcar: Collaborative consumption. *Harvard Business Review, 88*(10), 30. PMID:20607961

Botsman, R., & Rogers, R. (2011). *What's mine is yours-the rise of collaborative consumption*. HarperCollins.

Bray, J. J., Johns, N., & Kilburn, D. (2011). An exploratory study into the factors impeding ethical consumption. *Journal of Business Ethics, 98*(4), 597–608. doi:10.100710551-010-0640-9

Bryman, A., & Bell, E. (2003). *Business research methods*. Northamptonshire, UK: Oxford University Press.

Bucher, E., Fieseler, C., & Lutz, C. (2016). What's mine is yours (for a nominal fee) – Exploring the spectrum of utilitarian to altruistic motives for Internet-mediated sharing. *Computers in Human Behavior, 62*, 316–326. doi:10.1016/j.chb.2016.04.002

Bucher, E. F. (2016). What's mine is yours (for a nominal fee) – Exploring the spectrum of utilitarian to altruistic motives for Internet-mediated sharing. *Computers in Human Behaviour*, 316-326.

Buda, G., & Lehota, J. (2017). *Attitudes and Motivations of Consumers in Sharing Economy, Management, Enterprise and Benchmarking in the 21st Century*. Retrieved Sept 3, 2018, from KGK university: https://kgk.uni-obuda.hu/sites/default/files/02_Buda_Lehota.pdf

Casadesus-Masanell, R., & Heilbron, J. (2015). *The Business Model: Nature and Benefits*. Retrieved from https://www.hbs.edu/faculty/Publication Files/15-089_afa7e1c9-40d2-486d-9bd4-b8ea71de9058.pdf

Correa, T. (2010). The participation divide among 'online experts': Experience, skills and psycho-logical factors as predictors of college students' web content creation. *Journal of Computer-Mediated Communication*, *16*(1), 71–92. doi:10.1111/j.1083-6101.2010.01532.x

Cramer, J., & Krueger, A. (2016). Disruptive Change in the Taxi Business: The Case of Uber. *The American Economic Review*, *106*(5), 177–182. doi:10.1257/aer.p20161002

DaSilva, C. M., & Trkman, P. (2014). Business Model: What it is and What it is Not. *SSRN Electronic Journal*, *47*(6), 379–389. doi:10.2139srn.2181113

Davis, P. M. (2012). Trust is number 1 barrier to sharing. *DeskMag*. Retrieved from http://www.deskmag.com/en/trust-is-1-barrier-to-sharing-coworking-shareable-491/

Deci, E. L., & Ryan, R. M. (1985). *Intrinsic motivation and self- determination in human behaviour*. New York: Plenum. doi:10.1007/978-1-4899-2271-7

Downes, L. (2009). *The Laws of Disruption: Harnessing the New Forces that Govern Life and Business in the Digital Age*. Basic Book.

Economist.com. (2013). *The rise of the sharing economy*. Retrieved, 12 April, 2017, from http://www.economist.com/news/leaders/21573104-internet-everything-hire-rise- sharing-economy

Felson, M., & Spaeth, J. L. (1978). Community Structure and Collaborative Consumption: A routine activity approach. *The American Behavioral Scientist*, *21*(4), 614–624. doi:10.1177/000276427802100411

Forbes. (2019). Retrieved from https://www.forbes.com/

Galbreth, M. R., Ghosh, B., & Shor, M. (2012). Social sharing of information goods: Implications for pricing and profits. *Marketing Science*, *31*(4), 603–620. doi:10.1287/mksc.1120.0706

Goldstein, N. J., Cialdini, R. B., & Griskevicius, V. (2008). A room with a viewpoint: Using social norms to motivate environmental conservation in hotels. *The Journal of Consumer Research*, *35*(3), 472–482. doi:10.1086/586910

Government State Victoria. (2018). *Teach with digital technologies*. Retrieved 05 1, 2019, from Education.vic.gov.: https://www.education.vic.gov.au/school/teachers/teachingresources/digital/Pages/teach.aspx

Hamari, J., Huotari, K., & Tolvanen, J. (2015). Gamification and economics. In S. P. Walz & S. Deterding (Eds.), *The gameful world: Approaches, issues, applications* (pp. 139–161). Cambridge, MA: MIT Press.

Hamari, J., Sjoklint, M., & Ukkonen, A. (2015). The sharing economy: Why people participate in collaborative consumption. *Journal of the Association for Information Science and Technology*.

Hargittai, E., & Walejko, G. (2008). The participation divide: Content creation and sharing in the digital age. *Information Communication and Society*, *11*(2), 239–256. doi:10.1080/13691180801946150

Hars, A., & Ou, S. (2001). Working for Free? Motivations of Participating in Open Source Projects. *Proceedings of the 34th Hawaii International Conference on System Sciences*. 10.1109/HICSS.2001.927045

Hellwig, K., Morhart, F., Girardin, F., & Hauser, M. (2015). Exploring different types of sharing: A proposed segmentation of the market for sharing businesses. *Psychology and Marketing*, *32*(9), 891–906. doi:10.1002/mar.20825

Hennig-Thurau, T., Henning, V., & Sattler, H. (2007). Consumer file sharing of motion pictures. *Journal of Marketing*, *71*(4), 1–18. doi:10.1509/jmkg.71.4.1

Henten, A., & Windekilde, I. (2016). Transaction costs and the sharing economy. *Info*, *18*(1), 1–15. doi:10.1108/info-09-2015-0044

Jeune, S. L. (2016). *The Sharing Economy*. Retrieved June 2, 2019, from www.schroders.com: https://www.schroders.com/pl/sysglobalassets/digital/insights/2016/pdfs/responsible-investment/the-sharing-economy/the-sharing-economy-report-final.pdf

Joo, J. (2017). Motives for Participating in Sharing Economy: Intentions to Use Car Sharing Services. *Journal of Distribution Science*, *15*(2), 21–26. doi:10.15722/jds.15.2.201702.21

Joshi, A., Chandel, S., Kale, S., & Pal, D. (2015). Likert scale: Explored and explained. *Current Journal of Applied Science and Technology*, *7*(4), 396–403. doi:10.9734/BJAST/2015/14975

Kaplan, A. M., & Haenlein, M. (2010). Users of the world, unite! The challenges and opportunities of Social Media. *Business Horizons*, *53*(1), 59–68. doi:10.1016/j.bushor.2009.09.003

Kathan, W., Matzler, K., & Veider, V. (2016). The sharing economy: Your business model's friend or foe? *Business Horizons*, *59*(6), 663–672. doi:10.1016/j.bushor.2016.06.006

Keir, D. (2018). *Industry Spotlight: How the sharing economy is changing the face of business*. Retrieved June 2, 2019, from https://www.startupbootcamp.org/blog/2018/03/industry-spotlight-sharing-economy-changing-face-business/

Kim, Y. G., & Lee, J. N. Bock, G. W., & Zmud, R. W. (2005). *Behavioral intention formation in knowledge sharing: Examining the roles of extrinsic motivators, social-psychological forces, and organizational*. Academic Press.

Kotler, P. (1986). *The Prosumer Movement: a New Challenge For Marketers*. Retrieved 06 25, 2019, from http://www.acrwebsite.org/search/view-conference-proceedings.aspx?Id=6542

Lakhani, K. R., & Wolf, R. (2005). Why Hackers Do What They Do: Understanding Motivation and Effort in Free/Open Source Software Projects. In J. Feller (Ed.), *Perspectives on Free and Open Source Software*. Cambridge, MA: MIT Press.

Lin, K. Y., & Lu, H. P. (2011). Why people use social networking sites: An empirical study integrating network externalities and motivation theory. *Computers in Human Behavior*, *27*(3), 1152–1161. doi:10.1016/j.chb.2010.12.009

Lindenberg, S. (2001). Intrinsic motivation in a new light. *Kyklos*, *54*(2–3), 317–342. doi:10.1111/1467-6435.00156

MacroTrends. (2019). *Market Cap*. Retrieved June 1, 2019, from MacroTrends: https://www.macrotrends.net/stocks/charts/ETSY/

Magno, F., De Boer, M., & Bentoglio, B. (2016). Sharing economy: comparing users' and non-users' perceptions. In *19th Toulon-Verona International Conference* (pp. 277 - 285). Huelva: University of Huelva.

Miller, D. (2019). *The Sharing Economy and How it Is Changing Industries*. Retrieved June 30, 2019, from THE BALANCE SMB: https://www.thebalancesmb.com/the-sharing-economy-and-how-it-changes-industries-4172234

Miller, S. R. (2016). First principles for regulating the sharing economy. *Harvard Journal on Legislation, 147*(53), 149–202.

Mitchell, M., & Jolley, J. (2012). *Research Design Explained* (8th ed.). Wadsworth Publishing.

Nielsen. (2014). Retrieved from http://www.nielsen.com/us/en/insights/reports/2014/is-sharing-the-new-buying.html

Nov, O., Naaman, M., & Ye, C. (2010). Analysis of participation in an online photo-sharing community: A multidimensional perspective. *JASIST, 61*(3), 555–566.

Olofsson, L., & Farr, R. (2006). Business Model Tools and Definition. *Business*. Retrieved from https://www.researchgate.net/publication/272813909_Business_Model_Tools_and_Definition_-_a_Literature_Review

Ovans, A. (2015). *What Is a Business Model?* Retrieved 06 22, 2019, from HBR: https://hbr.org/2015/01/what-is-a-business-model

Ozcan, P., Möhlmann, M., & Krishnamoorthy, C. (2017). *Who shares and who doesn't?* Retrieved from https://www.wbs.ac.uk/wbs2012/assets/PDF/downloads/press/ResultsofUKSharingEconomyConsumerSurvery2017.pdf

Parameswaran, M., & Whinston, A. B. (2007). Social computing: An over- view. *Communications of the Association for Information Systems, 19*(1), 37.

Park, H. M., & Perry, J. L. (2008). Do campaign web sites really matter in electoral civic engage ment? Empirical evidence from the 2004 post-election Internet tracking survey. *Social Science Computer Review, 26*(2), 190–212. doi:10.1177/0894439307309026

Phipps, M., Ozanne, L., Luchs, M., Subrahmanyan, S., Kapitan, S., Catlin, J., ... Weaver, T. (2013). Understanding the inherent complexity of sustainable consumption: A social cognitive framework. *Journal of Business Research, 66*(8), 1227–1234. doi:10.1016/j.jbusres.2012.08.016

Prothero, A., Dobscha, S., Freund, J., Kilbourne, W. E., Luchs, M. G., Ozanne, L. K., & Thøgersen, J. (2011). Sustainable consumption: Opportunities for consumer research and public policy. *Journal of Public Policy & Marketing, 30*(1), 31–38. doi:10.1509/jppm.30.1.31

PWC. (2015a). *The sharing economy*. Available at https://www.pwc.com/us/en/technology/publications/assets/pwc-consumer-intelligence series- the-sharing-economy.pdf

PWC. (2015b). *Sharing or paring? Growth of the sharing economy*. Retrieved June 2, 2019, from PWC: https://www.pwc.com/hu/en/kiadvanyok/assets/pdf/sharing-economy-en.pdf

Rinne, A. (2013). Position Paper: Young Global Leaders Sharing Economy Working Group. *World Economic Forum Young Global Leaders Taskforce: Circular Economy Innovation & New Business Models Initiative*. Retrieved from http://www.slideshare.net/ CollabLab/ygl-sharing-economy-position-paper-final-june-2013

Sacks, D. (2011). *The sharing economy.* Fast Company 2011, April 11, Retrieved from http://www.fastcompany.com/magazine/155/the-sharing- economy.html

Statsta. (2019). *Ride Hailing*. Retrieved July 04, 2019, from https://www.statista.com: https://www.statista.com/outlook/368/100/ride-hailing/worldwide#market-revenue

Teece, D. J. (2010). Business Models, Business Strategy and Innovation. *Long Range Planning*, *43*(2), 172–194. doi:10.1016/j.lrp.2009.07.003

Toffler, A. (1980). *The Third Wave*. William Morrow.

Tussyadiah, I. P. (2015). An exploratory study on drivers and deterrents of collaborative consumption in travel. In I. Tussyadiah & A. Inversini (Eds.), *Information & Communication Technologies in Tourism 2015 Switzerland*. Springer International Publishing. doi:10.1007/978-3-319-14343-9_59

Tussyadiah, I. P. (2016). Factors of satisfaction and intention to use peer-to-peer accommodation. *International Journal of Hospitality Management*, *55*, 70–80. doi:10.1016/j.ijhm.2016.03.005

Tussyadiah, I. P., & Pesonen, J. (2015). Impacts of peer-to-peer accommodation use on travel patterns. *Journal of Travel Research*. doi:10.1177/0047287515608505

Van de Glind, P. B. (2013). *The Consumer Potential of Collaborative Consumption*. Utrecht: Utrecht University.

Verba, S., Schlozman, K. L., & Brady, H. E. (1995). *Voice and equality: Civic voluntarism in American politics*. Cambridge, MA: Harvard University Press.

Wallenstein, J., & Urvesh, S. (2017). *What's Next for the Sharing Economy?* Retrieved June 1, 2019, from BCG: https://www.bcg.com/publications/2017/strategy-technology-digital-whats-next-for-sharing-economy.aspx

Wang, C., & Zhang, P. (2012). The evolution of social commerce: The people, management, technology, and information dimensions. *Communications of the Association for Information Systems*, *31*(1), 105–127.

Wasko, M. M., & Faraj, S. (2000). It is what one does: Why people participate and help others in electronic communities of practice. *The Journal of Strategic Information Systems*, *9*(2), 155–173. doi:10.1016/S0963-8687(00)00045-7

Wasko, M. M., & Faraj, S. (2005). Why should I share? Examining social capital and knowledge contribution in electronic networks of practice. *Management Information Systems Quarterly*, *29*(1), 35–57. doi:10.2307/25148667

Wiertz, C., & de Ruyter, K. (2007). Beyond the call of duty: Why customers contribute to firm-hosted commercial online communities. *Organization Studies*, *28*(3), 347–376. doi:10.1177/0170840607076003

Yang, H., Cho, H., & Lee, W. (2015). Multi-dimensional emotional intelligence effects on intrinsic/extrinsic motivation and job satisfaction: Analysis using laborer perceived organizational support. *East Asian Journal of Business Management*, *5*(4), 13–18. doi:10.13106/eajbm.2015.vol5.no4.13.

## KEY TERMS AND DEFINITIONS

**Business Model:** A business model includes a set of activities (strategic choices, the value network, creating value and capturing value); scopes of business pillars (need, market technology customer interfaces, and financial aspects); elements (core capabilities, value configuration, revenue streams, cost structure, value proposition, customer segments, distribution & communication channels, partnerships, customer relationship,) and a range of actions (who, what, when, why, how and how much). a business model helps firms to structure their internal constituents (inbound, operations, R&D, marketing, distributions, services, and customer transactions) as well as external alignment with the suppliers, customers, distributors, and other external stakeholders.

**Consumer Motivations:** Intrinsic and extrinsic needs & drives that impel consumers to purchase and use product, services, ideas or adopt certain behaviors.

**Consumers:** Are individuals or organisation that purchase and exchange a product or services or value to satisfy their needs.

**Economic Benefit:** Are monetary, rational and functional benefits or values achieved by a consumer post-adoption, purchase and use of the product, services, ideas or certain behaviours.

**Purchase Intention:** The Sum total of cognitive, affective and behavioural towards adoption, purchase, and use of the product, services, ideas or certain behaviours.

**Revenue Streams:** A range of diversified sources or targets or products or offerings, spill-overs' or pricing methods; which are sources of a number of diversified incomes, fees, profits and benefits to an individual and organisation using a business model.

**Sharing Economy Business Model (SEBM):** A Sharing Economy business model (SEBM) may be defined as a strategic process that an organisation uses to create and capture customer values by making use of innovation, technologies, online sharing, peer-to-peer sharing, or collaborative consumption in order to reconstitute organisational internal core competencies, external alignment, & dynamic capabilities and thus achieving sustainable competitive advantages.

**Sharing Economy:** The sharing economy is an economy in which production and consumption are ensured via peer to peer collaborative consumption, shared knowledge, co-creation, co-production, prosumption, gigging, and using the technological platform, and such an economy is based on sharing the underutilised resources as collaborative consumptions with underpinned mutual trust.

**Technology Innovation:** Is a process, tools, and products of inventions, creativity, and modification that results in new ideas, products, process, solutions to existing or new needs,and disruption of industries, & its business models.

# Chapter 5
# Post-Truth and Marketing Communication in Technological Age

**Manpreet Arora**
*Department of Commerce and Management, Himachal Pradesh Kendriya Vishvidyalye Business School, Central University of Himachal Pradesh, Dharamshala, India*

## ABSTRACT

*The way by which the communication is done depends upon the purpose of the communication. The complex technology-driven environment is affected by a syndrome called post-truth. Post-truth scenario is marred with a situation where there are spread of lies, rumors, propaganda, and deceit. Human perception is distorted by the spread of lies and fake news. We struggle hard to decide whether any communication which we read, or listen to, or share is true or untrue. The strategic advancements aspired by any company are based more or less on the marketing tactics of the product or service. Many strategies of the organisations are based on the communicative interactions of the corporate world with the consumers. The era of post-truth is based on emotions, opinions, and distorted facts. False advertising tactics are hitting the emotions and sentiments of the public at large. Many social media players in the move to curb the menace of false news, misinformation, and false advertisements have opted for a voluntary code of ethics.This chapter analyses the marketing communication in the era of post-truth.*

## INTRODUCTION

Post-truth relates or demonstrates those circumstances where the objective facts are not important or worth enough for shaping public opinion. Appeals to emotion or personal beliefs play an important role than the objective analysis of the facts. Suddenly in 2016, a 2000% increase was seen by Oxford dictionaries in the usage of the word post truth. The social media, digital platforms, news articles, and blogs were full of the word, especially in the United States of America, that is why they chose post-truth as the word of the year in 2016. The word- post-truth became popular more particularly in US presidential elections and involvement of technology platforms like Facebook. In 2016 media was flooded with the news and

DOI: 10.4018/978-1-7998-0131-3.ch005

opinions regarding the fabrication of truth by Trump. The post-truth phenomena and is thus associated with fabrication of the truth, propaganda and lie, and most of the times via social media or digital media technologies. The truth is so fabricated in the world of media multiplicity that unfortunately there is no such thing anymore as a fact or truth.

The question arises why political issues and technological innovations are relevant to marketing and management. The business world is directly affected by the media and the reason is quite obvious there is no boundary or fence around politics. The opinions of politicians and their way of dealing with a particular phenomenon directly affect the business world and the strategies of a business. It is the opinion of the politicians which ultimately takes the shape of policy decisions. So, in one way or another it has a profound impact on the wider public at large. Therefore, it becomes utmost important that whether the political decisions are based on the foundations of truth, honesty and objective facts or whether they are contaminated by the post-truth, where there is no relevance of objective facts. One fabricated opinion of a business house can dupe millions of users. It can prove dangerous to millions at a simple instance. The technological innovations and spread of information, communication technologies have further brought complicated the issues of communications of the truth. Communication Technologies: also known as information technology & communication, refers to all equipment and programs that are used to process and communicate information. In the growing use of digital media and social media platforms, one can be duped by any misinformation in a few minutes. We have built only a laizzez faire attitude towards the truth and now nobody bothers whether something is true or not. The information particularly the digital one is the slippery slope, we most of the times are indecisive that whether we are standing on the firm foundation of the truth or it's just a slippery sham which can end up into a misleading, biased, untrue and fabricated piece of untrue statement.

## COMMUNICATION, TECHNOLOGY, AND POST- TRUTH

Communication: a process of creating, exchanging and receiving information, messages, and ideas, etc in order to influence or get a response from someone. Communication Technologies include all equipment and programs that are used to process and communicate information Every communication channel or each communication we do in our daily lives has its own dimensions and on different occasions, we require different types of communication. The way by which communication is done depends upon the purpose of the communication. It can be done verbally or non-verbally also. Firstly, we need to decide what will we communicate? We can communicate through various languages, expressions of languages, a mix of languages, of course, smiley's these days, jargons, local dialects, and buzzwords but how well the words are used plays an important role in it. Therefore, the choice and use of appropriate words in a particular situation determine the efficiency of the individual and the effectiveness of the communication. Gone are the days when sender and receiver were identified, and few types of identified noise played a role in distorting the communication.

The complex technology-driven environment is affected by a syndrome called post-truth. The post-truth scenario is marred with a situation where there are spread of lies, rumors, propaganda, and deceit. Human perception is distorted by the spread of lies and fake news. Fake News refers to nontruthful information, False news, hoax news, false information or propaganda published under the guise of being authentic news and mostly spread out using a range of media including social media with some ulterior motives and sometimes for the sake of fun, or influencing others opinions. We struggle hard to decide whether any communication which we read, or listen or share is true or untrue. The demarcation between true and objective facts between the lies and propaganda has become a serious disease where arguments, lies, distorted facts, power-politics influence, strategies, disregard to objective facts play crucial as well as disruptive role. False notions, affected by politics, power, media multiplicity, social media, and fraudulent media products are used as strategies for deception. They lead to propaganda, rumors, etc. Propaganda is a set of distorted information, especially of a biased or misleading nature. information, ideas, or rumors deliberately spread widely to promote a political cause or point of view or to help or harm a person, group, movement, institution, nation, etcNonsense communication overpowers the truth and relevance of truth are disrupted. There remains nothing as such truth. Stephen, Ullrich & John (2017), find the word post-truth and fake news to be the most prevalent in public discourse. Their article explored the increasing abundance of misinformation. They have also studied how the use of misinformation is affecting people, they also discussed the ways of countering it. Societal megatrends were the major factors responsible for the increased use of misinformation in their study.

Teaching values and ethics, the *Vedas, the Ramayana, the teachings of Geeta,* the researcher feels is the most challenging task these days. How to prove the authenticity of what is spread? Where a spate of new books have emerged, with the writers having own opinions and their availability on the internet must be affecting the human rationality to a larger extent. Personal beliefs are becoming stronger. The researcher really feels amazed that in childhood, it was taught that what is right and what is wrong. The concept of right and wrong, do's and don'ts, is this valid enough for us now in the era of post-truth?

Lies leading to hatred, deception, personal beliefs affected by false notions are hampering the human ability to think or behave rationally. The rationality is driven only by power, money and untrue facts. The most alarming, displeasing, and shocking fact of this era is disregard as well as disrespect to the objective facts. Yes, the communication is distorted; we are living in an era where conflicts arise as we are marred with a phenomenon called post truth. The conflicts are not only external they are intra-personal also.

## MARKETING IN POST-TRUTH SCENARIO

The pace and intensity with which post-truth has overwhelmed contemporary political and socio-cultural scenarios it is sure to have its effects on the corporate world. The strategic advancements aspired by any company are based more or less on the marketing tactics of the product or service. Many strategies of the organizations are based on the communicative interactions of the corporate world with the consumers using ICT. The era of post-truth is based on emotions, opinions and distorted facts. Social media, internet and the digitalization of every aspect have changed the scenario for marketing communication too. Now the objective facts are less important rather the propaganda plays a role in communication. The political scenario altogether in the world is now marked with post truth where objective facts are demeaned and the vague language plays a role. It is an evident fact that the political environment of a country or globe altogether has its effect on the corporate world. Social media are Web2.0 based e-platforms, that employ web-based technologies and mobile technology to create highly interactive platforms via which individuals and communities share, co-create, discuss, and modify user-generated content in order to identify, convert, share, show presence, and build relationships, reputation, and communities.The social media platforms like Facebook, What's up etc. are facing a huge challenge to manage fake news.

So, the question arises that while marketing the products aren't we mislead by short term goals influenced by global political environment? Truth is self-evident but just staying on truth does the companies achieve their strategic goals? Truth for one can be false for another. As we are living in the age of post-truth the opinions are framed on emotions rather than judgments. These days every person has his own definition of truth. The relative subjectivity in opinion forming overpowers the objectivity. Products like Maggie, Coca Cola, Johnsons and Johnsons are sold in the market by attaching them to the sentiments of consumers. This can happen indeed the era of post-truth.

In virtual parlance of ICT, the post-truth occurrence is like flickering signifiers/ concepts used heavily in spaces dominated by new media multiplicity. Another viewpoint of the post-truth phenomenon is that is sheer a half-truth which is used as ploy/ tricks. And people are made to believe in what is not. Post-truth can also be viewed as a ruse of a sort. Such kind of propaganda has a particular agenda. It can be used to deviate marginalized, deprived population across the world to believe the untrue. Matthew (2017), in his book, mentions that we are living in an era where trust has evaporated, and conspiracies play a big role. According to him emotions nowadays, matter more than facts. He also talks about this approach based on epistemology to analyze the declining value of truth.

False advertising tactics are hitting the emotions and sentiments of the public at large. They have many cultural and religious bearings also. After all, the cultural environment also has a direct bearing on the marketing of the products. Globalization still appears to be a myth as; the so-called global products had to adopt the regio-centric approaches to sell their product in the market.

The post-truth era has created an environment of confusion away from rationality. Therefore, the onus lies on the companies to adopt ethical standards in marketing communication.

Role of marketing is regarded much more than economic exchange. It is now much wider than that. Social marketing says, for example, can deal with social issues and ideas. Donald Trump is the biggest example in history for camouflaging the truth and approaching to the sentiments of the public at large. Similarly, widespread marketing campaigns can have serious implications on the society if not planned wisely. The innovations in marketing should be critically thought off in the light of post-truth era. There are some serious ethical questions which marketers face today. There arises some sort of serious responsibility in this creative and innovative marketing environment and only a critical discourse can provide us an insight into the antidotes of post-truth. How the use of fake or misleading information can affect the society at large is a question of debate. The Doctrine of Caveat Emptor though is a resort for the marketers, but there is an extent to which the consumers can use their rationale, agility, and logic. If the sheer target of the marketers is the sentiments, emotions, and opinions of the consumer then the reality is what is shown. It has become tough for the general public at large to distinguish between ethical marketing practices and ethical implications of the product being marketed.

TV advertisements also are creating an environment of confusion for the users in one way or another. The Kolkata based Emami sought an injunction restraining HUL and seven broadcasters to stop airing campaign on Men's Fair and Lovely fairness cream. The suit saying the campaign has "tarnished the goodwill, reputation and brand value" of its product, Fair and Handsome, making it appear "inferior, fake and counterfeit" which has impacted its sales was filed by Emami (Mukherjee, 2018). The ad war intensified, and the makers had to launch a new ad with the new brand face.

Thai and Zhang, 2013, tried to explore the real-life world situations to understand the present status of marketing. They analyzed different type of marketing strategies in the present era adopted by marketers. They are of the view that marketing has the capacity of raising the buyer's interest. Persuasive advertising can boost the buyer's confidence in quality. They found in the study that by the use of marketing strategies which hits the opinion, perceptions, and beliefs of the buyer, the companies have been able to accelerate the buyer behavior.

It has become considerably difficult in the era of post-truth to distinguish between facts from opinion. The personal biases may influence the quality or depth of the information which we receive in the digitalized world. It can take the form of videos or that of any multimedia content. Various new forms of misinformation have emerged. As we open our email box in the morning there are hundreds of emails regarding promotion of products, winning lotteries, new schemes of bank accounts, personal loan approvals and what not. It is extremely difficult for a layman to figure out which email of the marketer is genuine and which is a fraud. The nasty elements who are always in search of the opportunity to find out prey for looting are taking advantage of the digital media and befooling the public as fact-checking mechanisms are few. Even the central banks of some countries faced a threat due to false emails and text messages sent to the general public on their behalf and it was spreading panic in the economy.

Smith(2017), states that facing or encountering unreliable or false information is not a new phenomenon, but it has become more alarming now, the reason is straight forward which is the communication is too rapid these days. People have devised ways and means to craft misleading information for malafide reasons. The author states that the young generation can be easily duped by misinformation shared on the social media channels. He further stresses on the fact that reading, questioning, thinking critically can help the young generation to defend themselves against misinformation of all the forms. Another serious problem posed by the current post-truth scenario especially in the field of marketing is ethics. Maintaining and inculcating professional ethics in the field of marketing is challenging as well as difficult to maintain.

## Digital Platforms, Marketing, and Post-Truth

Digital Platforms are internet and web-based virtual spaces that are based on some kind of unique business models in order to exchange, information, knowledge, goods, ideas, or services, etc, either with financial or nonfinancial returns, Eg Google search engine, Facebook, Spotify, Youtube, Apple store, Amazon market place, Uber, Apple /Google Pay etc . The amount spent on mass media and social media advertising these days is an all-time high. Social Media Marketing: is a process of marketing promotion and communication that makes use of Web 2.0 or higher level internet technologies and a range of social media platforms to raise the visibility, and promote a brand, product, idea, service or a person or an organization by building social networks, and for exchanging ideas and knowledge. It may use, audio, videos, wikis, blogs, photo sharing, news, message boards, and posts on social networking platforms to reach a large or targeted audience.

In countries like America and now in India too, the social media platforms are used to do election campaigns. The reasons are simple people have easy access to such platforms, and more and more creative elements can be used in such scenarios. At one click thousands or even more than people can be targeted by such platforms. As the growing use of such platform increases, the possibilities of fake, untrue statements of advertisements have also emerged to a great extent. Advertisements have been regarded as the most controversial aspect of marketing (McGarry, 1958). Peters (2018), focused on the 'big lies' told by Donald Trump. He discussed how the use of media techniques helped him to win presidential elections and he through severe propaganda convinced the millions. He rightly tries to figure out how social media is playing a role in undermining our ability to recognize the truth. Higgins (2016), in her article, refers to post-truth as blatant lies which have become a routine for the society. She also gives reference to the tactics opted by Donald Trump in this context. McGarry, clearly stated in the year 1958, "Advertising as used today is primarily a type of propaganda". This statement holds good even today. He has viewed propaganda as a condition which deliberately attempts to influence people. It also contains persuasion. In his article, "The propaganda function in marketing", he further states, "In business, it is used primarily by sellers to obtain a market by conditioning people in the market to accept the particular products offered. The growth of new techniques of communication has greatly extended the range of propaganda penetration, has expanded the number of products advertised, and has increased the total amount of propaganda disseminated; but the aim of the messages carried is essentially unchanged since the beginning of civilization". The way the propaganda is used since ages appears so true today in this twenty-first century.

WhatsApp, the world's largest messaging platform, had to spend more than Rs 120 crore on print, television and radio advertising in just five months last year as it seeks to struggle the transmission of fake news, propaganda, lies through WhatsApp messages and were under legal scrutiny in India especially.

We all must have come across the latest advertisement of WhatsApp on almost all channels about not to spread fake news, and to respond against fake news. In an interesting move, in India before the general elections, many organizations came forward appealing to Election Commission of India to have a code of conduct and other guidelines for advertising on digital platforms. The organizations contend that the social or digital platforms are creating threats to the integrity of elections which is increasing day by day at alarming proportions. The news article also contends that the former election commissioner of India, states WhatsApp groups to be the most dangerous of all ("Internet Freedom Foundation", 2019).

Many social media players in the move to curb the menace of false news, misinformation, and false advertisements have opted a voluntary code of ethics. The major players include Facebook, Twitter, WhatsApp, Sharechat and Google. Before elections in India, in a major move to combat with the threat of fake news in the political scenario "Among other things, the code includes taking down objectionable posts within three hours during the 48-hour silent period ahead of elections and bringing transparency in political advertising"(Anumeha Chaturvedi,2019). Political Promotions uses a range of the communications models and methods used to influence a political debate, and ultimately voters to vote in favor of a case or a political party etc. Facebook has claimed that it is removing millions of fake accounts daily to stop, limit and slow down the mushrooming misinformation. These platforms are used by professionals like doctors, hospitals, lawyers, consultancy firms, etc to advertise, to share information or spread messages. Even sensitive conversations take place on digital platforms. In various parts of the world, police use it for investigations and report crimes. In such a scenario to combat with the post, truth scenario seems to be a challenging but impossible task. Article through certain quoted statements contends that a negative post takes around sixty minutes to enter into a viral category. It is followed by rapid sharing and seemingly so many comments from the followers.

Reuters, report that somewhat same scenario is threatening in the US. The fears of disrupting the 2020 count in the US are emerging again. The fake news campaigns are now the worry of the US Census Bureau, which has already requested Google, Facebook, and Twitter to combat with such fake news campaigns.

The digital platforms through the virals, fake news and media publicity are not only affecting the political scenarios, but they are also sometimes turning to be the platforms for national rivalries followed by hostile actions threatening national sovereignties'. India and Pakistan were in the limelight after Pulwama attack that killed 44 Indian Army men. After this attack, a vast variety of hostilities were exchanged between two countries and people repeatedly posted about military establishments, news, video, etc through various pages and shares in both countries. Facebook on request by the Indian government found many fake accounts on the name of the military by people in Pakistan. While all this happened, "Facebook said that this takedown included 24 pages, 57 individual accounts, 7 groups, and 15 Instagram accounts. It added that about 2.8 million accounts followed "one or more of these Pages", while about 4,700 accounts "joined one of these groups", and around 1,050 users followed "one or more of these Instagram accounts." These accounts and pages, Facebook said, had spent $1,100 on ads on its platform, paid for in US dollars and Pakistani rupees" (Venkat Ananth, Apr 02, 2019).

Just ten days before general elections in India WhatsApp announced that people in India can check whether the advertisement or news is fake or not on a WhatsApp tip line numbers. The company claims that the information will help them to create a database of rumors to study misinformation during elections.

Undoubtedly fake news has caused a ruckus in every aspect all over the world impacting every society. It has become a concern, particularly in digital marketing. Fake populist rhetoric's are taking place which is based on the firm's foundations of personal beliefs. Gradually the assumptions gain strength on the firm footings of logic and facts which hence are irrefutable. Traditional marketing methods are losing their relevance with the emergence of new digital modes of communication like blogs, YouTube, Facebook advertisements, and a single tweet possesses the power to mobilize masses in millions. Lies are becoming common and spread of fake news or propaganda is overpowering the digital world.

Marketing tactics were always been questioned on the name of ethics. It is not like it can be or should be equated with lying. However, it has always bee associated with manipulation. All these concepts now take refuge under the semantic umbrella of post-truth. Similarly, post-truth is not synonymous with lying; however, it is marred with a state where personal beliefs and the objective facts are losing their relevance.

Post-truth though as a term is generally associated with political scenarios but it has also very dangerously developed in advertising and in the corporate world. The transition of marketing from paper to digital media is essentially fabricated by the loss of professional ethics, manipulation, and propaganda leading to the abandonment of truth-telling. The notion of truth and search for it in the world of marketing is complex and has no end. It lays down a great duty on the marketers to preserve its true nature. In this world of consumerism, the most controversial is the stealth marketing. It is basically a practice of marketing to consumers without their awareness. It has become nearly impossible to avoid stealth marketing advertisements almost on all social media platforms and online shopping portals. They just happen to start encroaching in whatever we browse on the digital media. The consumer is not even aware that he is just a marketing ploy. Giants like FedEx, Prada/Vogue, Sony Erricson, WalMart, and Starbucks have been using this strategy widely through their appearances in famous blockbuster Hollywood movies.

The concept of stealth marketing can be well related to the overpowering post-truth conditions, where there are doubts, confusion, and manipulation overcasts the whole scenario. Many consumers can be found wondering as the public interest is aroused in such a manner that the consumer is not even aware of the tactic. He is just manipulated tactfully under the cover. That is why this concept is also regarded as buzz marketing by some. An appeal to general masses is the basic idea whereby online channels, blogs, websites are the major targets. Due to the low cost of such marketing strategies the product is widely publicized. Propaganda and gaining popularity are both present in post-truth and stealth marketing. Or we can say, the post-truth scenario has made propaganda and popularity an important element of marketing strategies.

Today marketers are facing serious challenges of coping with fake news too and trying hard to make their marketing messages received by the general public at large in true spirit. Nowadays consumers have exposed thousands of marketing communications done daily by countless companies. It has not only led to an unprecedented level of increase in the marketing clutter, but it has also led to a situation of confusion where emails message in boxes and phones are full of fake marketing messages. Many of us don't even open them and just delete it. On the same hand only, those companies are becoming successful who are responding to the innovative approaches of attaining customer attention. In such a situation stealth marketing or covert marketing is increasingly being used by the companies.

Martin and Smith 2008 tried to identify various ethical problems which are related to stealth marketing in the present day scenario. They have discussed case studies related to stealth marketing. Prominently they have discussed the Sony Ericsson's fake tourist campaign where they hired to 60 actors to pose as tourists on behalf of the company and the fake tourists were asking people to take photographs by a newly launched camera phone by Sony Ericsson. The actors who participated in the campaign did not identify themselves as the representatives of Sony Ericsson. This campaign was exposed in the Wall Street Journal and was criticized deeply for adopting deceptive practices by the company. The authors are of the view that in the case studies consumers were deceived and ultimately the information was hidden for the interest of the company. They also regarded it as an intrusion and violation of privacy in many cases. Considerably, stealth marketing creates a threat to customer groups of a wide variety. In many cases, it was found that the customers were abused, and stealth marketing can create a reversible distrust for future marketing initiatives of the company. Still in this environment where media multiplicity is there any truth has not remained to be the truth. Marketers are aggressively adopting the techniques of stealth marketing which are indeed increasing the pressure on the consumer to distinguish deception from truth.

Advertisement is a paid form of communication that employees a range of media channels to send out an open, non-personal message to inform, persuade and influence users of a product, idea, service or place or person the users. Balough (2012), in his article, states that the internet is playing an important role in marketing and false claims of advertising through the use of websites and social media are growing at a rapid pace. Even incidents have been reported where misleading domain names can give rise to false advertising claims. Petty and Andrews (2008), discusses covert marketing practices opted by the companies. They focused on the fact that masked marketing is one form of covert marketing and it involves marketing communication which seems independent of product marketers. They talk about six practices which are opted in masked marketing i.e., "Posers, Buzz and Viral marketing, Advertorials, Ad-results from a search engine or other query, Urgent ad-formation and Advertainment". Poser's technique of marketing leads to deception and playing with the sentiments of the consumers. As it happened in the case of Sony Ericsson as mentioned earlier where the company used 120 actors as fake tourists. Same is the case of Buzz and viral marketing where the company encourages word of mouth by consumers itself by opting certain tactics. Prominently, it is done by emails, blogs, and messaging. The companies opt the tactics for encouraging a "buzz" i.e a conversation or a talk about the product in the market. In this situation also, the marketing tactics are also unclear and somewhat deceptive that whosoever is creating a buzz in the market is the agent of the company or the consumer itself.

Nelson and Park (2014), consider publicity to be covert marketing where they believe that the audience is befooled under such marketing tactics. The audience is under the impression that the message was created by some third party but not the marketer himself. They further state that in covert marketing there is a potential as well as intention to deceive the customer on one ground or another. As the source is not disclosed to the customer and they are unaware of the tactics followed by the company to persuade them for a product thereby causing certain problems in regard to ethics. Bush, Venable & Bush (2000), surveyed marketing executives to understand their perceptions about, "regulations of the internet, the potential ethical issues via internet marketing facing their industry and the role of ethics and internet marketing in their organizations." Nearly 80% of their respondents indicate that there is a dire need of developing a code of ethics for the use of the internet by the organizations. Online marketing is considered to be more complex than traditional marketing. Various researchers have attempted to analyze the purchase likelihood effects of consumers who come to know about the covert practices opted by the companies and they found out that mixed moderate reactions of the consumers can be seen. Covert marketing practices are always been associated with the non transparent activities opted by the marketers to persuade them or induce their buying behavior. Milne, Rohm &Shalini Bahl (2009), in their article, "If it's legal, is it acceptable?"; talks about some serious implications of covert marketing practices. They conducted a conjoint scenario and a segmented study was conducted by them on the US consumers. In their study, they examined the impact on consumers purchase likelihood after learning about online covert marketing practices. Their findings suggest that while the consumers learn about the covert marketing practices it lowers the purchase likelihood. In the study, the purchase likelihood was reduced by 29.2%. A more negative reaction was shown by the consumers when the covert marketing practices were done to collect personal information of the consumer. Such deceits in actions by the companies also reduce trust in the company. Warrwn, Burns & Tackett (2012), state that consumers most of the times trust the brands and believe that they will not be deceived. But this trust is regularly/constantly threatened when the companies pursue their specific objectives to perform in the market. Such pressures in the market lead them to the situations of ethical failures thereby violating the trust of the consumer. Ultimately many stakeholders along with consumers prove to be victims.

Gaining popularity through various hit TV programs is another concept which sometimes dupes the audience. Product is being discussed at public forums and popularity is achieved at a global level. Companies find these modes to be much easier for launching their product. It becomes easier for them to plan and execute for that particular product. On the negative side, if such tactics are not used wisely it can harm the reputation of the company badly. The negative reviews can very well destroy the image of the company, When companies make use of false news to advertise or do excessive propaganda then false news may lead to customers losing trust in the brand. Creating a brand image is very tough but destroying the brand image is somewhat easy in this post-truth scenario. Any fake news about the brand can become viral in minutes. To spread a negative buzz is easier and it spreads quickly than the positive word of mouth.

Even some companies are able to make their product popular even before its launch. Apple is using this strategy combined with other strategies of marketing in India.

## Where Are We Heading?

The proliferation of social media channels are not only now being used to push our own beliefs, personal agendas but it has become an attitude of spreading lies, misconceptions in order to affect the public perception. It has become a tool to destroy the images of the brands which are competing against them. In fact, a study conducted by Statista found that 42% of the fake news in 2017 was generated and distributed through social media in the United States.

Fake news is regarded as the dark side of social media for marketers as well as users. The supporters of these digital platforms contend that this is not a new phenomenon as it can be traced back to famous hoaxes spread many times. The digital garbage is cluttering our minds, lives and overall perceptions. The truth has got diluted in the bad flood of misinformation. There has become a tendency of spreading misinformation. There were times when morality overpowered our decisions. Now nothing remained to be immoral. The demarcation between a truth and lie has become invisible. The truth of one becomes lie for another and vice-versa. The new generation has now been conditioned with fake news. The consequences of fake biases are unknown. Information received is multi-layered, multi-filtered. By the time it reaches us, it has already lost its significance. The digital clutter has mushroomed plenty of sources of distractions affecting our rationality and perceptions. Brands are now competing to feed us with certain deductive reasoning in order to sustain in the market. The spread of fake news is just like an everyday news. News channels are playing havoc in these scenarios. The clear association with political parties can be seen many times. They cook, and present lies to be true. The information is so publically circulated that it becomes impossible to figure out that it is fake or not. Strategies of deception based on self convenience are marring the digital markets. Distorting facts, blatant falsehood, news bubbles, fraudulent media products, and bullshit is conquering the world. All these things have brought an epochal shift in digital marketing.

Allcott & Gentzkow (2017), are of the view that the social media platforms especially Facebook has proved to be so powerful that one can relay the content to the users, "with no significant third-party filtering, fact-checking, or editorial judgment". They regard this mode to be even powerful that even if the person has no past track record of writing or any kind of reputation he can be noted by the major players like *New York Times, CNN, Fox News, etc.* Cerase and Santoro (2018), consider media hype to be the main reason for the spread of hoaxes. Even due to media hypes the same hoax or false news reoccurs in a few months. It is so powerful that even after years they have the capability of gaining people's attention.

The dark side of social media is affecting users as well as marketers. The solution lies in better incorporate checks, the spread of information but still, the onus lies on consumers, creators as well as marketers. It takes years and years, or you can say lifetime to create a brand image and gain a positive reputation. Shugan (2006), strongly propagate that marketers invented branding and trademarks for creating an environment of trust and honesty in the market. With the help of branding and appropriate strategies of brand building, the organizations can create a reputation in the market. Branding has been considered a medium or a mechanism through which the buyer is able to identify that an organization is taking responsibility for the good or bad quality of products in the market. Building up a positive reputation in one way or another signifies that consumer has trust in the brand and he looks forward to buying the products of it. Another dimension of trust building is earning revenue as well as stability for the organization. The organizations should work upon their positive image in the market as it helps them to sustain in the long run. These days' reviews on blogs or social media platform impact a lot. A negative comment or dissatisfaction shared or shown on social media platforms can be viral and it takes minutes to destroy the company image. The companies should never take such reviews lightly and should immediately take corrective actions to satisfy the consumer. Building a positive image of the brand and taking care of the needs of customers beforehand is a proactive measure which helps a lot to sustain in the post-truth era.

## COPING UP WITH MISINFORMATION IN POST-TRUTH SCENARIO

Coping up with misinformation and spread of false news have many implications for individuals, for companies as well as their customers. On the same hand, it is very challenging also. Fact checking can be one of the antidotes to the situation. One should try to find out the purpose of the information at the outset. Whether that information is to sell or to entertain, or it's a hoax or propaganda? We should keep these dimensions in mind while dealing with information. We need to do away with the habit of dealing with information very casually. The times have come where every body's tendency towards information is quite unpredictable and on the same hand casual. We forward or delete without evaluating the information on the parameters such as when was that information published? Who is the source of publishing information? Whether it was ever revised or updated? Is the information so shared or posted contains appropriate language, tone, unbiased statements, appear to be objective and impartial or not? Marketers along with opting appropriate proactive measures should work upon customers after sale service. Especially in the case of small businesses, the organization should opt the most effective measures to solve customer grievances, promoting the product honestly without using misleading information. A proper blend of creating an emotional bonding along with the transparent fact sharing should be seen in the advertisements then only trust building in customers in regard to the brand will be possible.

These days' companies are resorting to online reputation management strategies for enhancing their goodwill. Brands have dedicated budgets to ensure that proper information is spread, and they are transparent enough to combat the challenges posed by digital modes in the era of post-truth.

Many companies with any of their careless attitude are getting penalized also. These incidents should act as warnings for the other players of the market. Recently, India's food ordering sector is also facing challenges and so much competition among the players is leading to burn out of large amounts of cash to compete with each other. The Department for Promotion of Industry and Internal Trade (DPIIT) summoned Swiggy, Zomato, Foodpanda and Uber Eats following complaints from many restaurants, including Federation of Hotel & Restaurant Associations of India and National Restaurant Association of India that food aggregators are engaging in "deep discounting" and "predatory pricing". Such incidents can create a complicated situation for marketers. Multinationals have to opt for the corrective actions by the way of advertisements to deal with a negative reputation in the market otherwise survival is not possible. The example of Maggi is worth mentioning here, wherein *The Economic times (Jan 05, 2019),* news appeared that, "The Indian arm of Swiss food company Nestle SA is set to release advertisement campaigns highlighting the "trustworthy facts" about its instant noodles brand Maggi. It clearly indicates that a strong need is to create trust and faith of the consumers on the activities done by the companies. They may belong to any sector, it is immaterial, what important is that customer should not be misleading, deceived or cheated.

Many digital platforms have already started campaigns against false information. People are more or less realizing that truth is power, and we need to be agile and informed in this era of post-truth. We can't be just hovering around misinformation. Asmolov (2018), rightly disagree with various scholars who generally consider counter-fake initiatives to be the appropriate and effective remedies for combating disinformation campaigns. He is of the opinion that "Counter-fake initiatives could worsen the negative effects of fakes...".

WhatsApp has also announced measures to help users identify fake news. The company introduced a feature to identify whether a message was created by the sender or came from someone else by labeling forwarded messages. It gives the first impression that the sender is not sure about the authenticity of the message. Additionally, WhatsApp has declared that "it continues to strengthen antispam detection capabilities to ban accounts that engage in unwanted automated activity".

The only strong, convincing, objective, rational and intense fact in the post-truth era is an antidote to post-truth is speaking truth to power. The velocity and power with which post-truth has besieged contemporary political, social, cultural, economic and the marketing world including our daily lives; demands that this blight is countered by truth and truth alone.

## MANAGERIAL IMPLICATIONS

The epochal shift in the technology no doubt has given marketers as well as consumers a wide endless platform of communication but on the same hand it has created a state of being where strategies of deception, biased opinions, distorting facts, blatant falsehood, news bubbles, enigmatic remarks, bizarre behaviors, fake news, propaganda, and fraudulent media products have overcast our lives. There is a strong need for re-engaging with the audience at every level. We need to re-establish the lost trust in the marketing world. The proliferation of truth, transparent fact inclinations are required. The hoaxes and the inclination to spread fake, blatant dramas can be curbed by setting examples by the use of rational ethical marketing practices. Managers need to work upon the policy measures involving ethical, non-deceptive and transparent practices. The judgments should not exhibit ignorance of the truth; rather they should exhibit promotion of rationality and truth. Countering fake with more fake is not the solution; rather countering fake with the rational, creative, transparent, objective true fact is the first step to the ladder.

## CONCLUSION

Post-truth relates or demonstrates those circumstances where the objective facts are not important or worth enough for shaping the public opinion by appealing to emotion or personal beliefs rather than the objective analysis of the facts. The business world is directly affected by the media and the reason is quite obvious there is no boundary or fence around politics. The opinions of politicians and their way of dealing with a particular phenomenon directly affect the business world and the strategies of a business. It is the opinion of the politicians which ultimately takes the shape of policy decisions. The complex technology-driven environment is affected by a syndrome called post-truth. The post-truth scenario is marred with a situation where there are spread of lies, rumors, propaganda, and deceit. Human perception is distorted by the spread of lies and fake news.. Many strategies of the organizations are based on the communicative interactions of the corporate world with the consumers using ICT. The era of post-truth is based on emotions, opinions and distorted facts. Social media, internet and the digitalization of every aspect have changed the scenario for marketing communication too. Now the objective facts are less important rather the propaganda plays a role in communication. The way the propaganda is used since ages appears so true today in this twenty-first century. Many social media players in the move to curb the menace of false news, misinformation, and false advertisements have opted a voluntary code of ethics. The major players include Facebook, Twitter, WhatsApp, Sharechat and Google. WhatsApp, the world's largest messaging platform, had to spend more than £12 Million on print, television and radio advertising in just five months last year as it seeks to struggle the transmission of fake news, propaganda, lies through WhatsApp messages and were under legal scrutiny in India especially.

## REFERENCES

Allcott, H., & Gentzkow, M. (2017). Social Media and Fake News in the 2016 Election. *The Journal of Economic Perspectives, 31*(2), 211-235. Retrieved from http://www.jstor.org/stable/44235006

Anumeha. (2019, March 25). Social media code of ethics unlikely to tame fake news, say analysts. *The Economic Times*. Retrieved from https://economictimes.indiatimes.com/tech/internet/social-media-code-of-ethics-unlikely-to-tame-fake-news-say-analysts/articleshow/68531164.cms

Asmolov, G. (2018). The disconnective power of disinformation campaigns. *Journal of International Affairs, 71*(1.5), 69-76. Retrieved from https://www.jstor.org/stable/26508120

Balough, C. (2012). A Survey of False Advertising in Cyberspace. *Business Lawyer, 68*(1), 297–304. Retrieved from http://www.jstor.org/stable/23527095

Bureau, E. T. (2019, April 6). Election Commission urged to put check on digital platforms. *The Economic Times*. Retrieved from https://economictimes.indiatimes.com/news/politics-and-nation/election-commission-urged-to-put-check-on-digital-platforms/articleshow/68747932.cms

Bush, V., Venable, B., & Bush, A. (2000). Ethics and Marketing on the Internet: Practitioners' Perceptions of Societal, Industry and Company Concerns. *Journal of Business Ethics, 23*(3), 237–248. doi:10.1023/A:1006202107464

Cerase, A., & Santoro, C. (2018). From racial hoaxes to media hypes: Fake news' real consequences. In P. Vasterman (Ed.), *From Media Hype to Twitter Storm: News Explosions and Their Impact on Issues, Crises, and Public Opinion* (pp. 333–354). Amsterdam: Amsterdam University Press; doi:10.2307/j.ctt21215m0.20

d'Ancona, M. (2017). *Post-truth: The new war on truth and how to fight back*. Random House.

Higgins, K. (2016). Post-truth: A guide for the perplexed. *NATNews, 540*(7631), 9.

Lewandowsky, S., Ecker, U. K., & Cook, J. (2017). Beyond misinformation: Understanding and coping with the "post-truth" era. *Journal of Applied Research in Memory and Cognition, 6*(4), 353–369. doi:10.1016/j.jarmac.2017.07.008

McGarry, E. (1958). The Propaganda Function in Marketing. *Journal of Marketing, 23*(2), 131–139. doi:10.1177/002224295802300202

Miklós-Thal, J., & Zhang, J. (2013). (De)marketing to Manage Consumer Quality Inferences. *Journal of Marketing Research, 50*(1), 55-69. Retrieved from http://www.jstor.org/stable/42003065

Milne, G., Rohm, A., & Bahl, S. (2009). If It's Legal, Is It Acceptable? Consumer Reactions to Online Covert Marketing. *Journal of Advertising, 38*(4), 107–122. doi:10.2753/JOA0091-3367380408

Nelson, M., & Park, J. (2015). Publicity as Covert Marketing? The Role of Persuasion Knowledge and Ethical Perceptions on Beliefs and Credibility in a Video News Release Story. *Journal of Business Ethics, 130*(2), 327–341. doi:10.100710551-014-2227-3

Peters, M. A. (2018). Education in a post-truth world. In *Post-Truth, Fake News* (pp. 145–150). Singapore: Springer. doi:10.1007/978-981-10-8013-5_12

Petty, R., & Andrews, J. (2008). Covert Marketing Unmasked: A Legal and Regulatory Guide for Practices That Mask Marketing Messages. *Journal of Public Policy & Marketing, 27*(1), 7–18. doi:10.1509/jppm.27.1.7

Reuters. (2019, March 27). US Census enlists Internet giants to fight fake news. *The Economic Times.* Retrieved from https://economictimes.indiatimes.com/news/international/world-news/us-census-enlists-internet-giants-to-fight-fake-news/articleshow/68604823.cms

Shambhavi. (2019, Jan 10). A Rs 120-cr WhatsApp message to fight fake news. *The Economic Times.* Retrieved from https://economictimes.indiatimes.com/tech/internet/a-rs-120-cr-whatsapp-message-to-fight-fake-news/articleshow/67464732.cms

Shugan, S. (2006). Editorial: Who Is Afraid to Give Freedom of Speech to Marketing Folks? *Marketing Science*, *25*(5), 403–410. doi:10.1287/mksc.1060.0236

Smith, M. (2017). Arming students against bad information. *Phi Delta Kappan*, *99*(3), 56–58. doi:10.1177/0031721717739595

Venkat. (2019, April 02). Facebook takes down Pak military-linked pages targeting India ahead of Lok Sabha polls. *The Economic Times.* Retrieved from https://economictimes.indiatimes.com/news/elections/lok-sabha/india/facebook-takes-down-pakistan-military-backed-pages-targeting-india-ahead-of-ls-polls/articleshow/68668722.cms

Warren, H., Burns, D., & Tackett, J. (2012). The Likelihood of Deception in Marketing: A Criminological Contextualization. *Business & Professional Ethics Journal*, *31*(1), 109–134. doi:10.5840/bpej20123115

Writankar. (2018, June 20). Court issues restrain order on HUL's fairness cream ad on Emami petition. *The Economic Times.* Retrieved from https://economictimes.indiatimes.com/industry/cons-products/fashion-/-cosmetics-/-jewellery/court-issues-restrain-order-on-huls-fairness-cream-ad-on-emami-petition/articleshow/64667851.cms

## KEY TERMS AND DEFINITIONS

**Advertisements:** A paid form of communication that employees a range of media channels to send out an open, non-personal message to inform, persuade, and influence users of a product, idea, service, or place or person.

**Communication:** A process of creating, exchanging and receiving information, messages, and ideas, etc. in order to influence or get a response from someone.

**Communication Technologies:** Also known as information technology and communication, refers to all equipment and programs that are used to process and communicate information.

**Digital Platforms:** Are internet and web-based virtual spaces that are based on some kind of unique business models in order to exchange, information, knowledge, goods, ideas, or services, etc, either with financial or nonfinancial returns, Eg Google search engine, Facebook, Spotify, Youtube, Apple store, Amazon market place, Uber, Apple/Google Pay, etc.

**Fake News:** Refers to nontruthful information, false news, hoax news, false information, or propaganda published under the guise of being authentic news and mostly spread out using a range of media including social media with some ulterior motives and sometimes for the sake of fun, or influencing others opinions.

**Political Promotions:** A range of the communications models and methods used to influence a political debate, and ultimately voters to vote in favor of a case or a political party, etc.

**Post-Truth:** It relates or demonstrates those circumstances where the objective facts are not important or worth enough for shaping public opinion and appeals to emotion or personal beliefs play an important role than the objective analysis.

**Propaganda:** Distorted information, especially of a biased or misleading nature. information, ideas, or rumors deliberately spread widely to promote a political cause or point of view or to help or harm a person, group, movement, institution, nation, etc.

**Social Media:** Social media are Web2.0-based e-platforms that employ web-based technologies and mobile technology to create highly interactive platforms via which individuals and communities share, co-create, discuss, and modify user-generated content in order to identify, convert, share, show presence, and build relationships, reputation, and communities.

**Social Media Marketing:** A process of marketing promotion and communication that makes use of Web 2.0 or higher level internet technologies and a range of social media platforms to raise the visibility, and promote a brand, product, idea, service or a person or an organization by building social networks, and for exchanging ideas and knowledge. It may use, audio, videos, wikis, blogs, photo sharing, news, message boards, and posts on social networking platforms to reach a large or targeted audience.

# Chapter 6
# Millennials vs. Cyborgs and Blockchain Role in Trust and Privacy

**Hamid Jahankhani**
https://orcid.org/0000-0002-8288-4609
*Northumbria University, London, UK*

**Stefan Kendzierskyj**
*Northumbria University, London, UK*

**Ionuț Octavian Popescu**
*Northumbria University, London, UK*

## ABSTRACT

*Over recent years, technology has rapidly advanced and is accelerating the emergence to Industry 4.0, particularly due to the connectivity abundance, volume increase of smart devices, and a growing interconnectivity between humans and technology. Within the last two years, 90% of the data in the world today was generated and in the next few years the volume of IoT interactions is said to reach approximately 4800 per day, which equates to a human interaction every 18 seconds. This correlates well with research undertaken regarding how consumers are exchanging information through smart devices and behavioural changes due to the technology adoption. The Generation Y and Z demand for smart devices, consumer behaviour online, and almost immediate data experiences is seeing fast consumption and data exchange without any preconceived concerns of trust, privacy, security, data profiling, or how data is used without their knowledge by third parties. This chapter will also analyse technology innovations to better protect identity data and processing of data through blockchain technology.*

DOI: 10.4018/978-1-7998-0131-3.ch006

## INTRODUCTION

This chapter takes a deeper look into themes such as smart retailing in the internet era, the adoption of new technologies, and the differences between generations Y and Z and the notion of the millennial versus cyborg. There are differences between generations in terms of the decision-making process regarding smart retailing, which covers the comprehensive idea of young generations of consumers are behaving differently in the era of smart retailing. This also means how they access through devices in decision making and how freely data is given.

To help with an understanding of how generations are labeled, the following Table 1 gives the status and description of each:

## THEORIES AND PRINCIPLES AND EVOLUTION OF MARKETING CHANNELS IN DIGITAL ERA

It is useful to understand marketing transitions so human interactions may be further analysed. During the past couple decades, humanity has experienced the most revolutionary inventions such as the growth of the Internet and World Wide Web which had a very powerful impact on the printed press, eventually leading to the digitalization era. The development of new technologies imposed a powerful impact on organizations, transforming the strategies of the businesses and the way of creating awareness for products and services, moving from traditional advertising (TV ads, direct marketing, etc.) to a digital approach (Pomirleanu, 2013).

The development of new technologies created new opportunities and challenges for education and academic research, likewise for industry practitioners (Weiss, 2011), and the global adoption of digital marketing strategy, has automatically contributed to the growth of marketing for organizations and communication with individual consumers, receiving individual feedback to provide the optimum decision for actual and potential customers for goods and services (Simons, 2008).

"Traditional Marketing" evolved to "Digital Marketing", through the development of communication and marketing channels and has been described as a powerful adaptive process to promote brand awareness, to increase sales for an organization, to create a strong relationship with existent and potential customers, and to satisfy customer's needs (LexiconFT, 2018).

*Table 1. Labelling of generations*

| Type | Year of Birth | Description |
|---|---|---|
| **Baby Boomers** | 1944 - 1964 | After World War II, Population was enjoying new-found prosperity, so the term "baby boom." |
| **Generation X** | 1965 – 1979 | Illustrating the undetermined characteristics that followed Baby Boomers so why 'X' was used |
| **Generation Y** | 1980 – 1994 | Generation Y followed as alphabet but was coined by the phrase 'Millennials' and although tech-savvy not as fully reliant on smart devices as Generation Z |
| **Generation Z** | 1995 - 2015 | The newest Generation and different from Millennials as having truly grown up with in the hyper-connected world, heavily reliant on smart devices |

In Kung (2008) perspective, the digitalization of communication channels and media will impact a substantial change in the direction for communication and interactions, and the consumer behaviour and the development of technologies have always been the main elements of developmental direction in marketing strategy.

## Theories of Marketing Channels

Watson et al. (2015) describe that the evolution of marketing channels is divided in in two categories "Pre-1980" and "Modern Developments". Previous studies describe a marketing channel as "a set of interdependent organizations involved in the process of making a product or service available for use or consumption" (Palmatier et al., 2016), which is perceived as a flow of goods or services before 1980. In Modern Developments, the literature shows that theories from sociology, social psychology or political science has been adopted in marketing, emerging to a behavioural based approach illustrating the benefits of behavioural theories in marketing channels domain (Palmatier, Dant, & Grewal, 2007). Recent research describes a new era of marketing, reflecting the maturation and diversification of the domain, with the substantial disruption caused by the internationalization of marketing and the amplification of e-commerce approach (Grewal, Kumar, Mallapragada, & Saini, 2013). The development of marketing channels strategy is based on a range of *Marketing channels theories* (see Table 1) Based on Stern and Reve (1980) study, the evolution of marketing channels has been studied by using two different frameworks (see Table 2):

- **Economic**: To emphasize the performance and economic efficiency
- **Behavioural:** To understand the disagreements that develop from rational statements in an economic framework, as they are presented in Table 2 (Watson et al., 2015).

# TECHNOLOGY DEVELOPMENT AND ADOPTION THEORY

The development in technology or adoption of new technology is a key element for the process of growth and development, and for the unaccountable income in the world. However, any barriers implemented will not allow the process of development. Studies show that there are different types of barriers due to technology development such as cost-adoption (Leung & Tse, 2001) or "appropriate technology" concept for the slow diffusion of technology as a consequence of productivity differences across countries (Lahiri, Ding & Chinzara, 2018). Cobin and Hobijn (2010) state that, the diffusion of new technologies is the main contributor to economic development, and the differences in use cases of technology lead to inequality between countries.

The nature of products and services today has radically changed due to the adoption of digital technologies, implementing the digital capabilities that in the physical world will allow companies to reach new opportunities and for creating unique experiences for customers. Currently, in the era of digital transformation, products, services, and organization activity are controlling the world markets. To manage innovations in an unpredictable and highly dynamic environment, organizations have to understand the diffusion of developments to generate proper decisions, because innovations could become very quickly outdated, and competitors will create market advantage from this situation where organisations do not adapt quickly enough. Companies have to create products or services with a high level of adop-

*Table 2. Marketing channels theories (Source: Watson et al., 2015)*

| | |
|---|---|
| | ***Economic Framework*** |
| Transactions Cost Economics Theory | Describes the transaction-specific asset (TSA) as tangible and intangible with the purpose to exchange relationship at the end of the transaction (Heide & John, 1988). The channel design decisions should be targeted at minimizing transaction costs. |
| Agency Theory | Describes an efficient contract as one that delivers the leading outcome for the receiver of the contract with given constraints imposed by circumstances, with unrevealed information that refers to the agent knowledge which is favorable for the agent, and the receiver does not know (Bergen, Dutta, & Walker, 1992). The relationship between different levels of channels members can be seen as principle and agents based relationship. The relationship of different members of distribution should be determined and settled by considering the agency theory and any channel members' conflicts should be resolved accordingly. |
| Game Theory | State that all the possible actions or decisions in a game is defined as a strategy for the available options given to "the payoffs and expectations of other players actions" (Watson J., 2013). The channel strategies are a win/lose game. The options should be decided with a winning game move. |
| Resource-Based Theory | Illustrate the organization resources are valuable, rare and ineffectively imitable and other organization could exploit the resources to generate a considerable competitive advantage for potential competitors (Barney & Clark, 2007). The channel members and their skills, knowledge, culture, etc can create rare, non-copiable, value for the customers. Such values can be the basis of the core competency of a company. |
| | ***Behavioral Framework*** |
| Power Conflict and Dependence Theory | Describes the distribution of power among group members which could lead to conflicts, and the use and response to power are effective in explaining the outcomes such as performance and structure (Gaski & Nevin, 1985). The channel relationships can be determined as per this theory. |
| Relational Norms Theory | State that, norms are "expectations about attitudes and behaviors parties have in working cooperatively together to achieve mutual and individual goals" (Cannon, Achrol, & Gundlach, 2000, p. 183). |
| Commitment Trust Theory | Presents the commitment and trust as the fundamentals of intern-organizational performance, both promoting mutual goals and prevent the members of an organization to act in their own interest (Morgan & Hunt, 1994). The Supply chain relationship will enhance commitment, and trust and relationship of the channel members with the organisation. |
| Network Theory | Highlights the social structure and standardizing in which exchanges are fixed providing an appropriate approach to understand how one ecosystem part influence the others (Baron & Hannan, 1994). This theory explains and prescribes the basis of designing distributed channel networks, efficiently. |

tion to perform and guarantee profit and growth. This phenomenon of diffusion of technology without a clear understanding may lead to late adoptions generating a slow diffusion and can consequently create a loss of market share to competitors and negative financial outcomes. Hence, it is crucial to develop digital innovations with a high rate of advancement and to address to a wide market segment (Jahanmir & Cavadas, 2018).

During the development stage, organizations considered as decision makers/leaders, have to understand the problems that may influence the consumer's decisions by using a specific pattern or strategy. To understand why people, accept new technologies, researchers and practitioners have to create a better method for evaluation and prediction for users accepting new technologies (Dillon & Morris, 1996).

Theories and technology adoption frameworks have been applied in a wide range of sectors to analyse, understand, and predict the consumer's behaviour, to explain the adoption of new technologies and the cause that can influence the consumer's acceptance. Based on Venkatesh et al. (2003) research, eight models of adoption have analysed the differences and similarities regarding the information system, which all of these models had origins from communication, sociology, and psychology. These eight models are,

Theory of Reasoned Action, Social Cognitive Theory, Diffusion of Innovations Theory, Motivational Model, Technology Acceptance Model, Theory of Planned Behaviour, Model of PC Utilization, and mix between TAM and TPB in Figure 1 below (Taherdoost, 2018).

However, the *Unified Theory of Acceptance and Use of Technology* (UTAUT), is developed from the previous eight theories and has a construct on performance and effort expectations, social influence and facilitating conditions, anxicty, computer self-efficacy, and attitude towards technology adoption; which generate significant moderating variables such as age, gender, experience and action of use. These variables demonstrate the behavioural intention and certain use case (Venkatesh et al., 2003). In Bgozzi (2007) view, UTAUT consolidates aspects and functions of the Adoption Model with different models from IT adoption research but being extremely complex and the so applicability is difficult to appraise. Van der Haijden (2006) also believes that UTATUT is limited regarding the applicability in voluntary use of technology such as mobile applications, ecommerce and mobile banking.

Venkatesh et al. (2012) introduced an extension in the UTAUT model, specifically UTAUT2 by introducing hedonic motivation, habit and price value as independent variables to create a more suitable adoption model regarding use of technology for consumers. Hedonic motivation is considered as an important driver of behavioural intention. Therefore, the adoption model of UTAUT2 can be used to analyze the main determinants of e-commerce usage regarding different generations, specifically Y and Z, to contribute to the diffusion of e-commerce.

*Figure 1. Adoption theories (Bgozzi,(2007)*

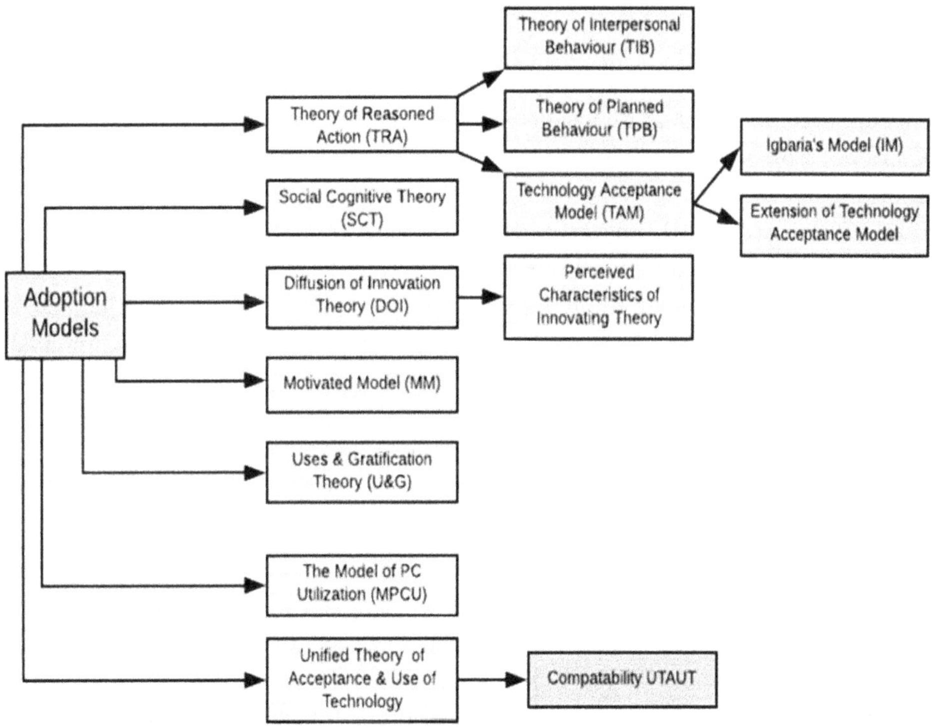

## Generations Y and Z And Adoption Of Smart Retail Interactions

During the Internet decade, retailing and communication technologies innovated the way of purchasing, allowing consumers to become technology-dependent (Zhitomirsky-Geffet & Blau, 2016). Retailing has changed due to development and adoption of new technologies in digital channels, specifically mobile and social media, having a very powerful impact on the customers and changing the perspective of shopping behavior and the business models of the organizations (Verhoef, Kannan, & Inman, 2015). Sorescu et al. (2011) state that, the customers started to behave differently, and many retailers have innovated the retail mix offered, according to the digitalization of marketing.

In a recent study, Fotiadis and Stylos (2017) analysed the way that consumers exchange information and interact through smart devices such as smartphones, laptops, tablets and PC's that resulted with online shopping developing as a continuous expansion of traditional services. Also, the customer experience improved, leading to better usability of the purchasing process and customer expectations. In contradiction, Kourafis (2003) states that the behaviour of online consumers is limited because it does not pursue the traditional consumer model. Moreover, Rigby (2011) described that brick-and-mortar stores offered a unique experience for customers, allowing touching and feeling the products, and in comparison, the internet retailers supply a wide range of items, products or services with a better price. Consequently, the "retailing industry evolves toward a seamless omnichannel retail experience, the distinction between physical and online will vanish, turning the world into a showroom without walls" (Rigby, 2011).

Smart retailing changed the consumer behaviour through the decision-making process stages (search, purchase, consumption, post-purchase) and moved towards an innovative approach for the growth of the businesses (Vrontis et al., 2017). Beyond the concept of smart retailing exists a high level of "smartness" in the application of modern technology being relatedtothe deployment of technology (Pantano & Timmermans, 2014). However, smart retailing has been defined as an "interactive and connected retail system which supports the seamless management of different customer touchpoints to personalize the customer experience across different channels and optimize performance over these touchpoints" (Roy et al., 2017).

Pantano and Timmermans (2014) describes that the perception of smart retailing will reflect on the use of technology for companies and consumers. This will recreate and reinforce a new role in economies, by enhancing the quality of customers shopping experiences. In other research conducted by Verhoef et al. (2015) it emphasizes on the importance of the customer experience and hedonic motivation, which plays a major part in retail strategy. When compared with traditional retail, smart retail brings both flexibility and challenges, as the consumer behaviour is evolving due to the process of technological changes and in the future, the interface of retail consumers may be completely different from current interactions (Roy et al., 2017).

Inman and Nikolova (2017) highlight that, from smart technologies, both customers and businesses can benefit, which will lead to business profitability and customer satisfaction. They described that mobile app, self-checkout, and scan and go technologies have a powerful impact on consumer's behaviour. However, the development of smartphones has innovated the way of purchasing, starting from mobile apps to geographic areas with same interests, creating a continuous connection with online environments which will change the consumer expectations and the ability to connect with consumers for retailers (Grewal et al., 2017). A recent study demonstrated the forecast of smartphone users worldwide increased from 1.57 bn in 2014 to 2.87 bn in 2020 which will further create the opportunity for companies to invest in smart technologies (Statista, 2018).

## Decision-Making Process and Cohort Theory on eCommerce

It is known that the decision-making process has at the foundation of it, a purchase decision with a particular pattern that a consumer will decide and follow, comparing the alternative viewpoints and opportunities to reach a decision (Erasmus, Boshoff, & Rousseau, 2001). In past research, Van der Heijden et al., (2003) adopted the Nicosia and Mayer (1976) framework for the online consumer behaviour methodology and established that the decision-making process follows next stages: recognition need, information search, alternatives, purchase and post-purchase. (Figure 2)

In the primary stage, recognition need, the consumers are aware of different needs or acknowledgment of certain types of products or services. The following stage, information search, consumers search and analyse the information to generate relevant decisions. The alternatives stage, consumers compare alternative products, prices or different retail websites to create appropriate judgments and suitable decisions. Furthermore, the purchase stage involves the consumer's actions or specific activities to accomplish the purchase process. The last stage, post-purchase, involves specific activities such as delivery process, reviews, ratings and recommendations for products or services, refunding or cognitive dissonance (Liang & Lai, 2002). This is the most common framework of consumer purchase behaviour and has been extensively used in consumer research, however, the decision-making process literature describes that "decision-makers are flexible and construct decision-making processes as they adapt and respond to decision tasks" (Karimi et al., 2018). Thus, this framework of decision-making process does not accurately display the complexity of the system is too simplistic and does not illustrate the modification in the process flow (Karimi et al., 2018), because while shopping online or in stores some decisions are spontaneously initiated (Grewal et al., 2017).

*Figure 2. Adapted online decision-making process framework (Karimi et al., 2015)*

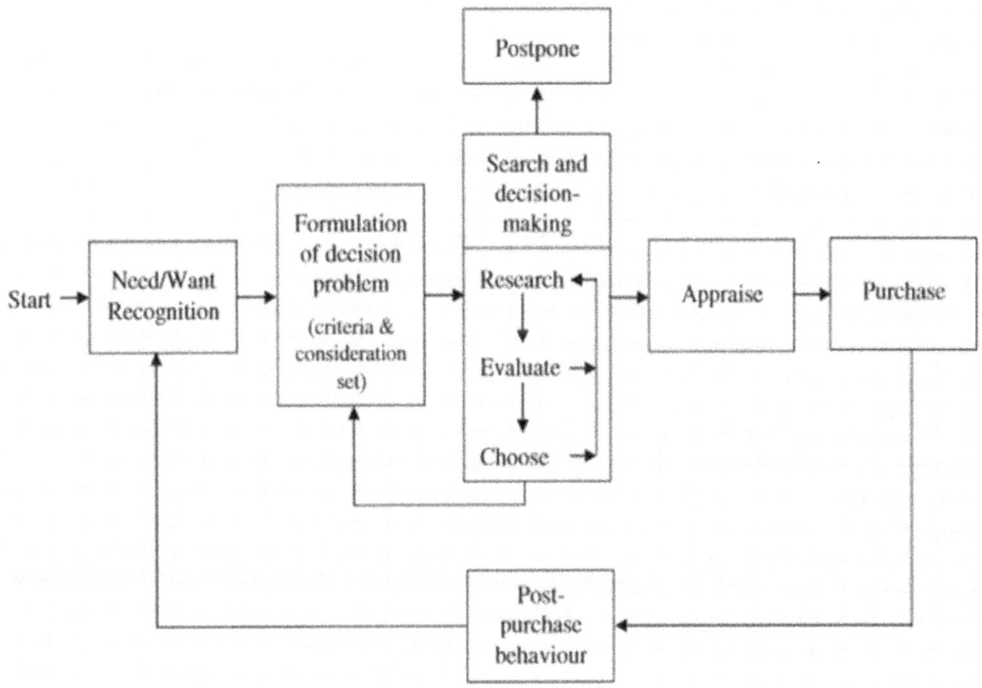

De Pelsmacker et al. (2005) highlights that cohort theory using generational cohorts will allow achieving a better understanding of the decision-making process for consumers who were born in distinct period with similar values, priorities, and experiences (Bento et al., 2018). In Lee (2009) perspective, the most important variable in the digital environment is age, which creates a distinction between categories of cohorts, with various assumptions. Furthermore, lifestyle, values or other priorities or social behaviour are uniquely relative from one cohort to another, and shopping behaviours are different regarding retail format, based on purchasing drivers (Gindi et al., 2016).

## Young Generations and Adoption of Technology

It's established that generation Y and Z are dominant in the Internet environment. The above-mentioned cohorts share same activities with different purposes such as, to meet and interact online, work, study, search for information, online shopping or to socialize on social media platforms (e.g. Facebook, Twitter, Instagram, YouTube). Compared with other generational cohorts, these generations are known as "leaders of technology", spending a considerable amount of time on web navigation, to verify the email inbox, social media profiles, new trends, to socialize with family and friends, or to complete academic projects (Issa & Isaias, 2016). Priporas et al. (2017) state that, both generations Y and Z, are oriented for online shopping, being dependent of intelligent gadgets (e.g. smartphone, tablets, laptops) and new technologies for smart retailing.

The young adults who were born in 1995 or later are known as generation Z (Bassiouni & Hackley, 2014), with a practical knowledge of smart technologies, high level of education, having innovative ideas and creative minds, considered the first generation born in the digital environment, spending time online and engaging with favourite brands. This generation is considered a challenge, by cause of the behaviour, acting differently than other cohorts which can lead to behavioural changes in consumer decision-making processes (Schlossberg, 2018). Brosdahl and Carpenter (2011) conducted research on the classification of generational cohorts and identified the adults who were born between 1981-1995 as generation Y. This cohort differentiates to others with one particular element, they have grown up during the technology development age and they are technology dependent relying on smart gadgets such as smartphones, tablets, and laptops (Çelikdemir & Tukel, 2015).

Recent research by Bilgihan (2016), describes generation Z as a young generation, being high consumers of customizable online shopping apps, with a perspective towards smart retailing, in which they extensively use technology for smart retailing. In Wood (2013) view, generation Z consumers had been characterized in four trends:

- **Innovation**: Interest in new technologies
- **Convenience:** Insistence in ease of use
- **Security**: Desire to feel safe
- **Escapism**: Desire to temporarily escape the reality they encounter.

Regarding social engagement, younger generations are using more often the features of social media platforms such as uploading photos, content writing, socializing and creating posts, compared with older generations (Hayes et al., 2015).

## Internet's Influence on Generations

Generations Y and Z are aware of local and global events, as they are connected to the internet, social media, cable television or other sources of information, and are obsessed with new technologies, devices, having an unmeasurable desire to obtain highly advanced knowledge and skills around them (Freestone & Mitchell, 2004). However, the internet could create challenges, opportunities, and threats for these cohorts, increasing their knowledge, developing their skills for study, work or social environment, leading to independence. On the other hand, it could lead to damaging health and cause stress, anxiety or depression (Issa & Isaias, 2016).

It's noted that the internet will facilitate the communication, collaboration, involvement, becoming more aware of local and global issues, and will replace the face to face interaction, cooperating to meet new people, developing relationships and maintain actual friendships (Sun, 2011). Additionally, most importantly it will allow developing independent learning, to become self-regulating learners possessing the ability to solve problems easily, allowing to perform well in their studies and work developing their communication, reading and writing skills (Pujazon-Zazik & Park, 2010). Contrarily, as mentioned before the internet could have a negative impact on people and, the influencing factors can be easily identified which is considered to be caused by computer addiction leading to isolation, stress and depression, since the interaction face to face is no longer present in a digital environment and people have fewer reasons to leave their homes (Tyler, 2002).

## Online Activities and Shopping Behaviour

Regarding online activities, both generations Y and Z are using, on a daily basis, Facebook, YouTube, and Instagram for pictures and fashion to access social media platforms and the preferred method to navigate online being through their own smartphone. However, there are more social media platforms, which they are accessing such as Snapchat, LinkedIn and various blogs. Most preferred posting across social media platforms such as lifestyle posts, while IT&C posts are more available on Facebook, beauty and personal care on YouTube and fashion-oriented on Instagram. Young generations select Facebook for promotional content adopting promotional articles, product trial, and presentation videos. Similarly, YouTube content related to video products, presentation videos and vlogs are preferred. After acknowledging the advertising on Facebook and YouTube young consumers are often searching for in-depth information on that particular product or brand and are most likely to recommend the products or brands they have seen online via advertisements (Starcom, 2018).

Concerning shopping behaviour, young generations are keen on online shopping, as a result of saving time to do other activities. However, on a weekly basis, neighbourhood stores and supermarkets are favourite places to purchase the necessary goods, being more reasonable to have a fast trip to the nearest shop to their living location, whenever they are in need for different goods. Furthermore, from typical ecommerce websites, young consumers purchase clothes, IT&C products, and books and from foreign websites, women purchase clothing and beauty care products. Young generations when they choose the online retailer, the first condition is price followed by terms of delivery. In terms of payment methods, men opt for online payment via the website and women prefer payment on delivery whether it is cash or card (Starcom, 2018).

## DIGITAL FOOTPRINTS AND THE VALUE OF DATA

Data is the new currency of value. Mostly all online activity captured either is a passive or active manner and users may not even be aware of the digital footprint they leave, how they can be targeted through ads, etc. It's willingly shared by users in a way that sometimes has no thought to the consequences and actually it is the data that is being left unintentionally that offers more value to those collating and profiling than the fixed type of data one might see for example on LinkedIn employment history. To help understand the differences between Passive and Active can be explained as follows:

**Passive:** This is usually data that organisations harvest in an admin function such as purchasing habits or browsing data, operating system used, etc. It's collected to build profiling on its audience and perhaps used for advertising targeting. VPNs may be a way around this issue to minimise footprint.

**Active:** This can be publicly traceable data which can be a cause of concern. This type of digital footprint is information shared on the web and can be as example Twitter or Facebook updates, messages or rants. A classic example of this may be prospective employers undertaking a search on a job candidate across these social media platforms to detect behaviours past anything a CV will tell about how a person may be.

### Data Harvesting and Mining

A huge amount of data and wealth of information is regularly generated about our lives with or without knowing. A digital footprint is established that stays forever and mostly cannot be erased. Whilst individuals think on obvious places such as credit card, banking, purchases, social interactions, etc., that builds this picture of preferences and routines, there is the aspect of data mining that is going on in the background that is more cause for concern. Forrester undertook research and output of a report in 2014, *Big Data's Big Meaning for Marketing*, and some highlights discussed by Kramer (2015) with regards to personal data protection, financial liabilities, and ethical dilemmas. Methods of protecting an individual's identity may not go far enough in the case of identity protection in the data mining process. Forrester outlines how Netflix released data after believing it had anonymised the data, but University of Texas researchers were able to identity Netflix users for anonymous reviews, but by knowing some parameters such as movies rented then it was possible to reverse-engineer the data and find out all viewing history; Pepitone (2010).

Whilst many would be in favor of healthcare providers mining data to ensure best-placed precision-based healthcare, where data mining is used to predict health needs. This sounds good but could raise ethical questions on privacy invasion. An example of Carolinas Healthcare System who manages 900 care centers and purchase data collected from credit card purchases, store loyalty programs, etc., to allow identification of high-risk patients in attempts to intervene prevention on any health issues developing, Kramer (2015). This identification by medical practitioners would enable gaining insight into patients' lifestyles and habits. A risk score is used so doctors can see flagged up issues. The data is collected from credit card purchases, store loyalty programs, and other public records. In theory, medical practitioners can learn more about their patients—and their patients' lifestyles—from their shopping habits than from brief, or sometimes non-existent, consultations. Although the data doesn't yet identify individual purchases, it does provide a risk score doctors can use to highlight potential problems. The issue could become a more trust-based issue between medical providers and patients if the data mining intrudes into the privacy and questions even healthy patients about their habits and digital footprints they leave. Or it may not take too long before insurance companies also start to review this mined data and risk score and that influences the service a patient receives, or worst case is refused if deemed too high a risk.

Or perhaps the case of Target, a retail organisation, that through a number of factors was able to identify and assign shoppers with a pregnancy prediction score (due to the array of 25 products when analysed together) and estimate a birth delivery due date to a small window. It allowed Target to provide coupons to the specific stages of pregnancy and highlighted a case of a dad who discovered his teen daughter was pregnant because Target mined her purchased data and sent her ads for baby products, Hill (2012).

## Social Media Data Misuse

The widespread success of online social networking sites (OSNS) such as Facebook is a tempting resource for businesses engaged in electronic commerce. Using personal information, willingly shared between online friends' networks, OSNS appear to be a natural extension of current advertising strategies such as word-of-mouth and viral marketing. However, the use of OSNS data for business marketing purposes has provoked outrage amongst social network users and highlighted issues over privacy. Within such environments, OSNS users disclose information that would be potentially rich sources of data mining for commercial organisations because it includes information that can personally identify an individual in rich detail (Krishnamurthy and Will 2010). Such 'personally rich' information includes attributes such as name, location (city), telephone numbers, email addresses, photos, interests, and purchases, etc. This rich online social network data together with electronic word-of-mouth (eWOM) communications of OSNS users represents a tempting resource for viral and word-of-mouth marketing unlike other online and offline data which has to be prepared before systematically explored for patterns of use meaningful to commercial organisations (Kohavi et al. 2002, Zhang et al. 2011). A qualitative investigation of 861 blog comments from 715 individual online users was collected during the launch of Beacon, an unsuccessful third party marketing initiative by Facebook. Results show that business integrity, transparency of data use, user control, automatic disclosure, and data leakage were key privacy concerns posing significant challenges to using business analytics in online social networks. However, attempts to leverage personal information and eWOM communications for commercial gain have provoked outrage amongst OSNS users because of privacy concerns. Privacy concerns of online social network users include use of personal information by unknown others for potential harmful purposes (e.g. by sexual predators), use and selling of personal information without notice and consent, access of personal information by unwanted audiences (Young and Quan-Haase 2009), involuntary disclosure of personal information, damaged reputation because of rumours and gossips, unwanted contact and harassment or stalking, third party use of personal information, and identity theft (Boyd and Ellison, 2008). Consequently, privacy concerns challenge the classic thinking outlined by Kohavi and Provost (2001) that online (social) environments are particularly suitable domains for data mining because of the rich and large volume of data publicly available. Rather, issues of privacy concerns have emerged that overshadow the commercial potential of OSNS data (Hoadley et al. 2010) and highlight the boundaries of acceptance and use of business analytics in social networks. Privacy concerns have emerged as a critical factor determining the willingness, or not, of internet users to divulge personal information to online companies. Many studies have used 'privacy concern' construct to understand privacy in online contexts. Therefore 'privacy concern' has become a central construct to study privacy in information systems research. Likewise, it is a useful construct for business analytics because it provides theoretical guidance in defining and measuring privacy-related issues in the context of mining social network data for business marketing.

Facebook's personalised marketing tool "Beacon" was initially withdrawn by Facebook due to users' backlash because of privacy concerns and ultimately shut down due to the settlement of a lawsuit of $9.5 million. What should have been a successful innovation, however, was damaged and ultimately withdrawn because the nature and form of privacy concerns in OSNS were poorly understood.

### Biohacking and the Arrival of the Cyborg

Biohacking, or sometimes labeled as 'do it yourself' biology, are essentially ways to enhance human abilities. This futuristic thinking has become a reality with more humans seeking to turn themselves into cyborgs with additions, for example, USB drives in their fingertips, or growing third ears on their forearms; Wainwright, 2015. The idea of the third ear which is part surgically modeled and partly has grown from the person's flesh is to turn this into a remote listening device and even add a GPS tracker so movements can be monitored and followed. This community of biohackers terms themselves as 'grinders' and information shared in how to attempt these practices are openly shared in online forums and wetware implants (biological equipment) offered. However, the term cyborg is not new as Professor Kevin Warwick was declared the worlds first cyborg in 1998 after he implanted an RFID tag in his arm and tracked his movements around the University campus, opened doors without physical touch and so on. His projects went further by implanting a 100 electrode chip into nerve fibers of his arm that transmitted signals from his wrist to computer, Warwick (2002).

There may be benefits to the advancement of humanity as some participate as a method for alternatives to large pharmaceuticals. Some may argue that trying to uncover drugs through biohacking can be undermining scientific research without following procedures to detect toxicity before patients would be administered any drugs. But the government are not able to stop individuals from experimenting on themselves even though there seems a lot of risks as the methods appear unregulated.

## THE ROLE OF PRIVACY AND TRANSPARENCY IN THE DIGITAL ERA

Data is growing at exponential rates and there is no sign of any slowing down or resistance to technology enablers, such as smart devices, Internet of Things, etc. There are also other considerations regarding interoperability of data interchange since data is mainly kept in silos and other factors that give rise to concerns of non-transparency due to the nature in the way that data is stored and accessed. There is also the risk of cyber-attacks that cause data breaches and identity data theft due to a number of reasons in the way data are managed by trusted third parties and types of sophisticated cyber-attacks and those who are undertaking the attack. The ownership of data is also becoming a question of trust and looks to have abuses and exploitation as part of daily normal activities.

However, the properties of blockchain can offer a solution to give immutability, audit trail, traceability, offer better security and importantly a method for transparency and privacy. If we consider the way millennials interact with data, especially in retail or social media, then there are concerns over exactly what type of data is kept or profiled on them and where that data is further sent or analysed. If blockchain can be the mechanism to protect identity then the purposes of these faster interactions by millennials may be more protected. This also covers protecting privacy in newer concepts such as 'smart cities or societies.'

## BLOCKCHAIN BACKGROUND

Blockchain is being viewed as a mechanism to provide further protection and enhance the security of data by using its properties of immutability, auditability, and encryption whilst providing transparency amongst parties who may not know each other, so operating in a trustless environment. In the view of Benchoufi & Ravaud (2017) some characteristics that have helped blockchain to withstand itself from the previous inventions arc that it has greater velocity, wider implications and vast areas of implementation enabling all the modern features of the technology. Clauson et al., (2018) added to this by stating that blockchain is counted as one of the top 10 trends in the business world relating to technological emulation, enabling a great platform for extending peer to peer decentralised connectivity. Blockchain can be a great way to enable and bring a dynamic and drastic change in the business world enhancing the productivity dynamics, changing the employment pattern and transforming the ways present industries operate. Hill (2018) added that the overall concept of blockchain is to create a unique platform towards a fully digitalised, flexible, secure, immutable and fixed way of making business operations that are expected to transform the sub-systems and support activities of the business to a large extent as well. This would take care of some of the issues hanging around the privacy and ownership of data. Particularly in the retail world where identity data is shared and re-shared across third parties and there appears to be a loss in the ownership of how the data should be used, what is being stored on individuals and impacts on how they are profiled or targeted.

### Forming Decentralization and Distributed Ledger

Blockchain is the method of maintaining digitalization and distributed way of data recording and handling. By implementing blockchain technology the retail business owners can effectively form a peer to peer communication hub reducing the costs regarding human resources and also allowing less intervention of the third parties. Blockchain can lead to a decentralized distributed ledger through creating unique nodes and safeguard the records of the ledger through enabling encryption option (Dixit, 2017). This can help the retail companies to reduce the roles of the third parties, reduce the theft of the trade secrets and handle the entire transactions in a more secure and safe way via soundproofing and verifying options. The best thing with the decentralized and distributed ledger is that it can protect the company for the manual modification of the records which can stop fraud and enable more transparency in the operation and also can enable the users to access the data from anywhere and anytime.

### Different Aspects of Blockchain Technology

According to Clauson et al., (2018), the context and aspects of blockchain technology are huge and difficult to cover as the use and application of the blockchain technology is immense. Many are familiar with blockchain being associated with cryptocurrency or financial transactions, but the real benefits look to be far wider and reaching into the different sectors. Santos (2017) listed some of the major companies that have already enabled different forms blockchain in the market by adding that Bitcoin, Ethureum, NEO, NEM, Qtum, Zcash, Hyper ledger, and Quorum are some of the forms of blockchain available in the market. Kaal (2017) mentioned that one of the major advantages of blockchain technology is the wide ranges of transformation provision that it provides and means it can be in different forms that allow taking advantage of the key properties of blockchain that suit to the specific task. Ishmaev (2017) added to this discussion by adding that though there can be different forms of blockchain technology, their implications remain almost similar as they allow the same sets of benefits but appear in different forms. Kaal (2017) mentioned while describing different aspects of blockchain technology not only can it be used in banks and financial institutions, but applied to manufacturing organisations, public services, hospitals/healthcare and so on. Blockchain offers some obvious benefits in banking and financial applications by bringing safer and faster transactions and in the manufacturing and retail sector blockchain is expected to bring changes in the supply chain management, utilising its traceability, transparency and saving costs, reducing wastages and deterring identity data thefts.

## Types of Blockchain

Asnit (2014) had the view that cryptocurrencies are going to change the entire face of banking transactions as it involves digital currency and fast transmission of the money peer to peer in real-time, without the intervention of the third party. It can also cover the world percentage that has no bank account or do not want to pay the higher transaction cost of trusted third parties. Casado-Vara, R et al (2018) noted that the main advantage of cryptocurrency is that it allows safer and faster transmission without any real transaction costs and help to facilitate cross-border trade in much faster and safer ways. The following are a few popular blockchain types.

## Ethereum

Ethereum is a version of blockchain technology that mainly involves smart contracts between parties in a safe, faster and flexible way by developing a unique set of algorithms that automatically creates a shared ledger and can be accessed by the parties involved from anywhere anytime. Cocco et al., (2017) mentioned the major advantage of a smart contract is that it removes the time lags and also helps to remove the transaction costs in the contract as well to a large extent. With regards to chronological ordering or time-stamping, this is extremely helpful for auditability and trackability.

## NEO

Dash & Behera (2017) mentioned that NEO is the latest addition of smart contract which is mainly China-based and the core aim of it is to facilitate the establishment of the smart economy by enabling faster and safer transaction through the use of smart contracts and deal. Dixit (2017) added that this technology involves the issuance of the business ICOs to the token owners and allow them fast peer to peer transaction to help to create a decentralised economy.

## NEM

In the view of Dos Santos (2017) NEM is an upcoming blockchain technology that is the idea which will lead to the creation of the smart asset based on the proof of algorithm through a fast, flexible and secure way. Halaburda (2017) suggests that NEM involves the record of the how many coins and transactions users do and also helps to establish smart pools of assets and systems that can have wider implications in the financial asset management, documents handling and supply chain-related operations.

### Qtum

Hayes (2009) stated that Qtum is a technology that has combined the Bitcoin and Ethereum technology together to form an improved all-around package for blockchain technology as it involves the use of smart contract through the UTXO technology and proof stake mechanism that can be customised for the enterprise functions. John (2017) mentioned that Qtum technology adds more areas of implementation for blockchain technologies in different industry segments.

### Hyperledger

Dos Santos (2017) mentioned one of the major advantages of the blockchain technology is the immutable record opportunity that it provides and Hyperledger is exactly the solution to it as it is an umbrella organisation formed by Linux that incubate different blockchain technologies in a single platform to integrate the use of blockchain technology in different operations. Dixit (2017) state that Hyperledger allows the instant and simultaneous safe and unbreakable recording of business transactions.

## BLOCKCHAIN IMPACTS IN DIFFERENT SECTORS

Kawa and Maryniak (2018) listed the major segments where blockchain can be implemented by articulating that blockchain can be used in supply chain management and manufacturing. Its main purposes for recording the transactions, stopping fraud and can be used for reducing the lags and delays in operations and give assurances to its traceability. This was also the case with Benchoufi & Ravaud (2017) who mentioned that in supply chain management blockchain can be very useful, allowing control and tracking of the inventories in every step of the supply chain and can be a great aid in stopping theft and inconsistencies while the shipment and storing of the goods can be effectively monitored.

Halaburda (2017) added that the major shipping companies have already shown their interest in the blockchain technology investing around $150m and it is predicted that the technology is going to reduce 85% of the paper use and 90% of the time delays helping the companies to save at least 10-15% costs in each transaction. Ishmaev (2017) explained the implications of the blockchain technology from the macroeconomic perspective by describing and marking it as a way of introducing digital currencies and already some emerging countries like Tunisia and Senegal have initiated their digital currencies such as E-Diner and E-CFA taking the concept from this technology.

## IMPORTANCE OF BLOCKCHAIN APPLICATIONS IN THE RETAIL SECTOR

The size of the UK retail market has grown significantly over the last few years and shows no sign of slowing down. See Figure 3 below that explains the growth cycle.

While commenting about the application of the blockchain technology in the retail segment, Ishmaev (2017) mentioned some of the major challenges that the retail companies are now currently dealing with, are regarding more transparency with their consumers whom more recently have become cautious on the origin of the goods, whom the products have been produced by and ethics concerning this. Tracking and traceability are relied upon in more conventional methods and where trust is not certain. Kaal

*Figure 3. Retail growth 2015-2020*

(2017) added that aside from the customer viewpoint blockchain has real use cases in some of the core operational areas for the retail companies especially in handling their supply chain management operation which is proven to be the most crucial for the retail companies. Contamination in the supply chain can be not just financially uncomfortable and damaging to credibility, but potentially fatal if processes are not tracked and provide the trust and immutability around this.

Kane (2017) added to this discussion by stating that blockchain can be an all-around solution for supply chain management enabling the companies to monitor and control their physical goods flow in the most effective way possible involving the companies with the entire journey and real-time monitoring. In the view of Stratopoulos (2018) blockchain can have countless positive consequences and can help the retail companies to connect with their customers more intensely, gaining trusts in their transparency statement.

However, on the other hand, the collation of retail data without fully understanding its intent or purposes can have significant effects in profiling consumers and assumptions made by those controlling the data sets.

The following sub sections discuss the properties of blockchain and use cases with examples of benefits.

## Transparency And Ethical Trading

One of the recent trends in the UK retail industry is that customers want to engage themselves with every stage of the production journey and requiring to ethically consume viable products. They want to know from where exactly the raw materials have been sourced, who is the producer and how it has been served and observe this information perhaps from a QR code on the packaging that is the immutable footprint of information stored on the blockchain. There have already been some situations where contamination of meat products has infiltrated the production line and ended up in the consumer purchase point. Such as the horse meat scandals by major UK retailers (Clowes, 2014). Companies and blockchain technology organisations are investigating this need for end-to-end traceability for its quality and assurance that what is being delivered is 100 percent and the single version of the truth.

## Authenticity and Intellectual Property Protection

Intellectual property rights or ownership are a concern as to how records are maintained and its authenticity. This is more apparent in the high street fashion retailers, as it has been noticeable that there have been many replicas of expensive fashion brands and it's become difficult for consumers to recognize the actual authentic product. Blockchain technology can become a potential solution for enabling consumers to have authentic and original products. An example of this is the popular fashion brand Babyghost, who is experimenting with the Chinese company Bitse to form NFC tags for each cloth to enable consumers to check the authenticity (Cocco, et al, 2017).

## Logistic Consideration

A study conducted by Dudek (2017) reveals that 15% of the total operating expenses of the top 5 retailers of the UK are derived from the theft and poor handling of the shipment and its workflow process. Blockchain can enable a better logistical solution as it can make the shipment easier to verify and any information regarding the status of the products at every stage of shipment with all rich data available around what happens at these milestone stages. For a retail business, this technology can effectively solve the food safety and contamination and give an added layer of prevention as blockchain can trace the temperature and airflow throughout the shipment journey and any issue is flagged and recorded. The blockchain technology has already been practiced by major retailers and there has been evidence that blockchain technology has potentially helped to overcome the UK egg crisis enabling the process to track the origin of eggs and handle and destroy them accordingly.

## Ecommerce, Payment and Ownership Verification

Cross-border transactions have always been lengthy and costly because of different documentation requirements and blockchain is expected to provide an alternative with the introduction of crypto-currencies in the transaction process and so can make the cross-border barter trade a lot easier. The introduction of cryptocurrency payment can make ecommerce more secure, fast and flexible way of handling the transactions as it can lead towards the creation of an immutable record of transactions, protecting the interest of the related stakeholders. Already companies have been experimenting with the crypto-currency payments as travel giants like Expedia is accepting hotel booking payments through the use of Bitcoin. E-commerce giants such as Shopify is also expecting the bitcoin payment (Dash, & Behera, 2017) to take place.

## Chronological Recording And Immutability And Security

One of the core reasons behind the poor customer satisfaction in the retail industry is that there is a great deal of time wasted in finding out the desired products and it happens as most of the retail business can't afford to make the chronological recording of the goods because of the flow of the huge product as found by study conducted by Dixit (2017). Blockchain can help to redeem this problem by allowing the effective categorisation and recording of the goods in a chronological manner. Another benefit that blockchain can provide to the retail companies is that it can help with the immutable record feature as once it is recorded on the blockchain platform, it is there forever. The data is protected by encryption and can only be accessed by those authenticated or allowed through the key exchange. This is one of the core reasons for the growing popularity of blockchain technology through its security properties. As retail businesses hold personal sensitive information, so hence the majority of this information always remains vulnerable to cyber-attacks. Blockchain solves this issue by enabling encryption option for the stored information and by not allowing any alteration and destruction of the recorded information at the same time, Hayes (2009).

## Transparency and Auditability

The transparency of data is a key aspect from both the context of the retailers and also from the viewpoint of the consumer. Blockchain solves this problem by allowing greater transparency through real-time control, time-stamping of data and chronological ordering. In the blockchain system, no third-party can enter into the system without the consent of the controlling parties or access the data without correct authentication approvals. The suitability and evaluation of the stored information become a lot easier in the blockchain system because it helps to represent the data in an organised and structured way with parties that have the authentication rights to view and access all data.

## Allowing Better Traceability and Faster Response Time

As there are millions of products and huge numbers of suppliers involved with the retail industry it becomes often difficult for the retail companies to exact trace which products have been received from which supplier. There is a great deal of cost factor associated with manual recording and data handling. The tracking of the shipment products has also become costly and difficult for the retail business as well. Blockchain technology can allow real-time traceability, removing the paper use and can ensure the just in time response regarding the status of the products of the retail business on an instant basis. Take the pharmaceutical retail industry, as an example, of where traceability is both key and important. It is mostly about the strong chain of custody in the manufacturing and supply of drugs to a patient and blockchain heralds itself as the answer to the issue where things have gone wrong and act as the block to fake drugs entering the supply chain. As it stands counterfeit drugs are estimated to be at 50% in low-income countries with a global market range of $200 billion (DrugPatentWatch, 2017). As well as counterfeit drugs being a failure to treat the patient, it may also kill/harm the patient. Blockchain will create a place where the ecosystem of a supply chain would interact and record all transactions without being able to tamper the records. The result is a transparent method to secure the chain of custody and data.

## Removal of Fraud and Quickening up the Pace of Tracking

Fraud, in the context of the retail business, happens mainly because of the selling from the expiry of the products, wastages, and theft of the goods in the shipment process and also theft from the store. A study conducted by John (2017) reveals that 2.5% of the global import gets counterfeited that amounts up to half a trillion dollars. Around 6% of the imported products get pirated and 24.72% of the major retail products such as handbags, perfumes, and chemicals get duplicated. From the research conducted by Kane (2017) shows that this rate can be reduced as low as 3% and 74% of the counterfeit trade can be stopped if blockchain can implement in the system as blockchain allows the quick tracking enabling optimum traceability and control from the source of intellectual property (IP) to its end point. Inventory management has also become a major cause of concern for retailers as the costs associated with it has become intensified and also companics arc facing difficulties in serving their customers according to their exact needs. Due to the constant demand fluctuations either retail businesses are facing the threat of over inventory storage or a shortage of inventory storing. A study conducted by Karame and Androulaki (2017) reveals that 25% of the overall operational costs for the retail business comes from the inventory management operation. As described earlier, blockchain can enable the provision for the digital flow of the physical goods allowing the companies with optimum inventory management operations. Another benefit that blockchain can enable in the context of retail business is that it can contribute to reducing the overall courier costs for the retail companies. Kane (2017) discusses how the implementation of the blockchain in the shipment of goods around the world can reduce the courier costs by 80% as it will effectively stop the time lags in delivery and the use of lengthy documentation. Kawa and Maryniak (2018) confirm that in a year almost £5billon is lost because of the poor documentation and also the failure of the timely delivery of products arising from this poorly kept documentation. The smart contracts feature helps to create digital documentation through the use of unique codes and the comprehensive blockchain software can enable the completion of the contract and detection of the contract with ease.

## DIGITAL IDENTITIES AND BLOCKCHAIN

The concept of digital identities is not an entirely new idea and has been approached with ID cards but this is not digital identity in a true sense. Digital identities originate from activity online or via the web and shadow data is generated as a collective body of data and recorded as individuals carry out various tasks that may be automated rather than intentionally purposed. This shadow data may mean a collation of data taken from IP surveillance, communication metadata, sensors and so on. This creates a risk in terms of data being clearly associated with an individual. With online activity, a normal interaction on a frequent basis means potentially many interactions where data is given without necessarily receiving or purchasing a product. For example, purchasing car insurance can require all identity data points before the individual selects a vendor from a series of quotes or smart data interactions in the concept of smart cities. This means there needs to be a greater demand for trust and security due to the highly mobile activity an individual undertakes.

Even in website login and creation of that initial registration either generating a new login ID and password on the site or through universal login features such as through Facebook or Google. Both methods carry a risk since the former can be subjected to a cyber-attack and identity data loss or in the latter case the data is being collated by the Universal login feature and not entirely known as to what action is being taken on the data being parsed through as third-party trackers embedded on the site are accessing this data as well. Also, the concept of KYC (Know Your Customer) presents an issue each time for due diligence a financial institution has to start afresh with onboarding the process of documents of identity and proof such as passport, identity card, driver's license, etc.

The concept of blockchain playing a part in securing digital identities looks a valid and viable option to offer enhancement of privacy and security. The choice is given more to the individual in that they can access it at anytime and cannot be accessed without their consent. There can be many use cases of how to incorporate digital identities into everyday activities. For government they could consider introducing into voting elections or in the case of KYC, blockchain makes it viable for financial institutions to access customer information without having to start from the beginning with taking in personal data. The same can be said for digital identities being used for loan requests, social media interaction and even in property auction where the example can be the buyer's identity being used as the digital identity and so not revealing true identity until a decision on purchase is agreed.

Digital identity systems look to provide the trust, privacy, and transparency a digital world will need to protect its citizens from events of cyber-attacks and loss of data. Also, to protect the invisible profiling undertaken so that sensitive personal data remains personal and not for public consumption without an individual's consent.

## CONCLUSION

This chapter looked at the main differences between the different generations and interactions made in how online activity is undertaken. Without a doubt, the volume of data is exponentially increasing and daily interactions with smart data becoming the normal mode of interaction. The gap between humans and technology has never been so close and now with the advent and acceptance of biohacking has made this transition to the term cyborg. However, so is the abundance of data being created around individuals from their online activity and retail interactions. This makes it more accessible for social media misuse and data profiling undertaken from analyzation that may use tools of machine learning and artificial intelligence. This is one of the reasons that blockchain is becoming more valued for its various use cases in industry and the retail sector is interesting since there is a high instantaneous response in data interactions (especially with millennials) that can cause a potential risk in how that data is profiled and used by third parties and other. The use of digital identities can make a layer of protection to offer better security and privacy. Using blockchain in a commercial way explained in this chapter also takes care of the transparency issues and with its properties of immutability, auditability, and traceability add to making this mechanism a powerful addition to any organisation.

## REFERENCES

Asnit, A. (2014). Collective Intelligence based Supply Chain Planning Process Considering Supply Chain Uncertainties. *Korean Journal of Logistics*, *22*(4), 15–26. doi:10.15735/kls.2014.22.4.002

Barney, J. B., & Clark, D. N. (2007). *Resource-based theory: Creating and sustaining competitive advantage*. New York: Oxford University Press.

Baron, J. N., & Hannan, M. T. (1994). The impact of economics on contemporary sociology. *Journal of Economic Literature*, *32*(3), 1111–1146.

Bassiouni, D. H., & Hackley, C. (2014). 'Generation Z' children's adaption to digital consumer culture: A critical literature review. *Journal of Customer Behaviour, 13*(2), 113–133. doi:10.1362/14753921 4X14024779483591

Benchoufi, M., & Ravaud, P. (2017). Blockchain technology for improving clinical research quality. *Trials, 18*(1), 335. doi:10.118613063-017-2035-z PMID:28724395

Bergen, M., Dutta, S., & Walker, O. C. Jr. (1992). Agency Relationships in Marketing: A Review of the Implications and Applications of Agency and Related Theories. *Journal of Marketing, 56*(3), 1–24. doi:10.1177/002224299205600301

Bilgihan, A. (2016). Gen Y customer loyalty in online shopping: An integrated model of trust, user experience and branding. *Computers in Human Behavior, 61*, 103–116. doi:10.1016/j.chb.2016.03.014

Brosdahl, D. J., & Carpenter, M. J. (2011). Shopping orientations of US males: A generational cohort comparison. *Journal of Retailing and Consumer Services, 18*(6), 548–554. doi:10.1016/j.jretconser.2011.07.005

Cannon, J. P., Achrol, R. S., & Gundlach, G. T. (2000). Contracts, norms, and plural form governance. *Journal of the Academy of Marketing Science*, (28): 94–180.

Casado-Vara, R., Prieto, J., la Prieta, F., & Corchado, J. (2018). How blockchain improves the supply chain: Case study alimentary supply chain. *Procedia Computer Science, 134*, 393–398. doi:10.1016/j.procs.2018.07.193

Çelikdemir, D. Z., & Tukel, I. (2015). Incorporating Ethics into Strategic Management with regards to Generation Y's view of Ethics. *Procedia: Social and Behavioral Sciences, 207*, 528–535. doi:10.1016/j.sbspro.2015.10.123

Clauson, K., Breeden, E., Davidson, C., & Mackey, T. (2018). Leveraging Blockchain Technology to Enhance Supply Chain Management in Healthcare. *Blockchain In Healthcare Today*. doi:10.30953/bhty.v1.20

Clowes, R. (2014). Thinking in the Cloud: The Cognitive Incorporation of Cloud-Based Technology. *Philosophy & Technology, 28*(2), 261–296. doi:10.100713347-014-0153-z

Cocco, L., Pinna, A., & Marchesi, M. (2017). Banking on Blockchain: Costs Savings Thanks to the Blockchain Technology. *Future Internet, 9*(3), 25. doi:10.3390/fi9030025

Dash, C., & Behera, P. (2017). Blockchain Technology: A Revolutionary Bitcoin Technology. *International Journal Of Information Science And Computing, 4*(1), 27. doi:10.5958/2454-9533.2017.00004.7

De Pelsmacker, P., Geuens, P., & Van den Bergh, J. (2005). *Marketingcommunicatie*. Amsterdam: Pearson Education Benelux.

Dillon, A., & Morris, M. (1996). User Acceptance of Information Technology: Theories and Models. *Annual Review of Information Science & Technology*, 3–32.

Dixit, R. (2017). Multi-Cloud for Improving Cloud Data Security. *International Journal For Research In Applied Science And Engineering Technology, 5*(11), 2696-2700. doi:10.22214/ijraset.2017.11371

Dos Santos, R. (2017). On the Philosophy of Bitcoin/Blockchain Technology: Is it a Chaotic, Complex System? *Metaphilosophy*, *48*(5), 620–633. doi:10.1111/meta.12266

DrugPatentWatch. (2017). *Can Blockchain Technology put an end to Counterfeit Drugs*. Available at https://medium.com/drugpatentwatch/can-blockchain-technology-put-an-end-to-counterfeit-drugs-c4087e652fe0

Dudek, D. (2017). Possibilities of using blockchain technology in the area of education. *Informatyka Ekonomiczna*, (45), 55-65. doi:10.15611/ie.2017.3.05

Erasmus, A. C., Boshoff, E., & Rousseau, G. G. (2001). Consumer decision-making models within the discipline of consumer science: A critical approach. *Journal of Family Ecology and Consumer Science*, *29*, 82–90.

Fotiadis, A., & Stylos, N. (2017). The effects of online social networking on retail consumer dynamics in the attractions industry: The case of 'E-da' Theme Park, Taiwan. *Technological Forecasting and Social Change*, *124*, 283–294. doi:10.1016/j.techfore.2016.06.033

Freestone, O., & Mitchell, V. W. (2004). Generation Y Attitudes Towards E-ethics and Internet-related Misbehaviours. *Journal of Business Ethics*, *54*(2), 121–128. doi:10.100710551-004-1571-0

Gaski, J. F., & Nevin, J. R. (1985). The Differential Effects of Exercised and Unexercised Power Sources in a Marketing Channel. *JMR, Journal of Marketing Research*, *22*(2), 130–142. doi:10.1177/002224378502200203

Gobo, G. (2014). Glocalizing methodology? The encounter between local methodologies. *International Journal of Social Research Methodology*, *14*(6), 417–437. doi:10.1080/13645579.2011.611379

Grewal, R., Kumar, A., Mallapragada, G., & Saini, A. (2013). Marketing Channels in Foreign Markets: Control Mechanisms and the Moderating Role of Multinational Corporation Headquarters–Subsidiary Relationship. *Journal of Marketing Research*, (50), 378-398.

Halaburda, H. (2017). *Blockchain Revolution Without the Blockchain*. SSRN Electronic Journal. doi:10.2139srn.3133313

Hayes, J. (2009). The clout of the cloud (cloud computing). *Engineering & Technology*, *4*(6), 60–61. doi:10.1049/et.2009.0611

Heide, J. B., & John, G. (1988). The Role of Dependence Balancing in Safeguarding Transaction-Specific Assets in Conventional Channels. *Journal of Marketing*, *52*(1), 20–35. doi:10.1177/002224298805200103

Hill, T. (2018). Blockchain for research [Review]. *Learned Publishing*, *31*(4), 421–422. doi:10.1002/leap.1182

Hofmann, E., Strewe, U., & Bosia, N. (2016). *Supply Chain Finance and Blockchain Technology*. Academic Press.

Inman, J. J., & Nikolova, H. (2017). Shopper-Facing Retail Technology: An Adoption Decision Calculus. *Journal of Retailing*, *93*, 7–28. doi:10.1016/j.jretai.2016.12.006

Ishmaev, G. (2017). Blockchain Technology as an Institution of Property. *Metaphilosophy*, *48*(5), 666–686. doi:10.1111/meta.12277

Issa, T., & Isaias, P. (2016). Internet factors influencing generations Y and Z in Australia. *Information Processing & Management*, *52*(4), 592–617. doi:10.1016/j.ipm.2015.12.006

Jahanmir, S. F., & Cavadas, J. (2018). Factors affecting late adoption of digital innovations. *Journal of Business Research*, *88*, 337–343. doi:10.1016/j.jbusres.2018.01.058

John, A. (2017). Blockchain and Its Applications. *International Journal of Recent Trends in Engineering and Research*, *3*(4), 143–145. doi:10.23883/IJRTER.2017.3123.ZS1WM

Kaal, W. (2017). *Blockchain Technology and Race in Corporate America*. SSRN Electronic Journal. doi:10.2139srn.3071378

Kane, E. (2017). *Is Blockchain a General Purpose Technology?* SSRN Electronic Journal. doi:10.2139srn.2932585

Karame, G., & Androulaki, E. (2017). *Bitcoin and blockchain security*. Academic Press.

Kawa, A., & Maryniak, A. (2018). *SMART Supply Network*. Cham: Springer.

Lee, S. (2009). Mobile internet services from consumers' perspectives. *International Journal of Human-Computer Interaction*, *25*(3), 390–413. doi:10.1080/10447310902865008

Leung, C. K., & Tse, C. Y. (2001). Technology choice and saving in the presence of a fixed adoption cost. *Review of Development Economics*, *5*(1), 40–48. doi:10.1111/1467-9361.00105

Lexicon, F. T. (2018). *Financial Times*. Retrieved from LexiconFT: http://lexicon.ft.com/Term?term=digital-marketing

Liang, T., & Lai, H. (2002). Effect of store design on consumer purchases: Van empirical study of on-line bookstore. *Information & Management*, *39*(6), 431–444. doi:10.1016/S0378-7206(01)00129-X

Morgan, R. N., & Hunt, S. D. (1994). The Commitment-Trust Theory of Relationship Marketing. *Journal of Marketing*, *58*(3), 20–38.

Nicosia, F. M., & Mayer, R. N. (1976). Toward a sociology consumption. *The Journal of Consumer Research*, *3*(2), 65–75. doi:10.1086/208653

Palmatier, R. W., Dant, R. P., & Grewal, D. (2007). A Comparative Longitudinal Analysis of Theoretical Perspectives of Interorganizational Relationship Performance. *Journal of Marketing*, *71*(4), 94–172. doi:10.1509/jmkg.71.4.172

Pantano, E., & Timmermans, H. (2014). What is smart for retailing? *Procedia Environmental Sciences*, *22*, 101–107. doi:10.1016/j.proenv.2014.11.010

Pomirleanu, N. S., Schibrowsky, J. A., Peltier, J., & Nill, A. (2013). A review of internet marketing research over the past 20 years and future research direction. *Journal of Research in Interactive Marketing*, *7*(3), 166–181. doi:10.1108/JRIM-01-2013-0006

Priporas, C.-V., Stylos, N., & Fotiadis, A. K. (2017). Generation Z consumers' expectations of interactions in smart retailing: A future agenda. *Computers in Human Behavior*, *77*, 374–381. doi:10.1016/j.chb.2017.01.058

Pujazon-Zazik, M., & Park, M. J. (2010). To Tweet, or Not to Tweet: Gender Differences and Potential Positive and Negative Health Outcomes of Adolescents' Social Internet Use. *American Journal of Men's Health*, *4*(1), 77–85. doi:10.1177/1557988309360819 PMID:20164062

Pujazon-Zazik, M., & Park, M. J. (2010). To Tweet, or Not to Tweet: Gender Differences and Potential Positive and Negative Health Outcomes of Adolescents' Social Internet Use. *American Journal of Men's Health*, *4*(1), 77–85. doi:10.1177/1557988309360819 PMID:20164062

Rigby, D. (2011). The Future of Shopping. *Harvard Business Review*, *89*(12), 65–76.

Rouse, S. V. (2015). A reliability analysis of Mechanical Turk data. *Computers in Human Behavior*, *43*, 304–307. doi:10.1016/j.chb.2014.11.004

Schlossberg, M. (2018). *Teen Generation Z is being called 'millenials on steroids', and that could be terrifying for retailers*. Retrieved from Business Insider UK: http://uk.businessinsider.com/millennials-vs-gen-z-2016-2

Simons, G. (2008). Marketing to postmodern consumers: Introducing Internet chameleon. *European Journal of Marketing*, *42*(3/4), 299–310. doi:10.1108/03090560810852940

Sorescu, A., Frambach, R. T., Singh, J., Rangaswamy, A., & Bridges, C. (2011). Innovations in Retail Business Models. *Journal of Retailing*, *87*, 3–16. doi:10.1016/j.jretai.2011.04.005

Starcom. (2018). *Starcom România lansează ediţia 2017 a studiului Consumer Report*. Retrieved from IQAds: https://www.iqads.ro/articol/40927/starcom-romania-lanseaza-editia-2017-a-studiului-consumer-report

Statista. (2018a). *eCommerce Romania*. Retrieved from Statista: https://www.statista.com/outlook/243/148/ecommerce/romania#market-age

Statista. (2018b). *Number of smartphone users worldwide from 2014 to 2020 (in billions)*. Retrieved from Statista: https://www.statista.com/statistics/330695/number-of-smartphone-users-worldwide/

Stern, L., & Reve, T. (1980). Distribution Channels as Political Economies: A Framework for Comparative Analysis. *Journal of Marketing*, *44*(3), 52–64. doi:10.1177/002224298004400306

Stratopoulos, T. (2018). *Blockchain Technology Adoption*. SSRN Electronic Journal. doi:10.2139srn.3188470

Sun, J., Yan, J., & Zhang, K. (2016). Blockchain-based sharing services: What blockchain technology can contribute to smart cities. *Financial Innovation*, *2*(1), 26. doi:10.118640854-016-0040-y

Sun, S. (2011). The Internet Effects on Students Communication at Zhengzhou Institute of Aeronautical Industry Management. Advances in Computer Science, Environment. *Ecoinformatics and Education*, *5*(11), 418–422.

Taherdoost, H. (2018). A review of technology acceptance and adoption models and theories. *Procedia Manufacturing*, *22*, 960–967. doi:10.1016/j.promfg.2018.03.137

Tyler, T. (2002). Is the Internet changing social life? It seems the more things change, the more they stay the same. *The Journal of Social Issues*, *58*(1), 195–205. doi:10.1111/1540-4560.00256

Van der Haijden, H. (2006). User Acceptance of Hedonic Information System. *Management Information Systems Quarterly*, *28*(4), 695–704. doi:10.2307/25148660

Van der Heijden, H., Verhagen, T., & Creemers, M. (2003). Understanding online purchase intentions: Contributions from technology and trust perspectives. *European Journal of Information Systems*, *12*(1), 41–48. doi:10.1057/palgrave.ejis.3000445

Venkatesh, V., Morris, M. G., Davis, G. B., & Davis, F. D. (2003). User acceptance of information technology: Toward a unified view. *Management Information Systems Quarterly*, *27*(3), 425–478. doi:10.2307/30036540

Venkatesh, V., Thong, J. Y., & Xu, X. (2012). Consumer acceptance and use of information technology: Extending the unified theory of acceptance and use of technology. MIS Quarterly: Management. *Information Systems*, *36*(1), 157–178.

Verhoef, P. C., Kannan, P. K., & Inman, J. J. (2015). From Multi-Channel Retailing to Omni-Channel Retailing: Introduction to the Special Issue on Multi-Channel Retailing. *Journal of Retailing*, *91*(2), 174–181. doi:10.1016/j.jretai.2015.02.005

Wainwright, O. (2015). Body-hackers: the people who turn themselves into cyborgs. *The Guardian*.

Warwick, K. (2002). *Project Cyborg 2.0: The next step towards True Cyborgs*. Available at: http://www.kevinwarwick.com/project-cyborg-2-0/

Watson, G. F. IV, Worm, S., Palmatier, R. W., & Ganesan, S. (2015). The Evolution of Marketing Channels: Trends and Research Directions. *Journal of Retailing*, *91*(4), 546–568. doi:10.1016/j.jretai.2015.04.002

Watson, J. (2013). *Strategy: an introduction to game theory* (3rd ed.). New York: W. W. Norton and Company.

Weiss, M. A. (2011). The use of social media sites data by business organizations in their relationship with employees. *Journal of Internet Law*, *15*(2), 16–27.

Wood, S. (2013). Generation Z as consumers: trends and innovation. Institute for Emerging Issues: NC State University.

Zhitomirsky-Geffet, M., & Blau, M. (2016). Cross-generational analysis of predictive factors of addictive behavior in smartphone usage. *Computers in Human Behavior*, *64*, 682–693. doi:10.1016/j.chb.2016.07.061

## KEY TERMS AND DEFINITIONS

**Biohacking:** Sometimes labelled as ‘do it yourself’ biology, is essentially ways to enhance human abilities.

**Blockchain:** This is viewed as a mechanism to provide further protection and enhance the security of data by using its properties of immutability, auditability and encryption whilst providing transparency amongst parties who may not know each other, so operating in a trustless environment.

**Cyborg:** The gap between humans and technology has never been so close and now with the advent and acceptance of biohacking has made this transition to the term cyborg.

**Data Harvesting:** A huge amount of data and wealth of information is regularly generated about our lives with or without knowing and through a set of preferences and routines using data mining a pattern can be harvested.

**Digital Footprint:** Is the track of data created and left behind while using the digital platforms.

**Digital Identity:** Digital identities originate from activity online or via the web and shadow data is generated as a collective body of data and recorded as individuals carry out various tasks that may be automated rather than intentionally purposed.

**Digital Marketing:** The digitalization of communication channels and media will impact a substantial change in the direction for communication and interactions, and the consumer behaviour and the development of technologies is the main elements of developmental direction in marketing strategy in the digital era.

**Social Media:** During the Internet decade the social arrangements made up of many actors in the virtual environment/ media which is called social media.

# Chapter 7
# Internal Marketing Cybersecurity-Conscious Culture

**Gordon Bowen**
*Northumbria University, London, UK*

**Atul Sethi**
*Ulster University, London, UK*

## ABSTRACT

*The chapter is putting forward the idea that internal marketing is a tool of which there are many to embed a culture to combat cybersecurity threats. This conceptual paper is suggesting that cybersecurity threats are multi-facet and although internal marketing is a major contributing factor in reducing the threats, other factors are in play. The shape of the organisation (i.e., bureaucratic or organic) has an important bearing on the implementation of a marketing-oriented culture, including that of internal marketing and, thus, the success of a cybersecurity-conscious organisational culture. Another significant factor in creating a cybersecurity-conscious organisational culture is the management willingness to empower and employees and their willingness to accept the responsibility to make decisions and be accountable, which requires acceptance of the authority.*

## INTRODUCTION

Cybercrime will cost societies $6 trillion annually by 2019, which is twice the cost of what was paid in 2015. Escalating at this rate requires serious action to be taken by organisations, society, and governments. To combat cybercrime currently, $1 trillion is spent on cybersecurity (radiusits.com). The focus of this paper is on the internal environment of the firm from the perspective of internal marketing to combat the internal threat of cybercrime and improve awareness of cybersecurity by using an internal marketing lenses.

DOI: 10.4018/978-1-7998-0131-3.ch007

The organisational landscape has a bearing on the effectiveness of combatting cybersecurity issues (Nye, 2017). Cybersecurity combines "public good" attributes, frequently associated with governmental responsibilities for private market goods and services, and private organisations with non-market, non-governmental resources, and information sharing. Management of governmental responsibilities requires a robust governance structure (Kuerbis & Badiei, 466, 2017). The paper suggests that not only governments and nations have responsibility for cybersecurity, but the organisation and employees have ownership of the governance structures internally to mitigate the effects of cybercrime. Furthermore, some of the responsibilities of government need to be cascaded down to organisations to gain the organisational commitment necessary for organisations to defend their organisation and employees against cybercrime. Shackelford & Kastelic, (2015) suggest there is a growing agreement that nations need to take responsibility for enhancing cybersecurity. Ultimately, governments and nations will require to engage organisations in cybersecurity, and organisations must shoulder more of the burden of cybersecurity. To ensure firms are ready to engage with the responsibilities of governance and activities related to cybersecurity, the paper contends that an internal marketing approach is necessary, because cybersecurity is everyone's responsibility, and employee responsibility is a key driver to guarantee cybersecurity safeguarding of the organisation.

## THEORETICAL CONCEPTS

### Determinants of internal marketing

"Market orientation", "market-driven" or "customer orientation" are used interchangeably and have a component of internal marketing orientation (IMO) (Naude´, Desai & Murphy,:1205, 2003). There is no agreed definition of the internal marketing construct (Rafiq & Ahmad, 2000). The use of marketing approaches within the organisation to create and publicise overall corporate values is an integral part of internal marketing (Hogg & Carter, 2000). The paper is positioning IMO as an important factor to embed a positive factor to embed employee engagement in detecting and preventing cybercrime within the organisation.

Schneider, (1990) and James el (1979) consider the perception of organisational climate is based on "person" and "situation" variables. Person x situation = perception of organisational climate. The Table 1 identifies the variables (Person and Situational) and the perception of the organisation (situation x person) (see *Table 1).*

Naude´, Desai & Murphy, (2003) develop the following hypotheses for the variables in Table 1:

1. IMO will vary by age – younger age groups and generations will have stronger attitudes and transfer the expectations to the organisation. A significant factor is an age as a determinant of IMO. This implies that younger people's attitudes would need moulding to the organisational cybersecurity policies and procedures to ensure consistency in the operational requirements.
2. IMO results from males (gender) will be positive. The results bear this out that there is a positive outcome between males and IMO. Females tend to be more critical than men. This particular variable is not significant as a determinant of IMO.

*Table 1. Possible determinants of internal marketing (Naude ́, Desai & Murphy, 2003)*

| Variables | | |
|---|---|---|
| **Person** | **Situation** | **Person x situation** |
| 1 Age<br>2. Gender<br>3. Level of education | 4. Location<br>5. Tenure<br>6. Function | 7. Organisational socialisation<br>8. Involvement<br>9. Commitment<br>10. Organisational satisfaction<br>11. Communication<br>12. Evaluation of local management<br>12. Evaluation of direct manager<br>13. Evaluation of colleagues |

3. IMO results will correlate to education i.e. the higher the level of education the more critical the individual. The higher the level of education the more negative the perception of the organisation. This particular variable was not significant as an influencer of IMO.
4. Different locations will view the organisation's IMO differently. This hypothesis is significant. This could be due to the different tasks being undertaken at different sites. This requires organisations to ensure the culture of cyber-security is consistent, so employees that locate from different locations with the firm will have a consistent approach to the threat of cybersecurity.
5. The length of tenure correlates positively with IMO. The length of service correlates positively with IMO and is thus significant. Once a cybersecurity culture is in place, then from an IMO perspective those with long tenure under this culture could be more critical of the new culture and become less vigilant on cyber-security threats, than new employees.
6. Different functions evaluate IMO differently. This is not a significant determinant of IMO.
7. Reviewing the person and situation variables only age, tenure and locations are significant determinants of IMO.
8. Organisational socialisation correlates positively to IMO. Organisational socialisation is defined " as the process by which an individual comes to appreciate the values, abilities, expected behaviours, and social knowledge essential for assuming an organisational role and for participating as an organisational member" (Louis, 1980, 229 -230). There is a correlation between IMO and organisational socialisation. However, higher levels of socialisation depend on the ability of the employees to cope positively with their work. The implication for cybersecurity is that employees that are less able to cope with their work, would be less able to exhibit the cybersecurity values and behaviours expected.
9. There is a positive relationship between the degree of involvement and a respondent's IMO. This appears to be the case that involvement has a high significance on IMO. Engaged and involved employees are more willing to exhibit the necessary behaviour expected in a cybersecurity environment.
10. Commitment is positively related to the perception of IMO. This hypothesis is significant in its effect on IMO. Commitment is related to organisational goals and the individual acceptance of the goals. Also, a sense of belonging is an attribute of commitment.
11. Organisational satisfaction is linked to three dimensions i.e. reward satisfaction, stimulation from work and workload. The three factors are positively related to IMO.

12. Communications construct has two dimensions openness and information accuracy, which are positively related to IMO. Accuracy of information is slightly more significant than openness.
13. Employees' perception of local management's IMO correlates positively to their overall perception of the organisation's IMO. The employees' perception of local management market orientation is positively linked to IMO scores.
14. Employees' perception of supervisors' level of IMO correlates positively with the individual's perception of the organisation's IMO. The employees' perception of their supervisors' market orientation is positively linked to IMO scores.
15. Employees' overall perception of the company's IMO correlates positively with their relationship to co-workers and their perception of their colleagues' market-oriented behaviour. The perceived level of market orientation of colleagues does influence other employees own perceived level of IMO.

The most influential variables on IMO are the location (which depends on job function), length of tenure and age. The person x situation variables show that local and direct management, socialisation and satisfaction factors are important contributors to IMO.

## Internal Marketing Tools

In any organisations, it is important that all departments act as integrated systems, so that they achieve the organisational goals in a coordinated way. this requires interdepartmental exchange of ideas, knowledge, activities and internal services. services are acts of performances that one party offers to other, and the activities are essentially intangible, non-ownable, non-storable, heterogenous, perishable and variable. The unique characteristics of services requires, a three-dimensional marketing approach. The three dimensions of service marketing are illustrated by service marketing triangle (see Figure 1), that argues for External Marketing, Internal Marketing and Interactive Marketing (Dabhade & Yadav, 2013).

The external marketing efforts are directed by the organisation towards understanding and exceeding its customers' expectations, the Internal marketing are the activities the organisation must carry on to train, motivate, and reward its employees m so the employees are able and willing to deliver the customer services to the customers; and the interactional marketing incudes those activities that involves interaction between the employees with the customers (Dabhade & Yadav, 2013). Unless the organisations market the ideas, knowledge, practices and procedures related to wide range of activities including that related to cyber security; it will not be possible to offer secure services to the customers.

Understanding internal marketing in terms of marketing principles and the context of employees has been researched for more than 30 years (Berry et al, 1976). Traditional communication techniques of promotion, such as advertising and personal selling are common approaches to promote products to external customers. These techniques are also used to communicate with employees (Berry, 1981). Berry et al, (1976) related internal marketing to employees (internal customers) and jobs as products. Munir (2015) suggests that internal marketing is not just about communications tactics, such as employee commitment, workplace posters, and employee meetings. Internal communication is a significant component of internal marketing. Furthermore, internal communication is a new employer-employee contract (Varey & Lewis, 1999). Effective management of internal communications could bring many organisational benefits (Piercy & Morgan, 1995).

*Figure 1. Service marketing triangle*

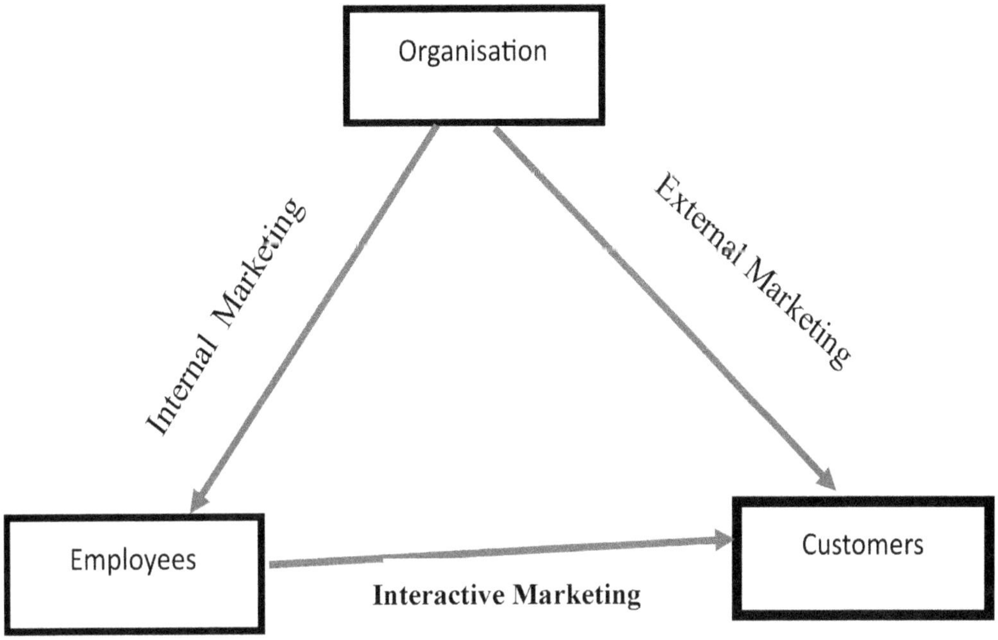


Internal marketing in many parts of the literature is associated with marketing techniques in a human resource management resource context to continuously improve employer-employee relationship to satisfy employees and customers (Kotler & Armstrong, 1991; Wildes & Parkes, 2005). Abzari, Ghorbani & Madani (2011) consider internal marketing as part of the human resource function.

Furthermore, research suggests that training is an underpinning dimension of internal marketing, which can be sub-divided into four categories, namely service standards, training, development programmes and rewards (Papasolomou & Vrontis, 2006). Lee & Chen (2005), further conceptualised that internal marketing as having five functions, namely recruitment, training, incentives, communications and retaining employees, all are human resource functions. 11 of the 42 internal marketing definitions focus on training apart from customer focus (Huang & Rundle-Thiele, 2015). Implementation of internal marketing requires employees with skills and information (Paraskevas, 2001). Internal marketing requires employee know-how and autonomy to meet their wants and needs (Ballantye, 1997).

Internal marketing research is an important starting point, which will be survey-based on internal marketing practices measurements (Huang & Rundle-Thiele, 2015). The type of data that could be collected include:

Supervisors clearly state their expectations of others (Bearden & Niemeyer, 1999); Receiving feedback from supervisors that informs the employees' progress (Bearden & Niemeyer, 1999); Supervisor clearly states expectations of me (Bearden & Niemayer, 1999); Supervisors do a good job of sharing information (Bearden & Niemayer, 1999; Naude´, Desai & Murphy, 2003; Tsai & Tang, 2008); Communication is weak between departments and employees (Peltier & Scovotti, 2005); Employees can reach managers easily (Chang & Chang, 2008); Employees have a solid understanding of the ways the organisation evaluates their work (Karasa et al, 2008; Chang & Chang, 2008); and Employees at all levels understand the direction and key priorities of the organisation (Huang & Rundle-Thiele, 2015).

In order to embed cybersecurity practices and governance, an internal marketing approach requires engagement with employees to create dialogue and understanding of the organisation and management expectations from the process and practices. Dialogue between employees and ensuring information is relevant and accurate will underpin the success of embedding cybersecurity practices. The model to embed cybersecurity practices includes internal communications, training and internal research. Although all dimensions are significant, training is the most important. Worth noting is that the model is based on western culture, and differences are likely to occur in eastern culture.

## Internal Marketing And Cybersecurity Environment

Data security and privacy are pressing issues facing marketing today (Ferrell, 2017). The domains that are suggested as important to marketers are related to consumers, organisational, ethical, and legal (Martin & Murphy, 2017). Consumers, organisations and regulators are important stakeholders. Organisations collect and use consumer data for marketing activities, which are required for marketing activities. Consumers sacrifice privacy so that marketers can understand their wants and needs, which is necessary for competitiveness (Romanosky, 2016). Organisations have a responsibility and opportunity to protect consumer data. The organisational culture should press for increase cybersecurity internally (opportunity for internal marketing and its ability to influence organisational culture) and externally. Consequently, organisations need to carry out a risk assessment on the use and protection of the data. Marketing research needs to investigate the interface between using and acquiring data. Marketing requirements for big data and data analytics suggest that most organisations are at risk (Ferrell, 2017). This suggests that cybersecurity is the responsibility both legally and ethically for organisations and they have a responsibility to develop and implement governance rules and processes for handling data internally.

Understanding the nature and properties of privacy ethic is a step in the right direction to prevent cybersecurity issues. Organisations interact with regulatory and legal bodies to ensure and develop compliance, but this interaction could lead to conflict (Martin & Murphy, 2017).

Decisions on cybersecurity are a strategic decision. Ferrell (2017) state that ethics form part and parcel of every strategic decision in the digital environment. Understanding the risks digital systems put on consumers is important. The systems contain diverse and sensitive information, such as credit card details and national insurance numbers. Understanding the risks associated with holding this data is paramount. Donaldson & Dunfee (1994) suggest research around stakeholder norms and based on integrative stakeholder theory using ethical perspectives and social contract theory is a requirement. However, the organisation may accept or comply with stakeholder norms, but they may also not wish to do so. Hypernorms (help to evaluate lower level norms that are applied to develop the roots of ethical acceptability) for stakeholders may be areas organisations may wish to avoid. Organisational norms will decide, which stakeholders are important and if data privacy is a top priority. Also, do they have the resources to protect consumers (Maignan & Ferrell, 2004)? Internal marketing or an internal marketing orientation culture cannot protect against cybersecurity issues if the organisation does not put the necessary resources in place and the nature of cybersecurity issues means resources must be sustained and developed and updated.

As stated earlier social contracts is an avenue to protect privacy but social contracts (all contracts) are based on fairness. Research on the harm an act or practice can cause, which gives rise to unfairness is document by Ohlhausen (2014). Unfairness could be applied to data privacy risk assessment and the prevention of data breaches (Ferrell, 2017). Frameworks suggested to reduce unfairness is justice theory and power responsibility equilibrium. The frameworks would be able to express fairness expectations (Martin & Murphy, 2017). Ferrell & Gresham (1985) developed a descriptive model for understanding ethical decisions in an organisation. Privacy decisions the model indicate individual values, and attitudes, organisational factors (impact of significant others) and opportunities (policies and compliance requirements). Specialised code of ethics for top financial and accounting officers improve the integrity of financial reporting (Ahluwalia et al, 2016). Specialised data privacy codes should help organisations develop a more effective data privacy culture thatsupports ethical decisions. Importantly, is an understanding of the risks to the organisation and consumers and the development of effective cybersecurity (Ferrell, 2017).

All organisations should have a privacy crisis management or a backup plan to minimise the risks from data breaches. The plan needs embedding in an ethic and compliance programme for data privacy and security. Those that think social contracts, values, policies, and norms can be an effective deterrent in cybersecurity has not consider external risk, which requires collaboration with other organisations (Ferrell, 2017).

Possibly one the greatest risk is complacency by the organisation and the consumer in protecting their data and privacy. Akhter (2014) found the self-efficacy influenced privacy concerns negatively. Privacy concerns impacts the frequency of online transactions, reasons why organisations must protect consumer privacy and data. Ferrell (2017) suggest that marketing research should evolve to include frameworks to address and raise awareness of issues that influence cybersecurity. The impact on cybersecurity on brand image, erosion of consumer trust and organisations reputation. Cybersecurity is an external threat and is uncontrollable making trust difficult to secure. Internal marketing is not a panacea to cybersecurity issues but is a stepping stone along with new techniques not yet developed.

## Internal Marketing and Firm's Performance

The empirical evidence gives limited support that is positive correlation exists between internal marketing practices, organisational effectiveness and organisational performance (Ahmed, Rafiq & Saad, 2003). Galpin (1997) coined the phrase "organisational influencer systems" are required to implement business strategy internally. The framework identified a number of factors to embed business strategy internally and could be designated the internal marketing mix. The factors are identified below:

- Strategic rewards;
- Internal communications;
- Training and development;
- Organisational structure;
- Senior leadership;
- Physical environment;
- Staffing, selection, and recruitment;
- Interfunctional coordination;
- Incentive systems;
- Empowerment; and
- Operational/process changes.

There is much similarity between this framework and others already discussed. It is worth noting that strategic rewards and incentive systems serve different purposes. Incentive systems are a basic requirement to motivate individuals' actions such as organisational culture, values and business activities behaviour (Pfeiffer, 1998), whilst strategic rewards are linked to motivating future performance to achieve business goals (Hale, 1998). Incentive systems are backward looking and strategic rewards is a forwarding looking factor. The previous discussion has linked cybersecurity to strategic decisions, which implies it is important for the future prosperity of the organisation. This, in turn, suggests that to influence cybersecurity behaviour the internal marketing factor of strategic rewards has an important part to play.

The paper by Ahmed, Rafiq & Saad, (2003) is proposing that the internal marketing mix developed by Galpin (1997) will lead to improved individual and organisational performance, by managing the interdependent elements in the internal marketing mix.

Organisational competitive advantage is discussed in two contexts, namely competitive forces (Porter, 1980; 1985) and resource-based view (Barney, 1991; Prahalad & Hamel, 1990). Supporters of the Porter view of strategy is that competitive advantage comes from analysis and understanding the industry environment to determine a unique position, which is known as "strategic position". Counter to this strategy is the resource-based view (RBV), which relies on "core competencies" or "distinctive competences" to develop a competitive strategy (Prahalad & Hamel, 1990). Core competences are organisational based capability according to Prahalad & Hamel (1990). Taking an RBV approach to strategy the organisational competencies that will improve a firm's performance is based on the three internal marketing constructs are Ahmed, Rafiq & Saad, (2003):

- Customer/market orientation;
- Employee satisfaction; and
- Specific/individual competencies.

The external marketing philosophy (market/customer oriented) and marketing tools will also mediate the relationship between internal marketing and the organisational competence constructs and the firm's performance (Ahmed, Rafiq & Saad, 2003). The research postulates the following:

There is a significant and positive relationship between the internal marketing mix and business performance.

Organisational competences mediate the relationships of internal marketing mix with business performance.

Application of marketing-like philosophy and application of marketing-like tools moderates the relationship between the internal marketing mix and organisational competencies.

All the above hypotheses were supported. The internal marketing mix is a method to support and facilitate organisational competencies. The results support the role of top management as the initiator of internal marketing (Barnes, 1989), and it requires continuous support (George, 1990). Gro¨nroos (1981) states make the point that internal management should be part of strategic management. The results are also supportive of the notion that senior management is an important driver of market orientation (Kohli & Jaworski, 1990).

## SKILLS TO REDUCE CYBERSECURITY ATTACKS

Skills are a combination of knowledge, experience, and abilities that the user can apply to be successful (Levy, 2005; Boyatzis & Kolb, 1991). The acquisition of skills is a multi-stage process and is a learning process linked to incremental stages (Gravill, Compeau, & Marcolin, 2006). Stage 1 is the initial acquisition of the skills (declarative knowledge). This type of knowledge is given by instruction and information to the recipient of the knowledge. The recipient receives fundamental knowledge (Gravill, Compeau, & Marcolin, 2006). Stage 2 is practicing the declarative knowledge to convert it into procedural knowledge (Neves & Anderson, 1981). In this stage, knowledge is organised and users can the knowledge to accomplish activities (Gravill, Compeau, & Marcolin, 2006). Stage 3 is the final stage and is characterized by autonomous and efficiency by practicing activities and gaining more experience. This improves skills further. Experience is a positive influence on computer usage, which reinforces the need for skills (Gravill, Compeau, & Marcolin, 2006). A generalisation of procedural knowledge and increase performance comes throughout the stages (Gravill, Compeau, & Marcolin, 2006). Skills honed over time become competences (Eschenbrenner & Nah, 2014).

Competence is a high level of skill that can be certified or allow a person to practice in a profession (Levy & Ramin, 2015). Maturing knowledge of a person improves skills, which develops the user's competency (Eschenbrenner & Nah, 2014). Competency (knowledge, experience, and abilities) is acquired once a skill is practiced over time (Levy & Ramin, 2015).

According to Goode & Levy (2017), IT (information technology) skills are those skills that relate to software, hardware, and programming in order to develop technical skills in IS (information systems). IT skills are becoming the norm in the work environment, as IT becomes a fixture in the workplace (Weigel & Hazen, 2014). Competence in IT empower users and has an impact on the users' workplace productivity and leadership effectiveness (Marcolin, et al, 2000).IT skills are essential for organisations to gain competitive parity, butthe management of those IT skills that enables the organisation to sustain a competitive advantage (Downey & Smith, 2000). The ability of a firm to have competences in cybersecurity, over and above current IT skills would enhance an organisation's sustain competitive advantage. Cybersecurity would move from an exclusively IT role to an organisation-wide responsibility, thus becoming part of the strategic decision making process in the organisation. Verizon Enterprise Solutions (2014) carried out a survey and the results suggested that data breaches are found by users armed with the necessary identification and reporting skills. The implication is that technology alone cannot guarantee security (Carlton, Levy & Ramim, 2018). Users' failure to take countermeasures when a breach is perceived to be responsible for interference in productivity (Choi, Levy, & Hovav, 2013). The most recurring data breaches since 2003 can be classified as miscellaneous errors, crimeware, insider misuse, and physical theft/loss. All are due to human error or misuse (Verizon Enterprise Solutions, 2015). Social engineering is a continuing cause for concern, "unfortunately, even the best security mechanisms can be bypassed through social engineering" (Winkler & Dealy, 1995:1). Social engineering is seen as a greater threat to organisations and people (Kvedar, Nettis, & Fulton, 2010). However, the top three security issues are namely, malware, use of stole personal information, and phishing (Verizon Enterprise Solutions, 2016).

Organisational competencies show a partial correlation as a mediator of organisational performance. However, marketing-oriented behaviour is an important mediator between internal marketing mix and business performance (Ahmed, Rafiq & Saad, 2003; Kohli & Jaworski, 1990; Narver & Slater, 1990). The internal marketing mix is a strong predictor of employee satisfaction, but employee satisfaction is not a significant mediator for internal marketing mix- performance relationship. The literature identifies that job satisfaction and customer perceptions of quality for UK financial advisers that no relationship exists (Ahmed, Rafiq & Saad, 2003; Herrington & Lomax, 1999). Market-oriented philosophy has a moderating influence on the internal marketing mix and organisational competences (Ahmed, Rafiq & Saad, 2003; Quester & Kelly, 1999).

Concluding from the research by Ahmed, Rafiq & Saad, (2003), firstly, improving organisational competencies improves business performance. Undoubtedly, improved cybersecurity is an organisational competence that has become more and more pressing due to the prevalence of the internet, and consequently, business performance will move forward. Market and customer orientation and individual and specific competencies are strong influencers on business performance. From their research job, satisfaction does not receive much support. Nevertheless, job satisfaction is an important factor. Secondly, the elements that build organisational competencies are empowerment, top management support, strategic rewards, physical environment, internal communication, interfunctional co-ordination and training, and development. Finally, managers can enhance the variables in the internal marketing mix that influence organisational competencies by adopting a marketing-centric philosophy towards human resource issues and use market type tools such as market research, segmentation, etc. for implementing human resource strategies.

## A Framework to Assess Cybersecurity

One cannot eliminate risk entirely so one needs to mitigate risk. Cybersecurity risk is associated with a disruption to the business and instantaneous loss caused by a malicious cyber situation (NIST, 2014). National Institute of Standards and Technology (NIST, 2014, 8 - 9) created a framework to assess cybersecurity with the following functions:

**Step 1. Identity:** Develop organisational understanding in these areas (assets, systems, data, and capability) to manage cybersecurity risks in asset management, business environment, governance, risk assessment, and risk management;

**Step 2. Protect:** Develop and implement appropriate safeguards to ensure delivery of critical infrastructure services, i.e. access control, awareness and training, data security, information protection processes and procedures, maintenance and protective technology;

**Step 3. Detect:** Development and implement the appropriate activities to identify the occurrence of a cybersecurity event, i.e. anomalies and events, security continuous monitoring and detection processes;

**Step 4. Respond:** Develop and implement the appropriate activities to identify to take action regarding a cybersecurity event, i.e. response planning, communications, analysis, mitigation, and improvements;

**Step 5. Recover:** Develop and implement the appropriate activities to maintain plans for resilience and restore any capabilities or services that were impaired due to a cybersecurity event, i.e. recovery planning, improvements, and communications.

The 5 functions are continuous cyclical and current in nature.

Research by Carlton, Levy and Ramim (2018) suggests non-IT professional should have opportunities to develop appropriate cybersecurity skills and to use a tool (Cybersecurity Index) to assess the cybersecurity skill level in the organisation. Application of the tool enables management to identify skill gaps in relation to cybersecurity and moves away from the survey approach to determine deficiencies. Gender, hours accessing the internet, job function, or other demographic determinants were not found to be significant factors in influencing the level of cybersecurity skills. Individual skills found to minimise cybersecurity threat are the following:

- Preventing the leaking of confidential digital information to unauthorized individuals Sk1;
- Preventing malware via non-secure websites Sk2;
- Preventing personally identifiable information theft via access to non-secure websites Sk3;
- Preventing personally identifiable information theft via email phishing Sk4;
- Preventing malware via email Sk5;
- Preventing credit card theft by purchasing from non-secure websites Sk6;
- Preventing information system compromise via USB or storage device exploitations Sk7;
- Preventing unauthorised information system access via password exploitations Sk8;
- Preventing personally identifiable information theft via social networks Sk9.
- The skills are categorised as follow leading to Cybersecurity Skills Index:
- Work Information Systems (Sk1, Sk7 & Sk8)
- Malware (Sk2, Sk5 & Sk6)
- Personal identifiable information (Sk3, Sk4, & Sk9)
- Overall Cybersecurity Skills Index based on the above categories.

Skills relating to reduction in unauthorised leakage of confidential information were significantly improved as a result of increased age, advanced education level and use of IT systems during the course of employment. Preventing personally identifiable information theft on social media improved with time spent on the internet, which is not unsurprising.

Cybersecurity awareness is a short-term solution that only provides employees with exposure. However, cybersecurity training and education that includes hands-on cybersecurity activities with scenario-building exercises, deliver knowledge, skills and deeper understanding that enable employees to develop the right cybersecurity skills (Whitman Mattord, 2018).

## Internal Marketing Implementation

Although internal marketing is a growing and important area of marketing for academic, there are few models that deal with its implementation (Ballantyne, 2003; Gilmore & Carson, 1995). The different approaches to the implementation of internal marketing include Woodruffe (1995) argues the principal elements of internal marketing programme are training and personnel development, effective internal communications, integration technique, and motivational programmes to increase knowledge and understanding of market orientation. Ballantyne (1996) suggests that a bank approach to internal marketing by focusing on customer orientation is an appropriate approach. The bank launched a "customer service improvement programme", with the desire to change staff attitudes by the use of formal communications and engagement of staff in policy and procedures changes. There are only a few internal marketing models on implementation (Papasolomou, 2006).

Implementation of internal marketing requires a supportive board of directors, chief executive and other top senior executives (Felton, 1959). Unless the organisation receives clear signals from top-management internal marketing will find it challenging to take root in the organisation culture. Coupled with this is the need for interfunctional co-ordination support, especially between marketing and HRM departments (Rafiq & Ahmed, 1993; Ahmed, Rafiq & Saad, 2003). Interaction between departments also facilitates information sharing, leading to responsiveness to customer needs in relation to quality, products, and services (Kohli & Jaworski, 1990; Narver & Slater, 1990). Another benefit of implementing internal marketing will improve the overall business process in the organisation (Ahmed, Rafiq & Saad, 2003; Varey, 1995).

Organisational structure influences how organisations adapt to changes in the external environment. Two organisational structures developed for two different environments developed by (Burns & Stalker, 1961):

1. The mechanistic model is suitable for stable and unchanging external environments. The emphasis is on rules, procedures, and dominated by a hierarchy of authority; and
2. The organic model is suitable for uncertain external environments. The emphasis is on free-flowing, decentralised, and more adaptive organisational system (Buchanan & Huczynski, 1991).

The mechanistic model of organisational design is associated with bureaucracy, which implies extensive departmentalism, high formalisation, a limited information network (downward communication), and not much participation by lower ranked employees in decision making (Robins, 1996).

Employee empowerment is the link to successful internal marketing. A formal marketing plan for an internal market is of little value if customer contact staff are not motivated and empowered to deliver the level of service quality required (Payne, 1993: 37). Gilmore & Carson (1995) state that the involvement and empowerment of employees to enable them to make decisions relating to customers is part of the internal marketing activities. Employee empowerment is paramount for service organisations. Pushing decision lower in the organisation and empowering people close to the customer is a crucial factor for internal marketing (French & Bell, 1995). One could argue that employees that are not empowered and cannot make decisions relating to customers they interact could lower morale and deliver inferior service to customers. Empowered employees are more committed, more productive, more competent, more satisfied and innovative, while they create high-quality products and service than non-empowered employees (Whetten, Cameron & Wood (1996); Greenberger & Strasser, 1991 & Spreitzer, 1992). A contrary view is that employee empowerment will result in higher labour costs, which could result in slower or inconsistent service delivery, and bad decisions on the part of employees (Bowen & Lawler, 1996). Consequently, it could lead to dissatisfied customers, negative word of mouth communications, and higher prices, which no organisation can afford.

An organisation's structure can facilitate or inhibit empowerment. Rigid organisational structures will limit empowerment, to minimise the effect of this type of organisation elimination of bureaucratic rules and in its place organisational support systems that encourage empowerment (Peters, 1988). Freedom to take risks, flexibility, and to make mistakes need embedding in the organisation structure so it becomes part of the market orientation culture. Implementation of internal marketing is to change the organisational culture and leverage the dimensions of internal marketing (image of the internal customer, training and development, internal performance standards, and rewards systems). Results from a bank that used the above dimensions to improve service quality and customer satisfaction led to dissatisfied customers and divisiveness amongst staff and ambiguity. In the background the bank is engaging in compulsory redundancy, the prospects for promotion or job rotation is stagnant and lack of employee empowerment in terms of decision making and organisational rigidities that stop staff from meeting expectations of internal and external customers. Bureaucratic and mechanistic structures in banks hinder the benefits of internal marketing and they need to move to organic structures that are supportive of marketing oriented environments. Empowerment alone cannot create a marketing oriented culture if employees are not given decision-making powers and are willing to take responsibility and authority (Papasolomou, 2006).

## IMPLICATION TO MANAGEMENT

Cybersecurity is a major threat to the internal workings of an organisation. The ability of the organisation to respond to the threat of cybersecurity depends on the organisational structure and how it engages and empowers its employees. In business, we tend to think of security issues as external i.e. keeping them out of the organisation, but cybersecurity is an internal threat that have entered the organisation from the external environment (outside the organisation). Cybersecurity issues can also be introduced by employees (Carlton, Levy & Ramim, 2018). The underlying assumption in this paper is that cybersecurity enters from the external environment and internal marketing is a tool to manage the internal/external interface of the threat. Effective management of the interface requires senior management support and facilitation and an organisational mind-set that puts the customer at the centre of the organisation, a customer-centric organisation. Internal marketing is a technique to manage the boundary between the external and internal environments. Senior management involvement is imperative, because cybersecurity decisions are strategic and require the right decision makers to be fully cognisant of the issues and have the strategic leverage to allocate the resources required in the implementation process. Cybersecurity makes internal marketing an organisational-wide activity, thus linking into the strategic planning process. However, the internal marketing technique and the management of interface might vary dependent on the organisational structure. A bureaucratic organisation will find a marketing orientation approach more demanding to implement than an adaptive organisation, the so-called organic model. One significant issue is to ensure the organisation is cybersecurity ready, which requires understanding where the deficiencies in cybersecurity knowledge and understanding lay within the organisation. This is the subject of the next paragraph.

Cybersecurity issues are not a constant and will mutate, which will require the organisation to adopt a flexible and nimble organisational structure. The organic structure would appear to be more adaptable to cybersecurity threats, but not all organisations can adopt such a structure due to the nature of the business. Firms that require a procedural approach to decision making may find it challenging to adopt an organic structure. Cybersecurity decision making requires an approach that is decentralised and autonomous approach to enable threats to be dealt with swiftly and in a timely manner. Cybersecurity threats as stated earlier is an organisational threat and internal marketing techniques must permeate across the organisation. Collaboration between different functions is an imperative and detection and prevention techniques shared continuously across the organisation. Sharing knowledge and information on cybersecurity internally solves the problem reactively. There is a need for collaboration across industries and other firms even competitors so that cybersecurity threats take on a proactive stance. This will enable organisations to alert others to new threats, sharing best practice improving internal marketing techniques by applying and developing models such as CSI, develop common training and development programmes and develop governance systems that integrate not only within the organisation, but across different organisations. Adoption of the collective approach to fighting cybersecurity means more resources are being marshalled and there is an economies of scale advantage for the participating organisations. More eyes watching cybersecurity activities helps to minimise the effect of social engineering, which is still the biggest threat to undermining cybersecurity governance. Bureaucratic organisation with the centralised approach to decision making may have to deploy autonomous cybersecurity groups that can make cybersecurity decisions proactively. These groups would have to be organisation-wide and communications between them seamless to share information and update programmes and activities. The cybersecurity grouping in a bureaucratic organisation must have a market orientation approach, which is the glue to make organisations become cybersecurity proof.

Internal marketing is an important determinant for detecting and defeating cybersecurity threats. Employee engagement is an important factor, which will lead to employee empowerment, but the organisational structure, procedures, and policies might inhibit this process. Research on inhibitors to employee engagement and market orientation will be a prerequisite to a successful cybersecurity strategy. The governance structure for cybersecurity should link to the strategic planning process and will influence HRM strategy in relation to IT skillsets, recruitment, retention, and strategic rewards. Awareness of cybersecurity issues will be sufficient for some staff, but to be effective engagement in training and development will be the only convincing way to give the organisation and employees the skills required to guard against cyber-threats. However, this will require additional expense, which not all organisations can afford or are willing to pay. There will need to be a trade-off, which will vary with the organisation. Cybersecurity needs to be recognised by the organisation as a team effort, so that strategic rewards are for the whole team and not for individual performance. The implementation of internal marketing will play an important role in achieving the desired objectives.

Cybersecurity tends to be the preserve of computing. Nevertheless, marketing needs to engage with research in this area, because it affects consumers in many ways from their behaviour, perception of the organisation and employees, brand integrity, customer satisfaction, customer relations to product and service quality. Marketing may be required to adopt appropriate governance procedures and policies on cybersecurity on how they deal with customers that have been compromised by cybersecurity threat. The TSB bank is returning money to customers taken from their bank account via cybersecurity action(s). Will more organisations have to relax customer rules and policies to offset and minimise the impact of cybersecurity threats?

## CONCLUSION

Cybersecurity cannot be departmentalised and communications localised. All staff must be engaged in cybersecurity activities and awareness training is not sufficient. Development training from training course to scenario activities to give the hands-on are necessary components to bring staff to the appropriate skillset to minimise the cybersecurity threat. Given the nature of cybersecurity requirements, it will not be a cheap exercise, and hence the strategic imperative needs to be factored in. Cybersecurity implementation will incur many costs from ensuring there is an internal marketing culture of market orientation, awareness training to extensive training and development in cybersecurity. To ensure there is value for the organisation cybersecurity needs to be more prominent in organisations so it has an effective governance system and is embedded the corporate strategy process, thus it becomes part of the strategic decision-making process. This will help to elevate its status to senior management, drive the necessary organisational and human resource management changes. Importantly, internal marketing alone cannot fix the cybersecurity threat, and the internal and external environments will be significant influencers. Cybersecurity safety is a multi-dimensional problem and requires many actors to come together to formulate an overarching strategy.

## REFERENCES

Abzari, M., Ghorbani, H., & Madani, F. A. (2011). The effect of internal marketing on organizational commitment from market-orientation viewpoint in hotel industry in Iran. *International Journal of Marketing Studies*, *3*(1), 147–155. doi:10.5539/ijms.v3n1p147

Ahluwalia, S., Ferrell, O. C., Ferrell, L., & Rittenburg, T. (2016). BSarbanes-Oxley 406 Code of Ethics for Senior Financial Officers and Firm Behavior. *Journal of Business Ethics*, *151*(3), 693–705. doi:10.100710551-016-3267-7

Ahmad, P. K., Rafiq, M., & Saad, N. M. (2003). Internal marketing and the mediating role of organisational competences. *European Journal of Marketing*, *37*(9), 1221–1241. doi:10.1108/03090560310486960

Akhter, S. H. (2014). Privacy concern and online transactions:the impact of internet self-efficiency and internet involvement. *Journal of Consumer Marketing*, *31*(2), 118–125. doi:10.1108/JCM-06-2013-0606

Ballantyne, D. (1996). Internal networks for internal marketing. In *Proceedings of 4th International Colloquium in Relationship Marketing*. Swedish School of Economics.

Ballantyne, D. (1997). Relationship marketing of services-perspectives from 1983 and 2000. *Journal of Marketing Management*, *13*(5), 343–366. doi:10.1080/0267257X.1997.9964479

Ballantyne, D. (2003). A relationship-mediated theory of internal marketing. *European Journal of Marketing*, *37*(9/10), 1242–1260. doi:10.1108/03090560310486979

Barnes, J. G. (1989). The role of internal marketing: If the staff won't buy it, why should the customer? *Irish Marketing Review*, *4*(2), 11–21.

Barney, J. B. (1991). Firm resources and sustained competitive advantage. *Journal of Management*, *17*(1), 99–120. doi:10.1177/014920639101700108

Bearden, W. O., & Netemeyer, R. G. (1999). *Handbook of Marketing Scales: Multi-Item Measures for Marketing and Consumer Behavior Research* (2nd ed.). SAGE Publications. doi:10.4135/9781412984379

Berry, L. L. (1981). The employee as customer. *Journal of Retail Banking*, *3*(1), 25–28.

Berry, L. L., Hensel, J. S., & Burke, M. C. (1976). Improving retailer capability for effective consumerism response. *Journal of Retailing*, *52*(3), 3–14.

Bowen, D.E. & Lawler, E.E. III. (1992). The empowerment of service workers: what, why, how, and when. *Sloan Management Review*, *8*(1), 31-9.

Boyatzis, R. E., & Kolb, D. A. (1991). Assessing individuality in learning: The learning skills profile. *Educational Psychology*, *11*(3/4), 279–295. doi:10.1080/0144341910110305

Buchanan, D., & Huczynski, A. (1991). *Organisational Behaviour: An Introductory Text* (2nd ed.). Englewood Cliffs, NJ: Prentice-Hall.

Burns, T., & Stalker, G. M. (1961). *The Management of Innovation*. London: Tavistock.

Carlton, M., Levy, Y., & Ramim, M. (2019). Mitigating cyber attacks through the measurement of non IT professionals' cybersecurity skills. *Technology Information & Computer Security*, *27*(1), 101–121. doi:10.1108/ICS-11-2016-0088

Chang, C. S., & Chang, H. C. (2008). Perceptions of internal marketing. *Journal of Advanced Nursing*, *8*(87), 92–100. PMID:19120584

Choi, M. S., Levy, Y., & Hovav, A. (2013), The role of user computer self-efficacy, cybersecurity countermeasures awareness, and cybersecurity skills influence on computer misuse. *Proceedings of the Pre-International Conference of Information Systems (ICIS) SIGSEC – Workshop on Information Security and Privacy (WISP) 2013*. Available at: http://aisel.aisnet.org/wisp2012/29

Donaldson, T., & Dunfee, T. W. (1994). Toward a Unified Conception of Business Ethics: Integrative Social Contracts Theory. *Academy of Management Review*, *19*(2), 252–284. doi:10.5465/amr.1994.9410210749

Downey, J. P., & Smith, L. A. (2011). The role of computer attitudes in enhancing computer competence in training. *Journal of Organizational and End User Computing*, *23*(3), 81–100. doi:10.4018/joeuc.2011070105

Eschenbrenner, B., & Nah, F. F.-H. (2014). Information systems user competency: A conceptual foundation. *Communications of the Association for Information Systems*, *34*, 1363–1378. doi:10.17705/1CAIS.03480

Felton, A. P. (1959, July). Making the marketing concept work. *Harvard Business Review*, 55–65.

Ferrell, O. C. (2017). Broadening marketing's contribution to data privacy. *Journal of the Academy of Marketing Science*, *5*(2), 160–163. doi:10.100711747-016-0502-9

Ferrell, O. C., & Gresham, L. G. (1985). A Contingency Framework for Understanding Ethical Decision Making in Marketing. *Journal of Marketing*, *49*(3), 87–96. doi:10.1177/002224298504900308

French, W. L., & Bell, C. H. Jr. (1995). *Organisational Development* (5th ed.). Englewood Cliffs, NJ: Prentice-Hall.

Galpin, T. J. (1997). Making strategy work. *The Journal of Business Strategy*, *18*(1), 12–14. doi:10.1108/eb039824

George, W. R. (1977). The retailing of services – a challenging future. *Journal of Retailing*, *53*(3), 85–98.

Gilmore, A., & Carson, D. (1995). Managing and marketing to internal customers. In W. J. Glynn & J. G. Barnes (Eds.), *Understanding Services Management* (pp. 295–321). Chichester, UK: John Wiley & Sons.

Goode, J., & Levy, Y. (2017). Towards empirical exploration of employee's cybersecurity countermeasures awareness and skills: differences in training delivery method and program type. *Proceeding of the Knowledge Management (KM) 2017 Conference, Faculty of Information Studies (FiS),* 18-30.

Gravill, J. I., Compeau, D. R., & Marcolin, B. I. (2006). Experience effects on the accuracy of self -assessed user competence. *Information & Management*, *43*(3), 378–394. doi:10.1016/j.im.2005.10.001

Greenberger, D. B., & Strasser, S. (1991). The role of situational and dispositional factors in the enhancement of personal control in organisations. *Research in Organizational Behavior*, *13*, 111–145.

Hale, J. (1998). Strategic rewards: Keeping your best talent from walking out the door. *Compensation and Benefits Management*, *14*(3), 39–50.

Herrington, G., & Lomax, W. (1999). Do satisfied employees make customers satisfied? An investigation into the relationship between service employee job satisfaction and customer perceived service quality. In *Marketing and Competition in the Information Age, Proceedings of the 28th EMAC Conference*. Humboldt University.

Hogg, G., & Carter, S. (2000). Employee attitudes and responses to internal marketing. In R. Varey & B. Lewis (Eds.), *Internal Marketing: Directions for Management* (pp. 109–124). London: Routledge. doi:10.4324/9780203207352.ch7

Huang, Y.-T., & Rundle-Thiele, S. (2015). A holistic management tool for measuring internal marketing activities. *Journal of Services Marketing*, *29*(6/7), 571–584. doi:10.1108/JSM-03-2015-0112

James, L., Gent, M., Hater, J., & Coray, K. (1979). Correlates of psychological influence: An illustration of the psychological climate approach to work environment perceptions. *Personnel Psychology*, *32*(3), 563–588. doi:10.1111/j.1744-6570.1979.tb02154.x

Karasa, A., & Akinci, F., EsatoElu, A.E., Parsons, A.L., & Sarp, N. (2008). An evaluation of the opinions of hospital employees regarding the contribution of internal marketing to the application of total quality management in Turkey. *Health Marketing Quarterly*, *24*(3), 167–187. PMID:19042534

Kohli, A., & Jaworski, B. (1990). Market orientation: The construct, research propositions, and managerial implications. *Journal of Marketing*, *54*, 1–18. doi:10.1177/002224299005400201

Kotler, P., & Armstrong, G. (1991). *Principles of Marketing* (5th ed.). Englewood Cliffs, NJ: Prentice-Hall.

Kuerbis, B., & Badiei, F. (2017). Mapping the cybersecurity institutional landscape. *Digital Policy. Regulation & Governance*, *19*(6), 466–492. doi:10.1108/DPRG-05-2017-0024

Kvedar, D., Nettis, M., & Fulton, S. P. (2010). The use of formal social engineering techniques to identify weaknesses during a computer vulnerability competition. *Journal of Computing Sciences in Colleges*, *26*(2), 80–87.

Lee, C., & Chen, W. J. (2005). The effects of internal marketing and organisational culture on knowledge management in the information technology industry. *International Journal of Management*, *22*(4), 661–672.

Levy, Y. (2005). A case study of management skills comparison in online MBA programs. *International Journal of Information and Communication Technology Education*, *1*(3), 1–20. doi:10.4018/jicte.2005070101

Levy, Y., & Ramim, M. M. (2015). An assessment of competency-based simulations on e-learners' management skills enhancements. *Interdisciplinary Journal of E-Learning and Lifelong Learning, 11*, 179-190. Available at: www.ijello.org/Volume11/IJELLv11p179-190Levy1958.pdf

Louis, M. (1980). Surprise and sense making: What newcomers experience in entering unfamiliar organisational settings. *Administrative Science Quarterly*, *25*(2), 226–249. doi:10.2307/2392453 PMID:10247029

Maignan, I., & Ferrell, O. C. (2004). CorporateSocialResponsibilityand Marketing: An Integrative Framework. *Journal of the Academy of Marketing Science*, *32*(1), 3–19. doi:10.1177/0092070303258971

Marcolin, B. L., Compeau, D. R., Munro, M. C., & Huff, S. L. (2000). Assessing user competence: Conceptualization and measurement. *Information Systems Research*, *11*(1), 37–60. doi:10.1287/isre.11.1.37.11782

Martin, K., & Murphy, P. (2017). The Role of Data Privacy in Marketing. *Journal of the Academy of Marketing Science*, *45*(2), 135–155. doi:10.100711747-016-0495-4

Munir, Z. A., Othman, A. A., Shukur, S. A. M., Ithnin, R., & Rusdi, S. D. (2015). Practices of internal marketing in small and medium industry. *International Journal of Social Science and Humanity*, *5*(4), 358–361. doi:10.7763/IJSSH.2015.V5.480

Narver, J. C., & Slater, S. F. (1990). The effect of market orientation on business profitability. *Journal of Marketing*, *54*(4), 20–35. doi:10.1177/002224299005400403

National Institute of Standards and Technology (NIST). (2014). *Framework for improving critical infrastructure cybersecurity (version 1.0)*. Available at: www.nist.gov/cyberframework/upload/ cybersecurity-framework-021214.pdf

Naude´, P., Desai, J., & Murphy, J. (2003). Identifying the determinants of internal marketing orientation. *European Journal of Marketing*, *37*(9), 1205–1220. doi:10.1108/0390560310486951

Nye, J. S. Jr. (2017). Deterrence and dissuasion in cyberspace. *International Security*, *41*(3), 44–71. doi:10.1162/ISEC_a_00266

Ohlhausen, M. K. (2014). Privacy Challenges and Opportunities: The Role of the Federal Trade Commission. *Journal of Public Policy & Marketing*, *33*(1), 4–9. doi:10.1509/jppm.33.1.4

Papasolomo, I. (2006). Can internal marketing be implemented within bureaucratic organisations? *Journal of Bank Marketing*, *24*(3), 194–212. doi:10.1108/02652320610659030

Papasolomou, I., & Vrontis, D. (2006). Using internal marketing to ignite the corporate brand: The case of the UK retail bank industry. *Brand Management*, *14*(1/2), 177–195. doi:10.1057/palgrave.bm.2550059

Paraskevas, A. (2001). Internal service encounters in hotels: An empirical study. *International Journal of Contemporary Hospitality Management*, *13*(6), 285–292. doi:10.1108/09596110110400481

Payne, A. (1993). *The Essence of Services Marketing*. Hemel Hempstead, UK: Prentice-Hall.

Peltier, J. W., & Scovotti, C. (2005). Relationship marketing and disadvantaged health care segments. *Health Marketing Quarterly*, *22*(2), 69–90. doi:10.1300/J026v22n02_05 PMID:15914375

Peters, T. (1988). *Thriving on Chaos*. New York, NY: Alfred A. Knopf.

Pfeiffer, J. (1998, May). Six dangerous myths about pay. *Harvard Business Review*, 108–109. PMID:10179647

Piercy, N. F., & Morgan, N. (1995). Internal marketing – the missing half of the marketing programme. *Long Range Planning*, *24*(2), 82–93. doi:10.1016/0024-6301(91)90083-Z

Prahalad, C. K., & Hamel, G. (1990). The core competence of the corporation. *Harvard Business Review*, (May/June): 79–91.

Rafiq, M., & Ahmed, P. (2000). Advances in the internal marketing concept: Definition, synthesis and extension. *Journal of Services Marketing*, *14*(6), 449–462. doi:10.1108/08876040010347589

Rafiq, M., & Ahmed, P. K. (1993). The scope of internal marketing: Defining the boundary between marketing and human resource management. *Journal of Marketing Management*, *9*(3), 219–232. doi:10.1080/0267257X.1993.9964234

Robins, S. P. (1996). *Organisational Behavior: Concepts, Controversies, Applications* (7th ed.). Englewood Cliffs, NJ: Prentice-Hall.

Romanosky, S. (2016). Examing the Costs and Causes of Cyber Incidents. *Journal of Cybersecurity*, *0*(0), 1–15.

Schneider, B. (1990). *Organizational Climate and Culture*. San Francisco, CA: Jossey-Bass Publishers.

Shackelford, S. J. (2014). Managing Cyber Attacks in International Law, Business, and Relations. In *Search of Cyber Peace*. Cambridge, UK: Cambridge University Press. doi:10.1017/CBO9781139021838

Spreitzer, G. M. (1992). *When organisations dare: the dynamics of individual empowerment in the workplace* (PhD dissertation). University of Michigan, Ann Arbor, MI.

Tsai, Y. F., & Tang, T. W. (2008). How to improve service quality: Internal marketing as a determining factor. *Total Quality Management*, *19*(11), 1117–1126. doi:10.1080/14783360802323479

Varey, R. J. (1995). Internal marketing: A review and some interdisciplinary research challenges. *International Journal of Service Industry Management*, *6*(1), 40–63. doi:10.1108/09564239510078849

Varey, R. J., & Lewis, B. R. (1999). A broadened conception of internal marketing. *European Journal of Marketing*, *33*(9), 926–944. doi:10.1108/03090569910285869

Verizon Enterprise Solutions. (2014). *Verizon 2014 data breach investigations report*. Available at: www.verizonenterprise.com/DBIR/2014/

Verizon Enterprise Solutions. (2015). *Verizon 2015 data breach investigations report*. Available at: www.verizonenterprise.com/DBIR/2015/

Verizon Enterprise Solutions. (2016). *Verizon 2016 data breach investigations report*. Available at: www.verizonenterprise.com/verizon-insights-lab/dbir/2016/

Weigel, F. K., & Hazen, B. T. (2014). Technical proficiency for IS success. *Computers in Human Behavior*, *31*, 27–36. doi:10.1016/j.chb.2013.10.014

Whetten, D., Cameron, K., & Woods, M. (1996). *Effective Empowerment and Delegation*. London: HarperCollins.

Whitman, M. E., & Mattord, H. J. (2018). *Principals of Information Security* (6th ed.). Boston, MA: Cengage Learning.

Wildes, V. J., & Parks, S. C. (2005). Internal service quality. *International Journal of Hospitality & Tourism Administration*, 6(2), 1–27. doi:10.1300/J149v06n02_01

Winkler, S., & Dealy, B. (1995). Information security technology? Don't rely on it: a case study in social engineering. *Proceedings of the Fifth USENIX UNIX Security Symposium*. Available at: www. usenix. org/legacy/publications/library/proceedings/security95/full_papers/winkler.pdf

Woodruffe, H. (1995). *Services Marketing*. London: Pitman. Retrieved from www.radiusits.com/5-startling-statistics-about-cybersecurity-in-2018/

# Chapter 8
# Cyber Threat Ransomware and Marketing to Networked Consumers

**Usman Javed Butt**
*Brunel University, London, UK*

**Maysam F. Abbod**
https://orcid.org/0000-0002-8515-7933
*Brunel University, London, UK*

**Arvind Kumar**
*Northumbria University, London, UK*

## ABSTRACT

*Marketing is a process of creating, capturing, and exchanging 'value' for the mutual benefits of marketers, customers, intermediaries, and other stakeholders. Such a transaction requires trust as it might be facing a range of online cyber risks. Modern cybercrimes have exponentially grown over the last decade. Ransomware is one of the types of malware which is the result of a sophisticated attempt to compromise the modern computer systems. The businesses, governments, and large corporations are investing heavily to combat this cyber threat against their critical infrastructure. New technological shifts help to improve marketing and business productivity and keep the company's global competitiveness in an overflowing competitive market. However, the businesses and the systems involved need security measures to protect integrity and availability which will help avoid any malfunctioning to their operations due to the cyber-attacks. There have been several cyber-attack incidents on several businesses such as healthcare, pharmaceutical, water cleaning, and energy sector.*

DOI: 10.4018/978-1-7998-0131-3.ch008

## INTRODUCTION

This chapter provides an introduction to risks in an online environment with a particularly its focuses on Ransomware cyber threat, how it impacts different enterprises, some recent incidents where businesses were targeted by this cyber-attack. Ransomware 'a type of malware used by attackers that first encrypts files and then attempts to extort money in return for the key to unlocking the files by demanding a ransom usually in Bitcoins'(Paul III, Spence, Bhardwa, & Coustasse, 2018). The ransomware attacks initially had targeted individual /customers, but now the trend is spreading towards corporate attacks by not only individual user's files but also encrypting the network files too.

The ransomware usually uses a route of emails to reach the targets. The users can be registered users of an eCommerce company and the users had registered with the eCommerce company for the smooth process of buying and payments etc. Now the Attackers can use a similar email (faking as originated from the Ecommerce company) and reaching and infecting the user's files and systems.

The users use the internet for a number of purposes including for buying products and services, The marketing companies use IT technologies to market their offerings. Marketing is a process of creating capturing and exchanging 'value' for the mutual benefits of marketers, customers, intermediaries, and other stakeholders. The' value' can be in the form of product, services, ideas, software, information or money. The process of exchange in an online environment requires e-transaction of value'. Such a transaction requires trust as it might be facing a range of online Cyber risks. The Ransomware attacks are a major threat, A study shows that there were around 2,673(2016) and 1,783(2017) complaints to FBI in the USA alone, causing around $2.4 Million loses each year(Simoiu, Symantec, Bonneau, & Goel, 2019).

The cyber-attacks has many potential costs, the cost of an initial response team, the loss of potential business while the response team restores backup, installs new equipment, and cost of new call center to answer questions about the attack, loss of reputations, legal claims by users for loss of personal data, and negative word of mouth resulting in future loss of the business and brand (Paul III et al., 2018).

The chapter also has a discussion on digital marketing a multidimensional growth for the business and how businesses are impacted by the latest ransomware attacks, most common computing and mobile platforms targeted by ransomware attacks, how to prevent ransomware attacks, and ways to recover. The failure of online security has a huge cost to its stakeholders

## CONCEPTS OF RISK AND TRUST IN ONLINE ENVIRONMENT

Ecommerce is the transaction of goods and services over the internet and it involves sharing, transferring and exchanging of information and value (Yazdanifard, Al-Huda Edres, & Seyedi, 2011)

Main issues with e-commerce transaction are issues of ensuring customer trust security, privacy, functionality and user-friendliness issues are considered to be barriers to online shopping and minimizing customers' risks of privacy and security is an issue in front of organisations (Gupta & Dubey, 2016). The privacy is related to customers' concerns regarding control of personal information and potential risk of stealing personal information and then subject to misuse by someone. Customer trust is the main barrier to the growth of eCommerce. So the key to the success of e-business is to ensure an e-environment in which various stakeholders can feel confident about any possible transactions and the process are smoothly running without undue blockages or obstructions.

The business has already adopted IT technologies in their different functional areas such as supply chain, operations, production, distributions, and transactions with the customers.

Thus the cyber-risk can affect any or all of the business operations. Online environment handles the transaction of values, information, and money. The monastery transactions happen via e-wallets, credit or debit cards, online banking, PayPal or other tokens methods. Mule, Trojan horse, malware, ransomware, and worms if launched against the exchange systems, pose the greatest threat to e-commerce privacy and security, as such virus, etc. can subvert most of the authorization and authentication mechanisms used in an eCommerce transaction(Gupta & Dubey, 2016). Previous research has also argued that trust is one's willingness to be vulnerable and accept the risk, managing risk relationships, and safer online environment (Lee, Warkentin, & Johnston, 2016). Thus maintain customer trust with the supplier organization's is paramount. Trust is the willingness of an individual to be vulnerable, and expectations and subjective believe in reliance and confidences in the other party; such a reliance can be Experiential (e.g., e-commerce experience, familiarity, Internet experience, etc.), Cognitive (e.g., system reliability, privacy protection, quality of information, security protection, brand image, etc.), Personality-oriented(e.g., disposition to shopping habits, trust, etc.) and Affective (e.g., presence of third-party seals, reputation referral, recommendation, buyers'' word-of-mouth, feedback, review comments, etc.) (Gupta & Dubey, 2016). Thus, the organization's must develop systems to build customer trust on those four dimensions, to enhance customer trust, customer relationship and ultimately revenue and profit.

The previous studies have developed various theoretical frameworks in a networked environment to explain the user's behaviour in an online environment. Lee et al., (2016) have cited a range of models consumer/retailer trust model (Jarena et al.'s 2000), privacy calculus model (Dinev and Hart, 2006), etc. as models of online risk and customer behavior. The consumer feels a risk or threat due to possible opportunistic behavior of the other party, which can exploit online vulnerabilities (Lee et al., 2016).

The organisation must attempt to build customer trust by addressing infrastructure vulnerabilities. A Trust is a governance mechanism that enables an exchange via an integrated model which provide information security awareness to the users of the online environment. Organizational mechanisms and cues can enhance customers and other stakeholders. From the point of view of the consumer decisions process, it means assuring the consumer at each stage of customer decisions process; before purchase (platform trust, e-word of mouth), information's search (reliability of sources), evaluations of alternatives(truthfulness and cost-benefit compassion trust), during purchase (privacy and transactional trust) and post-purchase (functional, emotional, social) warrantee trust (Lee et al., 2016).

Organizations should develop and use software to enhance safety and security including provisions for safety measures such as encryption, digital signatures, biometrics, virus protection, security seals, etc.(Yazdanifard et al., 2011) In additions by educating the users on security issues and how to protect their computers is also a positive step security implementation process. As per Protection motivation theory, a threatened individual is aware of the threat and is able to comprehend the noxious event and so such an individual can cognitively appraise the risk or threat sources with an understanding of potential threats (Lee et al., 2016). Information-security awareness is an antecedent to one's attitude, and a positive attitude drives one's intention to comply with information security policies or act safely. The purpose of this chapter is to increase understanding of various stakeholders about various types of ransomware and thus initiating appropriate precautions.

As computers evolved from floppy-disk bootable machines into more sophisticated workstation devices such as laptops and smartphones, Kaspersky suggests that so did malicious software technology or *malware* as most commonly known (Kaspersky, 2018). Kaspersky also suggests that malware was existent from information technology's infancy but only bloomed when the personal computer was accessible to everyone. Acknowledging that the first malware was called the "Elk Cloner Virus" (Tasril, et al., 2017), a few features of Elk Cloner Virus could give a clue that malicious technology transformed from simple motifs and techniques into a more serious and damaging consequence to computer devices. The virus was formed as a "prank" and did not do much harm except for the self-spreading feature which was done through manifestation using social engineering techniques such as floppy-disk insertions (Touchette, 2016). From there on, cybercriminals took advantage of cybercrime by maximising its growth and minimising the profitability of targets such as personal computers, industry devices, and businesses.

Cybersecurity is process and tools of protection of information, devices, and digital assets from compromise, theft or loss (The Australian Small Business and Family Enterprise Ombudsman, 2017) Cybersecurity is all about protecting business information assets from unauthorized access and protecting confidentiality, integrity, and availability of valuable business data. In the modern ear, intruders use different attack vectors to sabotage business operations. These attackers use malware as their source to penetrate into remote computers, among these malware family, Ransomware is the deadliest one, which not only takes control of the business computers but also demands digital currency in return. Cybercrime, which has once cost businesses 100 Billion USD, is classified accordingly to the types of malware that the industry produces. Kaspersky research has identified the types of malware through a diagram called "Malware Classification Tree" (Kaspersky, 2018).

Ransomware is a new kind of online security threat, which is of huge interest to business and marketing managers. For example, a ransomware ' CryptoWall3' had cost over $320 million in 2015(Simoiu et al., 2019).

# RANSOMWARE

## The Concept Of Ransomware

Ransomware is a kind of malware family, which compromise business operations by making computers un-accessible to its legitimate users, it encrypts all the data files available on the compromised machines and causes a denial of service to its user until demanded Ransomware is paid in the given time limit (Butt, et al., 2019). Ransomware is a dangerous 'form of malware that restricts an individual's access to their computer by encrypting and demands payment to restore functionality' (Simoiu et al., 2019). Ransomware uses strong encryption algorithm which makes it impossible to break, hence the user has no option to pay to get access to its valuable data unless backup data is available. Consumers most vulnerable victims as they have less awareness and they have less robust secure systems (Simoiu et al., 2019). The ransomware attacks motive is to hold a digital asset hostage, demanding and negotiations a ransom for releasing the digital assets (August, Dao, & Florin Niculescu, 2019).

A number of personal and non-personal factors has been attributed to the vulnerability to cyber-attacks. Some of the factors are user demography (e.g. gender, age, ethnicity, education), usage rate, user profiles (e.g. software developers, gamers, professionals, others) user's routine behaviours (social media use, software downloads, programming, shopping), 'deviant behaviour (e.g. VPN behavior, pirated media downloads, visiting adult websites), and having guardianship measures (e.g. having AntiVirus software, sharing passwords), and poor computer skill', poor awareness, lack of precautions in opening emails or websites, low-reputation sites, security hygiene (e.g. regular operating system updates) etc (Simoiu et al., 2019). The attack can be due to Hackers' motivations such as the desire for fame, economic benefits. vandalize, swindle, blackmail or demand ransom, curiosity, an anti-establishment motive, hacktivism cyberwarfare or nation-state actors' political motives, etc. (August et al., 2019)(Redstor, 2017).

The ransomware business model is moving towards pleasant "customer" experience, ease & support in online or bitcoin payments, telephonic support and .ransomware-as-a-service (ransomware virus for sale, or to run and administrate the ransomware operation on behalf of someone for a fee, etc.) (Redstor, 2017),

## Some of the Ransomware Attacks

Atlanta Ransomware Attack: A ransomware 'SamSam' attacked City of Atlanta Government site effecting and halting multiple services to people of the city until $7,000 was paid in Bitcoins. (Check Point Software Technologies, 2019). The city must spend $2.7 million to repair the damages from the cyber-attack.

Ukraine Energy Ministry: Exploiting vulnerability of Drupal 7, Ransomware attackers attacked the website of Ukraine's energy ministry and encrypt its files (Check Point Software Technologies, 2019).

WannaCry, Ransomware Attack: WannaCry, ransomware had affected over 230,000 computers across 150 countries in a single day in 2017. Boeing production plant in South Carolina was also attacked by WannaCry ransomware in 2018, raising concerns that the ransomware virus can even spread to airplane softwares too.

Small business are not less vulnerable to cyber-attacks such as ransomware. The studies have indicated that43% of cybercrimes involves small business, out of which around 22% are attacked with ransomware, at the same time majority of small business has not enough protection against cyber-crimes (The Australian Small Business and Family Enterprise Ombudsman, 2017).

## Types of Ransomwares

As already described the ransomware are 'kind of malware that attempts to deceive users by kerbing access to the user' device or data, either by locking the device or encrypting data' (Simoiu et al., 2019). There are different classification of Ransomware depending upon design and sophistication . The ransomware can be faking as law enforcement agencies or not so and further devising can be as such as Locker Ransomware and Crypto-Ransomware(Simoiu et al., 2019)s. One hand there is some fake ransom where the claim that data has been encrypted but actually it is not and on the other extreme are more sophisticated ransomware can use payload persistence, use strong encryption, irreversible, destabilize the system so as to disallowed restoring the older data (Simoiu et al., 2019). There are five different phases of Ransomware based upon the methodology used by the malicious threat to acquire, and infect files on the target machine, encryption standards used during file encryption process than installing the malware into the system to take command and control of the victim machine. The malicious intent to remove all the backup of victim's files and payment demand in return of data to the hostage target machine. Common attack vectors adopted by Ransomware either by virtual or physical means of manifestation to penetrate into the target machine such as emails, exploit kits and social engineering, various payment options accepted as a Ransomware.

According to the same report, these malware classifications are considered as "specific function" malware which means that these malwares are only capable of designated damage and does not produce a complex effect on devices. In contrary, cybercriminals have devised multi-dimensional and multi-functioning malware which now comprise 65.32% of *botnets* affecting devices and firms worldwide (34.68% for the combination of Trojans and Worms) (Soni, 2018).

*Figure 1. Malware Classification Tree of Kaspersky (Kaspersky, 2018)*

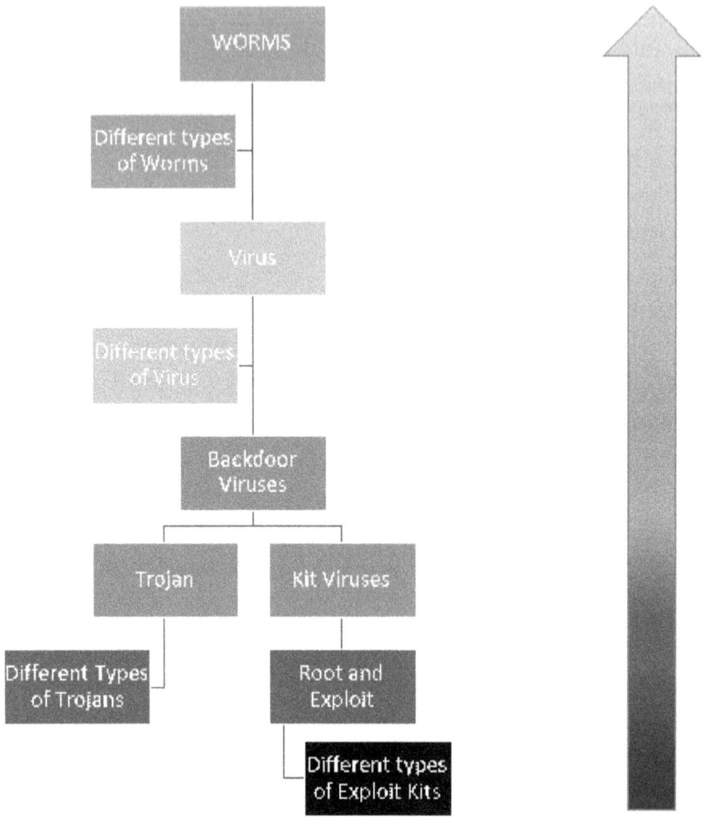


*Figure 2. Pie Chart of Multi-functional Malware vs Single-Function Malware (Trojans) (Soni, 2018)*

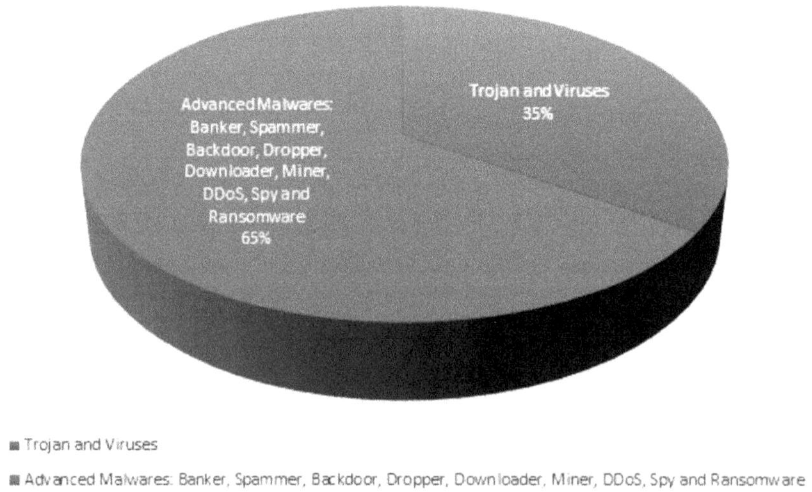

Cisco has classed this versatile malware as "Advanced Malwares" and has identified the most prominent advanced malwares affecting businesses as the following: Riskware, Spyware, Adware, and Ransomware with *Ransomware* being the deadliest due to its capabilities (Cisco, 2018).

These viruses affect every device in different manners, but these effects can be summed up to say that all of them breaches the "CIA" capability of a business affected. CIA triad namely

Confidentiality, Integrity, and Availability are a triad of information security model used by most businesses to assess the level of information security their firms possess (Imperial College UK, 2018). Confidentiality is achieved when businesses are able to give privacy to information which should not be accessed by unauthorized people like how banks do not allow anyone except the client him/herself to access their accounts. Integrity is achieved when businesses are capable of keeping the information of their clients as accurate as possible which is why as an example, FCA Regulation is strict with GDPR policies. And lastly, Availability is achieved when customers can view their information anytime they want and as an example, a website with personal information databases of clients should be accessible around the clock for the customers to check. Most viruses only affect one or two aspects of the security triad such as Riskware, since as ESET defines Riskware as a type of malware which increases security risk by using encryption methods to identify user procedure such as delivery and employee schedules and diverting the procedure into digital transaction without the user's discretion (Esset, 2018). In this scenario, the users' confidentiality was breached which is same for spyware since Spywares are types of malwares which from the name itself, collects data about the device, encrypts the information such as client information and sends the data back to the origin of the malware to be used for blackmailing (Stavrou, et al., 2010). On the other hand, Avast adds that Spywares are usually accompanied by Adwares where the user is bombarded with inappropriate and unwanted pop-ups or advertisements which is harmful to the device (Avast, 2018). In this scenario, both Confidentiality and Availability are abused since the user's confidential information is leaked whilst the availability of his/her information through their personal device is blocked.

Finally, an assumption could be done that when these features are combined together and are tailored for a bigger purpose, ***Ransomware*** is produced. With Ransomware, businesses are in danger of breaching all three of the information security model since clients of the businesses affected by ransomware will have their data breached, locked and possibly altered by the hackers.

An observation can be made that most of the Advanced Malwares are enhanced through the development of cybercrime which involves use of ciphering text and encryption. These malwares show the identity of evolving through the development of cryptovirology. which is part of an experiment done to identify if malicious software and hacking may affect the field of technology concerned with the use of ciphered text and encryption called cryptography (Young & Yung, 2017).

## Ransomware and It Impacts

Several Businesses and enterprises worldwide have been crippled by rans0omware attacks for paying an amount of money without actually gaining any benefits. Just like how Arran Brewery, a brewing company in Scotland recently paid 2 Bitcoins with an amount worth of 9,600 GBP to a group of anonymous hackers just to restore the company's system after locking down all the computers of the company (BBC, 2018). These incidents also occurred to the United States government when Pennsylvania Senate Democratic Caucus had to pay Microsoft to reconstruct the senate's IT Framework after being breached (Cimpanu, 2018). The same report states that hackers were demanding for 28 Bitcoins as payment which sums up to 30,000 USD but instead the government decided to reconstruct for a hefty price of 700,000 USD in order to discourage future attacks to government offices. And as just these incidents start to increase, attacks are reportedly getting worse. In the year 2019, reports have claimed that the same attacks are being planned to attack medium market businesses instead of public institutions since the demand of these attacks have shifted towards income-generating industries (Morrcraft, 2019).

Ransomware is a type of advanced malware where the victim is held at ransom for the infected files or documents. The files would not be available to the victim unless payment is given to the attacker in exchange for the attacker relieving the system from the malware (Young & Yung, 2017). Ransomware is believed to be one of the most effective malwares for the year 2018 with a total amount of more than 12 million malware counts and having an increase of 36% since the last quarter of 2017 (McAfee, 2017). The fact that ransomware accounts to 5 Billion US Dollars of loss in the global economy for the year 2017 made Europol considers ransomware as the most dangerous malware threat in their conference entitled "Internet Organised Crime Threat Assessment (IOCTA) 2018" (Walker, 2018).

## Severities of Ransomware

As Ransomware has turned into a booming business, ransomware authors have devised two types of ransomwares: *Locker Ransomware* and *Crypto-Ransomware* (Deloitte, 2016).

**Locker Ransomwares** are the types of ransomwares which do less damage since these ransomwares does not encrypt the files of the victim. Locker Ransomware is used to terrorise the victim by prompting the victim to pay for a fine charged for misusing the internet (i.e. duplicating other companies' spreadsheets or downloading illegal programs from torrents). These ransomwares usually come in an interface credible enough for the victim to believe that the warrant is legitimate by means of equipping the targeted user's sensitive data such as IP address and last viewed malicious website (Deloitte, 2016).

**Crypto Ransomwares (Crypto-Locker Ransomware)** are the types of ransomwares which does more damage to the device and to the financial stability of the victim. Crypto-Lockers are the type of ransomwares which infect a device and ***encrypt*** the victim's files until the ransom has been paid. Some of Crypto-Lockers even delete the back-up from the system making it harder to recover from the manifestation (Richet, 2016). Example of marketing business effected by crypto Ransomware.........

## Methodology of Ransomware

The word Ransomware comes from the words "Ransom" and "Malware". Defining the word Ransom, most people would think of payment or demand for the release of hostage of someone or something (Merriam-Webster, 2018). So, understanding the criticality of a malware capable of keeping virtual platforms on ransom and how the procedure is undertaken deems essential.

Ransomwares can reach a device or systems via number of ways such as ; Spasm emails and unsolicited email attachment, removable storage drives (flash drives and e hard drives), bundled together with other software applications that are downloaded and installed, a compromised or hacked website by using vulnerability of software or operating systems(Redstor, 2017).

Multiple kinds of research related to ransomware have pointed out that different ransomwares can have different approaches of propagation, but all ransomware follow a pattern of 5 phases in propagating the malware into the system. These five phases are the following (Brewer, 2016):

## First Phase: Acquisition, Utilisation, and Infection

Just as how each and every type of malware works, Ransomware manifestation starts by means of acquisition through different ways of malware transfers (Ali, 2017). In the business context, it could be an eCommerce website being surveillance by the attacker. Norton by Symantec suggests that there are five simple ways of acquiring regular malwares and these are the following (Norton, 2018):

- **Software Integrated Malwares:** This is when a user downloads a software which is tagged as "free" but actually comes with a hefty price of having a malware infection for the system.
- **Peer to Peer Virtual Sharing:** This is when a user shares files electronically like the use of BitTorrent, uTorrent, etc. This procedure does not only mean file sharing between familiar peers but also means the ***illegal*** download of applications via anonymous uploads.
- **Removable Media:** This is the most common way of malware acquisition since acquisition is done via electronic devices such as USB's, CD's, External HDD's, etc.
- **Network Acquisition:** This happens when a device connected to the internet comes across a website which has malicious cookies or pop-ups and the victim falls to the trap by exploring the links integrated into these digital platforms.
- **General Lack of Protection:** This happens when a device lacks security via software which offers protection from malwares.

## Attack Vectors of Ransomware

Although there are plenty of ways to be infected by malwares, researchers have identified that ***fortunately,*** there are only a few ways of acquiring ransomware. These vectors could be divided into virtual means of manifestation or physical means of manifestation.

### Virtual Means of Manifestations

**Emails** as the main source of Ransomware attacks. Statistics show that there are approximately 354.5 Billion emails delivered daily worldwide and 85.35 percent of these emails are spams which leaves 14.64 percent for legitimate emails (Cisco Talos, 2018). IBM estimates that there is a 350 percent increase in spam emails from January 2017 to December 2018 and alarmingly, despite the fact that not all spam emails contain malwares, the malware content on total spam counts is increasing. Malware containing spam mails were approximately just 10 percent of 100 percent in January 2018 and is already 210 percent of the total 450 percent increase in 2017 (IBM, 2019).

Symantec suggests that these malwares are spreading largely due to a botnet named Necrus which was established just to send out spam mails worldwide (O'Brien, 2017). Symantec also suggests that Ransomware, if acquired through email, can be activated through one of the following steps (O'Brien, 2017):

- Malicious attachments being opened
- Malicious attachments initiating third party JavaScript or PowerShell commands
- Malicious attachments initiating the download of **exploit kits**

*Figure 3. Volumes of malicious and non-malicious spam (IBM, 2019)*

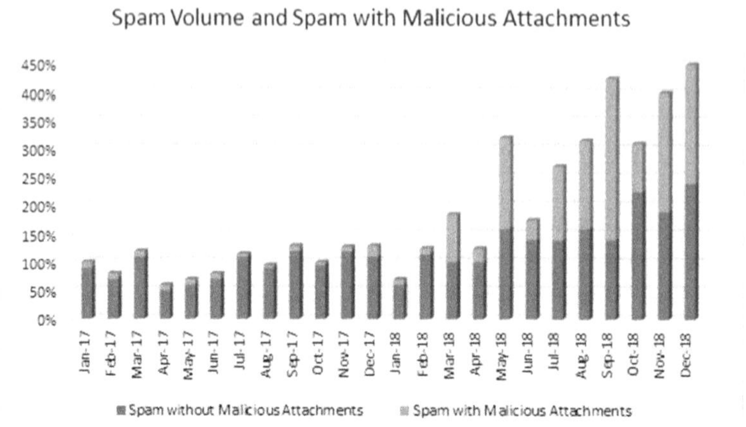


**Exploit Kits** which literally exploits the vulnerabilities of a computer. Exploit kits are used to take advantage of a particular device's weakness via web browsers, programs or operating systems. Most exploit kits are integrated into websites wherein once a user visit that particular site, the kit is activated in the user's device. The kit would then scan for vulnerabilities in the device and implement the malware in the device used to navigate the website. The website infected is not necessarily a malicious website since legitimate websites like BBC or Yahoo could be infested through advertisements as well (Monrose, et al., 2015). According to a study done by Malwarebytes, there is a 61 percent exploitation payload for ransomware amongst all exploit kits (Malwarebytes Labs, 2018).

## Physical Means of Manifestations

**Social Engineering** used as a sure but risky means of malware spreading. Social Engineering is the use of alteration of human psychology for an intended atrocious behaviour which may have a devastating effect on a person or a group of individuals. Researchers may call it "hacking" a human for an intended purpose (Mann, 2008).

Kevin Mitnick's Proposed Social Engineering Methodology (Gallegos-Segovia, et al., 2017):

- **Information Gathering:** This is the step where details of the victim are gathered by selected individuals.
- **Trust:** This is the step where the attacker establishes a deeper connection with the victim. This way more appropriate attack vectors could be defined by the attacker.
- **Exploitation:** This is where the attacker executes the plan of exploitation and manifest the ransomware in the device.
- **Reach:** This is where the system is finally compromised and usually the attacker is nowhere in contact with the victim.

*Figure 4. Exploit Payload Summary (Malwarebytes Labs, 2018)*

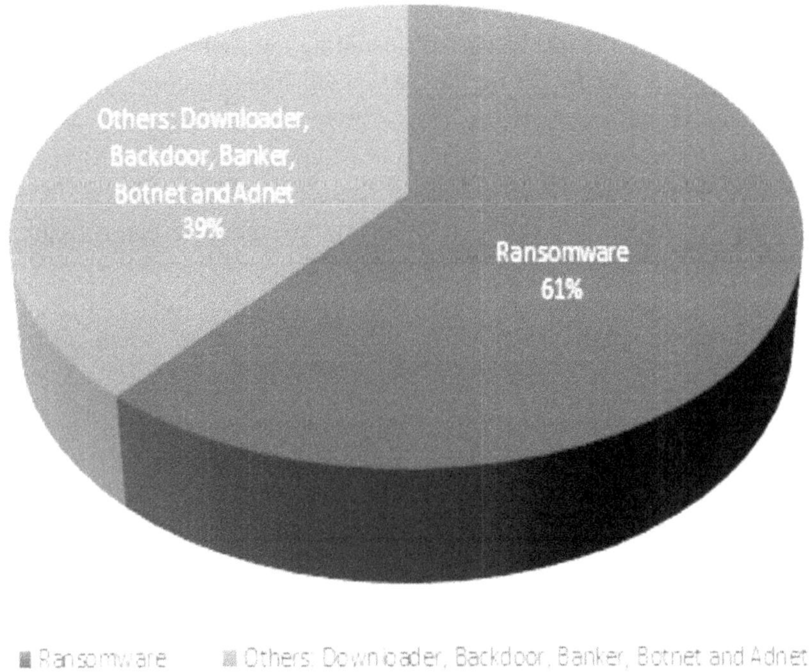


An example of this methodology is the *December 2015 Ukraine Power Grid Cyber Attack*. Numerous reports suggest that the incident was a well-planned attack on Ukraine's power company named Ukrenergo (BBC, 2017). Most investigators were amazed by how well the information and trust gathering was executed and further blaming the Russians for devising a way to Ukraine's SCADA system then manipulating the system through an infection caused by a USB (Zetter, 2016).

These proposed methodologies of Social Engineering can be further used to identify the different types of attacks that can be established, and these are the following (Gallegos-Segovia, et al., 2017):

- **Ego Attacks:** The attacker tries to create a personal contact with the victim by offering help and proving the reliability of the attacker's intelligence to the victim. Once a victim falls for a transparent manipulation, the attacker executes the ransomware into the system.
- **Sympathy Attacks:** The attacker would use emotional means of creating a connection with the victim. When the victim starts trusting the attacker, the attacker executes the ransomware into the system.
- **Bullying Attacks:** The attacker uses force, dominance or blackmailing to gather information. This is the most common and most effective type of social engineering attack.

## Second Phase: Consignment and Implementation

The next step for the ransomware is the process of installing the malware into the system, encrypting the ransomware program inside the device and further establishing a secure platform for the **upcoming** Command and Control network.

The ransomware uses a simple RSA asymmetric public key (Emsisoft, 2018) that will, later on, call a **GET** or **POST** request (Securonix Threat Research Team, 2018). The **GET** or **POST** request would consist of the following parameters to be collected (Securonix Threat Research Team, 2018) (Rajpal & Kotov, 2014):

- computer name
- processor information
- volume serial
- operating system
- active drives
- Public IP in a pattern of: { ipv4bot[.]whatismyipaddress[.] com}
- disk space

Researchers (Emsisoft, 2018) identifies the reasons why ransomware developers use RSA public key in coding ransomwares and these are the following:

- takes up lesser space for transportation and memory
- third parties or malware analysts surveying the network would only see plain texts and scrambled encrypted network traffic
- gives the malware authors a chance to use their own server during the communication with the deployed ransomware.

After identifying the victim through a unique hashed identity (using MD5 Algorithm), the ransomware would identify whether the process runs via **root or admin access** (Rajpal & Kotov, 2014). If the ransomware is running through either root or admin access, then further installation of the ransomware would take place through the following steps (Rajpal & Kotov, 2014):

*Figure 5. Ransomware installation procedures (Rajpal & Kotov, 2014)*

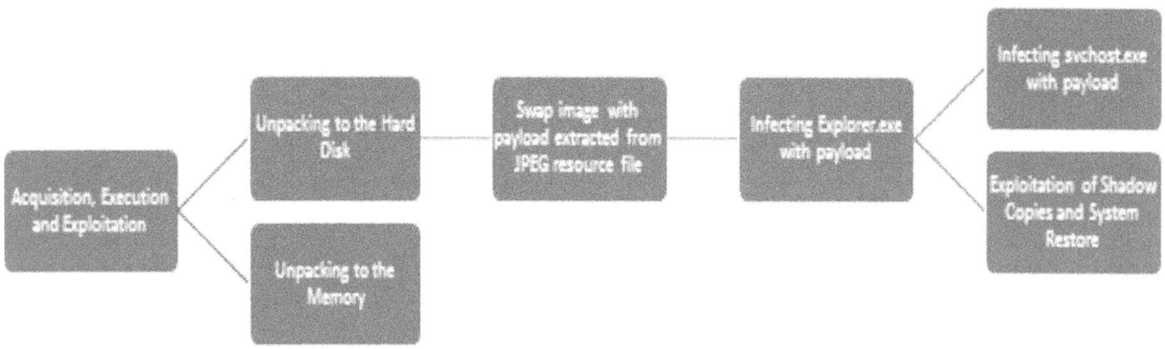

As shown in the flowchart, the ransomware executes itself and unpack in the memory of the device. The software would then create multiple copies of stage dropper and inject the payload into explorer. exe and svchost.exe. In the next *phases*, the ransomware would also delete all shadow copies, back up files and finally disable the device's ability to do any restoration of the system.

These processes normally take up only a few seconds to execute and usually is done without the user knowing that the process is being executed (Brewer, 2016).

## Third Phase: File Encryption and Command and Control (C2)

### Command and Control Establishment

This phase is the most important phase of a Ransomware since in this phase, whatever a ransomware is coded to do will take place. After making sure that all packages of the ransomware are successfully injected into the system, the ransomware platform in the device would now communicate to the command centre (host) via an RSA key pair (Brewer, 2016). A .bit namecoin would then be used to query .bit domain friendly DNS servers through the code: { ns1.corp[.] corp-servers[.]ru; a[.]dsnpod[.] com}. Once the connection is established, this is where the information gathered via **GET** or **POST** request would be sent to the host in a base 64 encoding format (Securonix Threat Research Team, 2018).

Researchers (Rajpal & Kotov, 2014) identified that over the past few years, ransomware developers have shifted from HTTP to the use of TOR and SSL during the communication of the command and control. The simplest reason is due to the complexity of decrypting TOR and SSL data in contrast to HTTP. RC4 encryption which is most commonly used through HTTP can be decrypted and fingerprinted using a simple *mathematical expression* [a-z]\=[a-z0-9]+ or also called *Regrex*. TOR and SSL's full encryption makes it difficult for developers to code a network signature for initial stage detection although TOR is less used due to multiple network restrictions (Rajpal & Kotov, 2014).

### File Encryption Process

Before encryption, the following files and folders are excluded:

- desktop.ini
- autorun.ini
- nuser.ini
- GDCB-DECRYPT.txt

These are excluded for the ability of the command server to connect to the device controlled (NJC-CIC, 2018).

Encryption of files is done through a combination of RSA 2048bit (public key) and AES 256bit (victim data) encryption. After data encryption, the ransomware is expected to encrypt the files by assigning a public-private key for the randomly generated symmetric key.

This type of encryption does not need any shared secret key which makes it easier for the attacker to keep the ciphered text and only give access once the ransom is paid (Emsisoft, 2018).

*Figure 6. Process of Encryption Used by Ransomware. (Emsisoft, 2018)*

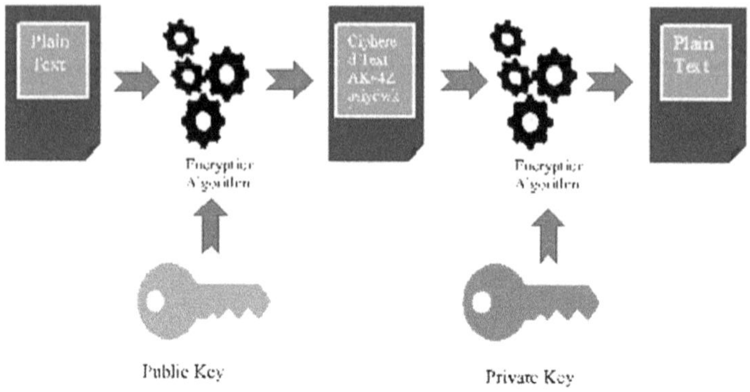


In most ransomwares, Virlock is commonly used for encryption. Virlock consists of two layers of encryption where in the **first layer** is the combination of XOR and ROL encryption which is backed up by a **second layer** of XOR encryption (Lindskog & Zavarskya, 2016). All encrypted files are converted into.GDCB or.KRAB files which then prompts a report back to the command centre using the same **GET** or **POST** request (Securonix Threat Research Team, 2018).

## Fourth Phase: Back-Up Corruption

Unlike most malwares which are usually designed just to implement the infection that the program is designed to spread, most ransomwares are designed to delete the back-up of the victim's files or at least the back-up of the ransomware (Brewer, 2016).

As shown in Object 5, Ransomwares usually ends by deleting the shadow copies of the victim's back-up file by either of two available methods: VSSAdmin service or WMI service.

## Fifth Phase: User Detection, Payment and Clean-Up

FBI has claimed that the Barack Obama Blue Blackmail Virus has been one of the biggest issues of USA due to numerous people logging in to their devices and suddenly seeing President Obama's face along with an FBI notice asking for a payment to a certain fine (Osborne, 2018). This news is a perfect example of an aftermath of a ransomware attack. Attackers demand for a certain amount of pecuniary reimbursement for the locked files and that too should be paid in a certain period of time.

Due to the advancement of technology, most attackers require victims to pay using bitcoins but there are other viable means of payment like credit or debit card payments, etc. (Rajpal & Kotov, 2014).

Table 1 suggests that most ransomware attackers require victims to pay from a range of 100 USD to 500 USD and 0.5 BTC (3,280 USD) to 0.8 BTC (5,250 USD).

Usually, these instructions are saved in the hard drive with file names such as "HELP_DECRYPT" for CryptoWall V3 or "HELP_YOUR_FILES" for CryptoWall V4. Once payment is given to the attacker, the attacker would decrypt the files and the ransomware will clean-up by itself (Brewer, 2016).

*Table 1: Payment Options (Data Gathered from Different Sources)*

| FAMILY | PAYMENT OPTIONS | PRICE OF DECRYPTING |
|---|---|---|
| TeslaCrypt | Bitcoin Payments are normally required but developers can also accept credit or debit card payments on the earlier variations. | 500 USD —increased to 1000 USD if not paid within the time frame (Kaspersky, 2018) |
| CryptoLocker | Started off with more options but eventually, narrowed down to Bitcoin | 300 USD (Cannell, 2013) |
| Petya or NotPetya | At this point, only Bitcoin is accepted by the criminals (Fruhlinger, 2017). | 0.3 - 0.5 BTC |
| WannaCry | Payments must be made in Bitcoin | Between $300 (£228) and $600 (Gibbs, 2017) |
| SimpleLocker | Payments via the Ukrainian MoneXy cash transfer system. | 260 hryvnias ($22, £13) (NJCCIC, 2016) |
| GandCrab | Dash or Bitcoin | 1200 USD —increased to 2400 USD if not paid within the time frame (Abrams, 2018) |

## Most Prominent and Latest Ransomwares in Market

As explained before, ransomware is an evolving business with malware developers as the vendors and cybercriminals as its customers. Due to this "booming" trend, plenty of variations of Ransomwares have been available in the market. The following is the top five strongest ransomwares in the last five years which is identified by an organisation of security decision-makers called CSO.

Top Five Strongest Ransomwares (Fruhlinger, 2017):

1. **CryptoLocker**: considered as the most generic variation of ransomware due to the capability of encrypting all the files inside the victim's device. These ransomwares use law enforcement themed GUI to threaten the victim into paying the ransom since decryption is near to impossible. All back-up files are deleted as soon as infection starts. (Cannell, 2013) CryptoLocker is usually defined as the "primitive ransomware" since the developers have not updated the features of the said ransomware (Fruhlinger, 2017).
2. **TeslaCyrpt**: considered as a subvariant of CryptoLocker when the ransomware started in 2015. This ransomware used gaming websites as the source of its infection and spreading which is why gamers were mostly affected by this ransomware. This ransomware only encrypted files with a file size lower than 268 MB (Kaspersky, 2018). The developers of the ransomware have decided to shut down operations and by doing so, the developers also posted the universal decryption key which helped infected devices to recover successfully (Koller, 2016).

The final message of TeslaCrypt including the master decryption key (Koller, 2016):

*Project closed! Master key for decrypt: 440A241DD80FCC5664E861989DB716E08CE627D-8D40C7EA360AE855C727A49EE. Wait for other people to make universal decrypt software. We are sorry!*

3. **SimpleLocker**: a ransomware effective on android platform which gathers IMEI, model number and manufacturer details for the command and control centre. Encryption is done through AES encryption method and the ransomware also access the camera to take a picture of the victim and threaten the victim more into paying for ransom (NJCCIC, 2016)

4. **WannaCry**: considered as one of the deadliest ransomwares to be developed. This ransomware shut down multiple hospitals across the United Kingdom and Ukraine. The developers of wannacry were able to detect the vulnerabilities of windows which was first discovered inside the United States National Security Agency. Symantec, later on, suspected that the developers originated from a North Korean linked group called Lazarus (Fruhlinger, 2018). This ransomware is also one of the latest. 6,912 appointments were canceled and 19,000 affected when wannacry affected NHS operations in the year 2017. This attack, despite being "unsophisticated" as Kingsley Manning suggests, became more successful due to the fact that the system of different NHS offices was "intertwined" with each other thus making the spread and effectivity of ransomware quicker (BBC, 2017).
5. **Petya** and **NotPetya**: launched after a week from Wannacry outbreak, this ransomware is the confirmation of the new age of ransomwares (Fruhlinger, 2017). Petya or NotPetya started with a tactic of sending a job application document via email in a pdf file format which is expected to be accessed by the company. NotPetya is the very first ransomware which does not need any spam emails or social engineering to infect and gain administrative access as long as there is a network connection in between the devices (Fruhlinger, 2017).

Aside from these famous ransomware attacks, there are a few other ransomwares making their name in the market but one of the most prominent recently is the GandCrab which just released the latest version 4 this past July 2018. GandCrab acts exactly like CryptoLocker and is also considered deadly since the ransomware converts files in.KRAB extension files once encrypted (Abrams, 2018).

## BUSINESSES AND MARKETING COMMUNICATION AND RANSOMWARE

In a video called "3,000 Years of Business History in Two Minutes" by (Schwedel, et al., 2017), the idea of the business was said to be established by the Indians at around eight century BC. Ever since then, the concept of business has been evolving and has actually changed throughout generations. This evolution leads to different ways of how business market their products and services. From simple orientation era in the 18$^{th}$ and 19$^{th}$ century to production and sales orientation era in the twentieth century further evolving into a greater marketing orientation era by 1960's (Bournemouth University, 2018), business marketing has now completely been transformed into a different field. With the advent of information technology, the business has seen itself dedicate into a multidimensional growth. This multidimensional growth is commonly referred to as "Digital Marketing" where which the name suggests it all, a concept of marketing which has more involvement of information technology (SAS, 2019).

A question may arise, how is digital marketing a multidimensional growth for business marketing? Digital marketing has been classified as growing multidimensional since the industry has been expanding the way it communicates with the clients. During the 1950s, (SAS, 2019) explains that marketing was mostly a one-way conversation.,

These one-way communications were primarily originating from the businesses and directed only to the consumers; communication was not even available for consumers towards the businesses. These one-way communications were monopolized through television, newspaper or poster advertisements. With the ease-of-access of the internet by the year, 1993 to late 1990s (Burkeman, 2009), two-way communication, by all means, was made easier. This gave birth to two-way marketing which was inexistent before.

This multidimensional growth of marketing helped consumers be able to communicate with the business and service providers electronically.

*Figure 7. One-way communication*

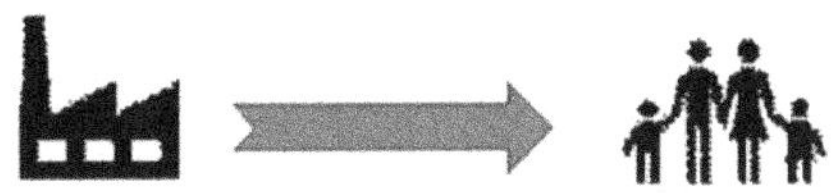

*Figure 8. Two-way communication*

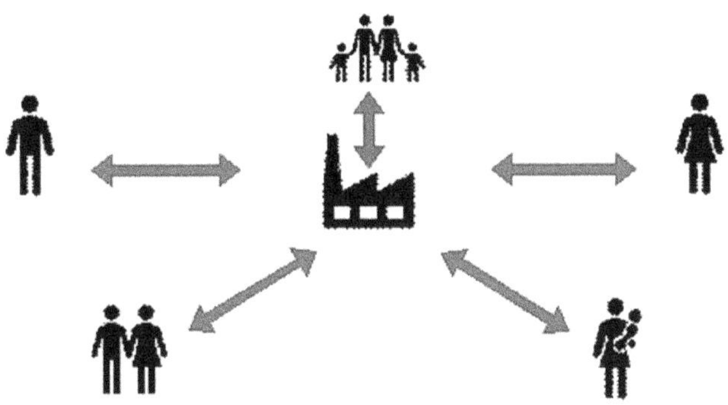

## The Issue of Access to Two-Way Communication

While businesses were maximising the advantage of being able to strengthen their public relations through digital marketing, hackers were keen to exploit the vulnerabilities of these businesses. On 1st of May 2004, the Sasser Worm was invented and was the very first worm to make serious damages to businesses such as Agenece France-Presse and Delta Airlines (Macrae, 2014) through the ports of their businesses. Despite the fact that plenty of famous business organisations such as Forbes suggests that one of the best ways to improve your business is through the use of online marketing (Kappel, 2017), the same platform can also be the downfall of any business. With a gross total of 22.7 percentage increase in cyberattacks between the years 2017 and 2018, the total cost of malware attacks is estimated to reach up to I Trillion USD by the year 2020 (Cyber Security Ventures, 2019). Among these numbers, there is an estimate of 4.13 million USD spending per medium to a large company just for the cybersecurity aspect of their businesses.

Although these figures by themselves already present a very big challenge to the potential victims, most businesses do not know that Ransomware in businesses is growing.

## The Effect of Cyber Risks to Marketing and Customer Trust

Knowing that there are plenty of issues with two-way communications, marketing especially digital marketing has been suffering from different malware attacks. Despite previously mentioning the financial effects of malwares to the business it is worth taking note that the financial side is not the biggest loss that a company has during malware attacks. With more people having less understanding regarding malwares (56%) security breaches are becoming more frequent (Help Net Security, 2016). The same report also informs us that due to the lack of understanding that people now have regarding malwares and cyber risks, people (59%) tend to *trust* less against companies who have been under any type of cybersecurity breach. 72% of the same survey emphasized that they have lost trust in social media and digital marketing as it is where most of the threat comes from (i.e. phishing related marketing and ransomware filled spam emails).

Once the trust between the client and business has been affected, the ability of a business to take full control in its Customer Relationship Management (CRM) can be partially or fully lost. Instead of having a data-driven growth in terms of sales, a company tends to have a malware-infested decline into losses. One may argue that CRM is just one facet of business procedures which can be true. But considering that CRM procedures in the companies have been growing by an approximate of 12.3% yearly (Columbus, 2016) and that the same management tool has been more digitalised through technology tools, it is as vital as any other component such as marketing.

## PLATFORMS AFFECTED BY RANSOMWARE ATTACKS

Malwares, in general, can affect multiple platforms of technology but recent studies have shown that ransomwares have only affected three platforms of computing technology so far. During the peak of *WannaCry* ransomware attacks, banks and bank users in India were falsely warned through circulating *Whatsapp* messages that the ransomware has actually breached ATM machines throughout the country. Through deeper investigation, all allegations were denied and were proven to be a hoax by one of the leading banks of India called Rural Bank of India (NDTV, 2017). Have this been true, ransomware could have been considered as a deadly terrorist weapon by the governments around the world?

Researchers have identified that ransomware has affected mobile platforms, computing platforms, IoT and Cloud Computing platforms with IoT and cloud computing platform is the most vital platform for security.

**Computing Platform:** computing platform has always been mostly affected by ransomwares. As previously discussed, ransomwares act on computers by infecting the system and encrypting the files until a certain amount of ransom is paid. A large number of ransomware attacks on computing platform are directed to home users comprising 86.87 percent of total ransomware attacks in 2018 (Kaspersky Lab, 2016).

**Mobile Platform:** with people dedicating more time to mobile phones, doctors have indicated that most people are suffering from mobile addiction (Walton, 2017). Having this in mind, cybercriminals have taken advantage of people being "addicted" to mobile phones.

*Android-* This has been the biggest target of ransomware attacks in the mobile platform this is mainly due to the "openness" of the android platform. With mobile ransomware increasing by 137.8% from first to the second quarter of 2017, SC Magazine predicts for a spike in mobile ransomwares in 2018 (SC Magazine, 2017). However, in Android and/or mobile ransomware overall, Cryptolockers are less spread since file encryption would be useless on mobile platforms due to the cloud backup feature that most mobile devices have. This is the reason why most android ransomwares lock applications with a coded GUI which where-in once the application is opened, a GUI showing the ransomware details would be shown (Snow, 2016). As a response for a better implementation of ransomware technology, the newest mobile ransomware specifically dedicated for android which is tagged as *Android.Lockroid.E* locks the whole mobile device instead of just locking the specific applications inside the mobile. This way, the user's mobile would be locked and unusable not until the ransom would be paid (Norton, 2018).

*iOS*- According to a report released by Symantec, iOS devices are mostly secured due to Apple's Technological and Security Ecosystem Structure. The only way that an iPhone is vulnerable to ransomware is when the mobile has undergone the process called "Jail-Break" (Savage, et al., 2015). Despite all the protection that Apple offers for iOS phones, researchers suggest that Proton Remote Access Trojan (RAT) has affected plenty of iPhones worldwide (SC Magazine, 2017).

## IoT and Cloud Computing Platforms

As previously discussed, the invention of NotPetya paved the way to a type of ransomware which does not need third party connections like spam emails or social engineering just to infect and gain administrative access to any device. This idea leads developers and researchers to think of the next step that ransomware is capable of. Although there has been no reported ransomware attack on any IoT or Cloud Computing platform, the implementation of this idea is not too far away especially that IoT is being plagued by DDoS attacks such as Mirai (Ismail, 2017). Since ransomware developers can now understand and create ransomware which can multiply by itself on a shared network, IoT technologies are not safe anymore since all IoT's share a common network which is the Cloud (Cobb, 2017). Although speculation about Microsoft 365 cloud-based technology being attacked by ransomwares named CERBER or RANSOM_CERBER.CAD has not been fully proven, TrendMicro researchers have stated that the ransomware can encrypt 442 file types using AES 265 and RSA encryption techniques. The said cloud ransomware seemed like the coding of cloud ransomware was just in its initial stages since the only command that the ransomware can successfully deliver was to play an audio message in a computer-generated (creepy) voice (Budd, 2016). These incidents may actually hint a growth of ransomware in the IoT and Cloud Industry.

## The Target of Ransomware Attacks

Ransomwares are not only built for a sole purpose of affecting normal users like regular citizens but are also built for a larger cause. Since malware development has been classified as an essential tool for money-making and has already been a booming business, malware developers have concentrated attacks on industries where more benefit could be taken. A report by Scientific American Magazines states that cybercriminals have been targeting and crippling important "institutions that everybody relies on" through different types of ransomware (Sneed, 2016). According to a report by CSO, the three industries which are mostly affected by Ransomware attacks include the following: Healthcare, Government and Education with *Healthcare* being mostly affected by all (Martin, 2017). These industries are targeted more since these industries run 24/7 thus these industries need their updated files all the time. Some are threatened regarding the institutional or organisational data being leaked and sold in the dark web which is why these industries tend to pay for the ransom quicker than the rest of the victims (Osborne, 2018).

Alarmingly, in an updated report of Cylance called 2019 Threat Report, businesses have obviously been targeted more after most healthcare have reportedly been secured by government agencies through anti-ransomware schemes.

Whilst there is significant drop on every industry that ransomware affects, only healthcare and businesses had an increase (14 percent for healthcare and 31% to business and finance related) in the total percentage of ransomware attacks over the span of a year (Cylance, 2019). Aside from the incident of Pennsylvania Senate, the report of Scientific American Magazine (Sneed, 2016) also states that police

*Figure 9. Industries impacted by ransomware (Cylance, 2019)*

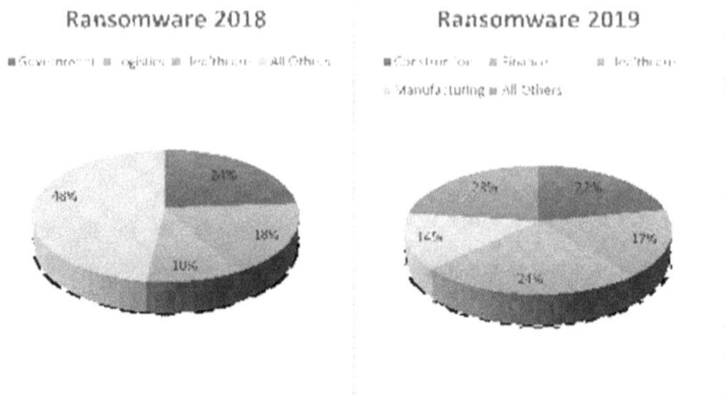


stations such as the Swansea Police Department (2013) and Fire Departments in Maryland (2015) have been struck by ransomwares due to the simple fact that these organisations hold sensitive and important data about the citizens which is vital for the government. The police department of Swansea (2013 incident) had to pay 750 USD just to recover the files but the Fire Department of Maryland opted not to pay which as they suggest could discourage further attacks.

In the report of Scientific American Magazine (Sneed, 2016), a clear message was actually delivered as a warning for those in charge of law enforcement and cybersecurity. These cyber-attacks are happening now with the industries concerning health and government, but a day would come when these malicious attacks could be directed towards bigger and worse attacks. Attacks like a breach to critical infrastructures such as dams, power grids or worse; Supervisory Control And Data Acquisition (SCADA) which are all frequent users of the internet for the daily basis of functionality. A report suggests cybercriminals have coded ransomware which is dedicated to infecting SCADA systems and this ransomware is named as LogicLocker (Kidron, 2017). This ransomware uses sockets API and manipulates weak credential authentication mechanism into infecting the workstation. After infection, the ransomware does not encrypt the files but instead deletes all current authentication passwords and let the command and control centre change the password to the attacker's choice. This way, the company affected needs to pay the ransom for the new authentication details (Kidron, 2017).

## RANSOMWARE IN BUSINESSES AND MARKETING

In the year 2017, Ransomware attacks grew 15 times bigger than the year 2015 (Fruhlinger, 2017) amounting up to 5 Billion USD (Walker, 2018) and multiple reports suggest that this trend is continuing in a growth pace of 350 percent annually. Although as previously discussed that the number one target of ransomware is the healthcare sector, (Cyber Security Ventures, 2019) reports that every 14 seconds, a new business falls into a ransomware attack. These businesses are not necessarily new to this attack since plenty of these businesses might have experienced ransomware for multiple times, but these businesses suffer greatly despite the number of attacks. Out of many industries, healthcare and financial services have been most vulnerable to ransomware attacks, due to the significance of the data they have as well as their capabilities to pay a ransom (Osterman Research, 2016). The organisations have reported that

*Figure 10. verizon's report on breaches on businesses (Verizon, 2017)*

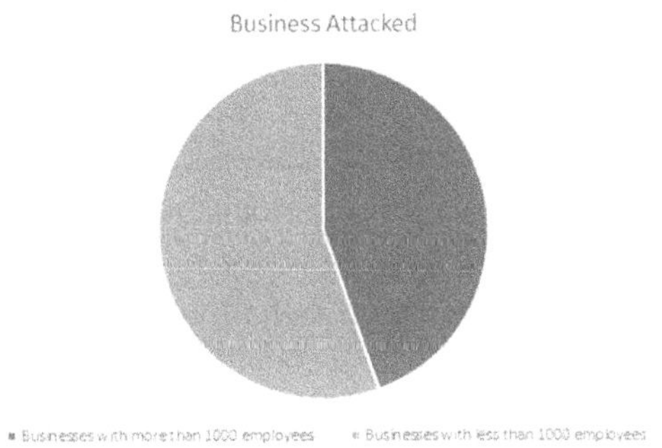


in the case of ransomware attacks customers or suppliers users were most affected (78%), it stopped business (125), the staff has to use personal devices in emergency for organisational purposes (11%),and organisations lose revenues (6%), (Osterman Research, 2016)

In conjunction with Verizon's report, smaller businesses are proven to be more vulnerable to these attacks since 61 percent of these attacks were targeted to companies which have a smaller workforce. An example of these ransomwares which targeted businesses is the *Ryuk* Ransomware. Ryuk ransomware is a copy of Hermes Ransomware, one of the latest types of ransomware, but instead designed to target businesses and enterprises. Ryuk ransomware was first used during the Christmas vacation of the year 2018, taking advantage of the lack of attention of businesses globally (Kujawa, 2019).

## Two Challenges That Businesses Marketing Face Due to Ransomware

Identifying the main challenges that ransomware pose to marketing would come from first understanding the deeper effect of two-way communication that occurs in the modern strategies of marketing.

Two-way marketing in the sense that the first step (Object 11, number 1) is a company advertising to citizens and trying to establish a public relationship. The second step, clearly (Object 11, number 2) is the company trying to gather the feedback of customers.

Knowing all the damages that ransomware does to a device, an examination of Object 10 diagram number 2 could be done. It could be a big possibility that after the efforts of companies to market their products, hackers can potentially disguise as regular customers and implant the ransomware virus through any form of feedback to the product. An example of this situation is how hackers are now targeting websites who do their marketing and advertisement through WordPress built websites (Bocetta, 2019). Hackers target advertisements and marketing strategies which involve the customer to leave either feedback or an

*Figure 11. Compounded two-way communication diagram*

email regarding a certain product. Once the email or feedback is opened, the ransomware virus would be spread in the victim's device and further infecting the network of computers linked into the system. This scenario is ***actually*** the least worrisome and least expensive for businesses if ransomware affects the company.

The next, biggest, most worrisome and most expensive challenge is actually the opposite situation. There is a possibility that if the company acquires the ransomware virus, whether through infection or through social engineering, the company might spread the virus to the clients without their full knowledge and approval. Knowing that emails are considered as both; most commonly used for advertisement of digital marketing and are also the biggest attack vector of Ransomware, a big threat is posed to the reliability of this platform. A scenario can be formulated wherein a certain company which actively does its marketing through the two-way communication process acquire a Ransomware virus through feedbacks and emails. This same Ransomware could now then be sent by the business as a part of their marketing materials without them even knowing. This scenario poses a bigger threat to businesses as they not only affect their businesses but also have affected their customer's devices. These customers may lose their trust in these companies or worse, may even sue the company and file claims for their losses due to the negligence presented by the company

## PREVENTING RANSOMWARE ATTACKS

One estimate is overall damage that businesses due to ransomware attacks could be around $11.5 billion in the year 2019(August et al., 2019).

The job of cybersecurity should not be left only to IT professional of an organoiron, it should be a joint effort of customers, employees, and all users and stakeholders. (The Australian Small Business and Family Enterprise Ombudsman, 2017). The organizations should Crete a culture of cybersecurity awareness, hygiene, corrective and preventing actions. It requires bringing everyone on the board, regular employee, customers, and other stakeholder training, developing security rules, guidelines and norms, know your vulnerability and use Security software like paid anti-malware (or antivirus) software(The Australian Small Business and Family Enterprise Ombudsman, 2017). Different companies, different researchers and different anti-virus brands have a different suggestion in preventing ransomware infection and spreading. Preventative actions such as regularly patching the stems, backup, firewalls, bargaining & deterrence strategies, matching the dynamics of targeted attacks (August et al., 2019)

Although multiple types of research have opposing steps in preventing ransomware, the approaches are the same. In one research the users were asked about the means they have used to cure their devices of ransomware attacks, the users stated that they have used a range of methods such as restarting the device, searching an online tool to remove ransomware, resorting device from backup, reformatting device, removed using Antivirus software, removed by experts and paid ransoms online etc (Simoiu et al., 2019) . The users often take a range of preventive moves such as use AV software, more careful browsing, backing up data, automated updates to software changes the operating system, changed default browser and encrypted hard drive, cloud storage, etc (Simoiu et al., 2019). The nature of prevention can be done in two simple ways: Human Prevention and Advance Prevention.

## Human Prevention

**Information Dissemination:** With the advancement of technology, people are now expected to gather information, be vigilant and ***educate*** themselves about the latest news in the digital society (Ali, 2017). Information about harmful software, not just *ransomware,* should be disseminated on the few different platforms so that more coverage of dissemination could be possible. These platforms are given as the following (Turpin & Harmsworth, 2001):

- **Mails** (Post Mails or Emails)
- **Newsletters**
- **Company or Educational Briefings**
- **Websites**
- **Reports**
- **Conferences**
- **Workshops**
- **Other Media** (Social Media etc.)

Although having the option of self-learning from these sources, people should be wise enough with the choices of sources from the following platforms. People should be wise enough that the news and newsletters sources, as well as the reports if being read online, should be from credible sources like the government or IEEE sources. Websites accessed for information regarding malware should ideally be from anti-virus company blogs such as Kaspersky, Avast, Asset, etc.

**Technical Prevention:** A few technical but simple steps are suggested by multiple types of research in the field of malware. These steps are subcategorized by different digital vectors and most of these steps could be looked up online.

**Back-up, Back-up, Back-up!** (Rajpal & Kotov, 2014)**:**

- *Regularly Back-up Data*: Back-up could be done in two different ways. Since there is a minimum chance of being hit by ransomware on your device and as well as in a selected cloud application, users are advised to use a cloud back-up for important and sensitive files. This is the same reason why mobile ransomware does not encrypt files inside the mobile but just locks the whole system instead.
- *External Hard Disk Back-up:* External hard disk can also be suggested as a back-up measure, but researchers suggest that after back-up, external hard disks should be unplugged from the computers (Ali, 2017)
- *Deploy User Account Control:* This will help limit the access of ransomwares since most ransomware procedures require administrative permissions.

**Email Security** (O'Brien, 2017)**:**

- *Prevent Downloads of Unknown Attachment files*
- *Do not open spam mails if the mail is sent by an unknown user*
- *Install special Email defender applications that have real-time the following link*
- *Disable macro scripts on the files received via emails* (O'Brien, 2017)

Anti-Virus

- *Anti-Virus should always be updated* (Ali, 2017)

  Other Important Preventive Measures:
- Disable remote services if not in use
- Disable Bluetooth services if not in use
- Limit accessing unreliable websites (i.e. porn sites)
- Limit clicking on links provided by colleagues instead type the full address on the link bar

**Prevention for Mobile Users** (Savage, et al., 2015)**:**

- Apps should only be installed from trusted application stores
- Check the permissions of the application being downloaded if the permissions are appropriate for the use of the application
- Try as possible not to jailbreak iOS platforms

### Advance Prevention

Multiple types of research online have given suggestions for different approaches that bigger companies can use in preventing ransomware attacks. A few of the most effective advance prevention techniques are listed as Advance Prevention with the use of (Carbon Black, 2018):

- Key Back-Up
- Process Monitoring on Android Platforms
- Connection Monitor and Connection Breaker
- Honeypot Techniques

## Ways to Recover from Ransomware Attacks

In terms of recovering from an **incomplete** ransom attack, this is when the user gets to know that there is a possible ransomware attack due to appearances of.KRAB and/or GDCB-DECRYPT.txt files but the files are not yet encrypted. The user is suggested to automatically run the anti-virus application for virus scanning of the system. A suggestion is also made that all devices infected with the ransomware should be disconnected from the network to protect cloud-based or external back-up files (Brewer, 2016).

In terms of recovering from a **successful** ransom attack, organisations and researchers always ask a common question: **To Pay or NOT To Pay?** There is a big reason why researchers and businesses ask the question and it all has to do with the rate of success of file recovery and eradication of the ransomware. A suggestion is done that in terms of eradicating the virus once the ransom is paid, the user can never be sure that there is no more residual file left in the system (Brewer, 2016). The ransomware residual files can actually hide in mailboxes or directories without the user knowing and these files can be triggered at any time that the user is logged in to the computer. Just in case that the user opts to pay for the ransom, as previously stated, the ransomware **should** delete itself and hostage files should be returned without any alterations. The article (Brewer, 2016) finally suggests that buying a newer device is wiser especially if files are backed up online since this would help lessen the fuel for ransomware developer's intentions to reproduce more ransomware applications.

## MANAGEMENT IMPLICATIONS

Cyber-attacks are one of the major challenges for the management in any businesses today. With the ever increase of computers and Internet in any business (Nishtha Kesswani, 2015), the cyber-attacks have seen massive growth in recent years, the attackers targeting individual and server machines to disrupt the operations of the businesses. This requires businesses to implement preventive controls, however, the management is always a concern with the return of investment in the form profits and gains, whereas cybersecurity implementation is always measured in terms of preventing losses to the business. Therefore the management requires a critical insight into the continuity of business operations planning to minimize the impact of any possible cyber-attack and establish a disaster recovery planning to recover from any cyber incidents.

The consumers as most vulnerable targeted may be protected by providing personalized educational resources and training, or discounted offers and could be motivated to adopt pre-emptive measures to protect any potential risks(Simoiu et al., 2019).

The increase compliance from regulatory bodies makes the business manager responsible for the information security management in any organization and require them to adhere with policies and procedures to successfully implement an effective information security controls which can prevent data loss and minimize any data breaches (Emmett Dulaney, 2018). This involves management to conduct a Business Impact Analysis (BIA) to identify risks to the business, allocate resources to mitigate them and ensure enough resources are made available for appropriate countermeasures in the form of physical controls and staff training. Management support and guidance is paramount for the implementation of successful information security management system (ISO, 2019)to meet business objectives ethically and protect information assets such as ecommerce website against malicious attacks such as Ransomware. This is normally achieved by implementing a hybrid security approach, which includes hardware controls and people education and awareness against the cyber threat.

## CONCLUSION AND SCOPE FOR FURTHER RESEARCH

Although Ransomwares are ranked as only the sixth most prominent malware in most Cybercrime reports, ransomware still makes a case of being a deadly malware to businesses. This is due to the fact that Ransomware has the capability to do damage by means of infecting a user's device and encrypting either all the files or the whole device. The damage would only stop until when the victim has paid for the ransom where in most cases there is a limited time given. If the ransom payment date passes, businesses would then be obliged to pay double the original ransom price. Multiple types of research also suggest that despite being able to pay the ransom price, there is no guarantee of the files being returned and/or the ransomware being eradicated completely from the system.

Most of the prominent ransomwares such as WannaCry, CryptoLocker, TeslaCrypt, SimpleLocker, GandCrab, Petya and NotPetya uses RSA 2048bit as the public key and AES 256bit for the victim's data encryption. Ransomware's most prominent feature aside from encryption is the command and control feature which actually gave birth to a new type of malware. This step made Kaspersky predict that the new trend for 2018 is to have a shift from ransomwares to ***crypto mining*** which most researchers suggest is just another variant of better ransomware.

Due to the two-way communication that the marketing industry possess, the industry is in a bigger danger of being infected and as well as infecting their clients. Especially after being reported that hackers have now planned to shift attention to targeting medium market businesses. If hackers study the way business and marketing is done, they may find a loophole and develop ransomware such as Ryuk which is solely dedicated to crippling businesses.

In terms of ransomware, human involvement is key since ransomware as a simple hard-coded software is **useless.** Ransomware could not spread and infect **by its own.** Human involvement actually gives life to ransomware and the procedures of how ransomware infects devices. Humans create the ransomware software and humans spread the virus. As previously stated, most acquisitions of ransomwares are done due to a human falling for the spam email trick set by hackers. Social Engineering which was previously discussed also play a vital part since human use psychology to gain illegal motifs. Humans are also responsible for activating the malware since most of the ransomware activation happens when .exe files disguised as pdf or word files are executed. Cybercriminals are also responsible for the encryption of files inside the victim's device and finally, once the trap is set, Humans are also responsible to choose whether **to pay** or **not to pay.**

Human empowerment along with proper information dissemination is key to know what ransomwares are and how to fight the attacks. With proper education about the topic, humans can actually find out how to at least lessen these types of cyber-attacks by means of early-stage prevention. Finally, these preventions can only be done if the **Human** factor in the computing environment would be willing enough to critically educate him or herself about the digital advancement about the different industries of computing.

## REFERENCES


Abrams, L. 2018. *GandCrab V4 Released With the New.KRAB Extension for Encrypted Files.* Available at: https://www.bleepingcomputer.com/news/security/gandcrab-v4-released-with-the-new-krab-extension-for-encrypted-files/

Ali, A. (2017). Ransomware: A Research And A Personal Case Study Of Dealing With This Nasty Malware. *Information Science Institute*, *14*(1), 87–99.

August, T., Dao, D., & Florin Niculescu, M. (2019). *Economics of Ransomware Attacks.* Retrieved from https://weis2019.econinfosec.org/wp-content/uploads/sites/6/2019/05/WEIS_2019_paper_60.pdf

Avast. (2018). *Adware.* Available at: https://www.avast.com/c-adware

BBC. (2017). *NHS 'could have prevented' WannaCry ransomware attack.* London: BBC.

BBC. (2017). *Ukraine power cut 'was cyber-attack.* London: BBC.

BBC. (2018). *Arran Brewery hit by ransomware attack.* Scotland: BBC Scotland.

Bocetta, S. (2019). *How ransomware targets WordPress sites.* Available at: https://marketingland.com/how-ransomware-targets-wordpress-sites-262939

Bournemouth University. (2018). *A brief history of marketing.* Available at: https://media3.bournemouth.ac.uk/marketing/02defining/01history.html

Brewer, R. (2016). Ransomware attacks: Detection, prevention and cure. *Network Security*, *2016*(9), 5–9. doi:10.1016/S1353-4858(16)30086-1

Budd, C. (2016). *Ransomware infects the cloud: What you need to know.* Available at: https://blog.trendmicro.com/ransomware-infects-the-cloud-what-you-need-to-know/

Burkeman, O. (2009). *Forty years of the internet: how the world changed for ever.* The Guardian.

Butt, M. (2019). Ransomware Threat and its Impact on SCADA. In *2019 IEEE 12th International Conference on Global Security, Safety and Sustainability (ICGS3).* London: IEEE.

Cannell, J. (2013). *Today the US Department of Justice (DOJ) announced an effort to disrupt the Gameover Zeus Botnet. In addition to this effort, the DOJ announced an another join.* Available at: https://blog.malwarebytes.com/101/2013/10/cryptolocker-ransomware-what-you-need-to-know/

Carbon Black. (2018). *Advance Your Ransomware Defenses*. Carbon Black.

Check Point Software Technologies. (2019). *Cyber Attack Trends Analysis Report.* Retrieved from http://www.snt.hr/boxcontent/CheckPointSecurityReport2019_vol01.pdf

Cimpanu, C. (2018). *Pennsylvania Senate Democrats paid $700,000 to recover from ransomware attack*. Zero Day Net.

Cisco. (2018). *What Is Malware?* Available at: https://www.cisco.com/c/en/us/products/security/advanced-malware-protection/what-is-malware.html

Cisco Talos. (2018). *Email & Spam Data*. Cisco.

Cobb, S. (2017). *RoT: Ransomware of Things.* Available at: https://cdn1.esetstatic.com/ESET/US/Newsroom/2017/03/ESET_Trends-and-Prediction_2017_Ransomware.pdf

Columbus, L. (2016). 2015 Gartner CRM Market Share Analysis Shows Salesforce. In *The Lead, Growing Faster Than Market*. Forbes.

Cyber Security Ventures. (2019). *Cybercrime Damages $6 Trillion By 2021*. Cyber Security Ventures.

Cylance. (2019). *2019 Threat Report*. Irvine, CA: Cylance.

Deloitte. (2016). *Ransomware Holding Your Data Hostage.* London: Deloitte Threat Intelligence and Analytics.

Emmett Dulaney, C. E. (2018). CompTIA Security+ Study Guide: Exam SY0-501 (7th ed.). Indianapolis: CompTIA Security+.

Emsisoft. (2018). *Spotlight on ransomware: Ransomware encryption methods.* Available at: https://blog.emsisoft.com/en/27649/ransomware-encryption-methods/

Esset. (2018). *Viruses, malware and remote attacks defined.* Available at: https://support.eset.com/kb186/

Fruhlinger, J. (2017). *Petya ransomware and NotPetya malware: What you need to know now.* Available at: https://www.csoonline.com/article/3233210/ransomware/petya-ransomware-and-notpetya-malware-what-you-need-to-know-now.html

Fruhlinger, J. (2017). *The 5 biggest ransomware attacks of the last 5 years.* Available at: https://www.csoonline.com/article/3212260/ransomware/the-5-biggest-ransomware-attacks-of-the-last-5-years.html

Fruhlinger, J. (2018). *What is WannaCry ransomware, how does it infect, and who was responsible?* Available at: https://www.csoonline.com/article/3227906/ransomware/what-is-wannacry-ransomware-how-does-it-infect-and-who-was-responsible.html

Gallegos-Segovia, P. L. (2017). *Social engineering as an attack vector for ransomware.* Pucon, Chile: IEEE. doi:10.1109/CHILECON.2017.8229528

Gibbs, S. (2017). *WannaCry: hackers withdraw £108,000 of bitcoin ransom.* Available at: https://www.theguardian.com/technology/2017/aug/03/wannacry-hackers-withdraw-108000-pounds-bitcoin-ransom

Gupta, M. P., & Dubey, A. (2016). International Journal of Computer Science and Mobile Computing E-Commerce-Study of Privacy, Trust and Security from Consumer's Perspective. *International Journal of Computer Science and Mobile Computing*, *5*(6), 224–232. Retrieved from www.ijcsmc.com

Help Net Security. (2016). *Impact of security breaches on consumer trust.* Help Net Security.

IBM. (2019). *IBM X-Force Threat Intelligence Index.* IBM.

Imperial College UK. (2018). *What is Security Analysis?* Available at: https://www.doc.ic.ac.uk/~ajs300/security/CIA.htm

Ismail, N. (2017). *Ransomware of IoT will become a new security nightmare in 2018.* Available at: https://www.information-age.com/ransomware-iot-new-security-nightmare-123470151/

Kappel, M. (2017). *5 Ways To Improve Your Small Business Marketing.* Available at: https://www.forbes.com/sites/mikekappel/2017/06/14/5-ways-to-improve-your-small-business-marketing/#1e7d00274969

Kaspersky. (2018a). *History of malicious programs.* Available at: https://encyclopedia.kaspersky.com/knowledge/history-of-malicious-programs/

Kaspersky. (2018b). *TeslaCrypt Ransomware Attacks.* Available at: https://www.kaspersky.co.uk/resource-center/threats/teslacrypt

Kaspersky. (2018c). *Types of Malware.* Available at: https://www.kaspersky.co.uk/resource-center/threats/malware-classifications

Kaspersky Lab. (2016). *KSN Report: PC ransomware in 2014-2016.* Kaspersky Lab.

Kidron, M. (2017). *LogicLocker Brings Ransomware to SCADA Networks.* Available at: https://blog.skyboxsecurity.com/logiclocker-brings-ransomware-to-scada-networks/

Koller, M. S. (2016). *TeslaCrypt Ransomware Developers Retire, Release Master Decryption Key.* Available at: https://www.dataprivacymonitor.com/cybersecurity/teslacrypt-ransomware-developers-retire-release-master-decryption-key/

Kujawa, A. (2019). *Ryuk ransomware attacks businesses over the holidays.* Available at: https://blog.malwarebytes.com/cybercrime/malware/2019/01/ryuk-ransomware-attacks-businesses-over-the-holidays/

Lee, J., Warkentin, M., & Johnston, A. (2016). A Broader View of Perceived Risk during Internet Transactions. *Communications of the Association for Information Systems*, *38*(8), 171–189. doi:10.17705/1CAIS.03808

Lindskog, D., & Zavarskya, M. P. (2016). Experimental Analysis of Ransomware on Windows and Android Platforms: Evolution and Characterization. *Procedia Computer Science*, (94): 465–472.

Macrae, D. (2014). *Everything you need to know about the Sasser worm.* CBR.

Malwarebytes Labs. (2018). *Ransomware dominates the threat landscape.* Available at: https://blog.malwarebytes.com/cybercrime/2016/06/ransomware-dominates-the-threat-landscape/

Mann, I. (2008). *Hacking the Human: Social Engineering Techniques and Security Countermeasures* (1st ed.). London: Routledge.

Martin, J. A. (2017). *Who is a target for ransomware attacks?* Available at: https://www.csoonline.com/article/3208111/security/who-is-a-target-for-ransomware-attacks.html

McAfee. (2017). *McAfee Labs Threat Report*. Santa Clara, CA: McAfee.

Merriam-Webster. 2018. *ransom.* [Online] Available at: https://www.merriam-webster.com/dictionary/ransom

Monrose, F. (2015). *Detecting web exploit kits by tree-based structural similarity search.* USA Patent No. US9723016B2.

Morrcraft, B. (2019). *Ransomware attackers set sights on middle market firms.* Insurance Business Aemrica.

NDTV. (2017). *ATMs Closed Due to WannaCry Ransomware? Experts Debunk WhatsApp Hoaxes.* Available at: https://gadgets.ndtv.com/internet/news/atm-closed-india-cyber-attack-whatsapp-wanna-cry-rumours-1694207

Nishtha Kesswani, S. K. (2015). *Maintaining Cyber Security: mplications, Cost and Returns.* ACM.

NJCCIC. (2016). *Simplelocker.* Available at: https://www.cyber.nj.gov/threat-profiles/ransomware-variants/simplelocker

NJCCIC. (2018). *GandCrab.* Available at: https://www.cyber.nj.gov/threat-profiles/ransomware-variants/gandcrab

Norton. (2018a). *Malware 101: How do I get malware? Simple attacks.* Available at: https://us.norton.com/internetsecurity-malware-malware-101-how-do-i-get-malware-simple-attacks.html

Norton. (2018b). *New variant of Android ransomware takes advantage of the lockscreen's user interface.* Available at: https://us.norton.com/internetsecurity-emerging-threats-new-variant-of-android-ransomware-takes-advantage-of-the-lockscreen-user-interface.html

O'Brien, D. (2017). *ISTR: Internet Security Threat Report- Ransomware 2017.* Symantec.

Osborne, C. (2018a). *Healthcare was a top target for ransomware families in 2017.* Available at: https://www.zdnet.com/article/ransomware-operators-select-the-healthcare-industry-as-a-top-target/

Osborne, C. (2018b). *Meet ransomware which wears the face of former president Barack Obama*. ZDNet.

Osterman Research. (2016). *Understanding the Depth of the Global Ransomware Problem Survey Report Spon*. Retrieved from www.ostermanresearch.com

Paul, D. P., III, Spence, N., Bhardwa, N., & Coustasse, A. (2018). *Healthcare Facilities: Another Target for Ransomware Attacksd the Health Information Technology Commons.* 54th Annual MBAA Conference, Chicago, IL. Retrieved from http://mds.marshall.edu/mgmt_faculty

Rajpal, M. S. & Kotov, V. (2014). *Understanding Crypto-Ransomware: In-Depth Analysis of the Most Popular Malware Families.* Bromium.

Redstor. (2017). *Ransomware*. Retrieved from https://www.ict4.co.uk/Ransomware_e-book_rev2.pdf

Richet, J.-L. (2016). Extortion on the Internet: The Rise of Crypto-Ransomware. *Harvard Researches*, *2*(1), 2–6.

S C Magazine. (2017). *Malware and the "Other" Platforms: Mac and Android Devices are Increasingly at Risk*. Available at: https://media.scmagazine.com/documents/314/malware_and_the_"other"_platfo_78268.pdf

SAS. (2019). *History of Digital Marketing*. Available at: https://www.sas.com/en_gb/insights/marketing/digital-marketing.html

Savage, K., Coogan, P., & Lau, H. (2015). The evolution of ransomware. *Security Response*, *6*, 57.

Schwedel, A., Root, J., & Allen, J. (2017). *3,000 Years of Business History in Two Minutes*. London: Bain and Company.

Securonix Threat Research Team. (2018). *Grandcrab Ransomware Attack*. Securonix.

Simoiu, C., Symantec, C. G., Bonneau, J., & Goel, S. (2019). "I was told to buy a software or lose my computer. I ignored it": A study of ransomware. *USENIX Symposium on Usable Privacy and Security (SOUPS) 2019.* Retrieved from https://5harad.com/papers/ransomware.pdf

Sneed, A. (2016). *The Most Vulnerable Ransomware Targets Are the Institutions We Rely On Most*. Scientific American.

Snow, J. (2016). *Ransomware on mobile devices: knock-knock-block*. Available at: https://www.kaspersky.com/blog/mobile-ransomware-2016/12491/

Soni, V. (2018). *Multifunctional malware becoming extensive in 2018, finds Kaspersky Lab report.* Available at: https://www.dailyhostnews.com/multifunctional-malware-becoming-extensive/

Stavrou, A. (2010). *Malware detector.* USA Patent No. US8935773B2.

Tasril, V., Ginting, M. B., Mardiana, & Siahaan, A. P. U. (2017). Threats of Computer System and its Prevention. *IJSRST, 3*(6), 448-451.

The Australian Small Business and Family Enterprise Ombudsman. (2017). *Cyber Security: The Small Business Best Practice Guide Cyber Security: A Small Business Best Practice Guide*. Retrieved from www.itsanhonour.gov.au

Touchette, F. (2016). The evolution of malware. *Network Security, 1*(1), 11–14. doi:10.1016/S1353-4858(16)30008-3

Turpin, S., & Harmsworth, S. (2001). *Creating an Effective Dissemination Strategy An Expanded Interactive Workbook for Educational Development Projects.* Available at: https://ajpp-online.org/resources/downloads/06-CreatingAnEffectiveDisseminationStrategy-AnExpandedWorkbook.pdf

Verizon. (2017). *DBIR 2017 Report.* Verizon.

Walker, J. (2018). *Ransomware remains biggest malware threat in 2018, says Europol.* Available at: https://portswigger.net/daily-swig/ransomware-remains-biggest-malware-threat-in-2018-says-europol

Walton, A. G. (2017). *Phone Addiction Is Real -- And So Are Its Mental Health Risks.* Available at: https://www.forbes.com/sites/alicegwalton/2017/12/11/phone-addiction-is-real-and-so-are-its-mental-health-risks/#527d531813df

Yazdanifard, R., Al-Huda Edres, N., & Seyedi, A. P. (2011). Security and Privacy Issues as a Potential Risk for Further E-commerce Development. *International Conference on Information Communication and Management.* Retrieved from https://pdfs.semanticscholar.org/01c5/5d28035e91cb5882bda08cb599cc63f44578.pdf

Young, A. L. & Yung, M. (2017). Privacy and Security Cryptovirology: The Birth, Neglect, and Explosion of Ransomware. *Communications of the ACM, 60*(7), 24-26.

Zetter, K. (2016). *Inside the cunning, unprecedented hack of ukraine's power grid.* London: Wired.

## KEY TERMS AND DEFINITIONS

**Botnets:** A compromised machine over the Internet which is controlled by hackers to carry out attacks on target machine.

**Cyber-Attack:** An illegal attempt by hacker to target an individual or an enterprise for harm or financial gain.

**Cybercrime:** A criminal activity which is carried out using computers to commit an offense.

**Malware:** A malicious software intentionally designed to harm computer systems or networks.

**Ransomware:** A kind of malicious software, it encrypts all the files on target machine, take control of it remotely and demands for virtual money to be paid as a ransomware.

# Chapter 9
# Impact of Supply Chain Digitalisation on a Connected Global Market

**Farooq Habib**
*Cranfield University, UK*

**Murtaza Farooq Khan**
*Independent Researcher, UK*

## ABSTRACT

*This chapter focuses on the impact of supply chain digitalisation on a connected global market. The first section focuses on the dynamic consumer requirements and preferences. The second section appraised the segmentation and mapping of digital technologies. The third section examines the contemporary application of digital technologies including: big data, blockchains, artificial intelligence, machine learning, and data analytics. The final section analysises the rules and regulations the form the basis of a contemporary framework for the governance of digital technologies.*

## INTRODUCTION

Across global supply chains, consumers are expressing evolving requirements and preferences. With the emergence of new technologies including Distributed Ledger Technology, the Internet of Things, Artificial Intelligence, Big Data and Cloud Computing, supply chain providers are in a unique position to better understand and cater to these dynamic consumer requirements and preferences.

Consumers express a desire for a greater degree of control, ownership and privacy of their data. This trend emerges from the fact that consumers' data, collectivised as Big Data, has been utilised by businesses, before the emergence of recent regulatory trends, to better understand and target individual consumer preferences, without users being appropriately informed or rewarded for the provision of their valuable data. With the emergence of regulatory trends, including the European General Data Protection Regulation (EU GDPR, 2019), supply chains are placed in a position where they must incentivise users to allow them to analyse and take advantage of data pertaining to their consumption.

DOI: 10.4018/978-1-7998-0131-3.ch009

Increasingly, consumers are also magnetised by ethical consumption. This trend finds its roots in consumers wanting to live more conscious lives, as well as health and safety concerns, particularly amidst growing concerns of food fraud. This need for greater traceability and proof of provenance within food supply chains is gaining political traction as well, with the French president Emanuel Macron recently calling for European standardisation of food produce tracking at the International Agricultural Affair in Paris during February 2019 (Vie Publique, 2019). Industries are following suit – In February 2019, Accenture announced a blockchain-based supply chain application to allow users to reward sustainable business models which conserve natural resources (Accenture, 2019). Partnered with Mastercard, Everledger and Mercy Corps, Accenture is seeking to create an application where consumers can track the provenance of the goods they consume, with verifiable certifications of sustainable practices incentivising adoption by producers. The initiative is enlisting the support of farming associations to act as cloud-based information nodes to act as proxy for small farmers themselves, users will be able to reward ecologically sustainable practices through either blockchain tokens or fiat currency through Mastercard.

With the emergence of the aforementioned technologies, consumer preferences have evolved to demand greater transactional efficiency. This trend finds ground within a desire for time and cost savings, as well as an individualised consumer experience. One of the more practical manifestations of this trend has been consumers' desire for end-to-end tracking in order to witness traceability across supply chains. This is increasingly important to consumers as we move away from a world based on physical to digital data exchange.

## IMPACT OF BRICKS VS CLICKS ON SUPPLY CHAINS

Traditionally, supply chains have been based off physical rather than digital infrastructure. As technology has evolved, so too have supply chains, with many digitalising various facets of their business operations. Even with the emergence of supply chain digitalisation, there is still the fact that many of the systems used by a variety of stakeholders within the supply chain do not always efficiently communicate with each other. The divergence between the consequences of physical and digital infrastructure can be analysed through the perspectives of data exchange, data analytics, traceability and supply chain integrity, efficiencies and the threat of fraud and loss.

In terms of data exchange, the first point of analysis is the fact that without digital data exchange, the process can be very time consuming for consumers and businesses, often resulting in calls, physical visits and paperwork which can create major inefficiencies across the supply chain. Additionally, physical records are more difficult to keep secure and immutable. Digitalisation has ebbed these consequences, however digital systems do not always work well together, and the fundamental issue therein is one of trust, as various stakeholders within the supply chain are not always willing to trust other stakeholders with their data. This can make data analytics difficult. Data analytics are important because they allow for the identification and solution to issues and inefficiencies within supply chains. Through digitalisation, particularly with the emergence of blockchain technology, data across supply chains can be standardised and secured; a major move away from the traditional trend of insular silos of data, which make analytics and improvements therefrom challenging.

Within traditional, physical infrastructure, there is also an issue of supply chain integrity and the loss of goods. Physical infrastructure requires human maintenance and therefrom can emerge the consequences of human error and fraud. This can be particularly damaging to supply chains as losses impact the bottom line, whether they emerge from inefficiencies or fraud, and fraud itself can significantly reduce the integrity of supply chains. With digitalisation, there has been an increase in the traceability of goods across supply chains, which improves confidence in performance metrics and in the reliability of representations made by stakeholders across the supply chain. Such traceability is useful for producers, consumers, shipping companies and government authorities. Additionally, with digitalisation, traceability is complemented by a variety of Internet of Things improvements, such as temperature control and gross mass sensors. Such developments allow supply chains to be more efficient and secure compared to those continuing to rely on physical infrastructure.

The advantages of increased efficiency and security within data storage and exchange networks, greater competency of data analytics, the prevention of fraudulent behaviour, and mitigation of administrative inefficiencies, resulting from technological evolution are not confined to the supply chain industry. A demonstrative example of this is Telefonica's collaboration with IBM's Blockchain Platform (Telefonica, 2019). The initial project between Telefonica and IBM seeks to aid with real-time tracking of the certainty of international calls and their attributes, primarily origin, destination and duration, in a decentralised environment to then provide stakeholders within the Blockchain with permissioned access. The incorporation of Blockchain technology is set to significantly enhance the accuracy and immutability of data generated by Telefonica's various services. Past this initial stage, Telefonica has also represented towards the incorporation of Blockchain technology in the operations of network operators, service providers and vendors to assist with the integrity of data consumption, authentication and storage. Data can be collected from a variety of sources and systems, with its traceability and veracity made immutable through the maintenance of decentralised and real-time ledger consensus. This move towards Blockchain technology has been motivated by a desire to improve the efficiency within Telefonica's business practices, including billing, accounting, reporting services. Additionally, Telefonica has identified that Blockchain technology will assist with the discovery and prevention of fraudulent behaviour, as well as streamlining operations between various stakeholders, particularly with a view towards dispute resolution and the mitigation of commercial losses emerging from uncollected revenues and discrepancies between information records.

## MODES OF CONNECTIVITY BETWEEN SUPPLY CHAINS AND CONSUMER PREFERENCES

Increasingly, Increasingly, there is a trend to build cohesion within the connectivity between consumers and supply chains. The underlying theme within this trend is to build accessibility to key data for consumers. This builds confidence in supply chains from the consumers' perspective. Additionally, increases in connectivity can mean costs and time savings for supply chains, as with an increase in accessibility of data, less direct communication is required by consumers to follow-up on the progress of goods across supply chains. The core technologies facilitating such increases in connectivity are the Internet of Things and Omnichannels, as complemented by the accessibility of immutable and reliable data records through the use of blockchain technology within supply chains.

An Omnichannel is a digital content strategy utilised by organisation to homogenise the various channels in their operations in order to enhance user experiences. Omnichannels combine channels including e-commerce, mobile applications, social media and physical locations to provide consumers with an all-in-one digital experiences, which widens the reach of supply chains to consumers who otherwise may not have the access to more physical channels within the supply chain. Omnichannels provide consumers with a dynamic experience and increasingly, are complemented by blockchain technology and the Internet of Things.

Blockchain technology has developed itself into a pivotal aspect of modern supply chains as it acts as infrastructure facilitating the collection, storage and exchange of decentralised, secure and immutable data records. This is useful both from a supply chain and a consumer perspective, as supply chains having access to that data can then provide permissioned access to consumers invested within the supply chain. This can make tracking goods and making payments accessible to consumers. Additionally, block chains are not limited to financial, transactional data and can also be used to store data derivative from Internet of Things technology. Internet of Things refers to the embedment of computing devices, connected by the internet, with everyday objects, in order to facilitate sending and receiving data. Internet of Things technology includes applications such as RFID, temperature and gross mass sensors (Tradelens, 2019a). Data from such technology can be securely and immutably recorded over block chains and can then be made accessible to consumers over Omnichannels. The marriage of these three technologies create major efficiencies across supply chains, increase the reliability of reliance by consumers upon supply chains and drastically enhances connectivity and communication efficiencies between consumers and supply chains.

A representative illustration of increases in the efficiency of communication between consumers and supply chains is Matqa Gateway (Maqta Gateway, 2019). It is the product of a partnership between The Port of Antwerp, Belgium and Abu Dhabi Ports. Their blockchain technology titled Silsal seeks to act as an open ledger with unique digital user identities. Silsal seeks to standardise and secure information exchange amongst port stakeholders, customers and governmental authority entities. Applications of this technology within the Port of Abu Dhabi's operations include licensing and vessel management, verifiable and traceable gross mass and an accessible payment gateway; all accessible through a Blockchain-backed omnichannel. In terms of the advantages realised, Silsal seeks to provide stakeholders, crucially consumers, with easy and public access to transaction status updates, a reduction in paperwork, calls and physical visits, increases in the efficiency of information exchange, real-time cargo tracking and costs savings on physical transport costs.

## THE CONNECTIVITY PERSPECTIVES – B2B; B2C; C2C

With the digitalisation of supply chains and the homogenisation of data silos within supply chains, there is an increasing connectivity between businesses and consumers, which can be analysed through the lenses of B2B, B2C and C2C connectivity. A useful and representative case study of the evolution of such connectivity is the partnership struck between Hewlett Packard Enterprise and Continental during February 2019 (Hewlett Packard, 2019). The two organisations are utilising blockchain technology to create a vehicle data sharing platform, with a focus on data security, transparency and efficiency. The goal for this partnership is to enable novel digital services to improve driver safety and convenience.

Even in the digital era, businesses often possess insular silos of data which remain disconnected from each other. This is problematic as businesses often lose the advantage of access to complementary data sets which can enhance their own provision of goods and services. Additionally, data monopolies stunt growth and innovation within industries. The partnership seeks to monetise the provision of data amongst car manufacturers and other stakeholders within the automotive industry. Monetisation creates an incentive for B2B connectivity. Additionally, the problem of trust is being addressed through decentralised blockchain infrastructure which allows data to be owned and controlled cooperatively by stakeholders with permissioned access to those the platform wishes to share data with.

The partnership also acts as a representative example on how B2B connectivity's advantages can then be transferred to B2C and C2C relationships. Consumers are fundamental to their business model as consumer data, both as a matter of best practice and legal compliance, may only be collected and analysed with consent. Consumers are incentivised to share their vehicular data through the provision of derivative services, which in this case include driver-assistance services allowing for drivers to avoid traffic hazards and the provision of efficient travel routes. Such information is collected through B2C connectivity, predominantly that between car manufacturers and drivers, which is them complemented by C2C connectivity as consumers data is the analysed and the solutions therefrom are redirected to other consumers within the network.

## SEGMENTATION AND MAPPING OF DIGITAL TECHNOLOGIES

### Segmentation of Digital Technologies

#### Segmentation of Digital Technologies

Technological developments within digital supply chains are best understood through Kraljic's supply matrix (See Figure 1). Peter Kraljic first published his revolutionary supply matrix in the Harvard Business Review during September 1983 (Kraljic, 1983). Kraljic's matrix is a useful tool for the identification of routine, leverage, strategic and bottleneck technologies being utilised within digital supply chains, as measured across supply risk and profit impact axes. Understanding the motivations behind usages of emerging technologies within these categories is useful for supply chains to identify immediate areas for evolution and improvement.

*Figure 1. Segmentation of Digital Technologies*

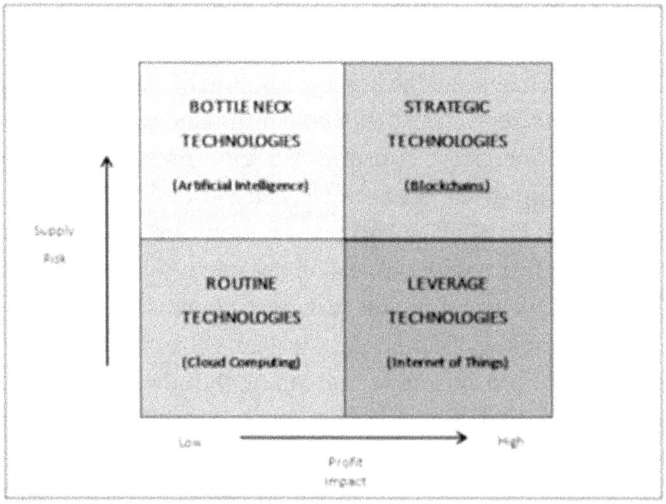

Supply risk emerges from the availability of supply, the number of suppliers, storage risks, price volatility, the probability of supply disruptions and are is also affected by the availability of make-or-buy and substitution opportunities. Profit impact is affected by the volume purchased, the technology as a percentage of total purchase cost and the impact such technologies will have on product quality and business growth.

Across these axes, four forms of technologies can be mapped – bottleneck, strategic, routine / non-critical and leverage technologies. Strategic technologies are associated with a high supply risk and a high profit impact. They are characterised by make-or-buy decisions in terms of their incorporation into business models and are generally an area for the development of long-term supply relationships, such as strategic partnerships. Bottleneck technologies also have a high supply risk, but their profit impact is low. Their supply should be ensured with backup plans in place should they prove unsustainable or impossible to procure. Leverage technologies come with a low supply risk and a high profit impact. Within the procurement of these technologies, owing to the multiplicity of suppliers, businesses should exploit the full extent of their purchasing power in order to minimise their costs. Lastly, routine / noncritical technologies are those with both a low supply risk and a low profit impact. Routine technologies can be simplified by businesses through product standardisation and efficient processing.

## Routine Technologies

It is essential for supply chain providers to determine how these forms of technology interlink. Routine technologies are an intrinsic part of business operations. However, they can be simplified or substituted as there is both an abundance of supply and a limited profit impact. Form a technological perspective, a representative example of a wide-spread non-critical technology is cloud computing. Cloud computing refers to the use of a network of remote servers to store, manage and process data, as opposed to the use of localised servers. Cloud computing allows supply chain providers, and businesses in a variety of other industries, to enact data storage and computing power in a far more globally efficient manner than localised storage. Cloud computing, while increasingly critical to business operations, can be viewed as non-critical, as the alternative of localised data storage and computing power does exist. Further, the market provides an abundance of enterprise-grade cloud computing service providers. The use of cloud computing service providers allows businesses to trade capital expense on data centres and servers for variable expenses, benefit from existing, massive economies of scale, increase the efficiency of IT operations, and provide savings in cost and risk associated with running data centres (Amazon, 2019a). Widely-used and well-established providers of this non-critical technology include: Microsoft Azure (Microsoft Azure, 2019a), IBM Cloud (IBM, 2019a) and Amazon Web Services (Amazon, 2019b).

## Leverage Technologies

Across the profit impact scale are leverage technologies. Such technologies are abundant in their supply and thus present a limited supply risk, however they can have a significant impact on product quality and business growth and are therefore associated with a high profit impact. Owing to the abundance of their supply, leverage technologies present an opportunity for supply chain providers to exert the full extent of their purchasing power in order to secure the best financial deal possible. Internet of Things technology (IoT) is a prime example of a leverage technology increasingly incorporated within supply chains to enhance connectivity and promote business growth. IoT has existed for a number of years, refers to a suite of devices which can be connected to the internet and programmed to interact with existing data networks. Increasingly, IoT is evolving to include existing technologies including sensors and video cameras, as well as blockchain and machine learning technologies. As IoT devices are abundant in their supply, supply chain providers need only follow a streamlined methodology in order to incorporate them into their operations. Intel's methodology for integrating IoT sensors into enterprises is as follows: build an IoT team, define the IoT system, determine the business value, acquire stakeholder agreement and funding, classify the sensor data, design the network infrastructure, review environmental conditions, define space and electrical power needs, secure IoT devices and data, align with corporate data governance policies, design for scalability, integrate and manage the IoT devices, establish a support model and plan resources for sustainability (Intel, 2019). Increasingly, supply chains are adopting similar methodologies to successfully integrate IoT sensors into their infrastructure. Common examples include video cameras, commodity trackers, temperature sensors, RFID trackers, gross mass sensors and chemical volume sensors. IoT can and does play an increasingly vital role within the industry; providing accurate, real-time, secure and verifiable information on the status of cargo across the supply chain. Such data, while easily obtainable through the incorporation of IoT devices which are abundant in their supply, can seriously promote business growth through the creation of both traceability and competitive advantage. For instance, verifiable proof of refrigeration temperatures and changes in gross mass is useful information for buyers as this data is integral to the contracts and guarantees entered into. A useful example illustrating this point is the requirement under the English Sale of Goods Act 1979, changes in the gross mass of commodities such as wheat must be borne equally by contracting parties. Having access to real-time changes in gross mass resulting from shrinkage can provide for legal and commercial efficiencies, thus promoting the business growth of the supply chain providers equipped with the IoT to facilitate this data exchange. Two providers of IoT include Samsara's cold-chain IoT sensors (Samsara, 2019) and NetGear Arlo's video capture devices (Arlo, 2019).

## Bottleneck Technologies

Bottleneck technologies present a low profit impact and a high supply risk. Representative examples of bottleneck technologies seeing increased use within the supply chain industry include the inter-linked Artificial Intelligence (AI) and Machine Leaning (ML) technologies. Used in conjunction with each other, AI – ML allows supply chains to analyse large data sets in order to identify and evolve recognition patterns to evolve business models in use-case specific ways. A demonstrative example of AI – ML in use is their application with Natural Language Processing (NLP) technology. AI – ML – NLP can be used to process large amounts of textual data in order to identify, for instance, the market sentiment surrounding a business more generally, as well as that deriving from business – specific news, for instance the impact a shipping delay had on market perception. This data can then be tied with, for instance, changes in stock price, to ascertain with accuracy the profit impact of inefficiencies across the supply chain, as well as steps which can be taken, based on market sentiment, in order to rectify and improve the public's perception of the supply chain provider. Additionally, AI – ML – NLP can be used to facilitate B2C communications, thereby saving time and labour costs, as well as standardising such communications. As is illustrated by the above, AI – ML technology presents a limited profit impact, primarily due to their technological infancy, as enhanced by a limitation of providers, and thus, falls squarely in the arena of bottleneck technologies. Two providers of enterprise-grade AI and ML technologies include IBM Watson (IBM, 2019b) and Microsoft Azure's ML Studio (Microsoft Azure, 2019b).

### Strategic Technologies

Finally and critically are strategic technologies. These are associated with a high supply risk, owing to a limitation of suppliers, and a high profit impact, as they can significantly enhance business growth and product quality. Strategic technologies present businesses with the option to either develop their own solutions or enter into strategic partnerships in order to take advantage of such technologies. One of the most well-known and widely-used forms of a strategic technology is blockchain technology. Blockchain technology acts as a decentralised and immutable ledger of data records, with the advantages of permissioned data exchange and increasingly, the addition of self-executing smart contracts. Blockchain technology is strategic for supply chain providers as it facilitates the efficient and secure storage and exchange of data, the insurance of data validity and immutability, the capacity to store both transactional and IoT data, and the ability to homogenise otherwise insular data silos to experience real advantages of end-to-end data analysis. Additionally, blockchain technology presents the notable advantage of operating through a decentralised governance structure which provides the capacity for network ownership to be equally and easily distributed amongst the supply chain's stakeholders. This helps ensure the integrity of the blockchain, as well as the provision of an accessible way for stakeholders to share secure data with each other. As a result of the above, blockchain technology presents a major impact on profits. At the same time, supply of blockchain infrastructure at an enterprise-level is severely restricted. While some business chooses to create their own blockchains, most tend to enter into strategic partnerships. Two notable examples of enterprise-level blockchain infrastructure providers include the IBM Blockchain (IBM, 2019c) and r3's Corda Platform (Corda, 2019).

## TECHNOLOGY MATURITY MAP

A useful way to understand the use of the aforementioned technologies is through the use of a Technology Maturity Map (TMM). A TMM provides a visual representation of the extent to which emerging technologies are being applied within the industry. For example, the TMM below (See Figure 2) looks at the incorporation of blockchain technology, across a range of industries, including: shipping and logistics, banking, food supply, automotive and telecommunication.

Among the businesses mentioned, the following have been discussed in Section 1: Accenture, Telefonica, Maqta Gateway and HPE. From these businesses, Telefonica has entered into a strategic partnership with IBM Blockchain, while the rest are developing their own proprietary blockchains, demonstrating the diverging approaches to strategic technologies across industries.

IBM Blockchain is one of the longest established providers of enterprise-level blockchain solutions, with hundreds of its clients reaping the advantages of efficient and secure transactions and information exchange. Partnering with the Official Monetary and Financial Institutions Forum (OMFIF), an independent think tank focused on central banking, economic policy and public investment, the two organisations surveyed 21 central banks between July and September 2017 and found that 8 of them were in the process of conducting trials around a digital central bank currency (OMFIF, 2019). Such a cryptocurrency would be used for intra and interbank transactions, with the report finding that this could lead to improvements in network and transaction efficiency and security, as well as a meaningful

*Figure 2. Technology Maturity Map (TMM) for Blockchain Technology*

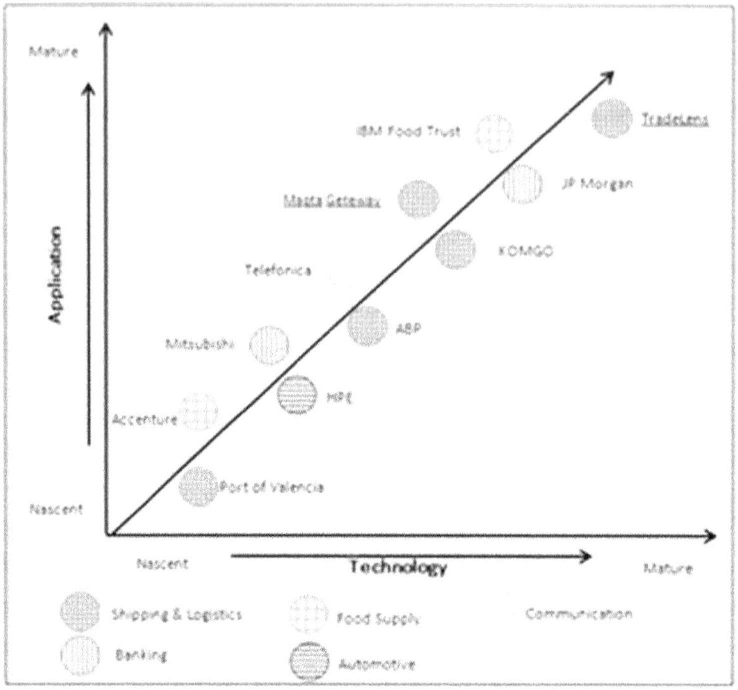


reduction in the cost and complexity associated with existing payment networks. Tethering and stabilising the value of the cryptocurrency to national currencies would eliminate credit risk, increase central banks' control over liquidity and aid transactional efficiency and security.

Understanding the emerging demand for blockchain technology in the banking sector, JP Morgan has been trialling its blockchain payment network dubbed Interbank Information Network (INN) since October 2017 (J.P. Morgan, 2019). During September 2018, JP Morgan announced the expansion of the Network into a live blockchain service, with more than 75 banks signing up to participate in the application of blockchain technology into its services. The Network aims to reduce friction in global payment processing thereby reducing costs. INN provides banks with the advantage of a reduction of in responding to compliance and other data inquiries which result in delays in payment. INN is powered by Quorum, a variant of Ethereum, developed by JP Morgan. The institution believes that INN will significantly reduce inefficiencies in cross-border payments and have published a full list of the 75 banks that have signed up, signalling a major shift in institutional attitudes towards blockchain technology and the advantages of adoption therefrom.

JP Morgan and IBM are not the only institutions seeking to incorporate blockchain technology into the banking sector. To their East, Mitsubishi UFK Financial Group, the largest bank in Japan and the fifth largest in the world as measured by total assets, announced in February 2019; the development of a joint blockchain-based venture with Akamai dubbed the Global Open Network (Mitsubishi, 2019). Mitsubishi shared that the payment network is expected to process over a million transactions per second, as well as the capacity to engage with the IoT, in order to enhance Mitsubishi's global outreach. The Platform is set to launch in the first half of 2020. With the VISA network handling, at most, 24,000 transactions per second, Mitsubishi, as an established retail bank, could significantly alter the global banking landscape (Visa, 2019a).

IBM's influence extends further than just banking and blockchain, and in fact, the IBM Food Trust Platform presents a fully-deployed, enterprise-grade blockchain solution assisting suppliers, wholesalers and retailers with end-to-end food produce tracking across their supply chains (IBM Block Chain, 2019). Launched in October 2018, the Platform seeks to minimise contamination and aid accountability via multi-directional traceability. Organisations that have signed up to the Platform include Carrefour, Kroger, Unilever, Walmart and Nestle. These business help demonstrate one of the models of incorporating blockchain technology as a key strategic technology into existing enterprise infrastructure. With advantages of efficiencies in data entry and exchange, traceability, sustainability and provenance certifications, and real-time demand forecasting, the Platform is revolutionising food supply chains across the world.

In terms of the shipping and logistics industry, KOMGO and Maersk's TradLens are the two global players, with the TradeLens having deployed a fully-functional and increasingly popular shipping platform. Maersk, the world's largest container shipping company operating in 130 countries with approximately 76,000 employees, through a strategic partnership with IBM, has created TradeLens; an entity applying blockchain technology to create a more efficient and secure global trade supply chain (Tradelens, 2019b). As part of the TradeLens early adopter programme, Maersk and IBM announced 94 organisations participating in the platform during October 2018 (IBM News Room, 2018). Since its inception in October 2018, TradeLens has capture over 390 million events, growing by 10 million events per week. Adopters of the TradeLens ecosystem include more than 20 global terminal and port operators, major freight forwarders and over 5 global customs authorities, including ones in Singapore and Australia. TradeLens is the product of a year-long trial. IBM and Maersk trialled dozens of ecosystem partners to identify preventable delays caused by documentation errors and information exchange delays. One example demonstrates that TradeLens can reduce the transit time of a shipment of packaging materials to the USA by 40 percent. TradeLens acts an end-to-end solution for shipping stakeholders across the board. TradeLens uses blockchain technology, including smart contracts, to empower shipping stakeholders to collaborate with each other through a single shared transaction view, with real-time access to shipping data and documents. TradeLens also utilises IoT within its blockchain framework, with sensor data ranging from container weight to temperature statistics. Its trade documentation module, dubbed ClearWay, further enables importers, exporters, customs brokers and government agencies to exchange shipping data backed by a secure and immutable audit trail.

KOMGO demonstrates a less well-developed yet equally promising solution to commodity shipping. Perhaps its comparative infancy may be attributed to the fact that KOMGO seeks to develop its own proprietary blockchain, rather than strategically partnering with IBM as Maersk and many others already have. KOMGO is an initiative seeking to revolutionise commodity trading using blockchain technology. Shareholder include Shell, Koch Supply, Guvnor, Mercuria, Citi, BNP Paribas and others (Komgo, 2019). The goal is to facilitate secure, decentralised and seamless data communication, with a focus on data security and exchange, between commodity trade institutions, corporations, inspection companies and 3rd parties. The network has a focus on end to end optimisation to lower the time and cost needed to manage data, and to enable multiple parties to seamlessly connect with each other.

Finally, in addition to Maqta Gateway, both the Associated British Ports and the Port of Valencia are separately looking into the incorporation of blockchain technology into their ports' operations. Interestingly, all three port providers are seeking to develop their own blockchains, rather than entering into strategic partnerships. The Port of Valencia in Spain, announced on 3rd October 2018, that it would be incorporating blockchain technology within its operations to evolve itself into a smart port (CCN, 2018).

The goal for the Port of Valencia is to use blockchain and cloud technologies to create the strategic option of end-to-end visibility of the logistics chain. Little is currently known as to the means through which this strategic technology will be incorporated into its operations and so it ranks at the lower end of the scale.

Similarly, on 19th September 2018, the Associated British Ports and Marine Transport International announced plans to create Europe's first comprehensive trial programme to examine the incorporation of blockchain technology to enhance cross-port connectivity (ABP, 2019). The partnership is promising given the utility presented by blockchain technology as testable across the Associated British Ports, which handles almost 100 million tonnes of cargo every year, operates 21 ports across the UK and handles 25% of the country's buoyant cargo. Currently, various stakeholders within the operation of ports utilise different systems which do not always communicate with the other efficiently. The aim is to use blockchain technology to deliver "trust, security and speed" across the logistics and shipping industry

Blockchain technology, as a representation of emerging technology, presents significant strategic advantages driving incorporation, both within and outside of the supply chain industry. Almost every enterprise can benefit from the immutability and traceability of blockchain-based data records, and many are also incorporating IoT into their operations, with data being stored and exchanged across blockchains. One of the most telling signs of blockchain technology as a strategic technology is the fact that there are two primary business models for its incorporation: proprietary development and strategic partnership. While proprietary development provides the advantage of longevity and complete ownership, doing so is time, cost and labour intensive. This is evidenced by the visible trend that most enterprises entering into strategic partnerships, primarily with IBM Blockchain, have already launched their operations, while most enterprises seeking to develop their own blockchains are still in their infancy. Time will tell which choice is wiser but for now, blockchain technology remains a key strategic technology which most large players across industries are keen to incorporate into their operations, with IBM Blockchain the most visible and widely-used enterprise-grade provider of the strategic technology.

## CONTEMPORARY APPLICATION OF DIGITAL TECHNOLOGIES

### Big Data

As businesses have evolved, so too has the data they generate. Big Data may be characterised as data which is ever-increasing in its volume, velocity, variety and complexity. Complex data sets emerging from modern data sources produced so much data that traditional storage hardware and processing software are ill-equipped to deliver efficiency. Through technological evolution the cost of data storage and processing has considerably decreased. Big Data is increasingly a source of real value for businesses and the accessibility to affordable data solutions equips businesses with the ability to make ever-precise business decisions.

The characteristics of Big Data are volume, velocity, variety and complexity. Volume refers to the fact that businesses today collect data from an abundance of sources, including transactional information, social media, IoT devices and Machine Learning applications. Velocity is a major factor as data streams in at unprecedented levels and must also be processed in a timely manner to maximise the value contained therein. For instance, RFID geo-tracking information and IoT sensor information can allow for predictive maintenance across supply chains but only if acted upon in a prompt manner. Variety in the context of Big Data, as distinct from volume and velocity, refers to the notion that data is collected in a variety of formats. These include unstructured data in the forms of financial data, maintenance logs and text documents, as well as the more traditional structured data sets such as numerical information housed within spreadsheets. Crucially, Big Data is complex due to the diversity of its sources and the combination of significant and inconsistent levels of volume, velocity and variety. As a consequence, Big Data must be linked, cleansed and standardised in order to correlate relationships to then take complete advantage of the value analytics can provide.

To cater to the need for businesses to efficiently store, process and analyse Big Data, a variety of enterprise-level solution providers have emerged. The bulk of these providers rely on open-source solutions, primarily the Apache Hadoop (Apache Hadoop, 2019) and its successor, the Apache Spark (Apache Spark, 2019), and the advantages these providers offer are unified platforms combining Big Data processing with cloud storage options and analytics' visualisation. Additionally, the prevalence of Big Data has significantly contributed to the uptick in reliance on Cloud Computing technology; storing and processing data across the cloud rather than on and through localised infrastructure is cost and labour efficient. In addition to the providers mentioned in Section 2, Oracle's Big Data Platform (OBDP) is a representative example of what the industry has to offer (Oracle, 2019a). OBDP assists with Big Data integration, management and analysis, and includes the functionality of cloud storage and the capacity to build models using ML and AI. Platforms like OBDP can assist businesses with product development, improving their customer experience, prevention of fraud, facilitation of timely compliance and the maximisation of operational efficiency (Oracle, 2019b)

## Blockchain

Blockchain technology is a form of Distributed Ledger Technology (DLT), wherein cryptographically linked data records are stored across distributed / decentralised infrastructure, often referred to as a Blockchain. Blockchain technology may be best understood through five lenses: data storage, data integrity, data transparency and exchange, decentralised / distributed governance and flexibility of operation.

Blockchain technology involves packaging data, transactional or otherwise (for instance, data from IoT sensors), into sets ("blocks") of data, which are then cryptographically computed to ensure their validity before being uploaded onto a distributed ledger of data records ("blockchain"). In its data storage capacity, blockchain is a prime solution to issues in Big Data management and can operate both through localised infrastructure, where enterprises construct their own blockchains, and cloud computing infrastructure, where blockchain providers, for instance IBM Blockchain or Ethereum are utilised.

Blockchain technology is increasingly useful because it maintains the immutability and integrity of data records and ensures their digital accessibility. Immutability of data records is intrinsic to Blockchains as it ensures freedom from tampering and fraud. This is incredibly useful for businesses involved in the supply chain sector given the large swarths of data accumulated. Data integrity and immutability is ensured through Proofs. Currently, there are two main Proof mechanisms – Proof of Work and Proof of Stake. The key difference between the two is that Proof of Work relies on computational power, while the latter allots an arbitrary computing power based on the amount of internal currency placed into escrow for the same purpose. Across cryptocurrencies, both Proof of Stake and Proof of Work participants are rewarded in a similar fashion – a percentage fee is awarded to the entity that successfully solves a cryptographic problem, either directly in the case of Proof of Work, or indirectly in the case of Proof of

Stake. Increasingly, Proof of Stake is a popular option, especially for enterprises such as those involved in the supply chain sector, which are looking to utilise blockchain technology for operational efficiency, rather than to generate revenue from distributing network ownership to the public.

Data transparency and exchange derive from the fact that data stored across a blockchain is immutable and tamper-free. Due to the fact that data records are digitalised prior to being uploaded onto the blockchain, data exchange is fluid. Additionally, blockchains allowed for permissioned access. What this means is that data stored on a blockchain can be as public or private as the entity utilising the blockchain wills. This can be useful where it would be of use to provide public access to the blockchain, for instance on a transaction-specific permissioned basis for customers in order to allow them complete transparency as to their orders.

Data transparency and exchange are meaningfully linked with the decentralised governance aspect of blockchain technology. The entity utilising the blockchain can decide whether it wants to retain complete control over the blockchain, or whether it might want to allow the public or business partners to own a stake of the network. The utility in decentralised infrastructure in this context is that there is a separation between data storage and network governance, which adds to the data transparency aspect. Additionally, as is the case with most supply chain providers entering into strategic partnerships which blockchain providers, a certain stake of network ownership is allotted to partners, with the rest being retained by the business.

Blockchain technology is flexible in its operation. Blockchains may be characterised by a high Transaction Per Second (TPS) count. For instance, Quark Chain provides existing Blockchain infrastructure with a stable 1 million TPS (QuarkChain, 2019). High TPS counts associated with Blockchain technology present a major advantage over existing retail infrastructure, with very few if any data providers crossing the 50,000 TPS count. For reference, the Visa network, at its best, is capable of managing 24,000 TPS (Visa, 2019b). In addition to this, Smart Contracts are increasingly a centrepiece within the Blockchain landscape. Smart Contracts are digital contracts which self-execute when certain conditions are met. They create significant advantages for commercial entities contracting with each other in terms of transactional efficiency and legal cost savings. ChainLink is taking this one step further by connecting Smart Contract technology with real world data, events and payments, rather than just events occurring on the Blockchain (ChainLink, 2019). Significantly, Blockchains do not solely house transactional data, and increasingly data from IoT sensors is being stored on them. VeChain utilises IoT devices to track metrics end-to-end in the cold-chain logistics industry, thereby increasing transparency, regulation, security and reliability within logistics operations (VeChain, 2019).

## Artificial Intelligence and Machine Learning

Artificial Intelligence (AI) refers to the process of training systems to think and react as a human would with the added efficiency of a computational device. Several applications have emerged from, most notably Natural Language Processing (NLP) and Machine Leaning (ML). ML involves providing systems with the ability to identify patterns and inferences from data, without explicit programming, in a self-evolutionary process. ML is useful as it does not require the provision of pre-defined data sets. NLP refers to the practice of computationally training systems to process and analyse natural language and speech data. It provides the meaningful utility of Sentiment Analysis. Neural Networks involve linking discrete AI and their applications together to enable Deep Learning from observational data. AI and its various applications have considerable utility within the supply chain sector, however few organisations are making use of the full capacity the technology has to offer.

Enabling AI to behave like a human requires provision of data. At its most basic level AI utilises pre-defined cause and effect relationships in order to do so. For instance, a common approach to NLP is the Lexicon Sentiment Approach, which involves the use of discrete sets of vocabulary to identify the semantic value of a piece of text. A representative example of the data sets available to facilitate the Lexicon Sentiment Approach is the Loughran – McDonald financial sentiment dictionary (SRAF, 2019). Such specialised word dictionaries are used to generate sentiment scores for textual data. Sentiment analysis deriving from NLP involves 4 main stages: the decomposition of raw text to remove stop words (such as "a", "but" and "how"), the use of Lemmatization techniques to covert different inflections of words for uniformity (e.g. "sleeping" and "slept" become "sleep"), the extraction of the associated score from the sentiment dictionary, and lastly, a sentiment score is created for each piece of textual data by taking an average of all individual word scores. NLP-based Sentiment Analysis is useful because it allows organisations to computationally calculate the market's sentiment towards them and has applications in analysis both news and social media data.

Machine Learning take AI's functionality even further. Using ML, unclassified data can be fed to an algorithm to enable the inference of functions to describe patterns and structure within the data. This is incredibly useful where there are large volumes of unclassified data to be analysed, for instance a backlog of transactional or IoT sensor data. ML can help identify areas for improvement by ascertaining otherwise undetected patterns. ML can also be used to enhance NLP by assisting with filtering and clustering relevant textual data, creating associations between seemingly unrelated news and the central entity, analysing and interpreting data for otherwise undetected contextual word associations, interpreting the impact of the data and mining historical data to refine pattern recognition capabilities.

Present industry leaders in the enterprise-level provision of AI functionality include Accenture's Applied Intelligence (Accenture, 2019a), IBM's Watson (IBM, 2019b) and Microsoft Azure's Machine Leaning Studio (Microsoft Azure, 2019b). AI presents a range of utilities making it a useful technology to adopt within the supply chain sector. These include applications in: customer service, contract governance, pattern recognition and the aforementioned sentiment analysis. AI can be used to conduct standardised, conversational customer interaction. This can help create scalable and reliable automated consistency within customer service, thereby generating time and cost savings. Further, AI, particularly ML, can be used to better compare, review and optimise contracts by training algorithms across a large volume of contractual data. Pattern recognition can help maximise value per customer by identifying and targeting services to buyers based on their usage habits, as well as streamlining marketing based on observable efficacy. In terms of supply chains, Accenture's Intelligent Supply Chain has reportedly helped realise $40M in benefits, representing the tip of the iceberg, given that there is significant utility in unlocking, processing and utilising unstructured data to automate to predict user needs, and the automation of flagging and resolving disruptions across the supply chain in real-time to save costs and business reputation (Accenture, 2019b).

## Data Analytics

Data Analytics (DA) is the science of processing and analysing raw data to infer conclusions from that data. Historically, DA were conducted manually, however the development of modern processes and algorithms has led to the optimised automation of such analytics. This is useful as it allows for the identification of patterns and statistics which would otherwise be lost in the bulk of data collected by organisations today. DA is also useful given the amount of time and consequent labour costs organisations would incur in having to manually sift through raw data. Data Analytics can help optimise business models in order to increase operational efficiency in a variety of ways and is of considerable advantage in the supply chain industry.

Broadly, Data Analytics involves six key steps (Oracle, 2019c). Firstly, the business must decide upon its end goals to be facilitated by data collection and analytics. Next, the business must identify the steps that can be taken to achieve these goals as without the existence of avenues for improvement, DA will not yield meaningful results. Thirdly, data must be collected, and often from a variety of sources including transactional data, consumer interactions with web pages and IoT sensors data. The data must then be cleaned for grammatical mistakes and to deal with missing information. This step is often automated and is necessary to prevent inaccurate conclusions. Once cleaned, the data must then be modelled by data analysts to correlate with the end goals to be achieved. This step is crucial as it involves linking DA with the business's tangible reality. Finally, the DA chain must be optimised and repeated, incorporating the results ascertained and further refining the process in order to witness the realisation of the idealised end goals.

In addition to these six steps, DA can take four primary forms: Descriptive, Diagnostic, Predictive and Prescriptive. Descriptive DA which provides an illustration of the data analysed. This can take the form of Key Performance Indicator dashboards and revenue reports. Diagnostic DA involves understanding problems arising in operations and can involve the exploration of themes such as delays within certain geographical zones. Predictive DA seeks to identify potential occurrences prior to their realisation and can be used for risk assessment and sales forecasting purposes. Finally, Prescriptive DA involves the ascertainment of more informed decision-making pathways and is where AI is used most frequently.

The use of DA presents significant advantages in the sphere of logistics and supply chain management (McKinsey & Company, 2016). In terms of sourcing, Predictive DA can be used to model costs and quantify benefits. In terms of production, Predictive DA can be used to optimise fault tolerances, as well as lot scheduling. For warehousing, Prescriptive DA can be used for efficient and dynamic warehouse spacing, stock location and worker allocation. In terms of transportation, Predictive and Prescriptive DA can be used for efficient routing. Additionally, Diagnostic and Predictive DA can be used to detect and prevent stock shortages, and in terms of consumer interaction, Diagnostic and Prescriptive DA can be used to detect and prevent fraudulent behaviour. In its totality, DA can equip supply chain providers with the enhanced capabilities of effective consumer need prediction, identification and resolution of supply chain inefficiencies, improvements towards reaction timing and traceability of goods.

## COMPLIANCE FRAMEWORK FOR THE GOVERNANCE OF DIGITAL TECHNOLOGIES

Regulatory compliance is essential to commercial certainty and consumer confidence. Legal systems across the world are developing novel ways of tackling emerging technologies, particularly the use of data and Blockchain technology. As supply chain providers begin to adopt these technologies into their operations, it is essential that they understand the regulatory environment they are entering into.

Most regulation relating to Blockchain relates to the use of security tokens. Cryptocurrencies sometimes use Initial Coin Offerings (ICOs) to raise capital. In an ICO, fiat currency (e.g. the British Pound) is exchanged for a token which is then converted into a cryptocurrency once the project Is fully developed. While this acts as a useful way to raise capital for projects innovating in an emerging technological sector, the lack of regulation has meant that some projects have not fulfilled their guarantees and investors have lost the money they had invested. As a result, tokens which are used to develop Blockchain projects are characterised as security tokens and fall under Securities' Regulations in most legal jurisdictions. Supply chain providers adopting Blockchain technology into their operations need not worry about classification of their internal cryptocurrencies as security tokens as these are not collateralising project development nor are they being offered to the public for investment purposes.

Similarly, Big Data, Data Analytics and Artificial Intelligence engage data protection regulations. Across the world there is an emerging trend towards data privacy and ownership, as is made clear by the recent European General Data Protection Regulation (GDPR), whereby users must opt into data collection for purposes other than those necessary for business operation. Further, under the European GDPR users can request copies and deletion of the data businesses collect on them. As supply chain providers seeks to take advantage of Big Data through Artificial Intelligence and Data Analytics, it is crucial that they employ substantial data protection policies to comply with the regulations applicable to them. As a matter of best practice, this can involve having a robust opt-in policy to ensure that users make a positive action of providing businesses with their data, as well as the functionality of efficiently removing user data from their processes in the case of users requesting the deletion of their data.

Owing to the evolving regulatory landscape governing data and blockchain technology, organisations have come to the forefront offering novel solutions and benefits of massive legal economies of scale. These include IBM Blockchain (IBM, 2019c) and r3's Corda (Corda, 2019) which provide legally compliant blockchain technology for supply chain providers and others to integrate into their operations. Furthermore, blockchain projects and cryptocurrencies have also developed enterprise-ready and legally-compliant solutions to bolster adoption. A notable example is Unbright, a German company creating a unified framework for DLT-based business integration (Unibright, 2019). The project has significant utility for supply chain providers wishing to incorporate DLT within its systems. Unibright primarily offers a visual workflow designer and a contract lifecycle manager to allow users to craft powerful DLT-based solutions and implement them through self-enforcing and reliable Smart Contracts. Use cases currently include multi-party approval for communications with suppliers, batch tracing from origin to end-consumer, asset lifecycle records, shipping process monitoring via ERP Systems and milestone-based project payment when the pre-defined conditions have been met.

## CONCLUSION

This chapter focuses on the impact of supply chain digitalisation on a connected global market. The first section focuses on the dynamic consumer requirements and preferences. The second section appraised the segmentation and mapping of digital technologies. The third section examines the contemporary application of digital technologies including: big data, blockchains, artificial intelligence, machine learning, and data analytics. The final section analysis the rules and regulations the form the basis of a contemporary framework for the governance of digital technologies.

## REFERENCES

ABP. (2019). *Early Adopter Programme*. Available at: https://www.abports.co.uk

Accenture. (2019a). *There's AI. And then there's Applied Intelligence*. Available at: https://www.accenture.com/gb-en/services/applied-intelligence-index

Accenture. (2019b). *Intelligent Supply Chain*. Available at: https://www.accenture.com/gb-en/services/applied-intelligence-index

Accenture. (2019c). *Accenture's New Blockchain App Lets Users Tip 'Sustainable' Producers*. Available at: https://www.coindesk.com/accentures-new-blockchain-app-lets-users-tip-

Amazon. (2019a). *What is cloud computing?* Available at: https://aws.amazon.com/what-is-cloud-computing/

Amazon. (2019b). *Open Distro for Elasticsearch?* Available at: https://aws.amazon.com/

Apache Hadoop. (2019). *The Apache™ Hadoop® project develops open-source software for reliable, scalable, distributed computing*. Available at https://hadoop.apache.org/

Apache Spark. (2019). *Apache Spark™ is a unified analytics engine for large-scale data processing*. Available at https://spark.apache.org/

Arlo. (2019). *Arlo Ultra: Enjoy total peace of mind with the ultimate home security camera*. Available at: https://www.arlo.com/uk/default.aspx

CCN. (2018). *Spanish Coastal City Valencia to Create a Smart Port with Blockchain Tech*. Available at: https://www.ccn.com/spanish-coastal-city-valencia-to-create-a-smart-port-with-blockchain-tech/

ChainLink. (2019). *Your smart contracts connected to real world data, events and payments*. Available at: https://chain.link/

Corda. (2019). *Corda Enterprise – A Next-gen Blockchain Platform*. Available at: https://www.r3.com/platform/

EU GDPR. (2019). *The EU General Data Protection Regulation (GDPR) is the most important change in data privacy regulation in 20 year*. Available at: https://eugdpr.org/

IBM. (2019a). *IBM Cloud is the cloud for smarter business*. Available at: https://www.ibm.com/cloud

IBM. (2019b). *Watson Discovery: A leader in AI Search*. Available at: https://www.ibm.com/watson

IBM. (2019c). *IBM Blockchain: Now Delivering Value around the World*. Available at: https://www.ibm.com/uk-en/blockchain

IBM Block Chain. (2019). *IBM Food Trust: A new era for the world's food supply*. Available at: https://www.ibm.com/blockchain/solutions/food-trust

IBM News Room. (2018). *Maersk and IBM Introduce TradeLens Blockchain Shipping Solution*. Available at: https://newsroom.ibm.com/2018-08-09-Maersk-and-IBM-Introduce-TradeLens-Blockchain-Shipping-Solution

Intel. (2019). *Integrating IoT Sensor Technology into the Enterprise.* Available at: https://www.intel.com/content/www/us/en/it-management/intel-it-best-practices/integrating-iot-sensor-technology-into-the-enterprise-paper.html

J. P. Morgan. (2019). *J.P. Morgan Interbank Information NetworkSM Expands to More Than 75 Banks.* Available at: https://www.jpmorgan.com/country/GB/en/detail/1320570135560

Komgo. (2019). *Komgo's digital network is a blockchain-based solution for data security and exchange in commodity trade.* Available at https://komgo.io/

Kraljic, P. (1983). Purchasing Must Become Supply Management. *Harvard Business Review.* Available at: https://hbr.org/1983/09/purchasing-must-become-supply-management

Maqta Gateway. (2019). *Digitalising Trade.* Available at: https://www.maqta.ae/

McKinsey & Company. (2016). *Big data and the supply chain: The big-supply-chain analytics landscape (Part 1).* Available at: https://www.mckinsey.com/business-functions/operations/our-insights/big-data-and-the-supply-chain-the-big-supply-chain-analytics-landscape-part-1

Microsoft Azure. (2019a). *Build your next great idea in the cloud with an Azure free account.* Available at: https://azure.microsoft.com/en-gb/free/cloud-services/

Microsoft Azure. (2019b). *Machine Learning Studio: Simple, scalable, cutting edge.* Available at: https://azure.microsoft.com/en-us/services/machine-learning-studio/

Mitsubishi. (2019). *MUFG and Akamai to launch Global Open Network, Inc. joint venture.* Available at: https://www.mufg.jp/english/vcms_lf/news/pressrelease-20190212-001-e.pdf

OMFIF. (2019). *Central Bank Digital Currencies.* Available at: https://thinktank.omfif.org/ibm

Oracle. (2019a). *22 Big Data Use Cases for the Modern Business.* Available at https://www.oracle.com/uk/big-data/

Oracle. (2019b). *What is big data?* Available at https://www.oracle.com/uk/big-data/guide/what-is-big-data.html

Oracle. (2019c). *Big Ideas.* Available at http://www.oracle.com/us/corporate/profit/big-ideas/index.html

Packard, H. (2019). *Hewlett Packard Enterprise and Continental launch blockchain-based data monetization platform.* Available at: https://www.hpe.com/us/en/newsroom/press-release/2019/02/hewlett-packard-enterprise-and-continental-launch-blockchain-based-data-monetization-platform.html

QuarkChain. (2019). *QuarkChain Resources: Get the latest on QuarkChain and the market.* Available at https://quarkchain.io/

Samsara. (2019). *Centralized, Wireless Refrigeration and Environmental Monitoring.* Available at: https://www.samsara.com/uk/industrial/cold-chain

SRAF. (2019). *Software Repository for Accounting and Finance.* Available at: https://sraf.nd.edu/textual-analysis/resources/#Master%20Dictionary

Telefonica. (2019). *Telefónica and IBM Collaborate to Apply Blockchain to Streamline Telco Processes*. Available at: https://www.telefonica.com/en/web/press-office/-/telefonica-and-ibm-collaborate-to-apply-blockchain-to-streamline-telco-processes

Tradelens. (2019a). *Digitalising the Global Supply Chain*. Available at: https://www.tradelens.com/

Tradelens. (2019b). *Early Adopter Programme*. Available at: https://www.tradelens.com/

Unibright. (2019). *The Unified Framework for Blockchain Based Business Integration*. Available at: https://unibright.io/

VeChain. (2019). *VeChainThor: The public blockchain that derives its value from activities created by members within the ecosystem solving real world economic problems*. Available at: https://www.vechain.org/

Vie Publique. (2019). *The Directorate of Legal and Administrative Information*. Available at: http://discours.vie-publique.fr/notices/197000414.html

Visa. (2019a). *Central Bank Digital Currencies*. Available at: https://usa.visa.com/run-your-business/small-business-tools/retail.html

Visa. (2019b). *Small Business Tools*. Available at: https://usa.visa.com/run-your-business/small-business-tools/retail.html

# Chapter 10
# Integrating Big Data Analytics Into Retail Services Marketing Management:
## The Case of a Large Shopping Center in London, UK

**Eleonora Pantano**
*University of Bristol, UK*

**Simona Giglio**
https://orcid.org/0000-0001-5386-234X
*University of Calabria, Italy*

**Charles Dennis**
*Middlesex University, London, UK*

## ABSTRACT

*This chapter aims at exploring the extent to which the recent trends in digitalization of marketing and related services are leading to a massive amount of consumers' information (big data) in order to suggest possible solutions and recommendations. To this end, the chapter will focus on the case of a large shopping center in London (UK) as meaningful example of how retailers might exploit big data analytics such as sentiment and image analytics to get useful consumers' insights to be successfully integrated into marketing strategies. Finally, the chapter discusses the implications for scholars and practitioners and proposes a future research agenda.*

DOI: 10.4018/978-1-7998-0131-3.ch010

## INTRODUCTION

Automation is increasingly becoming of fundamental importance in marketing and, more generally, in the service domain (Rust and Huang, 2014). The actual trend characterizing marketing management is to integrate more the technology in marketing activities to provide higher customized services, which involves the learning process of consumers' preferences and behavior and according responses (Grewal, Roggeveen, and Nordfält, 2017; Huang and Rust, 2017). For instance, in increasing diffusion of self-service technologies, robotic services or collaborative filtering allow the improvement of the efficiency of traditionally standardized activities that fulfil a given set of customer needs. Indeed, relational technologies, such as learning technologies and Artificial Intelligence (AI) are able to adaptively interact with customers (Huang and Rust, 2018). Thus, how marketing managers and retailers might use these technologies to collect and manage big data on consumers and adjust management strategies accordingly is emerging as a powerful line of inquiry (Bradlow et al., 2017; Pantano, Priporas, & Stylos, 2017; Balducci and Marinova, 2018; Hartman et al., 2019), with emphasis on their effect on store and customer-level strategies that will be more affected by technological forecasting and the emergence of big data (Kumar Anand, and Song, 2017). Indeed, the understanding of customers and markets that data generate supports effective decision-making in relation to all aspects of the marketing intelligence (Janssen, van der Voort, Wahyudi, 2017). They are of particular value in relation to segmentation and targeting as they allow marketing programmes to be personalized and support the maximisation of a consumer's life time value to an organisation. The growth of Data Science lead by the massive amount of unstructured data (including "big data") is seen as one of the most influential factors in contemporary marketing (Balducci and Marinova, 2018). Therefore, there is much interest in big data and how to successfully analyse it to gain competitive advantage. In other words, how to explore big data to get real-world business results and transfer them into successful strategies is becoming an important asset for today's marketing research and practice. To this end, new metrics to analyze this data are encouraged by recent studies (Ailawadi and Farris, 2017; Bradlow et al., 2017; Dindar and Yaman, 2018; Balducci and Marinova, 2018; Hartman et al., 2019; Pantano, Giglio and Dennis, in print.).

The aim of this chapter is to show how it is possible to transfer big data analytics into marketing management, in order to figure out both the extent to which these findings impact traditional marketing strategies and the opportunities emerging from the integration into marketing practice. To this end, the research reported in this chapter refers to the biggest Shopping Center in London: *Westfield London*, and data collected from two different social media, Twitter (for text) and Instagram (for images). The data are analysed through Wolfram Mathematica software for sentiment analytics for tweets analysis, and image analytics for pictures evaluation.

The chapter is structured in three main parts: (i) the background to recent innovation and technology in digital marketing, the emerging topic of big data in marketing intelligence and related issues and controversies, (ii) proposed solutions consisting of two new methodologies for big data analytics, and (iii) implications for marketers and scholars, and the future research agenda.

### Background: Recent Innovation And Technology In Digital Marketing

Innovation is widely considered to be the primary strategy for fostering organization growth (Cefis and Marsili, 2006; Volberda et al., 2013; Pantano et al., 2017), and retailers need to innovate to maintain their competitive advantage. However, the ability to implement successful the innovation processes relies on companies' abilities to change organizational forms, practices and strategies to leverage technological change (Volderba et al., 2013). The innovations introduced in retail settings are manifold, ranging from ad hoc mobile apps to the chips for contactless payments inserted in the credit card (with new credit card readers), to interactive displays and storefronts, and so on (Pantano et al., 2017; Pantano and Vannucci, 2019).

The intersection of retailing and innovation represents a fruitful research topic as the possibility to integrate new and more efficient digital technologies (digitalization) can be seen as an enabler fostering new models of retailing (Evanschitzky et al., 2015; Hagberg et al., 2016; Papagiannidis et al., 2017; Von Briel, 2018; Willems et al., 2017). Specifically, the phenomenon of digitalization is one of the most important transformations currently characterizing retailing (Hagberg, Sundstrom and Egels-Zandén, 2016; Pantano, Priporas, Dennis, 2018; Willems et al., 2017; Pantano and Vannucci, 2019). Indeed, this phenomenon is dramatically modifying business opportunities, business models, purchasing processes and traditional selling activities. Further, the diffusion of digital technologies leads to both new forms of consumption associated by the use of these digital technologies, and new services and interactions modalities between consumers and retailers (Hagberg, Sundstrom and Egels-Zandén, 2016).

Thus, the evolution of digital technology further triggers a dramatic transformation of retailers and of the competitive scenario where they perform (Willems et al., 2017). Factors triggering this change in retail settings include (i) the continuous technology push resulting in new efficient technology to support retail management at different level (Demirkan and Spohrer, 2014; Pantano et al., 2017; Williams et al., 2017), (ii) consumer demand for new shopping experiences (Evanschitzky et al., 2015; Roy et al., 2017), and (iii) competitors' pioneering innovation strategies (Pantano, Giglio, Dennis, in print). As a consequence, these elements also increase the complexity of the competitive marketplace.

Past studies agree that introducing digital technologies improves retail service quality from both consumers' and retailers' perspectives (Demirkan and Spohrer, 2014; Evanschitzky et al., 2015; Inamn and Nikolova, 2017). Other authors investigate the introduction of interactive technologies even in storefront windows to catch pedestrian attention and positively influence the entry decision (Pantano, 2016). Indeed, several authors suggest creating exciting and engaging in-store experiences, with emphasis on atmospherics, to realise the advantages of online and mobile channels (Shankar et al., 2011; Roy et al., 2017). Particular in-store digital technologies might include digital signage (Dennis et al., 2014; Roggeveen et al., 2016), ad hoc mobile apps (Chou, Chuang and Shao, 2016; Dacko, 2017; Wang et al., 2015), humanoid shopping assistants (Bertacchini, Bilotta and Pantano, 2017), and so on. In the emerging scenario, bricks-and-mortar retailers continuously face the challenges of dealing with new technologies, which also encourage the trend towards an omnichannel retail marketplace, which result into the successful combination of online, offline and mobile channels (Bell, Gallino and Moreno, 2018; Ieva and Ziliani, 2018; Razaei and Valaei, 2017). The aim of innovating in retail settings is to provide consumers with access to additional information on products to support them in finding, comparing, locating and buying goods, while enhancing their shopping experiences with new and efficient services. For instance, Zara introduced in late 2017 in few selected stores in London (UK) self-service cash desks directly in the fitting room area, to provide consumers with the possibility of immediately buying the products that they just tried (removing the alarm, paying by card and taking the bag), avoiding the traditional queue at the cashier in the payment area. Thus, digitalization of marketing and retailing is turning consumers into omnichannel customers who use digital (including mobile) and physical channels in the different stages of purchase behavior (Blom, Lange and Hess, 2017).

## BIG DATA AND MARKETING INTELLIGENCE

### Issues, Controversies, Problems

Over the last few years, the massive use of digital devices and the social media by users has led to the creation of millions of new data generated daily. Such data is called big data, defined as the growth and the simultaneous diffusion of huge amount of structured (text fields such as name and phone number) and unstructured (e.g. video, images, gestures, etc.) data in sizes that exceed the capacity of traditional tools to manage them satisfactorily (Chen & Zhang, 2014). For instance, the increasing use of voice systems for shopping (i.e. Amazon Echo) generates sonic (unstructured) data that companies should be able to analyse in order to understand consumers' shopping behavior in more depth.

In contrast with structured data, unstructured data are not in a predefined structure, thus are difficult to classify in a relational database. Nevertheless, big data enables enhanced decision making and process optimization (Siddiqa et al., 2016), and its analysis is applied successfully in different fields including marketing (Giglio et al., 2019; Dindar and Yaman, 2018; Bradlow et al., 2017; Balducci and Marinova, 2018; Pantano, Giglio, and Dennis, *in press*).

These data are characterized by the four "Vs": volume (the large quantity of data arising from digital technologies), velocity (the high-frequency of data), variety (types of data) and veracity (reliability and validity). A further "V" can be added to describe the value of data (Wedel and Kannan, 2016; Bradlow et al. 2017). This value can synthetize the opportunities and possibilities arising from big data in retailing. Such data in conjunction with analytical techniques for data acquisition might provide retailers with customer insights (Baxendale, Mcdonald and Wilson, 2015; Germann et al. 2014). While, big data analytics is the process of analysis of a massive amount of data in order to reveal hidden patterns, market trends, consumers' preferences and other business information useful to help companies to get the more accurate findings and to optimize business processes (Verma et al., 2016). For instance, Pantano and Dennis (*in print*) recently demonstrated to what extent the store building is a tourists' attraction through the analysis of tourists' photographs posted online (in Flickr) related to a luxury department store. In particular, they used machine learning algorithms to identify the geographical position of the department store, find the clusters and compare with the other attractions photographed in the same area.

Currently, companies might apply big data analytics in order to achieve better quality information regarding products and customer satisfaction (Zhao, Xu, and Wang, 2019), understanding customers' needs and preferences (Pantano, Giglio, Dennis, in print), making more detailed predictions on trends (Pantano, Priporas, Stylos, 2017), and so on. However, companies are still new to exploiting the true potential of big data that includes data originated from heterogeneous data sources (public and private) as well as the lack of organized data (Srinivasan & Swink, 2017; McAfee et al., 2012). Obstacles to big data analytics come from the lack of tools optimized for handling and processing unstructured data; software needed for these tasks are usually ad-hoc solutions that are not scalable (Sivarajah et al., 2017). Indeed, storing and retrieving this kind of data is extremely costly since it requires Petabytes of storage and cloud clustering unit processing. Furthermore, the number of highly skilled specialists trained for big data analysis is an issue as many firms are investing in the education and training of their employees yet, and the effects of training are unsatisfactory (Deng and Cao, 2018). In the context of marketing intelligence with new big data analytical tools, marketers might collect and analyse data to achieve insights on customer attitudes and preferences to transform the data into information for supporting marketing decisions. However, in the new big data scenario marketers face more challenges, such as understanding how to effectively transform data into useful insights, such as specific information on consumers preferences and needs (Fan et al., 2015). Thus, marketers need to: (i) mine consumers' generated contents (listening to what consumers say) and (ii) use these contents for forecasting (Balducci and Marinova, 2018).

Furthermore, since the amount of data and sources generating big data technology evolve continuously and formats and qualities of data will continue to grow and be digitized, the key for successful innovation in marketing intelligence is to invest in big data infrastructure including data scientists and big data platforms. For example, companies might solve these problems by developing and organizing the marketing analytical function within their organization or access third-party services, such as Google Cloud in order to acquire new knowledge and extract potential value from big data. For instance, Ocado (one of the largest UK online-grocery retailers) emerges as a clear example of how retailers started exploiting the opportunities offered by the analysis of large volumes of data. The company launched the Ocado Smart Platform as new hardware and software to host a shopping experience for large third-party retailers to sell online. Processing thousands of orders every day and generating thousands of data, Ocado considered Google the best partner to host the huge amount of data to be managed. The platform supports moving the data in the cloud while enabling Ocado managers to apply advanced data-driven analytics, which further supports business decisions and informs the supply chain in inventory control, logistics efficiency and demand prediction. Accordingly, Ocado uses the Google Cloud Platform (Google App Engine, Google Cloud Storage, Google Cloud Dataflow, Google Storage Nearline, Google BigQuery, Google Compute Engine, Google Container Engine) in online food retailing and uses big data (the large volume of data available online with high computing performances to be stored, accessed and managed) analytics and cloud storage to deliver groceries direct to the consumer, exploiting an amount of data available on consumers' profiles (including past orders and trends). However, one of the key concerns for companies is related to privacy and security data due to real-time production and complexity.

## SOLUTIONS AND RECOMMENDATIONS

London is considered to be one of the main capitals in the world for shopping (Centre for Retail Research, 2011; Morton and Redman, 2016), acquiring the attention of scientific research in consumer behaviour (Nobbs, Moore and Sheridan, 2012; Pantano and Vannucci). In this study we consider Westfield shopping center located in Shepherd's Bush in London (UK), containing 404 different stores (from fast fashion like H&M to luxury like Armani, from clothing to accessories, food, and so on). On TripAdvisor (the specialized platform for tourism information generated by tourists), it is considered to be one of the top destinations for shopping in the city and ranked at 213 in the list of things to do (out of 2,074). Moreover, shopping centers have been considered to be a hot topic for retail and retail planning literature for decades (Wrigley et al., 2019; Teller and Elms, 2010; Blut, Teller and Floh, 2018; Dennis, 2005; Dennis et al., 2002; Timmermans, 1982; Finn and Louviere, 1996; Merrilees and Miller, 2019; Calvo-Porral and Levy-Mangin, 2018).

The following paragraphs provide two examples of big data analytics and how the collected data can be transformed into consumers insights. The first relates to sentiment analysis as the systematic identification of the sentiments embraced in posts that consumers upload online (using Twitter as an example). The second concerns image analytics.

## Sentiment Analytics

Sentiment analytics is a process addressing the meaning of the words and the emotion behind the words (Pantano, Giglio, Dennis, in press.). It is becoming a popular method to mine consumers' opinions shared online, which requires systematic, automated procedures (Xu et al., 2011; Pantano, Giglio, and Dennis, in press). The aim of this analysis is to classify the polarity of a text determining if it is positive, negative or neutral. This kind of analysis allows computation of sentiment scores for each text (tweets), which can be used to quantify the positivity and emotional intensity with which people talk about a certain brand, product, service (Walasek et al., 2018), and shopping center as in the present research.

The first analysis concerns the collection of the tweets related to the *Westfield London* shopping center, posted in October 2018 by users, in a total quantity of 1,400 tweets. The tweets have been collected using Wolfram Mathematica software, a tool for computing, simulation, and mathematical modeling. To download the tweets we used the *ServiceConnect* module available in Wolfram Mathematica indicating the name of the shopping center as a hashtag - #westfieldlondon - (Figure 1) and connecting to Twitter.

Wolfram Mathematica generates a database with the full text of the tweet and other meta-data such as user ID, date of publication, language, etc. (Figure 2).

After collecting tweets, the software facilitates the sentiment analysis with the module *Classify* in order to recognise the emotions and opinions of the users in their experience in the shopping centre.

The *Classify* module is based on Machine Learning algorithms that are a relevant tool in our study. Machine learning algorithms are a set of tools for classifying a large amount of data that can predict different dynamics in several areas of interest. In particular, they involve several methods and tools such as object representation, optimization processes (Bayesian theorem), and neural networks. These tools aim to reduce the complexity of the data while searching for hidden patterns. To this end, these algorithms perform a basic cognitive function similar to the development of human cognition as the learning through experience. In other words, starting from the identification of a certain "law" on the scattered data, these algorithms create categories, similarly to the evolutionary processes occurring in childhood for the development of conceptual categories. This process allows the learning system to recognize the input data belonging to a certain category.

*Classify* is a pre-trained model. The training process uses a large dataset that makes the machine learn how to identify a different object or extrapolate a particular function between the data. This process is complete only when the algorithm achieves a good level of performance. In this case, the process aims at labelling each tweet into three categories: positive, neutral and negative. The *Classify* module uses the "Sentiment" built-in classifier (machine learning algorithm) to infer the sentiment of a certain tweet. Thus, the software systematically classifies each tweet under a positive, negative or neutral label, cor-

*Figure 1. Part of code used by Wolfram Mathematica software to collect the tweets*

```
twitter = ServiceConnect ["Twitter", "New"]

ServiceObject [ Twitter
                Connected ]

twitter ["TweetSearch", "Query" → "#westfieldlondon", MaxItems → 5000]
```

responding to the sentiment detected in the text. In particular, the software applies the function classify to each tweet and then return the sentiment detected. Figure 2 shows part of the code to perform this function for two specific tweets (resulting in neutral and positive respectively).

Findings indicate consumers' sentiments, synthetizing their evaluation for the shopping center. In particular, Wolfram Mathematica identified 1,050 positive tweets (75 percent of the total tweets), 300 neutral (21 percent of the total tweets) and 50 negatives (4 percent of the total tweets) (Figure 3).

This analysis figures out that Westfield customers are living very pleasant experiences related to the shopping center and associated services as the number of positive comments is much higher than the number of negative ones.

The sentiment analysis could be further conducted weekly or daily to achieve a more up to date understanding of the success of the marketing strategy and suggest if any action is needed.

## Image Analytics

Tourism literature considers pictures taken by tourists as rich data sources for tourism research (Balomenou and Garrod, 2019; Balomenou, Garrod, and Gerogiadou, 2017; Donaire, Camprubi, and Gali, 2014; Konijin, Sluimer, and Miras, 2016; Kim and Stepchenkova, 2015; Nikjoo and Bankhshi, 2019), by allowing understanding the perception of brand image (O' Connor, 2010), destination attractiveness (Perez- Vega et al., 2018; Jung et al., 2018), and quality of experience (Banrjee and Chua, 2016; Pantano et al., 2017). Since visual images based on their manifest content can be directly observed and quantitatively summarized with acceptable reliability (e.g. of co-occurrences and clustering) (Kim and Stepchenkova, 2015), algorithms for systematically identifying objects in pictures provide researchers with new analytical tools that can be applied successfully also in marketing. Therefore, the analysis of images (image analytics) is a process that facilitates the investigation of images identifying objects, places, and people in order to extract significant information. Image recognition is applied to perform several tasks, such as providing labels on the content images (Donaire Camprubí, and Galí, 2014; Lo and McKercher, 2015).

In the present case, the software automatically identifies the different objects included in each picture and assigns each of them to a reference category, creating the classification. Some manual categories have been developed to classify pictures on previous studies (Donaire et al., 2014). However, the software accesses to more than 10,000 different categories for the procedure.

The collection of pictures from the *Westfield London* Instagram Official page generated a total of 1,043 pictures shared by users, which have been saved in a folder, and then imported in Wolfram Mathematica.

The pictures are analysed with a specific machine learning algorithm for the image recognition process already available in Wolfram Mathematica software. This is a pre-trained algorithm that aims to label each picture into certain categories. In particular, this procedure uses the module *ImageIdentify*, to distinguish and classify the object of each pictures. All the pictures are labelled in different categories (Figure 4).

Table 1 shows the 10 most photographed objects in the shopping center according to the algorithm.

The most photographed elements emerging from this analysis are the shopping center environment (store, shopping center, courtyard), and some foods available in the foodcourt (coffee, pizza), while pictures related to specific stores highlight the store devoted to the nail polish and the flower boutiques (i.e. bouquets). These are the elements of Westfield that have so far achieved the highest interest from consumers.

*Figure 2. Classify function applied to tweets to determine sentiment polarity*

```
Classify["Sentiment", "Can you recommend anyone for this #job in #Westfield,
   MA? https://t.co/pDkr9FQshx #RN #NuurseLife #Nursing #Hiring"]
Neutral

Classify["Sentiment",
 "Eeeeek! Just 4 days to go!! Can you tell we are excited?😁 Have you entered
   our competition to win a £500 voucher to spend at Thérapie Clinic in
   @westfieldlondon? If not, head over to our Instagram page to enter!"]
Positive
```

Finally, Westfield could replicate both the above analyses for their main competitors' tweets and images (which are free accessible through Twitter and Instagram) to compare and contrast the data (emerging from similar open sources) for improving competitor intelligence.

## FUTURE RESEARCH DIRECTIONS

First, the present research uses data in aggregate forms, and these data do not include specific faces/persons. However, when collecting the images, companies do not need to store the images of individual people (which could raise privacy issues), rather it can count the number of images portraying people without storing them. Legal and ethical aspects are involved when the company collects and stores personal data on consumers, or combines data emerging from multiple sources to identify any individual consumer. Thus, future research should identify the main practical, legal and ethical challenges associated with the collection, management, and analysis of these data (tweets and images on Instagram) in order to provide detailed privacy guidelines.

*Figure 3. Findings of sentiment analysis for Westfield London shopping centre*

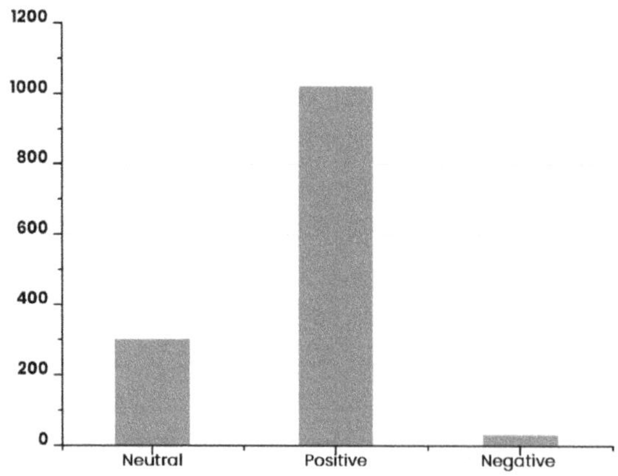

Second, the study conducted the sentiment analysis and the image analytics on two different sets of data. Thus, it does not associate the picture with the text, which renders impossible any understanding of whether a certain picture involved a positive, neutral or negative comment. Future studies might conduct the simultaneous analysis of pictures and text to also evaluate systematically if certain objects are more recurrent in the case of negative or positive comments. Although *Wolfram Mathematica* does not allow to do such an analysis with the extant algorithms, it provides the support to develop one's own algorithm drawing upon the existing *Classify* functions (machine learning) that can be combined for the new purpose. Thus, further studies might also provide new frameworks for the simultaneous collection and analysis of additional data.

Third, the choice of one specific department store in a very specific geographic context (London, UK) leading to the collection of 1,400 tweets and 1,043 pictures is another limitation that needs to be acknowledged. Future works might collect a larger data set with more department stores with similar characteristics in different countries. Similarly, the present study is focused on a shopping center only, new studies might conduct the same analysis in specialized retail agglomerations such as luxury department stores and designer outlet villages. Such a broader context is appropriate to study as different brands (.g. fast fashion versus luxury brands) and lower/higher price stores do not necessarily equate to lower/

*Figure 4. Part of the output for ImageIdentify module*

store, person, person, remote control, store, person, person, laptop,
bouquet, control room, clapperboard, person, business office, skateboard,
person, shopping cart

*Table 1. The ten most photographed elements in Westfield London shopping centre*

| Category | Number of pictures |
|---|---|
| Person | 135 |
| Store | 115 |
| Shopping center | 44 |
| work | 39 |
| courtyard | 12 |
| Paper chain | 11 |
| Coffee | 11 |
| Pizza | 10 |
| Nail polish | 10 |
| Bouquet | 10 |

higher satisfaction or quality of the service provided. New studies might compare the results in order to understand if these findings transcend the luxury experience to embrace a broader shopping experience. Also, new research can triangulate the data with information about the duration of the shopping activity that might impact the consumption experience in terms of the perception of quality and service.

Fourth, other researches might also consider additional data to be simultaneously collected and analysed to enhance the quality of recommendations for marketing managers, such as consumers' paths within a shopping center (data gathered from movements sensors), the locations with the highest number of shoppers (data gathered from thermal camera/thermal imaging technology), and so on.

Finally, since the methodology is based on the use of a machine learning algorithm provided by *Wolfram Mathematica* software, the percentage of error incorrectly classifying (recognizing) the different objects in the pictures may be related to the version of the software, advancements in computers science and subsequent updates in the software algorithms might lead to minor differences in future analyses.

## CONCLUSION

An increasing number of studies in tourism and marketing consider pictures (Balomenou and Garrod, 2019; Balomenou, Garrod, & Gerogiadou, 2017; Donaire, Camprubi, & Gali, 2014; Konijin, Sluimer, & Miras, 2016; Kim and Stepchenkova, 2015; Nikjoo and Bankhshi, 2019) and tweets shared online (Dindar and Yaman, 2018; Pantano, Giglio and Dennis, in print.; Walasek, Bhatia and Brown, 2018) as rich data sources for consumer research. Drawing upon these studies, our results demonstrate that big data analytics and machine learning algorithms support the extraction of consumers' insights in the context of luxury retailing. Thus, the study replies to the call for developing new analytics to understand how to extract value from the structured and unstructured data already available for retailers (Ailawadi and Farris, 2017; Bradlow et al., 2017; Dindar and Yaman, 2018; Balducci and Marinova, 2018; Hartman et al., 2019; Pantano, Giglio and Dennis, in print.).

The above proposed solutions in terms of methodologies for supporting big data analyses represent two examples of a systematic approach to accessing rich data on consumers' experiences and translating into insights. The procedures investigate part of the massive amounts of data that consumers upload continuously, how to detect data on their feelings concerning the brand/product/service (sentiment analytics) and the perceived main important elements of the brand/product/service (image analytics), all at a lower cost in terms of time and quantity of information collected and analyzed compared to traditional methods based on interviews and surveys.

The two exemplary procedures above are based on data available online to anyone, thus each company can conduct similar analyses for competitors and compare and contrast the insights, in order to improve competitor intelligence. However, our analyses that exploit big data extracted from two social media are not exhaustive. Although the sentiment analysis of the tweets allows Westfield to understand that customers are living very pleasant experiences related to the shopping center and associated service, additional analysis such as the ones related to the effective contents of the tweets (what effectively consumers say) would help the shopping center to focus more on the strengths of the provided experience for customers. Similarly, Westfield can collect pictures uploaded by consumers on Facebook in order to build a more comprehensive database resulting in a better overview of the elements that are interesting for consumers across a larger range of sources.

Nevertheless, our analyses are able to highlight the importance that digital data represent to create a more effective bridge between consumers and companies. Indeed, such data contributes to significant knowledge about consumers preferences and related online and offline behaviours (i.e. personal opinions related to certain products shared through a particular social medium or the times a consumer visited a physical store seeking specific products through the technologies available in the store, etc.). Such information could be helpful in driving changes to marketing strategy. In particular, the above frameworks of analysis provide functional tools to quickly leverage the potential of big data through artificial intelligence and machine learning algorithms to increase companies efficiency and find new customer solutions.

In agreement with Deng and Cao (2018), these analyses include a cost that transcends the cost of the software license. In this work, we demonstrated a few of the main analyses that can be conducted to support managers.

Marketing practitioners and retailers can benefit from new approaches like ours regarding how to collect consumers' insights from the data available online (i.e. on social media like Twitter). Thus, our results suggest that retailers might do more to meet consumers' expectations, by focusing simultaneously on systematic texts analysis and image analytics, through new approaches based on machine learning algorithms. However, the identification of appropriate techniques would need additional analytical skills and software knowledge that might be not already available in shopping centers or other retailers, suggesting a potential opportunity for staff recruitment and/or training.

## REFERENCES

Ailawadi, K. L., & Farris, P. W. (2017). Managing multi-and omnichannel distribution: Metrics and research directions. *Journal of Retailing*, *93*(1), 120–135. doi:10.1016/j.jretai.2016.12.003

Balducci, B., & Marinova, D. (2018). Unstructured data in marketing. *Journal of the Academy of Marketing Science*, *46*(4), 557–590. doi:10.100711747-018-0581-x

Balomenou, N., & Garrod, B. (2019). Photographs in tourism research: Prejudice, power, performance and participant-generated images. *Tourism Management*, *70*, 201–217. doi:10.1016/j.tourman.2018.08.014

Balomenou, N., Garrod, B., & Georgiadou, A. (2017). Making sense of tourists' photographs using canonical variate analysis. *Tourism Management*, *61*, 173–179. doi:10.1016/j.tourman.2017.02.010

Banerjee, S., & Chua, A. Y. (2016). In search of patterns among travellers' hotel ratings in TripAdvisor. *Tourism Management*, *53*, 125–131. doi:10.1016/j.tourman.2015.09.020

Baxendale, S., Macdonald, E. K., & Wilson, H. N. (2015). The impact of different touchpoints on brand consideration. *Journal of Retailing*, *91*(2), 235–253. doi:10.1016/j.jretai.2014.12.008

Bell, D. R., Gallino, S., & Moreno, A. (2018). Offline Showrooms in Omnichannel Retail: Demand and Operational Benefits. *Management Science*, *64*(4), 1629–1651. doi:10.1287/mnsc.2016.2684

Bertacchini, F., Bilotta, F., & Pantano, P. (2017). Shopping with a robotic companion. *Computers in Human Behavior*, *77*, 382–395. doi:10.1016/j.chb.2017.02.064

Blom, A., Lange, F., & Hess, R. L. Jr. (2017). Omnichannel-based promotions' effects on purchase behavior and brand image. *Journal of Retailing and Consumer Services*, *39*, 286–295. doi:10.1016/j.jretconser.2017.08.008

Blut, M., Teller, C., & Floh, A. (2018). Testing retail marketing-mix effects on patronage: A meta-analysis. *Journal of Retailing*, *94*(2), 113–135. doi:10.1016/j.jretai.2018.03.001

Bradlow, E. T., Gangwar, M., Kopalle, P., & Voleti, S. (2017). The role of big data and predictive analytics in retailing. *Journal of Retailing*, *93*(1), 79–95. doi:10.1016/j.jretai.2016.12.004

Calvo-Porral, C., & Levy-Mangin, J.-P. (2018). Pull factors of the shopping malls: An empirical study. *International Journal of Retail & Distribution Management*, *46*(2), 110–124. doi:10.1108/IJRDM-02-2017-0027

Cefis, E., & Marsili, O. (2006). Survivor: The role of innovation in firms' survival. *Research Policy*, *35*(5), 626–641. doi:10.1016/j.respol.2006.02.006

Centre for Retail Research. (2011). *World shopping capitals 2011 survey: which city is the biggest shopper?* Available at http://www.retailresearch.org/worldshoppingcapitals.php

Chen, C. P., & Zhang, C. Y. (2014). Data-intensive applications, challenges, techniques and technologies: A survey on Big Data. *Information Sciences*, *275*, 314–347. doi:10.1016/j.ins.2014.01.015

Chou, Y.-C., Chuang, H. H.-H., & Shao, B. B. M. (2016). The impact of e-retail characteristics on initiating mobile retail services: A modular innovation perspective. *Information & Management*, *53*(4), 481–492. doi:10.1016/j.im.2015.11.003

Dacko, S. G. (2017). Enabling smart retail settings via mobile augmented reality shopping apps. *Technological Forecasting and Social Change*, *124*, 243–256. doi:10.1016/j.techfore.2016.09.032

Demirkan, H., & Spohrer, J. (2014). Developing a framework to improve virtual shopping in digital malls with intelligent self-service systems. *Journal of Retailing and Consumer Services*, *21*(5), 860–868. doi:10.1016/j.jretconser.2014.02.012

Deng, M., & Cao, Y. (2018). Innovation and Effect Evaluation Model of Education and Training Outsourcing of State-owned Enterprises under Big Data. *Educational Sciences: Theory and Practice*, *18*(6). doi:10.12738/estp.2018.6.201

Dennis, C. (2005). *Objects of desire: consumer behaviour in shopping centre choices*. Palgrave McMillan. doi:10.1057/9780230509481

Dennis, C., Murphy, J., Marsland, D., Cockett, T., & Patel, T. (2002). Measuring image: Shopping centre case studies. *International Review of Retail, Distribution and Consumer Research*, *12*(4), 355–373. doi:10.1080/09593960210151153

Dindar, M., & Yaman, N. D. (2018). #IUseTwitterBecause: Content analytic study of a trending topic in Twitter. *Information Technology & People*, *31*(1), 256–277. doi:10.1108/ITP-02-2017-0029

Donaire, J. A., Camprubí, R., & Galí, N. (2014). Tourist clusters from Flickr travel photography. *Tourism Management Perspectives*, *11*, 26–33. doi:10.1016/j.tmp.2014.02.003

Evanschitzky, H., Iyer, G. R., Kenning, P., & Schutte, R. (2015). Consumer trial, continuous use, and economic benefits of a retail service innovation: The case of the personal shopping assistant. *Journal of Product Innovation Management*, *31*(3), 459–475. doi:10.1111/jpim.12241

Finn, A., & Louviere, J. J. (1996). Shopping center image, consideration, and choice: Anchor store contribution. *Journal of Business Research*, *35*(3), 241–251. doi:10.1016/0148-2963(95)00129-8

Germann, F., Lilien, G. L., Fiedler, L., & Kraus, M. (2014). Do retailers benefit from deploying customer analytics? *Journal of Retailing*, *90*(4), 587–593. doi:10.1016/j.jretai.2014.08.002

Grewal, D., Roggeveen, A. L., & Nordfält, J. (2017). The future of retailing. *Journal of Retailing*, *93*(1), 1–6. doi:10.1016/j.jretai.2016.12.008

Hagberg, J., Sundstrom, M., & Egels-Zandén, N. (2016). The digitalization of retailing: An exploratory framework. *International Journal of Retail & Distribution Management*, *44*(7), 694–712. doi:10.1108/IJRDM-09-2015-0140

Hartmann, N. N., Wieland, H., & Vargo, S. L. (2018). Converging on a new theoretical foundation for selling. *Journal of Marketing*, *82*(2), 1–18. doi:10.1509/jm.16.0268

Huang, M.-U., & Rust, R. T. (2017). Technology-driven service strategy. *Journal of the Academy of Marketing Science*, *45*(6), 906–924. doi:10.100711747-017-0545-6

Huang, M.-U., & Rust, R. T. (2018). Artificial intelligence in Service. *Journal of Service Research*, *21*(2), 155–172. doi:10.1177/1094670517752459

Ieva, M., & Ziliani, C. (2018). Mapping touchpoint exposure in retailing: Implications for developing an omnichannel customer experience. *International Journal of Retail & Distribution Management*, *46*(3), 304–332. doi:10.1108/IJRDM-04-2017-0097

Inman, J. J., & Nikolova, H. (2017). Shopper-facing retail technology: A retailer adoption decision framework incorporating shopper attitudes and privacy concerns. *Journal of Retailing*, *93*(1), 7–28. doi:10.1016/j.jretai.2016.12.006

Janssen, M., van der Voort, H., & Wahyudi, A. (2017). Factors influencing big data decision-making quality. *Journal of Business Research*, *70*, 338–345. doi:10.1016/j.jbusres.2016.08.007

Jung, T. H., Tom Dieck, M. C., & Chung, N. (2018). Determinants of hotel social media continued usage. *International Journal of Contemporary Hospitality Management*, *30*(2), 1152–1171. doi:10.1108/IJCHM-02-2017-0068

Kim, H., & Stepchenkova, S. (2015). Effect of tourist photographs on attitudes towards destination: Manifest and latent content. *Tourism Management*, *49*, 29–41. doi:10.1016/j.tourman.2015.02.004

Konijin, E., Sluimer, N., & Miras, O. (2016). Click to share: Patterns in tourist photography and sharing. *International Journal of Tourism Research*, *18*(6), 525–535. doi:10.1002/jtr.2069

Kumar, V., Anand, A., & Song, H. (2017). Future of retailer profitability: An organizing framework. *Journal of Retailing*, *93*(1), 96–119. doi:10.1016/j.jretai.2016.11.003

Lo, I. S., & McKercher, B. (2015). Ideal image in process: Online tourist photography and impression management. *Annals of Tourism Research*, *52*, 104–116. doi:10.1016/j.annals.2015.02.019

McAfee, A., Brynjolfsson, E., Davenport, T. H., Patil, D. J., & Barton, D. (2012). Big data: The management revolution. *Harvard Business Review*, *90*(10), 60–68. PMID:23074865

Merrilees, B., & Miller, D. (2019). Companion shopping: The influence on mall brand experiences. *Marketing Intelligence & Planning*, *37*(3), 465–478. doi:10.1108/MIP-08-2018-0340

Morton, C., & Redman, L. D. (2016). The best shopping cities in the world. *Condé Nast Traveler*. Available at: https://www.cntraveler.com/galleries/2015-01-03/best-shopping-cities-in-the-world-readers-choice-awards-2014

Nikjoo, A., & Bakhshi, H. (2019). The presence of tourists and residents in shared travel photos. *Tourism Management*, *70*, 89–98. doi:10.1016/j.tourman.2018.08.005

Nobbs, K., Moore, C. M., & Sheridan, M. (2012). The flagship format within the luxury fashion market. *International Journal of Retail & Distribution Management*, *40*(12), 920–934. doi:10.1108/09590551211274928

O'Connor, P. (2010). Managing a hotel's image on TripAdvisor. *Journal of Hospitality Marketing & Management*, *19*(7), 754–772. doi:10.1080/19368623.2010.508007

Pantano, E., & Dennis, C. (2019). Store buildings as tourist attractions: Mining retail meaning of store building pictures through a machine learning approach. *Journal of Retailing and Consumer Services*, *51*, 304–310.

Pantano, E., Giglio, S., & Dennis, C. (2019). Making sense of consumers' tweets: Sentiment outcomes for fast fashion retailers through Big Data analytics. *International Journal of Retail & Distribution Management*, *47*(9), 915–927.

Pantano, E., Priporas, C. V., & Dennis, C. (2018). A new approach to retailing for successful competition in the new smart scenario. *International Journal of Retail & Distribution Management*, *46*(3), 264–282. doi:10.1108/IJRDM-04-2017-0080

Pantano, E., Priporas, C. V., Sorace, S., & Iazzolino, G. (2017). Does the innovation-orientation lead to retail industry growth? Empirical evidence from patent analysis. *Journal of Retailing and Consumer Services*, *34*, 88–94. doi:10.1016/j.jretconser.2016.10.001

Pantano, E., Priporas, C. V., & Stylos, N. (2017). 'You will like it!' Using open data to predict tourists' response to a tourist attraction. *Tourism Management*, *60*, 430–438. doi:10.1016/j.tourman.2016.12.020

Pantano, E., & Timmermans, H. (2014). What is smart for retailing? *Procedia Environmental Sciences*, *22*, 101–107. doi:10.1016/j.proenv.2014.11.010

Pantano, E., & Vannucci, V. (2019). Who is innovating? An evaluation of the extent to which retailers are meeting the technology challenge. *Journal of Retailing and Consumer Services*, *49*, 297–304. doi:10.1016/j.jretconser.2019.01.019

Papagiannidis, S., Bourlakis, M., Alamanos, E., & Dennis, C. (2017). Preferences of smart shopping channels and their impact on perceived wellbeing and social inclusion. *Computers in Human Behavior*, *77*, 396–405. doi:10.1016/j.chb.2017.04.029

Razaei, S., & Valaei, N. (2017). Branding in a multichannel retail environment: Online stores vs app stores and the effect of product type. *Information Technology & People*, *30*(4), 853–886. doi:10.1108/ITP-12-2015-0308

Roy, S. K., Blaji, M. S., Sadeque, S., Nguyen, B., & Melewar, T. C. (2017). Constituents and consequences of smart customer experience in retailing. *Technological Forecasting and Social Change*, *124*, 257–270. doi:10.1016/j.techfore.2016.09.022

Rust, R. T., & Huang, M. H. (2014). The service revolution and the transformation of marketing science. *Marketing Science*, *33*(2), 206–221. doi:10.1287/mksc.2013.0836

Shankar, V., Inman, J. J., Mantrala, M., Kelley, E., & Rizley, R. (2011). Innovations in shopper marketing: Current insights and future research issues. *Journal of Retailing*, *87*(1), 29–42. doi:10.1016/j.jretai.2011.04.007

Sivarajah, U., Kamal, M. M., Irani, Z., & Weerakkody, V. (2017). Critical analysis of Big Data challenges and analytical methods. *Journal of Business Research*, *70*, 263–286. doi:10.1016/j.jbusres.2016.08.001

Srinivasan, R., & Swink, M. (2018). An investigation of visibility and flexibility as complements to supply chain analytics: An organizational information processing theory perspective. *Production and Operations Management*, *27*(10), 1849–1867. doi:10.1111/poms.12746

Teller, C., & Elms, J. R. (2010). Managing the attractiveness of evolved and created retail agglomerations formats. *Marketing Intelligence & Planning*, *28*(1), 25–45. doi:10.1108/02634501011014598

Timmermans, H. J. P. (1982). Consumer choice of shopping centre: An information integration approach. *Regional Studies*, *16*(3), 171–182. doi:10.1080/09595238200185201

Verma, J. P., Agrawal, S., Patel, B., & Patel, A. (2016). Big data analytics: Challenges and applications for text, audio, video, and social media data. *International Journal on Soft Computing, Artificial Intelligence and Applications, 5*(1).

Von Briel, F. (2018). The future of omnichannel retail: A four-stage Delphi study. *Technological Forecasting and Social Change*, *132*, 217–229. doi:10.1016/j.techfore.2018.02.004

Walasek, K., Bhatia, S., & Brown, G. D. A. (2018). Positional goods and the social rank hypothesis: Income inequality affects online chatter about high- and low-status brands on Twitter. *Journal of Consumer Psychology*, *28*(1), 138–148. doi:10.1002/jcpy.1012

Wang, R. J. H., Malthouse, E. C., & Krishnamurthi, L. (2015). On the go: How mobile shopping affects customer purchase behavior. *Journal of Retailing*, *91*(2), 217–234. doi:10.1016/j.jretai.2015.01.002

Wedel, M., & Kannan, P. K. (2016). Marketing analytics for data-rich environments. *Journal of Marketing*, *80*(6), 97–121. doi:10.1509/jm.15.0413

Willems, K., Smolders, A., Brengman, M., Luyten, K., & Schöning, J. (2017). The path-to-purchase is paved with digital opportunities: An inventory of shopper-oriented retail technologies. *Technological Forecasting and Social Change*, *124*, 228–242. doi:10.1016/j.techfore.2016.10.066

Wrigley, N., Wood, S., Lambiri, D., & Lowe, M. (2019). Corporate convenience store development effects in small towns: Convenience culture during economic and digital storms. *Environmental and Planning A. Economy and Space*, *51*(1), 112–132.

Xu, K., Liao, S. S., Li, J., & Song, Y. (2011). Mining comparative opinions from customer reviews for competitive intelligence. *Decision Support Systems*, *50*(4), 743–754. doi:10.1016/j.dss.2010.08.021

Zhao, Y., Xu, X., & Wang, M. (2019). Predicting overall customer satisfaction: Big data evidence from hotel online textual reviews. *International Journal of Hospitality Management*, *76*, 111–121. doi:10.1016/j.ijhm.2018.03.017

## ADDITIONAL READING

Garrod, B. (2008). Exploring place perception. A photo-based analysis. *Annals of Tourism Research*, *35*(2), 381–401. doi:10.1016/j.annals.2007.09.004

Kannan, P. K., & Li, H. (2017). Digital marketing: A framework, review and research agenda. *International Journal of Research in Marketing*, *34*(1), 22–45. doi:10.1016/j.ijresmar.2016.11.006

Li, H., & Kannan, P. K. (2014). Attributing Conversions in a Multichannel Online Marketing Environment: An Empirical Model and a Field Experiment. *JMR, Journal of Marketing Research*, *51*(1), 40–56. doi:10.1509/jmr.13.0050

Niemela, M., Heikkila, P., Lammi, H., & Oksman, V. (2017). Shopping mall robots- opportunities and constraints from the retailer and manager perspective. *Lecture Notes in Computer Science*, *10652*, 485–494. doi:10.1007/978-3-319-70022-9_48

Nunan, D., & Di Domenico, M. (2017). Big data: A normal accident waiting to happen? *Journal of Business Ethics*, *145*(3), 481–491. doi:10.100710551-015-2904-x

Pantano, E. (2014). Innovation drivers in retail industry. *International Journal of Information Management*, *34*(3), 344–350. doi:10.1016/j.ijinfomgt.2014.03.002

Pantano, E. (2016). Benefits and risks associated with time choice of innovating in retail settings. *International Journal of Retail & Distribution Management*, *44*(1), 58–70. doi:10.1108/IJRDM-03-2015-0047

Perez-Vega, R., Taheri, B., Farrington, T., & O'Gorman, K. (2018). On being attractive, social and visually appealing in social media: The effects of anthropomorphic tourism brands on Facebook fan pages. *Tourism Management*, *66*, 339–347. doi:10.1016/j.tourman.2017.11.013

Rodriguez-Torrico, P., San Josè Cabezudo, R., & San-Martin, S. (2017). Tell me what they are like and I will tell you where they buy: An analysis of omnichannel consumer behavior. *Computers in Human Behavior*, *68*, 465–471. doi:10.1016/j.chb.2016.11.064

Shen, X.-L., Li, Y.-J., Sun, Y., & Wang, N. (2018). Channel integration quality, perceived fluency and omnichannel service usage: The moderating roles of internal and external usage experience. *Decision Support Systems*, *109*, 61–73. doi:10.1016/j.dss.2018.01.006

Verhoef, P. C., Kannan, P. K., & Inman, J. J. (2015). From multi-channel retailing to omnichannel retailing: Introduction to the special issue on multi-channel retailing. *Journal of Retailing*, *91*(2), 174–181. doi:10.1016/j.jretai.2015.02.005

## KEY TERMS AND DEFINITIONS

**Artificial Intelligence (AI):** Technology able to adaptively interact with customers. It consists of the simulation of human intelligence by machines (computer systems) through different processes including learning (machine learning), reasoning and self-correction.

**Big Data:** Huge amount of structured (text fields such as name and phone number) and unstructured (e.g., video, images, gestures, etc.) data in sizes that exceed the capacity of traditional tools to manage them satisfactorily.

**Hashtag:** A particular type of metadata tag used in social networks (i.e. on Twitter and Instagram) and microblogging allowing users to apply a certain tag, which allows other users to easily find the messages with a specific theme or content (identified by this tag).

**Image Analytics:** A process consisting of the analysis of images that facilitates investigation of images identifying objects, places, and people in order to extract significant information. Image recognition is applied to perform several tasks, such as providing labels on the content images, in other words it assigns each object included in the image to a certain category (i.e., house, food, person, etc.).

**Machine Learning Algorithms:** A set of tools that classifying a large amount of data can predict different dynamics in several areas of interest through several methods and tools such as object representation, optimization processes (Bayesian theorem), and neural networks. These tools aim to reduce the complexity of the data while searching for hidden patterns. To this end, these algorithms perform a basic cognitive function of the development of human cognition as learning through experience. In other words, starting from the identification of a certain "law" on the scattered data, these algorithms create categories, similarly to the evolutionary processes occurring in childhood for the development of conceptual categories. This process allows the learning system to recognize the input data that belonging to a certain category.

**Marketing Intelligence:** A set of accurate information on consumers behavior (consumer intelligence) and competitors' behavior (competitor intelligence) that supports companies in the decision-making process to identify market opportunities and penetration strategies.

**Sentiment Analytics:** A process producing computing sentiment scores for each text, which can be used to quantify the positivity and emotional intensity with which people talk about a certain brand, product, service, and shopping.

**Wolfram Mathematica:** A tool for computing, simulation and mathematical modeling providing a computation environment through its already available functions (including machine learning algorithms, neural networks, image processing, visualization techniques, etc.).

# Chapter 11
# Technology-Enabled Marketing and Supply Chain Collaboration

**Abdul Ali**
https://orcid.org/0000-0002-3034-8628
*Northumbria University, London, UK*

## ABSTRACT

*The concepts of marketing and supply chain management, despite their intertwined heritage, are treated in isolation in the literature. Several recent studies have endeavoured to demonstrate the synergies between them. However, the need for technology-enabled marketing for SC collaboration is still in its infancy. This chapter outlines the supply chain management, supply chain collaboration, and technology-enabled marketing. The chapter also highlights the need for technology-enabled marketing for supply chain collaboration. This study also extended the relational view theory in the context of relationship orientation to form collaborative relationships in the supply chain. This study suggested that an organisation could harness the synergy through integrating marketing strategies and SC collaboration.*

## INTRODUCTION

The concept of inter-functional coordination to create superior customer value has long been the main goal of marketing. This concept has led the development of several research streams that includes relationship marketing and R&D, Marketing and finance and the integration of marketing with other interdisciplinary functions (Juttner *et al.,* 2007). It was argued that the customers' value could also be created through the integration of the other typically non-associated areas of Marketing (Ardito *et al.,* 2019).

The interactions between various disciplines that focus on the same customer and market segments considers the important functions and the way they add value to the organisation. Marketing is criticised generally for not being able to efficiently manage out of the box and interdisciplinary matters and hence confronted with various innovative concepts in the area of operations, manufacturing and technology. One of the concepts that have become the strategic priority for the companies in today's world is the SCM. Though the SCM concept was introduced in the early 1980s (Oliver & Webber, 1982) but it is early 199Os when it started becoming an important strategic priority for the businesses (Juttner et al.,

DOI: 10.4018/978-1-7998-0131-3.ch011

2007). The synergistic benefits between SCM and marketing are extensively recognised (Svensson, 2002), and this led to appreciating the importance of coordination between the disciplines to bring superior competitive performance.

Juttner et al., (2007) noted that the synergies between SCM and Marketing could be captured by demand chain management where customers' requirements will be fulfilled through designing the chain starting from customers to the manufactures and the suppliers, not the other way around. In today's market place this concept is becoming even more pervasive due to the technological development that facilitated real-time access to the customers on their accounts to change, amend, customise and communicate, and these will have an impact on the way supply chain is responding to fulfil customers' needs.

The purpose of this chapter is to present the role of technology-enabled marketing in supply chain collaboration. This chapter outlines the supply chain management, supply chain integration, and technology-enabled marketing. The chapter also highlights the technologies in supply chain management that can be used for improved marketing. Supply chain management is not a new concept rather a new terminology. The concept of movement of materials and information to fulfil customers' needs has always been there. Regardless of the industry and whether it is for the profitable or not-for-profit organisation, the concept of supply chain and the activities are at play. The supply chain also covers the wider concept of logistics, which is mostly linked with transportation and warehousing.

## BACKGROUND AND CONTEXT

Supply chain and supply chain management (SCM), which gained recognition in the 1980s, have drawn significant attention among the practitioners and the scholars alike. The businesses are in no illusion given the fact that the organisations in isolation cannot compete and withstand the ever-increasing competitive pressure in this globalised technology-enabled connected marketing era. Contemporary understanding of SCM portray its ever-increasing influences in the areas linked with the integration of supply and demand management (i.e. marketing) within and across organisations that includes greater integration and collaboration among the partners (i.e. customers, suppliers, logistics providers and other channel partners)in the chain (Mentzer and Gudnlach, 2010).

### Supply Chain Management

To understand supply chain management, it is worth looking at what is the supply chain? The supply chain can be described as the chain of supplies or the network of suppliers. In an organisation, there are a set of processes involved to create and deliver value to the customers. It starts with planning the entire processes to balance the demand and supply of what to create, where to get the raw materials from, how to make it and whether to make it in-house or outsource, how to deliver, manage the warehouse and deploy transportation and how to handle the returns. These concepts are well portrayed in the Supply Chain Operations Reference (SCOR) Model developed by supply chain council. SCOR framework is unique in the sense that it renders the business processes, performance metrics, and business practices in an integrated structure. A supply chain thus covers the wider aspects of organisational processes starting with extracting raw materials and ending with satisfied customers through creating, delivering and recreating value as a form of goods and services with the optimum quality and cost. Supply chain management (SCM) is the process to which upstream and downstream linkages of organisations are interconnected for creating value as a form of goods and services for the end consumers (Slack *et al.*, 2010). Hence, the SCM could to defined as the network of organisations working together to efficiently create, deliver and recreate value as a form of goods and services to consistently and resiliently satisfy customers' requirements at the right time with optimum quality and minimum cost.

Supply networks of a firm consider the market as a point of destination where raw materials flow from manufacture to intermediaries (i.e. wholesaler, retailer) or final consumers. In the supply network, information flows both directions from supplier customers and from customers to suppliers, whereas money and returns flow from customers to suppliers. Customer-centric organisations configure their supply network considering their customers' demand and work backwards to suppliers to make their supply network efficient. An organisation (the focal company) place themselves in the centre of the value network where they have the suppliers as well as the suppliers' suppliers in various tiers and the customers as well as customers' customers in various tiers. In a supply network, there are different partners involved that include the focal company, the suppliers, their suppliers' suppliers (1$^{st}$ tier, 2$^{nd}$), distributors, customers (customers' customer- tier 1, tier 2… final consumers). The more the tiers of suppliers and customer are, the more complex and challenging the supply chain is managed. The organisation needs to have a very good relationship with these partners to survive and thrive.

## Importance of Supply Chain Management

The role of supply chain management is hugely important for every organisation to be small and medium-sized enterprises (SMEs) or large multinational enterprises (MNEs). Supply chain management covers entire processes connecting all the partners (i.e. suppliers, suppliers' suppliers, customers, customers' customers, and so on) in the chain. Almost everything that an organisation produces or deliver, starting from sourcing the raw materials to satisfying final consumers are depended on how the supply chain is managed. Organisations are no longer competing against another organisation, rather the supply chain of another organisation. It refers to the importance that the stronger the supply chain of an organisation is, the better competitive edge it has in the market. It is important to understand that the firms' capability significantly depends on the capabilities of their suppliers and their supplier's capabilities also considerably depend on their suppliers and so on.

In the same way, customers' satisfaction and their customers' or consumers' satisfaction (depending on the tiers in the chain) depend on how their requirements are fulfilled. All these activities are interlinked, and an effective supply chain management can help a firm gain competitive advantage. Firms' success depends to a great extent on its partners in the chain. The firms will grow successfully only when the partners (i.e. suppliers and others) in the chain are growing.

## Supply Chain Collaboration

SC collaboration is the joint activities between the partners in the supply chains. It can be referred to as the relationship developed for a long time between supply chain members to lowering cost and risk as well as improving quality and market value (Gunasekaran *et al.*, 2015). A Supply chain is a network of activities among two or more firms (Slack *et al.*, 2010) where an individual firm cannot control the whole Supply chain. That is why it is crucial to have a healthy relationship with the key partners in the supply chains (SC). Once there is a strong relationship between the SC partners, then firms can collaborate to secure distinctive relational rents in the market. The more globalised a supply chain is the more challenges the SC is likely to face (Ali *et al.,* 2017) in sourcing, manufacturing and distributing products.

Collaboration is the joint activities between the partners in the supply chains. Gunasekaran et al. (2015) referred to Supply chain collaboration as the relationship developed for a long time between supply chain members to lowering cost and risk as well as improving quality and market value. Collaboration in the literature mostly focused on collaboration with the supplier, collaboration with customers, internal collaboration and some studies also looked at collaboration with other stakeholders including Universities, communities and local governments (Melander, 2018). The main stimulus for collaboration should come from the thrust of achieving competitive advantage.

Understanding the cultural integration, controlling the inventory, developing mutual trust, delivering customer value with optimum quality and efficient lead time are the challenges organisations face (Ali *et al.,* 2017). These challenges can be minimised through inter-firm collaboration. Firms in collaboration can do better than being in isolation because of the synergistic benefits. Once the firms are in collaboration, they have access to each other's resources, they share information, exchange knowledge, share reward and risk. However, a high degree of trust is crucial in a collaborative relationship. Also, the level of information is shared with the partners in the SCs is another concern. Nonetheless, collaboration helps the firm secure and maximise relational rents (improved performance) in supply chains has been previously researched, and it is prevalent in industrial practices as well.

Collaboration for competitive advantage is gaining popularity in the academic community and industrial settings. To achieve competitive advantage in the SCs, it is critical for the organisations to act collaboratively. It is noted that collaboration with the supplier will enhance mutual relationships and improve trust between the partners. In the long run, collaborating with suppliers, firms can improve their organisational practices, which will lead to achieving competitive advantage.

In the literature, supply chain collaboration and Supply Chain Integration (SCI) are being used interchangeably though they are not the same. While the SCI concentrates on integrating certain parts of the organisational activities or processes with other departments in the same organisation or with other organisations and SCC, which talks a long time to build the trust, involves in integrating all the activities of the organisation to achieve its pre-set goals. While both involve sharing information, however, collaboration requires much more than just information sharing with the partners. Integration is possible without collaboration; however, for collaboration, integration is essential.

Supply chain integration is defined as the degree to which a business strategically collaborate with its SC partners and collaboratively accomplishes intra and inter-firm processes, with a view to achieving effective and efficient flows of goods and services, information, finances, and decisions to deliver the supreme value to the customers(Flynn *et al.*, 2010).

In a basic supply chain, upstream partners of a focal company are suppliers, and downstream partners are customers, and for internal operations, there are employees. Collaborating with upstream partners in the supply chain facilitates firms in practising various activities in their supply chains, focal firm's operations and the upstream parts in particular, which may lead to competitive.

Relationship between customer-supplier collaboration results Improved mutual relationship between the buying firms and their suppliers and improved process control, which lead to achieving competitive edge (Ueki, 2016). Collaboration between the focal firms and other supply chain partners is necessary for product development, sustainability and innovation (de Vargas Mores *et al.*, 2018).

Collaboration in the supply chain has also become a strategic issue for gaining social, environmental and economic sustainability (Chen *et al.*, 2017). Most academics define collaboration in the supply chain as a partnership process where two or more independent entities in the supply chain work together to plan and implement SC operations to achieve set targets and mutual benefits (Cao and Zhang, 2011, Chen et al., 2017). Collaboration can be with the suppliers, customers or internal departments within the organisation or even it could be with the Universities, research institutes, governments or other stakeholders depending on the objectives of the collaboration. Collaboration with SC partners should be the key to initiate innovative practices in the supply chain, which will lead to having a better firm performance. Collaboration between partners in the SC is the common ways to share information, reduce overall costs and bring efficiency in inventory management and forming strategic alliances to improve performance (Soylu *et al.*, 2006). The overarching aim of collaboration in SC should be to secure a competitive advantage (Soylu et al., 2006; Cao and Zhang, 2010).

The Companies in this dynamic environment need to consider internal and external entities in the SCs to enhance their innovative practices, which will lead to achieving competitive advantage. Collaboration is a practicable means to balance the priorities between innovative practices and better performance (Chen et al., 2017).

The firms collaborate with their suppliers to secure various strengths and overcome weakness, eliminate threats and grab opportunities in the supply chain. Collaboration is formed based on the relationship and its strengths. This collaboration enhances mutual dependence between the firms and their activities. So, it became easier for both the firms to implement certain practices (e.g. innovative practices) they need. Therefore, SC collaboration influences firms overall performance. The collaboration between the partners is the strongest form of relationship. Supply chain collaboration, which is built on a strong mutual relationship, helps firms achieve relational rents (competitive advantage) through improved environmental, cost and social performance.

## MARKETING AND SCM TRENDS

Marketing is about how transaction (exchange) of values are conducted between the parties (Kotler, 1972) and hence, the marketing is particularly concerned with the way transactions are generated, encouraged, enabled and appreciated (Min and Mentzer, 2000). The purpose of marketing is to create exchanges, which satisfies customers. The trends of today's marketing are rather creating relational exchange using innovative technologies, which facilitate transactions over an extended period. This can be further elucidated because the relational exchanges can be traced back to previous interactions to reflect on current practices. The close and long term relational exchange facilitate better relationships between the partners (suppliers, customers, and others) in the chain. Hence, relationship marketing became an important aspect of marketing in today's world. Although relationship marketing does improve repeat purchase and supports retaining existing customers, it is worth considering that it goes further than repeating purchases and stimulus (Min and Mentzer, 2000).

Effective SCM needs firms to create and establish close long-term close relationships that base the strategic partnership between the trading partners in the chain. In this aspect, SCM put more emphasis on relational orientation to form a collaboration with the partners in the chain. Their success depends on the success of the entire supply chain. A strategic partnership among the associates in the chain (i.e. designers, suppliers, IT providers, manufactures and logistics vendors) will enhance functional integration in the supply chain. Another important trend in the supply chain is to be green and to be sustainable. Ali et al. (2017) noted that integrating environmental thinking into SCM is becoming a strategic issue for businesses to satisfy all stakeholders across the SCs.

Relationship marketing can be implemented through enhanced coordination and close inter-firm relationships (i.e. strategic alliances and joint ventures) between the partners for mutual planning, cost reduction, and inventory control- the activities of SCM. These activities can be better utilised with implementing latest technologies. Hence, the trends of today's marketing moving towards technology-enabled marketing in a relationship-oriented collaborative supply chain.

## Technology in Marketing Activities

Technology in the last couple of decades has fundamentally reconfigured the way we live, operate businesses, create and deliver value and markets goods and services. In the businesses and academia, there are irresistible tendencies in applying innovative technologies including big data, digital devices and artificial intelligence for crafting business and marketing strategies (Noci, 2019).

Digital technologies contributed significantly on business strategy, structure, and operations in understanding consumers, business to business customers and wider marketing practices. Usages of technologies including databases, data analytics, computers, internet, emails, marketing soft wares, social networking sites, mobile applications, instant messaging services, artificial intelligence, and the ever-growing list have changed how innovative marketing works. Marketing is one of the core functions that has been hugely influenced by technological advancement.

Edmund Jerome McCarthy has classified marketing functions as Product, place, price, and promotion or famously known as Marketing Mix or 4Ps of marketing. These 4Ps has later been extended with People, the physical environment and the processes. All these activities are collectively fulfilling marketing functions, and they should not be considered in isolation. Fulfilling all these activities require greater understanding and collaboration with the partners in the wider supply networks.

## Digital Marketing

Deployment of digital technologies in marketing and their management is referred to as digital marketing. It is an interesting debate to consider whether it should be called marketing in a digital world of digital marketing in the dynamic business world. The outstanding growth of ever-changing innovative digital technologies are continuously transforming the way business is operating and the way traditional marketing was conducted to grasp, flourish, enumerate and deliver value to the customers. It is not only the business organisations and the marketers whose practices are disrupted by innovative technologies but also the customers who are continuously becoming technology dependent. Technological advancement has also changed the way consumers behave, buy and react to promotional activities. Social media such as Facebook, Twitter, Instagram, YouTube, and others are playing a significant role in shaping consumers behaviour and their buying patterns.

## The Chemistry Between Marketing and Supply Chain Management

The synergy between marketing and supply chain management is demonstrated by satisfying customers' needs on time with the right specification, and these concepts are attributed to marketing success (Juttner et al., 2007). The purpose of marketing is creating demands for the goods and services the organisations offer, whereas the supply chain management is focusing on efficiently fulfilling that demands (Golgeci and Gligor, 2017). Much of the debate in SCM is centred on the area of Lean supply chain (Womack & Jones, 1996) or agile supply chain (Goldman et al., 1995).

While lean is focusing on minimising waste through cutting down nonvalue added activities in the operations including having minimised inventory and focusing on Just-in-time (JIT) method but the agile is designed for flexibility to responds the changing needs of the supply chain in terms of consumers demand volume and variety. Lean is useful for comparatively predictable demand, relatively high volume with low product variability. Christopher (2000) noted the features of the agile supply chain as volatile demand with higher variability in customers' requirements. Both the agile and the lean become important concepts in the face of increased product commoditisation, less brand loyalty, enhanced importance on product availability with minimised lead-time and deploying fewer resources. Although the SCM contributes to matching the supply with demand efficiently, however, SCM is criticised for not being able to recognise what constitutes value for the customers and how that value is translated to customer's value propositions. That means customers value and their satisfaction are not increased by the supply chain efficiency only. The concept of marketing to perceive customers value and translate them to customers' value propositions is needed to deliver value to the customers. Understanding the customers' value orientation is crucial for marketers today to evaluate product attributes, performance, and customers' expectations. Customers' value, which can vary within and across the customers, is dynamic. Hence, understanding customers' value and what drives the changes of value over time is important.

The success of marketing significantly depends largely on perceiving factors such as market and customers knowledge in which customers place value, understanding various market segments, developing customised products and services and marketing these with appropriate pricing, branding, communication and promotion techniques. A crucial strategic role of marketing is customer relationship management (CRM), which emphasises on structuring and preserving profitable long-term customer relationships.

While SCM emphasises on supplying efficiently with minimised cost, marketing, in contrast, focuses on generating enhanced revenue by concentrating on demand management. Hence, the synergy between SCM and Marketing contributes to the profitability of the company.

Scholars emphasised on establishing the link between SCM and marketing because of their roles in the organisation's success. According to Flint (2004), to have the marketing strategy successfully implemented, it is crucially to consider SCM because distribution part of a marketing approach significantly depends on it. Simultaneously, in a demand-driven SCM, to fulfil customers' requirements, the organisations need to match the supply with the demand (Sheth, Sisodia, and Sharan, 2000). A market-oriented company could secure sustained competitive advantage and provide superior value propositions to the customers through distinctive business processes to facilitate those (Kumar et al., 2000). The business processes are the activities necessary to source, make and deliver the customer value propositions is the SCM (Juttner et al., 2007). Supply Chain Management, along with CRM and new product development, is the main business practices that overtly contribute to creating and satisfying customer value (Srivastava, Shervani, and Fahey, 1999). While there are arguments and studies that suggested the extended role of marketing to incorporate these business processes but closer integration between the SCM and marketing has not been well acknowledged (Achrol & Kotler, 1999; Juttner et al., 2007). Prior studies in SCM however, acknowledged the importance of incorporating marketing concepts. Customer relationships management, customer Service and Demand management are seen as the key marketing related business processes linked with SCM that are useful to deliver value to satisfy customers' needs (Lambert and Cooper, 2000). Mentzer et al. (2001) a developed SCM model based on integrated business processes in the area of SCM and marketing and highlighted the necessities for future research in the domain to explore how effectively these activities can be synchronised. SCM in marketing plays a mediation role were ensuring the customers' requirements are fulfilled with the efficient flow of various products and materials in the marketplace (Fisher, 1997). For efficient implementation of SCM, the role of market orientation and relationship marketing is vital (Min and Mentzer, 2000). Within logistic departments, efficient consumer responses is an important approach that requires cross-functional activities between SCM and marketing (Juttner et al., 2007).

It is worth noted that the concepts of SCM, marketing, market orientation, and relationships management should not be considered in isolation; rather, these are inseparably connected (Min and Mentzer, 2000). Svensson (2002) argued that the concept of SCM is the reintegration of logistics and marketing functions, which were interlinked but alienated gradually. Marketing channel management is the most apparent interface between logistics or SCM and Marketing (Alvarado and Kotzab (2001). Even though there several studies that consider the SCM and Marketing, however, understanding SCM and Marketing require more studies in this domain (Juttner et al., 2007). In spite of having enormous importance in an integrated approach from both the supply side and demand side to deliver what customers want, the supply side of many organisations is yet to connect with the demand side of the chain. While supply chain coordination and collaboration between the partners in the chain is important but to facilitate this coordination, understanding the demand is paramount (Mentzer, 2004).

## Relationship Management in Supply Chain Management and Marketing

SCM can be described, from a marketing viewpoint, as internal and external customer relationships management, including channel of distribution through which the end-users receive their goods and services (Parente et al. 2008). Supply Chain relationship management in the literature is referred to as the incorporation of the management of the relationship between the supply chain partners (Choi and Wu, 2009; Lambert and Schwieterman, 2012). Sanders (2012) described it as the coordination, collaboration and information sharing between the partners in the supply chains. These activities help firms in joint planning and executions to achieve firms set objectives (Ashby et al., 2012; Seuring and Gold, 2013; Gualandris et al., 2014). A successful SRM requires trust and open communication, but mistrust, less communication or hiding information may lead to the transactional approach to a relationship or complete avoidance rather than collaboration approach. Tidy et al. (2016) Suggested having better supplier relationship management (SRM) firms can improve their performance.

## Importance of Supply Chain Collaboration in Marketing

Marketing is a set of activities and processes, including research, innovation, and advertising that firms undertake to promote and sales of products or services. The purpose of marketing is to keep finding, winning and retaining customers through innovative practices. The collaboration in the supply chain, which advocates for having aligned goals between the partners in the supply chain including upstream suppliers and downstream customers, is crucial not only to fulfil customers need but also to facilitate marketing team to reach out the customers with the right set of information and techniques. An organisation's stances are reflected based collaborative nature of the supply chain relationships that focuses on coordination between partners, units and departments (Jüttner and Christopher, 2013).

Marketers need to reach out to their customers, need to understand their channel of distribution which a part of logistics is, understand the processes and time to receive the raw materials and inputs which is covered by the sourcing in supply chain and need to understand the transformation process in the operations before selling it to the customers, so all these activities are supporting marketing as well to reach to their goal.

## Technologies in Supply Chain and Marketing

We have been through several industrial revolutions in the past couple of centuries. We also have been experiencing the exponential growth of the information technology, the manufacturing technology and the usages of technology almost every spare of life. We cannot even imagine spending an hour without the touch of technology. The businesses and the supply chain, in particular, is not immune to this ever-increasing effect. The technology has changed the landscape of the way businesses source, make, promote and deliver products and services to the targeted market segments. The fourth industrial revolution or the industry 4.0 as it is called in academia and the industry is the new revolution the world is experiencing and the much more is yet to come. This revolution has brought several emerging technologies, including those are increasingly becoming the determinants of organisations future. Industry 4.0 is also referred to as the term used in the literature as advanced manufacturing, digital manufacturing, digital age, the fourth industrial revolution, intelligent manufacturing, smart industry, smart manufacturing and so on. The increased competition in the market due to globalisation drive organisations to strive for competitiveness through implementing innovative technologies and business processes. Some of the technologies that are attributed to Industry 4.0 are the Internet of Things (IoT), Big Data, cloud computing, augmented and virtual reality, integrated wireless infrastructure and artificial intelligence (AI). Blockchain and Machine learning are also significantly contributing to the new industrial revolution.

Simultaneously, the way marketing is functioned dramatically been changed. The traditional way of marketing is no longer effective without integrating modern technology-Digital marketing. The marketing mix and the components of the marketing mix have different and extended meaning now than it had a couple of decades ago.

Marketing is mostly relying on data nowadays. Collecting, analysing, understanding and exploiting the massive amount of structured and unstructured data from everywhere paves the way for a successful marketing strategy for the connected consumers. This the processed data that helps understand the consumers' needs and deliver precisely what they need and when they need the right quality, quantity, and cost. So, these are the supply chain and marketing activities that can be combined with the blessing of the technology. So, collaboration with the partners in the supply chain facilitates technology-enabled marketing for connected consumers.

Marketing functions such as designing, making and delivering products and services should fulfil and exceed customers' expectation. So, the purpose of products or the services of the organisation should be not only to satisfy customers' requirements but also to provide extra elements that delight the customers. These can be done many ways that may include the offerings of various types of products or services, maintaining consistent appropriate quality, designing products or services aligning with customers' needs, adding features with the products or services that the customers find valuable, providing innovating packaging in various sizes with added services including guarantees, warranties, returns, rewards and so on. To fulfil these functions collaborating with the partners in the supply network is crucial to have an integrated approach starting from designing to delivering new products or services with different sizes, shapes, features, and packaging. All these activities in the supply network are facilitated by innovative technologies (i.e. 3D Printing, software, databases, and so on) that requires greater collaboration among the partners in the network.

The price element of the marketing function for the products or services has a significant impact on an organisation's profitability and overall success. The price should reflect the value of products/services in question. It should be done in such a way that attract customers minimising price-based competition and with a right margin for the company. It is imperative to understand the target customers and their psychology on products/service price and the elasticity of price changes. It is also essential to analyse the impact of discounts on prices on-demand using various data-driven technologies. To set the right prices across the supply network, it is essential to apply innovative technologies such as data analytics, big data, and so on. Application of all this is facilitated if there is better collaboration with the partners in the supply network. That means marketing functions are effectively executed through the effective SC collaboration.

Another essential marketing function is a promotion, which significantly depends on innovative technologies and their meaningful implementation. Promotion plays a substantial role in marketing activities through developing the messages and effectively communicate them with the target audience using appropriate tools (i.e. Technology). It includes integrated marketing commutation across the networks; fulfilling advertising, sales and promotional activities using various online and offline channels. The effectiveness of those promotional activities depends to a great extent to the customers and their feedbacks in the various level of the supply networks and deployment of various technologies (i.e. digital marketing). These promotional activities can better be communicated with the target audience when there is better communication with the partners in the supply networks.

Place refers to the channels in the supply networks that are used to disseminate information about the products/services among the targeted segments. There are various channels (i.e. online, mobile and offline) available to the marketers to market their products/services. Owing to the advancement of innovative technologies, marketers use different approaches in selling the products. Multi-channel marketing and omnichannel marketing become are becoming popular approaches to reach out to targeted customers. Multi-channels refer to the various channels that the marketers use to promote and advertise their products/services to their target segments. Omnichannel, however, is different than that of multi-channel marketing. Omnichannel works in an integrated platform where the aim is to provide a seamless shopping experience to the customers. In omnichannel, the customers can order going to the physical shops, can order using mobile phones or computers, can save products in online and visit the stores to check the products and before buying them. All these will be seamless when there is a better IT integration among the partners in the supply networks.

People elements in marketing as well as in SCM is highly valued, and unique resources without what execution of both the concepts and practices are impossible. It is the people and their capabilities that bring the uniqueness in the products/services offerings. It is crucial to have the right personnel and the right skill set for companies in today's globalised world to survive and compete in the market. Recruiting service personnel, motivating them and providing training should be in such a way that delivers the appropriate value to the customers. This is the employees who use technologies to deliver value for the customers. So, colleagues across the supply networks should be adequately trained to use those technologies that can, directly and indirectly, connect to the customers. Technologies, technological integration, and adaption across the channels in the chain significantly depend on the technical skills the personnel have in the organisation. It can be better coordinated and enhanced through SC collaboration.

Prior studies noted that the SCM and the marketing functions require mutual integration to fulfil customers' demand through matching that with the supply. Interactions between the businesses and the customers to deliver the products/services in every stage is covered by the process elements. Process design, self-service technologies, and controlling service variability in online, mobile and offline service processes are essential to set of activities in marketing. Having better relationships between the partners in the supply networks can enable marketers to effectively deploy various technologies in designing the processes and controlling the service variability. Simultaneously, in this dynamic business environment, merely the existence of a business is not enough for building a brand and achieve consumers trust. Hence, physical evidence is necessary. It could be as a form of products/service environment, webpages, catalogues, brochures, digital technologies, and so on. Having collaboration among the partners in the supply networks will facilitate better products/service offerings for the customers to shape their senses -sound, sight, smell, and touch. Hence, it is essential to understand that the marketing functions with enhanced technological integration help companies improve the collaborative relationship, which leads to sustained competitive advantage.

## Theoretical Concepts in Technology-Enabled Marketing and SC Collaboration

Despite acknowledging the vital disruptive variations in today's supply chain and highlighting the importance of extensive research in the area, the academics have depended on a limited number of theories to elucidate the interested phenomena (Gligor et al., 2019). There are several theories that are extensively used in management literature in general, and in supply chain management and marketing domain in particular to understand different phenomena. Gligor et al. (2019) have provided an extensive list of theories that are used in the areas of Supply Chain, Marketing and Management. Across the domain Resource-based view theory and its extensions such as Relational view, resource dependence theory, and others being extensively used in the literature.

Resource-based view theory (Barney, 1990) is used to apprehend the strategic resources that the organisation has to achieve sustained competitive advantage. The resources should have some unique characteristics that include valuable, rare, inimitable and non-substitutable to secure sustainable competitive advantage. While Resourced Based View theory (RBV) is a dominant theory for understanding the internal capabilities of an organisation, however, it has some limitations once the entire network organisation or supply chain is considered. Because RBV is mostly internal focused rather than inter-organisational focus (Leuschner et al., 2013), as this study is covering in the area of SCM and marketing that require collaboration between the partners in the Chain and hence there are other theories developed based on the RBV will be worth exploring.

Relational View (RV), which is the extension of RBV (Leuschner et al., 2013) is frequently known as capability development process (Dyer and Singh, 1998). Though RBV is widely used in various SC related research RV is gaining popularities in collaboration paradigm of operations and supply chain management; however, it mostly has been used in conjunction with other theories (e.g. RBV). So, it has been used as a supporting theoretical lens in the previous literature. RV supports the view that capabilities of a firm can be developed through combining or bundling its resources from various parts of the supply chains through inter-firm integration or a strategic partnership (Leuschner et al., 2013). Hence, forming an exchange relationship through organisational capabilities or resources become more accessible among various parts of the supply chain. This perception can be extended from a single firm to multiple firms who are on the same network and bundle them together. Dyer and Singh (1998) Consider this as network relationship or inter-organisational relationship. Whereas RBV considers internal strategic resources, the RV postulates that competitive advantage also comes from inter-organisational resources which cannot be achieved or possessed by an individual firm alone (Lavie, 2006, Leuschner et al., 2013). The RBV consider single firm, whereas RV takes inter-organisational collaboration aspects into account. This study believes that technology-enabled marketing leads to supply chain collaboration, which will facilitate a sustainable competitive advantage. So, RV as a guiding theoretical lens suits the needs for investigating the phenomenon of this study.

According to Dyer and Singh (1998), RV generates profits from relation-specific assets, inter-firm knowledge sharing activities, mutual availability of resources and efficient control. RV shifts focus from individual firm to an inter-firm relationship or network relationship, which suggest that firms share their resources and capabilities (i.e. technologies) with other partners in the supply chain. RV can enhance mutual relations between and among firms through mutual trust, communication exchanges, and knowledge sharing. Rivals find it hard to copy joint actions because of its collaborative nature with the firms and their partners through relation specific-investment, knowledge sharing, accumulating resources or capabilities and reducing transaction costs (Mesquita et al., 2008). These are possible because of the effective maintenance of a mutual relationship (Leuschner et al., 2013).

However, RV has some drawbacks relating to inter-firm resource sharing, scarcity of right allies and indivisibility of resources to develop relational rents. Inter-firm resource sharing and collaborating may create repetitive expectation because of previous relationship-specific activities between the partners. Also, selecting the right partners is an additional restraint to improve relational rent. Relational rent is created through collaboration with other partners having complementary strategic resources and relational capabilities to achieve desired objectives, but in many occasions, it is difficult to happen because the target partner may already have joint activities with other firms. Besides, Dyer and Singh (1998) mentioned that targeted partners might not be capable of harnessing sufficient relational skills, including knowledge sharing or investing in relation-specific assets. Moreover, firms' resources have specific features of distinctiveness in indivisibility, which hinders them in developing resources or capabilities.

However, these weaknesses can be minimised through an effective selection of the SC partners, develop them over time and deploying innovative technologies. Through mutual partnerships and collaboration, a firm can create unique resources which will bring differentiation in products or services (Mesquita et al., 2008). So, firms can develop relational rents successfully when they have collaborative relations and trusts with their partners. RV can be used to understand inter-organisational relationships in supply chains (Dyer and Singh, 1998). Inter-organisational collaboration creates win-win situations for the participating firms enhancing supply chain benefits by using difficult to copy specific resources, skills, and information (Leuschner et al., 2013). RV is essential for this study because technology-enabled marketing, knowledge acquisition, supplier collaboration in partnership specific assets and capabilities, and buyer-supplier relationship for mutual activities can be better elucidated deploying relational view theory. RV helps in justifying the decisions on technology-facilitated marketing to collaborate with suppliers or partners.

Based on a comprehensive literature search for this thesis only limited number of articles (Omar *et al.*, 2012, Sancha et al., 2015) considered RV as a single guiding theory to understand collaboration in the supply chain. Though RV is getting popular in collaborative supply chain domain, Chen et al. (2017) based on their recent comprehensive systematic literature review on collaboration for sustainability, found only one article deployed RV theory to comprehend collaboration for sustainability. Previous studies have not focused on this theory to understand technology integration in marketing for SC collaboration and improved performance. RV postulates that technology-enabled marketing facilitates SC collaboration, which will lead to sustained competitive advantage.

## The Influences of Technology-Enabled Marketing on Supply Chain Collaboration

Collaboration is the joint activities between the partners in the supply chains. Gunasekaran et al. (2015) referred to Supply chain collaboration as the relationship developed for a long time between supply chain members to lowering cost and risk as well as improving quality and market value. Collaboration in the literature mostly focused on partnership with the supplier, collaboration with customers, internal collaboration and some studies also looked at collaboration with other stakeholders including Universities, communities and local governments(Melander, 2018). The primary stimulus for collaboration comes from the thrust of achieving competitive advantage.

Firms in collaboration can do better than being in isolation because of the synergistic benefits. Once the firms are in partnership, they have access to each other resource, they share information, exchange knowledge, share reward and risk. However, a high degree of trust is crucial in a collaborative relationship. Also, how much information to share with the partners in the SCs is another concern. Nonetheless, collaboration helps the firm secure and maximise relational rents (improved performance) in supply chains has been previously researched, and it is prevalent in industrial practices as well. In the literature, supply chain collaboration and Supply Chain Integration (SCI) are being used interchangeably though they are not the same as the SCI concentrates on integrating certain parts of the organisational activities or processes with other departments in the same organisation or with other organisations. Supply chain integration is defined as the degree to which a business strategically collaborate with its SC partners and collaboratively accomplishes intra and inter-firm processes, with a view to achieving effective and efficient flows of goods and services, information, finances, and decisions to deliver the supreme value to the customers(Flynn *et al.*, 2010). While both involve sharing information, however, collaboration requires much more than just information sharing with the partners. Integration is possible without collaboration; however, for collaboration, integration is essential. To achieve or secure collaboration with the partners, it takes time.

IT-enabled marketing has a significant impact on SC collaboration. It was noted in the previous section that IT-enabled marketing facilitated digital marketing for companies to harness customers' requirements to fulfil their demand. To meet customers need or in other words to deliver the customers value requires partners in the chain (i.e. suppliers, manufacturer, distributor) to collaborate to ensure effective supply. IT plays a significant part in the entire chain starting from understanding customers' expectation through specialist software (i.e. AI), analysing their data and offer the customers with the products they need, until fulfilling their needs through feeding back the information along the supply chain to match demand with the supply.

## MANAGERIAL AND THEORETICAL IMPLICATIONS

As to the theoretical contribution of this research is the extension of marketing in SCM. Secondly, the elucidation of the concepts of marketing and technology-facilitated marketing for SC management in general and SC collaboration in particular. Most importantly, the amalgamation of Relational View (RV) theory to underpin the technology-enabled marketing and supply chain collaboration concepts should pave the way for future research. For managers, this study should help them understand the needs of technology in marketing, the role of relationship orientation and supply chain in general and SC collaboration in particular to deliver superior customers value. Understanding the requirements for integration between Marketing and SCM to survive and thrive in this ever-changing competition business environment is one of the key contributions this study can offer. It is crucial for the managers to understand that Marketing or SCM with isolated strategies may perhaps endure current challenges; however well not be equipped to compete in the technology-driven changing the environment. Hence, it is recommended for the mangers to integrate technology-enabled marketing and form a collaborative relationship between the partners in the chain to sustain competitive advantage.

## CONCLUSION

Finally, to conclude, this study endeavours to provide an inter-disciplinary perspective between marketing and SCM. The impact of innovative technologies on marketing and marketing functions to fulfil customers' needs are discussed. The concept of SCM and the SCM from a marketing perspective is explained and presented. The relationship orientation of Supply chain management that requires strategic partnership and improved collaboration are also discussed. It is crucial to recognise that the marketing and the supply chain should be considered an integral part of each other rather than isolated concepts. The organisation should harness the synergy through devising an integrated approach.

## REFERENCES

Achrol, R., & Kotler, P. (1999). Marketing in the network economy. *Journal of Marketing*, *63*(4_suppl1), 146–163. doi:10.1177/00222429990634s114

Ali, A., Bentley, Y., Cao, G., & Habib, F. (2017). Green supply chain management–food for thought? *International Journal of Logistics Research and Applications*, *20*(1), 22–38. doi:10.1080/13675567.2016.1226788

Alvarado, U., & Kotzab, H. (2001). Supply chain management— The integration of logistics in marketing. *Industrial Marketing Management*, *30*(2), 183–198. doi:10.1016/S0019-8501(00)00142-5

Ardito, L., Petruzzelli, A., Panniello, U., & Garavelli, A. (2019). Towards Industry 4.0: Mapping digital technologies for supply chain management-marketing integration. *Business Process Management Journal*, *25*(2), 323–346. doi:10.1108/BPMJ-04-2017-0088

Ashby, A., Leat, M., & Hudson-Smith, M. (2012). Making connections: A review of supply chain management and sustainability literature. *Supply Chain Management*, *17*(5), 497–516. doi:10.1108/13598541211258573

Barney, J. (1991). Firm Resources and Sustained Competitive Advantage. *Journal of Management, 17*(1), 99–120. doi:10.1177/014920639101700108

Cao, M., & Zhang, Q. (2010). Supply chain collaborative advantage: A firm's perspective. *International Journal of Production Economics, 128*(1), 358–367. doi:10.1016/j.ijpe.2010.07.037

Cao, M., & Zhang, Q. (2011). Supply chain collaboration: Impact on collaborative advantage and firm performance. *Journal of Operations Management, 29*(3), 163–180. doi:10.1016/j.jom.2010.12.008

Chen, L., Zhao, X., Tang, O., Price, L., Zhang, S., & Zhu, W. (2017). Supply chain collaboration for sustainability: A literature review and future research agenda. *International Journal of Production Economics, 194*, 73–87. doi:10.1016/j.ijpe.2017.04.005

Choi, T. Y., & Wu, Z. (2009). Taking the leap from dyads to triads: Buyer–supplier relationships in supply networks. *Journal of Purchasing and Supply Management, 15*(4), 263–266. doi:10.1016/j.pursup.2009.08.003

Christopher, M. (2000). The agile supply chain—Competing in volatile markets. *Industrial Marketing Management, 29*(1), 37–44. doi:10.1016/S0019-8501(99)00110-8

Christopher, M. (Ed.). (1992). *Logistics— the strategic issues*. London: Chapman and Hall.

De Vargas Mores, G., Finocchio, C. P. S., Barichello, R., & Pedrozo, E. A. (2018). Sustainability and innovation in the Brazilian supply chain of green plastic. *Journal of Cleaner Production, 177*, 12–18. doi:10.1016/j.jclepro.2017.12.138

Dyer, J. H., & Singh, H. (1998). The relational view: Cooperative strategy and sources of interorganizational competitive advantage. *Academy of Management Review, 23*(4), 660–679. doi:10.5465/amr.1998.1255632

Fisher, M. (1997, March/April). What is the right supply chain for your product? *Harvard Business Review*, 105–116.

Flint, D. (2004). Strategic marketing in global supply chains: Four challenges. *Industrial Marketing Management, 33*(1), 45–50. doi:10.1016/j.indmarman.2003.08.009

Flynn, B. B., Huo, B., & Zhao, X. (2010). The impact of supply chain integration on performance: A contingency and configuration approach. *Journal of Operations Management, 28*(1), 58–71. doi:10.1016/j.jom.2009.06.001

Gligor, D., Bozkurt, S., Russo, I., & Omar, A. (2019). A look into the past and future theories within supply chain management, marketing and management. *Supply Chain Management, 24*(1), 170–186. doi:10.1108/SCM-03-2018-0124

Goldman, S., Nagel, R., & Preiss, K. (1995). Agile competitors and virtual organisations: Strategies for enriching the customer. New York: Van Nostrand Reinhold.

Golgeci, I., & Gligor, D. (2017). The interplay between key marketing and supply chain management capabilities: The role of integrative mechanisms. *Journal of Business and Industrial Marketing, 32*(3), 472–483. doi:10.1108/JBIM-05-2016-0102

Gualandris, J., Golini, R., & Kalchschmidt, M. (2014). Do supply management and global sourcing matter for firm sustainability performance? An international study. *Supply Chain Management*, *19*(3), 258–274. doi:10.1108/SCM-11-2013-0430

Gunasekaran, A., Subramanian, N., & Rahman, S. (2015). Green supply chain collaboration and incentives: Current trends and future directions. *Transportation Research Part E, Logistics and Transportation Review*, *74*, 1–10. doi:10.1016/j.tre.2015.01.002

Juttner, U., & Christopher, M. (2013). The role of marketing in creating a supply chain orientation within the firm. *International Journal of Logistics: Research and Applications*, *16*(2), 99–113. doi:10.1080/13675567.2013.799636

Juttner, U., Christopher, M., & Baker, S. (2007). Demand chain management-integrating marketing and supply chain management. *Industrial Marketing Management*, *36*(3), 377–392. doi:10.1016/j.indmarman.2005.10.003

Kotler, P. (1972). A generic concept of marketing. *Journal of Marketing*, *36*(2), 46–54. doi:10.1177/002224297203600209

Kotler, P., & Keller, K. L. (2010).Marketing Management (15th ed.). Pearson Education.

Kumar, N., Scheer, L., & Kotler, P. (2000). From market driven to market driving. *European Management Journal*, *18*(2), 129–142. doi:10.1016/S0263-2373(99)00084-5

Lambert, D., & Cooper, M. (2000). Issues in supply chain management. *Industrial Marketing Management*, *29*(1), 65–83. doi:10.1016/S0019-8501(99)00113-3

Lambert, D. M., & Schwieterman, M. A. (2012). Supplier relationship management as a macro business process. *Supply Chain Management*, *17*(3), 337–352. doi:10.1108/13598541211227153

Lavie, D. (2006). The competitive advantage of interconnected firms: An extension of the resource-based view. *Academy of Management Review*, *31*(3), 638–658. doi:10.5465/amr.2006.21318922

Leuschner, R., Rogers, D. S., & Charvet, F. F. (2013). A meta-analysis of supply chain integration and firm performance. *The Journal of Supply Chain Management*, *49*(2), 34–57. doi:10.1111/jscm.12013

Melander, L. (2018). Customer and Supplier Collaboration in Green Product Innovation: External and Internal Capabilities. *Business Strategy and the Environment*, *27*(6), 677–693. doi:10.1002/bse.2024

Mentzer, J. (2004, May/June). Understanding demand. *Supply Chain Management Review*, 38–45.

Mentzer, J., DeWitt, W., Keebler, J., Min, S., Nix, N., Smith, C., & Zacharia, Z. G. (2001). Defining supply chain management. *Journal of Business Logistics*, *22*(2), 1–25. doi:10.1002/j.2158-1592.2001.tb00001.x

Mentzer, J. T., & Gundlach, G. (2010). Exploring the Relationship Between Marketing and Supply Chain Management: Introduction to the Special Issue. *Journal of the Academy of Marketing Science*, *38*(1), 1–4. doi:10.100711747-009-0150-4

Mesquita, L. F., Anand, J., & Brush, T. H. (2008). Comparing the resource-based and relational views: Knowledge transfer and spillover in vertical alliances. *Strategic Management Journal, 29*(9), 913–941. doi:10.1002mj.699

Min, S., & Mentzer, J. T. (2000). The Role of Marketing in Supply Chain Management. *International Journal of Physical Distribution & Logistics Management, 30*(9), 766–787. doi:10.1108/09600030010351462

Noci, G. (2019). The evolving nature of the marketing–supply chain management interface in contemporary markets. *Business Process Management Journal, 25*(2), 379–383. doi:10.1108/BPMJ-07-2018-0202

Omar, A., Davis-Sramek, B., Myers, M. B., & Mentzer, J. T. (2012). A global analysis of orientation, coordination, and flexibility in supply chains. *Journal of Business Logistics, 33*(2), 128–144. doi:10.1111/j.0000-0000.2012.01045.x

Parente, H. D., Lee, D. P., Ishman, D. M., & Roth, V. A. (2008). Marketing and supply chain management: A collaborative research agenda. *Journal of Business and Industrial Marketing, 23*(8), 520–528. doi:10.1108/08858620810913335

Sancha, C., Gimenez, C., Sierra, V., & Kazeminia, A. (2015). Does implementing social supplier development practices pay off? *Supply Chain Management, 20*(4), 389–403. doi:10.1108/SCM-07-2014-0239

Sanders, N. R. (2012). Supply chain management: A global perspective. Wiley Global Education.

Seuring, S., & Gold, S. (2013). Sustainability management beyond corporate boundaries: From stakeholders to performance. *Journal of Cleaner Production, 56*, 1–6. doi:10.1016/j.jclepro.2012.11.033

Sheth, J., Sisodia, R., & Sharan, A. (2000). The antecedents and consequences of customer-centric marketing. *Journal of the Academy of Marketing Science, 28*(1), 55–66. doi:10.1177/0092070300281006

Slack, N., Chambers, S., & Johnston, R. (2010). Operations management (6th ed.). Pearson Education.

Soylu, A., Oruç, C., Turkay, M., Fujita, K., & Asakura, T. (2006). Synergy analysis of collaborative supply chain management in energy systems using multi-period MILP. *European Journal of Operational Research, 174*(1), 387–403. doi:10.1016/j.ejor.2005.02.042

Srivastava, R., Shervani, T., & Fahey, L. (1999). Marketing, business processes, and shareholder value: An organizational embedded view of marketing activities and the discipline of marketing. *Journal of Marketing, 63*(4_suppl1), 168–179. doi:10.1177/00222429990634s116

Stolze, J. H., Mollenkopf, A. D., Thornton, L., Brusco, M. J., & Flint, D. J. (2018). Supply Chain and Marketing Integration: Tension in Frontline Social Networks. *The Journal of Supply Chain Management, 54*(3), 3–21. doi:10.1111/jscm.12169

Svensson, G. (2002). Supply chain management: The re-integration of marketing issues and logistics theory and practice. *European Business Review, 14*(6), 426–436. doi:10.1108/09555340210448785

Ueki, Y. (2016). Customer pressure, customer–manufacturer–supplier relationships, and quality control performance. *Journal of Business Research, 69*(6), 2233–2238. doi:10.1016/j.jbusres.2015.12.035

Womack, J. P., & Jones, D. (1996). Lean thinking: Banish waste and create wealth in your corporation. New York: Simon and Schuster.

Yu, W., Jakobs, M. A., Chavez, R., & Feng, M. (2016). The impacts of IT capability and marketing capability on supply chain integration: A resource-based perspective. *International Journal of Production Economics*, *55*(14), 4196–4211. doi:10.1080/00207543.2016.1275874

## KEY TERMS AND DEFINITIONS

**Digital Marketing:** Deployment of digital technologies in marketing and their management is referred to as digital marketing.

**Supply Chain Collaboration:** Supply chain collaboration can be defined as the relationship developed for a long time between supply chain members for mutual benefits and goals accomplishments including lowering cost and risk as well as improving quality and market value.

**Supply Chain Management:** The SCM could to defined as the network of organisations working together to efficiently create, deliver and recreate value as a form of goods and services to consistently and resiliently satisfy customers' requirements at the right time with optimum quality and minimum cost.

**Technology-Enabled Marketing:** Technology-enabled marketing can be referred to as the marketing activities that are facilitated by the usages of innovative technologies.

# Chapter 12
# Characteristics of Millennials and Technology Adoption in the Digital Age

**Imad Yasir Nawaz**
*Northumbria University, London, UK*

## ABSTRACT

*This chapter explores the attitude and behaviour of Millennials towards digital platforms. Millennial or Generation Y is the much talked about generation among business circles at the moment, and considering their ways of thinking, behaving, and preferences, organisations are altering their practices as they are the active workforce at the moment. In this chapter, the authors have tried to explore various aspects of Millennial life, preferences, practices, and attitudes including their behavior towards work practices, corporate social responsibility, cultural variations, education, buying patterns and technology, technological devices, and social/digital platforms. Millennial consumers' behaviours are affected many personal factors such as gender identity, income level, education, geography, political affiliations, and religion and non-personal factors, such as organisational effort, brand, technological factors, social pressures, and so on.*

## INTRODUCTION

The Consumer behaviour theories and models attempt to explain the consumer behaviour process, stages and relevant factors that influence the consumer decision process.

However, some studies indicate that the currently available consumer behaviour models are incomplete or are not able to address the needs of a new generation of consumers – the millennials. In 2016, there were around 1.8 billion Millennials worldwide (out of 7.4 billion people), and the estimation indicates that by 2020 around half of the world's workforce will be of Millennials and a buying power of $1000 billion (Newman, Kramer, & Blanchard, 2016).

DOI: 10.4018/978-1-7998-0131-3.ch012

Millennials receive information via ICT channel and have different lifestyles and value systems, hence the way the millennials search, prefer, chose, shop or use products or services are quite different than the previous generations (Cimperman, et al., 2018). Many organizations have responded to the needs of generation Y, but at the same time, there are organisations who are still using their traditional approaches to attract millennials which are proving ineffective. This chapter focuses on the consumer decision process and factor influence millennials' behaviours with a special focus on their online or digital platform usage related behaviours.

## LITERATURE REVIEW

Before discussing the preferences of Millennials or Generation Y consumers, it is worth exploring who Millennials are and what sort of key characteristics they possess which make them distinguished from the older generations.

### Characteristics of Millennials

As per the Generational theory (Karl Mannheim, 1959 cited by O'Connor, 2016), a generation becomes different from another generations due to some very significant historical and social context (e.g. world war, technical revolutions, big social changes) in which the individuals were raised This distinctive generation can be named as new generations due to their different characteristics, values & norms, etc. Such a generation's 'time - boundaries' (period) are formed when some new significant historical and social events occur that would have influenced and changed their values, norms, attitudes, behaviour and the life experiences (as different from other generations) of those people born during and after those significant events. For example generation of baby boomers was born during the period the World War II, generations X was formed post the TV and post-world war industrial growth, Generation y (Millennials) during the period of 'internet, mobile and ICT revolutions'. Thus each generation is unique and different from other generations due to different and significant life events and experiences, so the people born in different generations have different values, attitudes, traits and frames of reference and decision making processes (O'connor, 2016).

In compliance with the definition of Goffman (2017) that generations offer an opportunity to assess different groups of the population through their position in the work/life cycle, whether they are young adults, middle-aged or retired group of people born at different times. Thus, study of generations provides researchers with valuable information to analyse and understand visual changes in age-related groups' views, behaviours and characteristics over time, by looking at various indicators such as use of global technology, economic and social change, ageing process that shape the views of people (Blowfield & Murray, 2014).

There are no definitive birth Year delimitations of this generation as various authors claim that the Millennials were born between 1980 and 1996, or from the 1980s to year 2000s as depicted in *Figure 1* (Porral, et al., 2017). There is much contradictory age specification of Millennials but most of the definitions situate Millennials as a group of people in the age typically placed between 23-38 years old, born between 1980 to 1996 (See Figure 1) (Pew Research Centre, 2019).

*Figure 1. The generations defined*
*Retrieved from: https://www.pewresearch.org/fact-tank/2019/01/17/where-millennials-end-and-generation-z-begins*

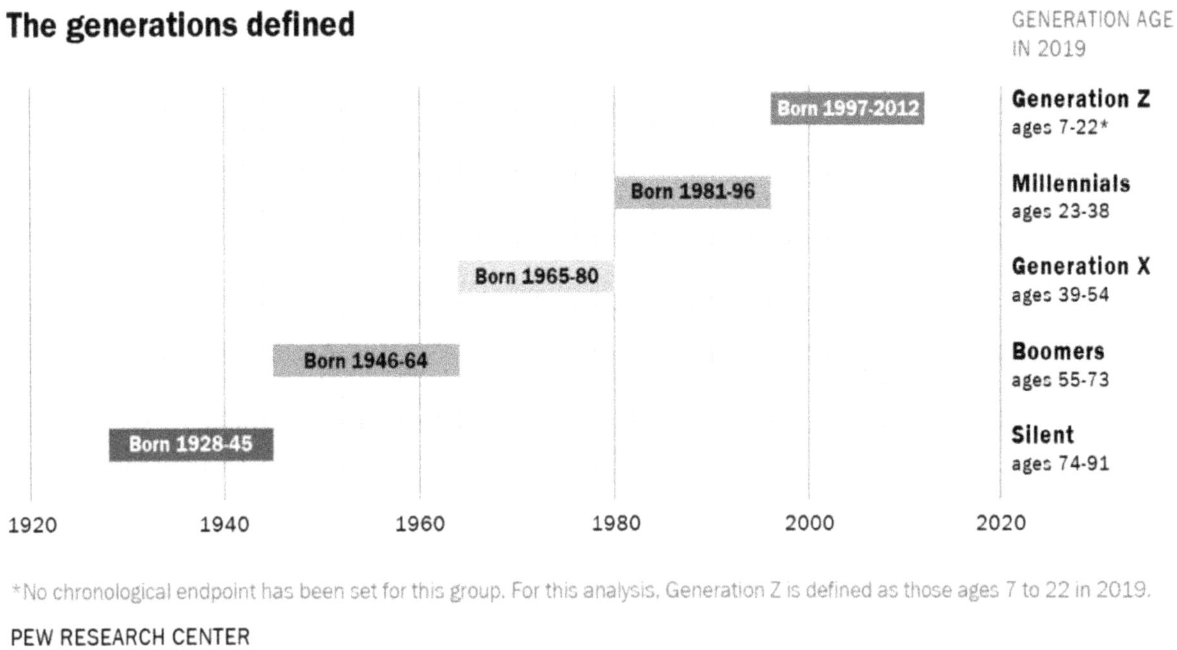


However, it would not be wrong to say that they are born in the era of mobile phones and when the internet spread was booming. The millennial generation is also known as Generation Y, Echo Boomers, Millennials, Why Generation, Gen Wired, Net generation, We Generation, DotNet Generation, First Globals, iPod Generation and IT, etc. (Dhanoa & Goyal, 2018).

Millennials also differ in terms of their communication and way of interactions, as they use more of mobile phones, active on social network sites, like games, music, pictures, email, and so on (Cimperman et al., 2018). Therefore, their decisions are influenced by social network platforms, online reviews and facilitating applications that must be considered by the organisations while developing new products and services as Generation Y has emerged as one of the key stakeholders in the market hence cannot be ignored.

In terms of buying behaviour Cimperman et al., (2018) opined that baby boomers buying process was initiated by developing trust with the retailers where the buying process of millennials starts with the trust of a product or brand and then they prefer the hassle-free online process of transactions. As they are heavy users of mobile phones and online shopping portals, therefore, millennials prefer platforms or Apps which are not only low in perceived risk, easy to use, compatible across platforms, useful but also provide them with fun and low cost (Cimperman et al., 2018). They also attain gratification by exploring products and services online, comparing their features, cost, and trustworthiness of the sellers as well. At the same time they are also the keen readers of past reviews on product and services but also make time to post reviews about their experiences regarding purchased products and services in order to help out other people to make more informed decisions which also shows that organisations are also not compelled to streamline their process, deliver products as per their expectations but also make every possible effort to collect positive online reviews for them. As Frederick (2018) opines that millennials spend more time online to search for product or service related honest & trustworthy information in order to make their purchase decisions and as they are natives to the technology they prefer user-generated contents (UGC) and online reviews to make their purchase decisions. (O'connor, 2016) . A study in Ireland has evidenced that millennials trust their peers more than brands and so they actively seek out recommendations from their peers by watching a variety of UGC on YouTube (O'connor, 2016).

Millennials grew up listening to CDs and renting movies from video stores, surfing internet occasionally, and many were already in their 20s when the iPod, iPod Touch, and iPhone first debuted and a majority of the millennials experienced Netflix, Amazon, Facebook, YouTube, and Twitter in their late 20s. (Newman et al., 2016) therefore they have witnessed immense technological transformation in the wider society which continuously influence their behaviours. In relation to the previous statement, one of the strongest attributes of Millennials is associated with highly developed technological skills due to post computer revolution of Generation X (Pew Research Center, 2019). Arora and Kshatriya (2017), defines Millennials as individuals who are focused on working in their own ways which makes them different from other past work societies. Brown (2017) recognised the unique working characteristics of Millennials i.e. use of digital working patterns, open communication, no division, less supervision at workplace and support for work-life balance from employers. Additionally, Storey (2016), express Millennials as the generation of digital natives, more significant, impatient, experimental learners, multitaskers who live the world of network connection and chooses selective, personalised and customised goods and services. However, McKenzie (2017) argues that Millennials are the most vulnerable group of modern work generation that grew up in a strongly socially-networked world.

Millennials also demonstrate extreme confidence, awareness, spend more time in the company of friends, engaged with social networking, influenced by personalized messages or word of mouth, more beauty conscious & much concerned of their physical appearance, have higher longing for individuality and are in large number with better purchasing power (Dhanoa & Goyal, 2018).

Millennials represent around 25% of the global population, and a study by Oracle found that these are in their 20s and are essentially making all of their household decisions with a total of $600 billion of purchasing power and driven by high quality, trustworthy and low-cost brands (Oracle, 2015). Oracle (2015) has identified five segments of Millennials. (*See Table 1*). The new digital technology can help organisation in acquisition, activation and ultimately advocacy from Millennials. As millennials are more inclined towards using mobile apps or mobile ordering systems, so any technology that is frictionless; anticipate demand; integrate online and in-store experiences, facilitate omnichannel commerce, track digital behaviour and trigger purchasing, deliver engaging dynamic content via web, social, email and mobile channels, personalize interactions and recommend relevant product and services in real-time, monitor social media and engage via social marketing and deliver a consistent service can leverage consumer insights to drive optimized and meet consumer expectations and trust which will be most significant factor for success (Oracle, 2015).

The consumer' attitudes, norms, values, aspirations and purchase behaviour developments are influenced by interpersonal influence. Social information plays an important role in consumer' purchase decisions and online social conversation is very significant influences of Millennials generation,.(Dhanoa & Goyal, 2018). Regarding millennials, need to be identified with others, or to enhance self -image, or willingness to conform to others expectations, or to seek information (normative, utilitarian value) and awareness from others, etc. might be the underlying drivers to use social information (Dhanoa & Goyal, 2018).

*Table 1. Segments of millennials source: adapted from (Oracle, 2015)*

| Segments of Millennials (born 1980-1996) | Characteristics |
|---|---|
| Up & Comers | a diverse segment of party-loving males, having a high income and more education levels, has high purchasing power low awareness of brands, etc |
| The Mavens | Mom segment in their 30s-with high income and a baby in tow and are brand aware & are a variety of seekers. |
| The Eclectics | Mostly females free spirits looking for the perfect deal, with a high level of brand and other awareness. |
| The Sceptics | Mostly video gamers, social media, sci-fi films, and fast food and IT stuffs and grab-and-go kind of customers. not easily swayed by TV ads, social media or traditional in-store experiences and have low awareness of brands. |
| Trendsetters | the youngest segment, start or adopt the new trend, latest entertainment gossip and have large social networks to stay connected and buy the widest variety of brands. |

## Millennials and Consumer Behaviours

The consumer behaviour is a process by which a consumer identify needs, searches for information, evaluate alternatives, chooses, buys, uses and disposes of a product or services. Many personal, psychological, Political, Economic, social, technological, ecological and organisational marketing related factors do influence consumer behaviour and consumer decision-making process (*see figure 2*) (Moreno, et al., 2017). As each generation of consumer is exposed to a range of different factors, so their buying process and decision making will be different. As the Millennials have many unique personal characteristics and they were born during and particular phase of political social and technological environments hence, their behaviour is dependent on those factors. The global political instability of 1990s such as Congo War (1997-2003), The Yugoslav Wars (1991-1995), The Chechen Wars (1994-ongoing), The Gulf, The Afghanistan War (2000songoing), Iraq War (2003–2011, Arab–Israeli conflict (2000s – ongoing),, Israeli–Palestinian conflict (2000s-ongoing) etc. and various terrorist attacks have influenced the values, attitudes, lifestyles opinions and norms of the Millennial generation (Anastasia, 2016). These situations have made them doubtful of political moves, media distrust, and apathy towards political activism so they demand more transparency and credibility from media and organisations.

Similarly, the concerns for ecology, environment degradations, and substantial development during the same period have made Millennials more concerned about corporate social responsibility, and suitable production and consumptions as exhibited in **Figure 2.**

The globalisation movements, human rights, and gender equality and other social movements of the 1990s has infused value of equality of gender roles in Millennials, thus they have become more accommodative for diversity, independence of individuals to make choices for themselves and at the time they show higher preferences for self-expression and freedom of speech etc. (Anastasia, 2016),

Similarly, the spread of internet and related technologies (pcs, mobile phones, smartphones, iPod, iPad, online music and video streamlines, social networking sites, Web 2.0 technologies) during the late nineties and early twenties has deeply affected the values frameworks, preferences, norms, lifestyles and behaviours of the Millennial consumers.

*Figure 2. Factors influencing millennial consumers' decision process*

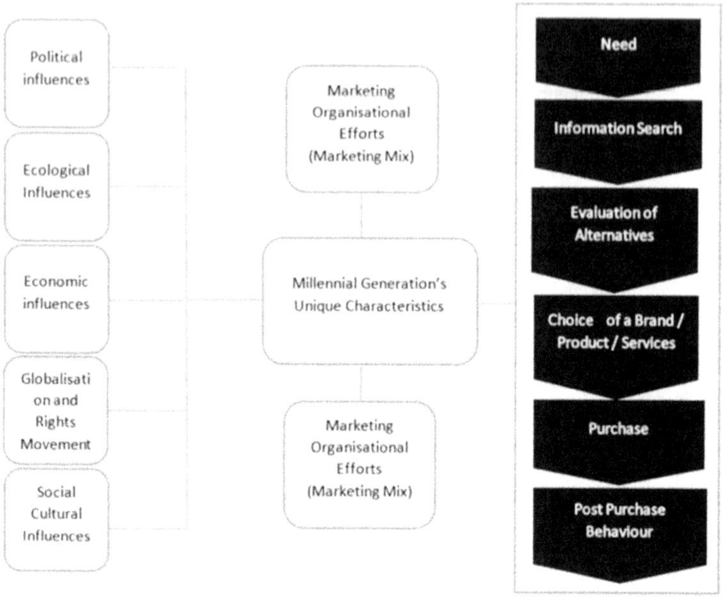


Millennial consumers' behaviours are affected by many personal factors; such as gender identity, income level, education, geography, political affiliations, and religion and also non-personal factors, such as organisational effort, brand, technological factors, social pressures, etc. also influence their behaviours (Newman et al., 2016).

The previous research has argued that Millennials are individualistic, technology-savvy, and as having high self-identity, self-esteem with unrealistic expectations, impatience, materialistic and narcissism, often group-oriented, highly responsible, independent, consumption-oriented and skeptical (Porral et al., 2017), thus the generations wants products or services which match their lifestyle and personality, and self-expression.

In order to understand the behaviours and retain Millennials either as employees or buyers, various studies by leading organisations and authors took place which includes "Beyond the Baby Boomers: the Rise of Generation Y", (KPMG, 2017), "Generation Y: Powerhouse of the Global Economy" (Deloitte, 2008), "Managing the Millennials: HR Survey of Recent Graduates" (PWC, 2011), "and "Millennials: Confident. Connected. Open to Change, (PEW, 2018) which all concluded that Generation Y possesses key characteristics including advanced technological skills, attitude towards work-life balance, social responsibility, highly value education and diversity (Bannon et. al., 2011). As the Millennials are also known as 'Echo Boomers' and 'Generation Y' who are entirely different from their previous generation are the drawing attentions of strategists, authors and researchers to understand how they influence the work practices (Macky et al. 2008) and what organisation need to do in order to attract them, galvanise them towards organisational goals and develop harmonised relationships with them (Cennamo and Gardner 2008; De Hauw & De Vos, 2010) as they are shaping up the market and emerging as one the prominent marketing force either in the form of workforce within organisations or as a customer and consumer in the market.

De Hauw and De Vos (2010) identified that the expectation of Millennials are influenced by factors such as careerism, optimism, and individual differences therefore in the situation of economic and political instability they will lower their expectation about the organisational environment and work-life balance. In addition to recent findings, Jenkin (2015), discovered that Millennials are more committed to values and ethics. Therefore, it is necessary for businesses to focus on corporate social responsibility practices as they not only support employee-employer relationship, assist in maintaining a safe and ethical working environment in order to attract potential Millennial workforce but they also create a positive image and gain an identity of 'brand of choice' which millennials prefer to get associated with as their customer or consumer. Today's, organisations are focused on attracting and retaining Millennials due to their fresh and innovative way of customizations and personalisation of goods and services and technological advancement.

The different factors and unique characteristics of Millennials require a different marketing approach to effectively create and captures customer values. They prefer a different kind of marketing promotional and communications channels which organisations can use to leverage their position.

## Millennials and Psychological Factors

The psychological contract is a mental or implicit contract (Kotter, 1973) between supplier and users which is established over the time period, based on the mutual relationship they have maintained, performed and expectations met for each other. Psychological contract informs guides what each party is expecting to give and receive in their relationship (Kotter 1973; Pant & Venkateswaran, 2019). Based on the written contract both parties share a harmonious relationship where both parties safeguard each other interests and meet expectations thus the psychological contract is established. De Vos et al. (2009) suggested that in the case Millennials it is anticipatory psychological contact which is defined as "individuals' pre-relationship beliefs about their future relationship, trust and keeping promises to each other's (De Hauw & De Vos, 2010, P 294). In terms of buying behaviour, Millennials prefer a range of products, however, their individualistic values and self-image conscious is leading towards a range of luxury products. The Millennials attitude towards buying luxury products (including affordable luxury products) is much influenced by ' quality of products, customised offering, online presence or platforms, digital content, social media, inspirational content, truly unique experiences, online word of mouth, celebrities and fashion influencers such as key opinion leaders (KOLs). They are looking for quality products, inspirational content and truly unique experiences (Com, 2017). The continuous connectivity to the internet creates plenty of opportunities for organisation to impact consumers' attention and behaviours but using contextual data and personalise interactions. Millennials attach high importance to their individual liberty, individuality and freedom, which shapes their expectation towards products and they prefer to get involved with an organisation where social connections, collaboration and cooperation is encouraged (De Hauw & De Vos, 2010).

Research also reveals that Millennials display a higher level of self-esteem and assertiveness but at the same time they also exhibit negative attributes such as narcissism as well (Twenge et al. 2008) which means higher level of narcissism also a reason for high self-esteem and assertiveness therefore appropriately designed products and information about products are regarded as psychological factors which promote self-esteem, autonomy achievement and recognition. Millennials like sharing economy platforms and believe in key opinion leaders more than the non-Millennials. Thus Innovation or disruptive innovation is way forward for organisations to market their goods and services therefore, organisations are using peer reviews, online opinion leaders, pop-up stores, etc. The organisation should understand that Millennials are not driven only by innovative products but also by functionality and the products ability to improve efficiency or make their lives more convenient (Com, 2017).

According to Parsa et al. (2015), opines that organiations can attain credibility and positive image in customer's eyes by making a contribution towards economic, social and cultural development of the society. Hence, it not only establishes better relations between orgnaisation and public but also make an immese contribution towards developing a favourable image people's mind. Involvement in corporate social responsibilities forms better bondage between organisation and its stakeholders therefore in order to promote oganisational identify, demonstrate commitment towards sustainable development and enhance stakeholder's engagement CSR initiatives play a significant role (Boxman & Flap, 2017; Klimkiewicz & Oltra, 2017).

In this regard, Ward (2016) conducted a survey which clearly indicates that 52% of people consider that CSR progrmames benefit both organisation and community where approximately 41% of people do not favour this stance. The close examination of the community and various groups reveals that young people often recognised as Millennials or Generation Y show the deepest sensitivity towards to corporate social responsibility and ethical practices as they strongly believe that such practices will help to make the world a better place for habitation (Connellet et al., 2012). Therefore they are more likely to work in organisations involved in CSR activities similarly they would consider CSR while buying products and services (Klimkiewicz & Oltra, 2017). As millennials are a significate segment of the market which cannot be ignored therefore companies shall formulate a consistent communication strategy to highlight their CSR initiative in order to attract them (Cone Communications, 2015).

## Millennials Media Habits

Though Millennials to some extent can be from the pre-internet, pre-smartphone and pre-online shopping world, however, they are power users and comfortable adopters of new technology. Except for a few specific tech-driven subcultures, they are comfortable with Mobile commerce, search, social channels, digital media, collaboration tools of an omnichannel ecosystem, though their world does not revolve around technology (Newman et al., 2016).

The Millennials are technological savvy, they like internet-based media, social media, video contents, however, they hate 'pop-up windows and other annoying content such as intrusive advertisements, Spams and too much-unwanted content (Anastasia, 2016). They want convenient and customized services but not at the cost of privacy and security, so they got a love-hate relationship with cookies or other tracking technologies. The millennial consumers use a range of media platforms such as Google search engine for searching, Instagram for pictures, social networking sites such as Facebook and Independent Reviews for customer reviews. They are also using YouTube for previous customer's experiences and product views, organisation's own website opening hours and prices, reviews of bloggers and celebrities, brand communities for engagements and sharing experiencing and so on.

According to the Independent Newspaper (August 2018), Millennials are 31.5% of the total world's 7.7 billion population which is three times larger than their predecessor Generation X. This huge population of Millennials are the active workforce working in various capacities in different organisations, shaping, reshaping and forming new ways to working, introducing new values and thinking patterns and labelled as "digital natives" (Shaw & Fairhurst, 2008) due to Internet, awareness, usage and adaptation of new technologies during their childhood and adolescence. The technological transformations have shaped not only their values but attitudes, behaviour, and preferences as well which has made them comfortable towards fast-paced, a high-tech environment which nurtured certain practices of communication, networking and extending their contacts beyond local proximities through social media platforms (Pew, 2010).

Besides the growth of science and technology, Millennials have grown in conditions where workforces across the globe are becoming more culturally diverse, people's mobility has increased than ever before, more and more people are switching their careers to follow their true aspirations, innovative organisations have not only made their way in the market and sustained but also posed a severe threat to existing established organisations and informal education focused on competences development are few among examples which have impacted on the attitude and behaviours of Millennials.

On the other hand political instability, terrorism, raging wars among countries, traumatic incidents, droughts, natural disasters, rogue leadership and organisational scandals impacted on their behaviours tremendously as well. Millennials consisting on both employees and customers are one of the significant players of today's economy who are challenging the existing traditional working practices and intend to change them (Bannon et. al., 2011) therefore, organisations need to enable conditions and identify a way to attract, retain and nurture this asset.

Millennials, are enthusiastic and positive to adopt technology for its more functional values, utility, and purpose-based reasons, they value digital technology that can offer them cheaper price options, free delivery, custom options, faster checkout, and smoother user experience or engage with it on social channels (Newman et al., 2016). This is evident via the initial low success of some innovative products like Google Glass, Apple watches as the generation of Millennials was searching for functional, purposeful and less for fun products. On the other hand, new generation Z (born after generation of Millennials) quickly adopted the same as well as many more new products.

Traditional advertising or marketing methods are not effective for Millennials due to their different media habits and usage patterns. The millennials use a number of devices, multiscreen, peer-influenced thus prefer only relevant and user-generated contents and videos, also they want to keep control on what they want to watch online and use advertisement blocking software (O'connor, 2016). This generation like a wide variety of online media, they read blogs, reviews, use social networking site regularly and update their online status, upload images and videos on social networks to openly express their interests and feelings (O'connor, 2016). The marketers need to consider the needs and media habits of this generation in order to reach them and offer customised products or services. Unlike generation X, who were TV lovers, the generation of Millennials is preferring Video on Demand services so they are becoming distant to the mainstream media and also getting increasingly resistant to advertisements. They like to rely more on social networks, friends, prefer fun, customisation, and authenticity in the messages, at the same time they prefer media or platforms of their own convenience and time (O'connor, 2016). Web 2.0 based online platforms give Millennials more power to generate and share customised content and information relevant to them. This new online word of Mouth (e WOM) is replacing the traditional word of mouth methods and is faster, wider and could be considered more independent by the Millennials. To trust information about a product or services the user check the quality of platform, transparency of the content and creator's balanced views or e-word of mouths, the credibility is also seen through the opinion lender's expertise in the area, number of followers they have and trustworthiness of the content creators and opinion leaders (O'connor, 2016 and De Hauw & De Vos, 2010). Though millennials being the younger generation currently has a lower income, but it going to increase significantly in the next decades, thus resulting in huge demand (Com, 2017).

## TECHNOLOGY AND MILLENNIALS

Previous studies have shown that that adoption of technology can be explained with Theories Of Reasoned Actions (TRA), Theories Of Planned Behaviours (TPB), Technology Acceptance Model (TAM) (Davis, 1989), Unified Technology Adoption Unified Theory of Acceptance and Technology-Use model or the UTAUT (Venkatesh, Morris, Davis & Davis, 2003), Gratification Theory (Katz, Blumler & Gurevitch, 1974, cited in Portal et al., 2017), and the Flow Theory (Csikszentmihalyi, 1977 cited in (Porral et al., 2017). TRA and TPB postulate that behavioural intentions are determined by consumers' attitude, social norms, and perceived behavioural controls. TAM and UTAUT models argue that acceptance depends on perceived ease of use, perceived usefulness, perceived self-efficacy, social norms, job relevance, etc. (Porral et al., 2017). The gratification theories argues that people use a product or technology for gratification, therefore, the main gratification with the use of technology includes information-seeking motives, seeking opinions, satisfying curiosity, novelty and socialization or social interaction for gaining insight into the circumstances of others, identifying with others and gaining a sense of belonging, while enabling connection with family, friends and society (Porral et al., 2017). The flow theory argues that use of new technology can also develop temporal detachment which is referred as an inability to register the passage of time while being engaged with technology due to deep involvement and focused immersion as the user finds it a highly enjoyable experience and fully immersed in the interaction with technology in a way that nothing else seems to matter. Porral et al. (2017) describes the flow experience as a seamless sequence of responses facilitated by interactivity and complemented by a loss of self-consciousness.

Millennials are recognised as Tech-Savvy Individuals who are heavily influenced by technology. O'connor (2016) describes millennials as a highly connected, technologically advanced and globally conscious generation which is open to experience new products and ideas than their previous generations. So Millennials have Techno-Philia - degree of love for using and adoption of technology thus, they tend not only to explore new technology, try new technology functions but also develop positive emotional and enduring associations with technologies as well as a positive motivational state towards technological use (Porral et al., 2017).

Millennial is a group which is born during the rapid booming of information and communication technologies (ICT), internets and mobile networks so are known as first digital natives and hence are much influenced by technological intervention marketing (Porral et al., 2017). They are technological savvy and readily technology adopters as well. They are the generation that has witnessed the swift technological transformation and experienced the globalised, post-digital and virtually connected face of the world. As per the research by PEW (2018) 92% (nine out of ten millennials) use smartphones, nearly 85% of them are actively using social media platforms where a vast majority of them is also using newly launched social media platforms including Instagram (52%), Snapchat (47%) as compared to their older generations.

The technologies are disrupting the sectors and consumers habits. The Millennial consumers, in turn, are disrupting the industries with their new demands of innovative, pragmatic products including luxurious products which led avenues for a variety of new emerging technologies such as smart cars, wearable watches, virtual reality and augmented reality, etc. (Com, 2017). In response to that organisations are adopting their online strategies e.g. integrating online and offline operations, using sharing economy models, developing new business models for monetization, go Omni-channels modes (conventional stores, websites, social media, webchats and mobile applications) to meet the needs of Millennials (Com, 2017).

*Figure 3. Technology adaptation among different generations Source: (PEW Research Centre, 2018)*

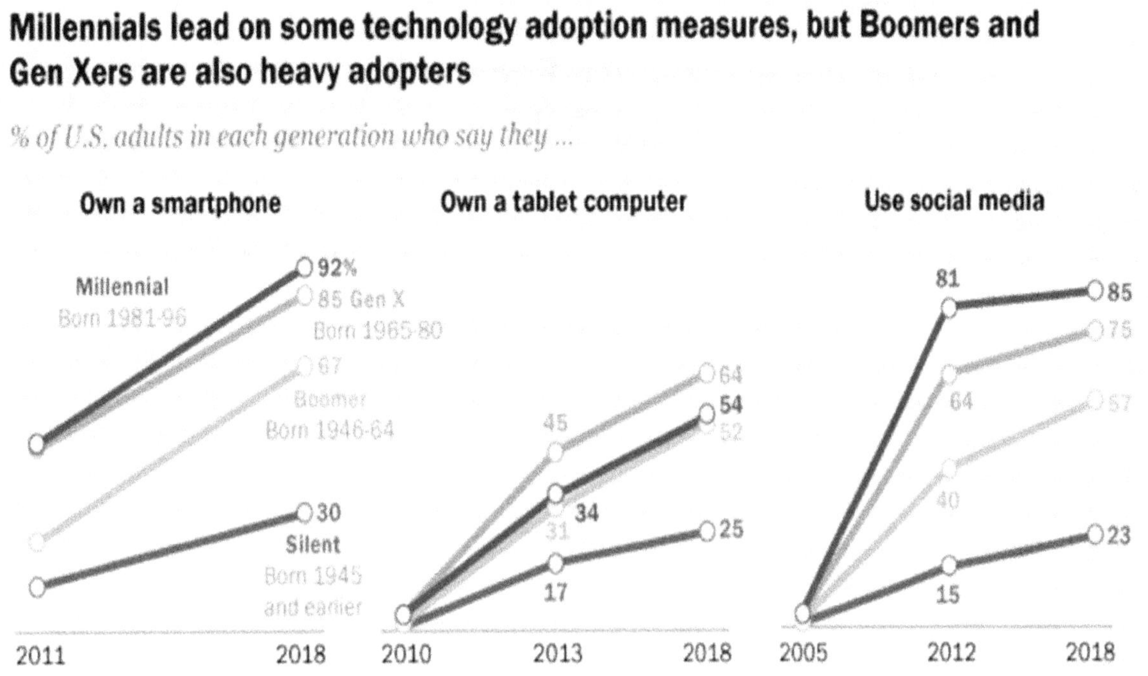


The below figure **(Figure 3)** clearly indicates that millennials are heavy users of smartphones and social media platforms as compare to their older generations however Generation X has outplaced Millennials in terms of adopting and owning a tablet where the Gap in this area is about 10% where 64% members of Generation X and 54% Millennials use and own a tablet.

Regarding social media platforms adaptation and usage Millennials are ahead of their older generations, however, Facebook usage among Millennials remained the same from 2012 to 2018 as shown in **Figure 4**, although the vast majority of Millennials are using newly developed platforms (see Figure 4). At the same time, more than 62% millennials are connected to the internet where 83% consider their cell phone as an extension of them, they tend to keep their phone with them 24 hours and spend most of their time playing video games both online and offline (Bannon, et. al., 2011).

The above trends clearly indicate results consistent to our expectations that Generation Y or Millennials are more inclined towards adaptation and usage of technological solutions as compare to Generation X, like staying connected and heavily rely on smartphones, internet and technological solution in their daily routine life such as travelling, finding places, staying connected to their peers, friends, family etc. this trends has also been confirmed by the research study conducted by National Centre for Sustainable Transportation by collecting responses from 2400 millennial respondents out of 3400 respondents that millennials exhibit "Travel Multitasking" as they tend to stay more online either through their smartphones or other devices (Circella, et. al., 2016). As the on-demand, technology-enabled transportation is on rise for number of reasons such as security, convenience, smartphone apps, transparency of tariffs, less waiting time, type of service, locations and payments methods thus preferred by the younger generation immensely across the world which has changed the traditional taxi trends and also paved a way for new technology-led firms to enter the market such as Lyft, Uber, Cream, Sidecar, etc. which extends short-

*Figure 4. Facebook usage among different generations Source: (PEW Research Centre, 2018)*

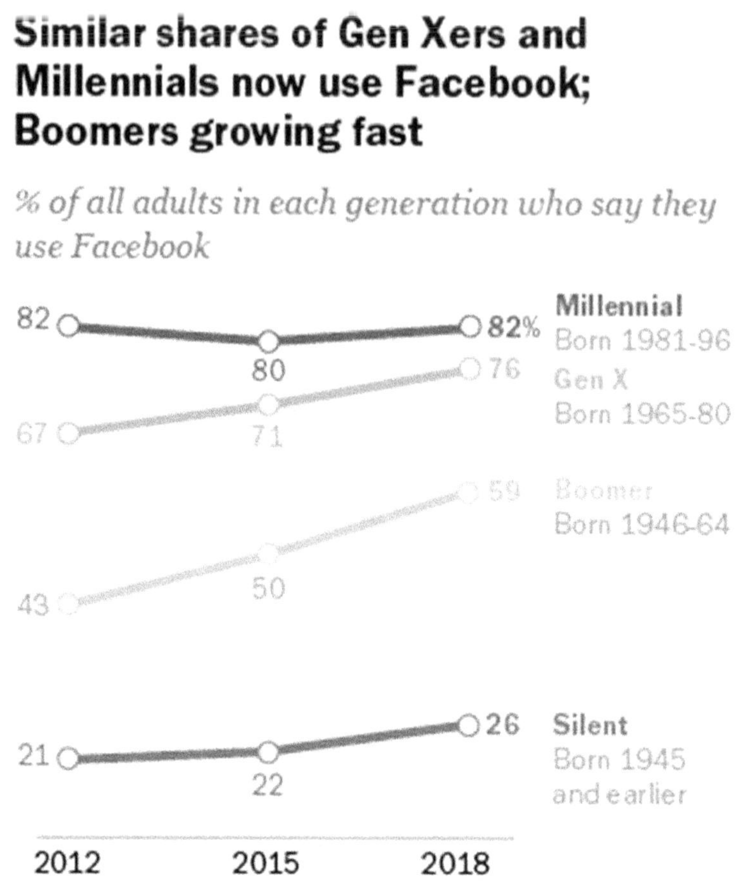


distance travel options. Rayle et al. (2014) stated that the technology-assisted traveling options through smartphones have not only facilitated 'real-time riders' but also created new employment opportunities for a number of people in the market and market is evolving constantly. Furthermore, the technology has also enabled people to 'split ride' to cut expenses by matching their origin and destinations via internet app as well. Research commissioned by Zipcar also endorses that millennials are more enthusiastic in using technology-assisted transport options than Generation X (Zipcar, 2013). In terms of traveling, technology is facilitating immensely and creating new social norms where the use of private cars is expected to decline which is good for the environment as Circella et al. (2016) suggest that millennials demonstrate stronger commitment towards environment protection.

The Millennials in a different part of the world has quite similarities in preferences of online platforms and online presence. For example, in China, Online shopping has effectively become a national pastime as around 77 percent of respondents picking it as their favourite leisure activity and for example, an annual Singles' Day bonanza created revenue of 25.3 billion US Dollars for Alibba.com (Com, 2017). The Chinese consumers shop online every week and their preferred stores include Tmall, JD.com, Alibaba.com, Amazon.com and VIP.com (Com, 2017).

*Figure 5. Factors influencing millennials' use of technology*

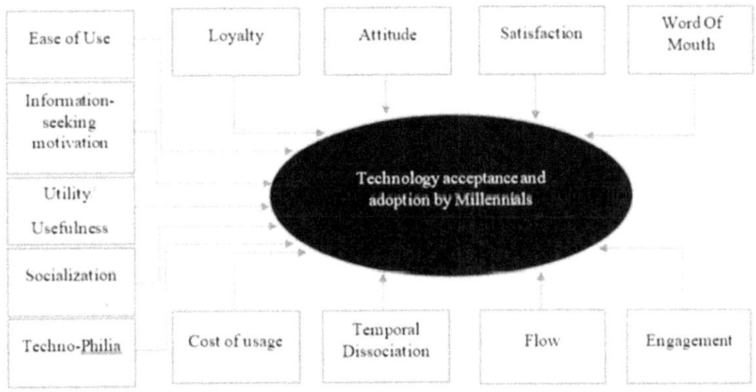


The main concerns in the e-commerce environment that are important to Millennials include inability to verify the authenticity and quality of items purchased online as well as offline, visual discrepancies price discrepancies, delivery issues, cumbersome return policies, electronic contracts and payments, dispute resolution mechanism, cybersecurity and unfair competition (Gupta & Dubey, 2016).

Thus, potential use of technology of millennials depends on many factors (as shown in *Figure 5*).

## A Case to Illustrate - Millennials and Use of Technology in the Education Sector

Every generation has certain unique characteristics which influence their assumptions, point of view to see the world, cultural and social values, etc. similarly millennials have experienced huge transition during their lifetime. They have seen developments from cassette players to MP3 Plyers to YouTube and Spotify, witnessed a journey from 2G, 3G to 4G internet and currently talking about 5G technologies means every department of life has been transformed in the last 2 decades which has not only influenced their attitude, ways of thinking, behaviour but expectations as well which is equally applied to the education sector as well. Therefore, they expect technology to play a vital role in teaching and learning where extensive and up to date information is accessible via different platforms and multimedia approaches tailored as per students' needs which facilitates in the learning process considering individual's learning styles (Chelliah & Clarke, 2011; Gibson & Sodeman, 2014). Therefore in this regard, various new developments have been noted such as the emergence of virtual learning platforms such as Moodle, Blackboard, etc. in order to facilitate learners beyond the classroom, helping them to learn at their own pace and encouraging more communication and connectivity between students and learners. At the same time, various other technologies have also been incorporated within these platforms which has enhanced the service quality further. Considering Millennials' aptitude towards technology and anticipating the future market demands, industry is also joining hands with higher education institutions to promote technology in the education system as Google generously donated funds to many Universities for technology promotion in their curriculum similarly in 2013 Microsoft donated 1.3 million dollars to University of Washington for studies related to Technology's role in Policy Making and promoting research and development on new technological devices (Hartley, 2011; Bishop, 2013).

The millennials are good team players, create good impact on the organisation, prefer open communication and open to adopt new ways of working and communicating through technology however, matter of fact is that they also lack soft skills and competencies such as literacy and numeracy especially in developed countries where the standard of education have improved as compare of previous generations (Myers & Sadaghiani, 2010; Au-Yong-Oliveira et al., 2018). It is an open secret that millennials have not only embraced technology in their daily routine life but also the heavily rely on that and are comfortable with technology, however, at the same time they have deficiency in their soft skills as Sahni (2014) defined as an ability to communicate oral and written competencies both, applying critical thinking, problem-solving skills and developing and harmonising better relationships with others. The findings of various researches even in developed countries including USA, UK, Australia, Canada, Hong Kong etc. clearly indicate that technology savviness is not a big concern for millennial but the biggest concern is the deficiency of their soft skills which is spanning over nearly all industries including Business, Finance, Engineering, Information Technology, Agriculture, etc. (Zaharim, et. al., 2009; Jackson, 2009; Sahni, 2011; Gibson & Sodeman, 2014).

As millennial students are having the good technical aptitude but lack in soft skills at the same time many Universities are facing a challenge that majority of their faculty has technology deficiency which is a hindrance in developing robust relationship between students and tutors as both need to speak the language (Johnson et. al., 2014). Educational Institutes are aware of this aspect; therefore, various organisational developmental measures are taken in this regard, tutors are offered a variety of learning and development programmes to enhance their capabilities on learning platforms and other relevant educational technologies. Additionally in order to support millennials and deliver them education as per their requirements the learning has been shifted from instructor-led teaching to student-centric education where exploring, learning, discovering, how to learn and apply learned knowledge practically beyond classroom has become more important therefore, identifying new way to teach considering students preferred learning styles, development of tutors and incorporating appropriate technology has become significant (Khan & Gouveia, 2017) which would be beneficial not only to millennial students but also for the educational institutions society at large. Teachers are also aware of the fact that in order to teach this generation of students they need to move away from traditional methods and adopt more innovative ways as millennials prefer working in collaboration, tend to participate in group discussions, link working in teams beyond classroom activities as well and they are not only open to express their ideas but less hesitant to experiments new ways of doing things. Therefore, activities shall be designed considering their learning styles, promote independent thinking, enable them to apply their innovative ideas and system should enable them to access and utilize resources remotely without any restrictions.

In recent times many free online learning platforms have also been surfaced and MOOCS is one of them which is adopted by a number of universities worldwide to offer courses online and it has also received very good response in the market by the students as it enables them to develop wider capabilities, extend their competences to best fit in the toughest job market ever and realise their dreams especially when fees are rising and education is becoming less affordable for most families all over the world. However, MOOCS is also not exempted from controversy as well as very many teachers are opposing the idea, even some educational institutions are reluctant to adopt it as they see this change a threat to their livelihood. Despite of all the reasons, the fact is that the transition is a reality and education sector is not an exception to it as Kessler (2013) noted that today organisations related to any industry or nature of business either they are researching on new drugs, involved in oil exploration, developing mobile applications, designing marketing campaigns, part of the financial industry or designing innovative environmentally friendly products – they all need graduates having strong cognitive skills, able to work in diverse cultural teams, detect the changing market patterns, competent to work in a virtual environment with different technologies and think strategically. In order to fulfill their needs, the only generation which these organisation can access and deal with is millennials who have grown up playing online games such as 'Call of Duty' therefore, their exposure to the technology while undertaking different courses also need to be enhanced.

They tend to be very career-oriented and expect rapid advancement and perks. They are very accustomed to being in the spotlight, receiving recognition for practically every achievement growing up no matter how trivial. Because of their skill at multitasking, millennials are likely to want to build parallel careers, not necessarily focusing on one job or profession at the exclusion of others. Thus, multitasking may ultimately take the form of continuous job-changing for millennials.

As the career development is one of the main priorities of millennials, they also expect swift advancement, accustomed to receiving recognition, value advancement and achievement even trivial in nature Research has also noted that the ability of multitasking enables millennials to develop parallel careers as well (Sandeen, 2008). Therefore, being career-oriented, able to multitask and work for parallel careers simultaneously encouraged a trend of continuing education while retaining their jobs has given rise to informal and online/distance learning programmes. Robinson (2008) stated that as millennials are tech-savvy and web-savvy and like to stay connected therefore distance learning mode of studies are attracting them, it provides them the flexibility to access instructions, materials, etc. 24/7 and also offer them more customised and personalised educational opportunities, however, they may also to be drawn towards face-to-face classroom-based learning as well. Sandeen (2008) suggested that in order to attract millennials for distance learning programmes, educational institutions can offer podcasts, webinars, extracts from tutor presentation, offering some perks and loyalty programmes will be effective as they expect to be treated special. Additionally marketing campaigns through social media platforms such as Facebook, Instagram, Twitter, Myspace, YouTube, LinkedIn, etc. can also play a vital role to attract them towards continuing education via distance/online learning modes.

## MARKETING TO MILLENNIALS

Buying Behaviour of Millennials Changing Traditional Marketing Practices. Remember that the millennial don't leave their mobiles away at any time, so these are their own preferred device to go online, hence any technology or apps design should first focus on design for smartphones. Two-thirds of Millennials expect a seamless omnichannel experience, so just 'doing digital' or 'doing mobile' is just not sufficient but connecting every channel, touchpoint, and experience—from discovery to purchase, and from unboxing to customer support, all the pieces should work, should be fit and all the pieces have to work together in perfect coherence and seamlessly (Newman et al., 2016).

The Millennial customer is market-savvy, hyper-aware, organized shoppers who easily jump from retailer to retailer in search of the best possible value, but they can be highly loyal to brands and retailers as associating to a brand is regarded as self-identity and self-image for social acceptance (Newman et al., 2016). The speed with which world is changing means the consumers will often have a feeling of nostalgia, for an instant the Millennials being a transitionary generation who have seen the world pivot from the early days of the internet to the mobile-first users to a new world of connected consumers. Hence the Millennials will have a high longing for nostalgic products, services and processes. The organisation can use technology to effectively scale, amplify, and deliver the answer to Millennial nostalgia and in this way, they have opportunity to become relevant and get attention among Millennial consumers (Newman et al., 2016).

Millennials have grown in an environment where technology provides a platform for personalization and immediate gratification in all aspects of life, hence marketers should use various digital marketing tools to enhance the inclusion of millennials in the needs arousal, search of information, consumption, personalisation, and development of particular offerings (Moreno et al., 2017).

Various forms of digital communication strategies such as online advertising and website features have been tried successfully on millennials. The online advertising strategies may include online advertisements, gamification advertisements, pop-up advertisements, emails, side-panel ads, coupons, YouTube videos, marketing channels and social media platforms (Smith, 2011). Those kinds of adds that engage consumers, provide relevant and customised information without information overloads will be liked by the Millennials similarly the website features include website layout, colour & graphics, personalisation, rewards, interactive, freebies, delivery, pricing, and return policy etc (Smith, 2011). The items that create a seamless experience, sense of flow and ease are liked by the consumers. Millennials find pop-ups, unclosable browser windows, flashing items, links to sponsors, mandatory software downloads, and other intrusive or distracting contents, etc. as annoying activities in an online environment (Smith, 2011). As such interruption can interfere with the temporal sense of flow experiences and works against the rule of consumer engagement, involvement and consumers' feelings of self-control.

The millennials want and use multiple channels to seek a product or brand-related information and evaluations of alternatives.

Millennials multitaskers, however, they are also short of time, thus Millennials seek 'chore vertical tasks' – the tasks that are necessary but aren't inherently empowering or rewarding such as banking and financial services, health care, bill paying, contacting a customer service representative, grocery shopping, auto repair, plumbing repair, and so on (Newman et al., 2016). The productivity or functional apps or platforms that save the customers time, enhance their digital experience, offer feature intuitive, convenience, speed, and give hurdle-free user interfaces with smartphone devices are very preferred by the Millennials (Newman et al., 2016).

The social networking sites are slowly losing it sheen for the millennials, due to the fact that during the initial phases of social media, it was overused for content delivery for customer engagements and now the customers have lost interest due to information overload and a brand being on social media has become banal or commodities for the customers (Newman et al., 2016). The purpose should be to create a deeper connection with customers and engage them with a real conversation with community and brand at multiple fronts with a social ecosystem. An effective social ecosystems shall use technology for social listening (human listening, AI listening, CRM, Big Data analytics and responses), create social community (community space, identity, activities, themes, peer to peer validation and rewarding community behaviour), develop and share social content (videos, live videos, blogs, Memes, podcasts, articles, pictures etc.) and develop deeper social engagement (human to human, human to machine AI, events, customer service, education, information and crowdsourcing etc.) with Millennials to create real shopper experiences and not just technology users' experience (Newman et al., 2016). It is important that technological applications provides natural shopping experience rather than interfere with that experience, thus technology should give them a state of a natural flow. For example a KFC shopper is a guest and an Amazon's shopper is a user, when the KFC shopper is given a menu, the shopper expect a consistent brand experience, similarly when an Amazon shopper is given a dashboard the shopper can expect a personalised experience but both of shoppers want real shopping experience, which is seamless, without discontinuity and a sense of social presence is delivered through their devices (Newman et al., 2016).

As Millennials also prefer luxury products such as clothing, shoes, jewellery, sports equipment, entertainment, health, beauty and food which appeal to hedonistic needs, social expressions, status-seeking and wealth show off or snobbing needs (Moreno et al., 2017).

Thus, in summary, Millennial consumer should be targeted with a marketing message which is visual and aesthetically fulfilling, appear the least commercial, address social and environmental issues, educate, empower and inspire the customer. This generation would prefer those communication channels, which is made of techno-social ecosystems. Such Tech - ecosystems are made up of integrations of social media platforms, blogs and review sites, featuring theme platforms and brand web-site, etc Also such a techno-social systems should offer community platforms, webinars, seminars, events, education, creativity workshops, sponsorship of role models, celebrities, to involve the customers in the brand development processes, etc. (Anastasia, 2016). As mentioned in their characteristics that they are impatient, impulse buyers, value time and seek value for money, hence they will prefer, low cost, fast delivery oriented omnichannel for watching and buying products or services.

## WAY FORWARD AND IMPLICATIONS FOR ORGANISATIONS

As compared to the previous generation of relatively passive consumers, the Millennials are more active who participate in the process of creation and development of products and services. Furthermore, the technology has enabled companies to capture consumer data through platforms and use this information to reshape the production process into an information loop between the Research & Development unit and consumers and finally engage and empower the Millennials in the whole process of value delivery networks (Com, 2017).

Launching Innovation in products and services, use of data analytics, artificial intelligence, customer-centric approaches, and customer engagement offer new opportunities for product co-creation and ultimately customization to Millennials (Com, 2017).

## CONCLUSION

This chapter provides a detailed discussion on the characteristics of millennials, analysis their key attitudes and behaviour, investigates millennials inclination towards technology, their preferences, decision-making process and also offers guidelines to organisations and marketers regarding developing relevant strategies to attract millennials.

Literature does not suggest a definitive birth year for millennials however according to some authors they were born between 1980 and 1996, and some argue that they fall between the 1980s to year 2000s (Porral, et. al., 2017). Millennials or Generation Y is possessed entirely different characteristics than their previous generation as they are heavy users of mobile phones and online shopping portals, therefore, prefer such digital platforms and application which are user-friendly, offer smooth services with less risk and provide fun at low cost (Cimperman et al., 2018). Research also noted significant aspects of millennials attitude as they are perfectionist, quality conscious, brans conscious and price-conscious but at the same time, they are an impulsive buyer and prefer novel fashions trends (Klein & Sharma, 2018).

As millennials are good with technology therefore they spend more time online to search and try finding trustworthy information about a product and service before buying and in this regard they usually take feedback and read online reviews given by other users (Frederick, 2018).

They are heavy users of smartphones and social media platforms as compare to their older generations. A vast majority of Millennials are using newly developed platforms and at the same time, more than 62% millennials are connected to the internet where 83% consider their cell phone as an extension of them which clearly indicate their attitude towards technology (PEW, 2018). Various Technology adaptation models are referred to analyse millennials attitude towards technology as O'connor (2016) describes them as a highly connected and technologically advanced which demonstrates a higher level of openness towards trying new ideas and experiencing new products. It is interesting to note that Generation Y across the globe illustrates more or less same sort of attitudes and behaviours which also distinguish them from previous generations. Like other fields, a huge transformation in the education sector has been noted where Millennials expect technology to play a vital role in teaching and learning as well. Therefore, education is not teaching-led anymore rather it is more student-centric was extensive and up to date information is accessible via different platforms and multimedia approaches tailored as per students' needs and their learning styles. Various contemporary educational platforms and flexible ways of learning have played an important role in widening participation and enabling masses to access education as per needs and convenience, in this regard MOOCS has made a huge contribution.

Similarly, marketers need to recognise that Millennials have experienced rapid technological transformation and have grown-up in an environment where technology delivers personalised and immediate gratification regarding the products and services they are looking for therefore, marketers need to establish such digital platforms which not only attract Millennials by tapping every phase of the decision-making process but also offer them more personalised services.

## REFERENCES

Anastasia, L. (2016). *Buying Behaviour Of Millennials Changing Traditional Marketing Practices*. Retrieved from https://www.theseus.fi/bitstream/handle/10024/107187/BachelorsThesisFinal.pdf?sequence=1&isAllowed=y

Arora, P., & Kshatriya, K. (2017). Millennials: The New Generation with High Employment Expectations. *International Journal (Toronto, Ont.)*, *5*(8).

Au-Yong-Oliveira, M., Gonçalves, R., Martins, J., & Branco, F. (2018). The social impact of technology on millennials and consequences for higher education and leadership. *Telematics and Informatics*, *35*(4), 954–963. doi:10.1016/j.tele.2017.10.007

Bannon, S., Ford, K., & Meltzer, L. (2011). Understanding Millennials in the Workplace. *The CPA Journal*, *81*(11), 61–65.

Bishop, T. (2013). *Can policy keep up with technology? New UW lab gets 1.7 million from Microsoft*. Retrieved from https://www/geekwire.com/2013/policy-technology-uw-create-lab-17mmicrosoft/

Blowfield, M., & Murray, A. (2014). Corporate responsibility. Oxford University Press.

Boxman, E., & Flap, H. (2017). Getting started: the influence of social capital on the start of *the occupational career*. In *Social capital* (pp. 159–181). Routledge.

Brown, G. (2017). The Millennials (Generation Y): Segregation, Integration and Racism, ABNF Journal. *Health Research Premium Collection*, *28*(1), 5–8. PMID:29873454

Cennamo, L., & Gardner, D. (2008). Generational differences in work values, outcomes and person-organisation values fit. *Journal of Managerial Psychology*, *23*(8), 891–906. doi:10.1108/02683940810904385

Chelliah, J., & Clarke, E. (2011). Collaborative teaching and learning: Overcoming the digital divide? *On the Horizon*, *19*(4), 276–285. doi:10.1108/10748121111179402

Cimperman, M. B., Harrison, A., Hatch, J., Pillar, K., & Snipes, T. (2018). Understanding the Millennial Buying Process in the Modern Digital Era - Secondary Research. *Honors Research Projects*. Available at: http://ideaexchange.uakron.edu/honors_research_projectshttp://ideaexchange.uakron.edu/honors_research_projects/546

Circella, G., Tiedeman, K., Handy, S., & Alemi, F. (2016). What Affects Millennials' Mobility? PART I: Investigating the Environmental Concerns, Lifestyles, Mobility-Related Attitudes and Adoption of Technology of Young. *National Center for Sustainable Transportation*. Retrieved from https://escholarship.org/uc/item/6wm51523

Circella, G., Tiedeman, K., Handy, S., & Alemi, F. (2016). *What Affects Millennials' Mobility? PART I: Investigating the Environmental Concerns, Lifestyles, Mobility-Related Attitudes and Adoption of Technology of Young*. National Center for Sustainable Transportation.

Com, M. (2017). *China' s Connected Consumers The rise of the Millennials*. Retrieved from https://assets.kpmg/content/dam/kpmg/cn/pdf/en/2017/12/chinas-connected-consumers-the-rise-of-the-millennials.pdf

Cone Communications. (2015). *Cone Communications Millennial CSR Study*. Retrieved from http://www.conecomm.com/research-blog/2015-cone-communications-millennial-csr-study#download-research

Connell, J. A., McMinn, N. E., & Bell, N. (2012). How will the next generation change the business world? A report on a survey. *Insights to a Changing World Journal*, *4*, 100–113.

Davis, F., Bagozzi, R. P., & Warshaw, P. R. (1989). User Acceptance of Computer Technology: A Comparison of Two Theoretical Models. *Management Science*, *35*(8), 982–1003. doi:10.1287/mnsc.35.8.982

De Hauw, S., & De Vos, A. (2010). Millennials' career perspective and psychological contract expectations: Does the recession lead to lowered expectations? *Journal of Business and Psychology*, *25*(2), 293–302. doi:10.100710869-010-9162-9

Deloitte. (2009). *Generation Y: powerhouse of the global economy Restless generation is a challenge–and a huge opportunity–for employers*. Deloitte Consulting LLP.

Dhanoa, R., & Goyal, N. (2018). Millennial Generations' Susceptibility to Interpersonal Influence: A Case of Personal Care Products Purchases. *International Journal of Management Studies*, (2). doi:10.18843/ijms/v5i2(6)/08

Frederick, W. C. (2018). Corporate Social Responsibility: From Founders to Millennials. In *Corporate Social Responsibility* (pp. [illegible]). Emerald Publishing Limited. doi:10.1108/S2514-175920180000002001

Gibson, L. A., & Sodeman, W. A. (2014). Millennials and Technology: Addressing the Communication Gap in Education and Practice. *Organization Development Journal*, 63–75.

Goffman, E. (2017). *Asylums: Essays on the social situation of mental patients and other inmates*. Routledge. doi:10.4324/9781351327763

Gupta, M. P., & Dubey, A. (2016). International Journal of Computer Science and Mobile Computing E-Commerce-Study of Privacy, Trust and Security from Consumer's Perspective. *International Journal of Computer Science and Mobile Computing*, *5*(6), 224–232. Retrieved from www.ijcsmc.com

Hartley, M. (2011). *Google unveils new research findings for University of Waterloo*. Retrieved from http://www.business.financialpost.com

Jenkins, R. (2015). 5 aspects of games to leverage for increased millennial engagement and retention. *HR Cloud*. Available at: https://blog.hrcloud.com/5aspectsofgamestoleverageforincreasedmillennialengagementretention

Jiang, J. (2018). *Millennials stand out for their technology use, but older generations also embrace digital life*. PEW Research Centre. Available at: https://www.pewresearch.org/fact-tank/2018/05/02/millennials-stand-out-for-their-technology-use-but-older-generations-also-embrace-digital-life/

Johnson, L., Becker, S., Estrada, V., & Freeman, A. (2014). *Horizon Report: 2014 Higher Education*. Austin, TX: NMC.

Kessler, A. (2013). Professors Are About to Get Online Education. *Wall Street Journal*. Retrieved from https://search.proquest.com/docview/1357479035?accountid=12860

Khan, S., & Gouveia, L. B. (2017). Is flipped classroom preferred learning style for the Millennials? An Exploratory Study. *IPASJ International Journal of Management*, *5*(8), 7–21.

Klein, A., & Sharma, V. M. (2018). German Millennials' Decision Making Styles and Their Intention to Participate in Online Group Buying. *Journal of Internet Commerce*, *17*(4), 383–417. doi:10.1080/15332861.2018.1463804

Klimkiewicz, K., & Oltra, V. (2017). Does CSR Enhance Employer Attractiveness? The Roleof Millennial Job Seekers'Attitudes. *Corporate Social Responsibility and Environmental Management, Wiley*, *24*(5), 449–463. doi:10.1002/csr.1419

KPMG. (2017). *Meet the Millennials: Produced under the umbrella of KPMG's "It's her Future" Programme*. Available at: https://home.kpmg/content/dam/kpmg/uk/pdf/2017/04/Meet-the-Millennials-Secured.pdf

Macky, K., Gardner, D., & Forsyth, S. (2008). Generational differences at work: Introduction and overview. *Journal of Managerial Psychology*, *23*(8), 857–861. doi:10.1108/02683940810904358

McKenzie, L. M. (2017). *The Stereotypes and Biases That Plague Millennial Leaders: Best Practices and Strategies for Job Promotion*. Pepperdine University.

Moreno, F. M., Gil Lafuente, J., Carreón, F. Á., & Moreno, S. M. (2017). The Characterization of the Millennials and Their Buying Behavior. *International Journal of Marketing Studies*, *9*(5), 135–144. doi:10.5539/ijms.v9n5p135

Myers, K. K., & Sadaghiani, K. (2010). Millennials in the workplace: A communication perspective on millennials' organizational relationships and performance. *Journal of Business and Psychology*, *25*(2), 225–238. doi:10.100710869-010-9172-7 PMID:20502509

Newman, D., Kramer, S., & Blanchard, O. (2016). *Marketing to Millennials*. Retrieved from https://futurumresearch.com/wp-content/uploads/woocommerce_uploads/2017/02/report_200117.pdf

O'Connor, F. (2016). *"Milennials & Youtube" An Investigation Into The Influence Of User-Generated Video Content On The Consumer Decision Making Process*. Retrieved from https://core.ac.uk/download/pdf/80766824.pdf

Oracle. (2015). *A New Perspective on Millennials Segmenting a Generation for Actionable Insights for Consumer Goods Companies and Retailers Sponsored by A New Perspective on Millennials*. Retrieved from http://www.oracle.com/us/industries/consumer/interbrand-cg-retail-cx-wp-2400662.pdf

Pant, J. J., & Venkateswaran, V. (2019). Exploring millennial psychological contract expectations across talent segments, Employee Relations. *International Journal (Toronto, Ont.)*, *41*(4), 773–792.

Parsa, H. G., Lord, K. R., Putrevu, S., & Kreeger, J. (2015). Corporate social and environmental responsibility in services: Will consumers pay for it? *Journal of Retailing and Consumer Services*, *22*, 250–260. doi:10.1016/j.jretconser.2014.08.006

Peter, O. (2018). Millennials Set to be Outnumbered by Gen Z Within a Year. *The Independent*. Available at: https://www.independent.co.uk/life-style/millennials-gen-z-outnumbered-2019-global-population-demographic-bloomberg-a8502251.html

Porral, C., Sanchez, P., Medín, F., & Clave, P. (2017). A Typology Categorization Of Millennials In their Technology Behavior. *Xxix Congreso De Marketing Aemark 2017 561 De 1617*. Retrieved from https://idus.us.es/xmlui/bitstream/handle/11441/78156/A_typology_categorization_of_millennials_in-their_technology_behavior.pdf?sequence=1&isAllowed=y

PWC. (2011). *PwC's NextGen: A global generational study: Evolving talent strategy to match the new workforce reality, Summary and compendium of findings*. Available at: https://www.pwc.com/gx/en/hr-management-services/pdf/pwc-nextgen-study-2013.pdf

Rayle, L., Shaheen, S., Chan, N., Dai, D., & Cervero, R. (2014). *App-Based, On-Demand Ride Services: Comparing Taxi and Ridesourcing Trips and User Characteristics in San Francisco*. Working Paper.

Robinson, T. (2008, March). Are You Courting millennials? *The Greentree Gazette*.

Sahni, L. (2011). The impact of soft skill training induction programme on new entrants. *Management Edge*, *4*(2), 40–47.

Sandeen, C. (2008). Boomers, Xers, and Millennials: Who Are They and What Do They Really Want from Continuing Higher Education? *Continuing Higher Education Review*, *72*, 11–31.

Sandeen, C. (2008). Millennials: Who are They and What Do They Really Want from Continuing Higher Education? *Continuing Higher Education Review*, *72*, 11–31.

Shaw, S., & Fairhurst, D. (2008). Engaging a new generation of graduates. *Education + Training*, *50*(5), 366–378. doi:10.1108/00400910810889057

Smith, K. T. (2011). Digital Marketing Strategies that Millennials Find Appealing, Motivating, or Just Annoying. Dr. Katherine Taken Smith Department of Marketing Texas A & M Univer. *Journal of Strategic Marketing*, *19*(6), 489–499. doi:10.1080/0965254X.2011.581383

Storey, D. (2016). *Understanding the small business sector*. Routledge. doi:10.4324/9781315544335

Twenge, J. (2007). *Generation Me: Why today's young Americans are more confident, assertive, entitled and more miserable than ever before?* Free Press.

Venkatesh, V., Morris, M., Davis, G., & Davis, F. (2003). User Acceptance of Information Technology: Toward a Unified View. *Management Information Systems Quarterly*, *27*(3), 425–478. doi:10.2307/30036540

Ward, J. (2016). *Keeping the family business healthy: How to plan for continuing growth, profitability, and family leadership*. Springer.

Zaharim, A., Yusoff, Y. M., Omar, M. Z., Mohamed, A., & Muhamad, N. (2009). Engineering employability skills required by employers in Asia. *Proceedings of the 6th WSEAS International Conference on Engineering Education.*

Zipcar. (2013). *Millennials & Technology: A Survey Commissioned by Zipcar*. Zipcar's Millennial Study.

## KEY TERMS AND DEFINITIONS

**Technology Savvy:** Well-informed, expert, or proficient in using modern technology especially internet technologies/computers, etc.

# Chapter 13
# The Role of Digital Advertising in Shaping Ideals and Consumption Choices in the Digital Era:
## Effectiveness of Digital Advertisements

**Lilit Baghdasaryan**
*Northumbria University, London, UK*

## ABSTRACT

*Digital advertising is one of the most dominant elements of a communication mix. Consumption choices refer to the journey where consumers make decisions based on the problem-solving attributes of the products and services. The choices are conditioned with the reality shaped around us and social processes that impose ideal, self-identity, self-concept, ideal self, gender identities, and consumer cultures via visual digital designs and celebrity portrayals. Organisations aim to build digital advertisement strategies and create awareness of certain goods and services, but at the same time, the advertisement plays a significant role in generating new needs, new identities for consumers, and new role expectations. Digital technologies enable marketers to predict consumption behaviour and measure the consumer responses on key metrics of advertisement effectiveness.*

## INTRODUCTION

Advertisement is a paid communication to announce and persuade customers that some product, services or ideas are available for sales. Citing *American Marketing Association*, Yakup (2011) defined advertising as 'the placement of announcements and persuasive messages in time or space purchased in any of the mass media by an organization with a purpose to inform and/ or persuade target market or consumers about their products, services, organizations, or ideas'. The definition highlights many elements or characteristic features of an advertisement; however, the main purpose is informing and

DOI: 10.4018/978-1-7998-0131-3.ch013

persuading. Informing and persuading requires crossing the boundaries of attentions and perceptions of the target consumers. Thus, the informing and persuading requires meeting the needs of attentions and favorable evaluations for the perceptions. The favorable evaluations happen if something fits with consumer's personal values systems Thus the effective advertisements tend to fit with customers values, believes and identities. The consumers will like a product or advertisement if it is congruent with the consumers# value systems and self-identities and desired self-images.

Advertising is one of the most dominant elements of a communication mix in marketing (Camilleri, 2018). Digital advertisements: is a paid form of communications, placed in an online, digital and virtual ecosystems in order to inform and persuade target consumers about a product, service or idea. Advertisement using digital technology is transforming the traditional advertisement industry. The advertisements use 'visual design' to aesthetics in an inspirational manner to attract viewers' attention to affect perception, persuasion, and ultimately behavior . This way the advertisement influence consumers visual values and visual cultures. The digital media has provided a lot of opportunities for marketers to create' effective 'visual design'.

The digital transformation enables marketers not just to track but also predict consumption behaviour (Erevelles, Fukawa, and Swayne, 2016). he ideological consumption structures or system of meanings are translated to consumers through the identities and lifestyle ideals portrayed in mass media and advertising (Üstüner and Holt, 2007). This has been widely observed through the exposure of identities on social media channels (Tuten, 2017; Ashley and Tuten, 2015; Bobkowski, Shafer and Ortiz, 2016). The self -concept is ' the totality of the individual's thoughts, perceptions, feelings and subjective evaluations that have reference to oneself as an object of thought (Yu, 2014). The advertisements', other people and the media can influence one's subjective evaluation of self. The research in marketing and advertisements have highlighted the importance of considerations of self-concept, self-evaluation, and self-comparison, etc. in consumer decision making(Ruiz and Sicilia 2004. DeBeer et al. 1973, Hong and Zinkhan 1995 & Malhotra 1988, etc. were cited by (Yu, 2014)). Also social comparison theory (Festinger (1954) argues that people make their decisions based on social comparison with others or role models (Yu, 2014)). There can be a number of motives for social comparison such as self-knowledge, role congruity, self-evaluations, self-improvement, self-enhancement, or improving self-image or self-status. And acceptance by others (reflective appraisals) The advertisement or social media is often driven to use and portraits role models. Celebrities, ideals, etc. to market and promote the image, awareness, and identity of their products and services. Thus, the advertainment can have an effect on our values, believes, roles, norms, status, customs, and bahaviours. All those are essential elements of one culture. Hence it can be inferred that advertisement has some role in influencing customers; cultures.

Consumer research pioneers often debate the extent of cultural interference on advertising design and delivery to the target audiences (Borgerson and Schroeder, 2002; Kravets, 2012). Historically, traditional advertising was positioned as a tool for creating meanings, shaping attitudes and consumption culture (Williamson, 2002). The opinion on the paradigm often overlap but also contradicts the notion of culture and cultural values which are believed to shape advertisement according to social needs and expectations (Lin and Yeh, 2013). Both streams of the research, however, acknowledge that advertising and culture constantly intermingle, create and employ cultural symbols to generate familiar concepts with the intention of selling products and services (De Mooij, 2018; Schroeder, 2005).

The self-esteem, self-identity self-culture, and self-image congruity are very significant drivers of consumer behaviour. This chapter explores the role of the self-identity in particular gender identity and their interactions with social media or digital portals of role models in the advertisements. The chapter also discusses consumer culture theory and visual culture theories as research methodologies of cultural studies. The chapter also discusses a marketing mix modeling (MMM) based model for measuring the effectiveness of Digital advertainments.

## LITERATURE REVIEW

Along with Campelo et al (2011) scholars state the role of advertisements is not just simply the delivery of direct information to consumers. We aim to build strategies and create awareness of certain goods and services, but at the same time advertisement plays a significant role with the aim of generating new needs for consumers, and therefore advertising creates meanings around those needs as a choice justification at the early stages of the consumption journey. Similarly, Borgerson and Schroeder (2002: 574) suggest that advertisements are a figurative system that yields meanings outside the realm of advertised product. In this sense, the ideological interpretation can be linked with Bourdieu's notion of symbolic power (Hesmondhalgh, 2006) that is indirectly imposed through cultural mechanisms (e.g. images, icons, symbols) it is claimed that historically shaped icons, images or symbols are used in contemporary advertising practice to deliver hidden meanings (Schroeder, 2006).

The purpose of digital marketing communication is to influence consumer behaviour. Any digital advertisements is a paid form of non-personal and online communications which is used to inform, persuade, reinforce and convince the target audience to purchase or use a product or services or an idea (Yakup, 2011). Digital advertisements is a paid form of communications, placed in an online, digital and virtual ecosystems in order to inform and persuade target consumers about a product, service or idea. It can be in the form of online advertisements, such as pop-up advertisements, social media advertisement, search engine optimized and pay per click optimized messages, etc.

The advertisements have a dual purpose, first to change consumer's attitude towards the advertisements itself and then about the product or the brand which is portraited in the advertisement(Çakır & Çakır, 2016). There are many factors such as message, intensity, reach, frequency, Location and Time, Interactivity, Competitive advertising, Media, celebrity, Incentive, credibility, believability, emotional appeals. Rational appeals, Product Involvement, Content Concreteness, etc. which that can determine the effectiveness of digital advertisements (Lakshmanan & Rabiyathul, 2015). The belief in, credibility and appeals of digital advertisements can be influenced by the customer's identification with the advertisements or the celebrity, which is shown in the advertisements. The content of advertising, advertising appeals are somewhat interrupted with self-identity and self-image congruity(Çakır & Çakır, 2016).

Thus, there are many principles and factors that should be considered while designing digital advertisements (see Figure 1).

This chapter focuses on the study of some of the principles and factors of digital advertainment. The focus of this chapter is on the effect of consumer identity & self-image, culture and ethical considerations gender portraits in digital and magazine advertisement (see Figure 2)

The congruity theory postulates that individual is motivated to minimize the gap between ones different self-images such ass Actual self-image", "ideal self-image", "social self-image" and "ideal social self-image" and one's possessions, products, and behaviors (Çakır & Çakır, 2016). Self-image congruence is the motivation that impels consumers to the match between consumers' self-concept (actual self, ideal self, etc.) and the user image of a given product, store, sponsorship event, etc. (Çakır & Çakır, 2016). The self-concept is the combination of multi-dimensional structure that might be determined by our sociol-

*Figure 1. Principles and factors of digital advertisement (Source: adapted from: (Charls & Costello, 2017)*

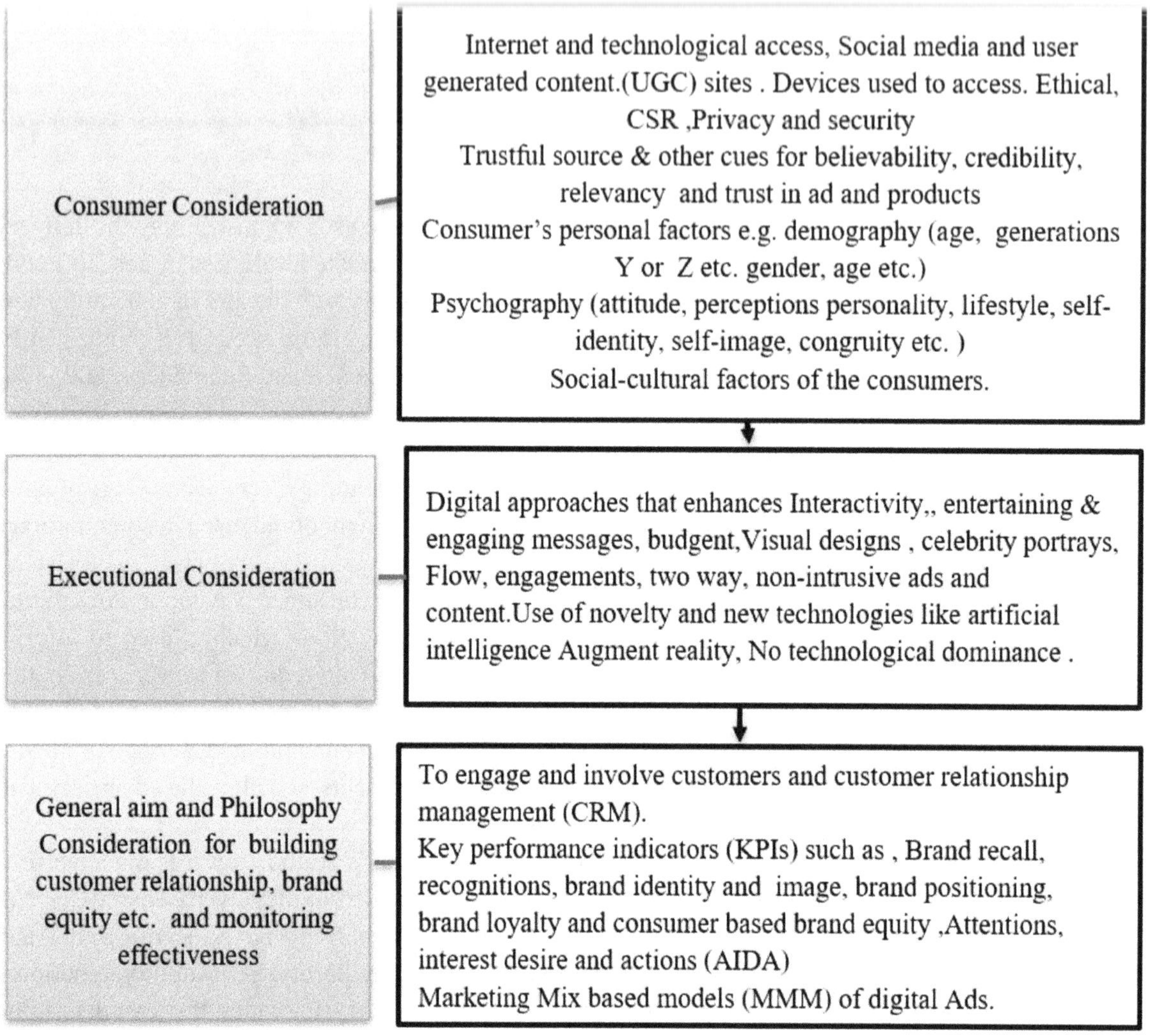


ogy and culture. This dynamic process of self-identity, self-concept, self-comparison, self-congruity, self-esteem, etc. creates new values norms, attitudes, customs, behaviors, etc. and culture. Thus, it can be inferred that the external factors such as media advertisements gradually influences towards new cultural expectations and in turn, is influenced by our exiting cultural expectations. The consumers tend to consume or buy the products, services, and media in order to feed, protect and maintain the self-concept (self-image, self-identity, self-worth, etc.).

Consumption choices refer to the journey where consumers make decisions based on the problem-solving attributes of the products and services (Liu and Mattila, 2017). Nonetheless, the choices are conditioned with the reality shaped around us and social processes that impose ideals (Papaoikonomou, Cascon-Pereira, and Ryan, 2016). The examination of the impact within the consumer culture theory predominantly place the importance within the interpretation of culturally accepted meanings, ideologies, sustained consumer identities (Bajde, Nøjgaard, and Sommer, 2019; Jhally, 2014, p. 4; Malefyt

*Figure 2. Role of visual design portraying self-identity & image, consumer culture visual culture in effectiveness of the digital advertisement*

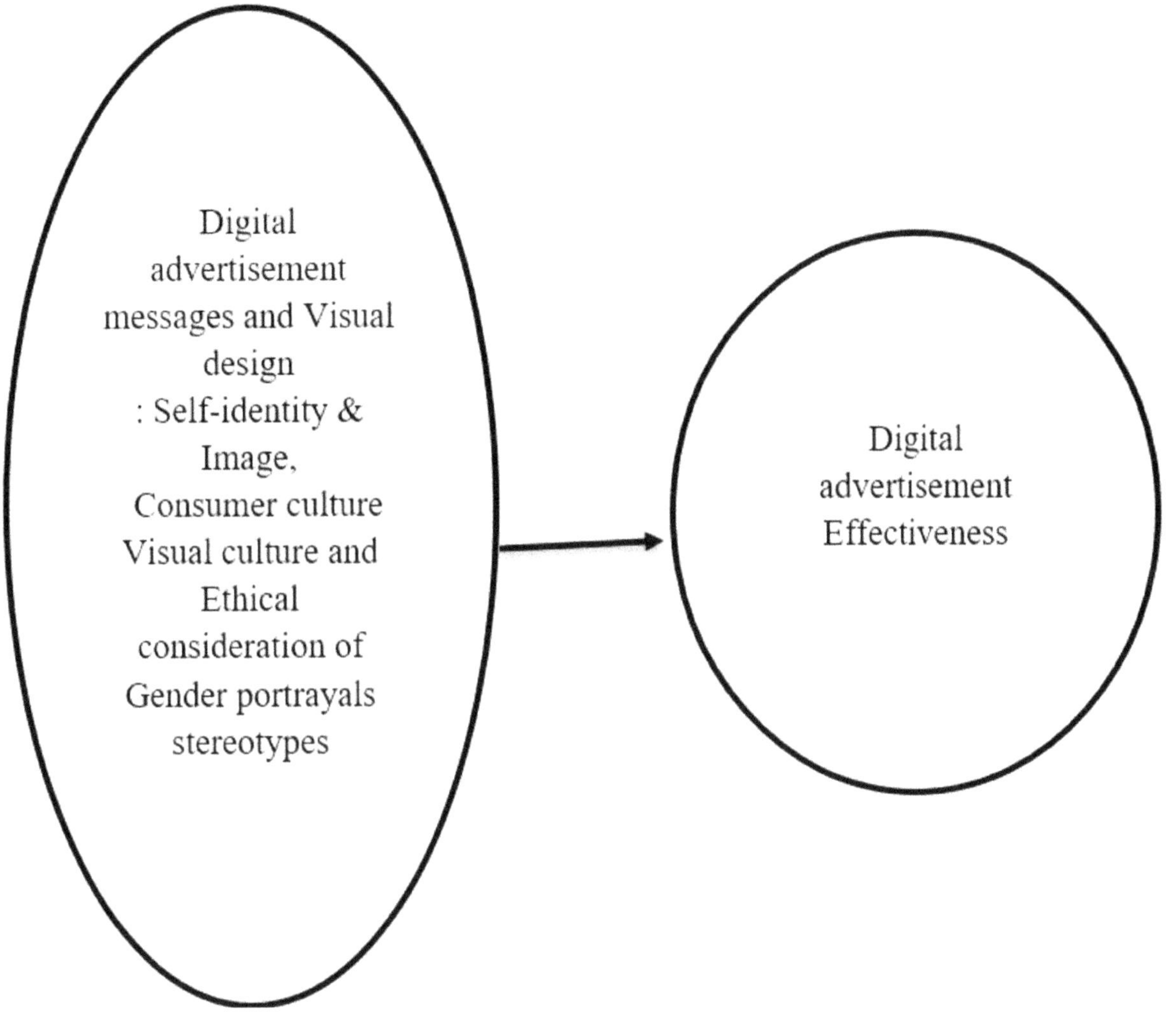


and Moeran, 2003) and the designs, codes and symbols employed to produce those meanings (Hackley, 2002; Schroeder 2005; Sherry, 1987).

## The Self-Concept and Self Identity

Individual's self-concept is the end product of a process of reflection on oneself as an object, thus the self-concept is one's totality of feelings, and thoughts having references to oneself as an object(Gecas, 1982). Many authors have used terms such as self-awareness, self-image, self-esteem, self-efficacy and other characteristics as immediate outcomes of self-concept. The attribution theory by Epstein views the self-concept 'as a theory of knower and believes that a person holds about oneself as an experiencing, functioning being in interaction with the world' (Gecas, 1982).

The authors have distinguished between self-conception (an Identity) and self-evaluations (self-esteem). Whereas self-Identity is about awareness and believes about self as an object or being, the self-esteem is the overall evaluations of one-self on emotional or affective dimension and rating oneself having; a sense of power, sense of self-worth, self-competence, or efficacy, self-virtue or moral worth (Gecas, 1982). This indicates that self-concept is a process of knowing self-identities and then evaluating its consequences in form of evaluative judgments about one's competence- worth (self-efficacy) and moral worth (self-worth). Competency-Based self-esteem is believing about one's own effective performance and is associated with self-attribution and social comparison processes(Gecas, 1982). The self -worth (moral or virtue worth) dimension of Self-esteem gives important to one's norms and values (justice, reciprocity, honor) concerning personal and interpersonal conduct (Gecas, 1982). Self-Esteem (self-efficacy + self-worth) can be formed due to a number of personal and external factors. Thus, there is a role of external factors like other people, social network, media, marketing organisation and advertainments in forming self-identity and self -image. The 'others appraisal' of someone can influence the someone's self-image, our looking glass self, ideal self-etc., unless the someone's; personal biases or self-defense mechanisms do not allow others' appraisal to influence nose's self-evaluations (Gecas, 1982).

Son, The social networking sites, media advertisements are such external other factors can have an effect on our self-identity and self-concept. As per self-awareness theory (Duval & Wicklund's, 1972), one's self-awareness of an incongruity between one's idealized self-concept and one's self-image can be a motivation to change self or self-concept (Gecas, 1982).

As per Festinger's (1954) theory, social comparison is 'a process of one's reality-testing in which individuals assess their own abilities and virtues by comparing them to those of others' is more profound when someone's knowledge about a self-attribute is ambiguous or uncertain' (Gecas, 1982). The reference groups or opinion leaders can become important source of social comparison and self-evaluations and a minority status can give rise to low self-esteem. A social class can effects one's on the self-esteem through four processes (reflected appraisals, social comparisons, self-attribution, ad psychological centrality) of self-concept formation (Gecas, 1982). Desired identities are the prizes sought or identities constructed which involve 'staging operations' and "impression-management'(Gecas, 1982). Naturally, the roles expected by others may let someone undertake sating operations and impression management by owning some products, process or showing certain desired behaviors. This explains the role of advertainment or social media in influences our desires and behaviors. Labeling theory (Lemert 1951, Wells 1978) argues that other social actors attitude towards and 'labeling of one individual's initial deviant behavior is the major factor in the systematization of deviance since it alters the self-concept and social identity of the person labeled so' (Gecas, 1982). Thus generated, self-Identities are viewed by the individual as internalized roles, also known as role identity. This is like seeing self-concept in the light of sociological social structures. The term "role" is a behavioral expectation associated with a position or status (either formal or informal such as father, gender, manager, boss, junior etc.) in a social system and the roles identities link a persons to social structures: ' the value aspects of roles connect persons to culture; the normative aspects of roles provide motivation to conduct and structure to social action; and the 'sense-making' or interpretive aspects of roles determine much of personal cognition, attitudinal predispositions, memories, and plan'(Gecas, 1982). The goal of identity theory tries to explain 'how society affects the self, and how the self-shapes society through social behavior as per social structures'(see Figure 3) (Hays, 2011). The social structure sets role boundaries (class, gender, race, roles, position, etc.) for an individual to behave in social interaction (see Figure 3) (Hays, 2011).

*Figure 3. Self identity theory-based structural interactions and role identity*

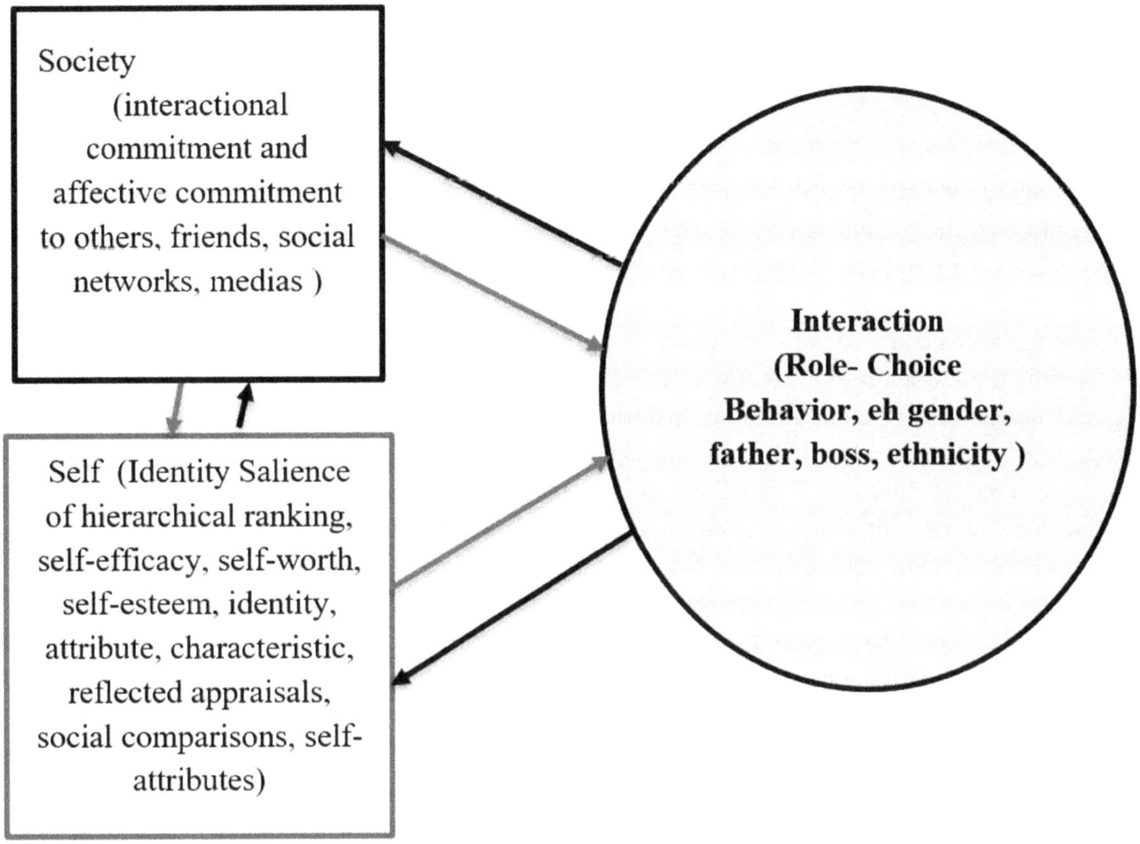


## Identity Structures in Women's Magazine Advertisements

The digital media has created a lot of options to create attractive visual portraits and visual designs. The visual designs are some total 'of form, shade, color, saturation, depth, and motion that is used to creating meaning or constructing a persuasive argument for moving a specific audience'(Negm & Tantawi, 2015). Advertisements can create impressions and longings in consumers through visual imagery or text-based imagery. The visual portrayals of male or female models in advertisements' can create motivation so for self-comparisons, self-conception, self-identity and self-image. The iconicity of visual images in such advertisements can elicit emotions by simulating the appearance of a real person or object(Negm & Tantawi, 2015)..

The traditional media advertising has always been one central topic of investigation in consumer research, but more dominant position was acquired by gender studies where feminine and masculine identities were looked like not just a social domain but a valuable drive on understanding the evolving consumption patterns (Hampel, Heinrich, and Campbel, 2012; Kemp, Bui, and Chapa, 2012; Mager and Helgeson, 2011). *Women's magazines* is a genre or category within the broader print media market primarily designed for women (Berns, 2017: 57; Holm, 1997; Endres and Luek, 1995). The content of the media varies from housekeeping, parenting, leisure, fashion, and many others. Historically women's magazines had the functionality of communicating with consumers, transmitting viewpoints on social problems and mirroring the changing roles and responsibilities of women in society (Berns, 2017: 57). In literature, the print media (predominantly women's magazine genre) is always respected as a powerful tool for reflecting constant changes in relation to historic shifts in women's status and roles within society and culture (Wolf, 2013, p. 64). Women's Magazine plays a dramatic role as powerful agents for transmitting ideologies and politically imposed structures. In contemporary globalisation women's magazines represent women's mass culture (Schug, et al., 2017; Shevelow, 2015). As consumers, women are influenced by the content conveyed to them through these print media channels and it impacts their identity construction and consumption behaviour (O'Brien, Myles, and Pritchard, 2016). In the last few decades, the content covered through this media channel became a rich source for qualitative and quantitative analysis. Scholars extended the research streams in decoding imagery representations, but also more broadly tried to interpret marketplace ideologies portrayed in magazine advertisements.

Unlike the majority of other mediums, historically women's magazine plays a significant role popularising popular feminist ideas to a larger and broader audience, but they produce both beauty myths and feminist content (Martens, 2016). They are an effective tool for reaching working-class, rural and less educated women with ideological messages. It is claimed that the content of the magazines covers aspects and fields where women function and want to be seen. The target audience consumes magazines not only as a leisure (or pleasure) activity but predominantly as a source of valuable information and instructions. They help to construct identities and contribute towards the development of prevailing 'femininities' that are often class and gender conditioned (McRobbie, 2007).

Magazines contextualise produce and reproduce women's roles, gender aspirations and evoke consumption needs. According to French sociologist Bourdieu (1984) consumers seek to acquire legitimate power and social position by consuming certain goods. The imagery display of consumer goods and information provided by media channels help to construct these lifestyle choices. Significant attention is paid to gender stereotyping in print media. Lindsey (2015: 415), for example, suggests that magazines portray, and project enrooted cultural beliefs and norms that are often preserved as stereotypes. The image portrayal not only projects stereotypical thinking but also builds upon the stratification and class conditioning within a society.

If we look back to the historical developments of gender portrayal in women's magazine, we can observe that since 1930 to late 1980 women were portrayed as happy housewives and worshiped as great mothers, as the socioeconomic changes impose the image of the ideal housewife with one or more children started shifting toward more independent and working mother images (Anderson, Johnson and Reckers, 1994). Unlike traditional images of women, the working women were often portrayed, hence perceived as unfeminine and dangerous for those who were in happy marriages (Horowitz, 2000; Meyerowitz, 1993). From late 90s gender stereotyping in magazines emphasised more victimised and passive, submissive features. The idea of masculine domination and female submissiveness as gender ideals suggested the emergence of advertisements in magazines that aim to objectify women (Ferguson *et al.* 1990; Nelson and Paek, 2005). Scholars critique that the imposed beauty myths as part of women's magazine ideology aimed to enslave women by portraying them as pleasure objects (Ballaster, 1991). The claimed objective of the given era was to enroot these ideals of womanhood (Wolf, 1999; 2013) and suggest new ways of consuming goods.

Women's magazines are part of mass media, the primary function and ideology of media are to transmit collective beliefs, shape identities, consumer's worldview and desirable objects/services that would trigger effective consumption patterns (McRobbie, 2004). Catterall, Maclaran, and Stevens (2013) view women's magazine as a means of articulating prescribed gender roles (womanhood, motherhood) that impact on consumer behaviour. It is suggested that the practice imposed by mass media help to legitimise politically, historically and culturally developed norms and women's rights/roles (Stevens, Maclaran and Brown, 2003: 35). Thus, it can be argued that women's magazines are an inseparable part of consumer culture, where dominant ideologies of femininity, sexuality, womanhood, and motherhood are circulated and promoted.

The digital interference in everyday life did not leave the magazines out either. Magazines adapted to technological trends and increased presence on the internet. Now print media shifted towards online media where magazine readers can subscribe and have electronic access to favourite magazines.

## Consumption Triggers and Gender Roles in Advertisements

Understanding gender and its role, portrayal and associated behavior in marketing have always been a central topic for discussion (Bettany, et al, 2010; Luyt, 2011; Eisend et al., 2014). Gender identity in Advertisements is the Portrayals of a gender-specific image, visual displays, values, customers and role identity and socially constructed expectations, etc. in an advertisement, which may impel consumers to identify themselves with the gender image shown in the advertisements. Marketing managers mostly focus on segmentation strategies where gender falls under the quantifiable category of demographic characteristics. In academic literature, the gender has been increasingly viewed from more interpretivist approach with a touch of sociology and psychological studies. One of the most prevalent themes for exploration in consumer research is 'the body', its objectification, representation and conception as *normalised* or *imaginative* ideals in the social field (Wang, Liaukonyte and Kaiser, 2015; Cortese, 2015; Featherstone, Hepworth and Turner, 1991). A noteworthy input in these studies was made through the placement of the body in the academic literature and marketing field (Featherstone, 1982). Feminist researchers had contributed towards the elaboration and critical evaluation of *bodily* associations and its impact on the identity construction that triggers consumption preferences (Freixas, Luque and Reina, 2012). Woodward (2008, p. 84) claims that embodiment incorporates the notion: *"...our bodies are who we are and are inextricably linked to an understanding of the self"*.

Identification with the people in the visual images may be the most common way in which visuals advertisements exploit their iconic relationship to our real world (Negm & Tantawi, 2015)Gender triggers associations, perceptions, stereotyping and assumptions, and these are more evident in the advertising practice. In the same manner, we perceive the body, some of the course from tradition. nal, neotraditional, liberal or feminist perspectives. That interpretation would project the reality around us and the way we interact with one another and in the marketplace. From a theoretical perspective, Judith Butler undoubtedly contributed towards the understanding of the body in a broader sense of "reproduction, differences of sex, labour wage, mothering, spectacle or even being invisible" (Butler, 2014: 124). Bourdieu (1989), on the other hand, referred to the body as a mixture of dispositions of class, gender, and race that are reproduced in everyday life (Bell, 1999: 119; Skeggs, 1997: 84). Bourdieu signified that the difference of class is demonstrated through physical manifestation, which is material and visible in this case through bodily dimensions, shape, forms (Bourdieu, 1984; McNay, 1999). The body in the process, such as movement and gestures, contributes towards the construction of social capital and aesthetic division of perceived reality (Bourdieu, 1984). The social construction of reality in its turn formulates consumer taste that is, as Bourdieu suggests, class conditioned and tightly linked with the symbolic power of the habitus (Bourdieu, 1979; Wacquant, 1993). Symbolic power in this sense is the effect of the bodily representations (which in its turn is argued to be shaped by dominant ideas of the society) and the effect of those body portrayals on the reproduction of the symbolic power by consumers' themselves.

The portrayals of gendered bodies in mass media have triggered greater attention of consumer culture theorists (Holt, 2002; Thompson and Hirschman, 1995). The arguments around body display in advertising, the way it conveys cultural and symbolic meanings and triggers desire in the consumer's mind are at the forefront of this (Joy and Venkatesh, 1994). Nonetheless, when positioned in a cultural context, advertising content reveals much more complex ideological structures, distributed through the production of identities and images (Grier and Deshpandé, 2001; Schroeder and Zwick, 2004).

## Consumers' Culture

The Consumer Cultural Theory (CCT) is a family of perspectives that explores the dynamic relationships between consumer actions, the marketplace, and consumer's cultural meanings(Arnould & Thompson, 2005). Thus, a consumer culture signifies a social arrangement in which markets mediate a relationship among the ways of life, lived culture, social resources, and the symbolic or material resources. Thus a consumer culture is jointly saclike constructed culture (of overlapping, flued, distributed and collective meanings of values,, norms, even conflicting practices, identities,) based on the markets, commercially produced images, texts, and objects (Arnould & Thompson, 2005). It is the study of consumption experiences, symbolic, and experiential aspects itself and not about the context in which the consumption occurs. Consumer culture theory explores 'the process via which consumers actively rework and transform symbolic meanings encoded in material goods, brands, retail settings, advertisements, or to manifest their particular personal and social circumstances and further their identity and lifestyle goals' (Arnould & Thompson, 2005) Undoubtedly, advertising generates knowledge but this knowledge is constantly reproduced from something previously acknowledged (Grier and Deshpandé, 2001). In the same vein, Williamson (1978: 99) claims that only if *the new* is already recognised as *known* can guarantee that what is newly *created* is *truthful.* In fact, Williamson position in the interpretation of the ideological consumption is summarized as follows:

*...constant re-production of ideas which are denied a historical beginning or end, which are used or referred to 'because' they 'already' exist in society and continue to exist in society 'because' they are used and referred to. (Williamson, 1978: 99)*

In a consumer culture, advertising and culture continuously interact, they create/recreate and circulate cultural symbols as demonstrations of largely recognizable concepts in order to sell products and services (Sherry, 1987; Hackley, 2002). Cultural symbols in marketing communications can be presented in different forms, such as logos, social stereotypes etc., and often can evoke the atmosphere of the past (Berger, 2015). Researchers in the past primarily focused on the textual meanings and associations, such as the use of *symbolic language* that is implied to indicate shared experiences or feelings through the circulation of ideas and information (Karo, 1975: 60). The rapid digitalisation of the consumption practice revolutionized methodologies traditionally imposed through textual meanings (Tammpuu and Masso, 2018). The digital platforms offer a plethora of options exposed to consumers via explicit use of imagery, voice search and virtual reality experiences (Hudders, Van Reijmersdal, and Poels, 2019;

Borgerson and Schroeder, 2018). The understanding and interpretation go well beyond the impact of textual emphasis or hidden textual meanings.

It is debated that the study stream in consumer research lacks in-depth evaluation of the digital reproduction of meanings by consumers themselves and its impact on consumption behaviour (Döveling, Harju and Sommer, 2018; Arnould and Thompson, 2005). In conjunction with this, Consumer Culture Theory offers a thorough investigation of the "relationship of consumers' experiences, the system of beliefs, practices that construct social reality and structures" (Arnould and Thompson, 2005: 876). The construction of social reality depends on media communication channels that convey the system of meanings in such a way to preserve dominant interests in society (Poster, 2018, p. 35; Schroeder, 2018; Hirschman, 1993). The reproduction of meanings has been diverted towards targeted communication channels where the recreation of meanings are associated with data tracking systems and strategies are built around what data provides as grounds for in-depth interpretation (Camilleri, 2018; Manser Payne, Peltier and Barger, 2017).

While research on the role of media in the construction of consumer culture and identity is a conventional topic in marketing and consumer research, there is a significant gap in innovative approaches towards the research design and analytical methods implemented (Kjeldgaard, 2002; Woodside, Sood and Miller 2008). Traditional methods in this realm explicate how media images (online, print ads) disseminate a plethora of meanings, signs and symbols amongst people and how such visual means contribute to people's sense of identity and lifestyle choices (Arnould and Thompson, 2005; Featherstone, 2006; Slater, 1997; Thompson, Arnould and Giesler, 2013). The nature for some of these studies is exploring the impact of advertisements on consumer attitudes and purchase intentions through quantitative research approach (Goffman, 1979; Chae and Hoegg 2013; Bush and Furnham 2013). Major emphasis on such methods on the production of advertising, design and codes are still within the visual rhetoric in marketing communications (Campelo et al., 2011; Rampley, 2005; Bulmer and Buchanan-Oliver, 2006). While acknowledging the constant digital shifts in the marketplace we also understand that images represent not just visual graphics, but represent culture, values and beliefs, so it is important to consider the context behind the image (Zappavigna, 2016; Wu and Memon, 1997). Upon the discussions related to the methods used in analysing advertising in cultural studies, semiotics stands upfront, which enables researchers to understand relationships of meaning within the text (Bell, 2001). In his early studies, Goffman (1979) saw advertisements as an exclusive segment of the real world and stimulating the individual's perceptions of a good life, gender roles and understanding of what is *right* and *good* in social reality (De Mooij, 2018; Wijaya, 2015; Belknap and Leonard, 1991). We use a number of techniques as discussed above to understand the meanings created around advertisement practice and evaluate its impact on the consumers' decision-making process. We unconsciously attach our identities towards the ideals imposed through diverse media channels and this in turn remains a constant challenge for marketers to position the advertising practice in the heart of the ideological shifts and create competitive advantage while delivering value and branded identities. The next subsection will build on the insights rendered from similarities and differences within the traditional magazine and more contemporary social media advertisements.

## The Role of Visual Cultural Consumption

The next aspects of interpreting identities are moving towards understanding visual culture and consumers as active agents who reproduce meanings through various consumption patterns and channels. The central notion in visual culture theory is the understanding of how or what images communicate and how consumers decode those images and reproduce meanings (Schroeder, 1998). Ideological discourse in consumer culture theory, predominantly in the field of advertising and media research studies, focuses on the interpretation of cultural codes and its impact on consumer perceptions and consumption behaviour (Schroeder, 2005; Hirschman and Thompson, 1997). The theorisation of visual consumption, which was developed by Jonathan Schroeder (2005), co-links with the CCT perspective of contextualising and historicising the consumption process. The core aspects of visual consumption (VC) are the images that circulate in everyday life and are part of cultural systems. Images, signs, icons, and symbols are an inseparable part of cultural and symbolic capital (Bourdieu, 1989). They produce and reproduce meanings and contribute to the construction of identity in the field of consumption (Schroeder and Zwick, 2004).

In this respect, aspects of mass-mediated ideologies have been viewed through the branding processes and meanings created using cultural codes (Brown and Patterson, 2003). Research into visual consumption shows that contextualisation of both branding and advertising depends on the perceived value of the cultural codes implied (Schroeder, 2009; Schroeder, Salzer-Mörling and Askegaard, 2006).

While visual consumption attempts to theories visual culture, its major contribution to consumer research is the new methodological perspectives and development of profound elements for critical visual analysis (Rose, 2016). Visual research methods are considered to be the most effective way of analysing the use of icons, identities and cultural codes produced and reproduced in advertising processes (Spencer, 2010). Over the decades, advertising has been researched as a powerful tool used to construct consumer identities and create a vision of the good life (Schroeder and Borgerson, 1998: 161).

*Advertising and mass media are the visual landscape that constructs the reality…it particularly shapes the gender identities. (Schroeder and Borgerson, 1998: 162).*

Schroeder argues that in traditional advertising research the focus is mostly concentrated on managerial implications rather than hidden cultural meanings, advertising imagery and the construction of identity (Schroeder and Borgerson, 1998: 163; Piller, 2001; Katz, 2003). In this sense, gender studies have been limited to the application of film theory, qualitative content analysis, photography and literary criticism on the use of female bodies in advertising (Castelnuovo and Guthrie, 1998; Bryman, 2015). This approach triggered profound criticism from feminist researchers due to it being limited and lacking critical discourse on female bodies in the marketing field (Bordo, 1993; Evans, Renaud, and Kamerow. 2006).

In his *Critical Visual Analysis* (VCA) Schroeder (2006) concedes that images are the key components of the marketing field, thus those images need to be analysed in an appropriate manner (Campelo, Aitken and Gnoth, 2011). He is convinced that images produced in contemporary advertising represent the strong power of cultural codes with "visual, historical and rhetorical presence" (Schroeder, 2006: 303). He reflects upon the identity differences in advertising and its representation of diverse socio-cultural context and pays particular attention to gender portrayal (Borgerson and Schroeder, 2002; Reichert and Lambiase, eds., 2013). Unlike previous gender studies, Schroeder does not limit the research to gender stereotyping. Moreover, one of the fundamental arguments of Schroeder is that advertisements are constantly "circulating information about the social world", (Schroeder and McDonagh, 2005; Borgerson and Schroeder, 2008). He suggests that gender and hidden meanings around it can be explored through the application of the following key variables in critical visual analysis: *description*, *subject matter*, *form*, *medium*, *style*, *genre,* and *comparison.*

The basic stage of critical visual analysis is to describe the image in terms of the "formal properties of the composition": colour, tone, contrast and the positioning of the images within a certain context (Bell, 2001; McQuarrie and Mick, 1999). The theory suggests that in order to have a complete understanding of the portrayed image, it is essential to recognise the design that is represented through the lifestyle and physical appearance, which ultimately is historicised through the hidden ideological or cultural meanings associated with certain settings and representations (Schroeder and Borgerson, 1998; Scott, 1994; Kang, 1997). This is also linked to the service and products being advertised, which supposedly should be linked to the whole design of the advertisement (Schroeder and Zwick, 2004). This perspective of critical visual analysis enables scholars to extend the content analysis of the visual imagery by incorporating interpretivist paradigms to bring more insights on visual consumption (Bell, 2001).

The main point with which Schroeder is constantly concerned is how the meaning is "visually constructed in ads". Schroeder seeks to explore how identities are presented and performed in consumer culture and why it matters. Reproduction of identity in cultural discourse is tightly correlated with advertising practice and image representation of female agency (Schroeder and Zwick, 2004; Schroeder and Borgerson, 1998; Stern and Schroeder, 1994; Borgerson, et. al., 2006; Valtonen, 2013).

Critical visual analysis in feminist research is concurrent with the broader scope of understanding the constitution of identity through representation of body (Butler, 2011; Butler and Scott, eds., 2013; Butler, 2004) and the effect of gender stereotyping on the construction of gender roles in a society (Goffman, 1976; 1979; Kang, 1997; Bell and Milic, 2002). In this vein, according to Judith Butler's philosophy, the body is objectified as performative iterations that refer to the natural or prescribed female agency in a society (Borgerson, 2005). Consumer culture theorists, on one side, argue for the iteration (or process of) 'recombinant culture' as a key component of reconstructing and preserving the illusion of '*natural*' categories of identity (Hirschman and Thompson, 1997). While Schroeder and Borgerson (2015: 1926), on the other side, suggest that those categories in advertising practice are "reconfiguring concepts of an ideal identity category" and consumers are acquiring the subject (image, icon, and symbol) that narrates to the ideal world.

Additionally, Schroeder (2006) proposes the concept of *'consuming difference'* that signifies the codes of identity such as ethnicity, gender, race, social class and how they create visual contrast (Schroeder, 2017). This construct brings us to Goffman's sociological understanding of gender relations as being visual conventions within the domain of marketing communications (Borgerson and Schroeder, 2005; Butler, 1988; Bell and Milic, 2002; Bell, 2001). It subsequently reproduces the power relations that are typical in mass-mediated marketplace ideologies (Arnould and Thompson, 2005). Schroeder and Borgerson (2015) oppose Goffman's gender disposition by stating that:

*Gender is much more than a demographic, personality, or 'individual differences' variable – it is a basic cognitive construct, cultural category and political concept that intersects with the entire realm of consumer behaviour.*

Goffman has revolutionised the whole methodological aspect of analysing gendered relations through images by introducing a structured coding framework for analysing images in the marketing context (Goffman, 1979; 1976). Through the frequency of the categories illustrated in the image, the researcher is able to conclude on gender roles and gender portrayals in advertising (Belknap and Leonard, 1991; Kang, 1997).

Many academics have been and are still inspired by Goffman's framework, mostly when the research is related to sexuality (Elliott and Wattanasuwan, 1998; Stern, 1999; Stern, 1999a; Baker, 2005), gender roles (Coltrane and Messineo, 2000; Masse and Rosenblum, 1988) and inequality (Bell and Milic, 2002; Smith, 1996). As such, the majority of previous studies are focused on gender stereotyping and linked to a comparative analysis of male and female contrasts observed in advertisements (Browne, 1998; Coltrane and Adams, 1997; Stern, 1999). Critical visual theory, in this instance, extends Goffman's perspective and proposes to move towards a much more in-depth interpretive approach of not just looking at the content illustrated in the image, but trying to contextualise and historicise it (Schroeder, 2006; Borgerson and Schroeder, 2005; Schroeder and Borgerson, 2015). It moves towards not just placing within the historical context, but also attempting to interpret the universal elements of the image and its coded meanings (Schroeder, 2005).

There are numerous amounts of multidisciplinary studies conducted on icons, iconography and archetypes (Panofsky, 1939; Gilman, 1985; Gill, 2008). However, this research will focus on the ideological aspect of the imagery (referred to in this research as iconography) in advertising practice (Williamson, 1978), and the hidden meanings (here referred to as archetypes) (Schroeder, 2005; Jung, 2014) that are rooted in consumer minds (Zaltman, 2003).

By reflecting on Schroeder's argument (2005) that the system of meanings is represented in consumption through images, icons, and symbols, this research further extends the argument that the *icon* is a primary substance in advertising (Davison, 2009) and *iconography* is a secondary level of coded meaning (Hasenmueller, 1978; Williamson, 1978) frequently used in contemporary marketing communications strategies (Schroeder, 2008; 2009; Puntoni et al., 2010; Stern and Schroeder 1994). Iconography has been described as the "symbolic content of images in artworks" (Panofsky, 1939; Sandywell, 2016). Iconography is also described as a study of subject matter in the art that requires knowledge of symbolic imagery to decode the images.

## Research Methodologies in Critical Visual Analysis

Two of the popular visual methods in consumer research are photography and video, which have several purposes, including analysing different environments, determining behaviour in a situational context and illustrating reflections of situational behaviour (Belk and Kozinets, 2005; Schroeder, 1998 b). It is claimed that the nature of these methods is to enrich the interpretation of consumer behaviour with visuals and to expose insights that can hardly be expressed without the intervention of the visual senses of participants (Harper, 2002; Duncum, 2004).

Photographic or video observation is considered to be a means of gaining visual information of a certain subject, object, service or action (Basil, 2011). What is interesting in the field of consumer research is that the verbal aspects of observation and interpretation have dominated the visual ones (Brooks and Poudrier, 2014; Hockey and Collinson, 2006). Photography, as a visual aid of observation, has been used in marketing and consumer research in both the philosophical camps of objectivist "positivism" and humanistic relativism. Visualisation techniques were initially developed for "empirical science and quantitative analytics" (Drucker, 2010). There are different perspectives on applying photography as a method. According to objectivists, photography records reality "written by light", meaning that "images reflect an omniscient recording of reality as it occurred and the camera acts simply as a mnemonic device that requires no special knowledge to interpret." (Barthes, 1981: 88). Conversely, the subjectivists argue that photography is "an intentionally constructed reality akin to the artistic "auteur" theory in film, where construction and interpretation of the image are necessary" (as cited in Basil, 2011: 247; Barthes, 1981).

At the beginning of the 1970s, visual anthropology started to grow and expand, especially in qualitative methods (Collier and Collier, 1981). It gained particular popularity in the fields of medicine, history, and marketing, more specifically within the camps of anthropology and sociology (Basil, 2011). Similarly, sociology expanded on visual interpretivism, considering images as a significant part of sociological research (Prosser, 2007; Spencer, 2010). This, of course, is related mainly to qualitative research (Basil, 2011). Photography and visual methods in marketing were mainly applied to the investigation of con sumption practices and aspects of social life (Spencer, 2010; Banks and Zeitlyn, 2015).

From a methodological perspective, visual culture combines elements of visual sociology, social semiotics and film theory (Dikovitskaya, 2005; Prosser, 2007). The main objective of this research tradition is to demystify, historicise and visualise the image (Schroeder, 2005; Schroeder, 2009). By using the image-based approach it is possible to understand consumer behaviour and image culture, hence, how people understand and decode images, and how those images circulate in culture (Schroeder, 2005). Critical visual methods are well integrated with consumer culture theory, which is well demonstrated with research questions, such as:

*how do images strategically communicate? How do images circulate in consumer culture? How do consumers understand advertising? How do images relate to brand meaning? What are some ethical and social implications for the reliance on images in marketing communications?" (Schroeder, 2006: 304).*

Spencer (2010: 24) argues that visual methods and images are the most effective way of exploring gender and power relations in media studies. For example, leading film theorist Laura Mulvey (2003: 44) studied the objectification of females in cinema narratives by referring to the psychoanalytical theories of Freud and Lacan, illustrating the dominance of male characters and the visualisation of the gaze on women as sexualised, subordinate and passive objects designed to be looked at. Naomi Wolf (1997), on the other hand, has been cited by Jones (2003: 415) when referring to the press and the visualisation of the female body in press propaganda.

It is claimed that through the use of visual methods it is possible to highlight the objectification of female bodies that are particularly designed for the male gaze and pleasure (Harper and Tiggemann, 2008; Patterson and Elliott, 2002). No doubt, when it comes to feminist studies, the application of visual methods enables greater illustration and exploration of gender implications in a consumer culture that might seem blurry and full of hidden ideological meanings (Schroeder, 1989; Schroeder and Borgerson, 1998; Gill, 2008).

*We consume with our eyes... (Willis, 1991: 31)*

One of the core aspects in marketing is consumer behaviour, and it is argued that buyer behaviour and consumption process rely mostly on images, including brand images, corporate images, artistic images, and digital images (Schroeder, 2006). In his canonical study *Visual Consumption,* Jonathan Schroeder (2005) explains how visual images function within a cultural system of meaning that is influenced by advertising, consumption, and marketing. Schroeder opens new insights into the visual aspects of consumption from an interpretive perspective (Balmer, 2008; Belk, ed., 2007).

In his *Critical Visual Analysis,* Schroeder (2006) guides the reader through the stages and key aspects to consider while conducting critical visual analysis. He is convinced that images produced in contemporary advertising represent the strong power of cultural codes through a "visual, historical and rhetorical presence" (Denegri-Knott and Molesworth, 2010; Schroeder, 2005; Campelo, Aitken and Gnoth, 2011). He reflects upon the identity differences in advertising and its representation of a diverse socio-cultural context (Borgerson and Schroeder, 2002). One of Schroeder's fundamental arguments is that advertisements are constantly "circulating information about the social world" (Schroeder, 2006: 303).

As part of essential critical visual analysis, he offers the following key variables: *description, subject matter, form, medium, style, genre* and historical *comparison (*Schroeder, 2006: 304). The basic stage of critical visual analysis is the descriptive element of the image in terms of "formal properties of the composition": colour, tone, contrast and then positioning the images within a certain context. The interpretation of the represented identity's image, lifestyle and physical appearance should be completed in accordance with the visual design, style of the advertising and finally the product/service advertised (Hartmann and Apaolaza- Ibáñez, 2009; Schroeder, 2004). The main aspect of visual consumption is to expose and understand how the meaning is visually composed of advertising (McQuarrie and Mick, 1999). With the application of critical visual analysis, I seek to position, historicise and contextualise the images produced in consumer culture and understand how that impacts on the consumption patterns (Schroeder and Zwick, 2004).

*Subject matter* follows the first phase of analysis. This phase is primarily concerned with the detailed description of the characters, objects, places, and events in the advertising (Barrett, 2007). The *Form* is how the subject matter is represented; it interprets whether there is an element of stereotyping, sexuality or another positioning. The *Medium* is related to the material that the images are made from (which is more relevant to the art). The *Style* 'indicates a resemblance among diverse art objects from an artist, movement, time period, or geographic location and is recognised by a characteristic handling of subject matter and formal elements' (Barrett, 2005: 35–6). The *Genre* indicates a *type* or *category* that is signified by subject matter and style, which requires more research related to the field.

The phases of analysis suggested by Schroeder were later extended, as they lacked generalisation, in-depth contextual and historic positioning that would help to understand of the actual patterns of consumption and the use of icons and symbols in representing hidden meanings (Wang, 2014; Borgerson, et al., 2006; Joy and Li, 2012).

In 2004 Schroeder and Zwick further extended the understanding of the visual genealogy of contemporary images that aid in contextualising and historicising images in modern visual consumption. By genealogy, the authors signify the meaning beyond the realm of the advertised product and refer to more cultural codes, symbols, and icons that generate meaning (Denegri-Knott and Molesworth, 2010; Schroeder and Zwick, 2004).

Notably, Schroeder (2006) and visual culture researchers are not simply interested in objects within the image and the meaning around those objects, rather they seek to explore how identities are presented and performed in consumer culture and why it matters. Visual culture theory also explores representations of identity in cultural discourses, including advertising; the role visual artists play in understanding identity and difference in consumer culture (Schroeder and Zwick, 2004; Mitchell, 2002; Schroeder and Borgerson, 2015). As an example, in one of his articles on '*consuming difference*' Schroeder (2006) highlighted the codes of identity that emphasise "difference"- ethnicity, gender, race, social class and how they create visual contrast and concluded that differences often function as branding techniques purported to represent "authentic subculture" or "diversity" (Schroeder, 2013).

## IDENTITY, VISUAL CULTURE CONSUMPTION, DIGITAL MEDIA, AND DIGITAL ADVERTISING EFFECTIVENESS

Digital Advertising Effectiveness

*You can't manage what you don't measure. (W. Edwards Deming)*

In 1906 Kellogg paid for a printed advertisement of corn flakes in a magazine and post advertisements the company observed that their sales increase from 500 cases to 2900 cases a day. The measurements of advertising effectiveness was quite obviously attributed to print advertisement and easy as the Kellogg's has done nothing else to promote the product except the printed advertisements. Fast forward spread of TV, newspapers, magazines and other outdoor indoor media, led to consideration of number of exposures as an indirect indicator of advertisements effeteness. In 1980s and 90s; The measurement of advertisements effectiveness moved beyond exposure and considered measurements on advertisement reach, advertisement frequency, brand effectiveness. Sales effectiveness etc.(IAB-Europe, 2018)But now the organisation do a lot of different things including a mixture of marketing mix (product, price, place, promotional mix – advertisements, publicity & PR, direct sales, sales promotions a, digital contents, user-generated contents and so on), hence it is difficult to isolate the effeteness of digital advertisement. Fast forward to digital era, a range of digital communication modes and varieties of online advertisement has spread too much, and the attributions of consumer responses to a particular advertisement have become very difficult. In digital eras, to prove the effectiveness of advertisement response requires answering a range of questions like; 'was ad viewed by the consumers? how many and how many times (reach, frequency)? whether that's a human viewing, noticing, engaging (engagement) with or clicking on an ad (interest & reactions)? Did the ad change their opinions, brand awareness (recognition & recall) brand image, purchase intentions (desire and actions) and brand loyalty, etc. ? ' (IAB-Europe, 2018). A range of KPI metrics related to ad impact, such as site visits (number), liking (number and % of visits), time spent on a page (time per consumer) purchase intentions (number & %), actual sales (number & %),and uplift in direct site visits (number & %) etc. has been used. Also, in each kind of digital media a range of KPIs can be used. For instant Social Media KPIs can include: number of shares, mentions, retweets, web traffic and followers etc.; in Content Marketing KPIs can include number of downloads, shares, leads, conversions et, and in an Email campaign related the KPIs can be number or frequency of open rates, Click-through rates (CTRs) and conversions etc..

However, the metrics still do not consider customer responses on those Key performance indicators (KPIs) based on consumer segments, profiles, devices and platforms types (IAB-Europe, 2018). With the digital technologies, artificial intelligence, and data analytics etc. it is possible now to measure, post, real-time and predict digital advertainments effects on a range of KPIs (see Table 1).

Marketing mix modeling (MMM) based models consider a range of metrics or KPIs such as shown in Table 1.

The key creative determinants of digital brand impact include branding, likeability, engaging, distinctiveness and relevance of digital advertisements (IAB-Europe, 2018).

Active engagement with social media sites, similar to the print media, have a significant impact on the construction of 'social' identity, sexuality and gender (Davis, 2018). People continuously interact on social media sites or social networking sites to establish relationships, build connections, peer interactions and project the self-built social identity (Pegg et al., 2018). Online technologies, as well as platforms,

*Table 1. Marketing mix modelling (MMM) based model of effectiveness of digital advertainments*

| KPI | Indicators Granularity |
|---|---|
| Display | Site, Placement, Creative Type, Creative, Media Type, Premium Vs Companion Vs Standard Banner, National Vs Local |
| Search | Keyword Group, Campaign, Targeting, National Vs Local, |
| Devices Specifics E.G. – Mobile | Site, Placement, Creative Type, Creative, Operating System, Media Type,, National Vs Local |
| Social Networking Sites (SNS) | Site, Placement, Creative Type, Creative, Media Type, Platform, National Vs Local. |
| Iptv | Reach, Frequency, Viewership, Placement, Creative Type, Creative, Media Channel, Vehicle,, Platform, National Vs Local. |
| Customer Segments Based Metrics | Segment Specific Reach, Frequency, Viewership, Placement, Creative Type, Creative, Media Channel, Vehicle,, Platform, National Vs Local. |

(Source Adapted From IAB-Europe, 2018).

play a vital role in shaping and influencing the way the younger generation in particular experience, share and self-legitimise their social and personal identities (Livingstone, 2011). Social identity has been conceptualised as a multidimensional construct, where social affinity can best be interpreted and validated through various dimensions or aspects characterizing diverse features of identification.

Digital Media creates a virtual environment for individuals where they can freely express emotions, thoughts, and interests, thus it proposes not just digitizing social revolution, but also creates a structural system of advantages for businesses to alter and customise content for visitors, users, and consumers. The technological developments indeed open up opportunities for better understand consumer behaviour and using a multichannel approach in achieving business objectives. However, the newly emerging communication channels remain dependent on traditional attributes of the previous system, meaning the communication strategies altered with new insights into segmentation and targeting. The social communities, in particular, enable a better understanding of the consumer insights through analysis and access to digitally created profiles and daily online activities.

The aggressively growing trend of social networking and online consumption opened up a new window for marketers to map consumers' activities and group them according to their online attitudes and behaviour. By analysing consumer online footprints across different online channels organisations generate large data sets and enable personalization and customization not just for products or services but also for activating the most relevant communication channels and with tailored content.

While in the previous sections the discussion was around the normalised or accepted identity structures imposed by the ideological dispositions that are in return bounded to society and culture, here the complexity of determining the ideals and consumption behaviour builds upon the digital identities. Some similarities with the traditional identity structures remain constant as the digital identity still remains within the framework of displaying accepted norms and beliefs largely characterised on virtual platforms. In contrast to the traditional mode of the legitimation where rules are not written, the online environment builds constraints and legal boundaries in terms of ethical interaction and self-expression. In both cases (print and digital media advertising) individuals are increasingly driven to visual representations which dominate in creation and recreation of identities, hence consumption choices.

## IMPLICATIONS FOR MANAGERS AND SCOPE FOR THE FUTURE RESEARCH

The chapter highlights the role of self-identity and self-image in designing persuasive advertisement campaigns. The advertisements are not only driven by culture, but they are also vehicles of creating and dissemination a new culture. Marketers can use this knowledge to visual design targeted campaigns to build brands images. The chapter also raises some ethical issues concerning the portrayal of genders in advertisements in general and in digital media in particular. The digital marketing executive can learn to apply marketing mix modeling (MMM) based model of the effectiveness of Digital advertainments.

The chapter also details the new kind of research methodologies such as consumer cultural theories and visual culture theories to explore the field of digital advertisements and the visual content of such advertisements. Future research may focus on establishing the role of self-identity, self-image, consumer culture, etc. in the design of effective advertisements in digital ecosystems. The researchers may like to use Consumer cultural theories and visual cultural theories to explore digital communications and effectiveness of digital user-created contents.

## CONCLUSION

The self-identity and consumer cultural considerations are very significant factors ineffectiveness of digital advertisements. The visual designs of advertisements using digital media can reinforce or portrait a consumer identity, consumer self-image, consumers and consumers culture. If adversities message is in congruence with consumers self-identity and self-cultural expectations, the advertisements might be more liked, believed, trusted as credible. The visual culture theory gives opportunities to both academics and practitioners to consider different aspects of consumption and gives insights into the hidden meanings. This particular chapter combined some definitions and interpretations of advertising both in print and digital media, highlighted the implications of visual analysis and gender roles in advertisements.

The digital advertisements are any paid form of online non-personal or personal, and mass or targeted communications to inform and persuade the targeted consumers. The consumer's perceptions can be used to convince consumers. The perceptions are used to evaluate the product and self. The congruity theory postulates that consumers tend to match their self-identity and self-image with their role expectations and their consumptions. Thus, the technology-enabled methods of creating visual design and gender identity role models have been used by marketers to persuade consumers The effectiveness of digital advertisements is controversial and multidimensional concept, it includes a number of KPIs, some of the best KPIs are based on Marketing mix modeling (MMM) of the effectiveness of Digital advertisements.

## REFERENCES

Arnould, E. J., & Thompson, C. J. (2005). Consumer Culture Theory (CCT): Twenty Years of Research. *Source: The Journal of Consumer Research*, *31*(4), 868–882. doi:10.1086/426626

Ashley, C., & Tuten, T. (2015). Creative strategies in social media marketing: An exploratory study of branded social content and consumer engagement. *Psychology and Marketing*, *32*(1), 15–27. doi:10.1002/mar.20761

Atkinson, L. (2014). Green moms: The social construction of a green mothering identity via environmental advertising appeals. *Consumption Markets & Culture*, *17*(6), 553–572. doi:10.1080/10253866.2013.879817

Bajde, D., Nøjgaard, M., & Sommer, J. K. (2019). Consumer Culture Theory and the Socio-Cultural Investigation of Technology Consumption. In Analytical Frameworks, Applications, and Impacts of ICT and Actor-Network Theory (pp. 171-190). IGI Global. doi:10.4018/978-1-5225-7027-1.ch008

Belk, R. W., & Costa, J. A. (1998). The mountain man myth: A contemporary consuming fantasy. *The Journal of Consumer Research*, *25*(3), 218–240. doi:10.1086/209536

Bettany, S. M., Kerrane, B., & Hogg, M. K. (2014). The material-semiotics of fatherhood: The co-emergence of technology and contemporary fatherhood. *Journal of Business Research*, *67*(7), 1544–1551. doi:10.1016/j.jbusres.2014.01.012

Birkhäuser-Oeri, S., (1988). *The mother: Archetypal image in fairy tales* (Vol. 34). Inner City Books.

Bobkowski, P. S., Shafer, A., & Ortiz, R. R. (2016). Sexual intensity of adolescents' online self-presentations: Joint contribution of identity, media consumption, and extraversion. *Computers in Human Behavior*, *58*, 64–74. doi:10.1016/j.chb.2015.12.009

Borgerson, J. L., & Schroeder, J. E. (2002). Ethical issues of global marketing: Avoiding bad faith in visual representation. *European Journal of Marketing*, *36*(5/6), 570–594. doi:10.1108/03090560210422399

Borgerson, J.L., & Schroeder, J.E. (2008). Building an ethics of visual representation: Contesting epistemic closure in marketing communication. *Cutting-Edge Issues in Business Ethics*, 87-108.

Borgerson, J. L., & Schroeder, J. E. (2018). Making skin visible: How consumer culture imagery commodifies identity. *Body & Society*, *24*(1-2), 103–136. doi:10.1177/1357034X18760987

Borgerson, J. L., Schroeder, J. E., Blomberg, B., & Thorssén, E. (2006). The gay family in the ad: Consumer responses to non-traditional families in marketing communications. *Journal of Marketing Management*, *22*(9-10), 955–978. doi:10.1362/026725706778935646

Butler, J. (2004). *Undoing gender*. Psychology Press. doi:10.4324/9780203499627

Butler, J. (2011). *Bodies that matter: On the discursive limits of sex*. Taylor & Francis. doi:10.4324/9780203828274

Çakır, V., & Çakır, V. (2016). The Role of Self-Esteem and Self Image Congruity with the Ad Spokespersons The Role of Self-Esteem and Self Image Congruity with the Ad Spokespersons in Ad Attitude. *International Conference on Changing World and Social Research*. Retrieved from https://www.researchgate.net/publication/292982423_The_Role_of_Self-Esteem_and_Self_Image_Congruity_with_the_Ad_Spokespersons_in_Ad_Attitude

Caldwell, M., Henry, P., & Alman, A. (2010). Constructing audio-visual representations of consumer archetypes. *Qualitative Market Research*, *13*(1), 84–96. doi:10.1108/13522751011013990

Camilleri, M. A. (2018). Integrated marketing communications. In *Travel marketing, tourism economics and the airline product* (pp. 85–103). Cham: Springer. doi:10.1007/978-3-319-49849-2_5

Campelo, A., Aitken, R., & Gnoth, J. (2011). Visual rhetoric and ethics in marketing of destinations. *Journal of Travel Research*, *50*(1), 3–14. doi:10.1177/0047287510362777

Cappellini, B., & Yen, D. A. W. (2016). A space of one's own: Spatial and identity liminality in an online community of mothers. *Journal of Marketing Management*, *32*(13-14), 1260–12. doi:10.1080/0267257X.2016.1156725

Catterall, M., Maclaran, P., & Stevens, L. (Eds.). (2013). *Marketing and feminism: Current issues and research*. Routledge. doi:10.4324/9781315010939

Chae, J. (2015). 'Am I a Better Mother Than You?' Media and 21st-Century Motherhood in the Context of the Social Comparison Theory. *Communication Research*, *42*(4), 503–525. doi:10.1177/0093650214534969

Charls, R. T., & Costello, P. J. (2017). International Digital Advertising- Lessons learned from around the world. In S. Rodgers & T. Esther (Eds.), *Digital Advertising: Theory and Research* (p. 466). Retrieved from https://books.google.co.uk/books?id=6CslDwAAQBAJ&pg=PA352&lpg=PA352&dq=digital+advertisement+,+culture+and+effects&source=bl&ots=w02730sON_&sig=ACfU3U368eqvM-l3AekNbdvWCp8tzum_6A&hl=en&sa=X&ved=2ahUKEwiv6NHlhozkAhV1SBUIHcvdDDg4FBDoATAFegQICRAB#v=onepage&q

Coskuner-Balli, G., & Thompson, C. J. (2012). The status costs of subordinate cultural capital: At-home fathers' collective pursuit of cultural legitimacy through capitalizing consumption practices. *The Journal of Consumer Research*, *40*(1), 19–41. doi:10.1086/668640

Davis, D. L. (1983). Woman the worrier: Confronting feminist and biomedical archetypes of stress: *Women's Studies. An Interdisciplinary Journal*, *10*(2), 135–146.

Davis, S. E. (2018). Objectification, Sexualization, and Misrepresentation: Social Media and the College Experience. *Social Media+ Society, 4*(3).

Davison, J. (2009). Icon, iconography, iconology: Visual branding, banking and the case of the bowler hat. *Accounting, Auditing & Accountability Journal*, *22*(6), 883–906. doi:10.1108/09513570910980454

De Mooij, M. (2018). *Global marketing and advertising: Understanding cultural paradoxes*. SAGE Publications Limited.

Douglas, S., & Michaels, M. (2005). *The mommy myth: The idealization of motherhood and how it has undermined all women*. Simon and Schuster.

Döveling, K., Harju, A. A., & Sommer, D. (2018). From mediatized emotion to digital affect cultures: New technologies and global flows of emotion. *Social Media+ Society, 4*(1).

Epp, A. M., & Velagaleti, S. R. (2014). Outsourcing Parenthood? How Families Manage Care Assemblages Using Paid Commercial Services. *The Journal of Consumer Research*, *41*(4), 911–935. doi:10.1086/677892

Erevelles, S., Fukawa, N., & Swayne, L. (2016). Big Data consumer analytics and the transformation of marketing. *Journal of Business Research*, *69*(2), 897–904. doi:10.1016/j.jbusres.2015.07.001

Feasey, R. (2016). From soap opera to reality programming: Examining motherhood, motherwork and the maternal role on popular television. Imaginations. *Journal of Cross-Cultural Image Studies*, *4*(2), 25–46.

Gecas, V. (1982). The Self-Concept. *Annual Review of Sociology*, *8*(1), 1–33. doi:10.1146/annurev.so.08.080182.000245

Glenn, E. N., Chang, G., & Forcey, L. R. (Eds.). (2016). *Mothering: Ideology, experience, and agency*. Routledge. doi:10.4324/9781315538891

Grau, S., & Zotos, Y. (2016). Gender stereotypes in advertising: A review of current research. *International Journal of Advertising*, *35*(5), 761–770. doi:10.1080/02650487.2016.1203556

Grier, S. A., & Deshpandé, R. (2001). Social dimensions of consumer distinctiveness: The influence of social status on group identity and advertising persuasion. *JMR, Journal of Marketing Research*, *38*(2), 216–224. doi:10.1509/jmkr.38.2.216.18843

Hampel, S., Heinrich, D., & Campbell, C. (2012). Is An Advertisement Worth The Paper It's Printed on?: The Impact of Premium Print Advertising On Consumer Perceptions. *Journal of Advertising Research*, *52*(1), 118–127. doi:10.2501/JAR-52-1-118-127

Hays, J. W. (2011). *Individual And Institutional Factors Affecting Identity Among Minority And Female Science Students*. Retrieved from https://etd.ohiolink.edu/!etd.send_file?accession=kent1322062127&disposition=inline

Herland, M. D., & Helgeland, I. M. (2017). Negotiating motherhood: Women with troubled upbringings and their self-conceptions as mothers. *Child & Family Social Work*, *22*(1), 47–56. doi:10.1111/cfs.12193

Hesmondhalgh, D. (2006). Bourdieu, the media and cultural production. *Media Culture & Society*, *28*(2), 211–231. doi:10.1177/0163443706061682

Hirschman, E. C., & Thompson, C. J. (1997). Why media matter: Toward a richer understanding of consumers' relationships with advertising and mass media. *Journal of Advertising*, *26*(1), 43–60. doi:10.1080/00913367.1997.10673517

Hudders, L., Van Reijmersdal, E. A., & Poels, K. (2019). Digital advertising and consumer empowerment. *Cyberpsychology (Brno)*, *13*(2). doi:10.5817/CP2019-2-xx

IAB-Europe. (2018). *Digital Advertising Effectiveness*. Retrieved from https://www.iab.it/wp-content/uploads/2018/09/IAB-Europe_Digital-Ad-effectiveness-White-Paper_September-2018-compressed.pdf

Jarvis, H., & Bonnett, A. (2013). Progressive nostalgia in novel living arrangements: A counterpoint to neo-traditional new urbanism? *Urban Studies (Edinburgh, Scotland)*, *50*(11), 2349–2370. doi:10.1177/0042098013478235

Johnston, D. D., & Swanson, D. H. (2003). Invisible mothers: A content analysis of motherhood ideologies and myths in magazines. *Sex Roles*, *49*(1), 21–33. doi:10.1023/A:1023905518500

Josephson, J. J., & Burack, C. (1998). The political ideology of the neo-traditional family. *Journal of Political Ideologies*, *3*(2), 213–231. doi:10.1080/13569319808420777

Jung, C. G. (2014). *The archetypes and the collective unconscious*. Routledge.

Kaplan, E. A. (1990). Sex, work and motherhood: The impossible triangle. *Journal of Sex Research*, *27*(3), 409–425. doi:10.1080/00224499009551569

Katz, J., (2003) Advertising and the construction of violent white masculinity. *Gender, race, and class in the media. A text reader*, 349-358.

Keller, K. (1994). *Mothers and work in popular American magazines*. Westport, CT: Greenwood Press.

Kemp, E., Bui, M., & Chapa, S. (2012). The role of advertising in consumer emotion management. *International Journal of Advertising*, *31*(2), 339–353. doi:10.2501/IJA-31-2-339-353

Kerrane, B., Bettany, S., & Kerrane, K. (2015). Siblings as socialization agents. *European Journal of Marketing*, *49*(5/6), 713–735. doi:10.1108/EJM-06-2013-0296

Kravets, O. (2012). Russia's "Pure Spirit" Vodka Branding and Its Politics. *Journal of Macromarketing*, *32*(4), 361–376. doi:10.1177/0276146712449627

Lakshmanan, D., & Rabiyathul, B. S. (2015). Factors Affecting the Effectiveness of Advertising in the Current Scenario "Advertising Factors are Immune to Business which Aspire to Inspire before You Expire." *International Journal of Science and Research*, *6*, 1264–1267. doi:10.21275/ART20163982

Lin, C., & Yeh, J. (2013). Modeling religious involvement: A qualitative integration based on female role visualization consumption. *Quality & Quantity*, *47*(1), 561–566. doi:10.100711135-011-9478-1

Liu, S. Q., & Mattila, A. S. (2017). Airbnb: Online targeted advertising, sense of power, and consumer decisions. *International Journal of Hospitality Management*, *60*, 33–41. doi:10.1016/j.ijhm.2016.09.012

Livingstone, S. (2011). Internet, children, and youth. In M. Consalvo & C. Ess (Eds.), *The handbook of internet studies* (pp. 348–368). Oxford, UK: Wiley Blackwell Publishing. doi:10.1002/9781444314861.ch16

Mager, J., & Helgeson, J. G. (2011). Fifty years of advertising images: Some changing perspectives on role portrayals along with enduring consistencies. *Sex Roles*, *64*(3-4), 238–252. doi:10.100711199-010-9782-6

Manser Payne, E., Peltier, J. W., & Barger, V. A. (2017). Omni-channel marketing, integrated marketing communications and consumer engagement: A research agenda. *Journal of Research in Interactive Marketing*, *11*(2), 185–197. doi:10.1108/JRIM-08-2016-0091

McNay, L. (1999). Gender, habitus and the field: Pierre Bourdieu and the limits of reflexivity. *Theory, Culture & Society*, *16*(1), 95–117. doi:10.1177/026327699016001007

McNeill, L., & Graham, T. (2014). Mother's choice: An exploration of extended self in infant clothing consumption. *Journal of Consumer Behaviour*, *13*(6), 403–410. doi:10.1002/cb.1489

Mirzaee, S., & George, B. P. (2016). Brand Archetypes: An Experiment with the Demeter. *Journal of Applied Economics & Business Research*, *6*(2).

Negm, E., & Tantawi, P. (2015). Investigating the Impact of Visual Design on Consumers' Perceptions towards Advertising. *International Journal of Scientific and Research Publications*, *5*(4). Retrieved from www.ijsrp.org

Neumann, E. (2015). *The great mother: An analysis of the archetype*. Princeton University Press. doi:10.1515/9781400866106

Nichols, T. R., Gringle, M. R., & Pulliam, R. M. (2015). You have to put your children's needs first or you're really not a good mother": Black Motherhood and Self-Care Practices. *Women, Gender, and Families of Color*, *3*(2), 165–189. doi:10.5406/womgenfamcol.3.2.0165

O'Donohoe, S., Hogg, M., Maclaran, P., Martens, L., & Stevens, L. (Eds.). (2013). *Motherhoods, markets and consumption: The making of mothers in contemporary western cultures* (Vol. 18). Routledge. doi:10.4324/9780203469729

O'Donohoe, S., & O'Donohoe, S. (2006). Yummy mummies: The clamor of glamour in advertising to mothers. *Advertising & Society Review*, *7*(3). doi:10.1353/asr.2007.0006

Papaoikonomou, E., Cascon-Pereira, R., & Ryan, G. (2016). Constructing and communicating an ethical consumer identity: A Social Identity Approach. *Journal of Consumer Culture*, *16*(1), 209–231. doi:10.1177/1469540514521080

Pegg, K. J., O'Donnell, A. W., Lala, G., & Barber, B. L. (2018). The role of online social identity in the relationship between alcohol-related content on social networking sites and adolescent alcohol use. *Cyberpsychology, Behavior, and Social Networking*, *21*(1), 50–55. doi:10.1089/cyber.2016.0665 PMID:28574719

Piller, I. (2001). Identity constructions in multilingual advertising. *Language in Society*, *30*(2), 153–186. doi:10.1017/S0047404501002019

Pinar, M. M. (2016). The Death of the Stereotype: Reclaim of Self in Angela Carter's "The Loves of Lady Purple. *International Journal of Social Sciences and Education Research*, *2*(1), 311–319. doi:10.24289/ijsser.279102

Poster, M. (2018). *The second media age*. John Wiley & Sons.

Schau, H. J., Russell, C., Crockett, D., Huff, A. D., Cotte, J., Bettany, S. M., ... Connell, P. M. (2012). Gender and Family Identity. *Advances in Consumer Research. Association for Consumer Research (U. S.)*, 40.

Schroeder, J.E. (1998). Consuming representation: A visual approach to consumer research. *Voices, views, and visions*, 193.

Schroeder, J. E. (2005). *Visual consumption* (Vol. 4). Essex, UK: Psychology Press.

Schroeder, J. E. (2006). 23 Critical visual analysis. Handbook of qualitative research methods in marketing. Academic Press.

Schroeder, J. E., & Borgerson, J. L. (1998). Marketing images of gender: A visual analysis. *Consumption Markets & Culture*, *2*(2), 161–201. doi:10.1080/10253866.1998.9670315

Schroeder, J. E., & Borgerson, J. L. (2015). Critical visual analysis of gender: Reactions and reflections. *Journal of Marketing Management*, *31*(15-16), 1723–1731. doi:10.1080/0267257X.2015.1077883

Schroeder, J. E., & Zwick, D. (2004). Mirrors of masculinity: Representation and identity in advertising images. *Consumption Markets & Culture*, *7*(1), 21–52. doi:10.1080/1025386042000212383

Schroeder, R. (2018). Towards a theory of digital media. *Information Communication and Society*, *21*(3), 323–339. doi:10.1080/1369118X.2017.1289231

Stevens, L., & Maclaran, P. (2007). Exploring the Celtic narrative in advertising: Goddess culture and the lexicon of perfumery. *Journal of Strategic Marketing*, *15*(1), 29–39. doi:10.1080/09652540601129973

Tammpuu, P., & Masso, A. (2018). 'Welcome to the virtual state': Estonian e-residency and the digitalised state as a commodity. *European Journal of Cultural Studies*, *21*(5), 543–560. doi:10.1177/1367549417751148

Thompson, C. J. (1996). Caring consumers: Gendered consumption meanings and the juggling lifestyle. *The Journal of Consumer Research*, *22*(4), 388–407. doi:10.1086/209457

Thompson, C. J. (2014). The politics of consumer identity work. *The Journal of Consumer Research*, *40*(5), iii–vii. doi:10.1086/673381

Thompson, C. J., & Üstüner, T. (2015). Women skating on the edge: Marketplace performances as ideological edgework. *The Journal of Consumer Research*, *42*(2), 235–265. doi:10.1093/jcr/ucv013

Tsai, S. P. (2006). Investigating archetype-icon transformation in brand marketing. *Marketing Intelligence & Planning*, *24*(6), 648–663. doi:10.1108/02634500610701708

Tsichla, E., & Zotos, Y. (2016). Gender portrayals revisited: Searching for explicit and implicit stereotypes in Cypriot magazine advertisements. *International Journal of Advertising*, *35*(6), 983–1007. doi:10.1080/02650487.2016.1189250

Tuten, T. L., & Solomon, M. R. (2017). Social media marketing. *Sage (Atlanta, Ga.).*

Wijaya, B. S. (2015). The development of the hierarchy of effects model in advertising. *International Research Journal of Business Studies, 5*(1).

Williamson, J. (2002). *Decoding Advertising: Ideology and Meaning in Advertisements*. London: Marion Boyars.

Yakup, D. (2011). A Theoretical Approach To The Concept Of Advertising In Marketing. *International Journal of Economics and Research*, *3*(2), 80–95. Retrieved from https://www.researchgate.net/publication/229987556_A_THEORETICAL_APPROACH_TO_THE_CONCEPT_OF_ADVERTISING_IN_MARKETING

Yu, H. (2014). College Students' Self-Concepts and Attitude toward Advertising; The Relationships among the Body-Esteem, Social Comparison, and the Perception about Diet Advertising. In Health Communication Research (Vol. 11). Academic Press.

Zaltman, G. (2003). *How customers think: Essential insights into the mind of the market*. Brighton, UK: Harvard Business Press.

Zappavigna, M. (2016). Social media photography: Construing subjectivity in Instagram images. *Visual Communication*, *15*(3), 271–292. doi:10.1177/1470357216643220

Zotos, Y. C., & Tsichla, E. (2014). Female Stereotypes in Print Advertising: A Retrospective Analysis. *Procedia: Social and Behavioral Sciences*, 148, 446–454. doi:10.1016/j.sbspro.2014.07.064

## KEY TERMS AND DEFINITIONS

**Consumer Cultural Theory (CCT):** The consumer cultural theory (CCT) is a family of perspectives that explores the dynamic relationships between consumer actions, the marketplace, and consumer cultural meanings.

**Consumer Culture:** A consumer culture signifies a social arrangement in which markets mediate a relationship among the ways of life, lived culture, social resources, and the symbolic or material resources. Thus, a consumer culture is jointly saclike constructed culture (of overlapping, flued, distributed and collective meanings of values, norms, even conflicting practices, identities,) based on the markets, commercially produced images, texts, and objects.

**Digital Advertisements:** Is a paid form of communications, placed in an online, digital and virtual ecosystems in order to inform and persuade target consumers about a product, service, or idea.

**Gender identity in Advertisements:** The portrayals of a gender-specific image, visual displays, values, customers, and role identity and socially constructed expectations, etc. in an advertisement, which may impel consumers to identify themselves with the gender image shown in the advertisements.

**Self-Concept:** Individual's self-concept is the end product of a process of reflection on oneself as an object, thus the self-concept is one's totality of feelings, and thoughts having references to oneself as an object.

**Self-Esteem:** Self-esteem is the overall evaluations of one-self on emotional or affective dimension and rating oneself having; a sense of power, sense of self-worth, self-competence, or efficacy, self-virtue, or moral worth.

**Self-Identity:** Self-identity is about awareness and believes about self as an object or being. Self-identities are viewed by the individual as internalized roles, also known as role identity.

**Visual Culture Theory (VCT):** Visual culture theory is the understanding of how or what images communicate and how consumers decode those images and reproduce meanings.

**Visual Designs:** The visual designs are some total of form, role models, shade, color, saturation, depth, and motion that is used to creating meaning or constructing a persuasive argument for moving a specific audience. The advertisements use 'visual design' to aesthetics in an inspirational manner to attract viewers' attention to affect perception, persuasion, and ultimately behavior.

# Chapter 14
# The Impact of Augmented Reality Advertisement on Customer Engagement in the Era of Connnected Consumers

**Azharul Islam**
*University of Wales Trinity Saint David, UK*

## ABSTRACT

*Innovation in technology is advancing by the day. As a latest and useful technology, augmented reality (AR) is drawing and getting attention from every sectors such as marketing, engagement, and user experience. Augment reality (AR) has become a recent trend for modern marketing. Marketers nowadays invest money and time in creation of new digital marketing platform for connected consumers. In this chapter, the researcher aims to discuss the impact of augmented reality advertisement on changing customer attitude towards brands. The purpose of this chapter is to discuss the impact of AR advertising on customer engagement and enhance user experience. Furthermore, this research has pinpointed the impact of augmented reality advertisement on cognitive, affective, and behavioural engagement.*

## INTRODUCTION

By adopting new approaches and technology a digital advertisement industry keeps moving forward to inventing more attractive ways of advertisement of products and services to the consumers. As an imperative part of the marketing communication, an advertisement can send non-personal messages about products and services with audio or visual effects to the consumers. Rogers and William (1990) stated that to develop the customer relationship. The fundamental role of the advertisement is to send the product information to consumers. Advertisement plays a vital role in every successful business. Over the years, marketers have followed the tools of traditional marketing; which includes print media, television, and radio or billboard advertisement. However, time has changed since digital marketing has penetrated the advertisement industry. Marketers nowadays are adopting new tools for digital market-

DOI: 10.4018/978-1-7998-0131-3.ch014

ing. More precisely, in this era of technology, almost everyone uses smartphones, tablets, and laptops and obviously using social media and blogs. Marketers have chosen social media and blogging sites as platforms to advertise their products and services. Advertisement, as well as the Mobile App's makers, firmly believe that the current generation of consumers spend most of their time on social media, blogging sites, virtual and augmented reality applications. The art of technology in advertising is to impress the target audience with products and services, that make them think after watching it. Moreover, the tools of the digital advertisement can influence a customer to make an impulse purchase decision. As part of the latest technology, Augmented Reality (AR) is getting popular in the field of digital advertisement. Augmented Reality based advertisements have the potential to change customer attitude towards a brand thus creating customer intentions to purchase. This chapter is intended to explain the impact of Augmented Reality Advertisements on customer attitudes towards brands through optimisation of customer engagement and enhancing user experience in the era of connected consumers.

## BACKGROUND OF AUGMENTED REALITY (AR)

In the era of the very connected consumers, the Augmented Realty (AR) in the advertisement is considered as the latest breakthrough technology. The AR is getting much attention for its extensive uses. Augmented Reality is a computer-assisted augmenting of perception by means of additional interactive information levels in real-time, such that the observer is immersed in the real and virtual world at the same time. Fundamentally, the AR is a combination of the virtual object and the real world that gives an opportunity to the audience to interact with this object in real-time (Vallio 1998). Moreover, it is an advanced concept of virtual reality (VR), in which the audience gets excess of the computer-based virtual environment. In addition, AR technologies work with interaction and integration with the real world with 3D technology in a virtual environment (Cascales et al., 2013; Mullen, 2011). AR is also described as the latest form of technology created on the sense of the integration, image, and clips of the real environment with the virtual environment through the 3D computer-based graphics and all the components measured by the computer (Etmeezi, 2010). By using the special system and methods AR technology merges the actual environment with the virtual environment. For example, during surgery using an augmented reality application, a surgeon can get all virtual information on areas of treatment (Nowfall, 2010). AR technology advanced step of the virtual reality with some variations, where with the support of the relevant application and graphical imposition audience experience the real world (Azuma, 1997). This creates a lot of interest, curiosity to the customers and can increase customer interest and involvement. Thus, the new form of technology and application AR considered to be the most buzzing concept in the advertisement industry.

For the non-technical readership, the notion of the AR technology in the advertisement appears relatively unknown somehow. *'By Augmented Reality, abbreviated to AR, we understand the computer-assisted augmenting of perception by means of additional interactive information levels in real-time. The distinction between AR and Virtual Reality: in the case of Virtual Reality, the user is totally immersed in a virtual world that has no connection with reality' (Buchholz, 2014)* Over the years through the gimmick (3D/webcam), simple experimentation phase (QR codes/SMS) and unnatural behaviour (location navigator) the classification of AR spectrum has evolved to more point of sales (POS) and more usefulness (Johnson 2014),. Furthermore, Johnson (2014) also believes the technology of the augmented reality is expanding in the areas of eye-tracking, AR contacts, and facial recognition, even the education system, etc. Augmented Reality Advertisements uses AR technology to enhance to visual, sensory and engagement effects of advertisements. Augmented Reality advertisement is a form of digital advertising or marketing with an interactive experience. Commenting about AR in advertisement Vong (2014) says that, *'with the new digital information and imaginary AR "augments" the viewer and surrounded by it. To that extent, AR may or may not mean much to the average consumer —a cool image is great, but it does not make a connection. Hence, augmented reality in and of itself usefully is not the aim of any advertisement campaign; the aim is to use Augmented reality technology in such a way that it constructs an interactive experience, through a rewarding and rich experience it is engaging the customer as well as change their attitudes towards brand'* According to Dunleavy and Dede (2006), augmented reality technology is the realistic synchronous integration of digital content from computer or software with the real world.

## THE PRINCIPLES OF CUSTOMER ENGAGEMENT AND AUGMENTED REALITY

The Augmented Reality may not be as exciting as the virtual reality gaming such as a roller coaster ride however this technology is proving to be important and is contributing in daily life. Augmented reality rapidly gaining popularity from social media filters, surgical procedure, etc, because AR brings the elements of the virtual world, into the real world, therefore enhancing the things that people hear, see and feel. When related to other reality technologies, AR lies in the middle which is called the "mixed reality spectrum" between the virtual world and real-world (Reality Technology, 2019).

Theories indicate that the customer engagement is very significant steps towards brand loyalty and creation of positive word of mouth. The customer engament is the level of customer absorption, deidication, vigour and interaction with a product or a barnd (Patterson et al. 2006). The absorption is the thought level of involvement and concentration with the product that the 'time flies off'. The dedication is a sense of emotional attachment and sense of belongingness with the product or a brand. The vigour is the level of energy and mental resilience while engaging on interaction with the brand, and interaction is two-way engagement and communication with the brand. Thus customer Engagement: is the proactive level of customer's rationale and emotional connection & involvement that results in behaviour towards a brand or brand or service, such orientations mean that a customer becomes a co-creator of value (Roderick, Hollebeek, Biljana, & Ana, 2011). The Customer engagement behaviour it generated due to a range of motivations such as word of mouth, blogging, custome to customer interactive, experiencing the service, emotion, creativity, collaboration, brand community engagement, other relational antecedents and advertisement etc. (Roderick, Hollebeek, Biljana, & Ana, 2011)

Moreover, Customer Engagement with advertising and/or specific media has been linked to superior advertising effectiveness (Roderick, Hollebeek, Biljana, & Ana, 2011).The media engagement motivates a customer to engage with a barnd, product or a services due to customers goal directed action, i.e. advertisement helps in achieving the goal of satisfying a need by using a brand, product or service (Patterson et al.'s, 2006). Customer engagement (CE) is a three-dimensional motivational state (cognitive, affective and behavioural) that occurs (and last in time with a sense of flow) by virtue of interactive co-creative, customer experiences with a focal agent/object/ brand in focal service relationships (Roderick, Hollebeek, Biljana, & Ana, 2011). Thus' Higher level of customer engagement results in more customer trust, commitment, self-brand connection, emotional attachment and brand loyalty (Roderick, Hollebeek, Biljana, & Ana, 2011). Higgins and Scholer's (2009) Regulatory Engagement Theory, refers to "a [consumer's] state of being occupied, fully-absorbed or engrossed," thus generating "a level of attraction to, or repulsion from, a focal engagement object."

Advertising is information that engages and persuade customers to shift their beliefs and preferences about a brand, product or its attributes (Dokyun, Hosanagar, & Nair, 2018).The social media advertisements are richer to persuade customers. The enjoyment with advertisement, trust in the information, level of involvement due advertisement's audio-visual content, interactions and word of mouth etc leads to higher level of engagement with a barnd.

Augmented reality advertisements enhance the advertainment content by mixing virtual experience with reality. Thus it might result in more customer enjoyment, involvement, flow and ultimately higher level of customer engagement. The varieties offered by AR ads further makes it potential more useful in advertainment contexts.

Augmented reality has various typologies such as; marker-based augmented reality, marker-less AR, projection-based AR, and superimposition-based AR. Marker-based AR (Image Recognition) uses some type of visual marker (QR/2D code) and a camera, to produce an effect. Marker-less AR is one of the most extensively implemented applications of AR, (also called GPS, location-based and position-based), it uses a digital compass, GPS, and an accelerometer or velocity meter. In order to provide data based on the location, it is normally embedded in the device (Reality technology, 2019). Projection-based AR functions by the projection of artificial light onto the surface of the real world. By transferring light onto the surface of real-world projection-based AR apps allow human interaction and sensing that interaction (i.e. touch) of that projected light. By distinguishing between the altered projection (caused by the user's interaction) and an expected (or known) projection it detects the user interaction. For example, Laser-plasma technology utilizes the projection-based AR to project a three-dimensional (3D) interactive hologram into mid-air (Reality technology, 2019). For the same object, with the newly augmented view, superimposition-based AR either fully or partially substitutes the unique view of an object. "*In superimposition-based AR, object recognition plays a dynamic role since the apps cannot change the original view with an augmented one if it cannot determine what the object is*" (Reality technology, 2019). A robust consumer-facing case of superimposition-based AR could be found in the IKEA's AR furniture's catalogue (See figure 1). By downloading an application and scanning designated pages in their digital or printed catalogue, users or customers can place virtual IKEA furniture in their own home with the support of AR technology (Reality technology, 2019).

## AR AND FUTURE MARKET IN SOCIAL MEDIA

The current market of social media is eagerly waiting to see what actually this technology has in store for them (Mentionlytics, 2019). By trying a new product, the Gen-Z and millennials will be amongst the fast adopters. Hence, businesses should keep up with the latest technology and emphasis on achieving their goal with the increase in sales and revenue-generation. Targeting for a new market and taking advantage of augmented reality in offering great user experience will be very beneficial to the marketers. There is no better place to do business than on the platform of social media. In addition, to succeed in their investments, the key marketers should develop suitable content for the markets using AR. In this technological era, advertisers will like to implement interactive content for their campaign in a competitive market. By developing appropriate content for the campaign advertisers should continue targeting the social media users (Mentionlytics, 2019).

*Figure 1. Example of AR*
*(source: Reality technology, 2019)*

The users of social media are no longer interested in traditional or typical TV-style advertisements (Mentionlytics, 2019). Eventually, the AR-based advertisement on the platform of social media would have a greater potential of touching the senses of the viewers. Consequently, To increase customer engagement and loyalty with a brand, one of the future social media trend would use AR/VR in advertisements (Mentionlytics, 2019).

## A CONCEPTUAL FRAMEWORK FOR AR ADVERTISING

Advertisements are paid a form of communication that employees a range of media channels to send out an open, non-personal message to inform, persuade and influence users of a product, idea, service or place or person the users (Kotler and Armstrong, 2006). AR advertisement uses AR technology to enhance to visual, sensory and engagement effects of advertisements. Attitude is a 'learned predispositions to respond to an object or class of objects in a consistently favourable or unfavourable way (Ferreira & Belem, 2017). Consumers' attitudes are accepted as a key driver of consumer behaviour. Consumers' attitude towards advertising is considered an important indicator to measure its effectiveness of the advertisement, as the research has indicated that a positive attitude towards an advertisement will lead to a positive attitude towards the brand shown in that advertisement (Kotler and Armstrong, 2006). However, the consumers may also see an advertisement as intrusive if the advertisement is un-interesting and untimely or irrelevant to the consumers' current interests (Ferreira & Belem, 2017). And studies have shown that interactive advertisements via social media (Ferreira & Belem, 2017) or via AR enhancement can be more interesting and will be not seen as intrusive by the consumers. The customer engagement is the level of customer's rationale and emotional connection & involvement that results in a behaviour towards a brand or brand or service etc. High customer engagement means that a customer becomes a co-creator of a product or brand. Hence, it can be broadly assumed an AR advertisement increases customers' engagement and enhance the experience, hence it can ultimately change consumer's attitude towards advertisement and the brand (see Figure 1) .

This literature review has evidenced that AR advertising has an impact on changing customer attitudes through optimising customer engagement and enhancing user experience. For this reason, it is very essential to have the conceptual framework that shows the relationship between the variables (see Figure 2).

*Figure 2. A conceptual framework for AR advertising*

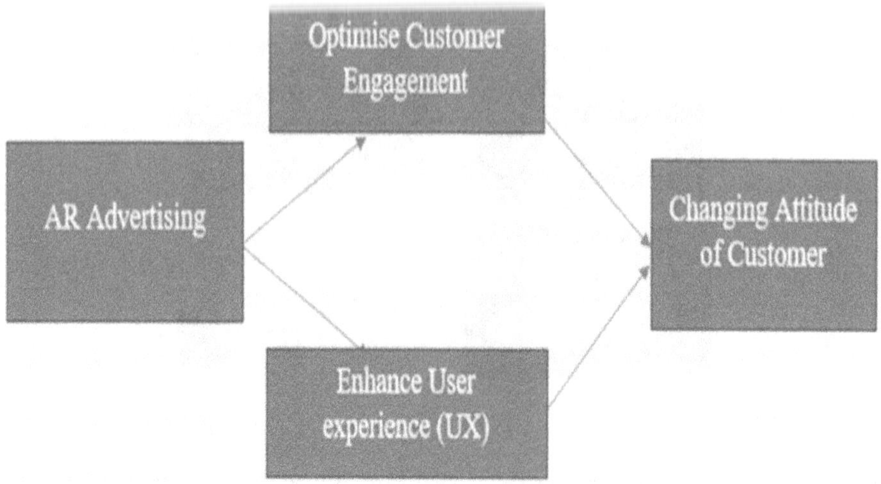


## Optimising Customer Engagement Through AR Advertisement

In terms of marketing and creating relationships with the target audience, customer engagement plays a vital role. According to Beatty, Vivek, and Morgan (2012, p133), the strong participation of an individuals with an organisation's offers and/or activities (either initiated by the customer or organisation), will create stronger relationships. With regards to customer engagement (online entities and computer-mediated), the cognitive and affective commitment of a customer with a company or brand is important for a stronger relationship. For, building and enhancing the customer relationship, customer engagement and consumer involvement in specific interactions and/or interactive experience is imperatives (Brodie, Ilic, Julic, & Hollebeek, 2013).Hollebeek (2011) state that, customer brand engagement is a brand-related, context-dependent state of mind at cognitive, emotional and behavioural levels towards a brand. Similarly, in the context of the media engagement and advertisement, customer engagement is seen as a multi-dimensional concept (example, attention, interaction, sensorial pleasure, dialogue, immediate activation, and emotion) to produce entire customer experience with the target customer. Brodie et al. (2011b) state that "customer engagement is a motivational idea of the psychological state".In addition, customer engagement has social and experiential dimensions. Hollbeck (2011) argued for three dimensions of engagement namely; affective, cognitive and behavioural customer engagement (see figure 3). Thus, as shown in the conceptual framework (figure 2); the AR advertising has an impact on customer attitude towards brand through optimising customer engagement. Hence, it is important to determine, how AR advertisement optimise the customer engagement in order to change customer attitude towards a brand. Based on the discussion it can be hypothesized that:

**H1:** AR advertisement has a positive association with customer engagement optimisation.

*Figure 3. Dimensions of optimising customer engagement (adapted from Hollebeek (2011)*

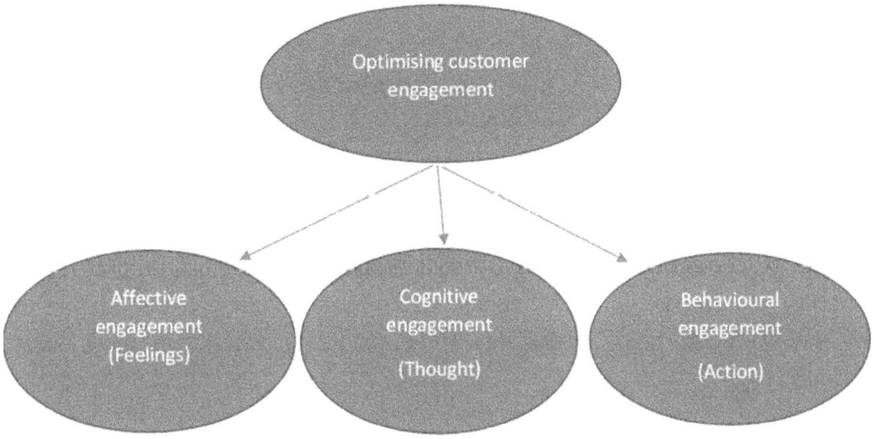


## Affective Customer Engagement

According to Hollbeck (2011), the effective engagement apprehends summative and enduring level of emotions experienced by the target audience through their engagements. Effective customer engagement is a long-lasting engagement rather than a one-off feeling. Hollebeck (2011), also mentioned as a dimension of customer engagement, affective engagement, has been widely used to measure customer engagement optimisation through traditional and digital advertisement media. However, it is still questionable whether augmented reality impacts customer engagement optimisation. The affective engagement has two sub-dimension those called enthusiasm and enjoyment (Hollebeck 2011). The enthusiasm of the affective customer engagement measures the instinct level of interest and feelings. AR advertisement creates *excitement* and *interest* in the product and services (Jovernick, 2015). Enjoyment as a sub-dimension of the customer engagement measures happiness, feeling, and pleasure of the customers. Many researchers have previously stated that advertisements create enjoyment and engagement. After the above discussion there should be a hypothesis to prove the statement, which can be:

**H1a:** AR advertisement has significant influences on affective customer engagement.

## Cognitive Customer Engagement

One of the key components of the customer engagement is cognitive customer engagement, which is an enduring and active mental state that a target audience experiences in relation to the principal objects of their engagement (Hollebeck 2013; Mollen and Wilson 2010). Cognitive customer engagement consists of two sub-components: absorption and attention (Hollececk, 2013). Many advertisement related researches have proved that visual advertisement increases the level of cognitive engagement. However, for the lack of research, it is still unsolved that the AR technology in the advertisement impacts the customer cognitively.

As a sub-component of the cognitive customer engagement, attention is considered as cognitive ability (Mollen and Wilson 2010) which is voluntarily dedicated to interaction with the audience or customer through the advertisement (Nambisan and Baron 2007). More precisely, as a part of the cognitive ability attention means how much time do customers want to spend to watch the advertisement? Also, how attentive are they to watch the advertisement? Thus, attention is important as a sub-components of cognitive engagement.

Absorption, as a sub-component of the cognitive customer engagement, implies the level of concentration and immersion of a focal object (Hollebeck 2013). In terms of the advertising, absorption means involvement/non-involvement, recalling memories, feels connected and awareness, etc. Thus, it could be assumed that:

**H1b:** AR advertisement has a significant impact on cognitive customer engagement.

## Behavioural Customer Engagement

Many researchers believe that behavioural customer engagement drives from customers' motivational aspects (Hollebeck 2011, MSI, 2010). More precisely, the manifestation of the behavioural customer engagement has brand focus resulting from the motivational drivers. According to the journal of the Marketing Science Institute (2010), behavioural customer engagement goes beyond the transaction. Hollebeck (2011) has stated that behavioural customer engagement consists of sub-components such as learning and sharing. To identify the impact of the AR advertisement on the behavioural customer engagement, it is important to find in what extent customer will able to learn about the product or services and their features also are they going to share the experience they got during the advertisement. It is a sub-components of the behavioural customer engagement, it provides experience, information, and ideas through the advertisement in order to create the opportunity of learning for customers (Hollebeck 2011).

Sharing is the process of passing information or experience with each other. It is another sub-dimension of the behavioural customer engagement (Hollebeck 2011). After experiencing any kind of interactive or attractive video advertisement customers normally share this with their friends and family. In terms of the AR advertisement and behavioural customer engagement, it can be hypotheses that:

**H1c:** Augmented reality advertisement has a significant impact on behavioural customer engagement.

## Enhancing User Experience Through the AR Advertisement

User experience is a process of the interaction between the audience and the world, it relates to a person's attitude and emotions about the product or services they used. User experience generates a new interaction through the intangible process (Davis, 2003). All interactions create several kinds of experiences, such as: cognitive, sensual, emotional, physical and atheistic (Forlizzi & Battarbee, 2004). The user experience expresses as a strange phenomenon that is implemented by the HCI (Human-computer-interaction). A user experience is a consequence of the user's perception (environment), user's interaction (organisation/ social setting, consequence of the activity and voluntariness of uses), user's internal state (predisposition, perception, mood, motivation and needs) and the characteristics of digital system (complexity, functionality, usability and purpose) (Hassenzahl and Tractinsky (2007). The user experience transfers beyond the usability (i.e. effective, efficient and satisfactory interaction) and can help in establishing the emotionally appealing relationship between the product/services and users (Desmet, Porcelijn, and Dijk 2007). Many authors and researchers have measured and described the user experience from different contexts and perspectives such as web-based advertisement, retail, online shopping, and gaming, etc. Also, they conceptualized and established many factors and components of the user experience. Hassenzahl (2007) described the multiplicity of user experience based on the pragmatic (goal-oriented) and hedonic (action-oriented) of the product (see figure 4). Hassenzahl (2007) also mentioned that user experience should be considered as an entire impression of a service or product to the audience. Moreover, it is called the judgment of users. It starts before touching, using and feeling the products. In addition, there is always transmit or change of impression before and after using the product or services. In summary, Hassenzahl and Tractinsky (2007) have argued that user experience is made up of pragmatic quality and hedonic quality (see Figure 4). So it can be drawn that:

**H2:** Augmented reality advertisement has significance effect on enhancing customer engagement.

## Pragmatic Quality of the User Experience

The attribute of the pragmatic quality represents the perceived usability of the product (Schaik and Ling, 2008). It is called usability because it is related to satisfaction, efficiency and effectiveness of the user experience (Butler, 1996). According to Norman (2004), "usability facet of the user experience covers the narrow opportunity of the user experience because it is not examined as a measure to evaluate user experience." The features of the product and services may include the size, weight, usability, usefulness, function, aesthetic and symbol that impact the user experience. Pragmatic quality comprises a portion of those interactions that highlight the utility and usability of the service and product in terms of the potential task (Hassenzahl 2007). The augmented reality advertisement has the potential to enhance the pragmatic quality of the user experience by revealing more information about the product or services. Thus AR advertisement facilitates customers to make a pre-purchase decision during shopping time (Kim and Forsythe, 2008a, 2008b) and decrease the consumer's anxiety (Huang and Hsu-Liu, 2014). The sub-dimensions of the pragmatic quality of the user experience are Perspicuity, Efficiency, and Dependability (Hassenzahl 2007). Perspicuity measures the users' experience, for example, easy/complicated features of the product, a clear/confusing attribute of the products or services, also understandable/non-understandable features of the product or the services (Hassenzahl 2007). Efficiency measures the fast and efficient way to use the product and services (Hassenzahl 2007). For this chapter, it is needed to discuss whether the AR advertisement working fast and efficiently to provide adequate information about the product and services to the customers. Dependability measures the user's experience on security, predictability, supportiveness, and meeting expectation (Hassenzahl 2007). After the discussion of the pragmatic user experience a conclusion can be that:

*Figure 4. User experience and its dimensions (adapted from Hassenzahl and Tractinsky,(2007)*

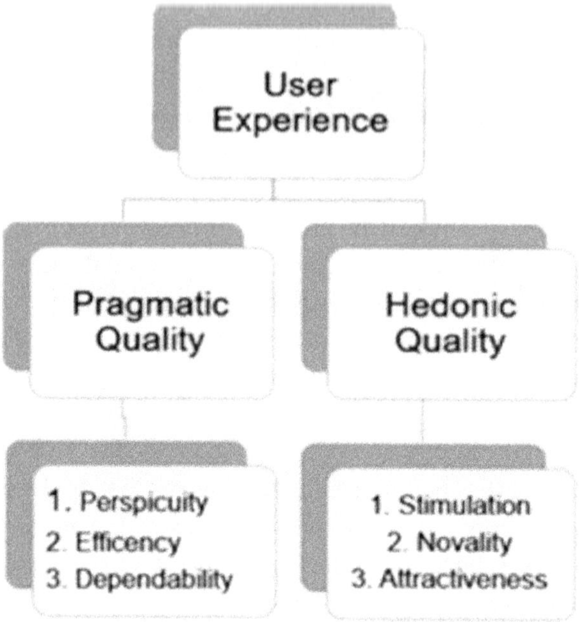


**H2a:** Augmented reality advertisement has a positive influence on the pragmatic quality of the user experience.

## Hedonic Quality of the User Experience

Hedonic quality of the user experience consists of the emotional reaction of a consumer towards brands, products or services (Hassenzahl &Tractinsky, 2006; Norman, 2004). More precisely, hedonic quality of the user experience of perceived ability of the of a product or services. The hedonic quality of the user experience provides the sensory pleasure to the users from service experience (Hassenzahl & Tractinsk, 2006) An AR advertisement facilitates many emotional benefits to customers, so it may affect the user's experiences and hedonic quality of the product (Kim & Forsythe, 2008b). The main value of the hedonic quality experience via AR is that it provides the opportunity to the users to share experience on the social or any other media in order to increase playfulness (Huang and Hsu-Liu, 2014).

The AR-based hedonic quality experience provides the impression and opportunity for the novel and challenging product or services (Hassenzahl 2007). Moreover, it can provide high stimulation due to novelty, fun and by offering an interesting way to interact through the advertisement. As a subdimension of the hedonic quality experience, the novelty of the creativity of advertisement can create a positive impression for the product and services. As such AR ads will be considered as unique, unexpected and divergent from other advertisements (Batra, Myers, &Aaker 1996; Belch &Belch 2004). Thus augmented reality advert creates novelty for the target users due to the unique feature and creative layout of AR. After discussing the hedonic quality, it can be hypothesized that:

**H2b:** An augmented reality advertisement has a positive influence on the hedonic quality of user experience.

## Customer Attitude Towards Brand

In terms of advertisement, customer attitude plays a critical role and has become popular topics for the research. Customer attitude is also considered as an obstacle and an advantage for the marketers. More precisely, during designing of advertisement and marketing strategy, if marketers ignore customer attitude, it will result in poor quality marketing/advertisement campaign. In the marketing and advertisement strategies, the customer attitude is significant as the attitude is a useful predictor of consumer behaviour(Mitchell & Olson 1981, Eagly & Chaiken 1993).

In terms of advertisement, customer attitude is considered as the general evaluation of a product or services. Customer attitude affects the shopping and buying habits of the customers as well as satisfy the personal motives of individuals (Las & Parnas 2010). The researcher also mentioned that -customer attitude consists of the feelings, behavioural intention, and belief towards some object or brands in the context of the marketing (Eagly & Chaiken 1993). Moreover, customer attitudes can be described as positive or negative feelings or beliefs of individuals towards the brands or products.

The functional model of Attitude (Daniel Katz, 1937) consists four parts that is "the value-expressive function (based on self-concept or central value), The utilitarian function (based on the produce happiness and ethical theory, pain/pleasure), The knowledge function (based on comparison and real market statistics) and the ego-defensive function (based on only self-image). The value-expressive and utilitarian function is commonly seen to measure the behaviour and attitude of the customer (Sirgy, 1991). Zinkhan and Fornell (1989), "The hierarchy of effects", model consists of two basic components which are high involvement of the standard hierarchy and low involvement of the hierarchy. The ABC model about the changing customer attitude is more straightforward, clear and widely used for making the advertisement strategy (Solomon, 2008). ABC model consists of three components which are affective, behavioural and cognitive (see Figure 5). This model illustrates and highlights the relationship between knowing-doing and feeling (Solomon, 2008). In terms of the product and services, it is mandatory to know about customers feels and act of action about those products and services from their point of view. In terms of the augmented reality advertisement, in this chapter author aimed to discuss how augmented reality technology in advertisement changing customer attitude towards the brand. So the hypothesis could be:

**H3**: Augmented reality advertisement has a positive significance on changing customer attitude towards the brand

## Cognitive Components of Customer Attitudes

Cognitive as a component of customer attitude measures the customer's opinion and the belief and thought about the product and services. It also consists of the evaluation of the entities of an individual which includes belief/disbelief or thought towards the brand (Homer,2008). It is consists of the knowledge and perceptions established by a combination of the direct experience of attitude and the interrelated experience objects from various sources. The belief and thought of the customer considered as the pre-perception of the product before purchase. According to Solomon, Grenier, & Stadler (2008, 2009),

*Figure 5. Customer attitude and sub-dimensions (adapted from Solomon, 2008)*

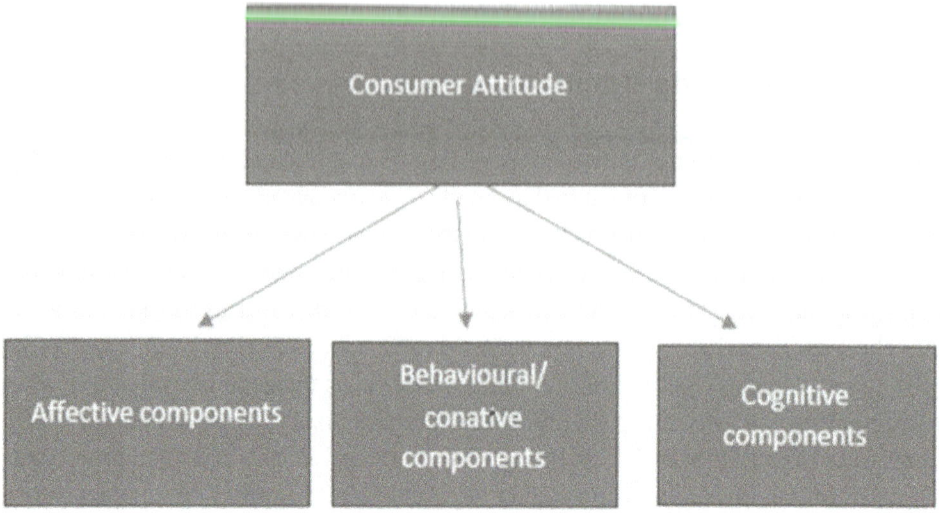


- "*the entire structure of belief of a brand epitomises the attitude's cognitive components towards the service or product.*" Knowledge helps to gives additional information about the product and services. It is considered to be important sub-components of the cognitive attitudes (Solomon and Homer, 2008). Thus in terms of the augmented reality advertisement, the hypothesis can be:

**H3a:** Augmented reality advertisement has a positive significance on changing customers cognitive attitude towards the brand

## Affective Components of the Attitudes

Affective components of the attitudes basically related to the emotional terms of the attitudes. Emotional components can be described in various ways (Cohen, Pham, & Andrade, 2008; Scherer, 2005). According to the theory of the affective components, it contains may terms such as, pleasure, feeling, psychological reaction, cognitive appeal, etc. (Russell, 2003; Scherer, 2001). Emotion can be triggered by many other directions however, the terms called feelings is one of them (O'Neill & Lambert, 2001; White & Yu, 2005 and Solomon,2008).In general. the feeling can be negative or positive. On one side, negative feelings always assessed the unfavourable features and other side positive feelings measured the favourable features (Bagozzi, Gopinath, & Nyer, 1999; Mano, 2004). According to the Lerner, Han, & Keltner (2007), - "*Consumer are persuaded to make their purchase decision by minimising the probability of experiencing the negative feelings*"

Previously, some augmented reality advertisement related research has concentred on the consumers' attachment or emotional feelings toward the brand by AR advert (Vincent, 2005). Moreover, Kolsaker & Drakatos, (2009) have mentioned that - "*only emotional attachment can bring potential benefits for the brand*". Regarding the augmented reality advertisement, the hypothesis can be:

**H3b:** Augmented reality advertisement has a positive significance on changing customers affective attitude towards the brand

### Behavioural intention

Behavioural intention is a tendency audience or customers in order to respond in a certain manner towards the brand. The actual behaviour of the consumer during the shopping can be related to the cognitive components as well (Russell, 2003; Scherer, 2001). In the marketing and advertisement sector, it is also known as the behavioural intention which is pretty much related to the purchase intention (Solomon, 2008). Purchase intention is an individual's buying tendency or action during the advertisement or shopping time also it is discrete from attitude (Bagozzi et al. 1979; Ostrom 1969) because intention works as a motivation which is driven by the attitudes (Eagly & Chaiken 1993, p. 168). The augmented reality advertisement changes the consumer attitude by behavioural tendency and increases purchase intention of customers through their behavioural action. So it can lead to a hypothesis:

**H4:** Augmented reality advertisement has a positive significance on changing customers behavioural attitude towards the brand

## METHOD AND METHODOLOGY

For this research researcher used the systematic literature review as well as quantitative analysis based on the online survey. The sample size was 75. The author has shown a video of IKEA and Nike's augmented reality advertisement on YouTube and social media to the participants and asked the questions. In the questionnaire author all the items from the sub-components of the independent variables. The questions were based on the Likert scale between 0-5 in weight. Ethical considerations as part of the axiology were kept in mind in terms of disclosing the data. After data collection, to check the internal consistency and validity of the data Cronbach Alpha has used also for the statistical analysis for this research correlation, regression and ANOVA test considered in order to check and examine the Impact of the augmented reality advertisement on changing customer attitudes towards brand through the enhancing user experience and increasing customer engagement.

## MAIN FINDINGS

### Correlation Between Augmented Reality Advertisement and Customer Engagement Optimisation

This research contains several hypothesis tests to check the impact of AR advertisement on changing customer attitudes. Each of the hypotheses synthesised to check the relationship between the variables. Person's correlation analysis has been used in this research in order to examine the degree of the correlation between the variables.

Table 1 shows that value of the Pearson's correlation coefficient *(r)* between Augmented reality advertisement (independent variable) and the different components of customer engagement (dependent variable) ; Affective (r=0.764, p<0.001), cognitive (r=0.743, p<0.001) and behaviour (r=0.682, p <0.01) and with overall engagement (r=0.805, p<0.001). Which shows there are significant associations exist between the variables. So H1 and related sub-hypotheses are accepted.

## Correlation Between the Augmented Reality Advertisement and User Experience

Table 2 shows the relationship between the augmented reality advertisement (independent variable) and user experience (dependent variables).

Table 2 shows that value of the Pearson's correlation coefficient *(r)* between the AR advertisement & user experience (dependent variable) and its dimensions, namely hedonic and pragmatic quality of user experience has been 0.77 and 0.82 respectively, which shows the significant correlation between the variables (p=0.00<0.01). So H2 and related sub-hypotheses are accepted.

## Correlation Between Customer Attitude And Customer Engagement

*Table 3* indicates the correlation between customer attitude (independent variable) and customer engagement (dependent variable). *Table 3* shows that the value of the Pearson's correlation coefficient *(r)* between Customer attituded and three kinds of engagements; affective customer engagement (r=0.74, p=0.00), cognitive customer engagement (r=0.76, p=0.00) and behavioural customer engagement (r= 0.79, p=0.00) as very strong and significant (p=0.00<0.01).Thus indicating a strong relationship among them. So H3 and related sub-hypotheses are accepted.

*Table 1. Correlation between augmented reality advertisement and customer engagement optimization*

| Correlations AR ads with Customer Engagements (with dimension) | | | | | | |
|---|---|---|---|---|---|---|
| | | AvgARads | AvgCE | AvgAffCE | AvgCogCE | AvgBehCE |
| AvgARads | Pearson Correlation | 1 | .805** | .764** | .743** | .682** |
| | Sig. (2-tailed) | | .000 | .000 | .000 | .000 |
| | N | 75 | 75 | 75 | 75 | 75 |
| **. Correlation is significant at the 0.01 level (2-tailed). | | | | | | |

*Table 2. Correlation between the augmented reality advertisement and user experience*

| Correlations AR Ads with Customer user experience (With dimensions) | | | | | |
|---|---|---|---|---|---|
| | | AvgARads | AvgUX | AvgPqUX | AvgHqUX |
| AvgARads | Pearson Correlation | 1 | .821** | .767** | .810** |
| | Sig. (2-tailed) | | .000 | .000 | .000 |
| | N | 75 | 75 | 75 | 75 |
| **. Correlation is significant at the 0.01 level (2-tailed). | | | | | |

## Correlation Between the Customer Attitude with User experience (UX) and Dimensions

The given Table 4 indicates the correlation between customer attitude (independent variable) and user experience (dependent variables).

Table 4 shows that the value of the Pearson's coefficient of correlation (*r*) for pragmatic quality of the user experience is 0.75, and the correlation between the hedonic quality of the user experience is 0.86 and the correlation of customer attitude with overall user experience is strong and significant (r= 0.84, p=0.00). this shows that hedonistic quality is more effected by the customer attitude as compared to the pragmatic quality of the experiences.

*Table 3. Correlation between customer attitude and customer engagement*

| Correlations of Customer attitude with Customer Engagements and dimensions | | | | | | |
|---|---|---|---|---|---|---|
| | | AvgCA | AvgCE | AvgAffCE | AvgCogCE | AvgBehCE |
| AvgCA | Pearson Correlation | 1 | .833** | .742** | .759** | .794** |
| | Sig. (2-tailed) | | .000 | .000 | .000 | .000 |
| | N | 75 | 75 | 75 | 75 | 75 |
| **. Correlation is significant at the 0.01 level (2-tailed). | | | | | | |

*Table 4. Correlation between the customer attitude with user experience (UX) and dimensions*

| Correlations of Customer Attitude with User experience and dimensions | | | | | |
|---|---|---|---|---|---|
| | | AvgCA | AvgUX | AvgPqUX | AvgHqUX |
| AvgCA | Pearson Correlation | 1 | .842** | .749** | .861** |
| | Sig. (2-tailed) | | .000 | .000 | .000 |
| | N | 75 | 75 | 75 | 75 |

**. Correlation is significant at the 0.01 level (2-tailed).

## DISCUSSION ON THE CONCEPTUAL MODEL AND FINDINGS

The marketers have started using the AR technology in their advertisement as a strategy to draw the attention of the target customers. More precisely, we are living in an era of technology, almost everyone has a smartphone and social media access in developed and developing countries.

### Impact of AR Advertisement on Customer Engagement

In the literature review, it was briefly discussed that customer engagement plays an important and crucial role in relationship marketing, digital marketing, and advertising. It was also discussed that the normal and traditional advertisement has an impact on customer engagement. Beatty, Vivek, and Morgan (2012), Mollen and Wilson (2010) and Brodie et al (2011), in their research have mentioned and discussed the different dimensions and model of the customer engagement. The other research of Gambetti, Grafigna, and Biragi, (2012), to measure the impact of advertisement on customer engagement optimisation they proposed social and experimental dimensions. However, Hollebeck (2011) mentioned cognitive, affective and behavioural engagement on her research to measure customer engagement. For this research, the researcher used the Hollebeck (2011) dimensions of the customer engagements in order to find and reach the conclusion about the AR advertisement on customer engagements. For each of these dimensions, the author used the items of the measurement like happy/not happy, interest/excitement, thought and beliefs, sharing/not sharing involvement/not involvements during the advertisement. As is mentioned previously, the research of Calder (2013), the impact of advertising on customer engagement has proven also measured by the scales of Hollebeck (2011). Similarly, in this research author has found the same result in terms of the AR advertisement. As the latest technology AR itself considered a new technology in the field of advertisement.

Tobais Hollerer and Dieter Schmalsteig (2015), has mentioned in their book called augmented reality: principles and practice, "*people are moving away from the desktop computer to experience the physical world as a new virtual experience.*" More precisely, augmented reality as a new innovation of the technology considered to helping the world with continuously innovate and connect as well as to improve the world of engagement ready. Then the "Pokémon Go" craze of the year 2016 can be a good example of engagement through the AR effect. That gaming app-connected people all over the world to catch the animated pokemon by visiting many places. After the success of that gaming apps, it has drawn the attention of the marketers and organisation to use that AR effect in the advertisement camping. On the other hand, the founder of the world largest social media Facebook Mark Zuckerberg (2016) has announced 10 years strategic plan which is "*The plan outlines within the next 10-years, virtual and augmented reality technology will be embedded throughout the entire Facebook platform*". Social media is the largest platform where people can talk, share and creates engagements, so that advert makers and marketers inspired to create adverts with the AR technology which can be implemented there advertise their product and optimise the engagement with the customers effectively, cognitively and behaviourally which may lead to change customer attitude toward the brand. During the survey of this research, the audience asked to answer some scale question which is based on the above items. Subsequently experienced the selected AR advertisement about IKEA and NIKE audiences articulated their perception about the advert also reaction towards the brand. The cause of the impact perhaps for the involvement, excitement, and likelihood, that augmented reality advertisement created for the participant as the latest technology. Maximum respondents have agreed to share with the content of the IKEA and NIKE's augmented reality advertisements to their friends and family also in the future they wanted to know more about the products from those brands. Eventually, the result of this research has verified that the augmented reality positive impact on customer engagement optimisation through cognitively, effectively and behaviourally. In the future to increase customer engagement, the implementation of AR technology in the advertisement campaign can be a good framework. For example: nowadays social media engaging people through social media especially with photo filters (Forbes, 2019)

## Impact of AR Advertisement on User Experience

In the literature review part, it was mentioned that any sort of visual advertisement has an influence on the customer user experience. Other research has mentioned, to enhance the customer experience, many types of experience such as cognitive, sensual, physical, emotional and aesthetic can interact with the audience (Forlizzi and Battarbee, 2004). Similarly, Desmet, Porcelijn, and Dijk (2007), the research of establishing emotional appeal between the product/services state the same consequences as Forlizzi and Battarbee, (2004) research in terms of the interaction with customers. However, for this study author used the Hassenzhal and Tractinsky (2007) user's experience concept as a heuristic device for this study. the Hassenzhal and Tractinsky (2007) concept of the user experience consists of two categories of the user experience as mentioned before which is the pragmatic and hedonic quality of user experience as dimension. In detail, the author has found that the pragmatic quality of the user experience consists of some sub-dimensions which is efficiency, dependability, and perspicuity. On the other hand, the sub-dimension of the hedonic quality user experience consists of the novelty, simulation, and attractiveness. All the sub-dimension of the user experience has items to measure the impact of AR advertisement on both the hedonic and pragmatic quality of the user experience (Hassenzhal and Tractinsky 2007). The sub-dimension of the user experience has been used in the survey question for this research to measure the AR impact.

"Buy or not to buy"- that is the final decision that customers make during the shopping time. User experience considered as the critical aspect of online shopping also helps to facilitate the transaction between the customers and business. Revolutionary technology like augmented reality improves and enhances user experience so that the marketers and advert makers adopting the augmented reality technology very quickly. First and foremost, augmented reality helps customers to make purchase decisions through product visualisation. By using the augmented reality mobile application enabled the social media/online outlets of a brand where the customer can choose and see the product and intersections them in their future environment. Swedish furniture brand and world-famous NIKE develop the augmented reality app for their advertisement campaign in their online outlets where they can promote their product with the latest technology and increase the user experience (Understanding e-commerce, 2018)

In this study, the survey results revealed the interesting results which are utterly similar to previously conducted research and literature. The result of the survey revealed that there is a significant impact of augmented reality advertisements on the user experience enhancement. However, the result also found that the augmented reality has more impact on the hedonic quality of user experience than pragmatic quality. The author found several reasons behind it. First, the participant might look for novelty in those given augmented reality advertisements. This means participants found augmented reality advertisements to be more innovative rather than conservative, creative not dull, or leading-edge rather than a typical advertisement. Furthermore, the audience might find it is a fun, valuable, and new way as well as interesting in terms of simulation. Ultimately, the audience might find it is an attractive way to present the products to customers and helps to create a brand image. In the pragmatic quality of user experience, the relation and result were acceptable but not least. The relationship is relatively lowered then hedonic quality since the audience might find it is less supportive, less efficient and a bit complicated to understand.

## Impact of Customer Attitude on Customer Engagement

In the part of the literature, review the author discussed that there is an association between customer engagement and changing customer attitude towards the brand. Numerous researcher such as Sirgy (1991), Shaughnessy (2010) and Novak (2010) have mentioned in their research, that there is an existence of the hierarchical influence of customer attitude on customer engagement through high and low involvement of the customer. Petty and Cacioppo (1981) exposed one of the popular theories of changing customer attitude called ELM (elaborate-likelihood-model). This theory also describes the two dimensions that are called 'Peripheral and Central route". These two routes persuaded the effect of content to the audience and emotional appeal. The researches have indicated if the customer involves/engages with the brand it will repeatedly impact customers to change their attitude and helps to increase purchase intention and faster decision-making. The ABC model in terms of measuring the customer attitude towards the brand is best suitable. This model itself has three dimensions which are cognitive, emotional and behavioural components of attitude. Each of the dimensions has sub-dimension such as thought and belief, knowledge, feelings, and purchase intention. Homer (2006) and Grenier and Stadler (2009) have mentioned in their research, "all the components are highly related, and they have impacts on customer engagement". Their findings of the research revealed that without the engagement of the customer it is very unlikely to change their attitude towards the brand.

Likewise, the survey results of this research found the same result as mentioned in the literature It shows there is a positive association between customer attitude and customer engagement. The main reason of this positive association could be high involvements of the customer towards brand through augmented reality advertisement, participants might have the constructive feelings for the brand after experienced the advert, their thought and belief stayed optimistic towards brands and they might get the additional information that they needed. Eventually, on the basis of the survey result author can say that there is a significant impact of augmented reality advertisement on the customer attitude which affected by customer engagement. The author firmly believes that the high involvement of the customer leading to change the customer attitude towards the brand. So, it was statistically proven that the impact of augmented reality advertisements on changing customer attitudes is driven by strong customer engagement in the era of prosumers.

## Impact of Customer Attitude on User Experience

As mentioned earlier, the research has suggested that the advertisement campaign can change customers attitudes by enhancing the user experience. Katz (1937) and Oskamp and Schultz (2005) have mentioned in their research the four factions' model to measure the attitude of customers. Those are The Value Expressive function (based on self-concept or central value), The Utilitarian function (based on, ethical theory, produce happiness and pain/pleasure), The Knowledge function (based on the fact-based comparison and real market statistics), The Ego Defensive function (based on self-image). These functions are vastly associated with the user experience; for example, The Utilitarian function based on happiness and pleasure/pain. According to Kim and Forshythe (2008), higher experience leads to increase purchase intention and pre-purchase decision, which indicates enhancing customer experience prominence to change the customer attitude towards the brand. However, for this research, the author found Hassenzahl (2007) model is the best suitable in terms of measuring the user experience of augmented reality advertisements towards the brand.

The survey result of this study also shows a significant association between the changing attitude and user experience. In the earlier part, it is shown that augmented reality advertisement increases user experience. This result also mentioned that if user experience enhances through augmented reality advertisement it changes the customer attitude as well. Also result of this survey represent that both augmented reality advertisement and changing customer attitude has the same result on the pragmatic and hedonic quality of the user experience. The reason for the similar result could be associated with Huang Hsu-Lie (2014) statements, - a participant may feel anxious to take immediate purchase decision or it was not information sufficient enough to think about the product instantly.

# CONCLUSION, MANAGEMENT IMPLICATIONS, AND RECOMMENDATION

The outcomes of this research have shown a constructive impact of the augmented reality advertisement on customer attitude towards the brand and that's driven by optimising customer engagement and enhancing user experience in the era of prosumers Customer engagement is considered to be a level that is related to motivation and brand and in terms of brand interaction, it is a context-dependent state of mind that is classified by an explicit level of cognitive, emotional and behavioural activities. Likewise, in the context of the Advertisement, media engagement and marketing customer engagement considers as the multi-dimensional concept that is a combination of the numerous elements such as attention, interaction, immediate activation, and sensorial pleasure emotion to generate a total brand experience with the customer.

Consumers like the new form of technology and prefer augmented reality in the advertisement, entertaining and interactive characters also valued and accept in the unique experience of augmented reality. Additionally, the participants of this survey research liked and enjoyed the features of augmented reality advertisement and felt involved with it. They also liked the concept of the integration process of virtual to the real-world real world as well and felt close to the environment which consequently optimise the customer engagement with the brand and perception of the users. In order to create any sort of exciting experience features augmented reality makes a significant impact on customer engagement. In the affective customer engagement, augmented reality advertisement has constructive influence since the result of this survey research revealed that the people getting more enthusiastic, interested and want enjoyment from the latest form of advertising media rather than typical. Similarly, cognitive engagement has shown the significant impact of AR advertising on it as participant already viewed the augmented reality advertisement responsively, shown the interest to spend their valuable time to experience it in future and participant also felt high involvement during the survey when they were watching given AR advertisement as a link in the survey page. The findings indicated a significant impact of augmented reality advertisement on the behavioural engagement since participants showed their interest in order to know and learn about the brand and products also moderate numbers of participant agreed with the statement that, they would like to share about augmented reality advertisement to their friends and family in future.

In some research, User experience described as the process of interaction between the audience and the world. Precisely, in human mind user experience generated through new interaction and process which is known as the intangible process. likewise, user experience is ta complete impression that a brand and product can creates on customers not only the current usages snapshot but also contemplated as the decision of the users starts before touching, feeling and using the services. The survey result for this study shows the augmented reality advertisement created the impression on participant and shown a significant influence on total user experience. In the pragmatic quality of the user experience augmented reality advertisement created a lesser amount of impact but not least rather than hedonic quality. Nevertheless, the result still significant because the context of the given augmented reality advertisement of that selected brands was not confusing but clear, it was efficient enough for them to get additional information from the given ad, it was considerably understandable according to the participant and moreover, it met their expectation. The result also indicates that there is also significant impact of the augmented reality advertisement on the hedonic quality and the result of the survey was notable, because participant has strongly agreed with the all statements correlated to hedonic quality since they found the augmented reality advertisements of this brands create fun and excitement when they are promoting their product. The augmented reality advertisement of IKEA and NIKE created the value of the product for the customer also participants would like to watch those kinds of an advertisement from the brand repetitively and those were creative advertisements not dull, that represents the novelty and attractiveness. The ABC model of customer engagement giving an overview and represent the relationship between knowing, feeling and act of actions about products of a brand.

In the part of cognitive components, this study has shown the customer attitude has positive association between customer engagements through the augmented reality advertisement because participant believes that augmented reality advertisements able to provides additional information, they will be benefited by the product and most of the participants believe they will consider thinking about switching the brand, that represent participants had high involvements with the brand through augmented reality advertisement. The study has shown that the AR impact on the effective components are positive as the participants got positive feeling motivated and felt engaged. Also, they have shown the high intention to make the pre-purchase decision that means there was a relationship with the behavioural component as well.

This research has found that customer attitude has an impact on the advertisement which is driven by the highest level of user experience. It is based on the knowledge function and utilitarian function which is almost linked to the pragmatic and hedonic quality of the user experience since they based on, expectation, pain/pleasure, and attractiveness, etc. The study also indicates that the respondent desired to experience more augmented reality advert from brands and believe it is an efficient and fastest way to get product information, participant thought it is a valuable way to represent the product of a brand also it drawn attention by attractiveness.

## REFERENCES


Azuma, R. T. (1997). A survey of augmented reality. *Computers & Applied Sciences Complete Presence*, *6*(4), 355–385. doi:10.1162/pres.1997.6.4.355

Bagozzi, R.P., Gopinath, M., & Nyer, P.U. (1999). The Role of Emotions in Marketing. *Journal of the Academy of Marketing Science, 27*, 184-206.

Beatty, Vivek, & Morgan. (2012). Consumer engagement in online brand communities: a social media perspective. *Journal of Product & Brand Management, 24*(1), 28-42.

Belch & Belch. (2004). Advertising & Promotion. An Integrated Marketing Communications Approach. *Corporate Communications*, *17*(3).

Brodie, R.J., Hollebeek, L.D., & Juric, B., & Ilic, A. (2011a). Customer engagement: Conceptual domain, fundamental propositions & implications for research. *Journal of Service Research*, *34*(10), 251–271.

Bryman, A., & Bell, E. (2007). *Business research methods* (2nd ed.). Oxford, UK: Oxford University Press.

Cacioppo, J., & Petty, R. (1982). The need for cognition. *Journal of Personality and Social Psychology*, *42*(1), 116–131. doi:10.1037/0022-3514.42.1.116

Cacioppo, J., & Petty, R. (1984). The Elaboration Likelihood Model Of Persuasion. *Advances in Consumer Research*, *11*(1), 673–675.

Calder, B. J., Malthouse, E. C., & Schaedel, U. (2009). Engagement with Online Media and Advertising Effectiveness. *Journal of Interactive Marketing*, *23*, 321–331. doi:10.1016/j.intmar.2009.07.002

Cascales, A., Pérez-López, D., & Contero, M. (2013). Study on parent's acceptance of the augmented reality use for preschool education. *Procedia Computer Science*, *25*, 420–427. doi:10.1016/j.procs.2013.11.053

Cohen, Pham, & Andrade. (2008). *Psychological testing and assessment: An introduction to tests and measurement* (7th ed.). Columbus, OH: McGraw-Hill Education.

Denscombe, M. (2007). *The good research guide: for small-scale social research projects* (3rd ed.)., Available at http://www.dawsonera.com/depp/reader/protected/external/AbstractView/S97803352

Desmet, P., & Dijk. (2007). A wheelchair can be Fun: a case of emotion-driven design. In *Proceedings of The International Conference on Designing Pleasurable Products and Interfaces*. New York: The Association for Computing Machinery.

Dokyun, L., Hosanagar, L., & Nair, H. (2018). Advertising Content and Consumer Engagement on Social Media: Evidence from Facebook. *Management Science*. Retrieved 7 7, 2019, from https://repository.upenn.edu/cgi/viewcontent.cgi?article=1353&context=marketing_papers

Dunleavy, M., & Dede, C. (2006). *Augmented reality teaching and learning*. Cambridge, MA: Harvard Education Press.

Eagly, A. H., & Chaiken, S. (1993). *The psychology of attitudes*. Orlando, FL: Harcourt Brace Jovanovich College Publishers.

Etmeezi. (2010). *Nuthom altaaleem alelektroni wadwatuh*. Phillipsburg, NJ: Phillips Publishing

Ferreira, F., & Belem, B. (2017). Consumers' attitude toward Facebook advertising. *Int Journal of Electronic Marketing and Retailing*, 46-57. Retrieved 7 10, 2019, from https://www.researchgate.net/publication/316054583_Consumers'_attitude_toward_Facebook_advertising

Fishbein, M. (1963). An investigation of the relationship between beliefs about an object and the attitude toward that object. *Human Relations*, *16*(3), 233–240. doi:10.1177/001872676301600302

Forlizzi, J., & Battarbee, K. (2004). *Understanding Experience in Interactive Systems*. Academic Press.

Forlizzi, J., & Ford, S. (2000). The Building Blocks of Experience: An Early Framework for Interaction Designers. In *Proceedings of the 3rd Conference on Designing Interactive Systems: Processes, Practices, Methods, and Techniques* (pp. 419–423). New York, NY: Academic Press. 10.1145/347642.347800

Foster, J. (2001). *Data analysis, using SPSS for window 8 and 10*. London: Sage Publication.

Gambetti, Grafigna, & Biragi. (2011). The Grounded Theory Approach to Consumer-Brand Engagement. *International Journal of Market Research*, *54*(5), 659–687.

Gambetti, Grafigna, & Biragi. (2012). The Concept of Engagement: A Systematic Analysis of the Ongoing Marketing Debate. *International Journal of Market Research*.

Grenier & Stadler. (2009). Presence and the sixth sense. *Presence (Cambridge, Mass.)*, *11*(4), 435–439.

Han, S., Lerner, J. S., & Keltner, D. (2007). Feelings and consumer decision making: The appraisal-tendency framework. *Journal of Consumer Psychology*, *17*(3), 158–168. doi:10.1016/S1057-7408(07)70023-2

Hassenzahl, M. (2007). The effect of perceived hedonic quality on product appealingness. *International Journal of Human-Computer Interaction*, *13*, 479–497.

Hassenzahl & Tractinsky. (2007). The thing and I: understanding the relationship between user and product. In *Funology* (pp. 31–42). From Usability to Enjoyment.

Hassenzahl. (2007). User experience (UX): towards an experiential perspective on product quality. In *Proceedings of the 20th International Conference of the Association Francophone d'Interaction Homme-Machine*. ACM.

Higgins, E. (2006). Value from Hedonic Experience and Engagement. *American Psychological Association, 113*(3), 439-460. Accessed via: http://cbdr.cmu.edu/seminar/Higgins.pdf

Holbrook, M., & Hirschman, E. (1982). The Experiential Aspects of Consumption: Consumer Fantasies, Feelings, and Fun. *Journal of Consumer Research*, *9*(2), 132-140.

Hollebeck. (2013). Demystifying Customer Engagement: Exploring the Loyalty Nexus. *Journal of Marketing Management, 27*(7–8), 785–807.

Homer, P. M. (2006). Relationships among ad-induced affect, beliefs, and attitudes: Another look. *Journal of Advertising*, *35*(1), 35–51. doi:10.2753/JOA0091-3367350103

Johnson, P., Buehring, A., Cassell, C., & Symon, G. (2000). Evaluating qualitative management research: Towards a contingent criteriology. *International Journal of Management Reviews*, *8*(3), 131–156. doi:10.1111/j.1468-2370.2006.00124.x

Kolsaker, A., & Drakatos, N. (2009). Mobile advertising: The influence of emotional attachment to mobile devices on consumer receptiveness. *Journal of Marketing Communications*, *15*(4), 267–280. doi:10.1080/13527260802479664

Mollen & Wilson. (2010). *Boundaries of the mind: the individual in the fragile sciences—cognition.* Cambridge, UK: Cambridge University Press.

Mullen. (2013). The best uses of augmented reality in the travel industry. *TourismLink*. Available at: http://www.tourismlink.eu/2013/08/the-best-uses-of-augmented-reality-in-the-travel-industry

Nambisan, S., & Baron, R. A. (2007). Customer environments: Relationship management. *Journal of Interactive Marketing*, *21*(2), 42–62. doi:10.1002/dir.20077

Norman, D. A. (2004). *Emotional Design: Why We Love (or Hate) Everyday Things*. New York: Basic Books.

Novak, Hoffman, & Yung. (2000). Measuring the Customer Experience in Online Environments: A Structural Modeling Approach. *Marketing Science*, *19*(1), 22–42.

Nowfal, K. (2010). *Teknologia alwaqea alefteradi wistekdamatuh altalemeya* [Virtual reality technology and its educational uses]. Amman, Jordan: Dar Al Manahej for Publishing & Distribution.

Oskamp, S., & Schultz, P. W. (2005). *Sociology, Attitudes and Opinions*. Lawrence Erlbaum Associates. doi:10.4324/9781410611963

Ostrom, T. M. (1969). The Relationship between the Affective, Behavioural, and Cognitive Components of Attitude. *Journal of Experimental Social Psychology*, *5*(1), 12–30. doi:10.1016/0022-1031(69)90003-1

Patterson, P., Yu, T., & de Ruyter, K. (2006). Understanding Customer Engagement in Services. *Advancing Theory, Maintaining Relevance, Proceedings of ANZMAC 2006 Conference*.

Reality technology. (2019). *Augmented Reality*. Retrieved from https://www.realitytechnologies.com/augmented-reality/

Robert, J.-M., & Lesage, A. (2011). From usability to user experience with user interfaces. In G. A. Boy (Ed.), *Handbook of Human-Computer Interaction: A Human-Cantered Design Approach* (pp. 303–332). Ashgate.

Roderick, B. J., Hollebeek, L. D., Biljana, J., & Ana, I. (2011). Customer Engagement Conceptual Domain, Fundamental Propositions & Implications for Research in Service Marketing. *Journal of Service Research*, *14*(3), 252–271. doi:10.1177/1094670511411703

Rogers, J. C., & Williams, T. G. (1989). Comparative advertising effectiveness: Practitioners' perceptions versus academic research findings. *Journal of Advertising Research*, *29*(5), 22–37.

Rubin, A., & Babbie, E. R. (1993). *Research methods for social work*. Pacific Grove, CA: Brooks/Cole.

Russell, J. A. (2003). Facial expressions of emotion: What lies beyond minimal universality? *Psychological Bulletin, 118*, 379–391.

Russell, J. A. (2003). Core affect and the psychological construction of emotion. *Psychological Review*, *110*(1), 145–172. doi:10.1037/0033-295X.110.1.145 PMID:12529060

Sakr, S. (2011). *Augmented Reality Goes Beyond Gimmicks For Business*. Accessed via http://www.bbc.co.uk/news/business-13262407

Saunders, M., & Lewis, P. (2012). *Doing research in business and management: an essential guide to planning your project.* Harlow, UK: Financial Times Prentice Hall.

Scherer. (2005). Changes in EEG alpha power during simulated driving: a demonstration. *International Journal of Psychophysiology, 37*(2), 155–162.

Sirgy, M. J. (1991). Self-Concept in Consumer Behaviour: A Critical Review. *The Journal of Consumer Research*, *9*, 287–300.

Solomon, M. (2008). Consumer behaviour: a European perspective (3rd ed.). Lars Parner.

The International Organisation of the Standardisation. (1998). *Ergonomics of human system interaction - Part 210: Human-cantered design for interactive systems (formerly known as 13407)*. Author.

The Mentionltyics. (2019). *Future augmented reality and social media*. Available at: https://www.mentionlytics.com/blog/how-augmented-reality-will-influence-future-social-media-trends/?fbclid=IwAR19EVpTUA1FfeOO2ANV--XG-tzjDebkZlxRXjm23kG3Shu9prTAzr-zkpc

Tractinsky, N. (2007) Aesthetics in Information Technology: Motivation and Future Research Directions. In Human - Computer Interaction in Management Information Systems: Foundations. M.E. Sharpe.

Tseng-Lung, H., & Hsu, L. F. (2014). Formation of augmented-reality interactive technology's persuasive effects from the perspective of experiential value. *Internet Research*, *24*(1), 82–109. doi:10.1108/IntR-07-2012-0133

Vallio. (1998). Disruptive technologies: The new reality will be augmented. *Customer Relationship Management Magazine*.

Van Schaik, P., & Ling, J. (2008). The role of context in perceptions of the aesthetics of web pages over time. *International Journal of Human-Computer Studies*, *67*(1), 79–89. doi:10.1016/j.ijhcs.2008.09.012

Vincent. (2005). Exploring consumers' attitude towards relationship marketing. *Journal of Services Marketing, 29*(3), 188-199.

Wells, W., Burnett, J., & Moriarty, S. E. (2003). *Advertising: Principles & practice*. Upper Saddle River, NJ: Prentice Hall.

White, C., & Yu, Y.-T. (2005). Satisfaction emotions and consumer behavioural intentions. *Journal of Services Marketing*, *19*(6), 411–420. doi:10.1108/08876040510620184

Woods, A (2009). *Augmented reality Revolution*. Business Source Complete. EBSCOhost. (14605953)

Zinkhan & Fornell. (1989). Advertising Research and Advertising Practice. *Journal of Advertising*, *22*(1), vii–viii.

## KEY TERMS AND DEFINITIONS

**Augmented Reality:** A computer-assisted augmenting of perception by means of additional interactive information levels in real-time, such that the observer is immersed in the real and virtual world at the same time.

**Augmented Reality Advertisements:** AR advertisement uses AR technology to enhance to visual, sensory, and engagement effects of advertisements.

**Attitude or Consumer Attitude:** A learned predisposition of a consumer to respond to an object or class of objects in a consistently favourable or unfavourable way. It is a sum total of thinking, feeling, and action towards an object, product, or brand.

**Behavioural Intention:** Is a tendency audience or customers in order to respond in a certain manner towards the offerings, value, product, or a brand.

**Customer Engagement:** Is the level of active customer's rationale and emotional connection and involvement that results in behaviour towards a brand or brand or service, such orientations mean that a customer becomes a co-creator of value.

**User Experience:** Is a process of the interaction between the audience and the world, it relates to a person's attitude and rational and emotions about the product or services they used.

# Chapter 15
# The Effect of Blogging on Fashion Consumption

**Daniel Hagan**
*Northumbria University, London, UK*

## ABSTRACT

*The value of the clothing industry in the UK was estimated at £57.7 billion in 2017 and is forecasted to experiment a slow growth of 3.8% reaching £68.69 billion in 2022. Currently, blogging has become one of the most common ways to communicate as well as share information. Fashion blogging has grown considerably over the years and is one of the major topic areas covered by bloggers. This phenomenon is composed of young women displaying their fashion outfits and styles, as well as their interests in fashion. Fashion blogging started around 2000 with the desire of young women to have a distinct place to share their passion and interest for fashion as well as expressing their thoughts on fashion trend with others.*

## INTRODUCTION

The value of the clothing industry in the UK is currently estimated at £57.7 billion in 2017 and is forecasted to experiment a slow growth of 3.8% reaching £68.69 billion in 2022 (Mintel, 2017). Currently, blogging has become one of the most common ways to communicate as well as share information (Mortara and Roberti, 2017). Fashion blogging has grown considerably over the years and is one of the major topic areas covered by bloggers (Marwick, 2013). This phenomenon is composed of young women displaying their fashion outfits and styles, as well as their interests in fashion (Marwick, 2013). Fashion blogging started around 2000 with the desire of young women to have a distinct place to share their passion and interest for fashion as well as expressing their thoughts on fashion trend with others (Fernandez and Karhawi, 2015). However, the apparition of these types of blogs has created a micro-revolution within the fashion industry and the way fashion practitioners communicate and interact with their audiences. Traditionally, fashion-related information was controlled and strategically disseminate only by members of the fashion industry through fashion magazines, television and fashion week event, giving the impression that being a member of fashion and couture community is something reserved only to a privileged few (Crewe, 2013; Marwick, 2013). Consequently, fashion blogging has changed

DOI: 10.4018/978-1-7998-0131-3.ch015

the old notions of "insider" and "outsider" and allowed those passionate about fashion to be connected to the fashion world (Luvass, 2013; Marwick, 2013). This period of fashion blogging is named "the first-wave" style of blogging. During this period there was not really any professionalization of fashion bloggers or connection with fashion companies for clothes and items placement.

Although there is plenty research concerning social media and blogging, few studies have been conducted in the area of fashion blogging and the influence on fashion consumers' choices (Esposito et. al. 2015; McCormick and Livett, 2012). The aim of this chapter is to explore the effect of blogging on how contemporary consumers consume fashion. It discusses the increasing interactivity, social networking, the culture of sharing and identity construction social media have engendered and how the spectre of social media in general and blogs, in particular, have created a micro-revolution within the fashion industry, and how fashion practitioners communicate and interact with their audiences.

The combination of fashion and technology no longer exclusively belongs to a fantasy world rather it has become the focus of a new wave of innovators eager to change the course of fashion. The long-term implications of colliding technology and fashion are expected to go as far as to how we market fashion products. New technological developments, materials, and designs appear in rapid succession, making it challenging to demarcate the boundaries of this elusive thing. Mobile and portable technology such as smartphones and tablets have radically transformed our ways of navigating, perceiving, communicating, eating, learning, and living over the past few decades (see, for example, Goggin and Hjorth eds. 2014).

The evolution of digital marketing can be traced back to the publication of AT&T banner on a platform that would become Wired.Com later in 1994. Based on this establishment, Felix *et al.* (2017) argued that digital space has fundamentally changed since its inception. With the advent of a digital platform, marketers are facilitated to gauge where the audience clicked, the way they behaved. Therefore, social media practically closed the loop, availing marketers to connect deciphered dots of identity as never before. The evolution of social media can further be traced back to early 2000, where social media pioneers such as Facebook considered collaborating with American colleges to display advertisements. In 2006, Facebook emerged as a prime player in social media marketing as it signed its first primary advertisement deal, a certain display partnership with JP Morgan chase, for promoting Chase Credit Credits (Schivinski and Dabrowski, 2016). The trend further continued through YouTube, launching its very firsts ads within its own eco system.

Hence, by this point in time, it was well understood that social media platforms would aid in monetizing their respective content along with display advertising. Coming back to the topic, Schivinski and Dabrowski (2016) identified that Instagram has become an obvious choice for most fashion brands. This is attributed to the fact that Instagram has been growing in an astounding manner and has acquired more than 1 billion users. Tuten and Solomon (2017) considered Instagram to be a highly appealing and visual medium that avails the companies to present the products from superior most perspective. As of now, fashion brands such as Burberry as well as Mark & Spencer have become masters of Instagram marketing, illustrating their products through curated content, targeted ads and carefully planned search engine optimisation (SEO) procedures. For instance, Burberry illustrates behind the scenes footage on their respective Instagram pages.

Social media have transformed and facilitated the search for both fashion information and fashion products. Fashion blogs provide information about clothing, fashion trends and other related issues and are posted or written by fashion bloggers on social media platforms that enable them to reach a wide audience of followers. Web 2.0 allows users to create and exchange content, share opinions, experiences, and build relationships with like-minded people. This happens on social media platforms (e.g.

Instagram, Facebook, Youtube, Twitter, and Tumblr) when users interact and communicate with each other which facilitate networking between users. Furthermore, social media platforms have been used as new channels by online retailers to promote their businesses and to gain a superior competitive edge as well as benefits. Social media is the ideal place where retailers can have bidirectional communication with users and reach more users or consumers, as the number of users of the internet and social media has been growing continuously globally. Fashion bloggers are becoming popular, who use blogs and social media platforms to post videos or photos and interact or communicate with the users, primarily utilising social media platforms, which can create eWOM and trigger the pre-purchasing decision for fashion products among users (Moe and Trusov, 2012).

## INFORMATION TECHNOLOGY IN FASHION

Information Technology (IT) in fashion has become a commonplace phenomenon nowadays (Baskerville and Myers 2009). IT in fashion has been defined as "a transitory collective belief that information technology is new, efficient, and at the forefront of practice". When such a belief becomes widespread, the technology can be described as "in fashion." An organisational innovation is a structure, practice, or technology new to the organisation adopting it. Diffusion is the process by which an innovation spreads over time among organisations (Rogers 2003).

Fundamental to the concept of diffusion of innovations is about why organisations adopt innovations. There are two main schools of thought. The first school of thought is the concept ofan economic rationalist. The economic rationalistic perspective is focused on organisational performance, which refers to the extent to which an organisation realises its objectives, often measured in financial or economic terms. Researchers from the economic–rationalistic perspective maintain that organisations recognise performance problems and then search and adopt innovations to solve the problems efficiently, consequently improving performance (Cyert and March 1992). The second school of thought is the concept of institutional perspective which emphasises organisational legitimacy, which refers to a generalised perception or assumption that the actions of an organisation are desirable or appropriate within the organisation's socially constructed environment of norms, values, and beliefs (Suchman 1995). Institutional researchers argue that organisations adopt innovations that are taken for granted as legitimate practices in order to gain organisational legitimacy, regardless of the actual impact of the innovation on the performance of particular organizations (Meyer and Rowan 1977).

There is a progressive adaptation of the IT communications strategies deployed by brands and companies, defined according to influence marketing plans in which the focus falls on specific individual targets (opinion leaders), that best adjust to the characteristics of the brand/campaign and that display the capacity to exert influence over potential consumers. According to Taylor and Strutton (2016), social media have contributed to this situation transforming the nature and scope of social networks and allowing users to express their identities. In turn, the companies still increasingly investing in these media (Vries *et al.*, 2012). According to Hudson *et al.* (2015), through social media, marketing professionals can obtain rich and unadulterated consumer insights, faster than ever before, and can promote loyalty through networking. Within this context, blogs and other communication platforms have emerged that effectively give a "voice" to individuals on the most varied of themes and also enabling relationships to flourish between the brand-blogger-consumer in which the communication sharing takes place swiftly and proves able to influence the target public. Blogs have thus become one of the most commonly deployed platforms by influence marketing given that they have the capacity to provide a brand with a channel for conveying the message that it wishes to get recognised

## BLOGGING IN THE FASHION INDUSTRY

The term blog comes from the contraction of two words "web" and "log." Blogs are Internet sites where individuals frequently articulate their thoughts on a specific subject or issues. The written texts, which are called posts appear ante-chronologically and are generally published with images, and, from time to time, videos and music. Blogs date back to the mid-1990s. However, until the end of the decade blogging was not a very common practice (Lovink 2008). In 1999, there were about fifty blogs, but by 2005 the number reached 8 million (Kaye 2007: 128). At the time "about 27% (32 million) of all Internet users accessed blogs and 12% had posted comments or links on these sites"1 (2007: 128). In 2008, the blogosphere—the Internet space comprising of all blogs—counted 184 million blogs and 346 million readers (Technorati 2008). Since their appearance at the beginning of the millennium, fashion blogs have become key players in the field of fashion. Personal fashion blogs, where bloggers post pictures of themselves documenting their style, has become a central form of fashion blogging. By bringing together various technologies of the self the author argues that blogs represent a significant space of identity construction. If the launch around the mid-1990s of platforms such as Blogger.com and Blogspot.com, which provide Internet users with ready-to-use blog templates, allowed for their multiplication, the 9/11 attack on the World Trade Centre is often identified as having heralded their rapid proliferation (Bruns 2005: 175; Tremayne 2007b: xii). Indeed, blogs' ability to quickly report on an event and update readers on its evolution on a frequent basis lends itself particularly well to the constant desire for new information key events generate, while the presence of a "commentary" section that allows readers to join in a discussion constitutes an important platform for dialogue and communion around such events.

Blogs do not deal with key historical moments and other public events only. Rather, recent studies have shown that they are chiefly devoted to their authors' everyday life, to the ordinary practices and moments it is made of. A survey conducted by AOL, for instance, reveals that in 2005, 50 percent of American bloggers used blogs as a therapeutic tool, against 7.5 percent only who were interested in politics (Sundar et al. If the launch around the mid-1990s of platforms such as Blogger.com and Blogspot.com, which provide Internet users with ready-to-use blog templates, allowed for their multiplication, the 9/11 attack on the World Trade Centre is often identified as having heralded their rapid proliferation (Bruns 2005: 175; Tremayne 2007b: xii). Indeed, blogs' ability to quickly report on an event and update readers on its evolution on a frequent basis lends itself particularly well to the constant desire for new information key events generate, while the presence of a "commentary" section that allows readers to join in a discussion constitutes an important platform for dialogue and communion around such events. Blogs do not deal with key historical moments and other public events only. Rather, recent studies have shown that they are chiefly devoted to their authors' everyday life, to the ordinary practices and moments it is made of. A survey conducted by AOL, for instance, reveals that in 2005 50 percent of American bloggers used blogs as a therapeutic tool, against 7.5 percent only who were interested in politics (Sundar et al. 2007: 87). A 2006 national telephone survey carried by the Pew Internet Project also shows that: most are focused on describing their personal experiences to a relatively small audience of readers and that only a small proportion focus their coverage on politics, media, government, or technology. Blogs, the survey finds, are as individual as the people who keep them. However, most bloggers are primarily interested in creative, personal expression—documenting individual experiences, sharing practical knowledge, or just keeping in touch with friends and family (Pewinternet 2006, cited in Lovink 2008: 260).

In spite of this, the few academics who have looked into blogs (see, for instance, Bruns 2005; Carlson 2007; Tremayne 2007a) have tended to privilege sites devoted to topics such as politics and current affairs (see also Sundar et al. 2007: 87), topics that are often perceived as "noble," in contrast with other fields, such as fashion, seen as trivial and unworthy of academic inquiry. However, with more than 2 million bloggers listed, in July 2010, by Blogger.com as being "with an industry of fashion" (Blogger 2010), and following the launch in 2003 of the first fashion blog—*nogoodforme* - the fashion blogosphere has asserted itself as a key space for the production and the circulation of fashion discourse. Blogs, although it encompasses a wide variety of sites, it can be split into two main categories: independent blogs and corporate blogs. The former includes a broad range of genres. Examples are blogs that focus on street fashion (e.g. *face hunter*; *the sartorialist*), on celebrities (e.g. *cocosteaparty*; *red carpet-fashion awards*), or on a particular type of commodity (shoes, for instance, with *seaofshoes*; *shoeblog*). They are usually run by one individual only, as opposed to corporate blogs, which are the voice of a fashion institution whether it be a magazine (see, for instance, *vogue.co.uk/blog*; *wmagazine.com/w/blogs/editorsblog*), a brand (see, for instance, *paulsmith.co.uk/paul-smith-blog*; *americanapparel.net/press-center/dailyupdate*) or a store (see, for instance, *blogs.colette.fr/ colette*; *topshop.com/webapp/wcs*).

There are independent blogs, specifically a subgenre sometimes referred to as "personal fashion blogs" or "personal style blogs" in reference to those blogs whose authors post pictures of themselves to document their outfit on a regular basis. Although some are run by and for men (see, for instance, *stylesalvage*; *dennysworld*; *fashionbitsandbobs*), the following pages focus on blogs created by women. *Stylebubble*, *karlascloset*, *tavi-thenewgirlintown*, *veckorevyn*, *thecherryblossomgirl*, *jestemkasia*, *theblondesalad*, *kertiii* are a few only of the numerous personal fashion blogs to have emerged on the World Wide Web in recent years. Their authors display their new acquisitions, their rediscovery of an old piece of clothing, or their new way of mixing things together on their body. The bloggers are usually featured in their bedroom, their living room, or their back garden. The setting is often unadorned, the props minimal.

The author argues that by bringing together new and old technologies of the self—screen and blog, on the one hand, photography, and fashion on the other—personal fashion blogs assert themselves as a privileged space of identity construction. Exploring the idea of computer screens as mirrors, and the presence of mirrors in the self-portraits posted on personal fashion blogs, blogs have become a space for the articulation of a panoptic gaze that reproduces blogger's position as specular objects, but also as a space of empowerment through the control it grants bloggers on their own image, as well as through the alternative visions of empowerment it allows them to circulate.

## SOCIAL MEDIA AND FASHION BLOGGING

Social media use within the fashion industry has facilitated average customers and regular people to have superior interaction with fashion designers, along with increased access to high-end shoes, clothing, and accessory. However, Choi *et al.* (2010) argued that unlike numerous traditional advertising platforms such as magazine ads, billboards ads and television commercials, social media marketing aids in comprehending recent customer trends by tracing the comments, like, dislikes and recent customer demand trends. The marketing endeavours in social media platforms of companies such as Louis Vuitton and even Burberry address that social media marketing is far from adequate if not considered in an appropriate manner. Based on these aspects, this research intends to explore certain determinants and crucial factors that render superior effectiveness to social media marketing strategies of these fashion firms. These factors, once detected, may leverage the British fashion enterprises in the context of designing fitting social media marketing strategies.

Internet and social media play an important role in brand marketing activities nowadays. There is much evidence about the importance of this platform for retailers to market and advertise their products and services and for the users to use them for their convenience (time, place, accessibility, etc.) and information searching purposes (Grewal, Roggeveen, Runyan, Nordfält, and Lira, 2016). Retailers also can learn about consumer behaviours and consumers' purchasing decision via the internet and social media data (Marian, 2015). In the fashion industry, successful influential fashion bloggers have become fashion opinion leaders, who have high involvement in fashion and the ability to persuade their followers or other consumers to buy or use the same style of fashion. Fashion bloggers play important roles to deliver messages to their followers or readers regarding fashion products or brands (Workman and Cho, 2012). It is important for bloggers to be a good storyteller, whether in text, images, or videos, to convince their followers or readers for communication and marketing purposes (De Valck and Kretz, 2011) Currently, famous fashion bloggers have amassed huge numbers of followers on the internet, post about their personal style: inspiring their followers with what they wear or collaborate with other fashion brands. Moreover, fashion bloggers who are involved in many fashion-related activities become fashion opinion leaders. As well, famous and established fashion bloggers are hired by companies as endorsers for fashion brands to promote their brands, such as Susie Lau (H&M, Gap and Urban Outfitters) and Chiara Ferragni (Chanel, Calvin Klein, and Louis Vuitton). The number of fashion bloggers is rising (IFB, 2015) and although some studies have been done on this topic, more issues need to be discussed in this relatively new topic, for example, consumer behaviour towards fashion blogs and fashion bloggers and how the fashion bloggers influence purchase decision for fashion products. Six key types of influences of fashion bloggers towards purchasing decision for fashion products for using social media platforms can be identified as democratisation of opinion, dialogic co-creation value, online community engagement, eWOM, celebrity endorsement and opinion leader endorsement (e.g. Choi and Rifon, 2012; Crewe, 2013; Hsieh and Hsieh, 2015).

1. **Democratisation of opinion** gives power for ordinary consumers' voices to be heard on the internet; by sharing and expressing the experience about the products which helps retailers to develop brand strategy and also influences consumers' purchasing decision (Crewe, 2013).
2. **Dialogic co-creation value** happens when consumers communicate with retailers; consumers evaluate the experience of the products as a value in context and retailers aim to satisfy them by providing goods or improve innovations based on consumers' evaluations (Hsieh and Hsieh, 2015).
3. **Online consumer engagement** is the bidirectional interaction; consumers share experiences, opinions or knowledge with retailers or brands by participating in the conversation on Web 2.0 platforms such as social media, has the ability to influence and improve shopping behaviour and consumer purchasing decisions (Powers, Advincula, Austin, Graiko and Snyder, 2012).
4. **Electronic word of mouth** (eWOM) is a communication or interaction between online or internet users which spreads information amongst them. This influences users' or consumers' decision making process and purchasing decision by referring to the information received and shared on the internet (Goodrich and de Mooij, 2014).

5. **Celebrity endorsement** refers to the practice of famous people who use their prestige and reputation to promote brands, products or services, which has significant influence on their fans or followers [30]. Hence, celebrity endorsers have the power to influence the consumers and trigger their purchasing decision (Choi and Rifon, 2012).
6. **Opinion leader endorsement** refers to the practice of opinion leaders, who have wide knowledge about the topic they are involved in, not only sharing their opinions or experience with others, but also having a major impact on consumer purchasing decision [28] and convincing others to get involved in the same thing (Shen, Wang, Lo and Shum, 2012).

Since their birth in the late 1990s, blogs have presented fundamental elements of novelty in communicative relations between broadcaster and audience, showing the potentialities of Web 2.0—a journalistic label introduced by Tim O'Reilly (2005) to describe Internet evolution toward increasing interactivity, social networking, and the culture of sharing. This participatory nature, which lowers entry barriers to publishing a personal point of view for a potentially worldwide audience has been welcomed as a communicational revolution, similar to the invention of printing by Gutenberg (Hewitt, 2005), due to the capacity of blogging to transfer the power of the media to ordinary citizens. First appearing in 2001, fashion blogs are now eighteen years old but they still represent some relatively uncharted territory for some fashion journalists and part of the corporate world, and fashion studies only recently started to be interested in the phenomenon. Due to the importance gained by blogs in the communicational scene, it has become necessary today to consider blogging as a key theme in fashion media research, as well as in more traditional branches such as fashion writing, photography and fashion images, gender representation through media (Crewe 2003), and fashion journalism (Moeran 2006, 2008). Body of the academic literature has focused on three principal issues. First, the relation between fashion blogging and information. In line with enthusiastic Web 2.0 readings, blogs are often the object of celebratory interpretations, due to their democratizing potential. In this way, a street style blog such as The Sartorialist, has been described as a "case study in media democracy" (Khamis and Munt 2010: 3) and a "form of social documentary" encouraging "a dialogue that reinforces fashion of the street as a democratic arena, where the general public, rather than models, celebrities or designers, can be at the forefront of fashion-making" (Berry 2012: 129). Some readings go as far as defining fashion blogging as a countercultural and anti-hegemonic practice, alternative to mainstream fashion and able to oppose the classical trickledown effect of mainstream power to produce a trickle-up movement (Bandlien, 2012).

## Influence of Social Media on Fashion

Brown and Fiorella (2013) refer to how the marketing of influence, as a strategy, emerged out of a variety of practices and recent studies in which the focus falls on the specific individual targets (or groups of individuals) rather than approaching the overall market. Influence marketing sets out by identifying those individuals able to wield influence over potential consumers and structuring the subsequent marketing strategies around these influential persons. The authors refer to how the term "influence" remains both complex and poorly interpreted. This "influence" essentially reflects the "power" generated by a person or entity in relation to (or over) another person.

Reality is now experienced through a hyper-connected world with an enormous abundance of data spanning news, advertisements and opinions. The Internet and the virtual communities have established a universe in which everybody may serve as a source of information, as opinion leaders and potential influencers (Halvorsen *et al.*, 2013). Hence, influence marketing correspondingly stems from the convergence of different sources of knowledge and practices such as word-of-mouth, digital marketing, social marketing or even neuromarketing. This studies the social dynamics of a particular community, identifies those with influence in these environments before designing and developing platforms for the dissemination of stories and constantly measuring the results throughout the entire process with the objective of altering consumption habits and the perception of the values of brands, products or services.

Consequently, is very common to associate the concept of influence marketing to social media tools. These communication instruments include a wide set of online tools and technologies, as such the blogs, chat rooms, discussion forums, service ratings websites, internet discussion boards, moblogs and social networking websites (Ngai *et al.*, 2015). Up until a certain time, influence marketing practices were thus relatively simple and direct. However, the appearance of the Internet and social network broke up the direct channel of communication between the brand, the influencers, and their followers. With virtual communities then fostering and encouraging the exchange of information and opinions, all their users have become

influential. Therefore, to marketeers, ascertaining just which influencers are appropriate to each brand and type of campaign and, subsequently, just which strategy to adopt has become the crucial questions (Brown and Fiorella, 2013). The range of influence marketing essentially extends to bloggers, YouTubers, and public figures. The effectiveness of each influencer type varies in accordance with the product undergoing communications and the target communities with the blogs currently holding the greatest weighting in the brand dynamics and still remaining, in general terms, a "very feminine" world both in terms of the type of content and the followers. This communication tool not only offers advantages to the users but is also an increasingly important new reality for marketeers that impacts on the definition of their marketing strategies (Gremler *et al.*, 2001). With the appearance of the Internet and Computer-Mediated Communication (CMC), electronic word-of-mouth emerged (eWOM) with bloggers a correspondingly integral part of this universe (Mutum and Wang, 2011). Consequently, the fact of consumers constantly generating and sharing opinions about products on the Internet has meant that eWOM proves substantially faster and wider-reaching than traditional word-of-mouth (Han *et al.*, 2009).

eWOM can be defined as any positive or negative opinion made by the current or previous clients about a product, service or company, which is made available to large audiences through the internet (Abubakar et al., 2016; Hennig-Thurau et al., 2004). eWOM is capable of influencing consumers' attitudes as well as their purchase decisions. Additionally, it is considered very persuasive, which can be partially explained by its perceived credibility and trustworthiness (Chatterjee, 2001). As such, the brands are particularly motivated to understand the eWOM, because the conventional forms of communication appear to be losing their effectiveness (Abubakar *et al.*, 2016). According to Kulmala (2011) and Gruen et al. (2006), eWOM holds influence over consumers and steadily gaining an increasing level of recognition as a relevant and reliable channel of communication to the consumer. The growth of eWOM has gained in relevance in conjunction with the proliferation of User Generated Content (UGC) created by individuals and disseminated immediately across various Internet platforms both easily and effectively (Christodoulides *et al.*, 2012). The social platforms existing on the Internet, especially virtual communities, social networks and blogs drive the growth in communications oriented towards socialisation with their content created by the users themselves and remaining accessible to everybody. There is effectively a change in the ways people communicate and interact online with the Internet an increasingly dynamic and social tool (Amaral, 2012). In the case of blogs that constitute the main focus of this chapter, they may be defined as a website on which one or more authors regularly

## BLOGGING AS A CONSUMER BEHAVIOUR

A new kind of consumer behaviour has emerged online in the past decade. The web has made it possible for ordinary consumers to reach a mass audience within a market or globally. More consumers now have more opportunities to reach thousands of other consumers than ever before. This novel phenomenon has not yet received much theoretical attention. The author draws on Turner's (2010) idea of a "demotic turn" in contemporary culture to situate blogs and other means whereby ordinary consumers acquire a mass audience. Fashion blogs are an example of the web phenomenon to be explained. Among the first fashion bloggers to reach a mass audience was a 13-year-old girl (Rosman 2009); by 2010 this blogger had been profiled in the Wall Street Journal, the Guardian, and other publications, and her blog posts were read by tens of thousands. This blogger got hold of the megaphone by means of her actions—not by birth or through institutional position. Fashion bloggers are ordinary consumers who build a sizable audience for their blogs. The phenomenon is not limited to the fashion context or blogging. Chocolate and Zucchini is a food blog whose author was not trained as a chef and did not work for a food magazine before starting the blog; she was employed in the computer field. Her posts may receive over 100,000 views. Tight Ass Little Apartment is a blog about interior design and home decoration. This blogger was not trained in design or employed as a designer before starting the blog. Setting blogging aside, Yelp.com, a site that hosts reviews of local businesses, each year deems some of its most active reviewers to be Yelp Elite. A multiyear member of the Elite may post hundreds of restaurant reviews, receive thousands of compliments, and be read by tens of thousands, without ever having owned a restaurant, worked for a food publication, or been a chef; these online reviewers have got hold of the megaphone. Likewise, "user-generated content" on YouTube and elsewhere, such as haul videos (Smith, Fischer, and Yongjian 2011), provides ordinary consumers opportunities to grab the megaphone (Burgess and Green 2009; Snickers and Vonderau 2009). Research indicates that bloggers began blogging as ordinary consumers outside of the fashion system (Mcquarrie, Miller and Phillips 2012). McCracken (1986) describes the fashion system as composed of the designers and manufacturers of fashion clothing and accessories, the media institutions that promote such clothing in editorials and advertising, and the social elite, especially celebrities, who engage in the vast public relations machine of television and movie roles, special event appearances, and talk show and gossip magazine placements (cf. the "gift system" defined in Giesler [2006]). These are the traditional, professional sources that govern the determination of what is fashionable, also recognized by Bourdieu (Rocamora 2002).

However, blogs need not concern consumption, and online behaviour consists of much else apart from consumers grabbing hold of the megaphone: social media, content that goes viral, avatars in virtual worlds, and so forth all represent phenomena beyond the remit of this book (Boellstorff 2010; Jenkins 2006; Miller 2011). The megaphone effect, as treated here, is specific: it occurs when ordinary consumers, defined as individuals lacking professional experience and not holding an institutional or family position, post to the web about consumption and acquire a mass audience for these posts. Blogging represents consumer behaviour. The blog posts, reviews, and user-generated content of interest are primarily concerned with consumption objects: fashion, food, home decor. Consumer bloggers achieve an audience that historically was only available to institutionally located professionals (McCracken 1986), but they achieve this audience by means of publicly consuming: choosing, evaluating, and engaging with clothing (in our focal example) and posting accounts of this consumption that garner a large audience of strangers.

This new consumer phenomenon, made possible by the web, is not well explained by existing theory. During the period studied, anyone who wished to share thoughts with others could do so on Facebook or other social media sites. Hence, when an individual chooses instead to generate content for a mass audience of strangers, the phenomenon is not readily understood as sharing (Belk 2010; Giesler 2006). Moreover, the fashion bloggers studied generally do not display clothes they sewed by hand but mass-marketed, branded goods; likewise, food bloggers do not only show meals cooked from scratch, and online reviewers do not only write about craft breweries and artisan bakeries. Hence, the phenomenon cannot readily be understood as presumption (Campbell 2005). One could label the phenomenon electronic word of mouth and call these bloggers opinion leaders or market mavens (Feick and Price 1987; Kozinets *et al.* 2010), but this obscures what is new and different about their consumer behaviour: ongoing communication by ordinary consumers to a mass audience of strangers.

Turner (2010) provides a conceptual framework that situates the megaphone effect within a larger cultural movement that he terms the "demotic turn," which embraces such phenomena as talk radio and reality television in addition to various forms of online behaviour (Rose and Wood 2005). The demotic turn is defined as an increase in opportunities for ordinary people to appear in the media. Normally only media professionals, other occupants of powerful institutional positions (e.g., government officials or business leaders), and designated celebrities appear on television or otherwise gain a mass audience. Moreover, celebrities became that way by prior successful performances in a credentialed institutional setting (entertainment, sports, etc.). Until very recently, ordinary individuals lacked access to the mass media and could only gain that access by successful performances in specified institutional settings—however extraordinary their individual motivation or skill. These restrictions began to loosen with the spread of reality television. Here the media began to create celebrities, rather than mediate between existing celebrities and the mass audience. Turner (2010) notes, however, that the celebrity gained by successful reality television participants is not gained by their independent action or even owned by them (his discussion of exploitative contract terms is bracing). Reality television celebrity thus remains an institutionally mediated phenomenon in which the owners of mass media determine which ordinary citizens are to be granted access to an audience. What distinguishes the megaphone phenomenon within the larger context of Turner's demotic turn is that in certain consumption spheres, consumers can grab the megaphone for themselves, without institutional certification or enablement. Unlike reality television participants, a successful blogger gains her audience directly, by blogging in such a way that large numbers of other consumers begin to follow her posts. Once a consumer gains a large audience, this can be converted into institutional access and further leveraged thereby, but prior institutional mediation is no longer required for audience access.

However, not every blogger succeeds in gaining an audience (Lovink 2008). What must be theorized is the process that allows a small number of fashion bloggers to realize the newfound possibility of building a mass audience for an ordinary individual's acts of consumption. There is a sociological explanation of this process that centres on taste judgments and the accumulation of cultural capital (Bourdieu 1984, 1986), buttressed by an application of Goffman's (1959) analysis of social action in terms of performance for an audience. In principle, fashion bloggers could deploy taste in either its horizontal or its vertical sense. Clothing choice-taste as preference can readily be used to identify the community or (sub)culture to which the wearer belongs: hipsters or clubbers or indie rockers (Elliott and Davies 2006; Goulding, Shankar, and Elliott 2002). Fashion blogs would then draw their audience from among consumers pursuing related identity projects, and the clothing and accessories most likely to be displayed on the blog would be those that send a strong signal about the particular community and subculture to which the blogger belongs (Berger and Ward 2010). Goffman's (1959) work provides a basis for an alternative account of fashion blogging that emphasizes taste leadership rather than taste preference. Goffman applied a dramaturgical metaphor to everyday life, arguing that participants in social encounters could be parsed into actors and audience, with actors striving to put on a front and convey a certain persona, and audiences accepting successful actors seeming as they wish to be seen. In Goffman's account, no social actor is ever authentic in his or her behaviours toward an audience; authenticity, to the extent it is possible, is reserved for the private or intimate sphere. To an audience, one shows a persona, rather than revealing one's identity. Goffman (1959, 58) draws on Simone de Beauvoir for support: "the least sophisticated of women, once she is 'dressed,' does not present herself to observation; she is, like . . . the actor on the stage, an agent through whom has suggested someone not there, that is, the character she represents, but is not."

Blogging, especially the visual self-presentations found in fashion blogging, can be theorized as Goffmann's dramaturgical metaphor. Unlike in face-to-face interactions in everyday life, or conversing with known friends on Facebook, a fashion blogger gains the capacity to represent a persona that may be far removed from her "real" self, a persona she can rehearse and rewrite until she gets it right. Display of such a persona seems ill suited to the construction of an authentic self. Blogging must then represent authoritative performance (Arnould and Price 2003). But if so, it is a novel kind, insofar as it is an individual rather than a collective act and a matter of fashion rather than tradition. Fashion blogging thus points the way to an expansion of the category of authoritative performances to include an individual's successful enactment of style—the authority of her taste. Rather than a means to seek affiliation with a community of like-minded consumers, through exhibiting taste preferences useful for drawing boundaries, blogging would point to its suitability for exercising taste in the vertical sense, as a means of drawing a mass audience of strangers.

## Blogs as Symbolic Power

Are blogs really instruments for the redistribution of symbolic power? Not everybody agrees with this interpretation. Chin and Hills (2008) and Arnold (2012) maintain that the shift of power from traditional media to new media is more rhetorical than substantial, and that blogging actually enforces the dominant positions of the fashion field's insiders, without becoming an effective instrument for the rewriting of hierarchy between "media people" and "ordinary people." Influenced by Tavi Gevinson, Chiara Ferragni, Bryanboy, and other successful bloggers' stories, we may forget that the majority of voices in the blogosphere remain unheard and that the traditional media exercise their agenda-setting power by popularizing a wide but restricted number of bloggers. Such a focus on blogs as (apparently revolutionary) informational websites leads us to the so-called "citizen-journalist debate," which wonders essentially about two sub-issues. Does blogging change the laws of the journalistic field? Can bloggers be considered journalists or, at least, knowledge-creators and gatekeepers of information? As to the former question, many opinions are optimistic, and look at bloggers as protagonists of "alternative" (Forde, 2001) and "networked" journalisms (Russell, 2011) more similar to conversation than to dictation, no longer centralized but "profoundly more grass-roots and democratic" (Gillmor. 2006: xxiii), and shaped by the creative control of the public.

As to the latter, interpretations of blogging as an extension of traditional journalism and, in the specific case of fashion, as a "parallel force in fashion media" (Khamis and Munt 2010: 3), do not erase differences between blogger and journalist. Despite their typical journalistic activities, such as fact-checking and reporting, bloggers often work alone and with limited resources, outside an organization where work is normally divided between editorial staff (from editor-in-chief to art directors and stylists) and publishing (or advertising) employees devoted to managerial, advertising, and financial tasks. This distinction, like that between culture and the business economy, is normally absent from blogs, where an individual often does everything alone, sometimes supported by someone who takes pictures of outfits. The comparison with journalism takes us to the second issue: the degree of bloggers' autonomy. Blogs inherited the "Janus-faced structure" (Moeran 2008: 269) of fashion magazines, that is, their twofold cultural and commercial nature. As happens in fashion magazine-based journalism, the relation between blogging and financial support is ambiguous and recalls the problem of balance between an independent editorial line and the influence of companies that buy (or decide to stop buying) advertising space. Without the supporting network of publishers and editors, bloggers are particularly exposed to the influence of corporate resources and to the loss of editorial independence: through invitations to events and fashion shows, proposals to collaborate with fashion brands to organise giveaways or product promotions, advertising in blogs, the sending of free samples and other economic and social incentives, the fashion blogosphere is exposed to a process of commodification by companies that understand its potential as a "marketing medium" (Pulizzi and Barrett 2009) and eWom instrument ("electronic word of mouth"; see Corcoran 2010; Hennig-Thurau *et al.* 2004: 39; Kulmala *et al.* 2013).

## Fashion Blogs as Identity Construction

Blogs have sociological aspects to it which focuses on the fashion blogosphere as an identitarian and discursive space. Blogs are instruments for identity construction, "new technologies of the Self" (Rocamora 2011: 410), where recent digital devices meet existing tools (e.g. photography) by allowing people to express their identities on an individualized space (the computer screen); at the same time blogs are also "spaces of surveillance, by oneself and by others" (Rocamora 2011: 418), where computer screens act as mirrors. Blogging cannot be fully understood, incidentally, without analysing the effects that the myriad of single bloggers' voices have on the field of fashion media— and on the field of fashion in general. The blogosphere, beginning as a simple discursive space for fashion amateurs has subsequently structured itself as a "keyspace for the production and the circulation of fashion discourse" (Rocamora 2011: 409), able to enhance a "hyper-textual fashion" (Rocamora 2012) where the system of links and the possibility of nonlinear reading are not only technical characteristics of Web space, but also a representation of the relational network in which the blogger is involved. A blog and its author are hence a node within today's very extensive network, specifically, a subfield of the field of fashion media internally characterized by struggles between established players and newcomers, and externally by an attempt of legitimization by the traditional owners of power (fashion journalists and brands).

In making such an analysis, care must be taken over breaking with both ordinary and scientific common-sense readings, which have become split along two dominant narratives: a communicational reading of blogs as a new fashion communication frontier able to challenge the power of journalists and the top-down circulation mechanism of fashion communication; and a commercial reading of blogs as mere marketing instruments (in their dual function as instruments manipulated by brands or as the bloggers' strategy for self-marketing). But what is a "field," according to Pierre Bourdieu? In which ways may this concept be useful in our study of fashion blogging? In short, a field is a "network, or a configuration, of objective relations between positions" (Bourdieu and Wacquant 1992: 97) that works as an (extremely serious) game: social agents participate in a social competition using their winning cards, which are forms of available capital in order to ensure themselves a stake that consists in the control of the field itself. The main advantage of a field approach may be summarized through Bourdieu's words: "To think in terms of field is to think relationally" (Bourdieu and Wacquant 1992: 96), analysing social agents as carriers of specific interests and different levels of resources, which are used to give "access to the specific profits that are at stake in the field" (Bourdieu and Wacquant 1992: 97). The struggle to control the field creates domination, submission, or homology between agents participating in the game, structuring the field upon a hierarchy differentiating those who have central positions from those who try to depose dominant players. Studying the blogosphere in terms of the field will shift our attention towards relations (collaborative or conflicting) that are produced within this social space, between bloggers, but also between bloggers and the traditional sources of power and legitimization within the field of fashion, that is, brands and journalism.

What we may ask ourselves is: how is it possible that ordinary consumers and fashion-lovers can become significant speakers in the institutionalized field of fashion? Why do some of them succeed and others do not? How is the field internally differentiated? To answer these questions I believe it is important to concentrate on bloggers' careers—what Bourdieu would call their "trajectory"—on the resources (forms of capital) used by bloggers to build their position, which increases as they gain dominant positions, and relational strategies with other bloggers, journalists, and fashion brands. Eventually, this analysis will allow us to speculate about which laws are working in the fashion blogging subfield.

## CONCLUSIONS AND MANAGERIAL IMPLICATIONS

Intrinsic to this chapter is a depiction of the web as a causal factor that makes available new forms of consumer behaviour through blogging. Past consumer research has tended to treat online consumer behaviour as an analog of some corresponding offline consumer behaviour and to conceptualize the web simply as a new location where pre-existing consumer phenomena unfold much as before. Therefore, marketplace communities can be established online the same as offline (Muniz and O'Guinn 2001), norms of reciprocity govern online communities the same as offline (Giesler 2006; Mathwick et al. 2007), and consumers' postings online correspond to word of mouth offline (Kozinets et al. 2010). By contrast, a focus on consumers' newfound capacity, courtesy of the web, to acquire a mass audience requires a new theorisation. Ordinary consumers did not have access to such an audience before the web. For consumers, there is no offline equivalent of a verbal-visual blog, a Yelp restaurant review, or user-generated video content. Before the web, only professionals holding an institutional position could publish their writing or disseminate video. Ordinary consumers were confined to participation in their immediate social networks and communities; they could not take the megaphone and acquire a mass audience of strangers for their acts of consumption. As a consequence, the value some consumers place on acquiring a large audience of strangers, and the value other consumers place on participating as a member of such an audience had not been theorised in consumer research.

The distinctiveness of the megaphone effect, as manifest in fashion blogging, may emerge more clearly through contrast with earlier studies of online consumer behavior by Giesler (2006) and Schau and Gilly (2003). In their study of personal websites constructed before blogging had diffused as a widespread practice, Schau and Gilly found consumers who undertook to communicate to an unknown public without institutional support. The key difference is that the websites in their study were ultimately intended to reach individual unknown others in order to set up a dyadic interaction, as, for instance, with future romantic partners or potential employers. Giesler's (2006) study of peer-to-peer file sharing through Napster is also an important predecessor to this study, in that it defines a gift system, parallel to what we, following McCracken (1986), refer to as the fashion system. For Giesler, a gift system is not merely a set of dyadic gift-giving relationships, or a bounded community of reciprocal give and take, but an overarching sociocultural structure that rests on, and provides an opportunity to demonstrate, social distinction (cf. Bourdieu 1980, 98–101). Likewise, this chapter represents the fashion system as a site in which ordinary consumers, by means of the web, can attain distinction. The key difference here is that taste leadership played no role in the file-sharing gift system studied by Giesler (2006), whereas the author argues that it is a taste that determines a blogger's distinction within the fashion system. The effect of the adaptation of Bourdieu is to highlight the role of taste in consumption, particularly online consumption, even as it shifts the emphasis away from existing theorisations of how taste operates. Current conceptualisations focus on what might be called the horizontal operation of taste: the ways in which taste preferences group consumers together and serve to divide a Us from a Them distinction-between (Lamont 1992).

It is important not to oversell the megaphone effect as instanced in fashion blogging. A particular concern of Turner (2010) was to debunk the idea that the demotic turn represents any kind of democratization of power. With Lovink (2008) and Pham (2011), he calls into question the utopian cast of some early celebrations of the web as an emancipatory medium that would place power in the hands of the people. For Turner, there is no relinquishment of political or institutional power consequent to the demotic turn; what changes is who gets access to a mass audience. There is a democratization of communication opportunities, not a change in who exercises power. Likewise, the fashion bloggers we studied did not break free of McCracken's (1986) fashion system and certainly did not break it up; they broke into it. What is distinctive about the megaphone effect is the absence of institutional mediation: these fashion bloggers acquired their initial audiences by dint of their own actions. This distinguishes the megaphone effect from reality television on the one hand and fast fashion on the other (Crane and Bovone 2006; Ferdows, Lewis, and Machuca 2004). In fast fashion, a clothing manufacturer an institution—seeks out fashion innovations on the street among the people and puts certain of these street fashions into production. As with reality television, originally demotic elements get picked up and presented to a mass audience, but in each case, the pertinent media and manufacturing institutions control the process. Fashion blogging, online reviewing, and user-generated content represent something different, insofar as these endeavours reduce the role of institutions by making them ancillary rather determinative. But the megaphone effect remains a matter of access to an audience, not accession to the ranks of power.

Consumer researchers have learned a great deal about consumers' pursuit of identity projects (Arnould and Thompson 2005; Parmentier and Fischer 2011), the role of community in supporting identities formed in opposition to the mainstream (Thornton 1996), and the ways in which authenticity can be claimed or disputed (Arnould and Price 2003). Less is known about the practices consumers engage in to improve their social position, how mainstream success may be pursued through acts of consumption, or the processes whereby an ordinary consumer can gain preferment over others outside of an institutional path. This chapter suggests that many fashion consumers wish to join audiences, as well as participate in communities; that a select few ordinary consumers desire to acquire an audience for their acts of consumption; and that both of these actions can readily be observed online. Hence, the time seems ripe to pursue more sociological formulations of online consumer behaviour (Nicosia and Mayer 1976).

In this regard, Muniz and O'Guinn's (2001) innovative treatment of the existence and prevalence of community in consumption marked a swing of the pendulum in social history. As originally conceived by German sociologists such as Tonnies, the marketplace was portrayed as the antithesis of community and, in fact, the agent of its destruction. Following Muniz and O'Guinn, consumer research has explored how consumers construct and participate in diverse kinds of marketplace communities, including virtual communities (Mathwick et al. 2007). That work has served as a much needed corrective to individually centred and purely psychological accounts of consumption. But the gist of the sociological perspective advanced in the current research is that consumers do not the only affiliate with communities— they also seek positions in society, which is to say, vis-a-vis a mass of strangers. These positions may not only the shape but are shaped by, and even attained by, acts of consumption. In fact, courtesy of the web, a new kind of social position has emerged: that of the tasting leader who takes hold of the megaphone builds an audience for her consumption and thereby gains a position. This rich new vein of web-enabled consumer behaviour awaits further exploration.

## REFERENCES


Abubakar, M., Ilkan, M., & Sahin, P. (2016). eWOM, eReferral and gender in the virtual community. *Marketing Intelligence & Planning*, *34*(5), 692–710. doi:10.1108/MIP-05-2015-0090

Amaral, I. (2012). Participação em rede: Do utilizador ao consumidor 2.0 e ao prosumer. *Comunicaçãoe Sociedade*, *22*(0), 131–147. doi:10.17231/comsoc.22(2012).1278

Arnold, A. M. (2012). *The Illusion of Increased Democracy in the Digital Age of Fashion Journalism* (Master's project). Stanford University. Retrieved from http://goo.gl/yqiIhQ

Arnould & Thompson. (2005). Consumer Culture Theory (CCT): Twenty Years of Research. *Journal of Consumer Research, 31*, 868-82.

Bandlien, C. B. (2012). On the Style Site: Face Hunter as Node and Prism. In J. Berry (Ed.), *Fashion Capital: Style Economies, Sites and Cultures* (pp. 115–128). Oxford, UK: Interdisciplinary.

Baskerville, R. L., & Myers, M. D. (2009). Fashion Waves in Information Systems Research and Practice. *MIS Quarterly, 33*(4), 647-662.

Belk, R. W. (2010). Sharing. *The Journal of Consumer Research*, *36*, 715–734. doi:10.1086/612649

Berry, J. (2012). Street-Style: Fashion Photography, Weblogs, and the Urban Image. In J. Berry (Ed.), *Fashion Capital: Style Economies, Sites and Cultures* (pp. 129–148). Oxford, UK: Interdisciplinary.

Blogger. (2010). Retrieved from http://www.blogger.com/profile-find.g?t=j&ind=FASHION

Boellstorff, T. (2010). *Coming of Age in Second Life*. Princeton, NJ: Princeton University Press.

Bourdieu, P. (1984). *Distinction: A Social Critique of the Judgment of Taste*. Cambridge, MA: Harvard University Press.

Bourdieu, P. (1986). *The Forms of Capital.* In G. John (Ed.), *Handbook of Theory and Research for the Sociology of Education* (pp. 241–258). Richardson: Greenwood.

Bourdieu, P., & Wacquant, L. (1992). *An Invitation to Reflexive Sociology*. Chicago, IL: University of Chicago Press.

Brown, D., & Fiorella, S. (2013). *Influence marketing*. Indianapolis: Que Publishing.

Bruns, A. (2005). *Gatewawatching*. New York: Peter Lang.

Burgess, J. E., & Green, J. B. (2009). *YouTube: Online Video and Participatory Culture*. Cambridge, UK: Polity.

Campbell, C. (2005). The Craft Consumer: Culture, Craft and Consumption in a Postmodern Society. *Journal of Consumer Culture*, *5*(1), 23–42. doi:10.1177/1469540505049843

Carrera, F. (2009). *Marketing digital na versão 2.0*. Lisboa: Edições Sílabo.

Chin, B., & Hills, M. (2008). Restricted Confessions? Blogging, Subcultural Celebrity and the Management of Producer-fan Proximity. *Social Semiotics*, *18*(2), 253–272. doi:10.1080/10350330802002424

Choi, S. M., & Rifon, N. J. (2012). It is a match: The impact of congruence between celebrity image and consumer ideal self on endorsement effectiveness. *Journal of Psychology & Marketing*, *29*, 636–650.

Choi, T. M., Liu, N., Liu, S. C., Mak, J., & To, Y. T. (2010). Fast fashion brand extensions: An empirical study of consumer preferences. *Journal of Brand Management*, *17*(7), 472–487. doi:10.1057/bm.2010.8

Christodoulides, G., Michaelidou, N., & Argyriou, E. (2012). Cross-national differences in e-WOM influence. *European Journal of Marketing*, *46*(11/13), 1689–1707. doi:10.1108/03090561211260040

Corcoran, C. T. (2010). Marketing's New Rage: Brands Sponsoring Influential Bloggers. *WWD*. Retrieved from http://goo.gl/u4kJmq

Crane, D., & Bovone, L. (2006). Approaches to Material Culture: The Sociology of Fashion and Clothing. *Poetics*, *34*(6), 319–333. doi:10.1016/j.poetic.2006.10.002

Crewe, L. (2013). When virtual and material worlds collide: Democratic fashion in the digital age. *Environment & Planning*, *45*(4), 760–780. doi:10.1068/a4546

Cyert, R. M., & March, J. G. (1992). *A Behavioral Theory of the Firm* (2nd ed.). Cambridge, UK: Blackwell Business.

De Valck, K., & Kretz, G. (2011). *Pixelize me: Digital Storytelling and the creation of archetypal myths through explicit and implicit self-brand association in fashion and luxury blog*. Research in Consumer Behavior.

Elliott, R., & Davies, A. (2006). *Symbolic Brands and Authenticity of Identity Performance*. In J. E. Schroeder & M. Salzer-Morling (Eds.), *Brand Culture* (pp. 155–170). London: Routledge.

Feick, L. F., & Price, L. L. (1987). The Market Maven: A Diffuser of Marketplace Information. *Journal of Marketing*, *51*, 83–97. doi:10.1177/002224298705100107

Felix, R., Rauschnabel, P. A., & Hinsch, C. (2017). Elements of strategic social media marketing: A holistic framework. *Journal of Business Research*, *70*, 118–126. doi:10.1016/j.jbusres.2016.05.001

Ferdows, K., Lewis, M. A., & Machuca, J. A. D. (2004). Rapid Fire Fulfillment. *Harvard Business Review*, *82*, 104–117.

Forde, S. (2011). *Challenging the News: The Journalism of Alternative and Community Media*. New York: Palgrave Macmillan. doi:10.1007/978-0-230-36096-9

Giesler, M. (2006). Consumer Gift Systems. *The Journal of Consumer Research*, *33*, 283–290. doi:10.1086/506309

Gillmor, D. (2006). *We the Media: Grassroots Journalism by the People, for the People*. Sebastopol, CA: O'Reilly.

Goffman, E. (1959). *The Presentation of Self in Everyday Life*. New York: Anchor.

Goggin, G., & Larissa, H. (2014). *The Routledge Companion to Mobile Media*. New York: Routledge. doi:10.4324/9780203434833

Goodrich, K., & de Mooij, M. (2014). How 'social' are social media? A crosscultural comparison of online and offline purchase decision influences. *Journal of Marketing Communications*, *20*(1-2), 103–116. doi:10.1080/13527266.2013.797773

Goulding, C., Shankar, A., & Elliott, R. (2002). Working Weeks, Rave Weekends: Identity Fragmentation and the Emergence of New Communities. *Consumption Markets & Culture*, *5*(4), 261–284. doi:10.1080/1025386022000001406

Gremler, D. D., Gwinner, K. P., & Brown, S. W. (2001). Generating positive word-of mouth communication through customer-employee relationships. *International Journal of Service Industry Management*, *13*(1), 44–59. doi:10.1108/09564230110382763

Grewal, D., Bart, Y., Spann, M., & Zubcsek, P. (2016). Mobile Advertising: A Framework and Research Agenda. *Journal of Interactive Marketing*, *3*, 3–14. doi:10.1016/j.intmar.2016.03.003

Gruen, T. W., Osmonbekov, T., & Czaplewski, A. J. (2006). eWOM: The impact of customer-to-customer online know-how exchange on customer value and loyalty. *Journal of Business Research*, *59*(4), 449–456. doi:10.1016/j.jbusres.2005.10.004

Halvorsen, K., Hoffmann, J., Coste-Manière, I., & Stankeviciute, R. (2013). Can fashion blogs function as a marketing tool to influence consumer behavior? Evidence from Norway. *Journal of Global Fashion Marketing*, *4*(3), 211–224. doi:10.1080/20932685.2013.790707

Han, M., Jang, Y., & Park, H. (2009). *Bloggers' intrinsic motivation and electronic word- of-mouth marketing*. Working Paper. Korea Advanced Institute of Science and Technology.

Hennig-Thurau, T., Gwinner, K. P., Walsh, G., & Gremler, D. D. (2004). Electronic word- ofmouth via consumer-opinion platforms: What motivates consumers to articulate themselves on the internet? *Journal of Interactive Marketing*, *18*(1), 38–52. doi:10.1002/dir.10073

Hewitt, H. (2005). *Blog: Understanding the Information Reformation That's Changing Your World*. Nashville, TN: Thomas Nelson Books.

Hsieh, J. K., & Hsieh, Y. C. (2015). Dialogic co-creation and service innovation performance in high-tech companies. *Journal of Business Research*, *68*(11), 2266–2271. doi:10.1016/j.jbusres.2015.06.009

Hudson, S., Roth, M., Madden, T., & Hudson, R. (2015). The effects of social media on emotions, brand relationship quality, and word of mouth: An empirical study of music festival attendees. *Tourism Management*, *47*, 68–76. doi:10.1016/j.tourman.2014.09.001

Jenkins, H. (2006). *Fans, Bloggers, and Gamers*. New York: New York University Press.

Kaye, B. (2007). Blog Use Motivations: An Exploratory Study. In M. Tremayne (Ed.), *Blogging, Citizenship, and the Future of the Media* (pp. 27–148). New York: Routledge.

Khamis, S., & Munt, A. (2010). The Three Cs of Fashion Media Today: Convergence, Creativity & Control. *Scha Journal*, *7*(2), 1–17.

Kozinets, R. V., de Valck, K., Wojnicki, A. C., & Wilner, S. J. S. (2010). Networked Narratives: Understanding Word-of-Mouth Marketing in Online Communities. *Journal of Marketing*, *74*(March), 71–89. doi:10.1509/jmkg.74.2.71

Kulmala, M. (2011). *Electronic Word-of-Mouth in Consumer Fashion Blogs* (Master thesis). School of Management, University of Tampere.

Lovink, G. (2008). *Zero Comments: Blogging and Critical Internet Culture*. New York: Taylor & Francis. doi:10.14361/9783839408049

Marian, P. (2015). Are you ready to create your own social media network? *WGSN*. Accessed on 18 October 2015, at http://www.wgsn.com

Mathwick, C., Wiertz, C., & de Ruyter, K. (2007). Social Capital Production in a P3 Community. *The Journal of Consumer Research*, *34*, 833–849.

McCracken, G. (1986). Culture and Consumption: A Theoretical Account of the Structure and Movement of the Cultural Meaning of Consumer Goods. *The Journal of Consumer Research*, *13*, 71–84. doi:10.1086/209048

McQuarrie, E. F., & Mick, D. G. (1996). Figures of Rhetoric in Advertising Language. *The Journal of Consumer Research*, *22*, 424–438. doi:10.1086/209459

Meyer, J. W., & Rowan, B. (1977). Institutionalized Organizations: Formal Structure as Myth and Ceremony. *American Journal of Sociology*, *83*(2), 340-363.

Miller, D. (2011). *Tales from Facebook*. Cambridge, UK: Polity.

Mintel. (2017). *Who's innovating?* Available from: http://academic.mintel.com/display/848837/?highlight#hit1

Moe, M., & Trusov, M. (2011). The Value of Social Dynamics in Online Product Rating Forums. *JMR, Journal of Marketing Research*, *48*(3), 444–456. doi:10.1509/jmkr.48.3.444

Moeran, B. (2006). Elegance and Substance Travel East: Vogue Nippon. *Fashion Theory*, *10*(1–2), 225–258. doi:10.2752/136270406778051012

Moeran, B. (2008). Economic and Cultural Production as Structural Paradox: The Case of International Fashion Magazine Publishing. *International Review of Sociology: Revue Internationale de Sociologie, 18*(2), 267–281. doi:10.1080/03906700802087944

Muniz, A. M. Jr, & O'Guinn, T. C. (2001). Brand Community. *The Journal of Consumer Research, 27*, 412–432. doi:10.1086/319618

Mutum, D., & Wang, Q. (2011). *Handbook of research on digital media and advertising: user generated content consumption*. University of Warwick.

Ngai, E., Moon, K., Lam, S., Kee, L., Chin, E., & Tao, S. (2015). Social media models, technologies, and applications. An academic review and case study. *Industrial Management & Data Systems, 115*(5), 769–802. doi:10.1108/IMDS-03-2015-0075

Nicosia, F. M., & Mayer, R. N. (1976). Toward a Sociology of Consumption. *The Journal of Consumer Research, 3*, 65–75.

O'Reilly, T. (2005). *What Is Web 2.0*. Retrieved from http://goo.gl/r4yY

Parmentier, M-A., & Fischer, E. (2011). You Can't Always Get What You Want: Unsustainable Identity Projects in the Fashion System. *Consumption Markets and Culture, 14*(1), 7–27.

Pewinternet. (2006). Retrieved from pewinternet.org/Reports/2006/Bloggers.aspx

Pham, M.-H. (2011). Blog Ambition: Fashion, Feelings, and the Political Economy of the Digital Raced Body. *Camera Obscura, 26*(1), 1–37. doi:10.1215/02705346-2010-013

Powers, T., Advincula, D., Austin, M. S., Graiko, S., & Snyder, J. (2012). Digital and social media in the purchase decision process: A special report from the Advertising Research Foundation'. *Journal of Advertising Research, 52*(4), 479–489. doi:10.2501/JAR-52-4-479-489

Pulizzi, J., & Barrett, N. (2009). *Get Content Get Customers: Turn Prospects into Buyers with Content Marketing*. New York: McGraw-Hill.

Rocamora, A. (2002). Fields of Fashion: Critical Insights into Bourdieu's Sociology of Culture. *Journal of Consumer Culture, 2*(3), 341–362. doi:10.1177/146954050200200303

Rocamora, A. (2011). Personal Fashion Blogs: Screens and Mirrors in Digital Self Portraits. *Fashion Theory, 15*(4), 407–424. doi:10.2752/175174111X13115179149794

Rogers, E. M. (2003). *Diffusion of Innovations* (5th ed.). New York: Free Press.

Rose, R. L., & Wood, S. L. (2005). Paradox and the Consumption of Authenticity through Reality Television. *The Journal of Consumer Research, 32*, 284–296. doi:10.1086/432238

Rosman, K. (2009, September 11). Fashion's Secret Helpers. *Wall Street Journal*.

Russell, A. (2011). *Networked: A Contemporary History of News in Transition*. Cambridge, UK: Polity.

Schau & Gilly. (2003). We Are What We Post? Self-Presentation in Personal Web Space. *Journal of Consumer Research, 30*, 385 404.

Schivinski, B., & Dabrowski, D. (2016). The effect of social media communication on consumer perceptions of brands. *Journal of Marketing Communications*, *22*(2), 189–214. doi:10.1080/13527266.2013.871323

Shen, C., Huang, C. Y., Chu, C. H., & Liao, H. C. (2010). Virtual community loyalty: An interpersonal-interaction perspective. *International Journal of Electronic Commerce*, *15*(1), 49–73. doi:10.2753/JEC1086-4415150102

Smith, A. N., Fischer, E., & Chen, Y. (2011). *Value Creation in Brand-Related User-Generated Content on YouTube*. Paper presented at the Association for Consumer Research Conference, St. Louis, MO.

Suchman, M. (1995). Managing Legitimacy: Strategic and Institutional Approaches. *Academy of Management Review*, *20*(3), 571-610.

Sundar, S., Hatfield Edwards, H., Yifeng Hu, H., & Stavrositu, C. (2007). Blogging for better Health: Putting the 'Public' back in Public Health. In M. Tremayne (Ed.), *Blogging, Citizenship, and the Future of the Media* (pp. 83–97). New York: Routledge.

Taylor, D., & Strutton, D. (2016). Does Facebook usage lead to conspicuous consumption? The role of envy, narcissism and self-promotion. *Journal of Research in Interactive Marketing*, *10*(3), 231–248. doi:10.1108/JRIM-01-2015-0009

Technorati. (2008). Retrieved from www.technocrati.com/blogging/state-of-the-blogosphere

Thornton, S. (1996). *Club Cultures: Music, Media, and Subcultural Capital*. Middletown, CT: Wesleyan University Press.

Tremayne, M. (Ed.). (2007a). *Blogging, Citizenship, and the Future of the Media*. New York: Routledge.

Tremayne, M. (2007b). Introduction: Examining the Blog-Media Relationship. In M. Tremayne (Ed.), *Blogging, Citizenship, and the Future of the Media* (pp. x–xvi). New York: Routledge.

Turner, G. (2010). *Ordinary People and the Media: The Demotic Turn*. Los Angeles, CA: Sage.

Tuten, T. L., & Solomon, M. R. (2017). Social media marketing. *Sage (Atlanta, Ga.)*.

Vries, L., Gensler, S., & Leeflang, P. (2012). Popularity of brand posts on brand fan pages: An investigation of the effects of social media marketing. *Journal of Interactive Marketing*, *26*(2), 83–91. doi:10.1016/j.intmar.2012.01.003

Workman, J. E., & Cho, S. (2012). Gender, fashion consumer groups, and shopping orientation. *Family and Consumer Sciences Research Journal*, *40*(3), 267–283. doi:10.1111/j.1552-3934.2011.02110.x

## KEY TERMS AND DEFINITIONS

**Blog:** A blog or weblog is a personal online journal or experiences, or observations, or opinions discussion or informational website published on the world wide web consisting of discrete, often informal diary-style text entries that are frequently updated and intended for general public consumption.

**Blogging:** The act of writing blogs.

**Fashion:** A trend, or popular or the latest style of personal accessories, clothing, hair, decoration, or behaviour.

**Marketing:** A process of conception, creating, communicating, distributing and exchanging the values, products, services, or ideas.

**Social Media:** Is computer-based technology that includes electronic communication, that uses Web 2.0-based technologies (websites, social networking, and microblogging, video) through which users create online communities to share information, ideas, personal messages, and other content.

# Chapter 16
# Using Social Media and Digital Marketing Tools and Techniques for Developing Brand Equity With Connected Consumers

**Pawan Kumar**
*Department of Marketing, Mittal School of Business, Lovely Professional University, India*

**Gursimranjit Singh**
*Department of Marketing, Mittal School of Business, Lovely Professional University, Phagwara, India*

## ABSTRACT

*This chapter provides a theoretical analysis on the role of digital marketing, social media, and digital marketing tools and techniques (DMTT) in developing customer-based brand equity (CBBE). The chapter discuses different types of digital marketing tools and techniques. The review has found that the consumer's behavioural engagement with brands via social media has a positive effect on customer-based brand equity. Digital media has a positive effect on buyer's intentions because it creates a strong connection between customers and business. Web 2.0-based technologies let users create and collaborate and exchange information and values. This has further led to consumers participating in the process of production of goods and services, as co-creators. Customer engagement, co-creating, and sharing of information via online platforms enhances customer relationship and brand equity.*

## INTRODUCTION

The advent of Digital media and social media has brought in various challenges and opportunities for marketers throughout the globe. Social networking sites such as Facebook, Linked In, Instagram, Twitter, You-Tube has revolutionized business environment. Marketers are using brand pages on social media

DOI: 10.4018/978-1-7998-0131-3.ch016

for connecting with then customers (Acker, Grone, Akkad, Potscher, & Yazbek, 2011). Organizations are getting closer to their customers through continuous interactions on social media (Hutter, Hautz, Dennhardt, & Fuller, 2013). Over the years there is an exponential growth of social media users and it is predicted to increase about 300% in the coming years (Dossier 2014). This growth has motivated marketers to include social media into their marketing strategy for promoting their brands to reach their customers (Mangold & Faulds, 2009; Korschun and Du, 2013).

Earlier organizations used one-to-many marketing communications, to reach their consumers (Hoffman and Novak 1996) but with the revolution brought by the internet, customers are also participating in the functioning of the organization, thus it requires many to many marketing (Kuksov, Shachar, and Wang 2013).

Social media has empowered the customer to raise their voice against the organizations which are not redressing their issues. For instant is a case of Dave Carroll, whose guitar was broken by baggage handler of United Airlines. The Canadian singer sang a song by the name "United breaks Guitar" and uploaded its video on social media platform You-tube. Without social media, the story of Dave Carroll would have got little response, however, with the help of social media the video went viral and as on April 2019, the video has roughly 19.1 million views and 152,000 likes. These stories are directly associated with the image of the brand (Holt 2003) and according to the public press, the episode of Dave Carroll with United Airlines had a negative financial impact on United Airlines through increased negative word-of-mouth (McCarthy 2009).

## LITERATURE REVIEW

The term "social network" is synonymous with Facebook, although the big-picture concept applies to most major social sites. The purpose of social media like Facebook, LinkedIn, Twitter, Instagram, Pinterest, Imgur, Snapchat and video sharing sites are Youtube,Vimeo, etc. is to provide users with a platform to connect with others. Boyd and Ellison (2007) defined social network sites "as web-based services that allow individuals to (1) construct a public or semi-public profile within a bounded system, (2) articulate a list of other users with whom they share a connection, and (3) view and traverse their list of connections and those made by others within the system."

### Social Media and Digital Marketing

Digital marketing is a 'form of direct marketing which links consumers with sellers electronically using interactive technologies like emails, websites, online forums and newsgroups, interactive television, mobile communications, etc.' (Kotler and Armstrong, 2009). It has its very own attributes and elements, which ought to be comprehended so as to have the option to choose viable showcasing strategies and methodologies. Advanced directs can be grouped in different ways. One approach to group the channels is to show them dependent on the perspective of which gathering controls the correspondences (the organization or the intended interest group) and whether interchanges is the single direction or two-way.

In recent times social media marketing is the manner in which promoting practices are done; the conventional showcasing rehearses by and large are negatively affecting the firm (Hennig-Thurau et al., 2013). As per Mangold and Faulds (2009), online lives have pushed customary media on the back foot for learning search. Customers view web-based social networking as a reliable and trustworthy premise of learning than customary promoting rehearses (Foux, 2006). The prime focal point of showcasing correspondence is to pull in customers towards their image. Thus, the associations put different endeavors exploiting online networking stages to accomplish their objectives (Kim and Ko 2012). There are sure elements of internet-based platforms advertising that may affect firm execution. The initial one is the manner by which the firm speak with its customers through web-based platforms. Also, how a firm can request and circulate the aggressive condition and assess it through online life. The firm ought to have the option to gauge the future and answer the present market needs by overseeing internet based life (Hoffman and Fodor, 2010). Digital marketing is an approach to manage cutting edge segments (Jarvinen et al., 2012; Liu, Karahanna and Watson, 2011; Rowley, 2008). It has its own qualities and components, which should be understood to have the choice to pick practical approaches.

## Online Environment and Consumers

The expansion in the use of the internet has forced the organizations to think in a creative method of associating with Customers (Cheong and Morrison, 2008). According to Hamid et al. (2007) "internalization" alludes expanding the selection, dispersion, and arrangement of web-based advancements. Web-based platforms are picking up and have become a significant part in the business segment and people lives. The organisations are utilizing web-based platforms particularly social media as a channel for supporting, engaging and making mindfulness among customers (Kaplan and Haenlein, 2010). Social networking sites like Facebook and Twitter are becoming robust tools to build a brand among young customers, (Vukasovic, 2013).

Online networking has moved toward becoming a need for individuals to speak with one another In addition, they collaborate with items, administrations, and associations. The study conducted by Kim and Ko (2010) in South Korea revealed that internet based life can dramatically affect a brand's notoriety. Online life can't be comprehended without first characterizing Web 2.0: a term that portrays manner by which end customers utilize the World Wide Web (Kaplan and Haenlein 2010). "It is much more to do with what individuals are doing with the innovation than the innovation itself (Campbell et al. 2011). Web 2.0 has advanced from basic data recovery to intelligence, interoperability, and joint effort (Campbell et al. 2011).

The development of online networking platforms has made it possible for customer to-purchaser quickly and efficiently (Duan et al., 2008). Mangold and Faulds, (2009) argue that Social media has affected shopper behavior on data sharing and purchasing. Similarly, research work by Media, M. (2011), concluded that social media platform such as You-Tube gives the highest exposure to brands. Similarly, Poecze, Ebster, and Strauss (2018) found that that the videos which are re-posted on You-Tube gained fewer likes, shares, and comments, whereas photos gained additional followers generated actions as compared to other types of post. Moreover, the user-generated content contribution is lesser, when there is negativity among followers. Additionally, the authors suggested utilizing natural language processing technique to maximize social media brand communication. Shojaee et al. (2013) also found that social media positively influenced brand awareness.

Social media has a positive effect on buyer's intensions because it creates a strong connection between customers and business(Alexandra, 2014). The wide accessibility of the web has furnished individuals with a stage to utilize online life bringing about a move from email to long range interpersonal communication destinations and to cooperate without the requirement for physical gatherings (Gruzd et al. 2011). Customers collaborate and share their encounters via web-based networking media bringing about making shared implications for brands (Guinn and Muniz, 2009). Internet-based platforms empower business to draw in existing customers and pull in new customers and produce more deals (Gilfoil, 2012) by structure brand mindfulness along these lines upgrading brand loyalty (Palmatier et al. 2007) and brand image (Bruhn et al. 2012). Schivinski and Dabrowski (2013) revealed that that social media communication positively affects the consumer mindset and brand evaluation.

The consumer's behavioral engagement with brands on social media has a positive effect on customer-based brand equity (Schivinski et, al. 2019). In addition, brand association influences the involvement and consumption of brand-related social content. Moreover, the creation of social media content related to the brand is influenced by brand loyalty.

Internet-based platforms empower buyers to assume a functioning job rather than an aloof one in the showcasing procedure for making brand mindfulness (Cizmeci et al. 2011). Hwang and Cho (2018) found that gratification of both entertainment and social interaction and perceived ease of use have a positive impact on the user's intention towards continue using networking site Instagram. Not only about the product characteristic, but also price awareness through social media has a significant positive effect on brand image and recognition and brand equity (Hyan, 2015).

## Social Media, Digital Marketing and Brand Equity

The social idea of brands (Muniz and O'Guinn, 2001) and the pertinence of connections in co-making brand esteem (McAlexander et al., 2002; Fuller et al., 2012) improve the significance of computerized showcasing and internet-based life as a promoting channel. The expansion of web-based social networking in the daily life of buyers has led to ever increased potential of social networking sites to be used for showcasing brands. Thus, online networking impacts brand observations and brand-related choices of customers. Singh and Singh (2018) proposed a conceptual framework for understanding communication by brands on social media and finally leading to customer intention to purchase.

Web 2.0 based technologies let users create and collaborate and exchange information and values. This has further lead to consumers participating in the process of production of goods and services, as co-creators. Co-creating with the customers utilizing online platforms prompts customer relationship and. Brand mindfulness. Brand mindfulness builds the likelihood that a brand will be thought about while choosing among different brands (Chakravarti et al., 2003). In addition, Tugbu (2014) posits that social media determinant of brand value. It suggests that consumers with experiences with a specific brand's social media sites are likely to have a higher evaluation of the brand. Similarly, Ali et al. (2015) posit that both traditional, as well as modern marketing strategies such a social media, positively influence brand awareness. As social media has essential networking and connection facilities, so it has dramatically impacted the relationship between consumer and business. Machado et, al. (2019) revealed that brand knowledge has an influence on customer-based brand equity through brand love and customer-brand engagement. Social media lets customer share their feelings about a brand by using emojis. The companies can use new emoji-based metrics to monitor customer's emotions towards brands on social media (Moussa, 2019).

Internet-based life of users portrays online assets that individuals use to share 'content': video, photographs, pictures, content, thoughts, knowledge, humor, conclusion, tattle, news, etc. These assets incorporate websites, video blogs, interpersonal organizations, message sheets, digital broadcasts, open bookmarking and wikis. Most loved instances of web-based life applications incorporate Flickr (online photograph sharing); Wikipedia (reference); Bebo, Facebook and MySpace (organizing); flavorful (bookmarking) and World of Warcraft (web-based gaming). Social media sites like Facebook, Twitter and Youtube and so forth have made a huge impact on interaction with the end customers. The web based life and advanced promoting are changing regular showcasing of brands. Traditional brand correspondences that were recently controlled and directed by brand and showcasing supervisors are steadily being molded by shoppers due to their online presences. In comparison between web-based media gives intelligent correspondence among customers and brands by enabling them to talk and share data among themselves. Internet-based systems empower customers with the opportunity to spread positive or negative news rapidly, encouraging cooperation's, and sharing of substance, in a quick, viral, and minimal effort way. Online life and platforms present brands with huge reach and perpetual conceivable outcomes. It enables brands to develop into a universe of the companion to peer exchanges. Similarly, Bhant (2011) uncovered how organizations utilize web-based life for advancing their offerings and brand image. Social media can also create positive or negative word of mouth and such customers leave a range of online reviews. Consumers find social media a cheaper, accessible and faster means of communication for complaining and requesting addressal of complaints (Mogaji, Ukpabi, & Olaleye (2018).

These days, brands are the organization's most significant resources, increasing the value of its owners and brands have been considered as the second most significant resources for a firm after customers. The idea of brand value has pulled in significant enthusiasm among advertising scientists and experts over the most recent two decades; the brand value idea was first presented in showcasing writing in the 1980s. The enthusiasm for brand value is as yet dynamic up to this point with more articles appearing continually. Higher brand value prompts higher customer inclinations and buying expectations.

Online and computerized Marketing Solutions offer a superb marking hotspot for our necessities. Different electronic devices are utilized to provide engaging advertisements. With the expansion of rivalry, among different organizations, there is clearly expected to think of improved advertising activity and innovation in advertisements and communications. Due to the various tool of online promotions, customer engagement, customer co-creation facilities, etc., the overall brand equity of the organization is enhanced.

## DIFFERENT TYPES OF DIGITAL MARKETING TOOLS AND TECHNIQUES *(DMTT)*

Digital marketing tools and Techniques (DMTT) are a range of ICT technology-related methods, tools, procedures, etc., which can be used to place and promote a product or a brand to the target audiences. The value of the brand; i.e. brand awareness, perceived quality, brand identity, brand associations, brand response, and brand loyalty, etc., can be enhanced by using DMTT in an online environment (Niculescu, Dumitriu, Purdescu, & Ana-Maria Popescu, 2019). One view to look at the brand value is looking at a brand from the customers' point of view. Keller (1993) has proposed a customer-based brand equity model(CBBE), that includes six building blocks (brand Salience, Image, performance, feeling, judgment, and brand resonance) arranged in four stages (brand identity, brand image, brand response, and brand resonance). The organization uses a number of digital marketing tools and Techniques (DMTT) such as Search engine optimization, Affiliated marketing, viral marketing, content marketing, social media platforms, email marketing, PR tools, etc. to enhance Customer-Based Brand Equity (see Table

*Table 1. Digital marketing tools & techniques (DMTT) and their impacts on Consumer-based brand equity (CBBE)*

| Digital Marketing tools & techniques (DMTT) | Impacts on CBBE stages (Brand Identity, Brand Image, Brand Response, Brand Resonance) |
|---|---|
| Search Engine Optimization (SEO) | Brand recognition and also bring a brand to the top of search preferences<br>To enhance customer awareness of new customers and thus effects the brand identity of the CBBE model |
| Pay per Click (PPC) | Brand awareness, more interest by exiting customers and brand identity and customer response (sales) |
| Email Marketing | Engaging and involving the customers<br>Influencing perceived service quality and brand loyalty and this can translate into brand associations, response and may be brand resonance |
| Web 2.0 and Social Media Platforms | Customer engagement in co-creating brand identity, meaning, and resonance.<br>Can enhance Brand awareness, perceived quality, loyalty as customer co-Create brand messages.<br>to enhance brand awareness, brand image & associations, brand response and brand resonance via social brand communities |
| Public Relations (PR) | High credibility to create and enhance brand awareness, brand image & associations, brand response, and brand resonance via social brand communities and independent experts. |
| Content Marketing | Appeal to emotions, associations, feelings, and judgments about a brand.<br>Can enhance received quality, brand loyalty by creating continuous interest in the brand.<br>Caters to multiple levels of CBBE, i.e. to brand meaning, brand response and brand resonance |
| Influencer Marketing | Enhance brand's associations, personality, engagement and so brand relationship and response by making use of brand advocates, who has large followings. |
| Affiliate Marketing (AM) | The brand gets more visibility (awareness), positive sales responses and possibly credibility |
| Viral Marketing (VM) | Utilizes the power of word of mouth among a mutually known and trustworthy network via an electronic network,<br>so, such communication can create a positive brand identity and brand image, higher brand trust, a positive response, and create resonance with the customer |

(source adapted from Zikeeva, 2017)

1). Table 1 summarizes the impacts of different DMTT on customer-based brand equity (CBBE). The discussions are given in the following sections.

## Search Engine Optimization (SEO)

Search Engine Optimization (SEO) is a process of content creations, in such a way that it becomes faster and easier for a search engine (such as Google, Yahoo, etc.) to search and find the relevant content about a brand, product, idea or information. The main focus of the concept of Search Engine Optimization (SEO) is providing leverage to a certain website to appear in the top result, for a website to move up to top result many different factors are involved (Enge et, al 2012). Search engine optimization is generally related to keywords, phrases, blogs, and pictures that are appropriate to take attention of users. To optimize a web site in accordance to search engine some technical conditions should be suitable to it (Cui and Hu, 2011) The process makes it easier for search engines, users and customer to search for products or brands of their choice. As search engine are also empowered to search for synonymous and related words, such a search can further help in brand recognition and also bring a brand to the top of search preferences. The SEO can be seen as a tool to enhance customer awareness of new customers and thus effects the brand identity of the CBBE model

## Pay per Click (PPC)

Pay Per Click (PPC) is a process that let marketers bid for sponsored or paid place in the web place and this let's search engine bring the relevant web page in front of the customers (Zikeeva, 2017). To drive traffic to websites, pay per click model of internet advertising is used, in which publisher is paid by an advertiser who is basically a website owner, or a network of websites, etc. when the ad is clicked (Mahdian & Tomak, 2011). Google Ads and Bing Ads are some exampless of pay-per-click. Advertisers bid on keywords which are pertinent to their target market. Social networking sites like Facebook, Twitter are using pay-per-click strategy to generate revenue (Pan et, al 2011).PPC is mostly targeted at exiting customers or competitive marketing. Thus, PPC improves website performance and so this is also a tool for brand awareness, more interest by exiting customers and identity.

## Email Marketing

It is a direct online communication method of interacting with targeted customers with a personalized message, which leads to a better understanding of their needs and subsequent satisfaction (Zikeeva, 2017). Email marketing is the display of sending a business message, generally to a social gathering of individuals, utilizing email. In its broadest sense, each email sent to a potential or current customer could be viewed as email showing (Sterne and Priore, 2000). The term normally suggests sending email messages to improve a seller's association with the present or past customer, empowering customer enduring quality and rehash business, getting new customers or persuading current customers to buy something quickly, and sharing outsider notification (Kent and Brandal, 2003). As email marketing is personalized and direct communication, so it has more potential for engaging and involving the customers. Hence, an email marketing could be targeting at influencing perceived service quality and brand loyalty and this can translate into brand associations, response and may be brand resonance.

## Web 2.0 and Social Media Platforms

In Web 2.0, is technology to create user greeted content, wherein all of the users can co-create and modify content in a participatory and collaborate way (Narkiniemi, 2013). Social media networks are also Web2,0 based platforms that allow users to create, share and discuss the content actively, some of the most well-known examples of social media are Facebook, Twitter, LinkedIn, YouTube, Instagram, Pinterest and MySpace, etc. (Narkiniemi, 2013). The social network sites have a strong influence on customers' purchasing all over the world, but it is the strongest in the Asian Pacific, Latin America, Middle East, and Africa regions (Nielsen's survey 2012:13, cited by Narkiniemi, 2013). Social media lets consumers to interact with a brand and increases their involvement in the brand buying decision process, such co-created content can become viral leading to more awareness, and such kind of brand interaction can create positive judgments and feelings towards a brand i.e. a positive response and ultimately all that can lead to higher brand loyalty and relationship (Zikeeva, 2017). .Thus, social media platforms have great potential to enhance brand awareness, brand image & associations, brand response, and brand resonance via social brand communities.

## Public Relations (PR)

The concept of public relations works on monitoring the reach of the information among individual and organization (Kent and Taylor, 1998). With the help of public relation organizations as well as individuals gain experience about their audience using topics which are of public interest and not requires direct payment. This ability of public relation separates it from advertising. The blogs, Social media sites, YouTube video, and media content, etc. might be used as a tool of public relations. The main focus of public relation is to create free customer coverage rather than advertising or marketing it. Public relations aim is to inform the public, partners, employees, prospective consumers and ultimately influence them to maintain an optimistic view of the organization. The basic responsibilities of public relation include writing a news release, designing communication campaign, etc. To be successful in the domain of public relation a proper understanding and concern for each stakeholder is required (Giannini 2009). As PR could use third party's view on a brand, so PR has high credibility to create and enhance brand awareness, brand image & associations, brand response, and brand resonance via social brand communities and independent experts.

## Content Marketing

Content marketing works on the philosophy of attracting prospects and converting those prospects into consumers by sharing and creating non-paid content (Holliman and Rowley 2014). The main benefit which content marketing provides is of creating brand loyalty, giving information, and creating an intention to purchase. Content marketing is that management process that is responsible for anticipating, recognizing, and satisfying consumer's requirement through the electronic channel (Rowley, 2008). Content marketing aids in focused targeting the customers with relevant and engaging content, thereby triggering constant interest in brand offers, perceived brand quality, brand loyalty(Zikeeva, 2017). Relevant content can appeal to emotions, associations, feelings, and judgments about a brand. Thus, Content marketing caters to multiple levels of CBBE, i.e. to brand meaning, brand response and brand resonance.

## Influencer Marketing

Influencer Marketing is a process of using key brand advocates to drive a brand message to the larger market in an organic way, the brand advocates are the people with large social followings who have sway over your target audience (Dawson, 2000). The impact of Web 2.0 based sites, wikis and other web-based systems is that those can engage new influencers to disperse brand essence. Organization pour billions of pounds each year into influencing what they accept are their influencers (Pickett-Baker and Ozaki, 2008). The tool can enhance brand's associations, personality and so brand relationship and response by making use of brand advocates, who has large followings.

## Affiliate Marketing (AM)

Affiliate marketing is a kind of referral process of earning a commission by promoting other organizations brands or products by the third party/person who initially liked the brand (Duffy, 2005). In AM, there are three participants ; An "Advertiser" who sells products or services, which is usually an e-commerce site (e.g. e-bay, Amazon, Expedia); an "Affiliate" whose website displays a link to the Advertiser's e-commerce site, usually as a text hyperlink or as a banner advertisement (who get a commission fee, for generating visitor traffic to the Advertiser's site); and an Affiliate Network, which is a specialized third-party platform that offers tracking technology using HTTP cookies etc. (Amarasekara & Mathrani, 2016). Affiliate marketing is a methodology in the online business appears to have more solid potential than direct on-line publicizing. An affiliate acts like of inventive web publicists, who gets commission by publicizing the deals of many other on-line brands (Duffy, 2005). Marketing specialists achieve the benefit of promotion cost. Thus, an afflicted marketing tactic that lets a product owner increase sale by allowing 'others' targeting the same audience— 'affiliates'—to earn a commission by recommending the product to others (Libai et, al. 2003). Because of the involvement of third person affiliates/opinion leader, the brand gets more visibility (awareness), positive sales responses and possibly credibility. Hence AM is a good driver of CBBE.

## Viral Marketing (VM)

Viral Marketing (VM) is an electronic extension of word of mouth (eWOM) and is a ' strategy and process of encouraging individuals to create, receive, send, pass-on, or forward virus marketing messages to others, thus creating potential for exponential growth in messages' exposure and influence (Rakic & Rakic, 2014). Viral promoting is a method that uses existing casual networks to propel marketing. Its name suggests how customers spread information about a brand with different people in their casual networks, much also that contamination spreads starting with one individual then onto the next (Leskovec, 2007). A viral message can be created by an organisation or by a customer and then it is spread to the network. Viral marketing is spread to networks of near & dear and, the organization does not pay for defusing of such message (Chan et, al. 2010). A large portion of viral messages on the web are promotions paid by an organisation or by means of electronic systems such as YouTube, email or a blog, page or online life profile. Viral marketing may show up as video cuts, wise Flash beguilements, advergames, computerized books, brandable programming, pictures, texts, email messages, or pages (Esomba, 2013). Viral marketing is also known as e-WOM, interactive marketing, internet WOM, Word of Mouse, stealth marketing, referral marketing, and buzz marketing (Rakic & Rakic, 2014). The most transmission vehicles for viral messages ca be income based, inspiration-based, famous based, and secret based, etc. Simplicity, speed,and coverage of message and mutual trust among receivers make viral marketing effective and interesting (Rakic & Rakic, 2014). Social networking sites such as Facebook, Twitter, Instagram and even video sharing site such as YouTube, etc. are very significant vehicles for viral marketing. As the viral messages are shared and spread the network of people & friends, who know each other, hence such messages have more credibility and trustworthiness (Rakic & Rakic, 2014). As Viral marketing utilizes the power of word of mouth among a mutually known and trustworthy network via an electronic network, so such aa communication can create positive brand identity and image, higher brand trust, a positive response, and resonance with the customer. Hence, Viral marketing has the potential to positively influence all of the four levels of CBBE. Viral Marketing message spread faster, covers more targets, acts as a two-way dialogue, and its content can be controlled by the initiator, hence the viral messages are more efficient and effective means of building customer-based brand equity (Rakic & Rakic, 2014).

## DIGITAL MARKETING AND CONSUMER BASED BRAND EQUITY

Social media include a set of connectivity-enabled applications and platforms that facilitate interaction and the publication, exchange, and co-creation of information among organization and their connected users, and social media include social networks, weblogs, social blogs, wikis, podcasts, pictures, video, rating and social bookmarking, etc.(Pham & Gammoh, 2015). Social media marketing is the process of generating viral communication, that uses social media channels to create, communicate, deliver, and exchanging of information, and value (Pham & Gammoh, 2015). Social media marketing is identified with relationship building and making associations with the consumers (Erdogmus and Cicke, 2012). In addition, the development in web-based society and the rise of social media has a positive effect on brand purchases (Kim and Ko, 2012). As Schivinski and Dabrowski (2014) posited that online networking platforms are associated with relationship building and making associations with consumers (Erdogmus and Cicke, 2012).

The current customers use technical platforms for buying products and services. The customers are well connected with each other, and they can ask questions, give suggestions, compare products and prices online, read and give reviews about brands, watch videos and even share the experience of brands via virtual reality, etc. Thus the traditional methods of marketing as 'one to many marketing models' needs to be changed to 'Many to Many marketing models' (Skute, 2014). .As a result, digital marketing tools such as; website, social media communication are predominately are adopted, adapted and implemented by the organization to deliver superior value and engage customers with a brand (Zikeeva, 2017). The interconnected consumers must be well engaged with multiple mechanisms and 'many to many' networked relationship engagements strategies(Skute, 2014)The organizations have to think themselves as 'platform moderators', and execute collaborate strategies to keep their networked customers well engaged with their products and brands. Such customer engagement strategies need to also target at engaging and managing social brand communities(Skute, 2014). The 'social community of brand' consist of a group of brand loyal customer base, and who create, share forward information about a brand with each other. Such brand engagement can enhance brand identity, brand image, brand value, brand loyalty, and brand equity. Brand equity is a tangible and intangible value (function, or emotional or behavioral) that a brand provides to an organization, its products, its services, and its bottom-line derived from consumer knowledge, perceptions, and experiences with the brand (Zikeeva, 2017).

A brand value is based on 'customer attitude to positive brand attributes and favorable consequences of brand usage and is made up of: a set of perceptions and consumer associations caused by a brand (description of a brand); degree of consumer loyalty towards the brand (strength of a brand); the total value of the brand (American Marketing Association, 2014 & Feldwick 2002 as cited by Zikeeva, 2017). Consumer-based Brand equity (CBBE) is a differential (cognitive, emotional and behavioral) effect that a brand knowledge exerts on customer response to the marketing of that brand (Keller, 1993). The brand awareness and brand image are the essential ingredients of brand knowledge, which aids in recognition, recall also creating a favorable as well as a unique association with the brand and ultimately a favorable response towards that brand (Keller, 1993; Skute, 2014). Social media can be effectively used to enhance the values of those assets of a brand. A few definitions depend on the money related point of view and stress the estimation of a brand to the firm (Simon and Sullivan, 1993). From the buyer's point of view, brand equity is the estimation of a brand's power to influence purchase intentions (Aaker, 1991). Keller (1993) argued for brand equity as a customer-based brand value and characterized it as 'the differential effect of brand knowledge on consumer response to the marketing of a brand'. Keller (2013) has put forward a CBBE pyramid model made up of six components; as brand salience, brand performance, brand imagery, brand judgments, brand feelings, and brand resonance. According to Keller(2013), the process of building a brand consist of four stages: First: creating a brand identity; Second: creating the appropriate brand meaning through strong, unique and favorable brand associations; Third: eliciting positive brand responses; and fourth: building brand relationship with customers leading to brand loyalty(Akinyemi, 2013) . The customer perceived value of a brand results from a complex interactions of various elements, such as product quality & performance, prominence, image, communication, price, emotional value, and brand's presence in online/offline environment through the use of digital marketing tools and techniques (Niculescu et al., 2019). The brand awareness and brand image can be improved through enhancing customer engagement and co-creation on social media networks, thus resulting in more brand loyalty, customer engagement, customer interactions and finally overall brand experience and feeling of the customers(Pham & Gammoh, 2015).

Digital marketing is a branch of marketing that uses digital channels place, and promote products or brands in order to attract and maintain customers(Narkiniemi, 2013). Digital marketing emerges as a very significant means of building consumer-based brand equity. A digital marketing is an online, data-driven system of processes, people, technology, customer insight, and decisions process, which allows organizations to offer customized solutions to the customers and hence it creates deeper, personalized interactions and exchange with the customers and ultimately continuously enhances customer experience of a brand or product (Garnerv 2016, cited by Zikeeva, 2017). Thus, digital marketing uses digital technology to promote, place and exchange, products, services, and values. The ultimate goal of digital marketing is to involve and engage consumers in a variety of unique, personalized and tailored online experiences, which can add value to customers' decisions about a brand at different stages of the buying process(Zikeeva, 2017).

The digital media facilitate the processes of connecting businesses to consumers, building customer relationships and engage users with active roles to manage those processes(Pham & Gammoh, 2015). Customers love to create, contribute, and joining communities to fulfill needs of belongingness, and enjoying interactions with other like-minded members and consumers; also like to co-create brand stories so they can feel that they control their brands (Laroche et al. 2012, cited by Pham & Gammon, 2015). As Digital media offers, variety, diversity, intensity, and connectivity to the consumers; naturally such an online environment is very suitable for consumer-based brand equity creation. The previous research has shown that digital media marketing activities have a strong influence on brands' image, brand trust, brand relationship, positive word of mouth and Brand equity (Chen et al., 2011; Chevalier and Mayzlin, 2006, Kim and Ko, 2012; cited by Pham & Gammoh, 2015). The digital media can be paid media (banner ads, pay-per-click advertisement, and sponsored social media contents), owned media (content a brand creates by itself say via website, blog, and its own social media contents) ; Earned media (how a brand is represented in digital space by third parties; press coverage, social media mentions, shares and retweets, product or company reviews, and independent blog). A sum total of digital media creates brand awareness, brand salience, brand performance, brand imagery, brand judgments, brand feelings, and brand resonance. The organization and brands need to factor in the impact of web-based platforms on buyers and better comprehend the degree to which social media impacts brand purchase intentions (Schultz and Peltier, 2013). The studies have shown that unknown brands can benefit from positive online reviews & e-Word of Mouth (e WOM), also consumers may develop a new brand image based on online reviews and eWOM.

A significant part of marketing aims at building brand value (Keller, 1998). With the expanded online options for consumers to converse with different customers around the world, organizations are not the only source of information about a brand (Bruhn et al., 2014). Online environment enhances customer's brand associations and social media has changed brand associations into a multi-party discussion as opposed to a brand-managed monolog (Deighton and Kornfeld, 2009). Thus, researchers have noticed the need for research into the field of customer's association with brands (Bowden, 2009) and brand-buyer commitments in an online social setting (Brodie et al., 2011). Research has found a positive impact of internet-based advertising on brand value and on customers intentions (Kim and Ko, 2012). In fact, the basic premise of customer-based brand equity (CBBE) model is that 'the power of brands lies in the minds of customers and relies on what customer have learned, felt, seen, and heard about the brand over time' (Keller, 2001).

The new digital technological developments have allowed increased connectedness and empowerment of social media users, which has led to the development of brand communities (Skute, 2014). Such brand communities collaborate to share brand-related information and values, The consumers engage in and maintain social networks and become deeply involved in immersive virtual web experiences. Brand community work in collaboration, pooling knowledge and constructing content that is shared between them. The social media aids in higher customer engagement, involvement, collaboration, thus co-creating the brand's social media equity, which will ultimately drive CBBE (Skute, 2014). Strategic brand engagement by social media community stimulates enhanced buyer-seller relationships, thus leading to higher brand equity, which further impacts positive behavior (retention rates, favourable e-Word-of-Mouth) towards the product/service (Skute, 2014). Thus digital media helps in increasing brand awareness, brand recall, a favorable brand image, positive brand response, and brand resonance and relationship with the social media community, On the basis of the above discussion conceptual model is proposed (see Figure 1). So, based on the discussions on in the previous sections, it can be concluded that digital marketing can enhance Consumer-based brand equity (see figure 1).

There are many instants, where the brands have used social media and digital tools to improve their brand image. For example, Coca-Cola propelled what they allude to as the 'Coca-Cola TV venture' battle, basically carrying live stimulation to its intended interest group through numerous online networking directs and gadgets in a year-long undertaking fundamentally went for crowds in Latin America. Paul McCartney's free show in Mexico was spilled live on Coca-Cola TV, with viewers urged to drive discussions via web-based networking media channels.

Another example is a 'Coca-Cola Happiness Machine' A YouTube video (https://www.youtube.com/watch?v=lqT_dPApj9U). In this case of viral marketing, Coca-cola has placed a special Coke machine in the middle of a college campus. When a customer paid to buy one can of coke, at that vending machine, the customer gets surprisingly good things, e.g. many coke bottles instead of one, Boquete of flowers, Birthday balloons, a Pizza, and a very long burger, etc. All these free gifts from the Coke happiness machine had created a very happy and sharing atmosphere at the college canteen. This Youtube video further became viral (more than 10.1 million hits) due to its innovativeness and 'sense of happiness & sharing) that represents the coke brand (YouTube, 2010). The viral campaign has reinforced Coke's brand image, led to a positive brand response and has let the brand personality resonance with its target customers; Thus, enhancing Coke's Customer-based brand equity (CBBE).

All the more as of late, Topshop joined forces with Facebook to permit audiences of its live-spilled style show to impart photos of their preferred outfits to their companions. The show was additionally the first historically speaking style show to be spilled live on Twitter, with watchers urged to condense the

*Figure 1. A model of digital marketing tools and techniques and CBBE*

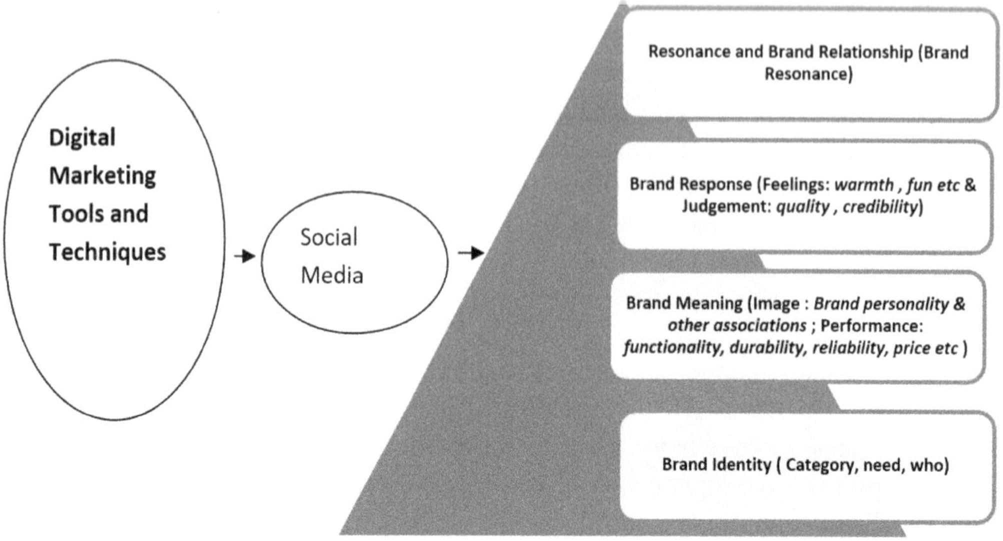


show in the customary 140 characters. As per the brand, it was viewed by more than 2 million watchers from more than 100 nations. The crusade brought about a phenomenal degree of traffic to Topshop.com, and in a few of the gathering's things being sold out inside 60 minutes.

## MANAGERIAL IMPLICATION OF DIGITAL MARKETING AND BRANDING

Social media is an effective and efficient means of advertisers for developing strong brand awareness. To utilize a range of benefits of the Internet, including building CBBE, an organization must make use of digital media for interaction and information to customers. The traditional 'push marketing' strategies aren't exceedingly feasible with a new generation of customers. Marketers are joining new generation customers (Millennial) on the internet to form customer association and ultimately a long-lasting healthy relationship.

Digital media and DMTT can be used to promote their brand by making use of a range of digital tools to spread positive informal interactions (e WOM) among customers. As social media platforms are attracting web customers, firms should think about making full use of social frameworks. Organisation should clearly realize whether digital marketing is a substitute or a reinforcing gadget of marketing. Potential energies of online interpersonal communication should be meticulously investigated and effectively managed.

Finally, firms should continually develop customer insight by monitoring target consumers and users' behaviors, preferences towards brands. The managers should draw strategies to create digital online brand communities, who will ultimately develop CBBE.

## CONCLUSION

There is a huge potential of using Digital media tools and Techniques (DMTT) in developing customer-based brand equity (CBBE) using the electronic peer to peer communication via digital media platforms to engage customers and build brands. The advancements in technology have brought a phenomenal increase in usage of digital media through instruments such as smart phones, tablets, smartwatches, smart TV, etc. to co-create, share, discuss, and modify user-generated content about brands. The organization should make use of a range of digital tools and techniques such as email marketing, search engine optimization, referral marketing, content market, and viral marketing, etc., in order to enhance brand equity. Consumers who are rationally, emotionally and behaviorally attached to a brand have a stronger urge to purchase the brands and show continuous brand loyalty.

## REFERENCES


Aaker, D. A. (1991). *Building brand equity*. New York: The Free.

Acker, O., Gröne, F., Akkad, F., Pötscher, F., & Yazbek, R. (2011). Social CRM: How companies can link into the social web of consumers. *Journal of Direct Data and Digital Marketing Practice*, *13*(1), 3–10. doi:10.1057/dddmp.2011.17

Alhaddad, A. A. (2015). The effect of advertising awareness on brand equity in social media. *International Journal of e-Education, e-Business, e- Management Learning*, *5*(2), 73.

Amarasekara, B. R., & Mathrani, A. (2016). Controlling risks and fraud in affiliate marketing: A simulation and testing environment. *14th Annual Conference on Privacy, Security, and Trust, PST 2016*. 10.1109/PST.2016.7906986

Boyd, D. M., & Ellison, N. B. (2007). Social network sites: Definition, history, and scholarship. *Journal of Computer-Mediated Communication*, *13*(1), 210–230. doi:10.1111/j.1083-6101.2007.00393.x

Brodie, R. J., Hollebeek, L. D., Jurić, B., & Ilić, A. (2011). Customer engagement: Conceptual domain, fundamental propositions, and implications for research. *Journal of Service Research*, *14*(3), 252–271. doi:10.1177/1094670511411703

Brown, J. D. (2010). High self-esteem buffers negative feedback: Once more with feeling. *Cognition and Emotion*, *24*(8), 1389–1404. doi:10.1080/02699930903504405

Bruhn, M., Schnebelen, S., & Schäfer, D. (2014). Antecedents and consequences of the quality of e-customer-to-customer interactions in B2B brand communities. *Industrial Marketing Management*, *43*(1), 164–176. doi:10.1016/j.indmarman.2013.08.008

Bruhn, M., Schoenmüller, V., Schäfer, D., & Heinrich, D. (2012). Brand authenticity: Towards a deeper understanding of its conceptualization and measurement. *Advances in Consumer Research. Association for Consumer Research (U. S.)*, 40.

Chakravarti, A., & Janiszewski, C. (2003). The influence of macro-level motives on consideration set composition in novel purchase situations. *The Journal of Consumer Research*, *30*(2), 244–258. doi:10.1086/376803

Chen, W., Wang, C., & Wang, Y. (2010, July). Scalable influence maximization for prevalent viral marketing in large-scale social networks. In *Proceedings of the 16th ACM SIGKDD international conference on Knowledge discovery and data mining* (pp. 1029-1038). ACM. 10.1145/1835804.1835934

Chen, Y., Fay, S., & Wang, Q. (2011). The role of marketing in social media: How online consumer reviews evolve. *Journal of Interactive Marketing*, *25*(2), 85–94. doi:10.1016/j.intmar.2011.01.003

Cheong, H. J., & Morrison, M. A. (2008). Consumers' reliance on product information and recommendations found in UGC. *Journal of Interactive Advertising*, *8*(2), 38–49. doi:10.1080/15252019.2008.10722141

Çizmeci, F., & Ercan, T. (2015). The Effect of Digital Marketing Communication Tools in the Creation Brand Awareness By Housing Companies. *Megaron, 10*(2).

Cui, M., & Hu, S. (2011, September). Search engine optimization research for website promotion. In *2011 International Conference of Information Technology, Computer Engineering and Management Sciences* (Vol. 4, pp. 100-103). IEEE. 10.1109/ICM.2011.308

Dawson, J. (2000). Retailing at century end: Some challenges for management and research. *International Review of Retail, Distribution and Consumer Research*, *10*(2), 119–148. doi:10.1080/095939600342325

Deighton, J., & Kornfeld, L. (2009). Interactivity's unanticipated consequences for marketers and marketing. *Journal of Interactive Marketing*, *23*(1), 4–10. doi:10.1016/j.intmar.2008.10.001

Duan, A., Wang, M., Lei, Y., & Cui, Y. (2013). Trends in summer rainfall over China associated with the Tibetan Plateau sensible heat source during 1980–2008. *Journal of Climate*, *26*(1), 261–275. doi:10.1175/JCLI-D-11-00669.1

Duffy, D. L. (2005). Affiliate marketing and its impact on e-commerce. *Journal of Consumer Marketing*, *22*(3), 161–163. doi:10.1108/07363760510595986

Enge, E., Spencer, S., Stricchiola, J., & Fishkin, R. (2012). *The art of SEO*. O'Reilly Media, Inc.

Erdoğmuş, İ. E., & Cicek, M. (2012). The impact of social media marketing on brand loyalty. *Procedia: Social and Behavioral Sciences*, *58*, 1353–1360. doi:10.1016/j.sbspro.2012.09.1119

Esomba, S. D. (2013). *Advertising and the spread of Business, Democracy and Knowledge*. Lulu.com.

Etemad, H., Wilkinson, I., & Dana, L. P. (2010). Internetization as the necessary condition for internationalization in the newly emerging economy. *Journal of International Entrepreneurship*, *8*(4), 319–342. doi:10.100710843-010-0062-x

Foux, G. (2006). Consumer-generated media: Get your customers involved. *Brand Strategy, 8*(202), 38-39.

Giannini, G. T. (2009). *Marketing public relations*. Pearson Education India.

Gilfoil, D. M. (2012). Mapping social media tools for sell vs buy activities into emerging and developed markets. *International Journal of Management & Information Systems (Online)*, *16*(1), 69.

Godes, D., Mayzlin, D., Chen, Y., Das, S., Dellarocas, C., Pfeiffer, B., ... Verlegh, P. (2005). The firm's management of social interactions. *Marketing Letters*, *16*(3-4), 415–428. doi:10.100711002-005-5902-4

Gorgios, T., & Sergios D. (2014). *Brand strategies in social media*. Academic Press.

Gruzd, A., Wellman, B., & Takhteyev, Y. (2011). Imagining Twitter as an imagined community. *The American Behavioral Scientist*, *55*(10), 1294–1318. doi:10.1177/0002764211409378

Hamid, M. R. A., Amin, H., Lada, S., & Ahmad, N. (2007). A comparative analysis of Internet banking in Malaysia and Thailand. *Journal of Internet Business*, (4).

Hennig-Thurau, T., & Hansen, U. (Eds.). (2013). *Relationship marketing: Gaining competitive advantage through customer satisfaction and customer retention*. Springer Science & Business Media.

Hoffman, D. L., & Fodor, M. (2010). Can you measure the ROI of your social media marketing? *MIT Sloan Management Review*, *52*(1), 41.

Hoffman, D. L., & Novak, T. P. (1996). Marketing in hypermedia computer-mediated environments: Conceptual foundations. *Journal of Marketing*, *60*(3), 50–68. doi:10.2307/1251841

Holliman, G., & Rowley, J. (2014). Business to business digital content marketing: marketers' perceptions of best practice. *Journal of Research in Interactive Marketing, 8*(4), 269-293.

Holt, N. L. (2003). Representation, legitimation, and autoethnography: An autoethnographic writing story. *International Journal of Qualitative Methods*, *2*(1), 18–28. doi:10.1177/160940690300200102

Hutter, K., Hautz, J., Dennhardt, S., & Füller, J. (2013). The impact of user interactions in social media on brand awareness and purchase intention: The case of MINI on Facebook. *Journal of Product and Brand Management*, *22*(5/6), 342–351. doi:10.1108/JPBM-05-2013-0299

Hwang, H. S., & Cho, J. (2018). Why Instagram? Intention to continue using Instagram among Korean college students. *Social Behavior and Personality*, *46*(8), 1305–1315. doi:10.2224bp.6961

Hyan, D.(2015). *Determinants of brand image in social media*. Academic Press.

Kaplan, A. M., & Haenlein, M. (2010). Users of the world, unite! The challenges and opportunities of Social Media. *Business Horizons*, *53*(1), 59–68. doi:10.1016/j.bushor.2009.09.003

Karam, A. A., & Saydam, S. (2015). An analysis study of improving brand awareness and its impact on consumer behavior via media in North Cyprus (A case study of fast food restaurants). *International Journal of Business and Social Science*, *6*(1).

Keller, K. L. (1993). Conceptualizing, measuring, and managing customer-based brand equity. *Journal of Marketing*, *57*(1), 1–22. doi:10.1177/002224299305700101

Keller, K. L. (2001). *Building customer-based brand equity: A blueprint for creating strong brands*. Cambridge, MA: Marketing Science Institute.

Keller, K. L. (2013). *Strategic Brand Management: Building, Measuring, and Managing Brand Equity*. Upper Saddle River, NJ: Pearson Education.

Kent, M. L., & Taylor, M. (1998). Building dialogic relationships through the World Wide Web. *Public Relations Review*, *24*(3), 321–334. doi:10.1016/S0363-8111(99)80143-X

Kent, R., & Brandal, H. (2003). Improving email response in a permission marketing context. *International Journal of Market Research*, *45*(4), 1–13. doi:10.1177/147078530304500404

Khan, F., & Siddiqui, K. (2013). The importance of digital marketing. An exploratory study to find the perception and effectiveness of digital marketing amongst the marketing professionals in Pakistan. *Journal of Information Systems & Operations Management*, 1.

Kim, A. J., & Ko, E. (2010). Impacts of luxury fashion brand's social media marketing on customer relationship and purchase intention. *Journal of Global Fashion Marketing*, *1*(3), 164–171. doi:10.1080/20932685.2010.10593068

Korschun, D., & Du, S. (2013). How virtual corporate social responsibility dialogs generate value: A framework and propositions. *Journal of Business Research*, *66*(9), 1494–1504. doi:10.1016/j.jbusres.2012.09.011

Kotler, P. (2009). *Gary Armstrong, Principles of Marketing*. Tehran: Learned Nshrasly (1379).

Kuksov, D., Shachar, R., & Wang, K. (2013). Advertising and consumers' communications. *Marketing Science*, *32*(2), 294–309. doi:10.1287/mksc.1120.0753

Leskovec, J., Adamic, L. A., & Huberman, B. A. (2007). The dynamics of viral marketing. *ACM Transactions on the Web*, *1*(1), 5. doi:10.1145/1232722.1232727

Libai, B., Biyalogorsky, E., & Gerstner, E. (2003). Setting referral fees in affiliate marketing. *Journal of Service Research*, *5*(4), 303–315. doi:10.1177/1094670503005004003

Liu, Y., & Li, H. (2010). Mobile internet diffusion in China: An empirical study. *Industrial Management & Data Systems*, *110*(3), 309–324. doi:10.1108/02635571011030006

Machado, J. C., Vacas-de-Carvalho, L., Azar, S. L., André, A. R., & dos Santos, B. P. (2019). Brand gender and consumer-based brand equity on Facebook: The mediating role of consumer-brand engagement and brand love. *Journal of Business Research*, *96*, 376–385. doi:10.1016/j.jbusres.2018.07.016

Mangold, W. G., & Faulds, D. J. (2009). Social media: The new hybrid element of the promotion mix. *Business Horizons*, *52*(4), 357–365. doi:10.1016/j.bushor.2009.03.002

Mangold, W. G., & Faulds, D. J. (2009). Social media: The new hybrid element of the promotion mix. *Business Horizons*, *52*(4), 357–365. doi:10.1016/j.bushor.2009.03.002

Mogaji, E., Ukpabi, D., & Olaleye, S. (2018, July). Examining Consumer-Brand Relationships in the UK Energy Sector: A Social Media Perspective. In *Academy of Marketing Annual Conference Proceedings*. University of Stirling.

Narkiniemi, J. (2013). *Using Digital Marketing to Develop a Modern Marketing Strategy for a Startup*. Retrieved from https://core.ac.uk/download/pdf/38098424.pdf

O'Guinn, T. C., & Muniz, A. M., Jr. (2009). Collective brand relationships. Handbook of brand relationships, 173-94.

Otugo, N. E., Uzuegbunam, C. E., & Obikeze, C. O. (2015, May). Social media advertising/marketing: A study of awareness, attitude and responsiveness by Nigerian youths. In *International Conference on Communication, Media, Technology and Design* (*Vol. 1*, No. 2, pp. 1-17). Academic Press.

Palmatier, R. W., Dant, R. P., & Grewal, D. (2007). A comparative longitudinal analysis of theoretical perspectives of interorganizational relationship performance. *Journal of Marketing*, *71*(4), 172–194. doi:10.1509/jmkg.71.4.172

Pan, B., Xiang, Z., Law, R., & Fesenmaier, D. R. (2011). The dynamics of search engine marketing for tourist destinations. *Journal of Travel Research*, *50*(4), 365–377. doi:10.1177/0047287510369558

Pham, P. H. M., & Gammoh, B. S. (2015). Characteristics of social-media marketing strategy and customer-based brand equity outcomes: A conceptual model. *International Journal of Internet Marketing and Advertising*, *9*(4), 321–337. doi:10.1504/IJIMA.2015.072885

Pickett-Baker, J., & Ozaki, R. (2008). Pro-environmental products: Marketing influence on the consumer purchase decision. *Journal of Consumer Marketing*, *25*(5), 281–293. doi:10.1108/07363760810890516

Poecze, F., Ebster, C., & Strauss, C. (2018). Social media metrics and sentiment analysis to evaluate the effectiveness of social media posts. *Procedia Computer Science*, *130*, 660–666. doi:10.1016/j.procs.2018.04.117

Rakic, M., & Rakic, B. (2014). Viral Marketing. *SSRN Electronic Journal*, *60*(4), 179–187. doi:10.2139srn.2561237

Richardson, M., & Domingos, P. (2002, July). Mining knowledge-sharing sites for viral marketing. In *Proceedings of the Eighth ACM SIGKDD international conference on Knowledge discovery and data mining* (pp. 61-70). ACM. 10.1145/775047.775057

Rowley, J. (2008). Understanding digital content marketing. *Journal of Marketing Management*, *24*(5-6), 517–540. doi:10.1362/026725708X325977

Schein, R., Wilson, K. & Keelan, J. (2010). *The effectiveness of the use of social media a report for peel public health.* Academic Press.

Schivinski, B. (2011). Effects of social media communication on brand equity and brand purchase intention. *Interdisciplinary Journal*, *2*, 157–162.

Schivinski, B., & Dabrowski, D. (2016). The effect of social media communication on consumer perceptions of brands. *Journal of Marketing Communications*, *22*(2), 189–214. doi:10.1080/13527266.2013.871323

Schivinski, B., Muntinga, D. G., Pontes, H. M., & Lukasik, P. (2019). Influencing COBRAs: The effects of brand equity on the consumer's propensity to engage with brand-related content on social media. *Journal of Strategic Marketing*, 1–23. doi:10.1080/0965254X.2019.1572641

Shojaee, S., & Azman, A. B. (2013). An evaluation of factors affecting brand awareness in the context of social media in Malaysia. *Asian Social Science*, *9*(17), 72. doi:10.5539/ass.v9n17p72

Singh, G., & Singh, M. (2018). Social Media Ambiance Can Make Strong Message for Consumer Brand Purchase Behavior. *International Journal of Online Marketing*, *8*(4), 38–48. doi:10.4018/IJOM.2018100103

Singh, S., & Sonnenburg, S. (2012). Brand performances in social media. *Journal of Interactive Marketing*, *26*(4), 189–197. doi:10.1016/j.intmar.2012.04.001

Skute, I. (2014). Brand Equity and Co-Creation Potential in the Social Media Environment: An Analysis of Brand Engagement with Community Influencers. In *3rd IBA Bachelor Thesis Conference* (pp. 1–18). Retrieved from https://pdfs.semanticscholar.org/bbca/f99ce0bb43acaabc8bd0da60a200ca79c9ab.pdf

Sterne, J., & Priore, A. (2000). *Email marketing: using email to reach your target audience and build customer relationships*. John Wiley & Sons, Inc.

Trusov, M., Bucklin, R. E., & Pauwels, K. (2009). Effects of word-of-mouth versus traditional marketing: Findings from an internet social networking site. *Journal of Marketing*, *73*(5), 90–102. doi:10.1509/jmkg.73.5.90

Vukasovic, T. (2013). Building a successful brand by using social networking media. *Journal of Media and Communication Studies*, *5*(6), 56.

Zikeeva, M. (2017). *The Study Of Digital Marketing Solutions Effect On Customer-Based Brand Equity In Cosmetic Industry In Russia*. Retrieved from https://dspace.spbu.ru/bitstream/11701/9542/1/Zikeeva_MasterThesis.pdf

## KEY TERMS AND DEFINITIONS

**Affiliate Marketing:** A kind of referral process of earning a commission by promoting other organizations brands or products by the third party/person who initially liked the brand.

**Brand Equity:** Brand equity is made of a set of assets and liabilities linked to a brand, its name, and symbol that add something to the value provided by it. The assets or liabilities a brand include; brand recognition, perceived quality, brand associations, brand loyalty, and some other unique intangible assets such as trademarks, patents, formula and customer relationships, etc.

**Content Marketing:** A philosophy of attracting prospects and converting those prospects into consumers by sharing and creating non-paid content.

**Customer-Based Brand Equity Model (CBBE):** A model to measure brand's strength and brand equity from customer's point of view, and it includes six building blocks (brand Salience, Image, performance, feeling, judgment, and brand resonance) arranged in four stages (brand identity, brand image, brand response, and brand resonance).

**Digital Marketing Tools and Techniques:** Digital marketing tools and techniques (DMTT) are a range of ICT technology-related methods, tools, procedures, etc., which can be used to place and promote a product or a brand to the target audiences. Such tools can include Search engine optimization, Affiliated marketing, viral marketing, content marketing, social media platforms, email marketing, PR tools, etc.

**Influencer Marketing:** Is a process of using key brand advocates to drive a brand message to the larger market in an organic way, the brand advocates are the people with large social followings who have sway over your target audience.

**Pay Per Click (PPC):** Is a process that let marketers bid for sponsored or paid place in the web place and this let's search engine bring the relevant web page in front of the customers.

**Search Engine Optimization (SEO):** Is a process of content creations, in such a way that it becomes faster and easier for a search engine (such as Google, Yahoo, etc.) to search and find the relevant content about a brand, product, idea or information.

**Social Media:** Include a set of connectivity-enabled applications and platforms that facilitate interaction and the publication, exchange, and co-creation of information among an organization and their connected users, and social media include social networks, weblogs, social blogs, wikis, podcasts, pictures, video, rating, and social bookmarking.

**Social Media Marketing:** Social media marketing is the process of generating viral communication, that uses social media channels to create, communicate, deliver, and exchanging of information, and value.

# Chapter 17
# Digital Trends in Education Operations and Marketing

**Trevor Gerhardt**
https://orcid.org/0000-0002-4478-4594
*GSM London, UK*

## ABSTRACT

*This chapter explores education as a business. It considers the various functional factors of education within a knowledge economy and the importance, in order to maintain competitive advantage, of knowledge management. It also considers more specifically technological innovation within this sector and the implications to marketing. Within the management of knowledge, the chapter analyses the higher education institutions producing knowledge, the staff who deliver this knowledge, and the students who purchase and engage in this knowledge. The chapter therefore also explores student enrolment, retention and outcomes, staff development, and product innovation.*

## INTRODUCTION

Education has changed (Gerhardt, 2015). Some of the factors responsible for these changes are "the internationalisation, expansion, and massification of HE [Higher Education], and concomitant heterogeneity of students' profiles at all levels of study" (Santos et al, 2016, p.58). One result is that HE has now become demand-driven (O'Donnell, 2018), and increased collaboration with business may result in better graduate outcomes i.e. employability. This chapter will consider the functional areas of education as a business and the digital trends that accompany changes within the sector.

### The Knowledge Economy

Education was seen as formation by the introduction to the forms of the real in the great symbols, narratives, rituals, doctrines, and theories of a great tradition (Tracy, 2002). In the 19th century, Newman considered sound intellectual formation an end in itself. In other words, education is not a product to be sold or consumed. He saw such intellectual formation as needing no other utility to make it a good worth

DOI: 10.4018/978-1-7998-0131-3.ch017

pursuing. Intellectual formation only becomes itself – only becomes formation rather than deformation, and only becomes truly intellectual – to the extent that it leads towards that end (Higton, 2012). This *paideia*, an ideal of the shaping of the whole person, argues Collini (2012, pp.47, 51), besides not actually being true, is no longer prevalent in modern Universities, which are more concerned with their contribution to the economy (Heap, 2012). In other words, education has now become a recognised product, sold by universities and consumed by students and universities are agents of knowledge exchange and development (Crawford-Lee and Moorwood, 2019). The significant trends that have created this shift include the change from an industrial economy to an economy influenced by technology and innovation. The consequential result of this shift is an emphasis upon employability within these new labour markets (Benda et al, 2019) and the internalization of education as a product (Cheong et al, 2018). This raises challenges for Higher Educational Institutions (HEIs) to keep abreast with these sector developments, such as incorporating smart systems fuelled by research methodologies, data, and technology learning methods (Nair and Munusami, 2019). The technological innovations have caused labour demand shifts from low-skilled labour to high-skilled labour i.e. an impact upon employability expectations (Benda et al, 2019). Knowledge, produced by HEIs, and therefore the management (knowledge management) of this intellectual capital has become pivotal functions in HEIs (Nair and Munusami, 2019). The reality of social learning in a digital age and the tensions these create will be explored (Crawford-Lee and Moorwood, 2019).

These tensions are important, because the introduction of, for example, digital trends within a changing expectation and value of what education is, allows insight into knowledge management and how to maximise educational products and services within the knowledge economy. Furthermore, changes in the demands of the volatile labour market means HEIs have to respond to these market forces. Understanding these forces requires a conceptual understanding of human capital theory, signalling theory and job competition theory (Brenda et al, 2019). Broader narratives surrounding neoliberalism and the increasing competitive nature of academia also need to be considered in terms of the impact these narratives have on decision-making at both system and institutional levels (Suggs and Jevons, 2018).

The dichotomy between education in its own right and education as a vehicle to supply employees for the economy is captured in the city metaphor of Athens versus Jerusalem - the rational pursuit of learning versus learning for profit. Or it can be captured in the tension between the academy and praxis – knowledge versus the practical value of that knowledge to the economy. Or it can be captured in the metaphor of monastery or marketplace – is it about forming citizens or providing for the economy (Haldane, 1994). Or it can be captured in what Pirsig (1974) called the real University and the other university – the real University being a state of mind, the continuing body of reason itself, whereas the other university is the physical branch of the state, a legal corporation, receiving money and responding to legislative pressures in the process (Gerhardt, 2015). This other university is echoed in the Browne report when it declared, 'higher education must serve the economy' (Heap, 2012, p.16), in contradiction to the aspirations that the university should go beyond any form of economic return (Collini, 2012). Higton (2012) suggests that the university is about employability but also about the forming of citizens. These views may, however, be informed by stable economical markets. Benda et al (2019) confirm that during economic downturns (such as in and after 2008), the likelihood of the more educated displacing the less educated increases and places yet again an increased emphasis on increasing trends that education must respond to market forces and active labour market policies. HEIs are now viewed as key to the economic, cultural and social development of countries (Nair and Munusami, 2019).

Collini (2012, p.19) suggests, that the university has three goals: to produce future employees, through research to contribute to narrow fields of development such as medicine and to preserve, cultivate and transmit cultural traditions, the latter goal linking to the idea of intelligent citizenship. However, Nair and Munusami (2019) argue that HEIs create knowledge for the knowledge economy through functions such as research, the dissemination of that knowledge through teaching and learning, research and development, communication and the dissemination of science and as such create jobs. In other words, knowledge creation, dissemination, and transfer. Knowledge gaps identified, therefore, provide HEIs a competitive advantage in the knowledge economy.

The objectives of the chapter are to explore the various factors that make education a competitive market and sector by exploring the various variables involved. Targeted marketing can then be applied to the segmentation.

## BACKGROUND

### Higher Education as Producer of Knowledge Product

In this knowledge economy, universities are facing the need to validate the previous experience and education of students and offer different and more competitive options of getting a higher education, a competition previously common only to businesses (Saginova and Belyansky, 2008). "Active labour market policies try to reduce unemployment by improving the quality of the supply side through upskilling and by reducing hiring risks associated with disadvantaged social groups on the demand side" (Benda et al, 2019, p.277). As such, knowledge management (KM), recognised as one of the determining factors for innovation and competitive advantage, plays a dynamic role in HEIs (Nair and Munusami, 2019). KM involves effective planning, organising, monitoring and coordinating of HEIs intellectual capital. New occupations and the internationalisation of education has brought about a thriving private HEI sector such as a 118 percent increase in Malaysia between 1995 and 1999, especially where public HEI provision and standards have fallen (Cheong et al, 2018, p.88). Growth of transnational education is directly related to this expansion. The process of KM in HEIs generates value from these intellectual and knowledge-based assets or products (Nair and Munusami, 2019). Another example considering Australia, reveals that although universities within Australia are rated highly in the global university rankings, scholarship of marketing education and publication of this knowledge in marketing journals lack high ranking (Snuggs and Jevons, 2018).

In the UK, recognising the Fourth Industrial Revolution (referring to digital innovation), a new apprenticeship agenda, incorporating vocational and academic programmes, started in 2017 (Crawford-Lee and Moorwood, 2019). Productivity in the UK forms a key part of government policy and employers now demand both technical and professional qualifications (Hughes and Saieva, 2019). These degree apprenticeships helped attract new talent, addressed stereotyping, encouraged inclusion and widening participation, reduced student debt and offered a significant new way for HEIs to engage with employers (Crawford-Lee and Moorwood, 2019).

## The Business Operations of Higher Education in the Knowledge Economy

The productivity of universities is measured through benchmarks, rankings, and audits (Suggs and Jevons, 2018). Knowledge management is therefore pivotal. KM, according to Nair and Munusami (2019), includes a set of tools and practices developed and implemented to gather, store, share, protect and use, through projects and training these knowledge assets. Broadly, these include the knowledge products such as research, innovation and teaching and learning technologies, student engagement including enrolment, retention and employability and staff delivering these services such as the use of innovative teaching practices and their contribution to scholarship. Mohammed et al (2019) add that talent management and development is a critical resource of differentiation and sustainable competitive advantage.

Increased research reveals that digital trends in education come with challenges. Gerhardt and Mackenzie-Philps (2018) in their research of e-efficacy among mature adults in education indicate that not everyone is in favour to embrace technology. They found that VLE use was poor and the use of social media was plagued with fear. Fleming et al. (2017, p.78) highlighted that significant negative relationships were found between age and internet self-efficacy; however, they found that these perceptions are changed depending on the ease of use of new technology and the availability of technological support, i.e. emotional factors related to risk and failure. Higher Educational Institutions face challenges regarding the cost of the product, the cost of services such as Wi-Fi or internet connection and products and services related to the technology. In addition, there are cost and time challenges to train staff in the use of these technologies, in their use but also in the service offered to users.

## Recruitment for the Knowledge Economy: Providers and Consumers

Knowledge as intellectual capital, in the knowledge economy is about those who deliver (staff), the product (programmes) and those who purchase the product overall as consumers (students). KM therefore as a systematic management of the HEIs knowledge assets for the purpose of creating value and competitive advantage includes objectives at operational, tactical and strategic levels (Niar and Munusani, 2019). Enrolment on online courses and programmes far exceeds campus-based enrolments but retention remains a challenge (Palloff and Pratt, 2013). Increased HE competitiveness is associated with the strategic importance of talent management as it assists in increasing rankings and profits in the talent economy dependent upon knowledge, networks, and information (Mohammed et al, 2019). This includes increasing in skills in the use of technological innovation.

In the workplace, Clements (2013) reports that just 26% of UK employees use social media for work, compared with 76% who use it for personal purposes and almost 61% who use a mobile digital device for work. Mobile Technology and their use in the classroom are now being posited as the next pedagogical innovation within the lecture room commonly referred to as M-learning. Students no longer rely on the knowledge of the lecturer and oral traditions of knowledge transfer. In contrast, students expect more engaged, action-orientated learning and they are more empowered as knowledge searchers and finders. Google Scholar, Virtual Learning Environments, Open Access Journals and the use of Talis (online books) within library services have all empowered the learner with access to knowledge not reliant on the lecturer as the holder and transmitter of that knowledge. New technologies have created powerful, global conversations. Through the internet, people are discovering and inventing news ways to share relevant knowledge with blinding speed according to Levine et al. (1999). ICT systems that maximise information but reduce overload are educational marketing 'hot-cakes'. As such transformations in education can be product innovations, new technologies, and new markets, particularly within Higher Educational Institutions (HEIs) (Saginova and Belyansky, 2008). "Global economic, technological and pedagogical currents are interweaving to produce paradigmatic changes that challenge many of the traditional practices and environments of HEIs" (Pates and Sumner, 2016, p. 159).

For example, Donelan (2016), in her research, was interested in how social media was being used to take advantage of now online accessible professional networks in order to gain social capital. She identified four categories of users based on their usage intensity, namely, lurkers, personal, active and habitual. Understanding these consumer usage descriptions allows the market to target the appropriate products and services to the appropriate users and enable a transition among them if they are only lurkers and personal consumers onto more active and habitual users and thereby securing a recurring consumptive market.

## ICT In Educational Operations

As ICT becomes increasingly mainstream, even Higher Educational Institutions (HEIs) will want to harness digital opportunities and so require an "e-readiness" audit, such as the research by Chipembele and Bwalya (2016) indicates. They defined e-readiness as the rubrics between people, processes and technology. These are important factors in marketing educational ICT products and services. The impact of ICT cannot be avoided. "Using ICT is indispensable in contemporary societies" (Bencivenga, 2017, p. 11) and this includes the educational sector. HE educators, therefore, too are exploiting ICT platforms to better communicate with their students and enhance their learning, although some HEIs remain within a traditional lecture-based model (Baytiyeh, 2017). You could suggest as an institution they remain lurkers.

Many researchers have investigated this emerging/emergent digital culture and how it has created for example generational differences. Cocquyt et al. (2017) referring to digitally illiterate adults within this ICT revolution has coined the term "non-natives". Similarly, Bencivenga (2017) has used the terms "non-digital natives" or "analog natives" to describe this ICT generational divide. He used this term to refer to people born before 1960. In addition, he referred to "digital immigrants" as people born between 1960s-1970s who grew up surrounded by analog technology (e.g. televisions) but who are now used to technological innovations. My opening account of my experience describes a time after this category but before the next. This next category, his final categorisation is that of "digital natives", describing those born post-1980. They are the first generations to grow up with digital technology. In a recent study by Panteli and Marder (2017, pp. 295-296) on how different generations interact with Social Networking Sites (SNSs) such as Facebook, they found that "normality is enacted differently by different age groups". Middle-aged samples used SNS less self-consciously, mainly among friends and family. Fleming et al. (2017, p. 78) highlighted that significant negative relationships were found between age and internet self-efficacy; however, they found that these perceptions are changed depending on the ease of use of new technology and the availability of technological support, i.e. emotional factors related to risk and failure. Cathro et al. (2017) concurred with the need to provide students with support for different ICT tools. It is these factors that have led the market to target certain generations, with certain products and services and other generations with different products and services.

Besides generational differences in terms of how digital trends are adopted and used by consumers there are also differences among various professions. Research conducted by Gerhardt and Mackenzie (2018) among a specific cohort of Church of England priests to investigate their e-efficacy revealed that during their Higher Educational studies many did not engage with the Virtual Learning Environment and other educational digital trends. Similar research among qualified Church of England priests revealed that many avoided SNSs due to concerns about the information or ethical breaches which would result in unwelcome press coverage. The context within with education occurs is vital to understand how digital trends impact in such a marketplace.

Flipped models of teaching also capitalise on ICT use by placing information transfer material online outside the classroom in order to allow assimilation of information activity to take place within the class (Baytiyeh, 2017). "Non natives" ("analog natives") experience a higher increase in social inclusion and social capital, aspects of self-efficacy according to Cocquyt et al. (2017) which means flip classroom pedagogy enables the best of both worlds. The interaction with others (peer learning), identified as crucial for the formation of online communities is a vital component of WIL and can either be initiated through online forums or social networking tools, as well as through the directed and organised supervision of students by respective WIL mentors. Learning communities allow for new learning formats, so that the material becomes internalised, according to Porterfield and Isaac-Savage (2013), allowing the student to have a relationship with it and for the material to become a part of the student's independent developmental achievement and shared communal experience. However, creating online communities through the use and interaction of digital media is challenging. At GSM London students have mostly relied on WhatsApp groups but some have also used Slack and Trello in order to enhance communication, coordinate tasks and by default build an online community. Intentional online communities need to generate and appropriate a shared repertoire of ideas, commitments, and memories in relation to digital technologies. Examples of the benefit of online communities, highlighted by Cottrell and Morris (2012), include making a connection with students on your course, students on similar courses in other universities, study support groups, academic staff teaching the course, other academics and other professionals. The changing culture of social media does represent new challenges, where for example "non-digital natives" need to be taught "digital literacy" to ensure they behave in what employers would consider an appropriate way online. Petra et al. (2016) argued that programmes that encourage autonomous learning prepare students for a complex and challenging world and this is possible through the use of autonomous web-based learning which also supports collaborative learning.

## SOLUTIONS AND RECOMMENDATIONS

### Operations and Delivery of Education

The marketing of HE as a separate discipline emerged in the United States of America (USA) in the mid-80s, adapting the traditional marketing of promotion by segmenting the market, implementing market research and positioning the university, the strategic dimension of marketing and relationship marketing (Hall and Witek, 2016). Social media and information technology are of particular importance among university inbound marketing tools.

A study in the USA by Steelcase Education (n.d.) among 10 schools and 6 colleges about the impact of technology-empowered learning revealed that technology is significantly changing the relationship between student and teacher. The use of such technology is increasing within education maximising according to Steelcase (n.d) personalised, self-directed blended learning approaches. Palloff and Pratt (2013, p.157) provides a number of principles to ensure success with potential virtual students:

*Teach students how to learn online; provide students with an online orientation specially to ensure that what is on offer is inclusive and accessible by all, variate teaching styles to incorporate different learning styles and ensure a good balance between action and reflection; foster self-directed learning through collaboration; pay attention to changes in participation and address these promptly; and stay present*

The benefits can be significant according to Steelcase (n.d.) which found teachers spent less time lecturing and more time working with groups and individuals. From their research, they add six insights about working with technology-driven learning methods:

*Person-to-person connections remain essential; technology is supporting richer face-to-face interaction and deeper cognitive learning; requires flexibility and activity-based spaced planning; spatial boundaries decrease/loosen; spaces must be able to capture and stream information, and high-tech and low-tech will coexist*

As such, Palloff and Pratt (2013, p.185) provide further tips for online classroom dynamics:

*The instructor is a facilitator and so there is an expectation that participants interact; students will move through different phases of activity and so facilitation is key; assume good intent by students; teach online etiquette including you waiting 24 hours before responding to what you may perceive as a personal attack; facilitate control and emergence of activity; expect conflict; don't mistake confusion for conflict; support and help; and be careful about off-line/sidebar communication as it creates dependency on you*

Virtual learning environments (VLEs) or learning management systems are popular among students as they coordinate many different aspects of the course and can generally be used in flexible ways, when and where students and staff may choose (Cottrell and Morris, 2012). A VLE, used well, can facilitate communication, resources, self-testing, teaching material and assessment portals. As mediating tools they can also support inter-action and intra-action, collaboration and training (Nguyen, 2017).

Popular VLE choices on the market are Moodle and Blackboard. These services then have further added applications, for a cost, that can further enhance learning and the student experience. These could include marking portal applications and other digital teaching resources. TurnItIn, a plagiarism tool used by most Universities, has just recently started trialling and producing an addition to their service which is an application that can detect contract cheating. These ICT tools are standard expenses on most HEI budgets. Examples of simulations would include CESIM, The Business Strategy Game, Corporation, Praxis-MMT, and Capstone. Some simulations are free for basic use with costs added for more enhanced functions such as ArcGIS and the Financial Times Portfolio.

MOOC and Future Learn are examples of online courses and open knowledge gateways inviting multitudes to engage with knowledge (Daellenbach, 2018). Many of these courses are free but certification as proof of completion is charged. Due to the importance of WIL students being more self-directed learners and therefore needing to self-organise their learning, they are most likely to rely more on technology and the flexible access to information courses like this provides (Helyer, 2015). A study among students in Slovenia regarding e-learning found that the most significant factor was the year of study, with those in their later years being more pervasive and expressing self-efficacy regarding ICT use (Aristovnik et al., 2017). Research like this provides key data for strategic marketing of these products and services. Open-based learning (OBL) such as this in education has yielded substantial benefits for adult learners providing flexibility, accessibility and affordable and improved pedagogy (Cocquyt et al., 2017). OBL helps students to study more inter-actively allowing students to learn from each other and from guidance by the teacher in offline and online learning (Nguyen, 2017). The Apple IObserve as a product is a good example. Students can be recorded using defined learning outcomes being indicated on a time-line within the recording. Every time they fulfil them, the tutor taps the screen to indicate in real time recording where the learning outcome was fulfilled. The student can then review the footage and visually assess their capability in doing the task. A tool such as this is valuable for example for sports students, drama and speaking assignments. Time flexibility and innovation in delivery modes, especially ICT modes are valued among students (Chernikova and Varonis, 2016).

The use of SNSs can further enhance learning, collaboration, and engagement and can include forums, weblogs, social networks, video, images and podcasts (Helyer, 2015). The development of Augmented Reality is impacting upon these tools and teaching resources. There are numerous YouTubers designing AR PowerPoints and other creative learning tools for use in education and training. A few renowned universities have started using guest speakers in the form of Holograms. I have not seen it yet, but it won't be long for Einstein to appear in such a form, lecturing students on quantum physics. As it has already been discussed, technology does allow more flexibility in learning, enabling personalisation, the integration of theory and practice, motivated learning, monitored learning and it does save time and money (Pullen and Varley-Winter, n.d.).

Researching future educational trends, Lopez-Catalan and Banuls (2017) discovered that mobile learning was the number one trend with greater diffusion and a better cost-impact ratio. However, they raised serious concerns about ICT literacy. "Awareness of the importance of ICT knowledge", according to Bencivenga (2017, p. 11), "is one aspect of the category of 'ICT pervasiveness' ". He argued that there is a reciprocal influence in that increased awareness of ICT pervasiveness encourages a higher desire to be ICT competent and being more ICT competent drives greater ICT pervasiveness. In their research of OBL, Cocquyt et al. (2017) argued that older learners invest more time online, resonating with Bencivenga's concept of ICT pervasiveness. However, they did find that there was a distinctive difference between online and blended learners.

The new, fast and changing digital age are not just about generational challenges but also about the modern workplaces evolving in order to remain competitive (Fleming et al., 2017) such as what we will discuss in this chapter amongst Higher Educational Institutions. Some universities are now using hologram lecturers to present lessons. The introduction of technology such as simulations with the combination of different pedagogical approaches such as work-based learning (WBL) has made education big business. Digital trends are here to stay and are set to increase and continue to change the educational landscape.

By 1999, according to internet livestats.com, there were just over 14 million people globally with an internet connection. By 2016, this figure had risen to a staggering 3.279 billion. This technological revolution, as argued by Waddington (2015) means we have seen the biggest upheaval in organisational communication in the past 20 years since the dawn of civilisation itself. To illustrate just how things have changed, measured in 2015, the impact of social media meant that social media platforms such as Facebook had 1.55 billion monthly active users (Statista, 2015a, b), the microblogging service Twitter had 307 million monthly active users (Statista, 2015a, b) and LinkedIn.com boasted over three million members (LinkedIn.com, 2016). The result is that "Information and communications technologies have transformed professional and workplace activity", affecting "how people communicate, collaborate, and find and share information" (Donelan, 2016, p. 708). It also means that these developments provide profitable marketing opportunities such as advertising within social media platforms or educational products. Educational technological developments have also contributed to changes in society because these technological developments have created profound social change and economic opportunity (Lopez-Catalan and Banuls, 2017).

## Virtual Reality and Augmented Reality

Morpus (2018) in his article about '5 Experiential Learning Augmented Reality (AR) Apps for Education' argues that experiential learning (learning by doing) as what is found in Augmented reality has a 75% retention rate among students. "Augmented reality is a new technology that projects digital objects onto a real-world surface (like a hologram)" (Morpus, 2018). He continues to describe the top five AR Apps within education: Augment Education which is free; Aug That! which is $5 per student per year; Sky Map (a specialized app for classrooms learning about the solar system and astronomy) which is free; Human Anatomy Atlas which is $24.99 and Learning Alive which is priced as individual programs at $995/each, while the bundled suite goes for $1,495. Technology has significantly changed education and has opened up a new exciting market. New product innovation and IT support continue to grow within this new educational trend. As McKean (2018) states, "In the same way that machines changed the lives of our ancestors in the 19th century, so technology is transforming our world in the 21st century. Here, we imagine a day in the life of a further education principal in a few years' time".

## Digital and Pedagogical Trends: Work-based Learning

Work-based learning (WBL) is learning by working, by the actual undertaking of work activities (Helyer, 2015). In institutions that use WBL and incorporate these pedagogies within their modules, the use of simulations, for example, are common place. One such example is the Greenwich School of Management in London. They use two simulations from CESIM, a Finish based company, for their level 5 projects module called Project Placement Design and Implementation (PPDI). Human Resource student's management a hotel as part of the simulation called CESIM OnService and Business Management students engage in weekly project management tasks in their simulation called CESIM Project Management. Work published back in 2006 by Moratis et al. already mentions the widespread use of managerial decision-making simulations within firms, universities and business schools. Their uses in teaching-learning processes have shown encouraging results such as absorption, implementation of knowledge, motivation, and performance (Arias-Aranda and Bustinza-Sanchez, 2009). The advancement of technology such as Augmented Reality and Virtual Reality will drive the re-development of these simulations in new undiscovered ways in the future, if not already now.

Helyer (2015) confirms the increased use of ICT in universities and particularly within WBL programmes, with some courses being offered totally online. She encourages WBL students to hone their digital skills in order to take maximum advantage of the opportunities, especially the opportunity to progress in their studies from wherever they may be which is described as an online advantage. The active and experiential learning experienced by using such technology enables students to learn from a simulated work experience, as if it were real. As such, using these kinds of methods and pedagogies, congruent with digital technologies, allows WBL to question the more traditional notion that knowledge is held and transferred by the privileged few through formal situations in pre-determined ways (Helyer, 2016). WBL, therefore, is congruent with the new technology age where information is available to all and can be experienced and accessed by all. It is a teaching pedagogy that embraces digital trends rather than trying to defend traditional modes of knowledge.

WBL is best placed to take advantage of such digital changes and innovations. WBL enables accelerated access through transferable skills, initial professional preparation for the "real world", explicit contextual professional development and the use of problem-based learning (Allan, 2015). It is distinctive in contrast to workplace learning (WPL) and work-related learning (WRL) because of its link to academic learning and programmes (Allan, 2015), i.e. Higher Education (HE) which is the focus of the chapter. WPL and WRL are more associated with training activities such as continuing professional development (CPD) courses. They all incorporate experiential forms of learning as a means to develop employability skills through a hands-on experience such as on the job training, internships, work experience, service experience, etc. (Hollister et al., 2017). Research by Allan (2015) confirms that these terms are used extensively interchangeably with conflicting conceptualisations in most literature. Australian institutions of HE use a more encompassing term called work integrated learning (WIL). WIL will often involve online and blended learning (OBL) modes of delivery (Cocquytet al., 2017) and multimodal learning (Maclean and Cahillane, 2015) allowing working adults access to learning anywhere at any time (Porterfield and Isaac-Savage, 2013). Working adults in this context resonates with the previous discussion regarding generations. This again leads to products and services which in the educational landscape can become profitable marketing opportunities. According to Isaac et al. (2017), studies indicate a positive correlation between technology usage and the individual development of skills, knowledge, and productivity, i.e. self-efficacy and e-efficacy. WIL becomes another educational space (Pates and Sumner, 2016) within which profitable marketing strategies can be defined and redefined.

Bencivenga (2017) highlighted that several studies regarding older adults' attitudinal shifts to ICT have already taken place. Some of these studies found ICT an aid to older adults, enhancing creativity and promoting personal growth, impacting upon life-long learning, access to information and rehabilitation. However, Palloff and Pratt (2013) state that adults are twice as likely to drop out of online courses due to their adult life constraints. Marketing tools within this online environment to sustain online communities and increase retention are valuable and solutions will be highly valued products and services. The connection to employability and getting adults ready for a workplace that may require ICT skills as a given are also worth mentioning at this point.

A helpful contribution is made by Dafoulas and Shokri (2016) when they suggested the use of an e-moderation model to understand the impact of ICT and SNS on teaching and learning. They highlighted five stages, namely, access and motivation; online socialisation; information exchange; knowledge construction and development. However, the common challenge remains regarding a lack of digital media literacies amongst staff and students impeding the adoption of such technologies (Pates and Sumner, 2016). I have often heard many of my colleagues in HE, resisting the use of ICT such as webinars, saying, "and of course, due to the nature of our students, they prefer X and Y rather than webinars (or some other ICT)".

## MARKET SEGMENTATION AND STRATEGIES IN AGE OF ICT

### Higher Educational Institutions (HEIs)

The first significant market for digital products and services are the HEIs themselves. They operate very complicated systems in order to process for example student registrations, timetables, and assessments. Companies market their IT systems and service for such purposes such as Power BI (https://powerbi.microsoft.com). Power BI provides services on desktops, mobiles and even report servers. They position their costs from free, to pro, to premium. Marketing of the HEI itself is also pivotal and up to date systems are a part of the 'sell'. HEIs are competitive in a 'glocal' market by considering their programme positioning, their target consumers and the most convenient channel of distribution which implies academic mobility, internationalisation of study programmes, transnational education and other various forms of export of education (Saginova and Belyansky, 2008). This increased market means that many private universities have entered the knowledge economy increasing competition between private universities and that with public universities. Nair and Munusami (2019) confirm that there is an unprecedented growth of private HEIs offering high quality courses. However, they argue that the design of a strategy to facilitate the creation, sharing and transfer of their knowledge as a product will give their HEI the competitive advantage. One such sharing and transfer of knowledge is the rise of micro-credentialing and associated digital badges as recognitions for smaller 'bites' of subjects (Daellenbach, 2018).

### Educational Products and Services

HE providers are made up of public, private and corporate institutions. An example of the latter is Motorola University being one of the earliest and most extensive, established in 1979 with 100 sites in 24 countries (Shaw, 2005). The aims of a corporate university are to nurture new corporate learning needs, ensure corporate intellectual property and comprehensive organisational resourcing (Dealtry, 2002, p.257). As such it is an endeavour that falls with HRM operations. In the UK, Higher Education Institutions (HEIs) not receiving educational funding through the Higher Education Funding Council of England (HEFCE) are known as alternative providers also known as private universities. In 2017, this included 112 such providers (National Audit Office, 2017). HE in the UK has seen many significant changes (Tudor & Mendez, 2014) such as changes in student funding and the increase of private universities (Watson, 2018). Universities educate graduates to meet the UK and global demand for higher-level skills, generate world-class research that transforms lives and drives innovation that supports local and national economic growth (Tudor, et al., 2014). Students have become consumers of education (a consumption experience) according to Arif & Hameed (2013) in a knowledge economy with the HEI as a contributor i.e. HE third stream activity (Muscio et al, 2013), the 'new work order' (Gustafsson & Thang, 2017, p.35). As a provider of 'experienced goods' (skilled graduates), HE has become more customer-centric (driven by service quality) ensuring the excellence of service that meets 'customers' expectations and their required levels of satisfaction (Arif, et al., 2013; Zacharakis, et al., 2016). One of the consequences of these and many other changes is an increase in stress within the sector. Research by Bothwell (2018) revealed longer hours were taking their toll on academics. Christie (2018) concurs stating the system (HE) is a mess. Pells (2018) reports that Anderson, having complained about excessive workloads to the management of, for example, being expected to mark 418 exam papers in a 20-day period, decided to take his own life.

Where there has been a negative impact on the demands of the educational sector on staff who deliver the services, proactive talent management is required as well as marketing interventions. In the example by Friedmann (2018) of the lack of women in the STEM industry, they suggest a social marketing strategy. This will address attitudes, beliefs, and behaviours of individuals and/or organisations and will stimulate sustainable change across targeted audiences compared to other educational interventions. Talent management and development impact upon university rankings, aligned with the talent of high-performing employees, and talented individuals which all contribute significantly to a university's performance by recruiting new students, conducting professional teaching, conducting high-level research and securing research funding (Mohammed et al, 2019).

The growing popularity of entrepreneurial courses, among others, has increased the demand of digital storytelling technology applications. For example, the Greenwich School of Management in London are using Articulate Storyteller to design their online course content. Other important digital learning tools are listed by Sousa et al. (2018) as web-based video (such as YouTube), computerised environments (such as WebQuests), spatial science technology, slow-motion, narrated slow-motion animation, generic modelling language, digital video, simulation, computer-based teaching and webinars. In addition, Sousa and Rocha (2018) list other disruptive technology such as Internet of Things, Cloud Technology, Big Data, Mobile Technologies and Artificial Intelligence and Robotics. They argue that these are sub-divided into internal and external technologies. The former includes analytics, search engine optimization, competitive intelligence and social media monitoring while the latter includes the platforms used to reach customers and deliver content such as websites, ads, emails campaigns, landing pages and apps of all kinds. Palloff and Pratt (2013) remind us that within online learning and technology there is a distinction between synchronous activity (in real time) and asynchronous activity such as using a recorded video or email. Other digital Web 2.0 Technologies would include Blogs, Google Docs, wikis, Podcasts (such as Audacity) and Second Life. Open knowledge gateways would include MOOC, the Khan Academy, EdEx, MITx and Google Analyics (Daellenbach, 2018).

## CONCLUSION AND FUTURE DIRECTIONS

The discussion from operational and marketing perspective have emphasised the extent to which education has become a competitive business and how digital trends have substantially increased within the world and more specifically within education to add to this internationally competitive sector. This prolific increase has created a diverse and lucrative educational marketplace. Within this marketplace, Higher Education provides a pluriform of opportunities. One sector within Higher Education has been considered namely WBL and hybrids forms such as Higher Degree Apprenticeships in the UK. This segment of the market was explored in terms of adult learners' e-efficacy, motivation, and expectations. As such, a number of digital trends and tools were listed and discussed and implicit strategies therefore in their marketing use were derived. HEIs require greater knowledge management strategies and this includes diversifying their products and talent management of their staff in order to increase student enrolment, retention and outcomes such as employability.

It was suggested that two specific markets would be of interest, namely the institution itself and the digital tools used in teaching within these institutions. Both these markets are extensive in their demographics and although a number of products and services have been listed, the marketing value and strategy for each differ dependent on the kind of pedagogies applied within the institution. An awareness of the educational market and the diversity of its consumers are vital to ensure a successful marketing plan for these digital trends.

## REFERENCES

Allan, D. (2015). Conceptualising work learning: Exploring the educational discourse on work-based, work-related, and workplace learning. *E-Journal International*, *5*(1), 1–20.

Arias-Aranda, D., & Bustinza-Sanchez, O. (2009). Entrepreneurial attitude and conflict management through business simulations. *Journal of Industrial Management and Data Systems*, *109*(8), 1101–1117. doi:10.1108/02635570910991328

Arif, S., Iiya, M., & Hameed, A. (2013). Student satisfaction and impact of leadership in private universities. *The TQM Journal*, *25*(4), 399–416. doi:10.1108/17542731311314881

Aristovnik, A., Tomazevic, N., Kerzic, D., & Umek, L. (2017). The impact of demographic factors on selected aspects of e-learning in higher education. *The International Journal of Information and Learning Technology*, *34*(2), 114–121. doi:10.1108/IJILT-09-2016-0045

Baytiyeh, H. (2017). The flipped classroom model: When technology enhances professional skills. *The International Journal of Information and Learning Technology*, *34*(1), 51–62. doi:10.1108/IJILT-07-2016-0025

Bencivenga, R. (2017). The 'digital curious': First steps towards a new typology for mapping adults' relationships with others when using ICT. *European Journal for Research on the Education and Learning of Adults*, *8*(1), 55–76. doi:10.3384/rela.2000-7426.rela9117

Bothwell, E. (2018). *Work-life balance survey 2018: long hours take their toll on academics*. Retrieved from www.timehighereducation.com/features/work-life-balance-survey-2018-long-hours-take-their-toll-academics

Brenda, L., Koster, F., & van der Veen, R. J. (2019). Levelling the playing field? Active labour market policies, educational attainment and unemployment. *The International Journal of Sociology and Social Policy*, *39*(3/4), 276–295. doi:10.1108/IJSSP-08-2018-0138

Cathro, V., O'Kane, P. and Gilbertson, D. (2017). Assessing reflection: understanding skill development through reflective learning journals, *Journal of Education + Training*, *59*(4), 427-442.

Cheong, K., Hiil, C., Leong, Y., Zhang, C., & Zhang, Z. (2018). 'Parents just don't understand' – generational perceptions of education and work. *Journal of Higher Education Evaluation and Development*, *12*(2), 85–98. doi:10.1108/HEED-06-2018-0016

Chernikova, I. A., & Varonis, E. M. (2016). Designing and delivering online curriculum in higher education: Riding the perfect storm. *The International Journal of Information and Learning Technology*, *33*(3), 132–141. doi:10.1108/IJILT-09-2015-0026

Chipembele, M., & Bwalya, K. J. (2016). Assessing e-readiness of the Copperbelt University, Zambia: Case study. *The International Journal of Information and Technology*, *33*(5), 315–332.

Christie, S. (2018). *Don't pity stressed students too much – academics have it worse*. Retrieved from www.timehighereducation.com/blog/dont-pity-stressed-students-too-much-academivs-have-it-worse

Clements, S. (2013). *Social technology, social business?* CIPD survey report. Retrieved from www.cipd.co.uk/Images/social-technology-social-business_2013_tcm18-10323.pdf

Cocquyt, C., Diep, N. A., Zhu, C., De Greef, M., & Vanwing, T. (2017). Examining social inclusion and social capital among adult learners in blended and online learning environments. *European Journal for Research on the Education and Learning of Adults*, *8*(1), 77–101. doi:10.3384/rela.2000-7426.rela9111

Collini, S. (2012). *What Are Universities For?* London: Penguin Books.

Cottrell, S., & Morris, N. (2012). *Study Skills Connected: Using Technology to Support your Studies*. London: Palgrave. doi:10.1007/978-1-137-01944-8

Crawford-Lee, M., & Moorwood, S. (2019). Degree apprenticeships: Delivering quality and social mobility? *Journal of Higher Education, Skills and Work-Based Learning*, *9*(2), 134–140. doi:10.1108/HESWBL-05-2019-123

Daellenbach, K. (2018). On carrot cake and marketing education: A perspective on balancing skills for employability. *Australasian Marketing Journal*, *26*(2), 172–179. doi:10.1016/j.ausmj.2018.04.005

Dafoulas, G., & Shokri, A. (2016). Investigating the educational value of social learning networks: A quantitative analysis. *Journal of Interactive Technology and Smart Education*, *13*(4), 305–322. doi:10.1108/ITSE-09-2016-0034

Dealtry, R. (2002). Managing the corporate university watershed. *Journal of Workplace Learning*, *14*(6), 256–261. doi:10.1108/13665620210441216

Donelan, H. (2016). Social media for professional development and networking opportunities in academia. *Journal of Further and Higher Education*, *40*(5), 706–729. doi:10.1080/0309877X.2015.1014321

Fleming, J., Becker, K., & Newton, C. (2017). Factors for successful e-learning: does age matter? *Journal of Education + Training*, *59*(1), 76-89.

Friedmann, E. (2018). Increasing women's participation in the STEM industry: A first step for developing a social marketing strategy. *Journal of Social Marketing*, *8*(4), 442–460. doi:10.1108/JSOCM-12-2017-0086

Gerhardt, T. (2015). *The link between the training of curates in the Church of England and their future ministry and the nature of that relationship: nationally competent and Deployable?* (Unpublished doctoral thesis). University of Canterbury Christ Church, Canterbury, UK.

Gerhardt, T., & Mackenzie-Philps, L. (2018). The challenges and opportunities of ICT in WIL: A case study among priests exploring the correlation and trajectory between effective WIL and ICT pervasiveness, *Higher Education, Skills and Work-Based Learning*, *8*(4), 408–421. doi:10.1108/HESWBL-07-2017-0045

Gustafsson, J., & Thang, P. (2017). Workplace learning in Higher Education: two examples from a Swedish context. In T. Bowen & M. T. B. Drysdale (Eds.), *Work-Integrated Learning in the 21st Century* (pp. 35–49). Bingley, UK: Emerald. doi:10.1108/S1479-367920170000032002

Haldane, J. (1994). The context of education: monastery or marketplace? In *Philosophy of Education*. London: Continuum.

Hall, H., & Witek, L. (2016). Conditions, Contemporary Importance and Prospects of Higher Education Marketing on the Example of polish Universities. *Procedia Economics and Finance*, *39*, 206–211. doi:10.1016/S2212-5671(16)30314-8

Heap, S. (2012). *What are Universities good for?* Cambridge, UK: Grove Educational Series.

Helyer, R. (2015). *The Work-Based Learning Student Handbook* (2nd ed.). London: Palgrave. doi:10.1007/978-1-137-41384-0

Helyer, R. (Ed.). (2016). *Facilitating Work-Based Learning*. London: Palgrave. doi:10.1007/978-1-137-40325-4

Higton, M. (2012). *A Theology of Higher Education*. Oxford, UK: Oxford University Press. doi:10.1093/acprof:oso/9780199643929.001.0001

Hollister, J.M., Spears, L.I., Mardis, M.A., Lee, J., McClure, C.R., & Liebman, E. (2017). Employers' perspectives on new information technology technicians' employability in North Florida, *Journal of Education + Training*, *59*(9), 929-945.

Hughes, C. J., & Saieva, G. (2019). Degree apprenticeships – an opportunity for all? *Journal of Higher Education. Skills and Work-Based Learning*, *9*(2), 225–236. doi:10.1108/HESWBL-10-2018-0113

Isaac, O., Abdullah, Z., Ramayah, T., & Mutahar, A. M. (2017). Internet usage, user satisfaction, task, technology fit, and performance impact among public sector employees in Yemen. *The International Journal of Information and Learning Technology*, *34*(3), 210–241. doi:10.1108/IJILT-11-2016-0051

Levine, R., Locke, C., Searls, D., & Weinberger, D. (1999). *The Cluetrain Manifesto*. Retrieved from www.cluetrain.com/cluetrain.pdf

LinkedIn.com. (2016). *About LinkedIn*. Retrieved from https://press.linkedin.com/about-linkedin?trk=uno-reg-guest-home-about

Lopez-Catalan, B., & Banuls, V.A. (2017). A Delphi-based approach for detecting key e-learning trends in postgraduate education: the Spanish case. *Journal of Education + Training*, *59*(6), 590-604.

MacLean, P., & Cahillane, M. (2015). The human factor in learning design, research, policy, and practice. *The International Journal of Information and Learning Technology*, *32*(3), 182–196. doi:10.1108/IJILT-12-2014-0029

McKean, P. (2018). *What does the FE college of the future look like?* Retrieved from https://www.jisc.ac.uk/blog/what-does-the-fe-college-of-the-future-look-like-20-nov-2018

Mohammed, A. A., Hafeez-Baig, A., & Gururajan, R. (2019). A qualitative research to explore practices that are utilised for managing talent development in the higher education environment: A case study in six Australian universities. *Journal of Industry-University Collaboration*, *1*(1), 24–37. doi:10.1108/JIUC-02-2019-003

Moratis, L., Hoff, J., & Ruel, B. (2006). A dual challenge facing management education: Situation-based learning and learning about CSR. *Journal of Management Development*, *25*(3/4), 213–231. doi:10.1108/02621710610648150

Morpus, N. (2018). *5 Experiential Learning Augmented Reality Apps for Education*. Retrieved from https://blog.capterra.com/experiential-learning-augmented-reality-apps-for-education/

Muscio, A., Quaglione, D., & Vallanti, G. (2013). Does government funding complement or substitute private research funding to universities? *Journal of Regional Policy*, *42*, 63–75.

Nair, B.V., & Munusami, C. (2019). Knowledge management practices: An exploratory study at the Malaysian higher education institutions, *Journal of Research in Innovative Teaching & Learning*. Retrieved from doi:10.1108/JRIT-01-2019-0008

National Audit Office. (2017). *Follow-up on alternative providers*. London: Department of Education.

Nguyen, V. A. (2017). Towards the implementation of an assessment-centred blended learning framework at the course level: A case study in a Vietnamese national university. *The International Journal of Information and Learning Technology*, *34*(1), 20–30. doi:10.1108/IJILT-08-2016-0031

O'Donnell, R. (2018). *Education must shift to produce 'job-ready' grads*. Retrieved from www.hrdive.com/news/education-must-shift-to-produce-job-ready-grads/525859

Palloff, R. M., & Pratt, K. (2013). *Lessons from the Virtual Classroom* (2nd ed.). San Francisco: Jossey-Bass.

Panteli, N., & Marder, B. (2017). Constructing and enacting normality online across generations: The case of social networking sites. *Journal of Information Technology & People*, *30*(2), 282–300. doi:10.1108/ITP-06-2015-0134

Pates, D., & Sumner, N. (2016). E-learning spaces and the digital university. *The International Journal of Information and Learning Technology*, *33*(3), 159–171. doi:10.1108/IJILT-10-2015-0028

Pells, R. (2018). *Cardiff plans review after suicide of 'overworked' lecturer*. Retrieved from www.timehighereducation.com/news/cardiff-plans-review-after-suicide-overworked-lecturer

Petra, S. F., Jaidin, J. H., Perera, J. Q., & Linn, M. (2016). Supporting students to become autonomous learners: The role of web-based learning. *The International Journal of Information and Learning Technology*, *33*(4), 263–275. doi:10.1108/IJILT-05-2016-0017

Pirsig, R. M. (1974). *Zen and the art of motorcycle maintenance: an inquiry into values*. Toronto: Bantam Books.

Porterfield, M., & Isaac-Savage, E. P. (2013). The formation of online wisdom communities amongst ministerial students: A quantitative case study. *Journal of Adult Theological Education*, *10*(2), 116–131. doi:10.1179/1740714114Z.00000000018

Pullen, C., & Varley-Winter, O. (n.d.). Culture, coaching, and collaboration. *City & Guilds*. Retrieved from www.cityandguilds.com/~/media/Documents/about-us/broadsheetnews/Culture%20coaching%20and%20collaboration%20pdf.ashx

Saginova, O., & Belyansky, V. (2008). Facilitating innovations in higher education in transition economies. *International Journal of Educational Management*, *22*(4), 341–351. doi:10.1108/09513540810875671

Santos, L., Bago, J., Baptista, A. V., Ambrosio, S., Fonseca, H. M. A. C., & Quintas, H. (2016). The academic success of mature students in higher education: A Portuguese case study. *European Journal for Research on the Education and Learning of Adults*, *7*(1), 57–73. doi:10.3384/rela.2000-7426.rela9079

Shaw, S. (2005). The corporate university: Global or local phenomenon? *Journal of European Industrial Training*, *29*(1), 21–39. doi:10.1108/03090590510576190

Snuggs, E., & Jevons, C. (2018). Reconceptualising the scholarship of marketing education – SoME futurescapes. *Australasian Marketing Journal*, *26*(2), 180–186. doi:10.1016/j.ausmj.2018.05.003

Sousa, M. J., & Rocha, A. (2018). Skills for disruptive digital business. *Journal of Business Research*, *94*, 257–263. doi:10.1016/j.jbusres.2017.12.051

Souse, M. J., Carmo, M., Goncalves, A. C., Cruz, R., & Martins, J. M. (2018). Creating knowledge and entrepreneurial capacity for HE students with digital education methodologies: Differences in the perceptions of students and entrepreneurs. *Journal of Business Research*, *94*, 227–240. doi:10.1016/j.jbusres.2018.02.005

Statista. (2015a). *Number of Facebook users*. Retrieved from www.statista.com/statistics/264810/number-of-monthly-active-facebook-users-worldwide/

Statista. (2015b). *Number of monthly active Twitter users*. Retrieved from www.statista.com/statistics/282087/number-of-monthly-active-twitter-users/

Stealcase Education. (n.d.). *Technology Empowered Learning*. Retrieved from https://www.steelcase.com/research/articles/topics/technology/technology-empowered-learning-six-spatial-insights/

Tracy, D. (2002). On Theological Education: A Reflection. In R. L. Peterson & N. M. Rourke (Eds.), *Theological Literacy for the Twenty-First Century* (pp. 13–22). Grand Rapids, MI: Eerdmans.

Tudor, S., & Mendez, R. (2014). Lessons from Covey: Win-win principles for university-employer engagement. *Journal of Higher Education, Skills and Work-Based Learning*, *4*(3), 213–227. doi:10.1108/HESWBL-06-2014-0018

Waddington, S. (2015). *The internet is a conversation*. Retrieved from http://wadds.co.uk/2015/11/04/internet-conversation/

Watson, A. (2018). *Widening Options for Adult Learners*. Retrieved from https://www.openaccessgovernment.org/widening-options-for-adult-learners/54350/

## KEY TERMS AND DEFINITIONS

**Human Capital Theory:** Is how the status of the employability of a person is determined within the labour markets (supply and quality).

**Job Competition Theory:** Is about where in the labour queue people are and why.

**Knowledge Economy:** Is the sector of the economy which derives profits from the production and sharing of knowledge such as what is found among universities.

**Knowledge Management:** Is how strategic choices and planning are made to gather, store, protect and disseminate knowledge as a product.

**Private HEIs:** Are universities that do not receive government funding.

**Signalling Theory:** Is about signs such as qualifications which help potential employees minimise risk in employment.

# Chapter 18
# Innovative Trends in Technology for Marketing of Events

**Julian Joy**
*GSM London, UK*

**Sumesh Singh Dadwal**
*Northumbria University, London, UK*

**Philiph A. Pryce**
*GSM London, UK*

## ABSTRACT

*Technology is playing a pivotal role in shaping the operations and marketing and events industry. The modern event manager has understood that the event success or failure may depend on the technology used or the lack of it. An event is a set of activities with specific purpose goals and needs of the attendees. An event can be defined as an organised occasion, it provides some lived experience and meaning. The technology has the potential to be used at each stage of the consumers' experience of events. The chapter has taken a resource-based view and analysed how technology can be a tool for operations and service innovation and ultimately a strategics for creating core competencies and core capabilities. This chapter explores how technology can be used in the management event, technology in the value delivery network of events, and marketing of events. Various new technologies like block-chain technology, augment relativity, RFID, social media, digital promotional tactics are discussed.*

## INTRODUCTION

In this globalised world, companies can gain competitive advantage and improve their performances by continually improving their products, innovative operations and innovative strategies to reach their target customers(Ungerman, Dedkova, & Gurinova, 2018). The innovations mean creating something new and

DOI: 10.4018/978-1-7998-0131-3.ch018

it can be product innovation, process innovations, organisational innovations, and marketing innovations to attract exiting or new customer segments (Ungerman et al., 2018). Those four innovations could be due to technological or non-technological innovations. The current ICT revolution and digitalisations have further increased the speed of innovations. The use of ICT Technology is playing a pivotal role in shaping the marketing of many industries including events industry. The use of technology in any industry is also known as an industrial revolution or Industry 4.0 is enhancing organizational competencies (Ungerman et al., 2018). With the amount of research and development going on within the sector, new technology is being unearthed almost on a daily basis. The modern event manager has understood that the event success or failure may depend on the technology used or the lack of it. Marketing innovations are based on lateral thinking with the underlying principle of innovativeness, playfulness, boundlessness, and provocativeness(Ungerman et al., 2018)

Most services organisations are developing or using technologies to add further value and dimensions to their services, in particular, the organisation is using social element in their services(Trivedi, Adomako Asamoah, & Doran, 2018). The organisations can achieve suitable competitive advantages by adopting technology in the whole of the value delivery network.

Managers can use technology in operations and in the marketing of events by using the power of Web2.0 and social media platforms. Technology-enabled social elements (letting social connections or friendship, community development around a brand, person, product or service) built has allowed customers or users to create, post content, share information and directly interact with each other via Social media or other platforms(Trivedi et al., 2018). This implies customers (as co-creators) participate, involve and engage in the operations of creating, developing, delivery and consumption of the of services. Such added-value services have a direct and positive impact on customers' purchase intentions, loyalty and e Word of Mouth (Trivedi et al., 2018). The social elements of services are not only useful for customers but also are very important feedback and two communications routes for the organizing, as the organisation can use those feedbacks or customer review to contentiously innovate and enhance overall service designed and service experiences of the customers.

Thus innovation can be inbuilt into the organisation system by making use of social elements into operations of an organisation. The operations of events and marketing of events also require innovative approaches for sustainable marketing and competitive advantages. The new technology trends such as digital platforms, social media, Big data, blockchain augmented reality, and artificial intelligence, etc., are disrupting many industries and the event industry is not an exception. This chapter covers some of the technology-based innovations in the field of marketing and events and their applications for competitive advantage. Most of these are the trends in the events industry in the last decade or so.

## LITERATURE REVIEW

Due to technological and other innovation and functional excellence, the process of marketing has been evolving to innovative ways of marketing such as personal marketing, ambient marketing, environmental marketing, guerrilla marketing, ambush marketing, buzz marketing, viral marketing, product placement, mobile marketing, event marketing, word of mouth marketing, neuromarketing, eMarketing, behavioural marketing . Augmented reality marketing, Artificial intelligent marketing, Botchat marketing, etc (Ungerman et al., 2018). Thus a marketing innovation is a process of creating and capturing values by meeting customer needs with fundamentally new ideas, products, services, or technologies, etc(Ungerman et al.,

2018)s. The evolution of Industry 4.0 and its application in the Events industry means change in whole value chain of the event industry: a dramatic increase in labour productivity, better interconnection of the production process, development and after-sales service; di-intermediation of distribution channels; New media and effective communication through internet of things (IoT), social media, & Artificial Intelligence (AI); exponential growth of data (big data); Virtual currency (cryptocurrency)& payments; Engagement marketing, buzz marketing & Customer Relations Management (CRM); and overall competitive advantage (Ungerman et al., 2018). The events are combinations of tangible and intangible offerings, and innovative technologies will affect the whole process of event management.

## The Concept of Event and Event Management

The events industry is linked with the tourism industry and in fact, they complement each other. Hospitality is seen as a linking pin for events and travel and tourism. Events include hospitality and so does tourism. Hence the marketing efforts for events may be similar to the marketing activities for tourism.

Many events act as drivers for tourism. Festivals, sports events, business events and various other kinds of event are responsible for a lot of tourism across the globe. On the other hand, more tourism will lead to more events being staged in the destinations as well. Hence effective events management is a key prerequisite for successful tourism. Most of the successful tourist destinations will almost always have good event management.

An event is a set of activities with specific purpose goals and needs of the attendees An event can be defined as an organized occasion such as meeting, music testable, product/brand promotion, convention, conference, exhibition, special event, wedding, social gathering or gala dinner, and so on; and it is made up of several related activities and functions with the purpose of attending the specific needs of the attendees (Bikash, 2013). An event means ‘occurrence with a begin and end that happens at a given place, time and circumstances (Getz 2007, 18), is often transient with a unique blending of durations, seating, management and people (Vassilopoulos 2005, cited in (Bikash, 2013)). The events may be organized for touristic or other purposes such as entertainment, relaxations, competitions, customs & cultural celebration or brand building or the need to raise funds for charity, public/government purpose and so on.

Broadly events can be classified as planned or unplanned events.

The planned events are created with a pre-planned social, cultural, economic, or environmental purpose. ‘The planned events event planning involves the design and implementation of themes, settings, consumables, services, and programs that suggest, facilitate or constrain experiences for participants, guests, spectators, and other stakeholders. Every event experience is personal and unique, arising from the interactions of setting, program, and people’ (Getz, 2012).

Unplanned events are random, spontaneous and unpredictable activities probably set in motion by people (Agitators, publicity agents or social activists). Once it starts, the actions that follow are uncertain (Getz, 2012).

Based on size, form, and contents the various kind of events can be ; Local or community events (music programs, community meeting, fundraising program, BBQ parties,), Major events, Hallmark events (Kumbh Mela in India, Haj Visits, Carnival in Rio or London), Mega-events (2012 London Olympics and Queen’s Diamond Jubilee celebrations), Cultural events (wedding events, commercial music festivals, Art festivals Chinese New Year, Holi Festival, Kumbh Mela, Carnival of Rio de Janeiro, St. Patrick’s Day Festival,) Sports events (Football World cup, Olympics, The Ashes), Business events (product launches, making publicity stunts,) (Bikash, 2013).

## Event Management

Event Management is a process of planning, organising, coordinating, executing various activities at an event with effective use of all the event resources to meet the specific goals and objective of the event (Bikash, 2013). The planning is the pre-event process of identifying the target audiences and the needs of the target audiences, planning, and scheduling for activities and budgets and other resources. Coordination is a during -event process of coordination / linking different actors, agents and supplier organisations who come together to successfully complete an event. Executing and controlling involves implementing the events and monitoring their progress. The evaluation is the post-event process of comparing the target aims with an actually achieved goal. The innovation in technology can lead to a modification in the process of events playing and management by application of ICT, AI, big data and driverless vehicles, digital audio-visual systems and automated safety & security systems. Another way an event can be considered as a 'project' or temporary cluster of industries (Bénédicte, Rani, & Longhi, 2011). Thus, models and theories of project management or Porter's model of industrial clusters, etc can be used as a basis of effective event management. Most of the project management theories are equally valid for events management. Although events and projects have a few differences, they are largely similar. Both project and events have temporary in nature & life i.e. Both have short life from start to finish, and most people employed at events or projects are of temporary nature for a limited or Adhoc time. This adhocracy brings issues of managing uniform standards of quality, quantity, and costs, etc. The issues of events and tourism management can be agreed by taking a combinations project management, clustered development and system approaches to the management. Tourism and events production process includes a range of activities, products, and services offered by coordinated suppliers and agents (Bénédicte, Rani, & Longhi, 2011). The coordination of such a diverse set of suppliers, operations, processes, activities, and products is a challenge. Hence, the use of technology is a viable option and strategy for tourism and event planners. The emerging technologies like Cloud technology, Cognatic & Artificial intelligence, Blockchain, artificial & Virtual reality, Live apps, etc. has huge potential to change the events and tourism industry. Hence in the event or project management, it is important to manage the expectations of the stakeholders If the stakeholder expectations are set to be too high, the event outcome will not satisfy them and hence can lead to disputes and disagreements. The three cornerstones of the stakeholder expectations model are Feasibility, Viability, and desirability. The use of technology and ICT can be very useful to integrate different components of a project sniff then link those components with stakeholders' expectations. Tourism and events include many diverse activities dedicated to the satisfaction of tourists' needs and the process borrowed from multiple actors, organizations and activities (Bénédicte, Rani, & Longhi, 2011).

As the tourism industry uses dynamic innovation, and so can be seen as a 'sectoral system of innovation and production (SSIP) Citing Malherbe, 2001, Bénédicte, Rani, & Longhi, 2011) argue'. The researcher s(ibid.) further said that an SSIP is 'a set of new and established products for specific uses and the set of agents carrying out market and non-market interactions for the creation, production, and sale of those products. The agents have varying learning processes, competencies, organizational structure, beliefs, objectives, and behaviours. The agents or players or organisations interact through subsystems & processes of communication, exchange, cooperation, competition and command, and their interactions are shaped by systems and institution's rules and regulations (Getz, 2012).

## Events and Services Innovations

As the tourism and Event industry is services which consist of processes, & subsystems with many diverse activities/ The diverse activities are scattered in geography, space, time and in nature, thus to manage the events, it needs a combined effort of actors, stakeholders, and resources, who themselves are a part of the physical, organizational, as well as cognitive senses (Bénédicte, Rani, & Longhi, 2011). Thus, the process of events and tourism services delivery requires a lot of knowledge and resources movement and resource flow. The knowledge is quite dispersed in various suppliers or cluster of industry, who come together to manage an event. The use of innovations and technology could bring rescue to such challenges. Furthered to temporary and ad-hoc nature of events, the individual suppliers have lesser incentive to invest inhouse for innovation on products and services. So, innovation in such cases can fit with the idea of 'open innovation'. Open services innovations can enhance service quality and standard (Yang, Li, & Su, 2018). Services innovation means changing, improving and modifying characteristics, features, process, activities, offerings and business models of services, so as to create values for customers, owners, employees, suppliers and another stakeholder (Yang et al., 2018). Service innovation implies developing a new service or renewal, modification of existing services. Events and tourism products/services are quite a heterogeneous mix of many other products and services (transport, accommodation, music, leisure and entertainment, food, and so on), and also has heterogeneous agents, actors, and suppliers, thus, the use of technology and ICT is a fundamental solution for better services. (Bénédicte, Rani, & Longhi, 2011).The use of ICT will lead to effective services marketing. The service innovations require innovation management process: innovation strategy, innovation process, integration tools & systems, project learning, effective communications, customer experience management, customer information and brand differentiation (Yang et al., 2018).

Service innovation requires developing employees with innovative and creative thoughts. Adaptive theory postulates that service innovation is a predictable or definite process that can be taught to others by following some definite steps (Yang et al., 2018) The services can be innovated either using project-based innovation (end product focus) approach or process-based innovation (continuums s of activities, events, and encounter innovations) approach by using ICT tools, for integrations, tracing and internal communications and control (Yang et al., 2018). An event is a purposely designed set of activities and in its essence it provides some 'lived experience & meaning' individually and collectively to the attendees, thus an event and event management should be seen from the angle of multidimensional experiences (personal, existential and socio-culture, etc) to the consumers and actors (Vassilios & Nikolaos, N.D.). Hence innovations of events services should be also seen from a multidivisional point of view. The whole event experience consists of three-stage; anticipation before the event, involvement/engagement during the event and back to the normal life post the event ends. Hence managing experiences and engagements of the event attendees are very important in event service quality. The technology has great potential for using at each stage of the consumers' experiences of events. Csikszentmihalyi's (1975,1990) Theory of flow indicates that people want to enjoy 'a state of flow' in an event, it means an event experience including feelings of arousal and flow, deeper involvement and immersion in the activity and ultimately providing a sense of transformation or accomplishment to the event attendees (Vassilios & Nikolaos, N.D.).The performances at the events are seen as 'extraction of shared meanings' of symbols, rituals and social drama. The ICT, social media networks, social online communities can aid in extracting a shared meaning to an event. Previous research has shown that a guide-based service innovation practice can lead to increased service innovation performance(Yang et al., 2018). However, the change is how to engage internal and external stakeholders in the process of innovation, technology development, and technology adoption?

The innovations in travel and events service industry mostly originate externally from the partners, suppliers or agents and not necessarily in-house Research & Development (Bénédicte, Rani, & Longhi, 2011). For example, a global distribution system (GDS) can be shared by one organisation with other players of the travel and event industry for direct access to airlines, flights, hotel or any other locations or services. Similarly, mobile technologies and mobile apps offer many services ranging from locations, maps, and RFI, etc. However, in order to utilise the full potential of service innovation, it is important for managers and other stakeholders to understand the concept of innovations and adoptions of technology.

## Adoption of Innovation and Technology

An innovation as; an idea, practice or object that is perceived as new by an individual or another unit of adoption' (Rogers, 1995, p. 11). An innovation or new combinations of innovation mean, introduction or production of a new product or a new quality of a product,, a new production method or a new sales market etc (Moldaschl, 2010), other terms such 'as change, development and/or evolution, mutation, creation, growth (as a mode of development), modernization, reform, revolution, progress, discovery, imitation and invention' etc are also used as synonymous of innovation (Moldaschl, 2010).

Technology includes a *physical component* (products, tooling, equipment, blueprints, techniques, and Processes) and informational component (know-how in management, marketing, production, quality control, reliability, skilled labour, and functional areas)(Dilogini & Shivany, 2016). The customer can be better engaged via the use of technology in marketing. However, before this is important to understand the factors that drive the adoption of technology.

The diffusion, adoption, and adaptation of technologies in events industry require interactions and sharing among various agents, actors, players, and organisations of the travel and event industry (Bénédicte, Rani, & Longhi, 2011). Marketing communications are the' means by which organisations attempt to inform, persuade, and remind consumers products and brands that sell'(Kotler, 2006). Various theories have attempted to explain the use and adoption of technologies. For example theory of reasoned action (TRA) (Fishbein and Ajzen, 1975), the theory of planned behaviour (TPB) (Ajzen, 1985), technology acceptance model (TAM) (Davis 1989) and Unified TAM Venkatesh 2003)(are most important researches related to the]adoption of technologies. TRA and TPB and TAM postulate that individual decides based on perceived conciseness of their decision, and the decision is influenced by user's attitude towards innovation, social norms perceived control and utility and perceived ease of use of the innovation or new technology. The social influence theory (French and Raven 1959), postulates that individuals are influenced to make decisions based on the types of relationships they have with others and this can lead to adoption of innovations due to principles of mutual commitment consistency, reciprocation, instant influence, social proof, liking, authority, and scarcity, etc(Erin Cowell, Kelly Feeney, Elizabeth Feldman, Todd Glover, et al., 2005). The Concerns-Based Adoption Model (CBAM) postulates that individual rationally follows a systematic process and use relevant information to allay their concern before the adoption of innovations.

In 1962, E M Rogers developed the Diffusion of Innovation (DOI) Theory, (Rogers, 2003). This theory is considered as one of the oldest social science theories. Although originally this theory was developed as part of the understanding of marketing communication to explain how, over a period of time, a product or service may become more popular and gain the acceptance among the public. The underlying theory behind the diffusion of innovation theory was that any social system will take some time to accept a new idea, product or behaviour. Diffusion of innovation means an adoption process across a population over time and it includes a special form of communication that leads to the spread of innovation from one individual to the other ((Straub, 2009). Adoption here refers to a situation where the people change some aspect of their behaviour and do something differently from how they used to do it. This could mean the purchase of a new product or service or simply a change in the perception of a brand. If people perceive the idea, behaviour, or product as new or innovative, it would lead to adoption. It is only through this adoption, that the diffusion is possible. In a social system, not everyone would adopt technology at the same pace or time. Some people would rush to adopt the technology while others may take their own time and would join only when they are certain of the outcome. It has been found by researches that since people are different, their different characteristics would mean that some people would adopt the technology early and others would do it later.

Thus there can be different categories of adopters (e.g. Innovators, early adopters, early majority, late majority, and laggards) depending on the pace of adoptions of an idea or event. Perceived Characteristics of Innovating Theory (PCIT) model is an extension of the diffusion of innovation theory as it has identified three added features namely, Image, voluntariness, and behaviour as a precursor of adoptions. According to this theory, the human behaviour is very much influenced by the individual's perception of the voluntariness which has an effect on actual behaviour compared to voluntariness. Research has shown that the adoption rate and the demonstrability are positively correlated to each other and as demonstrability increases the adoption rate increase too. Individuals usually respond better while adapting to innovations as compared to the society, hence, only a small number of individuals can be considered as potential adopters in the cases when the innovation contradicting with the culture (Wejnert, 2002). (Helitzer, Heath, Maltrud, Sullivan, & Averson, 2003) argue that it is the youth market which is more likely to become an early adopter of new technology and the technology can usually be integrated into the youth lifestyle

The use of technology in marketing is an important antecedent of customer relationship management (CRM). The CRM requires strategies is to increase customer awareness, customer interactions, customer's' propensity to use technology, two way communications, customer involvement, customer trust 7 commitment and customer engagement (Dilogini & Shivany, 2016), Use of social media and digital technology can meet many of those strategic needs of effective CRM.

The events are experiences and technology can be a very significant tool to enhance customers' experience of the events. Citing Rogers (1995), Byron & Shooter, 2005) stated that innovation-decision process of stages through which an individual passes while adopting a technological innovations (knowledge of an innovation, attitude toward the innovation, to a decision to adopt or reject, implementation and use of the new idea, and confirmation of this decision). Faster adoption of innovation requires it to have five attributes namely; relative advantage, compatibility, lesser complexity, trialability, and observability(Byron & Shooter, 2005). Diffusion of an innovation or technology is a five-stage process (Knowledge, persuasion, decision to adopt, use and confirm), and this process has a number of antecedents such as personal factors of the user and social system Semanticscholar, n.d.). in summary, the technology adoptions though is a challenging and complex process, however, once the innovations and technology are adopted, it leads to better user engagement and overall positive experience.

## Technology, User Engagement, and Experience

Customer engagement means involving customers in the process of a service purchase, consumptions, and post-purchase behaviour. Engagement behaviour of a person means his/her internal occupancy with the activity or some external interactions or cognitive linked reactions to an external stimuli or that activity; and those reactions can also include attention of five sense organs, movements of eyes, hands, body, change in blood pressure or heart pulse, liking, going for that stimulus, etc (Trivedi et al., 2018). In ICT platforms, this kind of engagement can translate into login, page visits, eye tracking, average page views, bounce rate, conversation rates, conversion rates, average order value, loyalty meteoric or reviews and e word of mouth, etc (Trivedi et al., 2018).

A user can be assumed as engaged in an activity, when he/she thinks, feels, uses and refers to others a product or service with higher and positive energy. Customer engagement is core to customer purchasing and loyalty and organisational performance engaged customer are the main drivers of viral marketing via digital media. Social media tools, Virtual reality, and Augmented reality technology can be very useful for customer/user engagement. There are many reasons for usurers to engage in events, tourism or other services via ICT technologies due to a number of personal, environmental and technological factors. The engagement of a user can include a user's reaction to initiate, interact and show loyalty towards an event and its activities(Trivedi et al., 2018). There can be a number of personal, environmental and technological reason for user engagement in an activity or an event.

The self-identity theory postulate that individual prefers a behaviour which is consistent with his self-concept, self-image, self-esteem, and self-identity (Usual & Mazman, 2009). This explains many people's behaviour to share their online status on social networking sites such as Instagram and Facebook etc. Needs of belongingness (be involved with, accepted by, and valued by others), addictive tendencies (activity that becomes a forceful habbit due its power of mood modification, tolerance, withdrawal symptoms, conflict, and relapse; conveys an impression to others; are other main drivers of usage of social networking sites (Usluel & Mazman, 2009). Social media networks create many opportunities for users to create, share, forwards and viral the electronic word of mouth (e WOM) (Cao et al., 2013)., Thus the event-goers can discuss products, services or events with their friends and communities using social media. This many to many communication create viral marketing and thus increase information & awareness about events, interest in events, and involvement and engagement in the events WOM have positive effects on intentions to visit events and also loyalty towards events(Cao et al., 2013).

The customer engagement is evident via higher customer interactions, customer co-creation and collaboration (Brodie et al., 2011). customer engagement is the main antecedent of customer relationship management CRM, repeat patronage, retention and loyalty through affecting the customer experience(Hollebeek, 2011) The customer engagement means social, cognitive, emotional and behavioural 'connection', attachment, emotional involvement, participation, and social community development for a brand or product or an event (Brodie et al., 2011). The engagement is also evident through absorption or engrossed in the event, dedication, vigour or positive energy towards the event and two-way interaction and positive experience (Brodie et al., 2011). Digital media technologies have all of the relevant characteristics, that leads to higher customer engagement. Thus it can be inferred that technology is the main driver of customer or user engagement. (Sashi, 2012) has developed a customer engagement cycle and argued that customer engagements start with customer connection, interaction, satisfaction, retention, loyalty, advocacy, and ends with stronger engagement. The interactive nature of social media with its ability to establish conversations among individuals and involve customers in content generation and value creation led to more interest in suiting technology and social media for serving customers in the events industry (Sashi, 2012). The Customer engagement, relationship, and loyalty achieved by suing ICT can provide competitive advances to a firm in events; industry.

## Technology and Core Capability of Value Delivery Network

The discussion in the previous sections highlights that how the use of innovation and technology can lead to better customer engagements, loyalty and customer relationships, and ultimately all that can be a source of competitive advances for organisations in any industry in general and events services industry in particular. This implies that information technology can be seen as a source of competitive advantage and core strength or core competency of a company (Liang & You, 2009). This is in line with the Resource-based View (RBV) of the corporate strategy as proposed by Wernerfelt in 1984 (Barney 1991).).The resource-based view is opposite to industry or external environment based view, whereas the former postulates theta organisation's strategy and performance depends upon its own internal resources, the latter view gives argues that fit and adaptation to the external environment, competitions and industry is more important for strategic thoughts and performance of an organisation. (Pervaje, 2011). The RBV view of organisational strategies gives postulates that the organisational success and, performance is driven by its unique capability, strength or tangible/ intangible resources or core competencies; such resources add Value to the organisation, customers& another stakeholder, are Rare, difficult to Imitate and Non-substitutable (VRIN) (Barney 1991). The previous studies have found that innovation, technology, IT infrastructure, and intangible resources such as organisational culture, employee skill, and knowledge management, etc have been found as core capabilities of many organisations (Liang & You, 2009). CIT helps in integrating other tangible and intangible resources in the value delivery process, hence can be seen as complementary core capability or resource, as CIT not only exerts direct effects on the organisational performances, but ICT also has an indirect effect due to integration and synergetic effects of other resources due to use of ICT. The ICT not only enhances firm's internal capabilities (utilising own internal resources to enhance internal controls, cooperation, coordination's, relationships, capacity enhancement, efficiency and performance) but also is a very useful tool for external capabilities (ability to adapt to external environment, cooperation and coordination with external stakeholder such as supplies, customers(Liang & You, 2009). So for the Events industry, which has many operational challenges (due to the temporary nature of its components and suppliers) ns to enhance internal and external capabilities, use of technology can be a panacea. Even CIT based core competencies can vanish with the passage of time unless the firm continually innovates technology and technological applications in related fields like data analysis, big data, Artificial intelligence, machine language, and Blockchain technology, etc, and the employee continues technological innovations in their value chain (Pervaje, 2011). Three key resources – continue evolving competent IT human resources, an innovative IT infrastructure, and a strong IT Business Management relationship working in synergy will lead to core capabilities, create agile & effective organisation and thus provide sustainable competitive advantage (Pervaje, 2011). The Web 2.0 based technologies (social media, wikies, etc) provides opportunities for triangulating the IT synergies, as the social media provides opportunities for co-creation, collaboration and innovation, better interactions, relationship building and knowledge management(Pervaje, 2011). The use of Web2.0 based technology is possible for internal integrations of internal organisational functions and operations (value chain) as well as for external integration with supply chain management (SCM) and customer relationship management (CRM) (Pervaje, 2011). The discussion naturally put forward a case of employing innovations and technology in the value delivery network (supplier, Inbound logistic, purchasing production/operations, distribution, marketing, customer services, etc) of an organisation of an Events' industry.

The next sections discuss some of the applications of technology at different stages of value delivery network of an organisation in the Events industry.

## THE TRENDS OF USING TECHNOLOGY IN EVENT MANAGEMENT

Technology plays a very important role in modern events. Events professionals are using more and more technology in their events as this can leave a lasting impression in the minds of the audiences. The various phases of events planning can be well managed by using appropriate technology. Innovation in general and innovation using technology in the service sector and tourism industry has a very significant role (Bénédicte, Rani, & Longhi, 2011). Growth of Tourism is seen as the main driver in the use of internet technology, eCommerce and Web2, and vice versa.

### User Experiential Marketing

Event attendees, like other customers, nowadays give a lot of importance to experience. This experience may be before the purchase, during the purchase, during the consumption or even after the same product or service. Some of the technology-based innovations may go a long way in improving the overall customer experience. Consumers nowadays want a brand or product to connect with them not just through its features, but also through experience. The focus is on the consumer experience, not consumer satisfaction (Schmitt, 1999). Positive event experience leads to more loyal customers. The event professionals have understood the importance of experience and have geared up for using modern technology to create a memorable experience for the attendees. Active participation from attendees serves a lot better than passive participation and the event managers have started using technology around smartphones which almost all the attendees nowadays carry. Real-time information can be provided to the attendees based on their location in big events. Disneyland in Paris uses a smartphone application to provide a positive experience to their customers. The users are encouraged to download a free app and use it throughout their time in the theme park. The app gives them real-time waiting times etc. the overall customer experience has improved tremendously for the theme park since the launch of the app.

Thus, the application of information and communication technology (ICT) has significantly changed the way events or tourism is planned and managed. Some of the popular technology-based trends within events are discussed here:

### Technology at Supplier and Inbound Logistics Stage of Value Delivery Network

Inbound logistics is a stage of Value delivery network of a firm in the events sector include all of the operations to bring in resources, players, stakeholder and supplier organisation which participate to produce a final event.

*ICT technologies:* The temporary staff can be hired easily using online recruitments or even using social media announcements. The various suppliers and agents who come together to organise an event can be better coordinated using ICT technology, emails, mobile phones, WhatsApp and other communication tools. The various contracts can be efficiently signed using online contract forms.

## Technology at Operations Stage of Value Delivery Network

### Event Diagramming and Project Planning Tools Such as Prince 2

By using an event diagramming software, planners can map everything out visually. These cloud-based programs also provide accurate, customizable, and collaborative project planning that's accessible by all managing parties. The tools are easy to use, with drag-and-drop diagramming, 3D walkthroughs, and seating software. The event activities and schedules can be undertaken more efficiently and effectively by using Project Planning tools.

## Camera and Facial Recognition Devices

The facial recognition technology has become very common these days and the majority of the population has been using this technology through their smartphones, tablets or laptops. The secure entry, crowd management, and monitoring at the event locations have all become possible due to facial recognition technologies, cameras, and allied technologies. The use of such technology is becoming more and more popular. Another hugely popular trend is facial recognition. Many smartphones, tablets, and laptops manufacturing firms are already using this technology to make their products more secure. Surveillance cameras can be equipped with this technology especially in crowded events like music festivals, sports events, festivals, etc and this will empower the event managers by providing real-time information on any specific attendee.

Facial recognition can prove to be priceless in many event situations like:

- Participant's management
- Overall event security
- Crowd control
- Managing Problem creators in crowded events.

Companies like Google, Apple, Facebook and Snapchat have been using face recognition for some time now. Based on the information on its database, the users are prompted to tag the pictures and are given suggestions. Some very creative examples include advertisement screens installed in shopping malls where the screens were also capturing data like age, gender or even mood by facial recognition and using this knowledge to customise the advertisement broadcasted. Again, there are numerous possibilities for the smart event manager who can use this data for various marketing purposes. Events can use this technology to provide a faster and more secure check-in for the audiences. However, there are many calls for banning this technology from public events as this may be considered a breach of human rights by some activists. Hence unless this technology can become fool proof, the event managers must be very careful in using this technology. Sustainability is the need of the hour. It is not just a fad but has become an absolute necessity for any event. The use of paperless tickets using digital documents and the use of other Smart technology can save energy usages at the events. This can lead to more sustainable events in the future.

## 3D Projection Mapping

At the forefront of the technology-based innovations is Projection-Mapping, also known as 3D Projection mapping, 3D Mapping or 3D Video Mapping or Projection Mapping or 3-dimensional magical mystery (see Figure 1). In the early nineties, it was referred to as video mapping or special augmented reality (SAR). 3D projection mapping is a complex technology-enabled 'system of creating three-dimensional points to the two-dimensional plane and the projection is created in such a way, that 3D illusion is created, rather than a static, flat display'(Jake, 2011). A projection mapping is a technique where images or videos of building, mountains, fountains, etc are directly mapped onto surfaces giving the surface a three – dimensional visual effect (Furlong, 2018). Images and video are shown on surfaces, from buildings and mannequins to stages and water fountains such surfaces shape, texture, and combined graphic creates 3D sense (Furlong, 2018). The Projective mapping is a wonderful way of using technology to enhance a venue' create a unified and immersive experience for the audience, one that grabs attention and builds strong brand experiences' and tells a compelling brand story (Aleksandersen, 2019). Thus projective mapping is perfect will the theoretical model of customer engagement, as it can be sued for brand awareness, customer engagement, lasting impressions, viral marketing via social media, and an ultimately higher return on investment(Aleksandersen, 2019).

The marketing of brands and events of the product has used the projective mapping techniques very successfully to create three dimensional 'magical mystery in the air' around the brands or events. In Games of thrones, launch party event; the organisers (HBO) used four animated looks, inspired by the world of Westeros. The evening attendees saw 'a dragon gliding across the building, engulfing the facade in flames; a startling frozen tundra and the face of the Night King casting an icy glare; the faces of the show's stars appearing in character throughout the glacial expanse'(Furlong, 2018). Similar, Megavision Arts created an illusion of infinity Wall (see figure 2), for a Qatari Royal family wedding event to impress guest(Furlong, 2018). In another occasion Pixadoo a deodorant brand in India projected 16 buildings covering 3000 square meters of the area of a district, thus created a memorable, novel brand experience for its potential consumers (Aleksandersen, 2019). Projection mapping ensures a lasting impression on the viewers by creating magical lifelike projections and events can add to the experience that the viewers are going to receive. This works very well in scenarios where there is a huge number of people gathered to witness an event. Some more popular examples of projection mapping include Projection mapping for Adidas at the Olympic Park, London, Jennifer Lopez's performance on American Idol, Katy Perry at the Super Bowl 2015, etc. (projection-mapping.org, 2019).

Although Projection mapping leaves a mesmerizing impact on the viewers, it works through ordinary video projectors. The big difference is that unlike ordinary projectors, which projects on flat screens or surfaces, the image is mapped on any available surface, creating the life-like display (projection-mapping.org, 2019). The Projection mapping can mesmerize the audience, create engagement, engagement in the events, sharing awe on social media, can be useful for interactive advertisement, and memorable experience, however, the implementations of projection mapping may require huge budget, technical know-how, and also it can lose its sheen, big buzz, and novelty, once every brand would have adopted this approach of managing an event.

*Figure 1. Projection mapping, where a cathedral is used to project the image*
*(Source: pixabay.com)*

## Visual Experience: Virtual Reality (VR), Drone Streaming, and Augmented Reality (AR)

Virtual reality can give three-dimensional effects to normal two-dimensional photographs or videos. This technology can be used to market the event during pre-event booking as well as can be used to enhance event user's experiences during the actual events. Mixed reality uses technology to break down barriers and creates new opportunities for event professionals. Remote attendance is now more engaging than ever before (Julius, Ruud, Pádraic, & Nick, 2017).

*Drone Streaming is further extortion of virtual reality.* Many event planners are using cameras installed in drones for capturing video footage of the event. The drone mooted with Above 4K cameras provide alive, active and high-quality virtual touring streaming experience to the viewers of an event (Wu, Wang, & Yang, 2016) The process combines virtual reality technology to give a virtual tour of the events. The stereoscopic video produced by drone-mounted cameras is or can be controlled by viewers wearing VR headsets(Wu et al., 2016). Drones with 4K cameras and the ability to live stream on social channels

*Figure 2. The infinity wall projection mapping at weeding event of wedding event of the royal family of Qatar*
*[Source, Credit: Megavision Arts]*

are powerful engagement tools, as they can further contribute to VR and AR (Julius, Ruud, Pádraic, & Nick, 2017). Such footage not only gives another angular view of the events but can be viewed as live streaming as well as a live feed to the security office. Such an immersive experience will be memorable and very engaging to the viewer. One more trend of immersive expiative is the use of Augmented reality, wherein the virtuality and reality seem to merge and appears to become one.

*Augmented Reality* is 'an enhanced version of reality created by the use of technology to overlay digital information on an image of something being viewed through a device (such as a smartphone camera) (Merriam Webster, 2019),. The viewers get a feeling of being transported to another world, while all the time staying connected to the actual event. Augmented Reality uses some of the five senses that we humans have, namely sight, smell, hearing, taste or touch. Smart Event Organisers can choose the right mix of these senses along with the user's perception of reality and create a simulated environment which, then can be used for any marketing purposes. Augmented Reality provides endless opportunities for event professionals. AR can be used in collaboration with the gaming industry by providing an interactive augmented reality game, where the customers can actively participate. Who can forget the uproar the last *Pokémon Go* game created, when they merged the augmented reality into the gaming world? It has become a common practice among event organisers to create an app for any event that they organise. There are endless possibilities with the augmented reality and the event organizers can keep coming with new ideas to delight the customers.

## RFID Wearable Technology

RFID refers to ' radio-frequency identification' is 'wireless communication protocol using radio waves to identify an object at some distance' and this is one of the newest technologies being used within events (Gingrich, 2017). There are many examples of the use of RFID, if warning bell rings at a retail exit, when your car zooms through tollbooths, barriers, without pressing any button, then it is down to use of RFID sensors. Walt Disney World has been using wearable write 'Magic bands' to park guest, similarly many music feasible has been using this to decrease queening hassles and other entertainment areas like Entry points, cashless payments, coloured led light bands for brand implications or visibility and data capturing and integrated with live social media, etc (Gingrich, 2017).

RFID is an analogue technology but now the output can be converted to digital output, thus leading to more applications in transportation, healthcare, and events such as tracing event-goers track, time spends on each activity ore areas and inputting that information back to the system in real-time and creating live gamification experiences. Wearable technology mostly uses RFID technology in events, related to arts, culture, leisure, etc. The museum has started using RFID for gamification of museum visits and thus engaging visitors (Gingrich, 2017). The use of RFID in wearables have led to decreased waiting times in the ques, improved customer experience, customer enjoyment in the events, more social media engagement, and revenue by 15 to 30%, hence one estimates indicate that the RFID market will increase \$10.1 billion (2015) to \$13.2 billion by 2020 (Gingrich, 2017). The attendees could be given bands, badges or plastic cards which contain some computer chip with some digital data which can transmit back valuable information regarding the location of the attendee or event some other information like the time spent in various sections of a big event. This information can then be collected and analysed to get various projections regarding future events. This information gathered could be priceless as this is very unlikely to include human biases. Event organizers can now have a much better understanding of what are the most popular sessions within an event and what sections of the event interest their audiences. XOVIA a company in London has developed a unique "emotional technology" platform called XOX that uses a wristband equipped with biometric sensors to measure crowd excitement at an event (Gingrich, 2017). There is a big competition in the tablet and smartphone market and hence the event professionals are moving towards wearable technology which can do the same job. Successful event professionals will be able to make full use of the opportunity and will be able to stand out. A common example of RFID wearable tech is 'Fit Bit'. This is the most successful and revolutionary product in its product category which has become one of the most trusted consumer brands in health trackers. In the absence of the internet or WIFI, an RFID has let attendees make payments by mobile with exclusive information (Luxford & Dickinson, 2015)

RFID Wearable Tech can prove to be used in many event scenarios like:

- Participant's mapping
- Crowd control
- Opportunities for customized marketing based on the profile of the customer.
- Adding the food and beverage token to the wearable product
- Audience surveys
- Faster check-Ins

RFID has replaced the need for physical tickets and even the need to make payments multiple times in some cases. Overall it can be used in improving the customer experience.

## Chatbots

Chatbots have been around in the events industry for quite some time now. This is a chat-based tool which allows the users to chat with the event organisation at any point or time of the day. The users are given quick text or voice responses by a computer programme, regarding the queries made. This may ease the pressure on the event managers who are trying to organise an event within a tight budget.

Chatbots can be used on many platforms like smartphones, tablets or laptops. This gives the audiences a very good choice. These can be used for an event of any size and is a very cost-effective way of handling customer queries. The recent developments in chatbots are the Google Assistant and the Amazon Alexa. These brands have helped to bring chatbots to an average household.

## Mobile Applications for Events

Event Mobile applications (apps) are software applications that provide attendees access to event information, set up schedules, help attendees keep track of network connections and help post-event follow-ups. Mobile Apps retailor-made or customised software for mobile devices improve the user utility, functionality and experience(Laxford & Dickinson, 2015)

Mobile applications for events have been going around for some time now, however, it is still a growing market and more mobile apps come in the market each year as compared to the past years. It has become a common practice for event managers to create a mobile app for the event and encouraging the attendees to use the mobile app. Other kinds of Apps are Native apps which can work without an Internet connection as they have already incorporated a lot of information(Laxford & Dickinson, 2015). .The more often the attendees use the app, the better it is for the event organisers as they would then get more information from the attendees. Apps add to the usability of smartphones hence become very popular among users and users are spending more time on mobile apps (Luxford & Dickinson, 2015). As per Presence Theory in order to engage users at an event, a social presence- in form ' degree of human contact and face to face presence' is required. as such a social presence brings in dynamic in communications, gives sensory inputs, and assurance the users (Luxford & Dickinson, 2015).

Mobile apps are more like a 'One Stop Shop' for the audiences. Most of the apps nowadays are focussing on the audience engagement and does integrate Virtual reality and augmented reality into the app for better audience experience. Emotional and sensory stimulation lies at the heart users' of experiences at events, and it involves communities- "temporary together, egalitarian communities, removed from ordinary life, with common goals such as outside world experience, control and mastery over their experience and enjoyment' (Luxford & Dickinson, 2015). Mobile apps can be used to provide event schedule, programs, event speaker information, networking opportunities and other important information useful for the attendee. In return, the organizers and the sponsors can get valuable data from the attendees. These provide a plethora of possibilities for the events professionals. English Premier league uses a mobile app for its Fantasy Football League, which provides a much better user interface as compared to its desktop version and allows the users to use the app on the go. Some of the popular mobile apps for events include Eventbrite Onsite, Attendify, Pathable, Guidebook, Whova, FestApp, Eventbase, etc. The mobiles are expected to grow by 70-85% in coming years in the event industry, as Event planners use mobile apps to improve the drive traffic, experience, connivance of the attendees, engage attendees, keep pulse of the event, collect event metric, emergency notifications, for sponsorship, for competitive advantage, gamification, live polling, surveys, attendee networking, Event maps, and to save printing costs (DoubleDutch. & MPI, 2014). However contras of budget, technological knowledge, WIFI non-availability, a one seize fit App for all generations, and inter-platform form portability is limiting the use of Apps (Jake, 2011).

## Big Data, Data Analytics, and Cloud Commuting in Events

Due to the digitization of most of the devices, processes, Intern of things (IoT), social network platforms, Apps, blogs, use of sensors, digital devices, wearable and expanding use of internet and artificial intelligence etc a very large amount of data is being produced, such data is unknown as 'Big Data'-data produced 'in very high Volume, Variety, Veracity, Variability, Value density and Velocity' (Bhadani & Jothimani, 2016) . 'Big Data refers to a huge amount of both structured and unstructured data that cannot be stored and analysed using traditional database management techniques' (Bhadani & Jothimani, 2016).

Digital technology is being used more often than not in the recent past. Marketers analyses data to under stint consumer behaviour and insight, target marketing, designing marketing mix and so on. The event managers can now use data analytics to see the effectiveness of the money invested in the events. Big data analytics tries to simulate traditional techniques of data analysis and mining with help of new algorithms of grid/distributed data storage, cluster or parallel computing and in-memory computation and cloud computing, etc (Bhadani & Jothimani, 2016). The faster internet means other technologies can be used more effectively. Cloud technology and big data analytics can be used to understand crowd behaviours and the resources and systems can be allocated as per real-time needs at the events. Although the business of events management can be very stressful, successful event professionals are very good at coping with the stress using the technology at hand. Cloud computing can provide a lot of flexibility to event professionals. Cloud computing provides permanent connection and faster accessibility to all the important information, emails, or even the software. Cloud computing provides much more accurate data because of updated real-time data. The information is also much more secure as there is no danger of the computer crashing or the portable storage being lost or stolen. Hence, cloud computing can help the event professionals easily handle changes at a short notice, help them be more flexible to the needs of the clients and help them respond in very quick time to any of the client's requirements. Live Tech and data analytics include tools that are engineered to empower event professionals to quickly calculate data analysis and act as per requirements of dynamics of an event (Julius, Ruud, Pádraic, & Nick, 2017). However, the meetings and other corporate events take place in the real world and not over the digital technology, hence, the industry has lacked a clear vision on the value these events can generate.

## Sharing Economy and Crowd Sourcing

Using technology is an effective way to manage the sharing economy and use crowdsourcing or crowdfunding for the events. Not only that the ride-sharing services such as Uber, but Lyft and Airbnb are also increasingly helpful for transportations and accommodations for the attendees of an event (Bénédicte, Rani, & Longhi, 2011). Crowdsourcing and crowdfunding are on a rise and as the internet becomes accessible to more and more people around the world, it is becoming increasingly possible for event professionals to collaborate with other people through the internet for resources or funding. The Internet has provided a sound platform for people from different areas to work together.

## Artificial Intelligence (AI)

Artificial Intelligence (AI) is not the future, it is the present. Organisations are using Artificial Intelligence for a variety of purposes. The possibilities with AI are endless and the successful organisations are those who have found the best use of AI. Artificial Intelligence, mostly in the form of chatbots are used in events marketing and management online (Bénédicte, Rani, & Longhi, 2011). AI-based apps such as Cortana, Alexa or Siri style interface are becoming preferences for customers of an event. These Apps act as a personal assistant for booking, ticketing, recording, reminding and live updating of events as well as can be used to connect with event organisers. Services companies reported the highest expected benefits across all four domains, expecting significant value from AI through engaging customers and empowering employees, for example via improving resource and skills allocation across their large human capital pools. (n.d., 2018). Events is essentially a service industry; hence it may expect the highest possible benefits from AI.

## Blockchain Technology

Most people know Blockchain due to its initial applications in Cryptocurrencies bitcoins. Blockchain technology is 'an internet-based distributed ledger or accounting book technology' that can be used to verify the unique digital identity of the user and analogous to peer to peer connection, interaction n or transaction (Al-Saqaf & Seidler, 2017). Due to its ability to store peer to peer unique identities, the Blockchain technology can be used for more trustworthy, secure ticketing, payments and tracing of people and resources more securely and more flexibly, This technology is based on the core principles of principles – such as decentralisation, transparency, equality, and accountability, hence is seen as more secure and transparent, trustworthy, and egalitarian between parties involved (Al-Saqaf & Seidler, 2017).

No single node in the blockchain technology can defraud makes this technology-based application more secure in financial and other sectors. "Blockchain has the potential to change the way we buy and sell, interact with government and verify the authenticity of everything from property titles to organic vegetable." (Eventtia, 2019).A blockchain is a record of transactions, like any movement of money, goods, or secure data. It may be purchased at the grocery store or an official government ID. Blockchain is a very secure form of record and due to the security it provides, it is impossible to add or change any record without being detected. More secure and trustworthy digital contracts between different suppliers and users of events can be executed based on this technology and this obliviates the costly and complex use of law firm contracts.

## TECHNOLOGY AT EVENT MARKETING STAGE OF VALUE DELIVERY NETWORK

### Events Marketing

"Events marketing is about making your event attractive to staff, volunteers, sponsors, participants, the media and attendees. It addresses all of the detail which makes up the event experience, both that which the attendee sees and that which they are not necessarily aware of. Events marketing is also a tool used by marketers for how they can reach audiences, promote products and enhance their brands" (Jackson, 2013).

There are different types of events and there can be a number of ways to market these events. The events have three Es namely, entertainment, excitement, and enterprise (Bikash, 2013). Sometimes the term 'Event Marketing' is also used in the literature. The event marketing implies using the special event to market an organisation or brand. An event marketing is a form of marketing activities; trade show, digital experiences like virtual conferences, webinars, and live-streamed workshop in order to create live experiences that promote a brand, service, or product (Eventbrite, The Ultimate Guide to Event Marketing, 2019).

Event marketing includes tools, techniques, and channels as part of a promotional strategy that may involve face-to-face or virtual contact between companies and their customers at special events like concerts, fairs, and sporting events.

The events have characteristics of services, such as intangibility, perishability, labor-intensiveness, uniqueness, non-storability, fixed timescales, personal interaction, and also closer to values, ritual or ceremony(Getz, 2012). The characteristics of events make their marketing difficult. Again, various kinds of technologies help in marketing events more effectively. The use of ICT and related technology helps in adding a tangible dimension to an event. The problem of perishability and in- storability means mostly mismatch between demand and supply, again technology can aid in right demand estimation but also the right quantity of production too.

The events are labour intensive, that can bring in two major issues; how to recruit more temporary employees and how to make sure that service standards do not vary due to usage of human elements; The use of technology can solve both of these issues by replacing employees with machines and robots and also producing standardised services. The only drawback of using technology can be the reduced personal interactions and social presence at the events.

The marketing of events has three phases: Pre-event, during the event, and post-event marketing (Eventbrite, The Ultimate Guide to Event Marketing, 2019).

**Pre-Event Marketing:** This included a set of activities and process are undertaken before an event. This phase can make use of ICT technology for developing a teaser video, event calendar, digital media & social media campaign, blogs, videos, and hashtags, etc (Eventbrite, The Ultimate Guide to Event Marketing, 2019).

**Mid -Event Marketing:** Include a set of activities and process undertaken during an event. This could include, sharing live photos, videos, engaging the attendees in situ, hashtags and social media comments, live streaming and using apps to run live liking and polls, etc (Eventbrite, The Ultimate Guide to Event Marketing, 2019).

**Post-Event Marketing:** This includes a set of marketing activities post the event. The purpose is to follow up with attendees, stakeholders, and sponsors for feedback, thanking, reviews and creating social media buzz and reserves for the future (Eventbrite, The Ultimate Guide to Event Marketing, 2019).

There can be many types of events that can be employed for marketing purposes, as given below:

**Webinars:** The term webinar is made up of web and seminar. As the name suggests, a webinar is an event which is held on the internet and is solely attended by an online audience. This includes online live featuring or presentations of events with a moderator and guest speakers. Webinars are getting more and more popular due to the convenience they provide. The presenters and the audience do not have to be present at the same place but can still interact with each other with the help of a webinar.

**Conferences:** 'A conference is generally understood as a meeting of several people to discuss a particular topic. A conference is usually confused with a convention, colloquia or symposium. While a conference differs from the others in terms of size and purpose, the term can be used to cover the general concept. A convention is larger than a conference; it is a gathering of delegates representing several groups' (Evenues, 2019) .The purpose of the conference could be one of the following, e.g. an academic conference, trade conference, business conference or an unconference. Most of the conference will choose some eminent people in their respective fields as keynote speakers, which usually will be able to attract more audiences to these conferences. There are various types of conferences:

A *symposium* is usually a casual gathering which may include some refreshments and light entertainment.

A *seminar* is organized to discuss a specific topic. The objective of a seminar is usually to educate the audience

A *workshop* is usually participative in nature and it provides a hands-on experience for the participants with demonstrations and activities. Since it requires active participation, the speaker's time is very short.

Peers would usually come together in a *round-table conference* to discuss their opinions on a certain topic, usually political or commercial. The number of participants in a round table conference is limited as it would be impractical to hold such type of conference with a big group of people as the participants are required to face each other around a table.

**Workshops:** The workshops are usually much smaller events where some experts provide training to the colleagues regarding some specific aspects of a job. Although these meetings are formal but are conducted in a very relaxed environment. A well-planned workshop can go a long way towards saving time, money and efforts. These workshops usually involve participatory methods, which have been well known for being a very effective way of learning. Dramatic changes in attitudes or behaviour are possible if the workshop is managed well. A workshop is a time saving and very powerful activity as it can lead to drastic changes and innovations in the behaviour, in the collaboration and ability to mobilise energy and intelligence of diverse stakeholders and people. (EMF, 2010).A workshop is both time consuming and a time-saving activity. Time-consuming because it requires a great deal of organisational effort and meetings to make sure that all aspects are clearly prepared and ready, as in a party, a concert or any event where many people are involved.

**Roadshows:** The marketers are nowadays creating their own events. Instead of using the old-fashioned way of attending the events organised by other organizations, they can host their own events. Roadshows are not about the number of people attending the show but are about ensuring the right target customers attending the event. These may be the people who are most likely to buy the organisation's goods and services. According to (Vajre, 2016) the steps to planning your own roadshow are:

- Identify your prospects and customers in your CRM.
- Create a list of who you want to attend using your marketing automation system.
- Review the list for geographic locations where contacts are located to determine which cities might be the best fit for your show.
- Further, segment the list of contacts to determine which locations are closest to their hometown.
- Then start looking at a place within that city to host your awesome roadshow

**Account-Based Marketing Events:** According to ITSMA "Account-based marketing (ABM) is a strategic approach to designing and executing highly targeted, personalized marketing programs and initiatives to drive business growth and impact with specific, named accounts. "These are targeted and customized experiences designed to address the client's needs. The purpose of such events will be to ensure that the company understands the client's needs and the client understand the offering. Their meeting can be tailored to the specific needs of each account or client. The secret to the success of account-based marketing is that it involves human interactions. It is this human interaction, which makes the customisation possible. Companies these days are choosing to meet the clients face to face in a more conducive setting. These meetings could be Intimate breakfasts, lunches, or dinners. These types of meetings are rather small and informal events with a focus on networking. The informal aspect of the meeting is very important as this usually would help the client open more to the company representative. These events are usually very effective as the clients would feel valued. The budget on these events may depend on the importance of the client for the organisation.

**Contests and Discounts:** The various kind of contests can be organised for events marketing. By offering some discounts, free samples, charity alignments, or fun at an event the organisers can make their attendees feel special and expect reciprocal positive behaviours. For example, A brand like Coca-Cola, who position their brand with an image of peace, happiness, and pleasure, made an excellent choice by installing vending machines that dispensed "happiness" along with free soft drinks. Flowers, pizzas, etc at a college canteen. The campaign created a very big buzz on YouTube. Similarly, at the Sundance film festival, Ray-Ban sunglasses put on a truth-or-dare themed campaign, which was fun for participants and also translated into social media shares after the event was over.

**Tradeshows:** A tradeshow is a face to face event that brings together large groups of individuals or companies in a particular industry or profession to network and shows off new products. These may include the buyers and sellers in an industry. The sellers will use this event to showcase their offering and the buyers will usually compare the different offerings and learn more about the new trends in the market.

## The Digital Promotional Tactics for Events

The digital promotional tactics or 'touchpoints' for an event may include Omnichannel such as Email Marketing, marketing websites, Registration Sites, Social Media, Testimonials and Referrals, Video, Blogging and Content Marketing, etc. Further, it is important to monitor the effeteness of your campaigns using a range of metrics and Key performance indicators (KPIs) such as financial results, event attendance, lead generation, overall awareness, and post-event analysis, etc.

### Email Marketing

The email marketing can be targeted towards the chosen audiences and email marketers need data bank and list of target consumers. The use of event poster or photo in the email signatures can add more weight to the email. The senders have to make sure that the message in short, simple and engaging. Smart professionals make use of AIDA (attention- Interest- desire- action) model in designing the structure and flow of the message. A study quoted by Eventbrite found that by using targeted emails a company can improve conversion by 355% and revenue by 781%, but the email opening or reading rate might be as low as 26% (Eventbrite, Essential Guides: Event Marketing, 2017).

### SEO, Advertising on SEO and Other Paid Social Media Ads

The search engine optimisations help in bringing your event/ad on the front page of a search engine. SEO can be achieved by making use of some important actions. For example, making sure that the title tag that appears in the browser tab as well in your listing in Google has a clear name, location and a keyword for the event. The headline/title on a webpage (H1) should use the event name along with some additional keywords. The marketers must make use of Google's local search priority by inputting the location in keywords. SEO can usually increase event sales by 5-10%. In addition to search engine optimising (SEO), your content and website, you should also consider advertising your event on paid platforms such as Facebook ads, Search engines like Google, Yahoo, etc. Google AdWords auctions can help you target and reach your desired audiences on YouTube, Google Search, mobile apps, and over two million websites (Eventbrite, Essential Guides: Event Marketing, 2017).

### Marketing Websites and Event Apps

The Event website or Apps should have bespoke landing pages, clear benefits to attend the events, booking/ registering facilities, and forms, payments, etc. The option of third parties such as Eventbrite etc. should also be considered to target the event's audiences who attend events, as it is possible that those audiences will usually visit the event advertising sites, such as Eventbrite, Eventful, Goldstar, Spotify, Facebook Events, Bands Intown etc.(Eventbrite, Essential Guides: Event Marketing, 2017).

### Blogging and Content Marketing

The Content Marketing Institute, an online resource for information on all things content marketing related, defines content marketing as: "Content marketing is a marketing technique of creating and distributing valuable, relevant and consistent content to attract and acquire a clearly defined audience – with the objective of driving profitable customer action." (Steimle, 2019).Content marketing is still a very new approach to marketing in many parts of the world. Although it is a very powerful tool, it comes as a surprise that it is not used enough. Most of the people can understand and use it without much training. However, organisations often see a big risk in this kind of strategy. They are not comfortable with giving away valuable knowledge without being sure of receiving something of value in return. That is why many companies rely solely on traditional marketing methods. (Maczuga, Sikorska, & Jaruga, 2014)

## Videos

With the internet becoming so accessible, the customers find it very easy to watch and share the videos they like. The marketers must make full use of a range of promotional videos, YouTube, videos within the event App, Video Competitions, Teaser Videos and helping how to do Videos. The audiences love videos and a good video can help create the right buzz for the product, service or an event. The marketers are using the video-sharing technology to promote their offering because of its benefits which include,

- Multimedia makes compelling content
- New audiences
- Public outreach
- Education and training
- How To videos & audios to improve service & achieve the mission
- Cost savings

## Press Releases and Blogs

A press release is a description of the event and a blog is a story or description of what, why and how of an event. The blogs can be very useful pre-event and post-event marketing tools. The various search engines favour blog postings. Potential customers or interested parties often read and follow a blog. Thus, blogging can be a very useful tool for events marketing. Blogs could be written by amateur or professionals or celebrity-based blogs and each one of those may have its own effect.

## Testimonials and Referrals

It is significant to make use of reviews and ask people for reviews and even offer ethical incentives for honest reviews. The testimonial videos can be a very effective way to invite more people to the Events. Make it easy for the ambassadors or reviewers to share your event by providing a variety of downloadable content: audio, video, an article, graphics, updates (Twitter/Facebook/LinkedIn/Google+), email/blog posts and blurbs/newsletter updates. These testimonials have a far-reaching impact on the prospective customers. Many marketers reward their existing customers when they refer to the brand offering to a new customer. Referrals usually motivate customers to act fast due to the presence of the reward factor.

### Social Media

Use paid or non-paid social media to show the presence of event on social networks sites like Facebook, Twitter, LinkedIn, Snapchat and Instagram. The event planners should optimize your social media account bios, encourage colleagues and employees to connect to your brand on social media, create relevant video content & regularly vary it, consider SEO, live chats/streaming, beware of automated posts, add fun and call to action. On social media one should ensure the message is short and mobile-friendly. When you compare the social media advertising to TV and other expensive media channels, you will find that the social media advertising is more targeted, customizable and user-friendly (Eventbrite, Essential Guides: Event Marketing, 2017).

Now Marketing Automation, machine learning, and Artificial Intelligence-based platform are also available options. For example, platforms like Boostable, ToneDen, and Radario, etc can be used to automatically market your campaign via social media (Eventbrite, Essential Guides: Event Marketing, 2017). Do not forget to build momentum just before and during the event using social network platforms. The social media platforms become more effective with the usage of hashtags, contests, ambassadors, consistence and relevant postings, interactions with the followers and pictures. Use highlights from prior events, share bloopers, venue & surroundings, share photos of performers/speakers, activities and attendees with stories or quotes, etc in order to create curiosity, buzz, energy, and excitement. An event hashtag in the Bio (about) section of your social media page has a high potential of reach and customer engagement.

## IMPLICATIONS FOR MANGERS

Event Management is a process of planning, organizing, coordinating, executing various activities at an event with effective use of all the event resources to meet the specific goals and objective of the event, and the use of innovative technology can be a panacea for effective planning, organization, coordination, and control. The managers can make use of technology for process and service innovations. The chapter has also discussed the process and conditions of technology adoptions; hence, the chapter could be a good guide book for the managers working in the event industry. The technology adoption can lead to sustainable competitive advantages for an organization in events and travel and tourism industry. According to the resource-based view of the organization, an organization needs to develop its core capabilities continuously for winning over the customers and competitors. The technology adoption is a complex process, but by providing favourable conditions to employees, customers, and other stakeholders; an organization can manage an event more efficiently and effectively. The technology can be used in all of the stages of value delivery network of an organization. Managers can adopt and technology to the local requirements of its organization and its stakeholders.

## CONCLUSION AND SCOPE OF FURTHER RESEARCH

An event is a set of activities with specific purpose and needs of the attendees An event can be defined as an organized occasion such as meeting, music testable, brand promotion, wedding, social gathering and so on. An event is made up of several related activities and functions, hence the use of ICT is very important for perfect coordination of an event. Technology adoptions can create sustainable competitive advances. By using technology at different stages of its value chain and value delivery network, an organization in an event industry can attain core competencies and core capabilities. The diffusion of innovation as the process takes time and requires a number of favourable factor conditions. The use of technology is very important for service innovations. The technology and innovations help in better marketing of events too. The organization can use social media and another web 2. 0 technologies for customer engagements. A range of new technologies such as Augmented Reality, Drone-streams, 3-D mapping, social economy-based apps Blockchain technology, and new social media networks have been already experimented by many organizations in the events industry. However, there is a dearth of research to empirically know the adoptions, factors, cost-efficiency, and success of that technology. Hence future research may address those areas. Overall, this is certain that technology creates disruptive innovations in all of the sectors and industries, surely the events' industry will also not be left untouched due to technological revolutions.

## REFERENCES

Al-Saqaf, W., & Seidler, N. (2017). Blockchain technology for social impact: opportunities and challenges ahead. *Journal of Cyber Policy,* 1–18. doi:10.1080/23738871.2017.1400084

Aleksandersen, B. D. (2019). *Why is projection mapping so popular in events and marketing?* Retrieved July 31, 2019, from https://newsandviews.dataton.com/why-is-projection-mapping-so-popular-in-marketing

*Artificial Intelligence in Europe - Outlook for 2019 and beyond.* (2018). EY LLP Limited.

Barney, J. (1991). Firm Resources and Sustained Competitive Advantage. *Journal of Management, 17*(1), 99–120. doi:10.1177/014920639101700108

Bénédicte, A., Rani, J. D., & Longhi, C. (2011). Innovation in the tourism industry: The case of Tourism. *Tourism Management, 32*(5), 1204–1213. doi:10.1016/j.tourman.2010.08.010

Bhadani, A. K., & Jothimani, D. (2016). Big data: Challenges, opportunities and realities. In M. K. Singh & D. G. Kumar (Eds.), *Effective Big Data Management and Opportunities for Implementation* (pp. 1–24). Retrieved from https://pdfs.semanticscholar.org/0a45/69cfcb193a548de7445106135445bae5950f.pdf

Bijmolt, T. H. A., Leeflang, P. S. H., Block, F., Eisenbeiss, M., Hardie, B. G. S., & Saffert, P. (2010). Analytics for Customer Engagement. *Journal of Service Research, 13*(3), 341–356. doi:10.1177/1094670510375603

Bikash, G. (2013). *Marketing in Event Management. Laurea University of Applied Sciences, Laurea Kerava.* Retrieved 6 25, 2019, from https://www.theseus.fi/bitstream/handle/10024/76351/Gurung_Bikash.pdf?sequence=1

Brodie, R. J., Hollebeek, L. D., Jurić, B., & Ilić, A. (2011). Customer Engagement: Conceptual Domain, Fundamental Propositions, and Implications for Research. *Journal of Service Research, 14*(3), 272–271. doi:10.1177/1094670511411703

Cao, Y., Ajjan, H., & Hong, P. (2013). Using social media applications for educational outcomes in college teaching: A structural equation analysis. *British Journal of Educational Technology*, *44*(4), 581–593. doi:10.1111/bjet.12066

Dilogini, K., & Shivany, S. (2016). *Framework of Technology in Marketing World: A Theoretical Review*. Academic Press.

DoubleDutch., & MPI. (2014). *The State of Event Apps Official MPI Research*. Retrieved from https://www.hbaa.org.uk/sites/default/files/mpi-research-state-of-event-apps.pdf

EMF. (2010). *Workshop concept and Methodology*. Pro Ideal Plus.

Eventbrite. (2017). *Essential Guides: Event Marketing*. Retrieved June 2, 2019, from Eventbrite.com/blog

Eventbrite. (2019). *The Ultimate Guide to Event Marketing*. Retrieved June 2, 2019, from Eventbrite: https://www.eventbrite.com/blog/event-marketing-ds00/

Eventtia. (2019, July 11). www.eventtia.com. Retrieved from www.eventtia.com: https://www.eventtia.com/blog/blockchain-technology-and-events-what-will-change

Evenues. (2019, July 11). *evenues.com*. Retrieved from evenues.com: https://evenues.com/event-planning-guide/what-is-a-conference

Furlong, J. (2018). *How 4 Companies Wow Customers With Projection Mapping Ads*. Retrieved July 31, 2019, from https://www.businessnewsdaily.com/10529-projection-mapping-examples.html

Getz, D. (2012). *Event Studies: theory, research and policy for planned events*. London: Routledge.

Gingrich, R. (2017). *Wearables in the Performing Arts: An RFID Primer for Arts Managers*. Retrieved from https://www.idtechex

Harmeling, C., Moffett, J., & Carlson, B. D. (2016). Toward a theory of customer engagement marketing. *Journal of the Academy of Marketing Science*, *45*, 312–335. doi:10.100711747-016-0509-2

Helitzer, D., Heath, D., Maltrud, K., Sullivan, E., & Averson, D. (2003). Assessing or Predicting Adoption of Telehealth Using the Diffusion of Innovations Theory: A Practical Example from a Rural Program in New Mexico. *Telemedicine Journal and e-Health*, *9*(2), 179–187.

Hollebeek, L. (2011). Exploring customer brand engagement: Definition and themes. *Journal of Strategic Marketing*, *19*(7), 555–573. doi:10.1080/0965254X.2011.599493

Jackson, N. (2013). *Promoting ans Marketing Events*. New York: Routledge. doi:10.4324/9780203583166

Jake, H. (2011). *16 mind-blowing examples of big-brand projection mapping*. Retrieved July 31, 2019, from https://econsultancy.com/16-mind-blowing-examples-of-big-brand-projection-mapping/

Julius, S., Ruud, J., Pádraic, G., & Nick, B. (2017). *10 Events Trends for 2017*. Retrieved June 3, 2019, from Godmother: http://www.godmother.ro/wp-content/uploads/2016/04/10-Event-Trends-2017-v3.pdf

Liang, T.-P., & You, J. (2009). Resource-based View in Information Systems Research: A Meta-Analysis. *Pacific Asia Conference on Information Systems (PACIS) PACIS 2009 Proceedings*. Retrieved from http://aisel.aisnet.org/pacis2009/72

Luxford, A. M. Y., & Dickinson, J. E. (2015). *The role of mobile applications in the consumer experience at music festivals*. Academic Press.

Maczuga, P., Sikorska, K., & Jaruga, A. (2014). *Content Marking Handbook - simple ways to innovate your marketing approach.* Warsaw: cmex.eu.

Pelling, E. L., White, K. M., & White, K. (2009). The theory of planned behaviour applied to young people's use of social networking websites. *Cyberpsychology & Behavior, 12*(6), 755–759. doi:10.1089/cpb.2009.0109 PMID:19788377

Pervaje, A. (2011). *Resource-Based View of Social Media as a Source of Sustained Competitive Advantage*. Retrieved from https://core.ac.uk/download/pdf/4431941.pdf

Projection-mapping.org. (2019, July 7). Retrieved from http://projection-mapping.org/what-is-projection-mapping/: http://projection-mapping.org/what-is-projection-mapping/

Qi, J., Monod, E., Fang, B., & Deng, S. (2018). *Theories of Social Media: Philosophical Foundations.* Academic Press.

Rogers, E. (2003). *Diffusion of Innovations* (5th ed.). Simon and Schuster.

Schmitt, B. (1999). Experiential Marketing. *Journal of Marketing Management, 15*(1), 53–67. doi:10.1362/026725799784870496

SteimleJ. (2019, July 11). www.forbes.com. Retrieved from www.forbes.com: https://www.forbes.com/sites/joshsteimle/2014/09/19/what-is-content-marketing/#6f6bda8210b9

Trivedi, N., Adomako Asamoah, D., & Doran, D. (2018). Keep the conversations going: Engagement-based customer segmentation on online social service platforms. *Information Systems Frontiers, 20*(2), 239–257. doi:10.100710796-016-9719-x

Ungerman, O., Dedkova, J., & Gurinova, K. (2018). The Impact Of Marketing Innovation On The Competitiveness Of Enterpris-Es In The Context Of Industry 4.0. *Journal of Competitiveness, 4*(2), 132–147. doi:10.7441/joc.2018.02.09

Vajre, S. (2016). *Account-Based Marketing for Dummies*. Dummies.

Vassilios, Z., & Nikolaos, B. (n.d.). *Contextualizing Phenomenology in Event Management Research: Deciphering the Meaning of Event Experiences*. Retrieved Mqy 2, 2019, from http://eprints.leedsbeckett.ac.uk/143/1/Contextualizing%20Phenomenology%20in%20Event%20Management%20Research.pdf

Wejnert, B. (2002). Integrating Models of Diffusion of Innovations: A Conceptual Framework. *Annual Review of Sociology, 28*(1), 297–326. doi:10.1146/annurev.soc.28.110601.141051

Wu, C., Wang, Z., & Yang, S. (2016). *Drone Streaming with Wi-Fi Grid Aggregation for Virtual Tour.* Retrieved from http://www.lemondrone.com/blog/dji-lightbridge-

Yang, Y., Li, Z., & Su, Y. (2018). The effectiveness of service innovation practices to reduce energy consumption based on adaptive theory. *Sustainability (Switzerland), 10*(9). doi:10.3390u10093317

## KEY TERMS AND DEFINITIONS

**Customer Engagement:** Customer engagement means involving customers (internal occupancy with the activity or some external interactions or cognitive linked reactions to an external stimuli) in the process of a service purchase, consumptions, and post-purchase behaviour.

**Diffusion of Innovation:** Diffusion of innovation means an adoption process across a population over time and it includes a special form of communication that leads to the spread of innovation from one individual to the other.

**Event:** An event is an organized occasion made up of a set of activities with specific purpose goals and needs of the attendees An event can incudes occasion such as meeting, music testable, product/brand promotion, convention, conference, exhibition, special event, wedding, social gathering or gala dinner, and so on.

**Event Management:** Event management is a process of planning, organising, coordinating, executing various activities at an event with effective use of all the event resources to meet the specific goals and objective of the event.

**Events Marketing:** Events marketing is also a tool used by marketers for how they can reach audiences, promote products and enhance event experience.

**Innovation:** An innovation is an idea, practice, or object or a new product or a new quality of a product,, a new production method or a new sales market etc that is perceived as new by an individual or another unit of adoption.

**Projection Mapping:** A projection mapping is a technique where images or videos of building, mountains, fountains, etc. are directly mapped onto surfaces giving the surface a three-dimensional visual effect.

**Resource-Based View:** The resource-based view postulates theta organisation's strategy and performance depends upon its own internal unique capabilities and resources, and such resources and capabilities should add value, rare, non-imitable, and non-substitutable.

**Service Innovation:** Service innovation implies developing a new service or renewal, modification of existing services.

# Chapter 19
# Marketing Innovation in Tourism

**Vipin Nadda**
*University of Sunderland, London, UK*

**Ian Arnott**
*Univeristy of Sunderland, London, UK*

## ABSTRACT

*Tourism businesses have become virtual organisations linked to information technology available for innovation in marketing as well as using other platforms in the social media environment such as Facebook, Instagram, etc. This use of social media is creating innovation, as the tourists are becoming co-designers, co-producers, co-marketers, and co-consumers of tourism experiences. The branding strategies methods, tools, and process are changing since the adoption of digital technology in marketing and branding. The organisations are able to reach their tourism appeal through multisensory information that touches the five senses in a more effective way. The use of liquid branding and audio branding to introduce, enhance, and develop various audio and visual elements of the brand is a new trend in branding. Therefore, as brick and mortar or virtual organisations, the destination marketing organisation should innovate their marketing efforts and should respond to change within a dynamic business environment.*

## INNOVATION

Innovation is becoming one of the most important elements in modern society and the changing global nature of business. A lot of research has been carried on the kinds of innovation and marketing innovation found to be one of the main fields which when traced backed into the literature; is not explored in depth but has relatively huge benefits. It is simply defined as the new ways in which businesses can market themselves to their current and potential customers.

One of the main reasons that innovation is getting so much attention is that is the companies are becoming successful and are found being able to achieve a competitive advantage based on those innovative products, processes or services. In today's globally competitive environment, the key to be the

DOI: 10.4018/978-1-7998-0131-3.ch019

best and achieve the highest market share is to understand what the customers want and to cater them with the changing needs. Successful firms found being acknowledging the fact that engaging the customers is a two-way dialogue and this is something that is very critical for the long-term development and profitability of the company. Innovation combined together with marketing helps the company to grow by providing products and services that are valuable to the consumers. Marketing is all about the end consumers and especially the four marketing P's found to assure that the organisation would use innovation in all main areas.

The rapid pace, at which the world is developing, has changed the way people used to live and has created a need for change, thus making marketing innovation even more important concept to be studied and implemented. The current customers are always seeking new developments while the potential customers want a differentiating factor, which is one of the many areas under the umbrella of marketing innovation.

Companies have different perceptions when it comes to innovation and particularly when they deal with marketing innovation. Even though the underlying perception might be different for each organisation, the main point is that unless innovation is built in every single fabric of the system that the firm has, it is not possible to implement it. Every organisation in order to be successful requires being innovative and marketing innovation can help them from micro to the macro level, to gain the position that they dream about.

Innovation is not something new (Verloop, 2004) rather it dates back to pre-historic times when a man was able to transform ideas into realization. The innovations of humanity continued to develop over time with huge variations ranging from controlling fire (Goudsblom 1992) to the light bulb to the new medicine that has been recently developed (Achilladelis and Antonakis 2001). Defining the process of innovation, Jacobs and Snijder (2008) explain it as developing and selecting ideas for innovation followed by the transformation of these ideas into innovation.

Given the many forms of innovation, many authors argue that it is vital for organisations to innovate (Tidd and Bessant 2005, Mulgan and Albury 2003) and manage innovation at the same time. Innovation management has therefore been a widely studied area and according to Brinkshaw (2007), innovation management is the ongoing and conscious organisation, control and execution of activities leading to innovation.

The modern-day business theory states that companies must compete in order to retain or gain market share and in all this, innovation is thought to be the key for creating and achieving competitive advantage (Stalk, 2006). It has not linked with a competitive advantage in growing markets but also in mature markets and unlike the majority of the other business practices, innovation might change the competitive balance in the mature markets (Brown, 1992). Not only does innovation renders firm-specific benefits rather in the 1930s, but it also became closely associated with economic gain and competitive advantage. Besides, Letenyei (2001) mentions in his work that the theory of economic development by Joseph Schumpeter bases economic development on five types of economic innovations including setting up or discovering a new product, a new market, manufacturing process and setting up of a new organisation.

## THE CONCEPT OF INNOVATION

The innovation is a concept of interest in all fields and has been often associated with human evolution, commencing with the invention of agriculture, fire, the wheel and so on. Citing a range of authors, Ioan, Gheorghe, & Monica (2010), described innovation as; introduction or modifications of new idea, product or a service (Schumpeter,1930), introducing a new element to the customer (Howard and Sheth,1969), new changes (Mohr,1969, new use of existing products or a new markets for existing products or even a new marketing method (Simmonds, 1986), a creative process (Simmonds, 1986, introducing a new policy, structure, method, process(Nohria and Gulati,1996) and knowledge creation and diffusion of existing knowledge (Rogers, 1998).

Innovations can roughly vary along many dimensions including type and extent of the novelty of innovation, the type and size of organisation undertaking innovation and lastly the environment under which innovation took place. However, in terms of types of innovation, Baker (2002) classifies innovation into three types including process, product/service, and strategy. All these types are related to each other, for example, strategy innovation might lead to or require process or product innovation. These levels, however, did not differentiate between newness and impact but taking the concept of innovation a step ahead, Christensen (1997) unraveled the newness and impact characteristic of innovation as new innovations might not necessarily have a significant impact which is what also differentiates sustaining from discontinuous innovation. It focuses on improving the functionality and features of the existing products or services while process innovation is oriented towards improving internal capabilities (Johne, 1996). The market innovation deals with the careful choice of entry into new market segments unexplored by the company.

## MARKETING INNOVATION

Andrews and smith (1996) consider marketing innovation as a significant process that differentiated, and the firm will do everything to reach a specific goal.Clemmer (1998) on the other hand, explained that marketing innovation and creativity are the main elements that provide the key for success in an organisations business environment. Haddad and Algadeer (2004) are of the view that marketing innovation reflects the ability of the firm as to how the organisation continuously improves its products and services, which in turn are known to provide a pathway which will lead to huge benefits for the clients as these products and services will satisfy their needs in a unique way. It also covers the latest innovation in marketing ranging from how people alter the ways of getting their messages out to the new tools they use with the aim of retaining old customers while attracting new ones.

Shergill & Nargundkar (2005) analyzed the main concept behind marketing innovation. The main idea behind the concept of marketing innovation is to work on a new concept or a new strategy related to marketing. This needs to be different from the methods that already exercised by the company and are related to either alteration in the design or packaging or the product or related to pricing, promotion or distribution of the product. Manual (2005) defines it as the implementation of new marketing methods involving major changes in the product design, its placement, packaging, pricing, and promotion. Further, Kosak, Marko, et al., (2006) suggested that in the financial sector the concept of marketing innovation is the one that achieved by implementing very creative ideas and translating these ideas into technical specifications. These specifications are the ones that meet the customers and clients needs in a manner that way better than competitors do.

When working upon marketing innovation, companies are required to follow some principles (Li,2009). The foremost among the many principles is that marketing innovation should provide value to the customers. Another principle indicates that the marketing innovation should in turn help in competition. The third principle statesthat marketing innovation should be something that directly affects the organisation. Companies should not only pursue marketing innovation for the sole purpose of aspiration of innovation. Every single innovation designed by the organisation aims to generate profit for the company in the current scenario or for the future. The last but the most important principle is that marketing innovation requires sustaining. It requires continuous improvement and companies to survive needs to keep on innovating.

Alsamydia, et al.,(2010) studied the impact marketing innovation on the creation of sustainable competitive advantage for the fithe nancial sector. The sample consisted of 200 respondents that belonged to the mathe in commercial banks of Jordan. The result of the study shows a positive relationship among four variables that in turn will lead to sustainable competitive advantage. Moreira, et al., (2011) worked on the marketing innovation and their studies revealed that this concept is a result when a company introduced a set of different practices or there are even alterations introduced by the firm, the main concern is that several factors, in turn, influence these changes. These factors are both internal and external. Their study highlighted the main areas like technology, research and development and marketing activities that are in turn responsible for marketing innovation.

## MARKETING INNOVATION AND THE FOUR P'S

The marketing innovation concept can take various forms and some authors define it as innovating the firm's current marketing programs or methods including the 4 P's (Product, Price, Place, and Promotion) of marketing; while according to other authors, innovation is a new element of the marketing mix which provides many new and evident advantages to a company. Thus, for an organisation to be successful and to fulfill the needs and requirements of its stakeholders, it must invest in research and development of the products and services it offers. This can be done through marketing innovation. The literature shows that marketing innovation sometimes takes as innovation in the marketing methods and process and that includes the four Ps of the marketing mix. McCarthy (1978) discussed the four P's of marketing and how they can work towards creating a profitable institution. Marketing innovation in context to the marketing mix variable can help in targeting the customer and reaching the potential consumers. Tian (2007) explained the strategies in the field of marketing innovation. His study revealed that there are three main elements that constitute a market. These elements are people having demands, desire to purchase and people with the capacity to pay. In short, marketing innovation can work among these elements. The work by Tuan generated five aspects that lead to marketing innovation. These five aspects are as follows:

1. Innovation taking place in products all by itself.
2. Innovation in the objectives of the customers or in the marketing position.
3. Innovation in the geographical position. Innovation in a geographical position provides an opportunity so that to cater a new market, in case the already existing market is a saturated one, or other market offers less competition; changing the geographical position in this scenario will turn out to be in favor of the company.

4. Innovation in the distribution channel of the organisation. Many companies are founds ignoring this aspect, but the kind and quality of distribution channels are important factors in marketing innovation.
5. Innovation in the ways of sales promotion. This is the most popular of all areas as in recent years most of the companies are working on designing innovation related to promotion, prices and many more.

Marketing innovation is linked with improving the mix of target markets and how they can be used to serve the target market in a better manner. The main purpose of marketing innovation is to find out where the potential market exists and what the ways to serve the target market are. Then marketing innovation can be used to serve the identified and selected target markets (Johne, 1999). Using organisational innovation and marketing innovation, allows more room to conduct an extensive analysis of exactly the interactions that exist between the types of innovation. Identification of marketing innovations creates some space and allows for the analysis of the impact that takes place due to the interaction among all types of innovation. One of the very important characteristics of marketing innovation is that it has an orientation towards the market and the customers; at the same time, It keeps in view the main sales target as to improve the sales and the market share as well. Cooperstein (2011) considers innovation to be proactive in incorporating new idea in marketing plans since marketing innovation is the art of discovering and capitalizing on new business opportunities.

According to Tsai (2001), organisations are found working on innovative products or even a marketing process that they create to be profitable. These products and processes are the ones which are unique and are designed to meet the customer needs and create value for them. Here marketing innovation is an explicit act of what a firm creates, and this act has several dimensions. These dimensions include the launch of a new product, pricing, promotion, distribution channel and many new combinations that result in innovative marketing.

Technology is one factor that changes every day and the business needs to change its operating environment very drastically to optimize the opportunities. The results indicate that the performance of marketing innovation is not dependent on only one model because it depicts several other dimensions. Marketing innovation is not something that comes along in a flash, but it needs to be sustained, changes should be made with the innovation and should be increased with the passage of time.

## MARKETING INNOVATION IN TOURISM

In every sector of the service as the tourism industry, each organisation has been looking at how they can entice the consumer to buy into what they offer. Needless each organisation has had to look at and think outside of the box in their marketing approaches and be more innovative in what they are doing. Therefore, in tourism marketing, which comprises of numerous autonomous suppliers, yet consumers make purchase decisions based on the totality of the experience a destination (Palmer and McCole, 2000; Williams and Palmer, 1999).

Tourism-related services have emerged as a leading product category to be promoted and distributed to consumer markets through a variety method and using different electronic platforms (Connolly et al, 1998; Sussman and Baker, 1996; Archdale et al., 1992; Millman, 1998; Underwood, 1996) and ideologies. By using different platforms and, what could be argued, innovative approaches allow them to male electronic commerce offers with much greater flexibility for the tourism supplier who is now operating in greater and more volatile markets and an industry (Palmer and Cole, 2000) than ever before.

The tourism industry has been identified as one of the key industries for driving economic development and economic transformation (Rogerson, 2002a; Rogerson, 2002b). In many respects, the marketing challenges facing tourism businesses are unique in that these businesses cannot be promoted in isolation from their competing and complementary products (Middleton and Clarke, 2001; Bennett, 2000). Compounding this challenge is the fact the industry is part of the service sector and the tourism product is predominantly a service offering (Bennett, 2000; Middleton and Clarke, 2001; Palmer, 2001).

Tourism is in the forefront of information communication technologies (ICTs) adoption and e-business in e-marketing (E-Businesses Watch, 2006) because of having to embrace new technologies to facilitate their tourism services in with other intermediaries and distribution channels (Tsiotsou and Ratten, 2010). Although tourism businesses are considered early adopters of new technologies there is still today an under-utilization and under exploitation of these technologies in innovation from being used as a marketing tool.

The factors of the internet being used as a marketing tool have been discussed largely about aspects of physical goods (Powell & Dent-Micallef, 1997; Zhang & Lederer, 2006).

Nonetheless, the potential benefits of using the internet as a marketing tool in the tourism industry have been well documented (Gretzel, Yuan & Fesenmaier, 2000; Kasavanna, Knutson & Palonowiski, 1997; Walle, 1996). These benefits include cost-savings (for instance cheaper advertising and lower expenditure on physical retail sites), speed, accessibility, convenience, improved customer relationship management, improved target marketing, and a worldwide reach for even the smallest tourism benefit (Boshoff and Elliott, 2009) a view shared by Costea et al.(2013) where they highlight the internet that it has a global, interactive, flexible, dynamic, accessible to a broad audience and abounds in resources of all kinds (Grossek, 2006). What is evident from the arguments and rationale put forward that there is a clear link for tourism businesses using the platform for external commerce.

The use of this method for external commerce is very good in handling the clearance of perishability in a greater capacity close to the time in the use of managing yields effectively (Wolff, 1997; Connolly et al., 1996). Boshoff and Elliott (2009) further identified it as a resource for such a platform, which allows businesses to leverage generic information technologies and yields through the internet to give a 'Return on Investment' (ROI) (Mata, Fuerst and Barney, 1995). Having the internet in a virtual space must be now seen as a compulsory component of tourism activity for many reasons (Stanciu & Costea, 2012; Costea et al, 2013) as has been highlighted specifically for ROI and very good at targeting user segments and the presence in the online environment giving it credibility to a tourism organisation with the right modelling.

Durkin and Mcgown (2001) developed a theoretical model to describe the role and importance of the platform, through using it in innovative ways so that it can be utilised as a platform for the marketing of the tourism business which has already been discussed. The model explains the competencies that a tourism business would need to be able to migrate it from the initial concept and then the application of its innovative use through the internet as an effective marketing tool to ensure that it is successful through to its implementation stage as a platform (Boshoff and Elliott, 2009).

Firstly, the tourism organisation should have an "Innovative vision', of what the internet can achieve, and secondly, a competency defined by Durkin and Mcgowan (2001) as "value'. which implies that the owner-manager takes the innovative vision further and actually acquires the technology and technical competencies to utilise the medium, the third competency is that of 'technical ability' and the last competency proposed that of "innovation in control". This competency-based model implies that the tourism business manages the internet within the context of the marketing activities on a continuous basis, which means a high level of involvement on the part of owner-manager (Boshoff and Elliot, 2009; Durkin and Mcgowan, 2001). By using involvement in this type of modeling by using such approaches the customers benefit by gaining immediate gratification of their requests through a greater choice, multi-sensory, accurate an and up-to-date information and an easy to use interface (Pollock, 1996). Needless to say, it benefits tourism businesses by developing a coherent position in the marketplace; increasing their market share by getting closer to the customers (actual and potential); and subsequently by providing greater satisfaction (Sussmann and Baker, 1996).

Then the issue of simplifying choice process raises two important concerns in the adaptation of electronic commerce. First, the ability of electronic commerce to learn about the needs of individual consumers, and secondly the ability of individual tourism supplier to link together their websites to present a complete "virtual" tourism experience which is appropriate to individual's needs (Palmer and McCole, 2000). The internet, currently, provides the ideal situation now than ever before for tourism businesses to become a virtual organisation linked to this information technology available for innovation in marketing as well as using others such platforms in the social media environment such as Facebook, Instagram, Twitter, Pintrest and many more.

## SOCIAL MEDIA (SM)

The digital revolution and social media are considerably influencing the tourism-related industry (Sotiriadis, 2016; Benckendroff et al, 2014; Law et al, 2014), and particular the virtual phenomenon (Palmer and McCole, 2000). The major impacts have come through social media (SM) and mobile telephony (Leung et al, 2013; Sigala et al., 2012). The adoption of SM and sharing on these platforms are growing globally. What has been reported by the eMarketer, the number of SM users across the globe exceeds over 2.5 billion, and more than 30 percent of people worldwide used SM regularly in 2015 (e-Marketer). SM platforms have become a powerful social tool for online communications allowing tourists to interact and share their views, to collaborate and contribute to developing, extending, rating and commenting on tourism experiences (Sotiriadis, 2016; Gretzel and Yoo, 2013; Leung et al, 2013; Sigala et al, 2013).

The internet today provides the ideal situation than ever before for tourism businesses to become a virtual organisation linked to information technology available for innovation in marketing as well as using other platforms in the social media environment such as Facebook, Instagram, Twitter, Pinterest and many more. The digital revolution and social media (SM) is considerably influencing the tourism-related industry and, the virtual phenomenon.

Because of the use of SM in this manner innovation takes place through the tourists becoming the co-designers, co-producers, co-marketers, and co-consumers of tourism experiences (Sigala et al, 2012). Due to this SM's great popularity among consumers be creators in this way it must be a high corporate priority. However, there is a significant degree of uncertainty among the tourism industry with allocating efforts and budgets to SM (Paniagua and Sapena, 2015). According to the Social media Marketing Industry Report in 2013, 97% of marketers indicate that they participate in social media marketing, but one it four marketers claim that they can measure the return from their coal media activities (Chang, Chou, Yu-Wu and Wu, 2017). Additionally, regarding the effectiveness of Facebook marketing, 37%

of marketers agree that their Facebook efforts are effective, whereas the remainder is uncertain or has opposite opinions (Stelzner, 2013).

What is clear from some of the views that have been put forward (Sotiriadis, 2016; Bennckendroff et al, 2014; Law et al, 2014) that the way SM is used is most definitely becoming an innovative phenomenon and it is changing the face of how consumers plan and buy travel products, but also co-producers in engaging new customers to exit brands and new ones also which corporation are going must start acknowledging.

Corporate owned SM is now widely applied in smart tourism practices to maintain a tourist's emotional connections to a product (Wang, Li, and Li, 2013). Marketers can use owned social media as a source a customer voice and market information to learn about their experiences about tourism products, identify new tourism, identify new tourism destinations, or receive early warnings regarding certain products (Sun and Lee, 2017). Gaining insights from customers can also help tourism marketers engage customers to co-create tourism products or to simply improve existing ones (Chang et al, 2018).

STA Travel, the world's largest travel company for young adults, used their owned social media sites to enable customers to help one another solve product related problems. The company launched an 'Unexpected Europe' campaign by sending the company's most socially active customers under 30 years old on a six-city tour in Europe (Chang et al, 2018). These customers act as STA travel insider, providing unique travel tips and tour guidance and sharing their experience on STA Travels YouTube channel, blog, and insider's websites and social channels (PRWeb, 2016). Another example where social media platform have been used are through Finnairs; "Quality Hunters" campaign where it provides an example for product co-creation. In this campaign, seven people were selected as Quality Hunters whose mission was to travel around the world for 48 days and share their ideas and insights on how Finnair and Helsinki Airport could improve the flight and airport experience through the Finnair blog and Twitter. Visitors to the Quality Hunters website and its owned social media sites could set tasks for them, make comments and share them, while passengers at Helsinki Airport could drop by at Hunter's Lounge to exchange their opinions (Change et al, 2018).

Through this what has become clearly apparent that new technology applications such as mobile services (mobile TV, mobile WEB) and Web 2.0 constitute significant areas for tourism marketers and businesses to consider (Tsiotsu and Ratten, 2010). The resultant of this has changed consumer behaviour and tourism firms' management. New innovative technologies benefit tourism consumers because it minimises transaction costs, brings higher quality products to the market, and share market information, lower uncertainty and aid in distribution channel efficiently. For example, Web 2.0 is essentially altering the behaviour of tourism consumers in their search through mobile technology and also recommendations through social media in their decision making process and after consumption response (Tsiotsu and Ratten, 2010). Tourists no longer only receive information and consume tourism services but they are the producers of tourism feedback and destinations (Sigala et al, 2012). Because of Web 2.0, the collaboration of trip planning, social media, and its content enables network results in new products/ services and travelers involvement in business operations which has enabled the tourism consumer to move from passive to active prosumers (producers and consumers) of travel experiences (Tsiotsu and Ratten, 2010).

The SM helps in driving innovation through the tourism industry and its consumers. The connected consumers are playing an active role in supporting the identity of a tourism company's brand. Brand strategy is to differentiate the business and the different types of products and services, and to build economic value for both the consumer and the tourism businesses brand itself. There are a variety of different brands that are used in tourism marketing from travel agents, companies advertising tourism products such as hiking equipment to destinations such as Canada brand (Hudson and Ritchie, 2009). Brand equity in the use of social media has made an organisation more accessible than ever before through platforms such as Facebook, Instagram, Pintrest or Twitter. Therefore, this without a doubt adds value to the brand and also the reinforces the brands attributes such as reputation, symbols, associations, and names (Tsiotsu and Ratten, 2009). The use of social media in tourism businesses leads to more brand involvement and engagement. Therefore, within the organisation they need to link their thoughts within their marketing plans to such social media approaches including an innovative approach of liquid branding, which can further add value to a brand.

## Liquid Branding

The root inspiration for traditional branding is probably the Swiss Style that really dictated, clean use of logos in branding. Traditional branding guides strongly controlled how logos could be used; their size, the space around them, their colors). The rigid template guides allowed the consistent application of a brand by non-designers across business units – making this approach appealing within keep the businesses name being at the forefront, in particular in the Tourism industry. This branding process remains popular among Tourism brands today.

The expansion of the media choices is accelerating the need for branding to be more flexible. The old ways of crafting a fixed brand identity and rigidly controlling it are ending. Similarly, the quickening pace of consumer fatigue requires brands to be constantly interesting and agile. This leads to brands needing to continually reinvent themselves, which is the antithesis of classical branding strategies. Liquid branding implies that the various brand elements such as colors, size, backgrounds, and elements that create the brand can all be malleable, so that the brand can adapt and be fun and seemingly appear "new" to consumers without having to redesign the brand every few years (William, 2015). The earliest example of liquid branding is a case of MTV that had challenged the traditional constraints of fixed logo branding, and the logo and associated visuals elements were modified without worry – to represent – 'A cool, rock-n-roll image. The later other brands such as American online, 'Apple' also followed this trend of liquid branding (William, 2015).

The iconic branding of the past is morphing into a more expressive form within the industry today. Rather than relying on a single icon (the logotype) to capture a brand's identity, the iconography is going deeper. The overall style and elemental treatments are being used to carry the brand (see figure 1). An icon may still exist, but it's no longer sacrosanct. Its holistic design approach that's being used to communicate a company's core values- allowing for much more fluidity in the overall brand in the Tourism industry to ensure brand engagement.

Highly shared content greatly promotes brand engagement, and this strengthens brand value. Needless to brand engagement must be at the heart of every Tourism business and operator in the 21st Century within their marketing plan. What must also be understood is that the tourism consumer is no longer grounded in one spot, one medium or one homepage – and what is also become known as "liquid consumer" that demands "liquid creativity" from marketers within the tourism industry (Fine, 2019).

When this approach is used within a tourism brand campaign strategy, liquid content should be highly aligned to the tourism business with which it is associated. It may include direct references to the brand or seek to build strong engagement with the target audience (Edmonds, 2019). To use this approach, the tourism business must consistently reflect its brand.

As early as the 1990's, brand equity has been widely discussed, in particular in tourism destination marketing as a development (Sam-Liu and Chou, 2016). By using the liquid branding innovation helps play a very important role not only in establishing the tourism product characteristics but also the marketing segments and enhance tourist's loyalty. (Horng, Liu, Chou & Tsai, 2012). The development of this type of branding approach can assist in communicating information about tourism destinations with tourists, including attributes, benefits, value, culture and the personality of destination (Lockshin and Spawton, 2001). In addition, Liquid branding also helps in developing relationships among the various constructs related to brand equity such as personality, symbols, users, user image, and country of origin, organisational affiliations, emotional aspects and self-expression of interests (Aaker, 2009). Aaker and Joachimstahler (2009) sited in Liu and Chou (2016) noted that any means of promoting branding such as; name and symbols can serve as an advantage or disadvantage, these can either increase or decrease customer perceptions of the value of the product or in this case tourism service. Thus, liquid branding can be used to increase the financial performance of a tourism organisation, as the tourist will trust that brand more and exhibit a higher degree of loyalty (Aaker, 2009).

It must be recognised there is also liquid consumption associated with liquid branding of tourism products. The usefulness of liquid branding and its relationship with brand loyalty had inspired Bauman's (2000; 2007a) to research theoretical models of liquid modernity. In it, the author uses the metaphor of liquidity to explain how everyday life has moved from being stable and secure to be more uncertain and rapidly changing (Bardhi & Eckhardt, 2017).

Therefore, the tourism sector now needs to be more proactive in the ways it should market and build brands. A solid or fixed brand image consumption will not disappear due to liquid branding, however definitely the trend in picking (Bardhi and Eckhardt, 2017).

What must be noted that the other concept of liquid branding is still evolving, and it links an offering to 'freedom of a brand visual identity' and this, in turn, can influence consumption patterns! Liquid branding provides tourism companies more freedom than was possible before in using branding elements such as colors, size, backgrounds, and elements to make their brands more malleable to encourage consumption patterns in the tourist.

Tourism organisations can use the liquid brand to make it fun and seemingly appear 'new' to tourists without having redeveloped the brand every year. It also means that the discerning tourism business that they will have to work harder to identify what they are at their core and how they want tourists to perceive them- they'll have to actually figure out their brand's essence!

It must be noted that the essential challenge that a 'liquid branding' presents to the tourist company is that in order to do liquid branding, they have to do it the right way. Of course use of innovative technologies, ICT is of great help. However, the organisations have to employ the right kind of designer and a marketer that work together to create the liquid 'elements' while keeping the ' essence' of the overall tourism brand. It also means the brand does not have to fit into a carefully manufactured fixed grids and templates, and that it does not always have to be uniform. The brand can be flexible, and liquid provided the brand still remains true to its 'core identity'.

The liquid brand is more expressive and flexible, the broad adoption of liquid branding will probably be slower for many tourism organisations to resistant to change the traditional ways of branding. The innovating tourism organisations will eventually embrace the new approach in marketing and branding.

## Audio Branding

The technology has changed the ways consumers remember a brand and brand identity. All of us do remember, the ways an Intel advertisement will end with a unique tune, a bong' at the end, followed by the display of logo, 'Intel inside'. The brand touches the 'sense of hearing' and is recalled by the user as fun and music. The trend has been there since the audio has been used in brands in form of jingles, music or tunes, however, the inventions and innovations in technology and digital technology have to lead to expressive 'audio branding'. Audio Branding is a process of brand development and management that uses audible elements of the brand for communications so that a multi-sensory brand communication gives a unique brand identity and provides opportunities for a holistic brand design (ISA, 2019). Audio Branding aims at building a brand sound that represents the identity and values of a brand in a distinctive manner. The audio logo, branded functional sounds, brand music or the brand voice are the characteristic elements of Audio Branding. While audio branding can be expensive for most organisations, it has been around since the age of radio, when television came on the scene, audio branding slowly became an afterthought for tourism organisations because of expenses of TV Advertisements (Hayzlett, 2014). The emerging of new media and devices with built-in audio delivery, such as podcasts, streaming media or smartphones, expands the opportunities for audio branding.

Audio branding makes use of audible elements of brand within the framework of brand communication and reaches multiple senses (International Sound Awards, 2019 (ISA)). Using audio branding in tourism enables the organisation, such as; Virgin, Thomson and many others to build they're solidly a brand that represents the identity and values of a brand in a distinctive way that captures the consumer's attention and hopefully draws them in. The audio logo, branded functional sounds, brand music or the companies brand voice are characteristics elements of Audio branding can aid in optimizing brand communication and in designing a better sounding environment.

There are many examples where this platform has also been used by tourist boards such as the Vienna Tourist board and Airlines such as KLM(***Adapted from ISA, 2019***).

## CASE STUDIES OF AUDIO BRANDING

### Case 1: Vienna Tourist Board

**Agency:** Sound Strategy (Vienna, Austria)

The Vienna Tourist board developed this campaign in the year 2009/ 2010 for destination branding. It was used to check the current touristy view about Vienna and help them to potentially establish the future direction of the destination brand Vienna with 10,000 people from its target market and over 550 experts were rhythm, which creates an atmosphere of departure, which phrases musically the claim Now or Never. The Vienna Tourist Board Soundscape served to linger into the atmosphere of the brand can be self-similar adjusted to any particular point of contact. The acoustic elements are applied in the worldwide destination marketing of Vienna for touchpoints.

## Case 2: KLM

**Agency:** Massive Music (The Netherlands)

The KLM brand was helped to shape the brand identity by translating the KLM brand heritage and brand value into music and a sonic logo. Through the 9-step process of sonic branding, a shaped sound was created that was distinct to KLM's basic values and it helped KLM to communicate their brand in an effectively. The aim was to bring more consistency in KLM's use of music, to tell its heritage and make sure people could relate to the core values and of the organisation.

In establishing instrumentation, musical intervals and tempo were explored. Where some aspects did not prove valuable like when some typical Dutch instruments like the 'Freeport' (friction drum), turned out to be cartoonesque. Other aspects like a distinct first interval of the melody which was derived from the Dutch national anthem (het Wilhelmus) did work. The end result is a sonic logo that implies values like 'safety' has a human touch and symbolizes a flight.

The sonic logo plays an essential part of KLM's corporate identity and was implemented on and offline. To facilitate KLM's and its use of the sound logo and its various interpretations, Massive Music created a customized logo strategy which allowed them to use the sonic logo and translate it into longer musical scores as well as a dedicated online music bank (sound library) where all compositions containing the sound logo could be stored and ready to be used.

By using various technological platforms that are available today for tourism destinations/companies can enhance their brand value by using the techniques of 'audio branding'. Surely, the use of audio branding will play a vital role in marketing and reaching out to tourists. The tourist has access to many companies or when they are exploring a destination via the internet. The tourists will have access to visual information via 'Liquid branding as well as to 'audible information' by the use of; audio branding'.

Thus, a multi-sensory approach to branding will be more effective in building brand awareness, trust, loyalty, and ultimately brand loyalty. The multi-sensory information that is shared through a range of digital platforms needs to be developed by the team of eclogitic, creative and marketing experts

The new approaches of branding in the tourism industry will help the destination marketing organisation in not only retaining existing tourist bases but also in reaching out to new tourist.

## CONCLUSION

In the tourism industry marketing innovation have a significant role for any tourism organisation to remain competitive in an ever-changing environment. it will provide tourism companies and destinations a way of differentiating themselves from their competitors and gaining a competitive advantage. The innovation in the process of a tourism organisation in general and marketing, in particular, can enhance their growth further. The branding strategies a, methods, tools and process are changing since the adoption of digital technology in marketing and branding. The organisation is able to reach their tourism' appeal through multisensory information, that touches the five senses in a more effective way. The use of 'Liquid branding ' and audio branding to introduce, enhance and develop various audio and visual elements of brand is a new trend in branding. Therefore, as brick and mortar or a virtual organisation, the destination marketing organisation, should innovate their marketing efforts, and should respond to change within a dynamic business environment.

## REFERENCES


Aaker, D. A. (2009). *Managing brand equity*. New York: Simon and Schuster.

Aaker, D. A., & Joachimsthaler, E. (2009). *Brand leadership; Building assets in an information economy*. New York: Simon and Schuster.

Alsamydia, Alnawas, & Yousif. (2010). The impact of marketing innovation on creating a sustainable competitive advantage: The case of Private commercial banks in Jordan. *Asian Journal of Marketing*, *4*(3), 113-130.

Andrews, J., & Smith, D. C. (1996). In Search of the Marketing Imagination: Factors Affecting the Creativity of Marketing Programs for Mature Product. *JMR, Journal of Marketing Research*, *33*(2), 174–187. doi:10.1177/002224379603300205

Barnatt, C. (1997). Virtual organisation in the small business sector; the case of Cavendish management resources. *International Small Business Journal*, *15*(4), 36–47. doi:10.1177/0266242697154002

Chang, H. L., Chou, Y. C., Wu, D. Y., & Wu, S. C. (2018). Will firms marketing efforts on owned social media payoff? A quasi-experimental analysis of tourism products. *Decision Support Systems*, *107*, 13–25. doi:10.1016/j.dss.2017.12.011

Chris, E. (2010). *Innovation management; a literature review of innovation process models and their implications*. Available at: http://www.lectoraatinnovatie.nl/wp-content/uploads/2011/01/Innovation-management-literature-review-.pdf

Clemmer, J. (1998). Path to innovation; Spend at least 25% of your time with customers. *Executive Excellence*, *15*, 10–10.

Cooperstein, D. (2011). What'sImportant To CMOs In 2011? *Forrester Blogs*. Available at: http://blogs.forrester.com/david_cooperstein/11-01-10whats_important_to_cmos_in_2011

Elliott, R., & Boshoff, C. (2009). The marketing of tourism services using the internet: A resource based view. *South African Journal of Business Management*, *40*(3), 35–49. doi:10.4102ajbm.v40i3.543

Faull, J. (2018). *'We're full steam ahead': travel brands brush off Brexit concerns ahead of January marketing blitz*. Retrieved from www.thedrum.com

Haddad & Algadeer. (2004). An empirical investigation on the impact of innovation within organisations on marketing innovation. *Jordan Journal of Applied Science*, (7), 77-95.

Hayzlett, J. (2014). The language of Audio Branding. *Marketing Management: Agents of Change*, 18-19.

Horng, J.-S., Liu, C.-H., Liu, C. S., & Tsai, C. Y. (2012). Understanding the impact of culinary brand equity and destination familiarity on travel intentions. *Tourism Management*, *36*, 15–25. doi:10.1016/j.tourman.2012.11.002

Horng, S.-C. (1999). *Marketing Management*. Taipei: Shinlou Book.

Hudson, S., & Ritchie, J. R. B. (2009). Branding a memorable destination experience. The case of Brand Canada. *International Journal of Tourism Research*, *11*(2), 217–228. doi:10.1002/jtr.720

Innovating for the Rising Global Middle Class. (2011). Available at: http://bx.businessweek.com/innovation-in-marketing/view?url=http%3A%2F%2Finventionmachine.com%2Fthe-Sustainable-Innovation-Blog%2Fbid%2F79047%2FInnovating-for-the-Rising-Global-Middle-Class

Innovative Marketing. (2002). *Pharmaceuticals Policy and Laws*. Author.

Ioan, L. P., Gheorghe, P., & Monica, B. (2010). *A Theoretical Approach of the Concept of innovation*. Retrieved July 9, 2019, from ftp://ftp.repec.org/opt/ReDIF/RePEc/bbu/wpaper/151-156.pdf

Jacinta, M., & Jorge, S. (2011). M*arketing Innovation: study of determinants of innovation in the design and packaging of goods and services – application to portuguese firms*. Available at: http://academic-journal.org

Kemp, M. (2010). Define Your Marketing InnovationStrategy. *ForresterBlogs*. Available at:http://www.forrester.com/rb/Research/define_marketing_innovation_strategy/q/id/56829/t/2?cm_mmc=Forrester-_-Blogs-_-Related%20Research-_-5603

Kolle, S. (2006). Top ten trends in marketing innovation. *Future Labs*. Available at: http://www.futurelab.be/blogs/marketing-strategy-innovation/2006/10/top_ten_trends_in_marketing_in.html

Li, S. L. (2009). Marketing Innovation in Enterprises. *Commerce Modernization*, *37*(23), 45–49.

Lockshin, L., & Spawton, T. (2001). Using involvement and brand equity to develop a wine tourism strategy. *International Journal of Wine Marketing.*, *13*(1), 72–81. doi:10.1108/eb043371

Marko, K. (2006). *Development strategies for banks in Eastern European Markets; the role of IT systems*. Ljubljana: Faculty of Economics.

Medrano, N., & Olarte-Pascual, C. (2016). The effects of the crisis on marketing innovation: An application for Spain. *Journal of Business and Industrial Marketing*, *31*(3), 404–417. doi:10.1108/JBIM-02-2013-0048

Moreira, J., José, M., Jorge, S., & Gastao, S. (2011). Marketing innovation: study of determinants of innovation in the design and packaging of goods and services – application to portuguese firms. *International Conference on Marketing Studies.*

Palmer, A., & McCole, P. (2000). The role of electronic commerce in creating virtual tourism destination marketing organisations. *International Journal of Contemporary Hospitality Management*, *12*(3), 198–204. doi:10.1108/09596110010320760

Pros and Cons of Various Research Techniques. (n.d.). Available at: http://www.riger.com/know_base/research/pros.html

Research Methodology. (n.d.). *An Introduction*. Available at: http://www.newagepublishers.com/samplechapter/000896.pdf

Sam-Liu, C. H., & Chou, F. C. (2016). Tourism Strategy development and facilitation of integrative processes among brand equity, marketing and motivation. *Tourism Management*, 298–308.

Shergill, G., & Nargundkar, R. (2005). Market orientation, marketing innovation as performance drivers: Extending the paradigm. *Journal of Global Marketing*, *19*(1), 27–44. doi:10.1300/J042v19n01_03

Skinner, H. (2008). The emergence and development of place marketing's confused identity. *Journal of Marketing Management*, *24*(9/10), 915–928. doi:10.1362/026725708X381966

Sotiriadis, M. D. (2016). Sharing tourism experiences in social media; a literature review and a set of suggested business strategies. *International Journal of Contemporary Hospitality Management*, *27*(1), 179–225. doi:10.1108/IJCHM-05-2016-0300

Tian, F. J., & Li, Z. Y. (2007). Study on Choosing of Enterprise"s Market Innovation Domain and Its Venture-eluding. *Science and Management of S. & T.*, *28*(12), 68–72.

Tsai, M. T. (2000). *The research for influence of market information process and organisation memory on marketing innovation*. National Chengchi University.

Tsiotsou, R., & Ratten, V. (2010). Future research directions in tourism marketing. *Marketing Intelligence & Planning*, *28*(4), 533–544. doi:10.1108/02634501011053702

Wang, D., Li, X., & Li, Y. (2013). China's "smart tourism destination "initiative: A taste of the service-dominant logic. *Journal of Destination Marketing & Management*, *2*(2), 59–61. doi:10.1016/j.jdmm.2013.05.004

William, L. (2015). *Is your business ready for liquid branding?* Retrieved Jul 10, 2019, from Nevoniuom: https://www.nuvonium.com/blog/view/is-your-business-ready-for-liquid-branding

## KEY TERMS AND DEFINITIONS

**Audio Branding:** Is a process of brand development and management that uses audible elements of the brand for communications so that a multi-sensory brand communication gives a unique brand identity and provides opportunities for a holistic brand design.

**Innovation:** Innovation is knowledge-driven change process of introduction or modifications of a new policy, structure, method, process, a new idea, product or service or use of existing products or a new markets for existing products or even a new marketing method.

**Liquid Branding:** Is a technology-enabled process of branding such that the various brand elements such as colors, size, backgrounds, and elements are displayed dynamically and malleable, so that the brand can adapt and be fun and seemingly appear "new" to consumers without having to redesign the brand every few years.

**Marketing Innovation:** Is an ability and the process that an organisation follows in order to continuously improve its products and services, ideas as well as marketing process in order to satisfy the needs of its customers effectively.

**Social Media:** Electronic communication platforms such as websites and applications that enable users to create online communities to share information, ideas, personal messages, and other contents and to participate in social networking.

**Tourism:** It is a collection of activities, services, process, and industry that delivers travel experience to individuals or group of travelers; who will spend time away from home in pursuit of recreation, relaxation, and pleasure while making use of the commercial provision of service.

# Chapter 20
# Technology-Supported Marketing for Sustainable Tourism in the Himalayas

**Azizul Hassan**
*Tourism Consultants Network, The Tourism Society, UK*

## ABSTRACT

*The Himalayas are one of the trendy tourist attractions that actually developed a special interest tourism type: Himalayan tourism. A considerable number of research studies have so far covered Himalayan tourism from numerous perspectives. However, innovative technology-supported marketing for sustainable tourism in the Himalayas in practice has limited knowledge. The aim of this research is to outline aspects of innovative technology adoption for sustainable tourism marketing in the Himalayas. From the Nepal part of the Himalayas context, this conceptual research outlines the features of innovative technology adoption from Roger's theoretical understanding and incorporates with relevant debates and arguments. This research advocates for adopting innovative technologies to ensure and support sustainability concerns in the Himalayas. This research concludes that the adoption of innovative technology for tourism marketing in this part of the world can support sustainable practices in tourism.*

## INTRODUCTION

The Himalayan region has significant variation in people, resources and economic development to support tourism and tourism activities (The Daily Telegraph, 2016). Overall, population pressure and poverty remain the key features of tourism in this part of Asia. Because majority of the poor people live in Asia, the fragmentation of habitat, number of landless people is forcing people to move to relatively fragile ecological settings. The loss of habitat remains the most visible in the Indian sub-continent including the Himalayan region. This is obvious that tourism cannot be identified as the only responsible cause for this, but a number of other reasons can be attributed for the same. The Himalayas is in fact a human museum having mosaic of people with diverse ethnicity, cultures and traditional beliefs. The full Himalayan region has natural richness in terms of bio-diversity and flora and fauna. Every single part of

DOI: 10.4018/978-1-7998-0131-3.ch020

the Himalayas is an important tourist destination for diverse reasons. Roads are constructed for defence purpose, for accessing prominent pilgrimage places in the core of the Himalayas. These destinations are also used for summertime leisure and recreation activities encouraging the tourists to enjoy the rich bio-diversity, scenic beauty, and many forms of niche-tourism activities. There are many areas in Himalayas which have importance in religious tourism. Thus it is essential to realise the importance and potential of tourism in the Himalayas. The other fact is that the urbanisation process around the Himalayas and establishing highly industrialised capitals in the entire South Asia have adverse impacts on Himalayas.

Not only India but also Nepal is one of the most notable country in the Himalayan region shows wonderful exhibition of heritage and history supported by indifferent cultural expression, philosophy, thoughts and religion. This country remains the home to many world heritage sites with their exceptional architecture, religious associations and monuments. These all constitute tourism resources.

Many studies indicate the adoption of technology has positive impacts on sustainable tourism. Ali and Frew (2014) argues that balancing economic growth with protection of the environment is a challenge and so sustained tourism makes it highly attractive as a means of economic development of a region. A number of approaches such as marking indicators, eco-labelling, monitoring, and codes of conduct etc. has been used to create ssustaauible products, however still there is no very good progress made, hence there is a case for destination management through the innovative applications of information and communication technology (ICT) (Ali & Frew, 2014).

Very little known or almost no mentionable research has been carried out to contribute to this area of use of innovation and technology for sustainable tourism. This determines an existent knowledge gap. A research to contribute to this knowledge gap thus becomes valid.

## TOURISM IN THE HIMALAYAS

Being termed as the pride of the Asia, the Himalayas is famous for domestic and international tourism. Among many other mountain ranges in the world, the Himalayas is believed as the youngest of its class. The civilisation that emerged surrounding these mountains dates back to the very early of the human history. The Himalayas is so important that without it, the climatic set up of not only the Indian subcontinent but also of entire Asia would change. As believed by the researchers that once the Mount Kailash was the key centre of the world. The Brahmaputra, the Indus, and the Sutlej river systems actually originated from its snowy points. There are archaeological evidences that the very early urban civilisation was emerged in these river valleys that coursed from the Himalayan Mountains. Spectacular cities emerged in the Indus Valley's Mohenjo-Daro and Harappa. These mountains supposedly cover the world's one-fifth land surface area but are the habitat of the world's one-tenth population and supply essential resources to more than half of the global population. The Himalayas Mountains also act as the gene bank of flora and fauna species that are very important for human survival covering forestry, agriculture and mining. Many ethnic groups have turned the Himalayan Mountains as religious and cultural receptacles offering a range of tourist attractions that are completely different from the conventional ones. The folklore, myths, mystery, romance, and adventure in these mountains turn these tourists desperate for engaging in tourism activities in almost all seasons without considering involved risks. Hence there is a case of development but a sustainable development for Himalayas.

## Tourism in the Himalayas and Nepal

Nepal is a prominent Himalayan Hindu Kingdom. The country is landlocked between the Tibetan China in South Asia and India. The population of Nepal is significantly increasing. Nepal's terrain is rather mixed ranging from sub-tropical jungle to the icy Himalayas. This gives rise to the world's eighth highest mountains including the Everest. The different cultural landscape covers around 12 dominant ethnic groups. Nepal can relatively be a small country in terms of land area but this is an important country in South Asia. The county is famous for many forms of tourism activities including mountaineering/trekking, recreational and leisure events. As a result, Nepal gets huge number of international tourists from almost every parts of the world including Europe. The most recent initiatives of the Nepal government opened door for private sector collaboration in its tourism sector. The focus is revised on tourism product development and promotion of environmentally sound service and product offers to distribute equal economic benefits to all local communities that are generated from tourism (Cockerell, 1997).

Nepal has gathered sufficient multi-disciplinary data on identified tourism regions and resorts to understand quantitative impact research with advanced Alpine countries (Coppock, 1978; Pawson 1984; Pawson & Standford, 1984; Muqbil, 1985). Concern for the increasing degradation atop the Everest provoked SATA (South Asian Travel Awards) for preparing an Integrated Hill Development Project (IHDP) to overview interdependencies between tourism, regional market, and environment (Baumgartmer, 1978; Baumgartner, 1978; Mauch & Schwank, 1981). Baumgartner (1986) researched the socio-economic changes reinforced by tourism in the Rolwalling Valley in the Eastern part of Nepal. There are also some useful data generated from empirical research on diverse parks, trekking routes and tourist frequented areas (His Majesty Government of Nepal, 1977a, p. 2983; Pawson & Standford, 1984; Bjonnes, 1979; Bhattarai, 1985). The Government of Nepal's 1995 policy document for the tourism sector outlined its strategic importance and demand for converging with attached sectors. The policy particularly concentrated on ecotourism resources and activities. The institutional mechanisms were also strengthened and a new Nepal Tourism Board was created for operation following the guidelines from an advisory body named the Tourism Council having representatives from major public and private sector organisations. Even such efforts were insufficient and there is a visible sign as the recent trends shows that tourism in Nepal is seemingly dominated by mass tourism suffering from political disturbances. These are having negative effects on the Nepal tourism industry and discourages tourist arrivals that threatens this identified mainstay of Nepal's economy.

At least in the last three decades, international tourism witnessed a steady growth in Nepal mainly based on the popularity of mountaineering and trekking that accounts to almost 15%-20% of the total tourist arrival (Cockerell, 1997). The Ministry of Tourism and Civil Aviation with an aim to maintain such competitive advantage formulated an infrastructure in present mountain parks as well as opened new trekking areas for disperse new trekkers. Despite of this consciousness on carrying capacity, Nepal tourism experiences difficulties to manage the growth of tourism in their mountains. However, there is a lack of primary data and information in this regard (Lamba & Sherpa, 1994; Pobocik & Butalla, 1998).

For regulating mountaineers, "ecological damage permits" need to be collected from the Ministry of Tourism, Nepal to climb peaks in Sagarmatha National Park, Annapurna region, and Langtang National Park. On the other side, many other tourist areas in the mountains are protected by an annual quota system and increased fees for trekking. Nepal although has exceptional and attractive cultural and natural resources, the lack of relevant facilities and resources (i.e. access difficulties, unavailability of both inbound and internal airline seats, lack of similar infrastructure, and poor land based access) act as barriers for general tourism promotion in this country. Such slower pace of tourism outlines the control of the government in exercising main control over tourist's arrival in the country followed by their free movement within.

The socio-economic opportunities generated from tourism in most of the remote mountain areas of Nepal actually replaced the traditional forms of local livelihood generation (i.e. animal husbandry and agriculture) as the key economic mainstay of population in the Annapurna Conservation Area (His Majesty Government of Nepal, 1977b). Traditional farmlands followed by the trekking routes are covered with high value crops and fruits that actually highlight positive economic changes. The labour market has also experienced demand for tourism products changing the employment pattern. The number of local people employed in tourism has increased significantly. These people are mostly hired by group trekkers than by free and independent travellers (Upadhyay, 1984; Banskota & Upadhyay, 1991). These independent trekkers are outnumbered group trekkers in the Annapurna area that shows the opportunity for more employment creation by the local hotels and lodges for accommodation and food (Pobocik & Butalla, 1998).

## IMPACTS OF TOURISM IN THE HIMALAYAS

Tourism activities covering the mountains are important and rewarding in many locations across the world including the Alpine countries. A considerable number of research studies are conducted outlining the impacts of tourism in these particular areas. These research studies have revealed that the mountain eco-systems are comprised of fragile ecologies followed by restricted tolerance and carrying capacity limitations. Thus, mass or aggressive tourism can definitely raise serious issues. These particular research studies outline a constant tension between the ecology and economy accompanied by a development dilemma that actually expands the gap between the 'dependency and autonomy' (Brugger et al, 1984). The impacts of both winter and summer recreation in the mountain environment and in the climatic changes in Australia are revealed in some research studies (Buckley et al., 2012). These researchers thus reached the conclusion that tourism can have notable implications for managing the mountain land areas. Some other research studies point out that the mountain environment conservation through tourism in Greece depends on the local community involvement who actually maintained an acceptable ecological integrity and scale of the region. The community people ensured that primary infrastructure is offered to the tourists that resulted funding flow to strengthen the local economy. Amenity migration issue becomes an important concern in the delicate mountain areas. People primarily make visits to these mountains for leisure, adventure, and health recreation. These people in many cases return with a mind-set for a longest stay through purchasing their second house for escaping the stress that they gather from the urban areas (Price et al., 1997). Thus a number of the mountain experts suggest for a role model tourism that can properly integrate with agriculture and forestry (Messerii, 1987). This needs to be more than convenience matter to turn tourism more or less an ecological industry on the genesis of sustainability and ecotourism.

## TOURISM IN THE HIMALAYAS AND SUSTAINABILITY

A sustainable development implies meeting needs of the present generation without compromising the ability of future generation to serve their needs too (Ali& Frew, 2014). In line with triple bottom line argues that a sustainable destinations is such that there is aballance between needs of people, planet and Profit. In other words a sustainable or eco-friendly destination will balance the requirements of environment, economic and socio-cultural aspects of tourism development (Ali & Frew, 2014). Sustainability can be achieved when the triangle's all of the three elements –the economy, the ecology, and the society progress concurrently (Rieder & Wyder, 1997). As a result, sustainability in the mountains searches for specifying the present demands by retaining the natural capacity resources for fulfilling the long term demands without compromising both the environmental quality and social equity (Roe, 1996). Considering all of these concerns, this is quite normal that the UN General Assembly declared the year 2002 as the International Year for Mountains and Ecotourism with an aim that issues related to both the environmental quality and social equity would attain importance. Unluckily, the World Travel and Tourism Council (WTTC), World Tourism Organization (WTO) and the Earth Council in 1995 accepted an economic approach for sustainable tourism suggesting that sustainable tourism can only be attained through forms of economic development subject to huge tourist number.

The sustainability can be achieved by managing the factors related to sustainability such as carrying capacity, taxes & economic approach, self-regulation via code of conduct, education, monitoring the goals of ecotourism, government interventions and use of innovation and technology (ICT) (Ali & Frew, 2014).

The innovation and ICT technology can be of much use to manage all of the factors of sustainability. Citing a range of authors, Ali& Frew, (2014) argue that ICT can help in capacity management, dynamic taxing, knowledge based destination management systems, stakeholders' awareness & participation and in setting and monitoring indicators of sustainability (see Table 1 for details).

## TOURISM IN THE HIMALAYAS AND TOURIST'S TECHNOLOGY ADOPTION DECISION MAKING

Technology and innovation have huge importance in fostering a greener, low-carbon economy for ensuring sustainability. Thus, it is apparent that technology can offer better solution for sustainable tourism in Himalayas. However, the question is, would stakeholders in general and Destination Management Organisations (DMO) and consumers in particular adopt the technology in the process of buying and consuming the tourist products and services ?

The process of technology adoption for decision making is rather complex. In general, process is defined as 'A series of actions or steps taken in order to achieve a particular end' (Oxford Dictionaries, 2015). Process in this research is defined as a set of actions as logically attached with each other. A number of relevant theories are placed for explanation as discussed in the literature review chapter. The process of technology adoption for consumer decision making is rather logical consisting of a series of stages.

Theory of reasoned action (TRA) postulates that intention to use is determined by attitude towards the product/technology/behaviour and subjective norms (Fischbein & Ajzen, 1975). The Theory of Planned Behaviour (TPB) postulates that in addition to attitude, and social norms, the other factors namely perceived control and self-efficacy also have important role in adoption new technology or product (Ajzen,

*Table 1. ICT tools and sustainable destinations*

| Issue / Cause and Description. | ICT Based Tools |
|---|---|
| Capacity management and stakeholder involvement: Engages stakeholders (people, planet and profit) with consolidating and distributing a comprehensive range of tourism information and its carrying capacity etc. | Destination Management System |
| Community empowering and participation: Online information system that disseminates relevant information for community participation in the decision making. | Community Informatics |
| Information & monitoring: An ICT systems which integrate disparate environmental Information (tracking, waste monitoring, emissions and cost/benefit) to facilitate management. | Environment Management Information Systems |
| Knowledge based destination management: Information systems that can capture, store, manage, manipulate, analyse, integrate and display geographical data for proposed sustainable development. | Geographical Information Systems |
| Sensitisation & Promotion: Location-sensitive information to and from a mobile device to raise awareness and familiarise them with e.g. the culture, heritage and customs of a destination | Location Based Services |
| Location: Satellite-based navigation system that provides spatio-temporal distribution of tourists, their positioning, navigation and timing services to users. | Global Positioning System |
| Transpiration: Telematic systems, which provide detailed information on traffic and destination leading etc. the stakeholders. | Intelligent Transport System |
| Management decisions: Data warehouses that manage business critical information in order to provide quality decision making. | Tourism Information System |
| E-Tourism: Virtual tours may act as a full or partial substitute for destinations that have exceeded their carrying capacity | Virtual Tourism |
| Monitoring: Software used to monitor the economic impacts of tourism to balance economic activity with other needs. | Economic Impact Analysis Software |
| Monitoring energy consumed and carbon footprints: Energy usage and Emission monitoring for cleaner environment benefit for visitors and local community. | Carbon Calculator |

Adapted from Ali & Frew (2014)

1985). The perceived control is determined by perceptions of easiness of the task and one's ability to think that one can do the task i.e. self-efficacy.

Thus the Technology adoption also require skills, opportunities, resources, or cooperation for their successful execution. Tourism as an academic domain has similarity and differences as compared to other sectors, as both the market and the consumer characteristics in tourism are different. Thus there might be some differences between general consumers and tourists as consumers, in terms of product or service preferences, behaviours and purchase actions (Alegre & Garau, 2010).

Generally all consumers, who adopt technology for decision making tend to follow some logically related stages to adopt and use technology for purchase decisions (Alegre & Garau, 2010). There should be a series of stages logically tied to each other as process of technology adoption for decision making. TRA and TPB postulates that stages of adoption starts with three variables, (attitude, subjective norms and perceived behaviour control) leading to intentions to use technology and ultimately using the technology. Thus in proposing a Tourist's technology adopted decision model, this research uniquely blends current theories with opinions of tourism consumers and industry experts.

*Figure 1. The proposed tourists' technology adoption model*
*(source: adapted from of sources (Gretzel, 2000; Davis, 1989, Leue et al., 2014))*

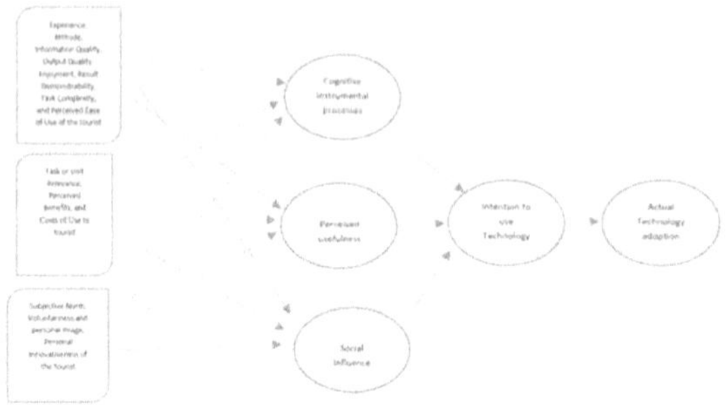

One of the pioneer studies in the adoption of technology was Technology adoption Model (TAM) that argued that perceived usefulness, perceived ease of use determines the intended and actual usage (Davis, 1989).Since then several alternatives has been developed based on TAM that includes more constructs such as perceived usefulness (job relevance, and benefits), social influence (subjective norm, voluntariness, and image) and cognitive instrumental processes (output quality, result demonstrability, and perceived ease of use) (Gretzel, 2000).Acceptance Model (TAM) represents innovative technologies as adopted for decision making by tourism consumers to purchase holiday in an advanced market setting of the United Kingdom.

In this research, the decision model appears combining factors and process of technology adoption for decision making for holiday purchase. This research is partly influenced by a similar research by Leue et al. (2014) where, a model of technology acceptance is proposed.

The model in Figure 1, is entirely based on existing literature while considering perceived usefulness. 'Personal Innovativeness', 'Perceived Benefits', 'Information Quality' and 'Costs of Use' as the basic antecedents to move towards 'Perceived Usefulness' and 'Perceived Ease of Use' leading to 'Attitude', 'Intention to Use technology' and 'Actual Usage Behaviour' to form the model.

The model (see Figure 1) is mainly based on the Technology Acceptance Model (TAM) as proposed by (Davis, 1986; Davis, 1989; Davis et al., 1989). The significance of the TAM (Davis, 1986; Davis, 1989; Davis et al., 1989) to use in this model is established by Wu et al. (2011) and Ayeh et al. (2013) where, Leue et al. (2014) believe that the TAM (Davis, 1986; Davis, 1989; Davis et al., 1989) is the most suited model to study technology acceptance. Then each element of the model is made supported by existing literature. 'Enjoyment' is seen as an important intention for using a new technology (Ha & Stoel, 2009; Wojciechowsk & Cellary, 2013) and also in the Technology Acceptance Model 3 (TAM3) as proposed by (Venkatesh & Bala, 2008). 'Perceived Benefits' as an element of the model is backed by (Amoako-Gyampah & Salam, 2004; Lopez-Nicolas et al., 2008; Olsson et al., 2012). 'Personal Innovativeness' is supported by (Lin et al., 2007; Morosan, 2012; Olsson et al., 2012; Yussof et al., 2011) and importantly by the Diffusion of Innovation Theory (Rogers, 1962). 'Information Quality' in the model is given importance by (Ha & Stoel, 2009; Olsson et al., 2012). Lastly, the 'Cost of Use' is explained by Parra-López et al. (2011) as important element of the model.

The model in Figure 1, is justified on the basis of existing literature and a limited number of theories and the TAM (Davis, 1986; Davis, 1989; Davis et al., 1989) in particular. However, the Technology Adopted Decision Model as outcome of this research is designed as more robust and explanatory. This model is to be based on reviews of more theories and literature of technology adoption and decision making to build the model with factors and process of AR adoption by tourism consumers. This chapter mainly focuses on use of eMarketing to promote sustainable tourism. The next section discuss this in more details.

## TOURISM IN THE HIMALAYAS AND eMARKETING

Marketing has been in existence for centuries to cater human centred demands that establishes the idea that marketing becomes operation as long as the humans started trading (Wang & Fesenmaier, 2006). However, the form of marketing has changed from one to another taking shapes from conventional to non-conventional and then online format. The methods of marketing have been changing gradually in terms of improvement and more efficiency. Delivering the messages of marketing has adopted efficient marketing techniques (Doolin et al., 2002).

eMarketing in its simplest manner can be defined as electronic marketing aimed to apply both techniques and principles of marketing through the use of electronic media and more precisely the Internet (Piccoli et al., 2001). The terms as Internet marketing, online marketing and eMarketing are very often granted as similar to each other. In more applied sense, eMarketing as a process is used by brands for marketing on the Internet (Leong, 2001). This type marketing involves both indirect and direct marketing components by using diverse technologies to connect customers with a particular business. Within this definition, this becomes evident that eMarketing involves almost all activities that a business can conduct by using the worldwide web for attracting, developing and retaining both new and existing customers (Mills et al., 2008; Wang & Russo, 2007). eMarketing is the outcome of modern and developed communication system; where, Internet stays as the key platform. This type marketing is entirely technology focused that replaced centuries old marketing principles and tactics. Recently developed, social media has been both popularizing and effecting eMarketing in relation to its application in complex market systems. According to El-Gohary (2012), five distinct roles of interactive technology are: activity tracing, thought tracing, property exchanges, social exchanges and cultural exchanges.

The factors related to using eMarketing are similar to digital marketing. The study outlines that, consumers can ensure efficiency, the better return of investment and increased profitability that leads to increased adopting of eMarketing. The campaigns in eMarketing generate online sales increment by attracting potential consumer bases and by minimizing negative risks. A range of promotional channels are the basic element to reach potential consumers; however, certain business strategies are required to let marketing and promotional channels remain fully operational and effective.

## TOURISM IN THE HIMALAYAS AND INNOVATIVE TECHNOLOGY AND EMARKETING

The adoption of innovative technology has encouraged tourists for visiting to challenging the mountain frontiers that were considered as remote once upon a time. The greater challenge at present now depends on creating unavoidable mountain tourism sustainable in terms of innovative technology supported marketing initiatives. There are evidences that innovative technologies are adopted in tourism (Hassan et al., 2017a; Hassan et al., 2017b; Hassan et al., 2017c; Shabani & Hassan, 2017; Hassan & Dadwal, 2018, Dadwal & Hassan, 2015).

The last section on technology adoption details a range of factors using TAM. Also the theory on diffusion of innovation postulates that the various influences that help spread the innovation can be thought of as lying on a continuum between pure diffusion (in which the spread of innovations is unplanned, informal, decentralised, and largely horizontal or mediated by peers) and active dissemination (in which the spread of innovation is planned, formal, often centralised, and likely to occur more through vertical hierarchies. When the mass media and other impersonal channels can create awareness of an innovation, interpersonal influence through social networks (defined as "the pattern of friendship, advice, communication and support which exists among members of a social system, Valente, 1996, p. 70) remains the dominant mechanism for diffusion. In order to help stakeholders adopt technology in vernal and eMarketing in particular a number of factors needs to be considered. Based on Rogers's overview on Diffusion of Innovation (Roger, 1995), and TAM; a number of components are identified related to the Diffusion of Innovation (DOI) and adoption of Technogym and marketing, as given in the next section:

- **Network Structure:** The adoption of innovations by individuals is powerfully influenced by the structure and quality of their social networks for strong indirect and moderate direct evidence (Fennell & Warnecke, 1988; Valente, 1996; West and Far, 1990).
- **Homophily:** The adoption of innovations by individuals is more likely if they are *homophilous meaning that*, they have similar socio-economic, educational, professional, and cultural backgrounds with current users of the innovation for strong direct evidence (Fennell & Warnecke, 1988; Fitzgerald et al., 2002; West & Far, 1990).
- **Opinion Leaders:** Some persons have a specific influence on the beliefs and actions of their colleagues (Becker, 1970). Expert opinion leaders exert influence through their authority and status, and peer opinion leaders exert influence through their representativeness and credibility (Fitzgerald et al., 2002; Locock et al., 2001). Opinion leaders can have either a positive or negative influence. If a project is insufficiently appealing (e.g. in clarity of goals, organisation, and resources), it will not attract the support of key opinion leaders (Locock et al., 2001; Rogers, 1995). Connecting the opinion leader's influence is also important. Even though the powerful impact of social influence like that of opinion leaders in naturalistic settings is well established, attempts for engaging such individuals in planned change efforts in many cases had disappointing results.

Champions: An innovation adoption by individuals in an organisation can possibly happen if the key individuals in their social networks are willing to support that particular innovation (Backer & Rogers, 1998; Markham, 1998; Meyer & Goes, 1988; Schon, 1963).

Boundary Spanners: An organisation is more likely to adopt an innovation if those people who have significant social ties both inside and outside the organisation are able and willing to link the organisation to the outside world in relation to this particular innovation. Such individuals play a pivotal role in capturing the ideas that will become organisational innovations (Rogers, 1995; Kimberly & Evanisko, 1981).

In tourism, eMarketing is particularly important because, business enterprises are required to become capable to understand the demands of both existing and potential consumers. Also, proper utilisation of business policies is essential and needs to be linked with effective marketing strategies. In many cases, eMarketing becomes an essential addition to an existing or potential business enterprise involved in tourism and hospitality industry. Thus, this study suggests that in practice, consumers define that digital marketing has clear dependencies on the Internet and very often pronounced as Internet marketing. E-mail marketing can be considered as highly effective as a form of digital marketing.

## CONCLUSION AND FUTURE SCOPE

This study argues that there is great need of developing sustainable tourist destinations and products. This requires a shift in adoption of technology by all stakeholders and use of eMarketing in tourism marketing strategies for the Himalayas tourism. This research aims to dig out innovative technology adoption aspects for sustainable tourism marketing in the Himalayas Mountains. The Nepal part of the Himalayas Mountains is the context. After critical explanations and arguments, this research supports the adoption of adoption of innovative technology to ensure sustainability in tourism in this part of the world. Considering the features of innovative technology adoption and TAM; this research critically discusses the significance of the factors such as; ease of use, usefulness, 'Network Structure', 'Homophily', 'Opinion Leaders', 'Champions', social norms and so on as relevant drivers for adoption of technology in the operational process and marketing of tourism. Various theoretical explanations are incorporated with relevant debates and arguments.

In practice also, tourism marketing in the Himalayas Mountains in recent years is somehow influenced by innovative technologies. As evidenced from the research findings, tourism product and service offers on innovative technology supported platforms are more often available than ever before. The tourists are allowed to have more access to innovative technologies and research findings spot the availability of innovative technology as the most influential factor. Easy access of the Internet on mobile phone device is a very positive development in this direction. The government's policy accelerates adoption of the innovative technology for the sustainable tourism. These policies would increase the Himalayan Mountains tourism at further level. This research notices a sharp growth of interest in the Himalayan tourism among general tourists who actually are well conversant with the most recent innovative technologies for tourism. The researcher of this chapter think that there is need for more research studies in the future to cover different aspects of tourism including sustainability in the Himalayan Mountains having supports from innovative technologies. One of the significant limitation of this study is the lack of primary data that possibly could have enriched the explanations and critical discussions. Thus, future research studies should present primary data and create a link between the primary and the secondary data to offer a comprehensive understanding of innovative technology adopted tourism in the Himalayas.

## REFERENCES

Alegre, J., & Garau, J. (2010). Tourist satisfaction and dissatisfaction. *Annals of Tourism Research*, *37*(1), 52–73. doi:10.1016/j.annals.2009.07.001

Ali, A., & Frew, A. J. (2014). Technology innovation and applications in Sustainable destination development. *Information Technology & Tourism, 14*(4), 265-290.

Amoako-Gyampah, K., & Salam, A. (2004). An extension of the Technology Acceptance Model in an ERP implementation environment. *Information & Management*, *41*(6), 731–745. doi:10.1016/j.im.2003.08.010

Ayeh, J., Au, N., & Law, R. (2013). Towards an understanding of online travellers' acceptance of consumer-generated media for travel planning: Integrating technology acceptance and source credibility factors. In L. Cantoni & Z. Xiang (Eds.), *Information and communication technologies in tourism 2013* (pp. 254–267). Heidelberg, Germany: Springer. doi:10.1007/978-3-642-36309-2_22

Backer, T. E., & Rogers, E. M. (1998). Diffusion of Innovations Theory and Work-Site AIDS Programs. *Journal of Health Communication*, *3*(1), 17–28. doi:10.1080/108107398127481 PMID:10947372

Banskota, K., & Upadhyay, M. (1991). *Impact of rural tourism on the environment, income, and employment in the Makalu-Barun area. Report 17, The Makalu-Barun Conservation project*. Kathmandu: Department of National Park and Wildlife Conservation, HMG Nepal and Woodlands Mountain Institute.

Baumgarnter, F. (1978). *Trekking Tourism in Nepal*. Zurich: Report of the INDEL Team.

Baumgartner, R. (1986). Tourism and socio-economic change: The case of Rolwaling Valley in eastern Nepal. In K. Seeland (Ed.), *Recent researches in Nepal* (pp. 199–217). Munchen: Weltforum Verlag.

Becker, H. S. (1970). *Sociological work: Method and substance*. Chicago, CA: Aldine.

Bhattarai, S. (1985). Environmental impact of tourism on mountain ecosystem. In *Proceedings of the International Workshop on the Management of National park and Protected Areas in the Hindukush Himalaya*. Kathmandhu: The King Mahindra trust Furniture Conservation (KMTNC) and International Centre for integrated mountain development (ICIMOD).

Bjonnes, I. M. (1979). *Impact on a high mountain ecosystem-recommendations for action in Sagramatha*. Kathmandu: N.P.W.C. Office.

Brugger, E. A., Furrer, G., Messerli, B., & Messerii, P. (1984). *The transformation of Swiss Mountain Regions*. Bern: Verlang Paul Haupt.

Buckley, R. (2012). Sustainable tourism: Research and reality. *Annals of Tourism Research*, *39*(2), 528–546. doi:10.1016/j.annals.2012.02.003

Chang, G., & Caneday, L. (2011). Web-based GIS in tourism information search: Perceptions, tasks, and trip attributes. *Tourism Management*, *32*(6), 1435–1437. doi:10.1016/j.tourman.2011.01.006

Cockerell, N. (1997). International Tourism Reports No.1 - Nepal. *Travel and Tourism Intelligence*, *1*, 40–57.

Coppock, R. (1978). *High season: The consequences and potential of tourism in the Region of Mount Everest*. Munich: German alpine Club.

Dadwal, S., & Hassan, A. (2015). The augmented reality marketing: a merger of marketing and technology in tourism. In N. Ray (Ed.), *Emerging innovative marketing strategies in the tourism industry* (pp. 78–96). Hershey, PA: IGI Global. doi:10.4018/978-1-4666-8699-1.ch005

Davis, F. D. (1986). *A technology acceptance model for empirically testing new end-user information systems: Theory and results*. Sloan School of Management, Massachusetts Institute of Technology.

Davis, F. D. (1989). Perceived usefulness, perceived ease of use, and user acceptance of information technology. *Management Information Systems Quarterly*, *13*(3), 319–340. doi:10.2307/249008

Davis, F. D., Bagozzi, R. P., & Warshaw, P. R. (1989). User acceptance of computer-technology - a comparison of 2 theoretical-models. *Management Science*, *35*(8), 982–1003. doi:10.1287/mnsc.35.8.982

Doolin, B., Burgess, L., & Cooper, J. (2002). Evaluating the use of the Web for tourism marketing: A case study from New Zealand. *Tourism Management*, *23*(5), 557–561. doi:10.1016/S0261-5177(02)00014-6

El-Gohary, H. (2012). Factors affecting E-Marketing adoption and implementation in tourism firms: An empirical investigation of Egyptian small tourism organizations. *Tourism Management*, *33*(5), 1256–1269. doi:10.1016/j.tourman.2011.10.013

Fennell, M. L., & Warnecke, R. B. (1988). *The diffusion of medical innovations: An applied network analysis*. New York, NY: Plenum. doi:10.1007/978-1-4684-5436-9

Fitzgerald, L., Ferlie, E., Wood, M., & Hawkins, C. (2002). Interlocking Interactions, the Diffusion of Innovations in Health Care. *Human Relations*, *55*(12), 1429–1449. doi:10.1177/001872602128782213

Gretzel, U. (2000). Tourism Managers' Adoption of Marketing Decision Support Systems. *Journal of Travel Research*, 172-181. Retrieved 6 30, 2019, from https://www.researchgate.net/publication/249700978_Tourism_Managers'_Adoption_of_Marketing_Decision_Support_Systems

Ha, S., & Stoel, L. (2009). Consumer e-shopping acceptance: Antecedents in a technology acceptance model. *Journal of Business Research*, *62*(5), 565–571. doi:10.1016/j.jbusres.2008.06.016

Hassan, A., & Dadwal, S. (2016). Search engine marketing – an outlining of conceptualization and strategic application. In W. Ozuem & G. Bowen (Eds.), *Competitive social media marketing strategies* (pp. 219–234). Hershey, PA: IGI Global. doi:10.4018/978-1-4666-9776-8.ch011

Hassan, A., Ekiz, A., Dadwal, S., & Lancaster, G. (2017a). Augmented Reality Adoption by Tourism Product and Service Consumers: Some Empirical Findings. In T. Jung & M. C. tom Dieck (Eds.), *Augmented Reality and Virtual Reality: Empowering Human, Place and Business* (pp. 47–64). New York, NY: Springer.

Hassan, A., Ekiz, A., Dadwal, S., & Lancaster, G. (2017b). Augmented reality adoption by tourism product and service consumers: some empirical findings. In T. Jung & M. C. tom Dieck (Eds.), *Augmented reality and virtual reality: empowering human, place and business* (pp. 47–64). New York, NY: Springer.

Hassan, A., Shabani, N., Ekiz, H. K., Dadwal, S., & Lancaster, G. (2017**c**). Augmented reality in tourism and factors for its adoption: an empirical study. In *The 22nd Annual Graduate Education and Graduate Student Research Conference in Hospitality and Tourism*. The University of Houston and The Hong Kong Polytechnic University. Available at: http://gradconfht.com/

His Majesty Government of Nepal. (1997a). *Economic survey of the fiscal year 1996/97*. Ministry of Finance.

His Majesty Government of Nepal. (1997b). *Statistical year book of Nepal*. Kathmandu: National Planning Commission Secretariat, Central Bureau of Statistics.

Kimberly, J. R., & Evanisko, M. J. (1981). Organizational innovation: The influence of individual, organizational, and contextual factors on hospital adoption of technological and administrative innovations. *Academy of Management Journal*, *24*, 689–713. PMID:10253688

Lama, W., & Sherpa, A. (1994). *Tourism development plan for the Makalu Base Camp Trek and Upper Barun Valley. Revised Draft Report*. Kathmandu: Makalu-Barun Conservation Project.

Leong, C. (2001). Marketing practices and Internet marketing: A study of hotels in Singapore. *Journal of Vacation Marketing*, *7*(2), 179–187. doi:10.1177/135676670100700207

Leue, M., tom-Dieck, D., & Jung, T. (2014). A Theoretical Model of Augmented Reality Acceptance. *e-Review of Tourism Research*. Retrieved from: http://3ws1wk1wkqsk36zmd6ocne81.wpengine.netdna-cdn.com/files/2014/02/enter2014_RN_93.pdf

Lin, C., Shih, H., & Sher, P. (2007). Integrating technology readiness into technology acceptance: The TRAM Model. *Psychology and Marketing*, *24*(7), 641–657. doi:10.1002/mar.20177

Locock, L., Dopson, S., Chambers, D., & Gabbay, J. (2001). Understanding the role of opinion leaders in improving clinical effectiveness. *Social Science & Medicine*, *53*(6), 745–757. doi:10.1016/S0277-9536(00)00387-7 PMID:11511050

Lopez-Nicolas, C., Molina-Castillo, F., & Bouwman, H. (2008). An assessment of advanced mobile services acceptance: Contributions from TAM and Diffusion Theory Models. *Information & Management*, *45*(6), 395–364. doi:10.1016/j.im.2008.05.001

Markham, A. N. (1998). Life online: Researching real experiences in virtual space. In C. Ellis & A. P. Bochner (Eds.), *Ethnographic alternatives book series*. Walnut Creek, CA: Altamira Press.

Mauch, S. (1979). *The estimating impact of I.H.D.P. programme components*. Zurich: Infras.

Mauch, S., & Schwank, O. (1981). *I.H.P.D. and tourism: Interdependencies between the L.J.R.P. tourism environment, regional market and I.H.P.D.* Zurich: Infras.

Messerii, P. (1987). The development of tourism in the Swiss Alps: Economic, social and environmental effects. *Mountain Research and Development*, *7*(1), 13–24. doi:10.2307/3673321

Meyer, M., Johnson, D., & Ethington, C. (1997). Contrasting attributes of preventive health innovations. *Journal of Communication*, *47*(2), 112–131. doi:10.1111/j.1460-2466.1997.tb02709.x

Mills, E., Han, J., & Clay, J. (2008). Accessibility of Hospitality and Tourism Websites: A Challenge for Visually Impaired persons. *Cornell Hospitality Quarterly*, *49*(1), 28–41. doi:10.1177/1938965507311499

Morosan, C. (2012). Theoretical and Empirical Considerations of Guests' Perceptions of Biometric Systems in Hotels: Extending the Technology Acceptance Model. *Journal of Hospitality & Tourism Research (Washington, D.C.)*, *36*(1), 52–84. doi:10.1177/1096348010380601

Muqbil, I. (1985). Himalayan tourism: Economics vs ecology. *Tourism Recreation Research*, *10*(1), 45–46. doi:10.1080/02508281.1985.11014361

Olsson, T., Kärkkäinen, T., Lagerstam, E., & Ventä-Olkkonen, L. (2012). User evaluation of mobile augmented reality scenarios. *Journal of Ambient Intelligence and Smart Environments*, *4*(1), 29–47.

Oxford Dictionaries. (2015). *Process*. Retrieved from: http://www.oxforddictionaries.com/definition/english/process

Parra-López, E., Bulchand-Gidumal, J., Gutiérrez-Taño, D., & Díaz-Armas, R. (2011). Intentions to use social media in organizing and taking vacation trips. *Computers in Human Behavior*, *27*(2), 640–654. doi:10.1016/j.chb.2010.05.022

Pawson, I. G., & Standford, D. D. (1984). Effect of modernization on Nepal's Khumbu Region: Changes in population structure 1970-1982. *Mountain Research and Development*, *4*(1), 73–78. doi:10.2307/3673172

Pawson, I. G., Stanford, D. D., Adams, V. A., & Nurbu, M. (1984). Growth of tourism in Nepal's Everest region: Impact on the physical environment and structure of human settlements. *Mountain Research and Development*, *4*(3), 237–246. doi:10.2307/3673144

Piccoli, G., Spalding, B. R., & Ives, B. (2001). A Framework for Improving Customer Service through Information Technology: The Customer-service Life Cycle. *Cornell Hotel and Restaurant Administration Quarterly*. *A*, *42*, 38–45.

Pobocik, M., & Butalla, C. (1998). Development in Nepal: The Annapurna Conservation Area Project. In C. M. Hall & A. A. Lew (Eds.), *Sustainable tourism: A Geographical perspective* (pp. 159–172). Essex, UK: Addison Wesley Longman.

Price, M. (1987). Tourism and forestry in the Swiss Alps: Parasitism or Symbiosis. *Mountain Research and Development*, *7*(1), 1–12. doi:10.2307/3673320

Rieder, P., & Wyder, J. (1997). Economic and political framework for sustainability of mountain areas. In B. Messerii & J. D. Ives (Eds.), *Mountains of the world: A global priority* (pp. 85–102). New York, NY: Parthenon Press.

Roe, E. M. (1996). Sustainable development and cultural theory. *International Journal of Sustainable Development and World Ecology*, *3*(2), 1–14. doi:10.1080/13504509609469919

Rogers, E. M. (1962). *Diffusion of innovations*. New York, NY: The Free Press.

Rogers, E. M. (1995). *Diffusion of Innovations* (3rd ed.). New York, NY: The Free Press.

Sacherer, J. (1976). *The Sherpas of Rolwaling Valley, North Nepal: A study in cultural ecology* (Unpublished PhD Thesis). University of Paris.

Schon, D. A. (1963). *Reflection of concepts*. New York, NY: Humanities Press.

Shabani, N., & Hassan, A. (2017). Augmented reality for tourism service promotion in Iran as an emerging market. In V. Nadda, S. S. Dadwal, & R. Rahimi (Eds.), *Promotional strategies and new service opportunities in emerging economies* (pp. 116–129). Hershey, PA: IGI Global. doi:10.4018/978-1-5225-2206-5.ch005

The Daily Telegraph. (2016). *The Himalayas: Trip of a Lifetime*. Retrieved from: http://www.oxforddictionaries.com/definition/english/process

Upadhyay, M. P. (1984). *Environmental impact on mountain ecosystem by trekkers and mountaineers: Mt. Everest Trek Route Survey Report*. Kathmandu: NAIS.

Valente, T. W. (1996). Social Network Thresholds in the Diffusion of Innovations. *Social Networks*, *18*(1), 69–89. doi:10.1016/0378-8733(95)00256-1

Venkatesh, V., & Bala, H. (2008). Technology Acceptance Model 3 and a Research Agenda on Interventions. *Decision Sciences*, *39*(2), 273–314. doi:10.1111/j.1540-5915.2008.00192.x

Wang, D., Park, S., & Fesenmaier, D. R. (2012). The role of smartphones in mediating the touristic experience. *Journal of Travel Research*, *51*(4), 371–387. doi:10.1177/0047287511426341

Wang, Y., & Fesenmaier, D. R. (2006). Identifying the Success Factors of Web-Based Marketing Strategy: An Investigation of Convention and Visitors Bureaus in the United States. *Journal of Travel Research*, *44*(3), 239–249. doi:10.1177/0047287505279007

Wang, Y., & Russo, S. M. (2007). Conceptualizing and evaluating the functions of destination marketing systems. *Journal of Vacation Marketing*, *13*(3), 187–203. doi:10.1177/1356766707077687

West, M. A., & Farr, J. L. (1990). Innovation at work. In M. A. West & J. L. Farr (Eds.), *Innovation and creativity at work: Psychological and organizational strategies* (pp. 3–13). Chichester, UK: Wiley.

Wojciechowski, R., & Cellary, W. (2013). Evaluation of learners' attitude toward learning in ARIES augmented reality environments. *Computers & Education*, *68*, 570–585. doi:10.1016/j.compedu.2013.02.014

Wu, K., Zhao, Y., Zhu, Q., Tan, X., & Zheng, H. (2011). A meta-analysis of the impact of trust on technology acceptance model: Investigation of moderating influence of subject and context type. *International Journal of Information Management*, *31*(6), 572–581. doi:10.1016/j.ijinfomgt.2011.03.004

Yussof, A., Ibrahim, R., Zaman, H., Ahmad, A., & Suhaifi, S. (2011). Users Acceptance of mixed reality technology. *Issues in Information Systems*, *7*(1), 194–205.

## KEY TERMS AND DEFINITIONS

**Diffusion of Innovation:** It is process of how, why, and at what rate an innovation, technology, or new idea spreads and reaches the users or consumers.

**eMarketing:** Process and activities involved in planning and executing the conceptions, distribution, Pricing and promotion of products, ideas and services in a computerized, networked environment using information communication technology.

**Innovation:** The process of converting or developing or implementing an idea or invention into a practical output or design, or good or service to the market that creates value for the stakeholders.

**Innovative Technology:** Technology that is innovative or used in an innovative way with considerations for improving value for the business or its stakeholders.

**Motivation to Use Technology:** A set of reasons, benefits, rationale for using a technology or innovations.

**Sustainable Tourism:** The development and use of tourism destination or products such that it not only meets needs of current stakeholders, but also it does not compromise the future needs of stakeholders in the future.

**Technology:** The application of scientific knowledge and skills for practical purposes, human welfare, or in industry. This might include, Information communication Technology (ICT), mobile technology, and design including robotics, artificial intelligence, computing, drones, and space exploration.

**Tourism:** It is collection of activities, services, process and industry that delivers travel experience to individuals or group of travelers who will spend time away from home in pursuit of recreation, relaxation, and pleasure, while making use of the commercial provision of service.

# Chapter 21
# Digitalisation of the Global FinTech Industry

**Muhammad Waleed Butt**
*Coventry University, UK*

**Usman Javed Butt**
*Brunel University, London, UK*

## ABSTRACT

*The digitalisation of global financial technology and marketing is central for the success of many banking organisations across the globe. Digital disruption is a change that occurs when new emerging digital technologies and business models affect the value proposition of existing goods and services for low end demanding customers or for new market customers. Digital banking or online or virtual banking is leading to the digitization of all the traditional banking activities, products, process, or services. It is needless to state that mere adaptation of digital media to comply with trends does not guarantee success. The digital trends in the banking industry has seen banks focusing on digitalization core processes, increasing awareness, financial inclusions, and undertaking sustainable practices. FinTech (i.e., financial technology) is competing with traditional financial methods in the delivery of financial services and reaching the unbanked segment of society, particularly in developing countries. There is a strong need to understand drivers and trends in the FinTech industry.*

## INTRODUCTION

With an increase in technological advancement, we are witnessing drastic changes across numerous disciplines that is disrupting the conventional means of doing business, practices or a general course of action in given scenarios; the digital advancement has become so rapid, that vast majority of innovations go unnoticed (Canales, 2018). In the light of convenience, the technological advancement has brought along, the word 'Digital' has become an indispensable element of our life. From latest gadgets that didn't exist two decades ago to applications facilitating online conferences, essentially connecting people from different continents, to digital watching monitoring pulse and stress level, all these not only

DOI: 10.4018/978-1-7998-0131-3.ch021

eliminate hassle but provide avenue for businesses to align themselves and make most the most out of it to maximize the success of their respective businesses.

The new innovations and technologies are disrupting existing industrial structures and leading to the disappearance of some industries and also the evolution of new industries. The disruption has to lead to disappearances of fax machines, real based cameras, floppy disks etc. and the digital output, digital prints cloud storage and a range of new online services have taken their place. The traditionally known as IT companies are now in the core field of retailing, transportations, logistics healthcare and so on. Uber car share, Uber foods, Airbnb, Apple Pay are some of the new companies that have crossed the boundaries of IT industry and landed in other industries.

The rapid technological advancement has 87% business executive believe that digital transformation is imperative (Gartner, 2018). With increased competition, businesses are being compelled to adopt digital trends, prefer digital marketing over traditional marketing, and rethink their business models while others are exploring ways to leverage technology to minimize operational costs (Gartner, 2018). The industries are trying to find new ways to create competitive advantages, increases efficiencies to reach customers at the lowest possible costs. For instance, banks are striving to reduce operation cost by a partner with FinTech who provide technology to essentially provide same services as it is provided at a branch, with the only difference is these services are readily available.

FinTech - short for Financial technology, means technology and innovation that aims to compete with traditional financial methods in the delivery of financial services. The Newly arising FinTech industry needs to understand the target audience and design products accordingly. The banks are already using a range of digital marketing tools to analyze customers' needs patterns, so as to come up with attractive products that may drive up the usage of the business. Likewise, Banks need to explore ways to mitigate the risk of future by analyzing historical data and predict the hindrance of the future. Apart from the vital changes in behavior amongst millennial, it is significant to note that a vast majority of millennial have experienced recession of 2009 in the U.S, the impression of which has consequently turned millennial into cautious investors or in other words risk-averse; However, this risk averseness may vary amongst millennial across the globe (Sloan, 2018). In addition to Banking sector's focus on digitalization of their process, and attempt to move away from paperwork, the banks are largely focusing on a branchless aspect of banking; also known as 'FinTech' industry thus realizing the future revenue streams in light of behavioral shift of the masses (Kendall, 2017).

## LITERATURE REVIEW

### Theory of Disruptive Innovation

The theory of disruptive innovation may help explain the race for digital technology adoption. While we are not oblivious to Bank's propensity to sell banking product every time it interacts with customers as figured by SVP of Cement's banking practice (Wisniewski, M. 2016), Clayton M. Christensen explains theory of disruptive innovation in the Innovator's dilemma (1997) which states that smaller companies with fewer resources can dethrone companies with substantial resources, better positioning and market share (Hutt, 2016).

Disruptive Innovation refers to innovation and technology whose application significantly affects the way a market or industry functions thus leading to either creation of a new market or new industry & value network and eventually disrupts the structure and makeup of an existing industry, market and value network. According to disruptive innovation theory, the big market players often focus on improving existing products, while new entrants focus on 'Foothold' market wherein customers are happy despite poor services (Raynor, M. E. 2011). Christensen observed that new entrants who merely replicated the existing model failed while the one wherein the existing model was tailored to serve underserved or less attractive market succeeded(Raynor, M. E. 2011). The theory of disruptive technology has been vastly misunderstood. It has been unusually linked with Uber's phenomenal success of its operations that continue to expand till date. However, Uber's success was by no means a disruption. For a company to be categorized as disruption, it has to comply with two tenets of disruption, with it being organization either serving low-end footholds or new market footholds (Clayton M. Christensen, 2015).

With digitalisation taking the world by storm, it is imperative to understand how industries are being shaped by rapid technological developments from a wider perspective. In the light of ever-increasing incorporation of digital technologies like artificial Intelligence, machine learning, & data analytics, a clear pattern of investors' interest has emerged in business that shed light on their digital initiatives (Suraj Srinivasan, 2019). From self-driving cars of Tesla to artificial Intelligence predicting inventory stocking, all these technologies, if used in the right way, could have a significant impact on financial indicators. This explains banks' thirst to adopt technology and focus on underserved or unbanked population (new market foothold) by means of using digital wallet accounts to create a market where It didn't exist before. Banks are rapidly adopting technology, partnering with FinTech and subsequently increase their outreach. For a bank to ensure that it is causing disruption, it may have to do the opposite of what Uber has done by serving an existing market in San Francisco where people were already acclimatized to booking rides.

Further, in this chapter, you will find the digitalisation aspect to better understand the constituents that are enabling the banking industry to cause disruption and adopt digital transformation to aid the same.

## Digital Disruption and Marketing Return on Investment (MROI)

Digital disruption is a change that occurs when new emerging digital technologies and business models affect the value proposition of existing goods and services. Such disruption are technology driven and give rise to new business models. It appears easier to understand how companies like Uber, Amazon, Google, Apple, and Lyft, etc. are disrupting industries, but it is not easy to recognise when disruptive technology appears on the horizon. The disruptive technologies create competitive advantages and first movers advantages. However, it is important to continually ' engage with any disruptive technologies as this will make a difference between survival or growth. Innovators not only have to innovate but also disrupt an organisation and industry, as they use innovation as a tool of normal competitive advantages and thus changing the organizational dynamics, strategic planning, investment priorities and the future technologies (Hill, 2017). The digital technologies can create core competencies as such technologies are virtual, embedded in the organisational systems, or appear from the outside normal horizon of organizational vision, however they add value to the stakeholders, can be rare, non-imitable, non-substitutable and widely applicable in a range of fields (VRIO). Previously many technology disruptions had been generally triggered by physical technologies such as PCs or ATMs, but now with some exceptions (robotics) the most digital disruptions are initiated in the virtual world, which makes them difficult to recognize, or imitate or understand(Hill, 2017). In the past, companies such as Facebook, Netflix,

Alphabet/Google, Amazon web service and Uber, etc. have used *BuTeInSo* model of disruption. Where *Bu* – means, Business (Market, Development, Pricing, Delivery, et); *Te* -Technology (invention, design, usage, etc.), *In*-Industry (processes, standards, methods, customers, etc.) and *So*- Society (change culture, habits, movements, etc.) (Hill, 2017).

In the present age, digitalization & digital transformation is amongst the most overused words, pretty much like strategy. One would often find executives using them in their day to day life without realizing its essence. This implies mere adoption of technology does not ensure businesses' success, rather the right use of technology by examining the disguised opportunities and translating into an action plan (Furr & Shipilov, 2019).

Businesses all across the world are implementing technology throughout its entire value chain; likewise, this has allowed banks to tweak their services to facilitate their customers. Since businesses are heavily reliant on customer data, almost all digital campaigns of products by banks are designed after developing an understanding of Consumer data, this is where marketing and finance are working together to create a meaningful return on investment -MROI on marketing efforts- a way of measuring the return on investment from the amount a company spends on marketing (Nichols, 2014).

It is needless to say that swift digital changes are causing change management issues amongst the organizations as some opt to make amends into business' value proposition by drastically changing it to cater new demands of the customers while the others prefer sticking with the existing value proposition, though opt to use the digital tools effectively (Furr & Shipilov, 2019). Kotter's theory of change management underlines that for change to occur, organizations have to understand its significance (Piirainen, 2016). Realizing the same, the companies are on varying stages of change management in their pursuit for digital adopting, while some are busy in creating a sense of urgency for digital implementation, others have institutionalized the change.

For instance, Maersk, a shipping container company which belongs to an industry that plagued by varying global trade barriers and lack of transparency. Maersk, however, partnered with governmental institutions and IBM to implement blockchain technology, allowing it to receive real-time data from sensors to lower administrative expenses, considerably improve risk assessment, which eventually is enabling it to serve the customer the right way (Furr & Shipilov, 2019).

In the past, unavailability of data posed a huge obstacle to marketing efforts for the bank to justify in front of stakeholders. For instance, in 2010 Intel began to work on the link between marketing and P&L. David Ginsberg who worked as VP insights. Brand and strategy at Intel realized the significance of analytics and bridged the gap between finance and marketing by highlighting the impact of the latter on sales (Nichols, 2014). This has led to financial accountability of marketing to come into prominence in addition to the availability of a platform with which testing of different scenarios may be checked and feedback that could be incorporated into performance strategies. To achieve successful implementation of distal disruptive technologies, not only requires leadership and change management, but it also requires an understanding of customers, their needs, and their reasons of adoption or not adoptions of technological innovations.

## Innovation Operational Model For Banks

For a bank to meet its business needs, it has three innovation operational model at its disposal: Centralized, decentralized & hybrid.

The centralized model is characterized by the presence of an innovation officer who scrutinizes with its innovation team to cater to business needs. The model banks on the need for innovation and consistently paves way for the bank to embrace new ideas and concept (EY, 2017). The Centralized model ensures better coordination amongst the departments, specifically with chief technology officer, etc. Despite the positives, the flip side is the team's lack of understanding for different business units. It is substantial to note that FinTech's may benefit from the support extended by centralized innovation model given it is successful. On the contrary, the business decision cycle may be thought about at length.

The decentralized model works well for small banks with each business unit running with tailored made governance processes, working favorably in favor of identifying problem and solutions. Like the rest of the operational innovation model, it has a flip side as the process may be plagued with the repetition of a task performed, varying processes and inconsistency. FinTech's may not have qualms working with organizations working along the lines of decentralized model since FinTech culture is characterized by quick decision making, drastic changes and rapid deployment of newer technology.

In the light of the pros and cons mentioned of Centralized and decentralized model, the suggested model is hybrid according to EY's research (EY, 2017). The need to have distinct innovation team that not only sets the right direction but leadership that backs and reinforces the benefit of innovation. The hybrid approach focuses on lessening the distance between innovator and business units but the transparency while the acquisition of technology on both sides is of utmost importance so as to avoid the FinTech from getting confused.

## GLOBAL INCLINATION TOWARDS FINTECH ADOPTION

As per theories of consumer behavior, many external and internal factors determine the adoption or use of a product or services. The researchers have used theories of reasoned actions, theories of planned behavior, theories of diffusion of innovations, etc. have been used to develop technology adoption model (TAM). In summary, those models have evidenced that user-related personal factors (demography, need, utility, ease of use, self-efficacy, comparative advantages and external factors (technology related, trends in mobile usage, social-cultural and environmental factors) determine the success of adoption of technology (Venkatesh, Thong, & Xu, 2012 and Lai, 2017).

FinTech is deemed as the next big thing which is luring market players from different industries to explore the prospects of tapping into FinTech. A detailed survey conducted by EY of developing & mature markets has identified a pattern in terms of feature usage offered by the FinTech (EY, 2017). The report extensively highlights the initial market traction the FinTechs have been able to garner in developing and mature markets by extending primary features of money transfer. The incentive in developing market is to capture the unbanked population that does not have access to banking facilities.

The theory of financial innovation by Siber (1983) may explain the phenomenal inclination of firms to enhance financial inclusion efforts and may be defined as the expansion of money benefit is central to financial inclusion (Michelle, 2016).

For an instant in Pakistan, the mobile phone ownership in Pakistan amongst people in the age group of 15-65 is 57% (Rizvi, 2018). Despite the fact that smartphone ownership stands relatively lower at 22 owing to less usage of internet and the much-delayed entry of 4g technology in Pakistan's market that has seen gradual interest of masses towards the internet, (Shahid, 2017), yet the future seems promising since many banks in Pakistan alone are focusing on partnering with FinTechs and working to bank the unbanked by extending almost the same services as what conventional banking has to offer. Likewise, in India where the electronic market size is rapidly growing at 41% and is poised to reach US $400 billion (IBEF, 2019), Paytm FinTech is growing by leap and bounds as it has reported a financial profit of $2.7 million (Anand, 2019).. Given the phenomenal response, the organization is contemplating to introduce further products and increase transaction on this platform (Anand, 2019). EY's report also indicates the highest adoption rate to be in China and India at 69% and 52% respectively while average adopting in the emerging market is at 46% (EY, 2017).

The next section discusses a range of external and internal drives for the adoption of FinTech.

## Social Media and Technology Adoption in the Banking sector

The FinTech has gained tremendous popularity over the years, not because it is merely a trend that has matched people's lifestyle but the lucrative opportunity for businesses to expand, capitalize on ease of doing business that comes along with it, for customers and businesses alike. The app-based banking solutions makes everything tap away, accessible wherever and whenever. In present times, the banks are competing with each other to capture market share in the digital sphere; however, the platform based organizations with the accurate know-how of local dynamics have potential to bring an element of surprise in the competition.

For example, Kaobank as a digital-first bank; launched in 2017 and successfully amassed over 300,000 subscribers in the first 24 hours of its operations, which now is poised to have over 10 million customers in South Korea with a population of over 50 million (EY). The idea of Kakaobank was conceptualized by Kakao Talk, a popular messaging platform which identified that underutilization of banking products since the products itself was not customer-centric. Understanding the gap, the Kakaobank began to dig deeper. The research conducted in collaboration with EY concluded that the decision of switching banking service provider majorly hinges on price; therefore, pricing was a priority to better cater to banking demand of the South Korean.

This is another classical case of local know-how which has been discussed extensively. With a major chunk of traditional bank's cost being attributed to running its operation, Kakao bank preferred a business model without physical branches, effectively slashing all costs so as to focus on offering banking products at a better price.

The Kakao Banking app does more than what typically FinTech apps have to offer. Besides providing option to instantly pay bills, transfer money and market place, it is offering option to get personal loans based on individual's need, transfer of money internationally at a reasonable interest, which has garnered interest of emerging technology companies to expand their horizons and unearth ways to diversify portfolio, thereby challenging the banking sphere into reassessing their value preposition (EY).

## The Spread of Mobile Phones, Youth Market and FinTech Adoption

With mobile phones becoming alarmingly common amongst the youth, one big reason for it being popular is the availability of social media applications on it. According to research, mobile phones are unimpressively popular amongst the youth in India (Vaidya, 2016), a country with the second-highest population. The addiction is a worldwide problem as in the U.K where the average age of children owning a mobile phone is 7 (Forster, 2017). Resultantly, it is leading to growing concerns in the U.K where parents are forced into sending their kids for Smartphone rehab over unfavorably high screen time and declining interest in other activities. However, in the U.S, children as young as 13 are undergoing treatment for digital technology addiction (Tsukayama, 2016).

The theory of self-presentation may explain the rising popularity of mobile phones amongst the youth, with theory stating people may share personal information that they may deem consistent with their perception which they wish to disclose to others (Goffman, 1959, Schau & Gilly, 2003). Although all these may indicate to a growing problem for parents and society in general, this may well work in favor of FinTech as 48% of FinTech users are in the age bracket of 25-34 (EY, 2017). With unprecedented number of mobile phone users being kids today, in a decade or so, the FinTech may have a huge influx of users for whom the tech giants may have to tailor product offerings in line with their lifestyle, with social media to spearhead in not only collection vital information to decide digital marketing ad run time but using it as a medium for viral marketing campaigns (Kaplan & Haenlein, 2011b)

The FinTech adoption will surge within the coming years, especially in the emerging market where people lack access to banking. A product offering that allows borrowing without having to go to the bank along with a feature to help in financial planning will certainly see a rise in the coming years. According to a report, Money transfer and payments will continue to dominate, something already highlighted earlier, with % of people engaging with tech applications for this purpose will stand at 50% (EY, 2017).

## Collaborative Models of FinTech & Banks Driving FinTech

With FinTech widely predicted to dominate the banking industry in the near future, the perception leading to big money being splurged by investors who are under the impression that reward for investment at this instance will be fourfold. According to an estimate, the FinTech industry has seen a staggering US $13.1 Billion VC back investment only in 2016 (EY, 2017). Considering the propensity of the digital sphere to evolve, the need for collaboration between FinTech and Banks becomes more and more evident.

According to the EY FinTech Adoption Index, consumers are more likely to uptake financial services offered by an innovative organization (EY, 2017). This also reflects that availability of latest technology may not cause disruption, rather the manner in which the technology is leveraged to capitalize in a given scenario. Likewise, With FinTechs' incessant reliance on customer data, increasing privacy concern coupled with regulatory requirement underscores the need for collaboration as customer acquisition and subsequent earning trust, building a reputation while striving to keep the customer experience at highest level poses a daunting task. In the light of this argument, FinTech is better suited complementing the traditional banks; however, the arduous procurement policy serves as the challenge besides implementing latest technology that is to run in parallel with bank's technology of the 1970s

The collaboration between FinTech & Banks will be a Win-Win scenario for both. For Banks, it will provide an opportunity to bring down the cost, and bolster profits while for FinTech, the customer acquisition, which apparently is by far the biggest hindrance, will be seamless which in turn will bring down operational costs, relatively easier to work in conformity with regulatory requirement and eloquently serve the customers. In Pakistan, the banks and FinTech appear to be following the strategy quite meticulously. While all Major Banks in Pakistan are focused on enabling customers to benefit from digital bank's application, the microfinance and commercial banking are striving to bring the digital wallet to customers, which enables customers to essentially sign up despite not having a bank account. Banks like FINCA, HBL, Telenor – A telecommunication organization with a Microfinance bank are all lured into this industry by the future potential. It is imperative that each bank has its own technology partners, overseeing the FinTech's operations.

FINCA has collaborated with Karandaaz whereby they will be rolling out digital financial services to reach low-income women who are involved in the cotton industry or industry work with an aim to expand financial inclusion in Pakistan (Karandaaz, 2018). This will not only enable them to have access to the contemporary digital wallet but will be extending nano loans by means of appointing community leader who will have access to loan no more than $ 100. The feedback from the year-long partnership has been phenomenal as the loan is extended by a community leader who identifies the low-risk borrower.

Furthermore, the community leader markets SimSim application, who not only assist people in signing up on the application but trains as to how an app could be used to take control of their digital financial requirement. Given the project becomes successful in Pakistan, it would reshape the digital sphere for the poor women in Pakistan. With digital wallets poised to connect 1.6 bn (Arnold, 2016), of which more than half will be women, this project will enable women to contribute to the country's GDP.

## Digital Product Substitutions as a Driving Factor

Digitalization is paying the way for FinTech to develop products that in future may successfully serve as a substitute for bank-branch based products. A digital product is an intangible and virtual asset or piece of media or a technological application or process automation and web-based services which can be sold and distributed repeatedly online without the need to replenish inventory. Banks are undergoing major changes themselves, and are adopting technology to improve value chain, and despite the lurking danger of digitalizing transgressing into boundaries of what conventional banking offers, the case of physical branch stands a strong case in the light of online scams, theft of credit information and phishing pages. It is superfluous to state that physical branches play a crucial role in ensuring that trust & credibility between customer and Bank are maintained (Frédéric Jacques, 2017). In a developing country like Pakistan where digital sphere has not built reputation, the presence of a physical branch hinges on success of the business, at least there is one such bank, U Microfinance Bank, who appear to be following this strategy as it recently inaugurated 170th branch after being injected with over Rs. 4 Billion to accelerate its growth (PTCL Pakistan, 2018).

In addition to providing convenience to customers to do a wide array of things in a branch, it is estimated that the network of branches in any given country is equivalent to millions of dollars to annual marketing. Despite the evident advantages, the global recession has dragged banks in a dilemma wherein it has become fundamentally vital to prioritize what bank's strategy is, whether it wishes to skew towards having physical branches and cater to preferences of customers or implement cost-cutting by relying on a digital medium (Frédéric Jacques, 2017). Mckinsey's latest survey outlines the challenges faced by banks in addressing the varying expectations of the customers. While 56% of customers in the U.S expressed their inclination in buying a product through digital means, another survey shows that 13% have actually bought a product digitally, which goes to show that much like the rest of the world, the physical presence of bank's branches are vital to maintaining customer base and subsequently catering them (Frédéric Jacques, 2017).In the U.S where purchase power to opt for high-end gadgets is high, the actual % of people buying banking products digitally represents the acceptance amongst the audience. On the other hand, in developing countries such as Pakistan where 33% of people have not heard of the word ATM (Gallup Pakistan, 2016), the need for having physical branches becomes top priority, especially in Microfinance Industry which is seeking to bank the unbanked by rolling out numerous schemes, with majority of them targeting SMEs and farmers by taking into consideration numerous factors. Another figure that makes the case of physical branch strong is people's inclination to trust a bank when it comes to making a financial decision irrespective of the bank one associated with (Gallup Pakistan, 2016).

## Investors' Inclination Towards Digital Initiatives and Adoption of FinTech

The investors' confidence in digital technologies is a significant driver for the growth of FinTech. According to a publication by Harvard business school which analyzed the financial indicators of non-listed companies, it was found that non-digital companies are rapidly working to get into the digital sphere, with over 22% non-listed digital companies reportedly going digital in 2017 (Wilbur Chen, 2019). Other stats indicate that firms going digital tend to have their valuation 7% to 21% higher than their peers (Suraj Srinivasan, 2019). Korn Ferry, an executive search management company that had introduced talent-related analytics in 2014 saw its valuation increase by over 60% (Wilbur Chen, 2019). In the same manner, a leading manufacturer of construction equipment, Caterpillar, invested substantially in analytics, which translated a 25% increase in its price to earnings ratio. The opportunities and threats offered by disruptive technologies are keeping the organisation on their toes. And adoption and adaptation to disruptive technology are becoming one of the main goals of the firms. The new innovations often create disruptions, so it will be significant to study the process and factors related to the adoption of disruptive innovations.

## New Players And Services Are Driving Adoption

As highlighted earlier, the future potential to earn big from this arena is translating in big players from different industries flocking to get their fair share from profitability. However, not everyone succeeds in devising a business model and the right strategy. In some cases, existing big player consolidate themselves to an extent where it simply precludes other players from being profitable like Paytm that is leading the market in India (Anand, 2019). Therefore, FinTechs are increasingly exploring additional products that may enable customers to differentiate on the basis of superior and diverse yet exciting product offerings. According to an estimate (EY, 2017), 50% of customers are using digital wallets for money transfer and payments. This is quite true in case of FinTechs in Pakistan who base their campaigns on utility bills payment and offer cashback in a bid to increase the transaction by the wallet account users. In present times, the cashback offers serve as a big incentive for consumers who flock to FinTechs with competitive promotions besides product offerings. (Mavadiya, Forbes, 25).

## A Case of Apple's Jump From Apple Pay to Credit Card

A common scenario with FinTech new entrant akin to that of Apple credit card is that they shoot to stardom initially only to struggle to perform in line with the expectations set earlier during the planning phase. **Apple Pay** is a mobile payments service and digital wallet app that utilizes Near Field Communication (NFC) to initiate secure payment transactions between contactless payment terminals and Apple iOS devices,

Apple, one of the leading big tech organization that designs, develops and sells consumer goods, with a huge market share in developed markets has unveiled its new product which makes it a banking player. Previously, Apple had unveiled 'Apple Pay' back in 2015 when it began serving as a substitute for bank's debit and credit card, reliving customers hassle of carrying a physical card, and likely protecting it from losing or misplacing it (Kelion, 2015). The introduction of pay saw industry-wide interest in the U.K with all major credit card and banks signing up to support new service.

In Apple's case, since the service has been launched only in America, it has received mixed feedback from Wallstreet investors (Fuscaldo, 2019). The Apple policy of cashback is under scrutiny. The 2% cashback digital marketing campaigns may be good enough but given the credit cards are on decline and 1% majority of the transaction to come in the realm of 1% cashback, the cashback may be merely viewed as acceptable (Fuscaldo, 2019). Moreover, the card is expected to generate $882 million which is not on part with what analyst had predicted so far. With Apple Pay flaunting product with unbelievable cashback, lowest interest rate, and free credit card, there are other FinTech who are more or less offering the same rewards. For instance, petal- a Network based FinTech that recently secured funding of $30 million, offer rewards that are quite similar to that of Apple's (Fuscaldo, 2019). With rewards being a differentiating factor for choosing credit card services, banks and FinTech alike have stepped up the reward scheme to preclude customer base from being lured away to the competitor.

Fast forward to 2019, Apple has taken another big stride which brings it heads on the competition with leading tech. The resultant success of Apple Pay now has paved way for launch for Apple card which makes it a banking player, with potential to wipe out competition in FinTech arena (Mavadiya, What Apple's Credit Card Means For FinTech, 2019). Behind Apple's latest venture into the banking, the arena is its partnership with Mastercard and Goldman Sachs with the value proposition of it providing 'Healthier financial life' (Mavadiya, What Apple's Credit Card Means For FinTech, 2019). With strategy to pursue customer and behavioral shift into using Apple's credit card and accordingly designing content marketing to given snapshot of products usage, it is also relying on its instant cashback of 2% on all transactions or 3% given it is spent on Apple products (Dans, 2019), something that many FinTech is working on with prominent example of Jazzcash & SimSim in Pakistan whereas Paytm in India. The cashback scheme captures the millennial trend meticulously by offering instant cashback and serves as viral marketing content for the organization. While Apple card's performance may not reflect as a threat for the credit card industry, it may set a precedent for other players from the smartphone industry to get their fair share of the industry's profitability. It is to be noted that in addition to Apple Pay, Samsung has its own version of digital payment 'Samsung pay' (Savvides, 2019). The Samsung pay works along the lines of Apply pay model, except the only threat Apple card may face is the staggering market share that Samsung has. According to the IDC report, Samsung leads the market with a share of 23% while Apple's share is almost less by half of Samsung's (IDC, 2019).

Apple's card is distinctive in a sense that unlike traditional credit cards issued by banks which involves extensive formalities, the Apple credit card is readily available to use. The Apple wallet requires few minutes for registration and its credit is at the user's disposal for use, a concept that is in its initial phase (Dans, 2019). In simpler words, it is a reinvention of credit card that comes with extra security, essentially preventing fraud. This is quintessentially a product that poses threat to emerging and existing FinTech as a market leader from another domain has successfully found a market which it is catering to rather differently and the very transaction is done Apple users at any given place is equivalent to the marketing of the product. Another benefit for the consumer from the Apple's credit card is that although it doesn't come with a CVV code or any number, losing it means that a user may immediately block that card and subsequently apply for a new one. The user may have to rely on card rarely since the smartphone payment is widely accepted, in 70% of establishments in the U.S (Dans, 2019). Another interesting policy linked to the card is the decline in interest, the more customer pays off the amount it owes, meaning thereby that it encourages paying less interest and above all else upholding privacy concerns of its customers.

## Digital Banking & Financial Inclusion Driving FinTech

**Digital banking** means either online or mobile or virtual banking or digitization of all the traditional banking activities, products, process services and programs that historically were only available to customers when physically inside of a bank branch. Without an iota of doubt, digital banking is the future for increasing financial inclusion. The average mobile usage amongst the youth coupled with the pace with which mobile manufacturer is increasing their outreach, it is evident that banking is being shaped gradually. However, tough questions to ask at this juncture are how digitalization would ensure that a poor household, with no access to banks, could benefit from the services it offers.

Financial inclusion means that individuals and businesses have access to useful and affordable financial products and services that meet their needs. financial inclusion means a process of ensuring that individuals (everyone, in particular, vulnerable people) or weaker section of society) and businesses have an easy, affordable and transparent access to useful and affordable financial products and services that meet their needs. With the spotlight being on FinTech, it is imperative to establish the difference between financial inclusion and financial data inclusion to better understand the scope it has the potential to serve. By virtue, financial inclusion is a strategy adopted by FinTech to reduce poverty by bridging the gap between unbanked and availability of finance. Though it is a separate discussion of the extent to which lower class may benefit from the service, but it is not the sole strategy to alleviate poverty. The government may partner with Philanthropist and charity organization to deal with pressing issues like poverty, availability of education and healthcare. Financial inclusion ensures the availability of financial services to unbaked, in other words, to all segments of the society whereby one is empowered to make sound decisions. As opposed to financial inclusion, Financial data inclusion is merging the entire population's biometric information to their bank account (Ozili, 2018). The merger and the resultant financial data inclusion may result in numerous benefits. It allows verification of digital transaction and may help in tracing transaction to the individual. Further insights may also be extracted on the basis of demographic. Participation of the general public in financial data inclusion may prompt greater financial inclusion as more individuals will have bank accounts log in linked with digital wallets that will allow masses to avail financial services. However, if the unbanked population refuses to participate, they will not only miss out using digital channels to carry out financial services but will perversely impact the financial inclusion indicators.

To examine the benefits of financial inclusion, it is imperative to understand the essence of digital financial inclusion which is defined as access to digital and usage of the same by underserved or excluded population (Timothly Lyman, 2015). With digital wallet services launched in over 80 countries (Clarie Penicaud, 2019), it is allowing poor customers to have access to financial services. These services cater poor in a sense that it empowers them, brings them in the center of decision making with respect to their finances, with the availability of financial services at a lower cost. The very financial inclusion assists in making sound decisions, allowing them to save for the future and possibly make the investment to increase their wealth. Given that banks are adopting technology and partnering with FinTechs to capture the market, the move to FinTech apps not only translates into favorable financial inclusion for the masses but also reduces stress on the banks (Rui Han, 2013) in terms of deposits. The more financial inclusion getters bigger in a country, it will see series of small savers whose accumulation of savings would reduce procyclicality risk, in other words, significantly reducing bank's dependence on non-core financing (Khan, 2011). The notion of forcing to get things done is existent in present days. Financial inclusion by force is expected to yield considerable benefits in the future, which is prompting governments to explore ways to impose measures that will ensure financial inclusion. It is to be noted that the more digital adoption is done voluntary, the better it is for financial inclusion as otherwise, it will merely impact financial data inclusion which is different from financial inclusion in its entirety.

One practice in Pakistan's bank links financial inclusion by force. FINCA Microfinance Bank, a subsidiary of FINCA International tends to transfer money of its employees in SimSim, a FinTech digital wallet, developed in collaboration with Finja, a technology partner for FINCA in Pakistan. In a market that has already seen banks introducing digital wallets to bank the unbanked and race to capture user base with active accounts, the idea of forcing employees may yield benefit in a way that they would be accustomed to it and what better than word of mouth about SimSim's Money transfer, IBFT, bill payment being spread by its own employees.

There are two strategies that FinTech and banks may opt for customer acquisition, one may be through relationship managers present in physical branches that will not only aid in establishing brand awareness but also credibility that comes along with it. The other strategy is customer acquisition through social media which for companies may account for 20% of their marketing budget (Christine Moorman, 2018) and reach the audience in far-flung areas with access to social media and bring them in the banking net through an easy and convenient app.Assuming that customer is acquired, the digital marketing's paid campaign may be availed to continually reinforce brand awareness, leverage it to get customer feedback and timely cope with product queries and issues (Christine Moorman, 2018).

Financial inclusion is inherently beneficial for the economy. Given banks put emphasis on catering lower end individuals, it may be immune to macro-economic shocks, which may, in turn, enhance the economy due to the level of high deposit, and may prevent financial crises (Hanning, 2011). Generally, it is assumed that the vast majority of people, the unbanked, have access to mobile phones. However, in order for financial inclusion to become a reality in emerging markets, the prerequisite is to have affordable internet connectivity.

## CRITICISM OF FINTECH AND DIGITAL MARKETING

While digital finance is a hot topic in the current business era, it has received its fair share of criticism. The view of the World bank encompasses the belief that higher use of digital finance may lead to high financial inclusion. However, the researchers suggest that instead of leading to higher financial inclusion, it rather leads to higher financial data inclusion (Accelerating financial inclusion in south-east Asia with digital finance, 2016).

According to a report by ITU, the usage of digital wallet may face impediments so as to create acceptance amongst vendors to set up a digital payment method (ITU, 2016) in emerging countries where setting up digital payment method is costly. As a result, the poor despite having access to digital wallet may not be able to carry out the transaction. The fact that poor individual may have a digital wallet set up indicates financial data inclusion, but as discussed earlier, higher financial data inclusion does not contribute to financial inclusion.

Aside from this, digital finance may not realize its full potential owing to concerns of digital marketing reliance on personal data. This scenario is generally more applicable on first world countries where data protection is of utmost importance, so much that companies inevitably have to hire data protection officers (Burt, 2019). While top companies like Facebook have been fined approx. $ 5 Billion for data branch and failure to comply with local laws (SHERR, 2019). In many countries where FinTechs are operating, the regulation relating to this are being developed following observing the implications that a FinTech service may have on the masses.

The digital sphere is evolving at an ever-increasing pace. The evolution is not jutted paving way of connectivity, access to finance and data to make an informed decision, it is also providing additional opportunities to hackers to attack computers, and potentially endanger customer's data. This is causing regulatory bodies to devise newer regulations to preclude any unforeseen incident from happening. An example cited earlier is of Facebook who failed to comply with regulatory bodies, resulting in a fine of $ 5 billion (SHERR, 2019). Moreover, with the enforcement of new regulations like having to hire data protection officer, the cost of protecting data for FinTech becomes more expensive than offering financial services, fundamentally putting regulators at odds with the FinTech firms.

In emerging countries, the regulations are not as stringent as in developed markets which coupled with people's perception of data being prone to hack, serves as a hindrance.

### Digitalization and Loss of Jobs as Arguments

In certain segments of society, the digitalization has been perceived negatively, looked down upon as it may lead to the impending loss of jobs. However, the fact that physical will be eliminated in its entirety is downright untrue as some part of physical may always exist (Furr & Shipilov, 2019). According to World economic form's report on 'The Future of Jobs', the adoption of new technology does not necessarily result in redundancies, rather it results in augmentation of jobs, creation of new jobs, drives business growth (World Economic Forum, 2018). The report states that 50% of companies foresee automation causing a reduction in workforce by 2022 that may also give rise to new jobs which may be performed by skilled contractors whom companies may have to deal in a far more flexible manner (World Economic Forum, 2018). 71% of total hours of work tasks are performed by humans in 2018 but this number is will dip by 2022, with 62% of data processing and similar tasks will be performed by machines (World Economic Forum, 2018). It is imperative to note that decline in some jobs may be offset by emerging jobs that will outweigh the number of jobs lost, roles that leverage human skills such as OD specialists, Culture professionals, Data analysts and software developers.

Furthermore, according to the World economic forum's report, a new job role of digital marketing has emerged (World Economic Forum, 2018). This is evident due to the constant evolving digital economy that has challenged the fundamentals of traditional economics and created a need for marketing on the digital medium. The emphasis on digital marketing's importance may be understood by numerous researches that reinforces the need to adopt digital marketing arena by incorporating marketing curriculum to cater to the requirement for digital initiatives (Wymbs, 2011).

## WAY FORWARD FOR FINANCIAL INDUSTRY AND SCOPE FOR FURTHER RESEARCH

Amidst the commotion to capture market share, digitalization and race to secure highest wallet transaction, the financial industry has to be meticulous at this juncture in adopting the digital technology and diligently use marketing campaigns to convey precise information. In the lights of factual arguments presented earlier, it would be in favor of the industry to adopt the financial revolution as overlooking may not only drive them out of the competition but will too much on the marketing front. According to Mckinsey, there will be a decline of 20- 60% of profits in the banking industry worldwide (Mckinsey, 2015). Moreover, the investors may have to change their expectation of the pace on which dividend is earned on the investment. The current system is based on a mechanism that intensely focuses on short term reward, which essentially inhibits the FinTech from realizing their full potential (Shaikh, 2017). A long term view is the only solution for FinTech and banks to collaborate and bank the unbanked. An example of what FINCA is doing in Pakistan.

Likewise, it is imperative for the financial industry to differentiate technology from innovation, for financial technology itself is a commodity. With the internet being bombarded with software, it is quite easy for anyone to acquire software, the real deal, however, remains the execution of the strategy to bring an industry-wide change. Banks will also have to take into consideration the hassle women entrepreneur have to encounter when looking for finances for their business. In order to have wider financial inclusion, the banks would have to cater to Women entrepreneur need by developing a product, much like what Karandaaz is working on for the upliftment of women. Moreover, banks will have to work on eliminating biases when considering financing inclusion applications. According to a research, women's access to capital with respect to another gender (Malin Malmstrom, 2018) and even if the loan application is approved, it comes tougher terms and conditions in comparison to males which indicated a clear case of gender bias in loan processing. It is advised for Banks, specifically FinTech to make financing decision centralized so as to prevent a female entrepreneur from being screened out which otherwise would put out of the formal economy.

In nutshell, the way forward for banks is collaboration as neither party alone could capture market, FinTech would be needing Banks to compliment and use its expertise in customer acquisition which is supposedly a tough ask while for banks who are working on near obsolete IT model, it needs FinTech to increase its outreach, allow it to move from conventional banking to branchless given the former deems it fit. Additional features in FinTech like availability of tailored made loan that are readily available based on one's risk assessment would go have the potential to gain sufficient traction.

The future research can focus on developing sensors or mechanism of innovations and recognizing the appearance of disruptive technology, the factors that lead to adoption or non-adoption of disruptive technologies. And how a company can create a culture for disruptive innovations and continues doing so! Research can also focus on to determine the boundaries of disruptive technologies and scopes of industry convergence etc. Also, future research can focus on FinTech as an economic tool of national development, etc.

## CONCLUSION

In the present times wherein the digital finance, social media coupled with mobile usage amongst people in general and teens, in particular, is spiking high on yearly basis, it is suggested to thoroughly utilize social media to gain insight and base decision pertaining to digital paid campaigns. The digital marketing has opened a new avenue for banks to unearth hard facts about the banking products, and general perception associated with a particular brand, with tools like businesses pages to address customer queries. The business leaders should be smart enough to sense the appearance of disruptive innovations, visionary to view- digital acuity, bold enough to challenge status quo, creative enough to create a culture of innovation and insight to determine customers' point of view.

Given the growing trend of digitalization and FinTech, digital marketing of present times requires to be data-driven to cater to the demand of contemporary businesses (Startsev, 2017). Prior to running any campaign for a product, it is more vital to ascertain the viability of the product and accordingly design campaigns on the basis on local know-how to make it work. For instance, Uber's introduction of cash payment feature enabled operate seamlessly and cater customers who have traditionally been comfortable with using cash (Uber, 2016).

While companies like Uber may succeed by introducing an additional payment option, it may as well underline an opportunity for digital finance to use digital marketing in its truest essence to capture the market gap. For instance, it is the established fact that banks and FinTechs cannot operate in silos, for it is next to impossible to operate and develop the expertise to comply with regulations of different industry and implement contemporary technology on system checks that are based on the technology of the 1990s. Furthermore, the development of innovative payment solutions like contactless payment and Apple's credit card serves as trendy marketing of the product that garners a thorough coverage from relevant industry reviewers.

Lastly, in banking context for digital marketing to succeed, it has to be increasingly data-driven as its paid campaign would be only meaningful as long as it reflects various KPIs like increase in impression to traffic onto the website and generation of business leads. This outcome for business may be further refined given its the digital marketing efforts are aligned with a global strategy to cater the unbanked, thereby could help in increasing user base who may, in turn, make financial decisions.

## REFERENCES

Accelerating financial inclusion in south-east Asia with digital finance. (2016). *Asian Development Bank*. Retrieved from https://www.oliverwyman.com/content/dam/oliver-wyman/v2/publications/2017/jan/Accelerating-financial-inclusion-in-south-east-asia.pdf

Anand, N. (2019, May 24). *QUARTZ India*. Retrieved July 21, 2019, from https://qz.com/india/1627121/vijay-shekhar-sharmas-paytm-bank-beats-jio-airtel-idea-fino/

Arnold, M. (2016, September 21). *Emerging markets urged to embrace digital finance*. Retrieved from https://www.ft.com/content/1f774952-7f5c-11e6-bc52-0c7211ef3198

Burt, A. (2019, January 3). *Privacy and Cybersecurity Are Converging. Here's Why That Matters for People and for Companies*. Retrieved from https://hbr.org/2019/01/privacy-and-cybersecurity-are-converging-heres-why-that-matters-for-people-and-for-companies

Bykea. (2019). *We're Solving a Real Problem*. Retrieved from Bykea: https://www.bykea.com/

Canales, K. (2018, August 21). *40 totally amazing technological advancements that we don't even notice anymore*. Retrieved 07 21, 2019, from https://www.businessinsider.com/amazing-technological-advancements-we-dont-even-notice-anymore-2018-8

Cascio, W. (2016). *How Technology Is Changing Work and Organizations*. Academic Press.

Christine Moorman, T. A. (2018, May). *Getting The Most Out of Social Media Investments*. Retrieved from The Wall Street Journal: https://deloitte.wsj.com/cmo/2018/05/18/getting-the-most-out-of-social-media-investments/

Clarie Penicaud, A. K. (2019). State of the industry 2013: mobile financial services for the unbanked. *Gates open Research*. Retrieved from https://gatesopenresearch.org/documents/3-1429

Dahir, A. L. (2018, August 24). *Uber's innovations in Africa have helped shape its global operations*. Retrieved from Quartz Africa: https://qz.com/africa/1368732/uber-in-africa-cash-payments-are-shaping-global-operations/

Dans, E. (2019, March 26). *Apple Reinvents The Credit Card*. Retrieved July 25, 2019, from https://www.forbes.com/sites/enriquedans/2019/03/26/Apple-reinvents-the-credit-card/#45d458047939

EY. (2017). *Four Themes driving FinTech Adoption by Consumers*. Retrieved from https://www.ey.com/en_gl/banking-capital-markets/four-themes-driving-FinTech-adoption-by-consumers

EY. (2017). *Unleashing the Potential of FinTech in Bank*. EY.

EY. (n.d.). *How a social media firm created Korea's fastest growing bank*. EY.

Forster, K. (2017, April 14). *Children as young as 13 attending 'smartphone rehab' as concerns grow over screen time*. Retrieved July 2019, 2019, from https://www.independent.co.uk/news/health/teenage-technology-addiction-smartphone-rehab-seattle-clinic-children-aged-13-mobile-devices-a7684356.html

Frédéric Jacques, M. N. (2017). *Reimagining the bank branch for the digital era*. Retrieved July 2019, 23, from https://www.mckinsey.com/industries/financial-services/our-insights/reimagining-the-bank-branch-for-the-digital-era

Furr, N., & Shipilov, A. (2019, July). *Digital Doesn't Have to Be Disruptive*. Retrieved July 21, 2019, from https://hbr.org/2019/07/digital-doesnt-have-to-be-disruptive

Fuscaldo, D. (2019, March 26). *Apple Card Fails To Impress Wall Street, Investors*. Retrieved July 25, 2019, from https://www.forbes.com/sites/donnafuscaldo/2019/03/26/Apple-card-fails-to-impress-wall-street-investors/#672305b625a8

Gartner. (2018, November 27). *Every Organizational Function Needs to Work on Digital Transformation*. Retrieved July 21, 2019, from https://hbr.org/sponsored/2018/11/every-organizational-function-needs-to-work-on-digital-transformation

Han, R. M. M. (2013). Financial Inclusion for Financial Stability: Access to Bank Deposits and the Growth of Deposits in the Global Financial Crisis. *e-library*. Retrieved from https://elibrary.worldbank.org/doi/abs/10.1596/1813-9450-6577

Hanning, A. (2011). *Financial Inclusion and Financial Stability: Current Policy Issues*. Retrieved from https://papers.ssrn.com/sol3/papers.cfm?abstract_id=1729122

Hill, J. B. (2017). *Gartner insights on spotting and responding to digital disruption Leading Through Digital Disruption*. Retrieved from https://www.gartner.com/imagesrv/books/digital-disruption/pdf/digital_disruption_ebook.pdf

IBEF. (2019). *Indian Consumer Market*. IBEF. Retrieved from https://www.ibef.org/industry/indian-consumer-market.aspx

IDC. (2019). *Smart Phone Marketshare*. Retrieved from https://www.idc.com/promo/smartphone-market-share/vendor

ITU. (2016). The Digital financial services ecosystem. *ITU*. Retrieved from https://www.sciencedirect.com/science/article/pii/S2214845017301503#bib25

Karandaaz. (2018, April 20). *FINCA Enters into a strategic partnership with Karandaaz Pakistan to launch 'Women Community Mobilizer' program*. Retrieved from https://karandaaz.com.pk/media-center/news-events/finca-enters-strategic-partnership-karandaaz-pakistan-launch-women-community-mobilizer-program/

Kelion, L. (2015, July 14). *Apple Pay: How will it work in the UK?* Retrieved July 24, 2019, from https://www.bbc.com/news/technology-33489066

Kendall, J. (2017, January 20). *FinTech Companies Could Give Billions of People More Banking Options*. Retrieved July 21, 2019, from https://hbr.org/2017/01/FinTech-companies-could-give-billions-of-people-more-banking-options

Khan, H. R. (2011). *Financial inclusion and financial stability: are they two sides of the same coin*. Academic Press.

Lai, P. (2017). Technology Adoption Models and Theories for the Novelty Technology. *Journal of Information Systems and Technology Management*, *14*(1), 21–38. doi:10.4301/S1807-17752017000100002

Malin Malmstrom, J. W. (2018, September 19). *Research: The Digitization of Banks Disproportionately Hurts Women Entrepreneurs*. Retrieved from https://hbr.org/2018/09/research-the-digitization-of-banks-disproportionately-hurts-women-entrepreneurs

Mavadiya, M. (2019, March 25). *What Apple's Credit Card Means For FinTech*. Retrieved July 24, 2019, from https://www.forbes.com/sites/madhvimavadiya/2019/03/25/what-Apple-credit-card-means-for-FinTech/#2b84884f4856

Mavadiya, M. (2019). *Forbes*. Retrieved July 24, 2019, from https://www.forbes.com/sites/madhvimavadiya/2019/03/25/what-Apple-credit-card-means-for-FinTech/#2b84884f4856

McKinsey. (2015). *The fight for the customer: McKinsey global banking annual review 2015*. Retrieved from https://www.mckinsey.com/industries/financial-services/our-insights/the-fight-for-the-customer-mckinsey-global-banking-annual-review-2015

McKinsey. (2019). *The Future of work in America. People & Places, today and tomorrow*. Author.

Michelle, A. M. (2016). *The Effect Of Digital Finance On Financial Inclusion In Kenya*. Academic Press.

Nichols, W. (2014, July 17). *How Big Data Brings Marketing and Finance Together*. Retrieved July 21, 2019, from https://hbr.org/2014/07/how-big-data-brings-marketing-and-finance-together

Ozili, P. K. (2018). Impact of digital finance on financial inclusion and stability. *Science Direct*. Retrieved from https://www.sciencedirect.com/science/article/pii/S2214845017301503#bib23

Pakistan, P. T. C. L. (2018). *PTCL injects PKR 4 Billion in U Microfinance Bank for growth*. Press Release. Retrieved from https://ptcl.com.pk/Home/PressReleaseDetail/?ItemId=654&linkId=130

Piirainen, L. (2016). *Digitalization of the financial sector and change management*. OULU University of Applied Sciences.

Raynor, M. E. (2011). Disruption theory as a predictor of innovation success/failure. *Strategy and Leadership*, *39*(4), 27–30. doi:10.1108/10878571111147378

Rizvi, J. (2018, November 9). *The NEws*. Retrieved July 24, 2019, from https://www.thenews.com.pk/print/391338-pakistan-s-urban-rural-mobile-ownership-divide-set-to-close-soon-study-shows

Savvides, L. (2019, June 22). *Samsung Pay: Everything you need to know (FAQ)*. Retrieved from https://www.cnet.com/how-to/samsung-pay-everything-you-need-to-know-faq-mobile-wallet/

Shahid, J. (2017, July 1). *DAWN*. Retrieved July 24, 2019, from https://www.dawn.com/news/1342511

Shaikh, N. (2017, July 17). *The Financial Industry Needs to Start Planning for the Next 50 Years, Not the Next Five*. Retrieved from https://hbr.org/2017/07/the-financial-industry-needs-to-start-planning-for-the-next-50-years-not-the-next-five

Sherr, I. (2019, July 25). *Facebook's $5 billion FTC fine is just the start of its problems*. Retrieved from https://www.cnet.com/news/facebooks-5-billion-ftc-fine-is-just-the-start-of-its-problems/

Sloan, J. (2018, October 2). *Why Financial Institutions Can Bank on Digital Innovation for Millennials*. Academic Press.

Startsev, D. (2017, April 25). *Data-Driven Marketing: Vision to Reality*. Retrieved from Wallstreet journal: https://deloitte.wsj.com/cmo/2017/04/25/data-driven-marketing-vision-to-reality/

Suraj Srinivasan, W. C. (2019, June 18). *Research: Investors Reward Companies That Talk Up Their Digital Initiatives*. Retrieved July 25, 2019, from https://hbr.org/2019/06/research-investors-reward-companies-that-talk-up-their-digital-initiatives

Timothly Lyman, K. L. (2015). What is Digital Financial Inclusion and Why Does it Matter? *CGAP*. Retrieved from http://www.cgap.org/blog/what-digital-financial-inclusion-and-why-does-it-matter

Tsukayama, H. (2016, May 21). *Internet addiction is costing young people their jobs and social lives*. Retrieved July 07, 2019, from https://www.independent.co.uk/life-style/gadgets-and-tech/this-dark-side-of-the-internet-is-costing-young-people-their-jobs-and-social-lives-a7041451.html

Uber. (2016, September 22). *Why we introduced cash payments*. Retrieved from Uber: https://www.uber.com/en-PK/blog/pkcash/

Uber. (2019). *Uber to Acquire Careem To Expand the Greater Middle East Regional Opportunity Together.* Author.

Vaidya, A. &. (2016). *Mobile Phone usage amongst the youth.*

Venkatesh, V., Thong, J. Y. L., & Xu, X. (2012). Consumer acceptance and use of information technology: extending the unified theory of acceptance and use of Technology. *Management Information Systems Quarterly*, *36*(1), 157–178. doi:10.2307/41410412

Venkatesh, V., Thong, J. Y. L., & Xu, X. (2012). Consumer acceptance and use of information technology: extending the unified theory of acceptance and use of technology. *Management Information Systems Quarterly*, *36*(1), 157–178. doi:10.2307/41410412

Wilbur Chen, S. S. (2019). *Going Digital: Implications for Firm*. Retrieved from https://www.hbs.edu/faculty/Publication%20Files/19-117_96a955bc-05ea-4252-94d8-6aecc539718a.pdf

Wisniewski, M. (2016). The Evolution Of Marketing. *American Banker Magazine, 126*(2), 7–8. Retrieved from http://search.ebscohost.com/login.aspx?direct=true&db=buh&AN=112775772&authtype=shib&site=ehost-live&scope=site

World Economic Forum. (2018). *The Future of Jobs Report.* World Economic Forum.

Wymbs, C. (2011). Digital Marketing: The Time for a New "Academic Major" Has Arrived. *Sagepub*. Retrieved from https://journals.sagepub.com/doi/10.1177/0273475310392544#articleCitationDownloadContainer

Yu, H. (2018, July 26). *For Some Platforms, Network Effects Are No Match for Local Know-How*. Retrieved July 2019, 22, from https://hbr.org/2018/07/for-some-platforms-network-effects-are-no-match-for-local-know-how

# Compilation of References

Aaker, D. A. (1991). *Building brand equity*. New York: The Free.

Aaker, D. A. (2009). *Managing brand equity*. New York: Simon and Schuster.

Aaker, D. A., & Joachimsthaler, E. (2009). *Brand leadership; Building assets in an information economy*. New York: Simon and Schuster.

ABP. (2019). *Early Adopter Programme*. Available at: https://www.abports.co.uk

Abrams, L. 2018. *GandCrab V4 Released With the New.KRAB Extension for Encrypted Files*. Available at: https://www.bleepingcomputer.com/news/security/gandcrab-v4-released-with-the-new-krab-extension-for-encrypted-files/

Abubakar, M., Ilkan, M., & Sahin, P. (2016). eWOM, eReferral and gender in the virtual community. *Marketing Intelligence & Planning*, *34*(5), 692–710. doi:10.1108/MIP-05-2015-0090

Abzari, M., Ghorbani, H., & Madani, F. A. (2011). The effect of internal marketing on organizational commitment from market-orientation viewpoint in hotel industry in Iran. *International Journal of Marketing Studies*, *3*(1), 147–155. doi:10.5539/ijms.v3n1p147

Accelerating financial inclusion in south-east Asia with digital finance. (2016). *Asian Development Bank*. Retrieved from https://www.oliverwyman.com/content/dam/oliver-wyman/v2/publications/2017/jan/Accelerating-financial-inclusion-in-south-east-asia.pdf

Accenture. (2019a). *There's AI. And then there's Applied Intelligence*. Available at: https://www.accenture.com/gb-en/services/applied-intelligence-index

Accenture. (2019b). *Intelligent Supply Chain*. Available at: https://www.accenture.com/gb-en/services/applied-intelligence-index

Accenture. (2019c). *Accenture's New Blockchain App Lets Users Tip 'Sustainable' Producers*. Available at: https://www.coindesk.com/accentures-new-blockchain-app-lets-users-tip-

Achrol, R., & Kotler, P. (1999). Marketing in the network economy. *Journal of Marketing*, *63*(4_suppl1), 146–163. doi:10.1177/00222429990634s114

Acker, O., Gröne, F., Akkad, F., Pötscher, F., & Yazbek, R. (2011). Social CRM: How companies can link into the social web of consumers. *Journal of Direct Data and Digital Marketing Practice*, *13*(1), 3–10. doi:10.1057/dddmp.2011.17

Adina, L. N., Valentin, T., Aurelian, S., Mihaela, F. T., & Rozalia, V. R. (2015). Exploring Gamification Techniques and Applications for Sustainable Tourism. *Sustainability*, 11160–11189.

Ahluwalia, S., Ferrell, O. C., Ferrell, L., & Rittenburg, T. (2016). BSarbanes-Oxley 406 Code of Ethics for Senior Financial Officers and Firm Behavior. *Journal of Business Ethics*, *151*(3), 693–705. doi:10.100710551-016-3267-7

Ahmad, P. K., Rafiq, M., & Saad, N. M. (2003). Internal marketing and the mediating role of organisational competences. *European Journal of Marketing*, *37*(9), 1221–1241. doi:10.1108/03090560310486960

Ailawadi, K. L., & Farris, P. W. (2017). Managing multi-and omnichannel distribution: Metrics and research directions. *Journal of Retailing*, *93*(1), 120–135. doi:10.1016/j.jretai.2016.12.003

Ajzen, I. (1985). From intention to actions: A theory of planned behavior. In J. Kuhl & J. Bechmann (Eds.), *Action Control: From Cognitions to Behavior* (pp. 11–39). New York: Springer-Verlag. doi:10.1007/978-3-642-69746-3_2

Ajzen, I. (1991). The theory of planned behavior. *Organizational Behavior and Human Decision Processes*, *50*(2), 179–211. doi:10.1016/0749-5978(91)90020-T

Ajzen, I., & Madden, T. J. (1986). Prediction of goal-directed behavior: Attitudes, intentions, and perceived behavioral control. *Journal of Experimental Social Psychology*, *22*(5), 453–474. doi:10.1016/0022-1031(86)90045-4

Akhter, S. H. (2014). Privacy concern and online transactions:the impact of internet self-efficiency and internet involvement. *Journal of Consumer Marketing*, *31*(2), 118–125. doi:10.1108/JCM-06-2013-0606

Alegre, J., & Garau, J. (2010). Tourist satisfaction and dissatisfaction. *Annals of Tourism Research*, *37*(1), 52–73. doi:10.1016/j.annals.2009.07.001

Aleksandersen, B. D. (2019). *Why is projection mapping so popular in events and marketing?* Retrieved July 31, 2019, from https://newsandviews.dataton.com/why-is-projection-mapping-so-popular-in-marketing

Alhaddad, A. A. (2015). The effect of advertising awareness on brand equity in social media. *International Journal of e-Education, e-Business, e- Management Learning*, *5*(2), 73.

Ali, A., & Frew, A. J. (2014). Technology innovation and applications in Sustainable destination development. *Information Technology & Tourism, 14*(4), 265-290.

Ali, A. (2017). Ransomware: A Research And A Personal Case Study Of Dealing With This Nasty Malware. *Information Science Institute*, *14*(1), 87–99.

Ali, A., Bentley, Y., Cao, G., & Habib, F. (2017). Green supply chain management–food for thought? *International Journal of Logistics Research and Applications*, *20*(1), 22–38. doi:10.1080/13675567.2016.1226788

Allan, D. (2015). Conceptualising work learning: Exploring the educational discourse on work-based, work-related, and workplace learning. *E-Journal International*, *5*(1), 1–20.

Allcott, H., & Gentzkow, M. (2017). Social Media and Fake News in the 2016 Election. *The Journal of Economic Perspectives, 31*(2), 211-235. Retrieved from http://www.jstor.org/stable/44235006

Alsamydia, Alnawas, & Yousif. (2010). The impact of marketing innovation on creating a sustainable competitive advantage: The case of Private commercial banks in Jordan. *Asian Journal of Marketing*, *4*(3), 113-130.

Al-Saqaf, W., & Seidler, N. (2017). Blockchain technology for social impact: opportunities and challenges ahead. *Journal of Cyber Policy,* 1–18. doi:10.1080/23738871.2017.1400084

Alvarado, U., & Kotzab, H. (2001). Supply chain management— The integration of logistics in marketing. *Industrial Marketing Management*, *30*(2), 183–198. doi:10.1016/S0019-8501(00)00142-5

Amaral, I. (2012). Participação em rede: Do utilizador ao consumidor 2.0 e ao prosumer. *Comunicaçãoe Sociedade*, *22*(0), 131–147. doi:10.17231/comsoc.22(2012).1270

Amarasekara, B. R., & Mathrani, A. (2016). Controlling risks and fraud in affiliate marketing: A simulation and testing environment. *14th Annual Conference on Privacy, Security, and Trust, PST 2016*. 10.1109/PST.2016.7906986

Amazon. (2019a). *What is cloud computing?* Available at: https://aws.amazon.com/what-is-cloud-computing/

Amazon. (2019b). *Open Distro for Elasticsearch?* Available at: https://aws.amazon.com/

Ambrosini, V., & Bowman, C. (2009). What are dynamic capabilities and are they a useful construct in strategic management? *International Journal of Management Reviews*, *11*(1), 29–49. doi:10.1111/j.1468-2370.2008.00251.x

Amoako-Gyampah, K., & Salam, A. (2004). An extension of the Technology Acceptance Model in an ERP implementation environment. *Information & Management*, *41*(6), 731–745. doi:10.1016/j.im.2003.08.010

Anand, N. (2019, May 24). *QUARTZ India*. Retrieved July 24, 2019, from https://qz.com/india/1627121/vijay-shekhar-sharmas-paytm-bank-beats-jio-airtel-idea-fino/

Anastasia, L. (2016). *Buying Behaviour Of Millennials Changing Traditional Marketing Practices*. Retrieved from https://www.theseus.fi/bitstream/handle/10024/107187/BachelorsThesisFinal.pdf?sequence=1&isAllowed=y

Andrews, J., & Smith, D. C. (1996). In Search of the Marketing Imagination: Factors Affecting the Creativity of Marketing Programs for Mature Product. *JMR, Journal of Marketing Research*, *33*(2), 174–187. doi:10.1177/002224379603300205

Anthony, D., Smith, S. W., & Williamson, T. (2009). Reputation and reliability in collective goods the case of the online encyclopaedia Wikipedia. *Rationality and Society*, *21*(3), 283–306. doi:10.1177/1043463109336804

Anumeha. (2019, March 25). Social media code of ethics unlikely to tame fake news, say analysts. *The Economic Times*. Retrieved from https://economictimes.indiatimes.com/tech/internet/social-media-code-of-ethics-unlikely-to-tame-fake-news-say-analysts/articleshow/68531164.cms

Apache Hadoop. (2019). *The Apache™ Hadoop® project develops open-source software for reliable, scalable, distributed computing*. Available at https://hadoop.apache.org/

Apache Spark. (2019). *Apache Spark™ is a unified analytics engine for large-scale data processing*. Available at https://spark.apache.org/

Ardito, L., Petruzzelli, A., Panniello, U., & Garavelli, A. (2019). Towards Industry 4.0: Mapping digital technologies for supply chain management-marketing integration. *Business Process Management Journal*, *25*(2), 323–346. doi:10.1108/BPMJ-04-2017-0088

Arias-Aranda, D., & Bustinza-Sanchez, O. (2009). Entrepreneurial attitude and conflict management through business simulations. *Journal of Industrial Management and Data Systems*, *109*(8), 1101–1117. doi:10.1108/02635570910991328

Arif, S., Iiya, M., & Hameed, A. (2013). Student satisfaction and impact of leadership in private universities. *The TQM Journal*, *25*(4), 399–416. doi:10.1108/17542731311314881

Aristovnik, A., Tomazevic, N., Kerzic, D., & Umek, L. (2017). The impact of demographic factors on selected aspects of e-learning in higher education. *The International Journal of Information and Learning Technology*, *34*(2), 114–121. doi:10.1108/IJILT-09-2016-0045

Arlo. (2019). *Arlo Ultra: Enjoy total peace of mind with the ultimate home security camera*. Available at: https://www.arlo.com/uk/default.aspx

Arnold, A. M. (2012). *The Illusion of Increased Democracy in the Digital Age of Fashion Journalism* (Master's project). Stanford University. Retrieved from http://goo.gl/yqiIhQ

Arnold, M. (2016, September 21). *Emerging markets urged to embrace digital finance*. Retrieved from https://www.ft.com/content/1f774952-7f5c-11e6-bc52-0c7211ef3198

Arnould & Thompson. (2005). Consumer Culture Theory (CCT): Twenty Years of Research. *Journal of Consumer Research, 31*, 868-82.

Arnould, E. J., & Thompson, C. J. (2005). Consumer Culture Theory (CCT): Twenty Years of Research. *Source: The Journal of Consumer Research*, *31*(4), 868–882. doi:10.1086/426626

Arora, P., & Kshatriya, K. (2017). Millennials: The New Generation with High Employment Expectations. *International Journal (Toronto, Ont.)*, *5*(8).

*Artificial Intelligence in Europe - Outlook for 2019 and beyond*. (2018). EY LLP Limited.

Ashby, A., Leat, M., & Hudson-Smith, M. (2012). Making connections: A review of supply chain management and sustainability literature. *Supply Chain Management*, *17*(5), 497–516. doi:10.1108/13598541211258573

Ashley, C., & Tuten, T. (2015). Creative strategies in social media marketing: An exploratory study of branded social content and consumer engagement. *Psychology and Marketing*, *32*(1), 15–27. doi:10.1002/mar.20761

Asmolov, G. (2018). The disconnective power of disinformation campaigns. *Journal of International Affairs, 71*(1.5), 69-76. Retrieved from https://www.jstor.org/stable/26508120

Asnit, A. (2014). Collective Intelligence based Supply Chain Planning Process Considering Supply Chain Uncertainties. *Korean Journal of Logistics*, *22*(4), 15–26. doi:10.15735/kls.2014.22.4.002

Atanassova, I., & Clark, L. (2015). Social media practices in SME marketing activities: A theoretical framework and research agenda. *Journal of Customer Behaviour*, *14*(2), 163–183. doi:10.1362/147539215X14373846805824

Atkinson, L. (2014). Green moms: The social construction of a green mothering identity via environmental advertising appeals. *Consumption Markets & Culture*, *17*(6), 553–572. doi:10.1080/10253866.2013.879817

August, T., Dao, D., & Florin Niculescu, M. (2019). *Economics of Ransomware Attacks*. Retrieved from https://weis2019.econinfosec.org/wp-content/uploads/sites/6/2019/05/WEIS_2019_paper_60.pdf

Au-Yong-Oliveira, M., Gonçalves, R., Martins, J., & Branco, F. (2018). The social impact of technology on millennials and consequences for higher education and leadership. *Telematics and Informatics*, *35*(4), 954–963. doi:10.1016/j.tele.2017.10.007

Avast. (2018). *Adware*. Available at: https://www.avast.com/c-adware

Ayeh, J., Au, N., & Law, R. (2013). Towards an understanding of online travellers' acceptance of consumer-generated media for travel planning: Integrating technology acceptance and source credibility factors. In L. Cantoni & Z. Xiang (Eds.), *Information and communication technologies in tourism 2013* (pp. 254–267). Heidelberg, Germany: Springer. doi:10.1007/978-3-642-36309-2_22

Azuma, R. T. (1997). A survey of augmented reality. *Computers & Applied Sciences Complete Presence*, *6*(4), 355–385. doi:10.1162/pres.1997.6.4.355

B'enabou, R., & Tirole, J. (2003). Intrinsic and extrinsic motivation. *The Review of Economic Studies*, *70*(3), 489–52. doi:10.1111/1467-937X.00253

Backer, T. E., & Rogers, E. M. (1998). Diffusion of Innovations Theory and Work-Site AIDS Programs. *Journal of Health Communication, 3*(1), 17–20. doi:10.1080/108107398127481 PMID:10947372

Bagozzi, R.P., Gopinath, M., & Nyer, P.U. (1999). The Role of Emotions in Marketing. *Journal of the Academy of Marketing Science, 27*, 184-206.

Bajde, D., Nøjgaard, M., & Sommer, J. K. (2019). Consumer Culture Theory and the Socio-Cultural Investigation of Technology Consumption. In Analytical Frameworks, Applications, and Impacts of ICT and Actor-Network Theory (pp. 171-190). IGI Global. doi:10.4018/978-1-5225-7027-1.ch008

Balducci, B., & Marinova, D. (2018). Unstructured data in marketing. *Journal of the Academy of Marketing Science, 46*(4), 557–590. doi:10.100711747-018-0581-x

Ballantyne, D. (1996). Internal networks for internal marketing. In *Proceedings of 4th International Colloquium in Relationship Marketing*. Swedish School of Economics.

Ballantyne, D. (1997). Relationship marketing of services-perspectives from 1983 and 2000. *Journal of Marketing Management, 13*(5), 343–366. doi:10.1080/0267257X.1997.9964479

Ballantyne, D. (2003). A relationship-mediated theory of internal marketing. *European Journal of Marketing, 37*(9/10), 1242–1260. doi:10.1108/03090560310486979

Balomenou, N., & Garrod, B. (2019). Photographs in tourism research: Prejudice, power, performance and participant-generated images. *Tourism Management, 70*, 201–217. doi:10.1016/j.tourman.2018.08.014

Balomenou, N., Garrod, B., & Georgiadou, A. (2017). Making sense of tourists' photographs using canonical variate analysis. *Tourism Management, 61*, 173–179. doi:10.1016/j.tourman.2017.02.010

Balough, C. (2012). A Survey of False Advertising in Cyberspace. *Business Lawyer, 68*(1), 297–304. Retrieved from http://www.jstor.org/stable/23527095

Bandlien, C. B. (2012). On the Style Site: Face Hunter as Node and Prism. In J. Berry (Ed.), *Fashion Capital: Style Economies, Sites and Cultures* (pp. 115–128). Oxford, UK: Interdisciplinary.

Banerjee, S., & Chua, A. Y. (2016). In search of patterns among travellers' hotel ratings in TripAdvisor. *Tourism Management, 53*, 125–131. doi:10.1016/j.tourman.2015.09.020

Bannon, S., Ford, K., & Meltzer, L. (2011). Understanding Millennials in the Workplace. *The CPA Journal, 81*(11), 61–65.

Banskota, K., & Upadhyay, M. (1991). *Impact of rural tourism on the environment, income, and employment in the Makalu-Barun area. Report 17, The Makalu-Barun Conservation project*. Kathmandu: Department of National Park and Wildlife Conservation, HMG Nepal and Woodlands Mountain Institute.

Barger, V., Peltier, J. W., & Schultz, D. E. (2016). Social Media and Consumer Engagement: A Review and Research Agenda. *Journal of Research in Interactive Marketing, 10*(4), 268–287. doi:10.1108/JRIM-06-2016-0065

Barnatt, C. (1997). Virtual organisation in the small business sector; the case of Cavendish management resources. *International Small Business Journal, 15*(4), 36–47. doi:10.1177/0266242697154002

Barnes, D., Clear, F., Dyerson, R., Harindranath, G., Harris, L., & Rae, A. (2012). Web 2.0 and micro-businesses: An exploratory investigation. *Journal of Small Business and Enterprise Development, 19*(4), 687–711. doi:10.1108/14626001211277479

Barnes, J. G. (1989). The role of internal marketing: If the staff won't buy it, why should the customer? *Irish Marketing Review, 4*(2), 11–21.

Barney, J. B. (1991). Firm resources and sustained competitive advantage. *Journal of Management*, *17*(1), 99–120. doi:10.1177/014920639101700108

Barney, J. B., & Clark, D. N. (2007). *Resource-based theory: Creating and sustaining competitive advantage*. New York: Oxford University Press.

Baron, J. N., & Hannan, M. T. (1994). The impact of economics on contemporary sociology. *Journal of Economic Literature*, *32*(3), 1111 1146.

Baskerville, R. L., & Myers, M. D. (2009). Fashion Waves in Information Systems Research and Practice. *MIS Quarterly, 33*(4), 647-662.

Bassiouni, D. H., & Hackley, C. (2014). 'Generation Z' children's adaption to digital consumer culture: A critical literature review. *Journal of Customer Behaviour*, *13*(2), 113–133. doi:10.1362/147539214X14024779483591

Baumgarnter, F. (1978). *Trekking Tourism in Nepal*. Zurich: Report of the INDEL Team.

Baumgartner, R. (1986). Tourism and socio-economic change: The case of Rolwaling Valley in eastern Nepal. In K. Seeland (Ed.), *Recent researches in Nepal* (pp. 199–217). Munchen: Weltforum Verlag.

Baxendale, S., Macdonald, E. K., & Wilson, H. N. (2015). The impact of different touchpoints on brand consideration. *Journal of Retailing*, *91*(2), 235–253. doi:10.1016/j.jretai.2014.12.008

Baytiyeh, H. (2017). The flipped classroom model: When technology enhances professional skills. *The International Journal of Information and Learning Technology*, *34*(1), 51–62. doi:10.1108/IJILT-07-2016-0025

BBC. (2017). *NHS 'could have prevented' WannaCry ransomware attack*. London: BBC.

BBC. (2017). *Ukraine power cut 'was cyber-attack*. London: BBC.

BBC. (2018). *Arran Brewery hit by ransomware attack*. Scotland: BBC Scotland.

Bearden, W. O., & Netemeyer, R. G. (1999). *Handbook of Marketing Scales: Multi-Item Measures for Marketing and Consumer Behavior Research* (2nd ed.). SAGE Publications. doi:10.4135/9781412984379

Beatty, Vivek, & Morgan. (2012). Consumer engagement in online brand communities: a social media perspective. *Journal of Product & Brand Management, 24*(1), 28-42.

Becker, H. S. (1970). *Sociological work: Method and substance*. Chicago, CA: Aldine.

Belch & Belch. (2004). Advertising & Promotion. An Integrated Marketing Communications Approach. *Corporate Communications*, *17*(3).

Belk, R. (2014). You are what you can access: Sharing and collaborative consumption online. *Journal of Business Research, 67*, 1595–1600. Retrieved from https://collaborativeeconomy.com/wp/wp-content/uploads/2015/05/Belk-R.2014.-You-are-what-you-can-access-Sharing-and-collaborative-consumption-online.Journal-of-Business-Research.pdf

Belk, R. (2001). You are what you can access: Sharing and collaborative consumption online. *Journal of Business Research*, *67*(8), 1595–1600. doi:10.1016/j.jbusres.2013.10.001

Belk, R. W. (2010). Sharing. *The Journal of Consumer Research*, *36*, 715–734. doi:10.1086/612649

Belk, R. W., & Costa, J. A. (1998). The mountain man myth: A contemporary consuming fantasy. *The Journal of Consumer Research*, *25*(3), 218–240. doi:10.1086/209536

Bell, D. R., Gallino, S., & Moreno, A. (2018). Offline Showrooms in Omnichannel Retail: Demand and Operational Benefits. *Management Science*, *64*(4), 1629–1651. doi:10.1287/mnsc.2016.2684

Beltrán, J., Sánchez, H., & Rico, M. (2016). Increase motivation in learning Java Programming Fundamentals using Gamified Moodle: CaseL Central University of Ecuador. *2016 11th Iberian Conference on Information Systems and Technologies (CISTI)*, 1-4. 10.1109/CISTI.2016.7521419

Benchoufi, M., & Ravaud, P. (2017). Blockchain technology for improving clinical research quality. *Trials*, *18*(1), 335. doi:10.118613063-017-2035-z PMID:28724395

Bencivenga, R. (2017). The 'digital curious': First steps towards a new typology for mapping adults' relationships with others when using ICT. *European Journal for Research on the Education and Learning of Adults*, *8*(1), 55–76. doi:10.3384/rela.2000-7426.rela9117

Bénédicte, A., Rani, J. D., & Longhi, C. (2011). Innovation in the tourism industry: The case of Tourism. *Tourism Management*, *32*(5), 1204–1213. doi:10.1016/j.tourman.2010.08.010

Bergen, M., Dutta, S., & Walker, O. C. Jr. (1992). Agency Relationships in Marketing: A Review of the Implications and Applications of Agency and Related Theories. *Journal of Marketing*, *56*(3), 1–24. doi:10.1177/002224299205600301

Berry, J. (2012). Street-Style: Fashion Photography, Weblogs, and the Urban Image. In J. Berry (Ed.), *Fashion Capital: Style Economies, Sites and Cultures* (pp. 129–148). Oxford, UK: Interdisciplinary.

Berry, L. L. (1981). The employee as customer. *Journal of Retail Banking*, *3*(1), 25–28.

Berry, L. L., Hensel, J. S., & Burke, M. C. (1976). Improving retailer capability for effective consumerism response. *Journal of Retailing*, *52*(3), 3–14.

Bertacchini, F., Bilotta, F., & Pantano, P. (2017). Shopping with a robotic companion. *Computers in Human Behavior*, *77*, 382–395. doi:10.1016/j.chb.2017.02.064

Bettany, S. M., Kerrane, B., & Hogg, M. K. (2014). The material-semiotics of fatherhood: The co-emergence of technology and contemporary fatherhood. *Journal of Business Research*, *67*(7), 1544–1551. doi:10.1016/j.jbusres.2014.01.012

Bhadani, A. K., & Jothimani, D. (2016). Big data: Challenges, opportunities and realities. In M. K. Singh & D. G. Kumar (Eds.), *Effective Big Data Management and Opportunities for Implementation* (pp. 1–24). Retrieved from https://pdfs.semanticscholar.org/0a45/69cfcb193a548de7445106135445bae5950f.pdf

Bharati, P., Zhang, W., & Chaudhury, A. (2015). Better Knowledge with Social Media? Exploring the Roles of Social Capital and Organizational Knowledge Management. *Journal of Knowledge Management*, *19*(3), 456–476. doi:10.1108/JKM-11-2014-0467

Bhattarai, S. (1985). Environmental impact of tourism on mountain ecosystem. In *Proceedings of the International Workshop on the Management of National park and Protected Areas in the Hindukush Himalaya*. Kathmandhu: The King Mahindra trust Furniture Conservation (KMTNC) and International Centre for integrated mountain development (ICIMOD).

Bijmolt, T. H. A., Leeflang, P. S. H., Block, F., Eisenbeiss, M., Hardie, B. G. S., & Saffert, P. (2010). Analytics for Customer Engagement. *Journal of Service Research*, *13*(3), 341–356. doi:10.1177/1094670510375603

Bikash, G. (2013). *Marketing in Event Management. Laurea University of Applied Sciences, Laurea Kerava.* Retrieved 6 25, 2019, from https://www.theseus.fi/bitstream/handle/10024/76351/Gurung_Bikash.pdf?sequence=1

Bilgihan, A. (2016). Gen Y customer loyalty in online shopping: An integrated model of trust, user experience and branding. *Computers in Human Behavior*, *61*, 103–116. doi:10.1016/j.chb.2016.03.014

Birkhäuser-Oeri, S., (1988). *The mother: Archetypal image in fairy tales* (Vol. 34). Inner City Books.

Bishop, T. (2013). *Can policy keep up with technology? New UW lab gets 1.7 million from Microsoft*. Retrieved from https://www/geekwire.com/2013/policy-technology-uw-create-lab-17mmicrosoft/

Bjonnes, I. M. (1979). *Impact on a high mountain ecosystem-recommendations for action in Sagramatha*. Kathmandu: N.P.W.C. Office.

Blackburn, R. A., Hart, M., & Wainwright, T. (2013). Small business performance: Business, strategy and owner-manager characteristics. *Journal of Small Business and Enterprise Development*, *20*(1), 8–27. doi:10.1108/14626001311298394

Blogger. (2010). Retrieved from http://www.blogger.com/profile-find.g?t=j&ind=FASHION

Blom, A., Lange, F., & Hess, R. L. Jr. (2017). Omnichannel-based promotions' effects on purchase behavior and brand image. *Journal of Retailing and Consumer Services*, *39*, 286–295. doi:10.1016/j.jretconser.2017.08.008

Blowfield, M., & Murray, A. (2014). Corporate responsibility. Oxford University Press.

Blut, M., Teller, C., & Floh, A. (2018). Testing retail marketing-mix effects on patronage: A meta-analysis. *Journal of Retailing*, *94*(2), 113–135. doi:10.1016/j.jretai.2018.03.001

Bobkowski, P. S., Shafer, A., & Ortiz, R. R. (2016). Sexual intensity of adolescents' online self-presentations: Joint contribution of identity, media consumption, and extraversion. *Computers in Human Behavior*, *58*, 64–74. doi:10.1016/j.chb.2015.12.009

Bocetta, S. (2019). *How ransomware targets WordPress sites*. Available at: https://marketingland.com/how-ransomware-targets-wordpress-sites-262939

Bocker, L., & Meelen, T. (2017). *Sharing for people, planet or profit? Analysing motivations for intended sharing economy participation*. Working Paper Series: Innovation Studies Utrecht.

Bock, G. W., Zmud, Kim, & Lee. (2005). Behavioral intention formation in knowledge sharing: Examining the roles of extrinsic motivators,Social-psychological forces, and organizational. *Management Information Systems Quarterly*, *29*(1), 87–111. doi:10.2307/25148669

Boellstorff, T. (2010). *Coming of Age in Second Life*. Princeton, NJ: Princeton University Press.

Boer, P. (2013). *Introduction to Gamification in Docent Online Marketing*. Academic Press.

Boer, P. V. (n.d.). *Introduction to Gamification*. Retrieved 07 10, 2019, from CD University: https://cdu.edu.au/olt/ltresources/downloads/whitepaper-introductiontogamification-130726103056-phpapp02.pdf

Bogost, I. (2011, August 8). Gamification is Bullshit. *Ian Bogost*. Retrieved January 8, 2019, from http://www.bogost.com/blog/gamification_is_bullshit.shtml

Borgerson, J.L., & Schroeder, J.E. (2008). Building an ethics of visual representation: Contesting epistemic closure in marketing communication. *Cutting-Edge Issues in Business Ethics*, 87-108.

Borgerson, J. L., & Schroeder, J. E. (2002). Ethical issues of global marketing: Avoiding bad faith in visual representation. *European Journal of Marketing*, *36*(5/6), 570–594. doi:10.1108/03090560210422399

Borgerson, J. L., & Schroeder, J. E. (2018). Making skin visible: How consumer culture imagery commodifies identity. *Body & Society*, *24*(1-2), 103–136. doi:10.1177/1357034X18760987

Borgerson, J. L., Schroeder, J. E., Blomberg, B., & Thorssén, E. (2006). The gay family in the ad: Consumer responses to non traditional families in marketing communications. *Journal of Marketing Management*, *22*(9-10), 955–978. doi:10.1362/026725706778935646

Bothwell, E. (2018). *Work-life balance survey 2018: long hours take their toll on academics*. Retrieved from www.timehighereducation.com/features/work-life-balance-survey-2018-long-hours-take-their-toll-academics

Botsman, R. (2013). *The Sharing Economy Lack a Shared Definition: Giving Meaning to the Terms.* Retrieved Sept 5, 2018, from Fast Company: https://www.fastcompany.com/3022028/the-sharing-economy-lacks-a-shared-definition

Botsman, R. (2015). *Defining the Sharing Economy: What Is Collaborative Consumption – And What Isn't?* Retrieved from http://www.fastcoexist.com/3046119/

Botsman, R., & Rogers, R. (2010). Beyond Zipcar: Collaborative consumption. *Harvard Business Review*, *88*(10), 30. PMID:20607961

Botsman, R., & Rogers, R. (2011). *What's mine is yours-the rise of collaborative consumption*. HarperCollins.

Bourdieu, P. (1984). *Distinction: A Social Critique of the Judgment of Taste*. Cambridge, MA: Harvard University Press.

Bourdieu, P. (1986). *The Forms of Capital.* In G. John (Ed.), *Handbook of Theory and Research for the Sociology of Education* (pp. 241–258). Richardson: Greenwood.

Bourdieu, P., & Wacquant, L. (1992). *An Invitation to Reflexive Sociology*. Chicago, IL: University of Chicago Press.

Bournemouth University. (2018). *A brief history of marketing*. Available at: https://media3.bournemouth.ac.uk/marketing/02defining/01history.html

Bowen, D.E. & Lawler, E.E. III. (1992). The empowerment of service workers: what, why, how, and when. *Sloan Management Review*, *8*(1), 31-9.

Boxman, E., & Flap, H. (2017). Getting started: the influence of social capital on the start of *the occupational career*. In *Social capital* (pp. 159–181). Routledge.

Boyatzis, R. E., & Kolb, D. A. (1991). Assessing individuality in learning: The learning skills profile. *Educational Psychology*, *11*(3/4), 279–295. doi:10.1080/0144341910110305

Boyd, D. M., & Ellison, N. B. (2007). Social network sites: Definition, history, and scholarship. *Journal of Computer-Mediated Communication*, *13*(1), 210–230. doi:10.1111/j.1083-6101.2007.00393.x

Bradley, A. J., & McDonald M. P. (2011). *The Social Organization*. Harvard Business Review Press.

Bradlow, E. T., Gangwar, M., Kopalle, P., & Voleti, S. (2017). The role of big data and predictive analytics in retailing. *Journal of Retailing*, *93*(1), 79–95. doi:10.1016/j.jretai.2016.12.004

Bray, J. J., Johns, N., & Kilburn, D. (2011). An exploratory study into the factors impeding ethical consumption. *Journal of Business Ethics*, *98*(4), 597–608. doi:10.100710551-010-0640-9

Brenda, L., Koster, F., & van der Veen, R. J. (2019). Levelling the playing field? Active labour market policies, educational attainment and unemployment. *The International Journal of Sociology and Social Policy*, *39*(3/4), 276–295. doi:10.1108/IJSSP-08-2018-0138

Brewer, R. (2016). Ransomware attacks: Detection, prevention and cure. *Network Security*, *2016*(9), 5–9. doi:10.1016/S1353-4858(16)30086-1

Brodie, R.J., Hollebeek, L.D., & Juric, B., & Ilic, A. (2011a). Customer engagement: Conceptual domain, fundamental propositions & implications for research. *Journal of Service Research*, *34*(10), 251–271.

Brosdahl, D. J., & Carpenter, M. J. (2011). Shopping orientations of US males: A generational cohort comparison. *Journal of Retailing and Consumer Services*, *18*(6), 548–554. doi:10.1016/j.jretconser.2011.07.005

Brown, D., & Fiorella, S. (2013). *Influence marketing*. Indianapolis: Que Publishing.

Brown, G. (2017). The Millennials (Generation Y): Segregation, Integration and Racism, ABNF Journal. *Health Research Premium Collection*, *28*(1), 5–8. PMID:29873454

Brown, J. D. (2010). High self-esteem buffers negative feedback: Once more with feeling. *Cognition and Emotion*, *24*(8), 1389–1404. doi:10.1080/02699930903504405

Brugger, E. A., Furrer, G., Messerli, B., & Messerii, P. (1984). *The transformation of Swiss Mountain Regions*. Bern: Verlang Paul Haupt.

Bruhn, M., Schnebelen, S., & Schäfer, D. (2014). Antecedents and consequences of the quality of e-customer-to-customer interactions in B2B brand communities. *Industrial Marketing Management*, *43*(1), 164–176. doi:10.1016/j.indmarman.2013.08.008

Bruhn, M., Schoenmüller, V., Schäfer, D., & Heinrich, D. (2012). Brand authenticity: Towards a deeper understanding of its conceptualization and measurement. *Advances in Consumer Research. Association for Consumer Research (U. S.)*, 40.

Bruns, A. (2005). *Gatewawatching*. New York: Peter Lang.

Bryman, A., & Bell, E. (2003). *Business research methods*. Northamptonshire, UK: Oxford University Press.

BT. (2019). *The history of radio in the UK*. BT.

Buchanan, B. (2005). A (Very) Brief History of Artificial Intelligence. *AI Magazine*, *26*(4), 53–60.

Buchanan, D., & Huczynski, A. (1991). *Organisational Behaviour: An Introductory Text* (2nd ed.). Englewood Cliffs, NJ: Prentice-Hall.

Bucher, E. F. (2016). What's mine is yours (for a nominal fee) – Exploring the spectrum of utilitarian to altruistic motives for Internet-mediated sharing. *Computers in Human Behaviour*, 316-326.

Bucher, E., Fieseler, C., & Lutz, C. (2016). What's mine is yours (for a nominal fee) – Exploring the spectrum of utilitarian to altruistic motives for Internet-mediated sharing. *Computers in Human Behavior*, *62*, 316–326. doi:10.1016/j.chb.2016.04.002

Buckley, R. (2012). Sustainable tourism: Research and reality. *Annals of Tourism Research*, *39*(2), 528–546. doi:10.1016/j.annals.2012.02.003

Buda, G., & Lehota, J. (2017). *Attitudes and Motivations of Consumers in Sharing Economy, Management, Enterprise and Benchmarking in the 21st Century*. Retrieved Sept 3, 2018, from KGK university: https://kgk.uni-obuda.hu/sites/default/files/02_Buda_Lehota.pdf

Budd, C. (2016). *Ransomware infects the cloud: What you need to know*. Available at: https://blog.trendmicro.com/ransomware-infects-the-cloud-what-you-need-to-know/

Bureau, E. T. (2019, April 6). Election Commission urged to put check on digital platforms. *The Economic Times*. Retrieved from https://economictimes.indiatimes.com/news/politics-and-nation/election-commission-urged-to-put-check-on-digital-platforms/articleshow/68747932.cms

Burgess, J. E., & Green, J. B. (2009). *YouTube: Online Video and Participatory Culture*. Cambridge, UK: Polity.

Burke, B. (2012). *Gamification 2020: What Is the Future of Gamification*. Gartner, Inc.

Burkeman, O. (2009). *Forty years of the internet: how the world changed for ever*. The Guardian.

Burns, T., & Stalker, G. M. (1961). *The Management of Innovation*. London: Tavistock.

Burt, A. (2019, January 3). *Privacy and Cybersecurity Are Converging. Here's Why That Matters for People and for Companies*. Retrieved from https://hbr.org/2019/01/privacy-and-cybersecurity-are-converging-heres-why-that-matters-for-people-and-for-companies

Bush, V., Venable, B., & Bush, A. (2000). Ethics and Marketing on the Internet: Practitioners' Perceptions of Societal, Industry and Company Concerns. *Journal of Business Ethics*, *23*(3), 237–248. doi:10.1023/A:1006202107464

Butler, J. (2004). *Undoing gender*. Psychology Press. doi:10.4324/9780203499627

Butler, J. (2011). *Bodies that matter: On the discursive limits of sex*. Taylor & Francis. doi:10.4324/9780203828274

Butt, M. (2019). Ransomware Threat and its Impact on SCADA. In *2019 IEEE 12th International Conference on Global Security, Safety and Sustainability (ICGS3)*. London: IEEE.

Bykea. (2019). *We're Solving a Real Problem*. Retrieved from Bykea: https://www.bykea.com/

Cacioppo, J., & Petty, R. (1982). The need for cognition. *Journal of Personality and Social Psychology*, *42*(1), 116–131. doi:10.1037/0022-3514.42.1.116

Cacioppo, J., & Petty, R. (1984). The Elaboration Likelihood Model Of Persuasion. *Advances in Consumer Research*, *11*(1), 673–675.

Çakır, V., & Çakır, V. (2016). The Role of Self-Esteem and Self Image Congruity with the Ad Spokespersons The Role of Self-Esteem and Self Image Congruity with the Ad Spokespersons in Ad Attitude. *International Conference on Changing World and Social Research*. Retrieved from https://www.researchgate.net/publication/292982423_The_Role_of_Self-Esteem_and_Self_Image_Congruity_with_the_Ad_Spokespersons_in_Ad_Attitude

Calder, B. J., Malthouse, E. C., & Schaedel, U. (2009). Engagement with Online Media and Advertising Effectiveness. *Journal of Interactive Marketing*, *23*, 321–331. doi:10.1016/j.intmar.2009.07.002

Caldwell, M., Henry, P., & Alman, A. (2010). Constructing audio-visual representations of consumer archetypes. *Qualitative Market Research*, *13*(1), 84–96. doi:10.1108/13522751011013990

Caloghirou, Y., Protogerou, A., Spanos, Y., & Papagiannakis, L. (2004). Industry-Versus Firm-specific Effects on Performance: Contrasting SMEs and Large-sized Firms. *European Management Journal*, *22*(2), 231–243. doi:10.1016/j.emj.2004.01.017

Calvo-Porral, C., & Levy-Mangin, J.-P. (2018). Pull factors of the shopping malls: An empirical study. *International Journal of Retail & Distribution Management*, *46*(2), 110–124. doi:10.1108/IJRDM-02-2017-0027

Camilleri, M. A. (2018). Integrated marketing communications. In *Travel marketing, tourism economics and the airline product* (pp. 85–103). Cham: Springer. doi:10.1007/978-3-319-49849-2_5

Campbell, C. (2005). The Craft Consumer: Culture, Craft and Consumption in a Postmodern Society. *Journal of Consumer Culture*, *5*(1), 23–42. doi:10.1177/1469540505049843

Campelo, A., Aitken, R., & Gnoth, J. (2011). Visual rhetoric and ethics in marketing of destinations. *Journal of Travel Research*, *50*(1), 3–14. doi:10.1177/0047287510362777

Canales, K. (2018, August 21). *40 totally amazing technological advancements that we don't even notice anymore*. Retrieved 07 21, 2019, from https://www.businessinsider.com/amazing-technological-advancements-we-dont-even-notice-anymore-2018-8

Cannell, J. (2013). *Today the US Department of Justice (DOJ) announced an effort to disrupt the Gameover Zeus Botnet. In addition to this effort, the DOJ announced an another join.* Available at: https://blog.malwarebytes.com/101/2013/10/cryptolocker-ransomware-what-you-need-to-know/

Cannon, J. P., Achrol, R. S., & Gundlach, G. T. (2000). Contracts, norms, and plural form governance. *Journal of the Academy of Marketing Science*, (28): 94–180.

Cao, M., & Zhang, Q. (2010). Supply chain collaborative advantage: A firm's perspective. *International Journal of Production Economics*, *128*(1), 358–367. doi:10.1016/j.ijpe.2010.07.037

Cao, M., & Zhang, Q. (2011). Supply chain collaboration: Impact on collaborative advantage and firm performance. *Journal of Operations Management*, *29*(3), 163–180. doi:10.1016/j.jom.2010.12.008

Cao, Y., Ajjan, H., & Hong, P. (2013). Using social media applications for educational outcomes in college teaching: A structural equation analysis. *British Journal of Educational Technology*, *44*(4), 581–593. doi:10.1111/bjet.12066

Cappellini, B., & Yen, D. A. W. (2016). A space of one's own: Spatial and identity liminality in an online community of mothers. *Journal of Marketing Management*, *32*(13-14), 1260–12. doi:10.1080/0267257X.2016.1156725

Carbon Black. (2018). *Advance Your Ransomware Defenses*. Carbon Black.

Carlton, M., Levy, Y., & Ramim, M. (2019). Mitigating cyber attacks through the measurement of non-IT professionals' cybersecurity skills. *Technology Information & Computer Security*, *27*(1), 101–121. doi:10.1108/ICS-11-2016-0088

Carrera, F. (2009). *Marketing digital na versão 2.0*. Lisboa: Edições Sílabo.

Carson, D., & Gilmore, A. (2000). Marketing at the Interface: Not 'What' but 'How'. *Journal of Marketing Theory and Practice*, *8*(2), 1–7. doi:10.1080/10696679.2000.11501863

Casadesus-Masanell, R., & Heilbron, J. (2015). *The Business Model: Nature and Benefits*. Retrieved from https://www.hbs.edu/faculty/Publication Files/15-089_afa7e1c9-40d2-486d-9bd4-b8ea71de9058.pdf

Casado-Vara, R., Prieto, J., la Prieta, F., & Corchado, J. (2018). How blockchain improves the supply chain: Case study alimentary supply chain. *Procedia Computer Science*, *134*, 393–398. doi:10.1016/j.procs.2018.07.193

Cascales, A., Pérez-López, D., & Contero, M. (2013). Study on parent's acceptance of the augmented reality use for preschool education. *Procedia Computer Science*, *25*, 420–427. doi:10.1016/j.procs.2013.11.053

Cascio, W. (2016). *How Technology Is Changing Work and Organizations*. Academic Press.

Cathro, V., O'Kane, P. and Gilbertson, D. (2017). Assessing reflection: understanding skill development through reflective learning journals, *Journal of Education + Training*, *59*(4), 427-442.

Catterall, M., Maclaran, P., & Stevens, L. (Eds.). (2013). *Marketing and feminism: Current issues and research*. Routledge. doi:10.4324/9781315010939

CCN. (2018). *Spanish Coastal City Valencia to Create a Smart Port with Blockchain Tech*. Available at: https://www.ccn.com/spanish-coastal-city-valencia-to-create-a-smart-port-with-blockchain-tech/

Cefis, E., & Marsili, O. (2006). Survivor: The role of innovation in firms' survival. *Research Policy*, *35*(5), 626–641. doi:10.1016/j.respol.2006.02.006

Çelikdemir, D. Z., & Tukel, I. (2015). Incorporating Ethics into Strategic Management with regards to Generation Y's view of Ethics. *Procedia: Social and Behavioral Sciences*, *207*, 528–535. doi:10.1016/j.sbspro.2015.10.123

Cennamo, L., & Gardner, D. (2008). Generational differences in work values, outcomes and person-organisation values fit. *Journal of Managerial Psychology*, *23*(8), 891–906. doi:10.1108/02683940810904385

Centre for Retail Research. (2011). *World shopping capitals 2011 survey: which city is the biggest shopper?* Available at http://www.retailresearch.org/worldshoppingcapitals.php

Cerase, A., & Santoro, C. (2018). From racial hoaxes to media hypes: Fake news' real consequences. In P. Vasterman (Ed.), *From Media Hype to Twitter Storm: News Explosions and Their Impact on Issues, Crises, and Public Opinion* (pp. 333–354). Amsterdam: Amsterdam University Press; doi:10.2307/j.ctt21215m0.20

Chae, J. (2015). 'Am I a Better Mother Than You?' Media and 21st-Century Motherhood in the Context of the Social Comparison Theory. *Communication Research*, *42*(4), 503–525. doi:10.1177/0093650214534969

Chaffey, D., & Ellis-Chadwick, F. (2019). Introduction – how has digital marketing transformed marketing? In *Digital Marketing* (7th ed.). Pearson.

ChainLink. (2019). *Your smart contracts connected to real world data, events and payments*. Available at: https://chain.link/

Chakravarti, A., & Janiszewski, C. (2003). The influence of macro-level motives on consideration set composition in novel purchase situations. *The Journal of Consumer Research*, *30*(2), 244–258. doi:10.1086/376803

Challco, C. G., Moreira, A. D., Bittencourt, I., Mizoguchi, R., & Isotani, S. (2015). Personalization of Gamification in Collaborative Learning Contexts using Ontologies. *IEEE Latin America Transactions*, *13*(6). 10.1109/TLA.2015.7164227

Chang, C. S., & Chang, H. C. (2008). Perceptions of internal marketing. *Journal of Advanced Nursing*, *8*(87), 92–100. PMID:19120584

Chang, G., & Caneday, L. (2011). Web-based GIS in tourism information search: Perceptions, tasks, and trip attributes. *Tourism Management*, *32*(6), 1435–1437. doi:10.1016/j.tourman.2011.01.006

Chang, H. L., Chou, Y. C., Wu, D. Y., & Wu, S. C. (2018). Will firms marketing efforts on owned social media payoff? A quasi-experimental analysis of tourism products. *Decision Support Systems*, *107*, 13–25. doi:10.1016/j.dss.2017.12.011

Charles, D., Charles, T., McNeill, M., Bustard, D., & Black, M. (2011). Game-based feedback for edu-cational multi-user virtual environments. *British Journal of Educational Technology*, *42*(4), 638–654. doi:10.1111/j.1467-8535.2010.01068.x

Charls, R. T., & Costello, P. J. (2017). International Digital Advertising- Lessons learned from around the world. In S. Rodgers & T. Esther (Eds.), *Digital Advertising: Theory and Research* (p. 466). Retrieved from https://books.google.co.uk/books?id=6CslDwAAQBAJ&pg=PA352&lpg=PA352&dq=digital+advertisement+,+culture+and+effects&source=bl&ots=w02730sON_&sig=ACfU3U368eqvM-l3AekNbdvWCp8tzum_6A&hl=en&sa=X&ved=2ahUKEwiv6NHlhozkAhV1SBUIHcvdDDg4FBDoATAFegQICRAB#v=onepage&q

Check Point Software Technologies. (2019). *Cyber Attack Trends Analysis Report*. Retrieved from http://www.snt.hr/boxcontent/CheckPointSecurityReport2019_vol01.pdf

Chelliah, J., & Clarke, E. (2011). Collaborative teaching and learning: Overcoming the digital divide? *On the Horizon*, *19*(4), 276–285. doi:10.1108/10748121111179402

Chen, C. P., & Zhang, C. Y. (2014). Data-intensive applications, challenges, techniques and technologies: A survey on Big Data. *Information Sciences*, *275*, 314–347. doi:10.1016/j.ins.2014.01.015

Cheng, C. C., & Shiu, E. C. (2018). How to enhance SMEs' customer involvement using social media: The role of social CRM. *International Small Business Journal*, *36*, 1–21. doi:10.1177/0266242618774831

Chen, H., Chiang, R., & Storey, V. (2012). Business intelligence and analytics: From big data to big impact. *Management Information Systems Quarterly*, *36*(4), 1165–1188. doi:10.2307/41703503

Chen, L., Zhao, X., Tang, O., Price, L., Zhang, S., & Zhu, W. (2017). Supply chain collaboration for sustainability: A literature review and future research agenda. *International Journal of Production Economics*, *194*, 73–87. doi:10.1016/j.ijpe.2017.04.005

Chen, W., Wang, C., & Wang, Y. (2010, July). Scalable influence maximization for prevalent viral marketing in large scale social networks. In *Proceedings of the 16th ACM SIGKDD international conference on Knowledge discovery and data mining* (pp. 1029-1038). ACM. 10.1145/1835804.1835934

Chen, Y., Fay, S., & Wang, Q. (2011). The role of marketing in social media: How online consumer reviews evolve. *Journal of Interactive Marketing*, *25*(2), 85–94. doi:10.1016/j.intmar.2011.01.003

Cheong, H. J., & Morrison, M. A. (2008). Consumers' reliance on product information and recommendations found in UGC. *Journal of Interactive Advertising*, *8*(2), 38–49. doi:10.1080/15252019.2008.10722141

Cheong, K., Hiil, C., Leong, Y., Zhang, C., & Zhang, Z. (2018). 'Parents just don't understand' – generational perceptions of education and work. *Journal of Higher Education Evaluation and Development*, *12*(2), 85–98. doi:10.1108/HEED-06-2018-0016

Chernikova, I. A., & Varonis, E. M. (2016). Designing and delivering online curriculum in higher education: Riding the perfect storm. *The International Journal of Information and Learning Technology*, *33*(3), 132–141. doi:10.1108/IJILT-09-2015-0026

Chin, B., & Hills, M. (2008). Restricted Confessions? Blogging, Subcultural Celebrity and the Management of Producer-fan Proximity. *Social Semiotics*, *18*(2), 253–272. doi:10.1080/10350330802002424

Chipembele, M., & Bwalya, K. J. (2016). Assessing e-readiness of the Copperbelt University, Zambia: Case study. *The International Journal of Information and Technology*, *33*(5), 315–332.

Choi, M. S., Levy, Y., & Hovav, A. (2013), The role of user computer self-efficacy, cybersecurity countermeasures awareness, and cybersecurity skills influence on computer misuse. *Proceedings of the Pre-International Conference of Information Systems (ICIS) SIGSEC – Workshop on Information Security and Privacy (WISP) 2013*. Available at: http://aisel.aisnet.org/wisp2012/29

Choi, S. M., & Rifon, N. J. (2012). It is a match: The impact of congruence between celebrity image and consumer ideal self on endorsement effectiveness. *Journal of Psychology & Marketing*, *29*, 636–650.

Choi, T. M., Liu, N., Liu, S. C., Mak, J., & To, Y. T. (2010). Fast fashion brand extensions: An empirical study of consumer preferences. *Journal of Brand Management*, *17*(7), 472–487. doi:10.1057/bm.2010.8

Choi, T. Y., & Wu, Z. (2009). Taking the leap from dyads to triads: Buyer–supplier relationships in supply networks. *Journal of Purchasing and Supply Management*, *15*(4), 263–266. doi:10.1016/j.pursup.2009.08.003

Choudhury, M. M., & Harrigan, P. (2014). CRM to social CRM: The integration of new technologies into customer relationship management. *Journal of Strategic Marketing, Taylor & Francis*, *22*(2), 149–176. doi:10.1080/0965254X.2013.876069

Chou, Y.-C., Chuang, H. H.-H., & Shao, B. B. M. (2016). The impact of e-retail characteristics on initiating mobile retail services: A modular innovation perspective. *Information & Management*, *53*(4), 481–492. doi:10.1016/j.im.2015.11.003

Chris Yapp. (2018). *The Road Ahead: Navigation AI's Pitfalls*. Oxford University Press; doi:10.1093/itnow/bwy008

Chris, E. (2010). *Innovation management; a literature review of innovation process models and their implications*. Available at: http://www.lectoraatinnovatie.nl/wp-content/uploads/2011/01/Innovation-management-literature-review-.pdf

Christie, S. (2018). *Don't pity stressed students too much – academics have it worse*. Retrieved from www.timeshighereducation.com/blog/dont-pity-stressed-students-too-much-academivs-have-it-worse

Christine Moorman, T. A. (2018, May). *Getting The Most Out of Social Media Investments*. Retrieved from The Wall Street Journal: https://deloitte.wsj.com/cmo/2018/05/18/getting-the-most-out-of-social-media-investments/

Christodoulides, G., Michaelidou, N., & Argyriou, E. (2012). Cross-national differences in e-WOM influence. *European Journal of Marketing*, *46*(11/13), 1689–1707. doi:10.1108/03090561211260040

Christopher, M. (Ed.). (1992). *Logistics— the strategic issues*. London: Chapman and Hall.

Christopher, M. (2000). The agile supply chain—Competing in volatile markets. *Industrial Marketing Management*, *29*(1), 37–44. doi:10.1016/S0019-8501(99)00110-8

Chui, M., Miller, A., & Roberts, R. (2009, February). *Six ways to make Web 2.0 work. The McKinsey Quarterly*.

Cimpanu, C. (2018). *Pennsylvania Senate Democrats paid $700,000 to recover from ransomware attack*. Zero Day Net.

Cimperman, M. B., Harrison, A., Hatch, J., Pillar, K., & Snipes, T. (2018). Understanding the Millennial Buying Process in the Modern Digital Era - Secondary Research. *Honors Research Projects*. Available at: http://ideaexchange.uakron.edu/honors_research_projectshttp://ideaexchange.uakron.edu/honors_research_projects/546

Circella, G., Tiedeman, K., Handy, S., & Alemi, F. (2016). What Affects Millennials' Mobility? PART I: Investigating the Environmental Concerns, Lifestyles, Mobility-Related Attitudes and Adoption of Technology of Young. *National Center for Sustainable Transportation*. Retrieved from https://escholarship.org/uc/item/6wm51523

Circella, G., Tiedeman, K., Handy, S., & Alemi, F. (2016). *What Affects Millennials' Mobility? PART I: Investigating the Environmental Concerns, Lifestyles, Mobility-Related Attitudes and Adoption of Technology of Young*. National Center for Sustainable Transportation.

Cisco Talos. (2018). *Email & Spam Data*. Cisco.

Cisco. (2018). *What Is Malware?* Available at: https://www.cisco.com/c/en/us/products/security/advanced-malware-protection/what-is-malware.html

Çizmeci, F., & Ercan, T. (2015). The Effect of Digital Marketing Communication Tools in the Creation Brand Awareness By Housing Companies. *Megaron, 10*(2).

Clarie Penicaud, A. K. (2019). State of the industry 2013: mobile financial services for the unbanked. *Gates open Research*. Retrieved from https://gatesopenresearch.org/documents/3-1429

Clark, M., Black, H. G., & Judson, K. (2017). Brand Community Integration and Satisfaction with Social Media Sites: A Comparative Study. *Journal of Research in Interactive Marketing*, *11*(1), 39–55. doi:10.1108/JRIM-07-2015-0047

Clauson, K., Breeden, E., Davidson, C., & Mackey, T. (2018). Leveraging Blockchain Technology to Enhance Supply Chain Management in Healthcare. *Blockchain In Healthcare Today*. doi:10.30953/bhty.v1.20

Clements, S. (2013). *Social technology, social business?* CIPD survey report. Retrieved from www.cipd.co.uk/Images/social-technology-social-business_2013_tcm18-10323.pdf

Clemmer, J. (1998). Path to innovation; Spend at least 25% of your time with customers. *Executive Excellence*, *15*, 10–10.

Clowes, R. (2014). Thinking in the Cloud: The Cognitive Incorporation of Cloud-Based Technology. *Philosophy & Technology*, *28*(2), 261–296. doi:10.100713347-014-0153-z

CNN Business. (2019). *Ford's delivery robot walks like a human*. CNN.

Cobb, S. (2017). *RoT: Ransomware of Things*. Available at: https://cdn1.esetstatic.com/ESET/US/Newsroom/2017/03/ESET_Trends-and-Prediction_2017_Ransomware.pdf

Cocco, L., Pinna, A., & Marchesi, M. (2017). Banking on Blockchain: Costs Savings Thanks to the Blockchain Technology. *Future Internet*, *9*(3), 25. doi:10.3390/fi9030025

Cockerell, N. (1997). International Tourism Reports No.1 - Nepal. *Travel and Tourism Intelligence*, *1*, 40–57.

Cocquyt, C., Diep, N. A., Zhu, C., De Greef, M., & Vanwing, T. (2017). Examining social inclusion and social capital among adult learners in blended and online learning environments. *European Journal for Research on the Education and Learning of Adults*, *8*(1), 77–101. doi:10.3384/rela.2000-7426.rela9111

Cohen, Pham, & Andrade. (2008). *Psychological testing and assessment: An introduction to tests and measurement* (7th ed.). Columbus, OH: McGraw-Hill Education.

Cohen, W., & Levinthal, D. (1990). Absorptive Capacity : A New Perspective on Learning and Innovation. *Administrative Science Quarterly*, *35*(1), 128–152. doi:10.2307/2393553

Collini, S. (2012). *What Are Universities For?* London: Penguin Books.

Columbus, L. (2016). 2015 Gartner CRM Market Share Analysis Shows Salesforce. In *The Lead, Growing Faster Than Market*. Forbes.

Com, M. (2017). *China' s Connected Consumers The rise of the Millennials*. Retrieved from https://assets.kpmg/content/dam/kpmg/cn/pdf/en/2017/12/chinas-connected-consumers-the-rise-of-the-millennials.pdf

Cone Communications. (2015). *Cone Communications Millennial CSR Study*. Retrieved from http://www.conecomm.com/research-blog/2015-cone-communications-millennial-csr-study#download-research

Connell, J. A., McMinn, N. E., & Bell, N. (2012). How will the next generation change the business world? A report on a survey. *Insights to a Changing World Journal*, *4*, 100–113.

Cooperstein, D. (2011). What'sImportant To CMOs In 2011? *Forrester Blogs*. Available at: http://blogs.forrester.com/david_cooperstein/11-01-10whats_important_to_cmos_in_2011

Cope, J. (2005). Toward a Dynamic Learning Perspective of Entrepreneurship. *Entrepreneurship Theory and Practice*, *29*(4), 373–397. doi:10.1111/j.1540-6520.2005.00090.x

Cope, J., & Watts, G. (2000). Learning by doing: An exploration of experience, critical incidents and reflection in entrepreneurial learning. *International Journal of Entrepreneurial Behaviour & Research*, *6*(3), 104–124. doi:10.1108/13552550010346208

Coppock, R. (1978). *High season: The consequences and potential of tourism in the Region of Mount Everest*. Munich: German alpine Club.

Corcoran, C. T. (2010). Marketing's New Rage: Brands Sponsoring Influential Bloggers. *WWD*. Retrieved from http://goo.gl/u4kJmq

Corda. (2019). *Corda Enterprise – A Next-gen Blockchain Platform*. Available at: https://www.r3.com/platform/

Corea Nana. (2011). *How to Play Jeopardy*. YouTube.

Correa, T. (2010). The participation divide among 'online experts': Experience, skills and psycho-logical factors as predictors of college students' web content creation. *Journal of Computer-Mediated Communication*, *16*(1), 71–92. doi:10.1111/j.1083-6101.2010.01532.x

Coskuner-Balli, G., & Thompson, C. J. (2012). The status costs of subordinate cultural capital: At-home fathers' collective pursuit of cultural legitimacy through capitalizing consumption practices. *The Journal of Consumer Research*, *40*(1), 19–41. doi:10.1086/668640

Cottrell, S., & Morris, N. (2012). *Study Skills Connected: Using Technology to Support your Studies*. London: Palgrave. doi:10.1007/978-1-137-01944-8

Court, D., Elzinga, D., Mulder, S., & Vetvik, O. J. (2009). *The consumer decision journey*. McKinsey.

Covin, J. G., & Slevin, D. (1989). Strategic management of small firms in hostile and benign environments. *Strategic Management Journal*, *10*(1), 75–87. doi:10.1002mj.4250100107

Coyle, J. R., Smith, T., & Platt, G. (2012). I'm Here to Help. *Journal of Research in Interactive Marketing*, *6*(1), 27–41. doi:10.1108/17505931211241350

Cramer, J., & Krueger, A. (2016). Disruptive Change in the Taxi Business: The Case of Uber. *The American Economic Review*, *106*(5), 177–182. doi:10.1257/aer.p20161002

Crane, D., & Bovone, L. (2006). Approaches to Material Culture: The Sociology of Fashion and Clothing. *Poetics*, *34*(6), 319–333. doi:10.1016/j.poetic.2006.10.002

Crawford-Lee, M., & Moorwood, S. (2019). Degree apprenticeships: Delivering quality and social mobility? *Journal of Higher Education, Skills and Work-Based Learning*, *9*(2), 134–140. doi:10.1108/HESWBL-05-2019-123

Crewe, L. (2013). When virtual and material worlds collide: Democratic fashion in the digital age. *Environment & Planning*, *45*(4), 760–780. doi:10.1068/a4546

CRR. (2019). Who's Gone Bust to end-March 2019. Centre for Retail Research.

Cuervo, A. (2005). Individual and environmental determinants of entrepreneurship. *The International Entrepreneurship and Management Journal*, *1*(3), 293–311. doi:10.100711365-005-2591-7

Cui, M., & Hu, S. (2011, September). Search engine optimization research for website promotion. In *2011 International Conference of Information Technology, Computer Engineering and Management Sciences* (Vol. 4, pp. 100-103). IEEE. 10.1109/ICM.2011.308

Curran, J., & Blackburn, R. (2001). *Researching the Small Enterprise*. London: SAGE Publications. doi:10.4135/9781849209847

Cyber Security Ventures. (2019). *Cybercrime Damages $6 Trillion By 2021*. Cyber Security Ventures.

Cyert, R. M., & March, J. G. (1992). *A Behavioral Theory of the Firm* (2nd ed.). Cambridge, UK: Blackwell Business.

Cylance. (2019). *2019 Threat Report*. Irvine, CA: Cylance.

d'Ancona, M. (2017). *Post-truth: The new war on truth and how to fight back*. Random House.

Dacko, S. G. (2017). Enabling smart retail settings via mobile augmented reality shopping apps. *Technological Forecasting and Social Change*, *124*, 243–256. doi:10.1016/j.techfore.2016.09.032

Dadwal, S., & Hassan, A. (2015). The augmented reality marketing: a merger of marketing and technology in tourism. In N. Ray (Ed.), *Emerging innovative marketing strategies in the tourism industry* (pp. 78–96). Hershey, PA: IGI Global. doi:10.4018/978-1-4666-8699-1.ch005

Daellenbach, K. (2018). On carrot cake and marketing education: A perspective on balancing skills for employability. *Australasian Marketing Journal*, *26*(2), 172–179. doi:10.1016/j.ausmj.2018.04.005

Dafoulas, G., & Shokri, A. (2016). Investigating the educational value of social learning networks: A quantitative analysis. *Journal of Interactive Technology and Smart Education*, *13*(4), 305–322. doi:10.1108/ITSE-09-2016-0034

Dahir, A. L. (2018, August 24). *Uber's innovations in Africa have helped shape its global operations*. Retrieved from Quartz Africa: https://qz.com/africa/1368732/uber-in-africa-cash-payments-are-shaping-global-operations/

Dans, E. (2019, March 26). *Apple Reinvents The Credit Card.* Retrieved July 25, 2019, from https://www.forbes.com/sites/enriquedans/2019/03/26/Apple-reinvents-the-credit-card/#45d458047939

Dash, C., & Behera, P. (2017). Blockchain Technology: A Revolutionary Bitcoin Technology. *International Journal Of Information Science And Computing*, *4*(1), 27. doi:10.5958/2454-9533.2017.00004.7

DaSilva, C. M., & Trkman, P. (2014). Business Model: What it is and What it is Not. *SSRN Electronic Journal, 47*(6), 379–389. doi:10.2139srn.2181113

Davis, P. M. (2012). Trust is number 1 barrier to sharing. *DeskMag*. Retrieved from http://www.deskmag.com/en/trust-is-1-barrier-to-sharing-coworking-shareable-491/

Davis, S. E. (2018). Objectification, Sexualization, and Misrepresentation: Social Media and the College Experience. *Social Media+ Society, 4*(3).

Davis, D. L. (1983). Woman the worrier: Confronting feminist and biomedical archetypes of stress: *Women's Studies. An Interdisciplinary Journal*, *10*(2), 135–146.

Davis, F. D. (1986). *A technology acceptance model for empirically testing new end-user information systems: Theory and results*. Sloan School of Management, Massachusetts Institute of Technology.

Davis, F. D. (1989). Perceived usefulness, perceived ease of use, and user acceptance of information technology. *Management Information Systems Quarterly*, *13*(3), 319–340. doi:10.2307/249008

Davis, F., Bagozzi, R. P., & Warshaw, P. R. (1989). User Acceptance of Computer Technology: A Comparison of Two Theoretical Models. *Management Science*, *35*(8), 982–1003. doi:10.1287/mnsc.35.8.982

Davison, J. (2009). Icon, iconography, iconology: Visual branding, banking and the case of the bowler hat. *Accounting, Auditing & Accountability Journal*, *22*(6), 883–906. doi:10.1108/09513570910980454

Dawson, J. (2000). Retailing at century end: Some challenges for management and research. *International Review of Retail, Distribution and Consumer Research*, *10*(2), 119–148. doi:10.1080/095939600342325

Day, G. (1994). *The capabilities of market-driven organizations. The Journal of Marketing*, 58, 37–52.

De Hauw, S., & De Vos, A. (2010). Millennials' career perspective and psychological contract expectations: Does the recession lead to lowered expectations? *Journal of Business and Psychology*, *25*(2), 293–302. doi:10.100710869-010-9162-9

De Mooij, M. (2018). *Global marketing and advertising: Understanding cultural paradoxes*. SAGE Publications Limited.

De Pelsmacker, P., Geuens, P., & Van den Bergh, J. (2005). *Marketingcommunicatie*. Amsterdam: Pearson Education Benelux.

De Valck, K., & Kretz, G. (2011). *Pixelize me: Digital Storytelling and the creation of archetypal myths through explicit and implicit self-brand association in fashion and luxury blog*. Research in Consumer Behavior.

De Vargas Mores, G., Finocchio, C. P. S., Barichello, R., & Pedrozo, E. A. (2018). Sustainability and innovation in the Brazilian supply chain of green plastic. *Journal of Cleaner Production*, *177*, 12–18. doi:10.1016/j.jclepro.2017.12.138

Dealtry, R. (2002). Managing the corporate university watershed. *Journal of Workplace Learning*, *14*(6), 256–261. doi:10.1108/13665620210441216

Deci, E. L., & Ryan, R. M. (1985). *Intrinsic motivation and self- determination in human behaviour*. New York: Plenum. doi:10.1007/978-1-4899-2271-7

Deighton, J., & Kornfeld, L. (2009). Interactivity's unanticipated consequences for marketers and marketing. *Journal of Interactive Marketing*, *23*(1), 4–10. doi:10.1016/j.intmar.2008.10.001

Deloitte. (2009). *Generation Y: powerhouse of the global economy Restless generation is a challenge–and a huge opportunity–for employers*. Deloitte Consulting LLP.

Deloitte. (2012). *Tech Trends 2012: Elevate IT for digital business*. Author.

Deloitte. (2013). *Tech Trends 2013: elements of postdigital*. Author.

Deloitte. (2016). *Ransomware Holding Your Data Hostage*. London: Deloitte Threat Intelligence and Analytics.

Demirkan, H., & Spohrer, J. (2014). Developing a framework to improve virtual shopping in digital malls with intelligent self-service systems. *Journal of Retailing and Consumer Services*, *21*(5), 860–868. doi:10.1016/j.jretconser.2014.02.012

Deng, M., & Cao, Y. (2018). Innovation and Effect Evaluation Model of Education and Training Outsourcing of State-owned Enterprises under Big Data. *Educational Sciences: Theory and Practice*, *18*(6). doi:10.12738/estp.2018.6.201

Dennis, C. (2005). *Objects of desire: consumer behaviour in shopping centre choices*. Palgrave McMillan. doi:10.1057/9780230509481

Dennis, C., Murphy, J., Marsland, D., Cockett, T., & Patel, T. (2002). Measuring image: Shopping centre case studies. *International Review of Retail, Distribution and Consumer Research*, *12*(4), 355–373. doi:10.1080/09593960210151153

Denscombe, M. (2007). *The good research guide: for small-scale social research projects* (3rd ed.)., Available at http://www.dawsonera.com/depp/reader/protected/external/AbstractView/S97803352

Denzin, N. K. (1997). Interpretive ethnography: Ethnographic practices for the 21st century. *Sage (Atlanta, Ga.)*.

Desmet, P., & Dijk. (2007). A wheelchair can be Fun: a case of emotion-driven design. In *Proceedings of The International Conference on Designing Pleasurable Products and Interfaces*. New York: The Association for Computing Machinery.

Deterding, S., Dixon, D., Khaled, R., & Nacke, L. (2011). From game design elements to gamefulness: Defining "gamification." In A. Lugmayr, H. Franssila, C. Safran, & I. Hammouda (Eds.), *Proceedings of the 15th International Academic MindTrek Conference* (pp. 9–15). New York, NY: ACM. 10.1145/2181037.2181040

Dhanoa, R., & Goyal, N. (2018). Millennial Generations' Susceptibility to Interpersonal Influence: A Case of Personal Care Products Purchases. *International Journal of Management Studies*, (2). doi:10.18843/ijms/v5i2(6)/08

Dicheva, D., Dichev, C., Agre, G., & Angelova, G. (2015). Gamification in education: A systematic mapping study. *Education Technology & Society*, *18*(3), 1–10.

Dillon, A., & Morris, M. (1996). User Acceptance of Information Technology: Theories and Models. *Annual Review of Information Science & Technology*, 3–32.

Dilogini, K., & Shivany, S. (2016). *Framework of Technology in Marketing World: A Theoretical Review*. Academic Press.

Dindar, M., & Yaman, N. D. (2018). #IUseTwitterBecause: Content analytic study of a trending topic in Twitter. *Information Technology & People*, *31*(1), 256–277. doi:10.1108/ITP-02-2017-0029

Dixit, R. (2017). Multi-Cloud for Improving Cloud Data Security. *International Journal For Research In Applied Science And Engineering Technology, 5*(11), 2696-2700. doi:10.22214/ijraset.2017.11371

Dixon, D. (2011). *Player Types and Gamification*. CHI, Vancouver, BC, Canada. Retrieved 07 10, 2019, from http://gamification-research.org/wp-content/uploads/2011/04/11-Dixon.pdf

Dodgson, M. (1993). Organizational Learning—A Review of Some Literatures. *Organization Studies*, *14*(3), 375–394. doi:10.1177/017084069301400303

Dokyun, L., Hosanagar, L., & Nair, H. (2018). Advertising Content and Consumer Engagement on Social Media: Evidence from Facebook. *Management Science*. Retrieved 7 7, 2019, from https://repository.upenn.edu/cgi/viewcontent.cgi?article=1353&context=marketing_papers

Donaire, J. A., Camprubí, R., & Galí, N. (2014). Tourist clusters from Flickr travel photography. *Tourism Management Perspectives*, *11*, 26–33. doi:10.1016/j.tmp.2014.02.003

Donaldson, T., & Dunfee, T. W. (1994). Toward a Unified Conception of Business Ethics: Integrative Social Contracts Theory. *Academy of Management Review*, *19*(2), 252–284. doi:10.5465/amr.1994.9410210749

Donelan, H. (2016). Social media for professional development and networking opportunities in academia. *Journal of Further and Higher Education*, *40*(5), 706–729. doi:10.1080/0309877X.2015.1014321

Doolin, B., Burgess, L., & Cooper, J. (2002). Evaluating the use of the Web for tourism marketing: A case study from New Zealand. *Tourism Management*, *23*(5), 557–561. doi:10.1016/S0261-5177(02)00014-6

Dos Santos, R. (2017). On the Philosophy of Bitcoin/Blockchain Technology: Is it a Chaotic, Complex System? *Metaphilosophy*, *48*(5), 620–633. doi:10.1111/meta.12266

DoubleDutch., & MPI. (2014). *The State of Event Apps Official MPI Research*. Retrieved from https://www.hbaa.org.uk/sites/default/files/mpi-research-state-of-event-apps.pdf

Douglas, S., & Michaels, M. (2005). *The mommy myth: The idealization of motherhood and how it has undermined all women*. Simon and Schuster.

Döveling, K., Harju, A. A., & Sommer, D. (2018). From mediatized emotion to digital affect cultures: New technologies and global flows of emotion. *Social Media+ Society, 4*(1).

Downes, L. (2009). *The Laws of Disruption: Harnessing the New Forces that Govern Life and Business in the Digital Age*. Basic Book.

Downey, J. P., & Smith, L. A. (2011). The role of computer attitudes in enhancing computer competence in training. *Journal of Organizational and End User Computing*, *23*(3), 81–100. doi:10.4018/joeuc.2011070105

DrugPatentWatch. (2017). *Can Blockchain Technology put an end to Counterfeit Drugs*. Available at https://medium.com/drugpatentwatch/can-blockchain-technology-put-an-end-to-counterfeit-drugs-c4087e652fe0

Duan, A., Wang, M., Lei, Y., & Cui, Y. (2013). Trends in summer rainfall over China associated with the Tibetan Plateau sensible heat source during 1980–2008. *Journal of Climate*, *26*(1), 261–275. doi:10.1175/JCLI-D-11-00669.1

Dudek, D. (2017). Possibilities of using blockchain technology in the area of education. *Informatyka Ekonomiczna*, (45), 55–65. doi:10.15611/ie.2017.3.05

Duffy, D. L. (2005). Affiliate marketing and its impact on e-commerce. *Journal of Consumer Marketing*, *22*(3), 161–163. doi:10.1108/07363760510595986

Dunleavy, M., & Dede, C. (2006). *Augmented reality teaching and learning*. Cambridge, MA: Harvard Education Press.

Durkin, M., McGowan, P., & McKeown, N. (2013). Exploring social media adoption in small to medium-sized enterprises in Ireland. *Journal of Small Business and Enterprise Development*, *20*(4), 716–734. doi:10.1108/JSBED-08-2012-0094

Dyer, J. H., & Singh, H. (1998). The relational view: Cooperative strategy and sources of interorganizational competitive advantage. *Academy of Management Review*, *23*(4), 660–679. doi:10.5465/amr.1998.1255632

Eagly, A. H., & Chaiken, S. (1993). *The psychology of attitudes*. Orlando, FL: Harcourt Brace Jovanovich College Publishers.

Economist.com. (2013). *The rise of the sharing economy*. Retrieved, 12 April, 2017, from http://www.economist.com/news/leaders/21573104-internet-everything-hire-rise- sharing-economy

Eisenhardt, K. M., & Martin, J. (2000). Dynamic capabilities: What are they? *Strategic Management Journal*, *21*(10–11), 1105–1121. doi:10.1002/1097-0266(200010/11)21:10/11<1105::AID-SMJ133>3.0.CO;2-E

El-Gohary, H. (2012). Factors affecting E-Marketing adoption and implementation in tourism firms: An empirical investigation of Egyptian small tourism organizations. *Tourism Management*, *33*(5), 1256–1269. doi:10.1016/j.tourman.2011.10.013

Elliott, R., & Boshoff, C. (2009). The marketing of tourism services using the internet: A resource based view. *South African Journal of Business Management*, *40*(3), 35–49. doi:10.4102ajbm.v40i3.543

Elliott, R., & Davies, A. (2006). *Symbolic Brands and Authenticity of Identity Performance*. In J. E. Schroeder & M. Salzer-Morling (Eds.), *Brand Culture* (pp. 155–170). London: Routledge.

EMF. (2010). *Workshop concept and Methodology*. Pro Ideal Plus.

Emmett Dulaney, C. E. (2018). CompTIA Security+ Study Guide: Exam SY0-501 (7th ed.). Indianapolis: CompTIA Security+.

Emsisoft. (2018). *Spotlight on ransomware: Ransomware encryption methods*. Available at: https://blog.emsisoft.com/en/27649/ransomware-encryption-methods/

Encyclopædia Britannica. (2019). *History of Publishing*. Author.

Enge, E., Spencer, S., Stricchiola, J., & Fishkin, R. (2012). *The art of SEO*. O'Reilly Media, Inc.

Epp, A. M., & Velagaleti, S. R. (2014). Outsourcing Parenthood? How Families Manage Care Assemblages Using Paid Commercial Services. *The Journal of Consumer Research*, *41*(4), 911–935. doi:10.1086/677892

Erasmus, A. C., Boshoff, E., & Rousseau, G. G. (2001). Consumer decision-making models within the discipline of consumer science: A critical approach. *Journal of Family Ecology and Consumer Science*, *29*, 82–90.

Erdoğmuş, İ. E., & Cicek, M. (2012). The impact of social media marketing on brand loyalty. *Procedia: Social and Behavioral Sciences*, *58*, 1353–1360. doi:10.1016/j.sbspro.2012.09.1119

Erevelles, S., Fukawa, N., & Swayne, L. (2016). Big Data consumer analytics and the transformation of marketing. *Journal of Business Research*, *69*(2), 897–904. doi:10.1016/j.jbusres.2015.07.001

Eschenbrenner, B., & Nah, F. F.-H. (2014). Information systems user competency: A conceptual foundation. *Communications of the Association for Information Systems, 34*, 1363–1378. doi:10.17705/1CAIS.03480

Esomba, S. D. (2013). *Advertising and the spread of Business, Democracy and Knowledge*. Lulu.com.

Esset. (2018). *Viruses, malware and remote attacks defined.* Available at: https://support.eset.com/kb186/

Etemad, H., Wilkinson, I., & Dana, L. P. (2010). Internetization as the necessary condition for internationalization in the newly emerging economy. *Journal of International Entrepreneurship, 8*(4), 319–342. doi:10.100710843-010-0062-x

Etmeezi. (2010). *Nuthom altaaleem alelektroni wadwatuh.* Phillipsburg, NJ: Phillips Publishing

EU GDPR. (2019). *The EU General Data Protection Regulation (GDPR) is the most important change in data privacy regulation in 20 year*. Available at: https://eugdpr.org/

Evanschitzky, H., Iyer, G. R., Kenning, P., & Schutte, R. (2015). Consumer trial, continuous use, and economic benefits of a retail service innovation: The case of the personal shopping assistant. *Journal of Product Innovation Management, 31*(3), 459–475. doi:10.1111/jpim.12241

Eventbrite. (2017). *Essential Guides: Event Marketing*. Retrieved June 2, 2019, from Eventbrite.com/blog

Eventbrite. (2019). *The Ultimate Guide to Event Marketing*. Retrieved June 2, 2019, from Eventbrite: https://www.eventbrite.com/blog/event-marketing-ds00/

Eventtia. (2019, July 11). www.eventtia.com. Retrieved from www.eventtia.com: https://www.eventtia.com/blog/blockchain-technology-and-events-what-will-change

Evenues. (2019, July 11). *evenues.com*. Retrieved from evenues.com: https://evenues.com/event-planning-guide/what-is-a-conference

EY. (2017). *Four Themes driving FinTech Adoption by Consumers*. Retrieved from https://www.ey.com/en_gl/banking-capital-markets/four-themes-driving-FinTech-adoption-by-consumers

EY. (2017). *Unleashing the Potential of FinTech in Bank*. EY.

EY. (n.d.). *How a social media firm created Korea's fastest growing bank*. EY.

Faull, J. (2018). *'We're full steam ahead': travel brands brush off Brexit concerns ahead of January marketing blitz*. Retrieved from www.thedrum.com

Feasey, R. (2016). From soap opera to reality programming: Examining motherhood, motherwork and the maternal role on popular television. Imaginations. *Journal of Cross-Cultural Image Studies, 4*(2), 25–46.

Feick, L. F., & Price, L. L. (1987). The Market Maven: A Diffuser of Marketplace Information. *Journal of Marketing, 51*, 83–97. doi:10.1177/002224298705100107

Felix, R., Rauschnabel, P. A., & Hinsch, C. (2017). Elements of strategic social media marketing: A holistic framework. *Journal of Business Research, 70*, 118–126. doi:10.1016/j.jbusres.2016.05.001

Felson, M., & Spaeth, J. L. (1978). Community Structure and Collaborative Consumption: A routine activity approach. *The American Behavioral Scientist, 21*(4), 614–624. doi:10.1177/000276427802100411

Felton, A. P. (1959, July). Making the marketing concept work. *Harvard Business Review*, 55–65.

Fennell, M. L., & Warnecke, R. B. (1988). *The diffusion of medical innovations: An applied network analysis*. New York, NY: Plenum. doi:10.1007/978-1-4684-5436-9

Ferdows, K., Lewis, M. A., & Machuca, J. A. D. (2004). Rapid Fire Fulfillment. *Harvard Business Review*, *82*, 104–117.

Ferreira, F., & Belem, B. (2017). Consumers' attitude toward Facebook advertising. *Int Journal of Electronic Marketing and Retailing*, 46-57. Retrieved 7 10, 2019, from https://www.researchgate.net/publication/316054583_Consumers'_attitude_toward_Facebook_advertising

Ferrell, O. C. (2017). Broadening marketing's contribution to data privacy. *Journal of the Academy of Marketing Science*, *5*(2), 160–163. doi:10.100711747-016-0502-9

Ferrell, O. C., & Gresham, L. G. (1985). A Contingency Framework for Understanding Ethical Decision Making in Marketing. *Journal of Marketing*, *49*(3), 87–96. doi:10.1177/002224298504900308

FIFA. (2019). *2018 FIFA World Cup Russia™ - News - More than half the world watched record-breaking 2018 World Cup*. FIFA.com.

Finn, A., & Louviere, J. J. (1996). Shopping center image, consideration, and choice: Anchor store contribution. *Journal of Business Research*, *35*(3), 241–251. doi:10.1016/0148-2963(95)00129-8

Fishbein, M. (1963). An investigation of the relationship between beliefs about an object and the attitude toward that object. *Human Relations*, *16*(3), 233–240. doi:10.1177/001872676301600302

Fisher, M. (1997, March/April). What is the right supply chain for your product? *Harvard Business Review*, 105–116.

Fitzgerald, L., Ferlie, E., Wood, M., & Hawkins, C. (2002). Interlocking Interactions, the Diffusion of Innovations in Health Care. *Human Relations*, *55*(12), 1429–1449. doi:10.1177/001872602128782213

Fleming, J., Becker, K., & Newton, C. (2017). Factors for successful e-learning: does age matter? *Journal of Education + Training*, *59*(1), 76-89.

Flint, D. (2004). Strategic marketing in global supply chains: Four challenges. *Industrial Marketing Management*, *33*(1), 45–50. doi:10.1016/j.indmarman.2003.08.009

Flynn, B. B., Huo, B., & Zhao, X. (2010). The impact of supply chain integration on performance: A contingency and configuration approach. *Journal of Operations Management*, *28*(1), 58–71. doi:10.1016/j.jom.2009.06.001

Folmar, D. (2015). *Game it up: Using gamification to incentivize your library*. Rowman & Littlefield.

Forbes. (2019). Retrieved from https://www.forbes.com/

Forde, S. (2011). *Challenging the News: The Journalism of Alternative and Community Media*. New York: Palgrave Macmillan. doi:10.1007/978-0-230-36096-9

Forlizzi, J., & Battarbee, K. (2004). *Understanding Experience in Interactive Systems*. Academic Press.

Forlizzi, J., & Ford, S. (2000). The Building Blocks of Experience: An Early Framework for Interaction Designers. In *Proceedings of the 3rd Conference on Designing Interactive Systems: Processes, Practices, Methods, and Techniques* (pp. 419–423). New York, NY: Academic Press. 10.1145/347642.347800

Forster, K. (2017, April 14). *Children as young as 13 attending 'smartphone rehab' as concerns grow over screen time*. Retrieved July 2019, 2019, from https://www.independent.co.uk/news/health/teenage-technology-addiction-smartphone-rehab-seattle-clinic-children-aged-13-mobile-devices-a7684356.html

Foster, J. (2001). *Data analysis, using SPSS for window 8 and 10*. London: Sage Publication.

Fotiadis, A., & Stylos, N. (2017). The effects of online social networking on retail consumer dynamics in the attractions industry: The case of 'E-da' Theme Park, Taiwan. *Technological Forecasting and Social Change*, *124*, 283–294. doi:10.1016/j.techfore.2016.06.033

Foux, G. (2006). Consumer-generated media: Get your customers involved. *Brand Strategy, 8*(202), 38-39.

Francisco-Aparicio, A., Guti'errez-Vela, F., Isla-Montes, J., & Sanches, J. (2013). Gamification: Analysis and application. In V. Penichet (Ed.), *New trends in Interaction, Virtual Reality and Modeling, Human Computer Interaction Series* (pp. 113–126). London: Springer-Verlag.

Franco, M., & Haase, H. (2009). Entrepreneurship: An organisational learning approach. *Journal of Small Business and Enterprise Development*, *16*(4), 628–641. doi:10.1108/14626000911000965

Frédéric Jacques, M. N. (2017). *Reimagining the bank branch for the digital era.* Retrieved July 2019, 23, from https://www.mckinsey.com/industries/financial-services/our-insights/reimagining-the-bank-branch-for-the-digital-era

Frederick, W. C. (2018). Corporate Social Responsibility: From Founders to Millennials. In *Corporate Social Responsibility* (pp. 3–38). Emerald Publishing Limited. doi:10.1108/S2514-175920180000002001

Freestone, O., & Mitchell, V. W. (2004). Generation Y Attitudes Towards E-ethics and Internet-related Misbehaviours. *Journal of Business Ethics*, *54*(2), 121–128. doi:10.100710551-004-1571-0

French, W. L., & Bell, C. H. Jr. (1995). *Organisational Development* (5th ed.). Englewood Cliffs, NJ: Prentice-Hall.

Friedmann, E. (2018). Increasing women's participation in the STEM industry: A first step for developing a social marketing strategy. *Journal of Social Marketing*, *8*(4), 442–460. doi:10.1108/JSOCM-12-2017-0086

Fruhlinger, J. (2017). *Petya ransomware and NotPetya malware: What you need to know now.* Available at: https://www.csoonline.com/article/3233210/ransomware/petya-ransomware-and-notpetya-malware-what-you-need-to-know-now.html

Fruhlinger, J. (2017). *The 5 biggest ransomware attacks of the last 5 years.* Available at: https://www.csoonline.com/article/3212260/ransomware/the-5-biggest-ransomware-attacks-of-the-last-5-years.html

Fruhlinger, J. (2018). *What is WannaCry ransomware, how does it infect, and who was responsible?* Available at: https://www.csoonline.com/article/3227906/ransomware/what-is-wannacry-ransomware-how-does-it-infect-and-who-was-responsible.html

Furlong, J. (2018). *How 4 Companies Wow Customers With Projection Mapping Ads.* Retrieved July 31, 2019, from https://www.businessnewsdaily.com/10529-projection-mapping-examples.html

Furr, N., & Shipilov, A. (2019, July). *Digital Doesn't Have to Be Disruptive.* Retrieved July 21, 2019, from https://hbr.org/2019/07/digital-doesnt-have-to-be-disruptive

Fuscaldo, D. (2019, March 26). *Apple Card Fails To Impress Wall Street, Investors.* Retrieved July 25, 2019, from https://www.forbes.com/sites/donnafuscaldo/2019/03/26/Apple-card-fails-to-impress-wall-street-investors/#672305b625a8

Galbreth, M. R., Ghosh, B., & Shor, M. (2012). Social sharing of information goods: Implications for pricing and profits. *Marketing Science*, *31*(4), 603–620. doi:10.1287/mksc.1120.0706

Gallegos-Segovia, P. L. (2017). *Social engineering as an attack vector for ransomware.* Pucon, Chile: IEEE. doi:10.1109/CHILECON.2017.8229528

Galpin, T. J. (1997). Making strategy work. *The Journal of Business Strategy*, *18*(1), 12–14. doi:10.1108/eb039824

Gambetti, Grafigna, & Biragi. (2011). The Grounded Theory Approach to Consumer-Brand Engagement. *International Journal of Market Research, 54*(5), 659–687.

Gambetti, Grafigna, & Biragi. (2012). The Concept of Engagement: A Systematic Analysis of the Ongoing Marketing Debate. *International Journal of Market Research.*

Garm, L., & Slinger, J. (2014). Gamification in Consumer Marketing - Future or Fallacy? *Procedia - Social and Behavioral Sciences*, 194 – 202. Retrieved 07 10, 2019, from https://core.ac.uk/download/pdf/82546276.pdf

Gartner. (2018, November 27). *Every Organizational Function Needs to Work on Digital Transformation.* Retrieved July 21, 2019, from https://hbr.org/sponsored/2018/11/every-organizational-function-needs-to-work-on-digital-transformation

Gaski, J. F., & Nevin, J. R. (1985). The Differential Effects of Exercised and Unexercised Power Sources in a Marketing Channel. *JMR, Journal of Marketing Research*, *22*(2), 130–142. doi:10.1177/002224378502200203

Gecas, V. (1982). The Self-Concept. *Annual Review of Sociology*, *8*(1), 1–33. doi:10.1146/annurev.so.08.080182.000245

Gee, J. P. (2005). The new literacy studies: From'socially situated'to the work. Situated Literacies. *Reading and Writing in Context*, *2*, 177–194.

Gee, J. P. (2007). *What video games have to teach us about learning and literacy* (Rev. Ed.). New York, NY: Palgrave Macmillan.

George, W. R. (1977). The retailing of services – a challenging future. *Journal of Retailing*, *53*(3), 85–98.

Gerhardt, T. (2015). *The link between the training of curates in the Church of England and their future ministry and the nature of that relationship: nationally competent and Deployable?* (Unpublished doctoral thesis). University of Canterbury Christ Church, Canterbury, UK.

Gerhardt, T., & Mackenzie-Philps, L. (2018). The challenges and opportunities of ICT in WIL: A case study among priests exploring the correlation and trajectory between effective WIL and ICT pervasiveness, *Higher Education, Skills and Work-Based Learning*, *8*(4), 408–421. doi:10.1108/HESWBL-07-2017-0045

Germann, F., Lilien, G. L., Fiedler, L., & Kraus, M. (2014). Do retailers benefit from deploying customer analytics? *Journal of Retailing*, *90*(4), 587–593. doi:10.1016/j.jretai.2014.08.002

Getz, D. (2012). *Event Studies: theory, research and policy for planned events*. London: Routledge.

Giannini, G. T. (2009). *Marketing public relations*. Pearson Education India.

Gibbs, S. (2017). *WannaCry: hackers withdraw £108,000 of bitcoin ransom.* Available at: https://www.theguardian.com/technology/2017/aug/03/wannacry-hackers-withdraw-108000-pounds-bitcoin-ransom

Gibson, L. A., & Sodeman, W. A. (2014). Millennials and Technology: Addressing the Communication Gap in Education and Practice. *Organization Development Journal*, 63–75.

Giesler, M. (2006). Consumer Gift Systems. *The Journal of Consumer Research*, *33*, 283–290. doi:10.1086/506309

Gilfoil, D. M. (2012). Mapping social media tools for sell vs buy activities into emerging and developed markets. *International Journal of Management & Information Systems (Online)*, *16*(1), 69.

Gillmor, D. (2006). *We the Media: Grassroots Journalism by the People, for the People*. Sebastopol, CA: O'Reilly.

Gilmore, A., & Carson, D. (1995). Managing and marketing to internal customers. In W. J. Glynn & J. G. Barnes (Eds.), *Understanding Services Management* (pp. 295–321). Chichester, UK: John Wiley & Sons.

Gilmore, A., & Carson, D. (1996). "Integrative" qualitative methods in a services context. *Marketing Intelligence & Planning*, *14*(6), 21–26. doi:10.1108/02634509610131126

Gingrich, R. (2017). *Wearables in the Performing Arts: An RFID Primer for Arts Managers*. Retrieved from https://www.idtechex

Glenn, E. N., Chang, G., & Forcey, L. R. (Eds.). (2016). *Mothering: Ideology, experience, and agency*. Routledge. doi:10.4324/9781315538891

Gligor, D., Bozkurt, S., Russo, I., & Omar, A. (2019). A look into the past and future theories within supply chain management, marketing and management. *Supply Chain Management*, *24*(1), 170–186. doi:10.1108/SCM-03-2018-0124

Gnizy, I., Baker, W. E., & Grinstein, A. (2014). Proactive learning culture: A dynamic capability and key success factor for SMEs entering foreign markets. *International Marketing Review*, *31*(5), 477–505. doi:10.1108/IMR-10-2013-0246

Gobo, G. (2014). Glocalizing methodology? The encounter between local methodologies. *International Journal of Social Research Methodology*, *14*(6), 417–437. doi:10.1080/13645579.2011.611379

Godes, D., Mayzlin, D., Chen, Y., Das, S., Dellarocas, C., Pfeiffer, B., ... Verlegh, P. (2005). The firm's management of social interactions. *Marketing Letters*, *16*(3-4), 415–428. doi:10.100711002-005-5902-4

Goffman, E. (1959). *The Presentation of Self in Everyday Life*. New York: Anchor.

Goffman, E. (2017). *Asylums: Essays on the social situation of mental patients and other inmates*. Routledge. doi:10.4324/9781351327763

Goggin, G., & Larissa, H. (2014). *The Routledge Companion to Mobile Media*. New York: Routledge. doi:10.4324/9780203434833

Goldman, S., Nagel, R., & Preiss, K. (1995). Agile competitors and virtual organisations: Strategies for enriching the customer. New York: Van Nostrand Reinhold.

Goldstein, N. J., Cialdini, R. B., & Griskevicius, V. (2008). A room with a viewpoint: Using social norms to motivate environmental conservation in hotels. *The Journal of Consumer Research*, *35*(3), 472–482. doi:10.1086/586910

Golgeci, I., & Gligor, D. (2017). The interplay between key marketing and supply chain management capabilities: The role of integrative mechanisms. *Journal of Business and Industrial Marketing*, *32*(3), 472–483. doi:10.1108/JBIM-05-2016-0102

Goode, J., & Levy, Y. (2017). Towards empirical exploration of employee's cybersecurity countermeasures awareness and skills: differences in training delivery method and program type. *Proceeding of the Knowledge Management (KM) 2017 Conference, Faculty of Information Studies (FiS),* 18-30.

Goodrich, K., & de Mooij, M. (2014). How 'social'are social media? A crosscultural comparison of online and offline purchase decision influences. *Journal of Marketing Communications*, *20*(1-2), 103–116. doi:10.1080/13527266.2013.797773

Gorgios, T., & Sergios D. (2014). *Brand strategies in social media*. Academic Press.

Goulding, C., Shankar, A., & Elliott, R. (2002). Working Weeks, Rave Weekends: Identity Fragmentation and the Emergence of New Communities. *Consumption Markets & Culture*, *5*(4), 261–284. doi:10.1080/1025386022000001406

Government State Victoria. (2018). *Teach with digital technologies*. Retrieved 05 1, 2019, from Education.vic.gov.: https://www.education.vic.gov.au/school/teachers/teachingresources/digital/Pages/teach.aspx

Granic, I., Lobel, A., & Engels, R. C. M. E. (2014). The benefits of playing video games. *The American Psychologist*, *69*(1), 66–78. doi:10.1037/a0034857 PMID:24295515

Grau, S., & Zotos, Y. (2016). Gender stereotypes in advertising: A review of current research. *International Journal of Advertising*, *35*(5), 761–770. doi:10.1080/02650487.2016.1203556

Gravill, J. I., Compeau, D. R., & Marcolin, B. I. (2006). Experience effects on the accuracy of self -assessed user competence. *Information & Management*, *43*(3), 378–394. doi:10.1016/j.im.2005.10.001

Grayson, K. A., Kotler, P., & Hibbard, J. D. (2019). *Marketing | business*. Retrieved from Britannica.com

Greenberger, D. B., & Strasser, S. (1991). The role of situational and dispositional factors in the enhancement of personal control in organisations. *Research in Organizational Behavior*, *13*, 111–145.

Gremler, D. D., Gwinner, K. P., & Brown, S. W. (2001). Generating positive word-of mouth communication through customer-employee relationships. *International Journal of Service Industry Management*, *13*(1), 44–59. doi:10.1108/09564230110382763

Grenier & Stadler. (2009). Presence and the sixth sense. *Presence (Cambridge, Mass.)*, *11*(4), 435–439.

Gretzel, U. (2000). Tourism Managers' Adoption of Marketing Decision Support Systems. *Journal of Travel Research*, 172-181. Retrieved 6 30, 2019, from https://www.researchgate.net/publication/249700978_Tourism_Managers'_Adoption_of_Marketing_Decision_Support_Systems

Grewal, R., Kumar, A., Mallapragada, G., & Saini, A. (2013). Marketing Channels in Foreign Markets: Control Mechanisms and the Moderating Role of Multinational Corporation Headquarters–Subsidiary Relationship. *Journal of Marketing Research*, (50), 378-398.

Grewal, D., Bart, Y., Spann, M., & Zubcsek, P. (2016). Mobile Advertising: A Framework and Research Agenda. *Journal of Interactive Marketing*, *3*, 3–14. doi:10.1016/j.intmar.2016.03.003

Grewal, D., Roggeveen, A. L., & Nordfält, J. (2017). The future of retailing. *Journal of Retailing*, *93*(1), 1–6. doi:10.1016/j.jretai.2016.12.008

Grier, S. A., & Deshpandé, R. (2001). Social dimensions of consumer distinctiveness: The influence of social status on group identity and advertising persuasion. *JMR, Journal of Marketing Research*, *38*(2), 216–224. doi:10.1509/jmkr.38.2.216.18843

Gruen, T. W., Osmonbekov, T., & Czaplewski, A. J. (2006). eWOM: The impact of customer-to-customer online know-how exchange on customer value and loyalty. *Journal of Business Research*, *59*(4), 449–456. doi:10.1016/j.jbusres.2005.10.004

Gruzd, A., Wellman, B., & Takhteyev, Y. (2011). Imagining Twitter as an imagined community. *The American Behavioral Scientist*, *55*(10), 1294–1318. doi:10.1177/0002764211409378

Gualandris, J., Golini, R., & Kalchschmidt, M. (2014). Do supply management and global sourcing matter for firm sustainability performance? An international study. *Supply Chain Management*, *19*(3), 258–274. doi:10.1108/SCM-11-2013-0430

Guha, S., Harrigan, P., & Soutar, G. (2018). Linking social media to customer relationship management (CRM): A qualitative study on SMEs. *Journal of Small Business and Entrepreneurship*, *30*(3), 193–214. doi:10.1080/08276331.2017.1399628

Gunasekaran, A., Subramanian, N., & Rahman, S. (2015). Green supply chain collaboration and incentives: Current trends and future directions. *Transportation Research Part E, Logistics and Transportation Review*, *74*, 1–10. doi:10.1016/j.tre.2015.01.002

Gupta, M. P., & Dubey, A. (2016). International Journal of Computer Science and Mobile Computing E-Commerce-Study of Privacy, Trust and Security from Consumer's Perspective. *International Journal of Computer Science and Mobile Computing*, *5*(6), 224–232. Retrieved from www.ijcsmc.com

Gustafsson, J., & Thang, P. (2017). Workplace learning in Higher Education: two examples from a Swedish context. In T. Bowen & M. T. B. Drysdale (Eds.), *Work-Integrated Learning in the 21st Century* (pp. 35–49). Bingley, UK: Emerald. doi:10.1108/S1479-367920170000032002

Haddad & Algadeer. (2004). An empirical investigation on the impact of innovation within organisations on marketing innovation. *Jordan Journal of Applied Science*, (7), 77-95.

Hagberg, J., Sundstrom, M., & Egels-Zandén, N. (2016). The digitalization of retailing: An exploratory framework. *International Journal of Retail & Distribution Management*, *44*(7), 694–712. doi:10.1108/IJRDM-09-2015-0140

Halaburda, H. (2017). *Blockchain Revolution Without the Blockchain*. SSRN Electronic Journal. doi:10.2139srn.3133313

Haldane, J. (1994). The context of education: monastery or marketplace? In *Philosophy of Education*. London: Continuum.

Hale, J. (1998). Strategic rewards: Keeping your best talent from walking out the door. *Compensation and Benefits Management*, *14*(3), 39–50.

Hall, H., & Witek, L. (2016). Conditions, Contemporary Importance and Prospects of Higher Education Marketing on the Example of polish Universities. *Procedia Economics and Finance*, *39*, 206–211. doi:10.1016/S2212-5671(16)30314-8

Halvorsen, K., Hoffmann, J., Coste-Manière, I., & Stankeviciute, R. (2013). Can fashion blogs function as a marketing tool to influence consumer behavior? Evidence from Norway. *Journal of Global Fashion Marketing*, *4*(3), 211–224. doi:10.1080/20932685.2013.790707

Hamari, J., Koivisto, J., & Sarsa, H. (2014). Does Gamification Work? A Literature Review of Empirical Studies on Gamification. *Proceedings of the 47th Hawaii International Conference*. Retrieved 07 10, 2019, from https://www.researchgate.net/profile/Michael_Armstrong6/post/What_empirical_evidence_is_there_for_various_gamification_techniques/attachment/59d61dcb79197b8077979ce0/AS:273513875738624@1442222197132/download/2014-hamari_et_al-does_gamification_work.pdf

Hamari, J., Huotari, K., & Tolvanen, J. (2015). Gamification and economics. In S. P. Walz & S. Deterding (Eds.), *The gameful world: Approaches, issues, applications* (pp. 139–161). Cambridge, MA: MIT Press.

Hamari, J., Sjoklint, M., & Ukkonen, A. (2015). The sharing economy: Why people participate in collaborative consumption. *Journal of the Association for Information Science and Technology*.

Hamid, M. R. A., Amin, H., Lada, S., & Ahmad, N. (2007). A comparative analysis of Internet banking in Malaysia and Thailand. *Journal of Internet Business*, (4).

Hampel, S., Heinrich, D., & Campbell, C. (2012). Is An Advertisement Worth The Paper It's Printed on?: The Impact of Premium Print Advertising On Consumer Perceptions. *Journal of Advertising Research*, *52*(1), 118–127. doi:10.2501/JAR-52-1-118-127

Han, M., Jang, Y., & Park, H. (2009). *Bloggers' intrinsic motivation and electronic word- of-mouth marketing*. Working Paper. Korea Advanced Institute of Science and Technology.

Han, R. M. M. (2013). Financial Inclusion for Financial Stability: Access to Bank Deposits and the Growth of Deposits in the Global Financial Crisis. *e-library*. Retrieved from https://elibrary.worldbank.org/doi/abs/10.1596/1813-9450-6577

Hanning, A. (2011). *Financial Inclusion and Financial Stability: Current Policy Issues.* Retrieved from https://papers.ssrn.com/sol3/papers.cfm?abstract_id=1729122

Han, S., Lerner, J. S., & Keltner, D. (2007). Feelings and consumer decision making: The appraisal-tendency framework. *Journal of Consumer Psychology*, *17*(3), 158–168. doi:10.1016/S1057-7408(07)70023-2

Hargittai, E., & Walejko, G. (2008). The participation divide: Content creation and sharing in the digital age. *Information Communication and Society*, *11*(2), 239–256. doi:10.1080/13691180801946150

Harmeling, C., Moffett, J., & Carlson, B. D. (2016). Toward a theory of customer engagement marketing. *Journal of the Academy of Marketing Science*, *45*, 312–335. doi:10.100711747-016-0509-2

Harrigan, P., Ramsey, E., & Ibbotson, P. (2011). Critical factors underpinning the e-CRM activities of SMEs. *Journal of Marketing Management*, *27*(5-6), 503–529. doi:10.1080/0267257X.2010.495284

Harrigan, P., Ramsey, E., & Ibbotson, P. (2012). Exploring and explaining SME marketing: Investigating e-CRM using a mixed methods approach. *Journal of Strategic Marketing*, *20*(2), 127–163. doi:10.1080/0965254X.2011.606911

Harrigan, P., Soutar, G., Choudhury, M. M., & Lowe, M. (2015). Modelling CRM in the social media age. *Australasian Marketing Journal*, *23*(1), 27–37. doi:10.1016/j.ausmj.2014.11.001

Harrison, R. T., & Leitch, C. M. (2005). Entrepreneurial learning: Researching the interface between learning and the entrepreneurial context. *Entrepreneurship Theory and Practice*, *29*(4), 351–372. doi:10.1111/j.1540-6520.2005.00089.x

Hars, A., & Ou, S. (2001). Working for Free? Motivations of Participating in Open Source Projects. *Proceedings of the 34th Hawaii International Conference on System Sciences.* 10.1109/HICSS.2001.927045

Hartley, M. (2011). *Google unveils new research findings for University of Waterloo.* Retrieved from http://www.business.financialpost.com

Hartmann, N. N., Wieland, H., & Vargo, S. L. (2018). Converging on a new theoretical foundation for selling. *Journal of Marketing*, *82*(2), 1–18. doi:10.1509/jm.16.0268

Ha, S., & Stoel, L. (2009). Consumer e-shopping acceptance: Antecedents in a technology acceptance model. *Journal of Business Research*, *62*(5), 565–571. doi:10.1016/j.jbusres.2008.06.016

Hassan, A., Shabani, N., Ekiz, H. K., Dadwal, S., & Lancaster, G. (2017**c**). Augmented reality in tourism and factors for its adoption: an empirical study. In *The 22nd Annual Graduate Education and Graduate Student Research Conference in Hospitality and Tourism.* The University of Houston and The Hong Kong Polytechnic University. Available at: http://gradconfht.com/

Hassan, A., & Dadwal, S. (2016). Search engine marketing – an outlining of conceptualization and strategic application. In W. Ozuem & G. Bowen (Eds.), *Competitive social media marketing strategies* (pp. 219–234). Hershey, PA: IGI Global. doi:10.4018/978-1-4666-9776-8.ch011

Hassan, A., Ekiz, A., Dadwal, S., & Lancaster, G. (2017a). Augmented Reality Adoption by Tourism Product and Service Consumers: Some Empirical Findings. In T. Jung & M. C. tom Dieck (Eds.), *Augmented Reality and Virtual Reality: Empowering Human, Place and Business* (pp. 47–64). New York, NY: Springer.

Hassan, A., Ekiz, A., Dadwal, S., & Lancaster, G. (2017b). Augmented reality adoption by tourism product and service consumers: some empirical findings. In T. Jung & M. C. tom Dieck (Eds.), *Augmented reality and virtual reality: empowering human, place and business* (pp. 47–64). New York, NY: Springer.

Hassenzahl & Tractinsky. (2007). The thing and I: understanding the relationship between user and product. In *Funology* (pp. 31–42). From Usability to Enjoyment.

Hassenzahl. (2007). User experience (UX): towards an experiential perspective on product quality. In *Proceedings of the 20th International Conference of the Association Francophone d'Interaction Homme-Machine*. ACM.

Hassenzahl, M. (2007). The effect of perceived hedonic quality on product appealingness. *International Journal of Human-Computer Interaction*, *13*, 479–497.

Hayes, J. (2009). The clout of the cloud (cloud computing). *Engineering & Technology*, *4*(6), 60–61. doi:10.1049/et.2009.0611

Hayes-roth, F. (1984). Expert Systems. *Computer*, *17*(10), 263–273. doi:10.1109/MC.1984.1658976

Hays, J. W. (2011). *Individual And Institutional Factors Affecting Identity Among Minority And Female Science Students.* Retrieved from https://etd.ohiolink.edu/!etd.send_file?accession=kent1322062127&disposition=inline

Hayzlett, J. (2014). The language of Audio Branding. *Marketing Management: Agents of Change*, 18-19.

Heap, S. (2012). *What are Universities good for?* Cambridge, UK: Grove Educational Series.

Heide, J. B., & John, G. (1988). The Role of Dependence Balancing in Safeguarding Transaction-Specific Assets in Conventional Channels. *Journal of Marketing*, *52*(1), 20–35. doi:10.1177/002224298805200103

Helitzer, D., Heath, D., Maltrud, K., Sullivan, E., & Averson, D. (2003). Assessing or Predicting Adoption of Telehealth Using the Diffusion of Innovations Theory: A Practical Example from a Rural Program in New Mexico. *Telemedicine Journal and e-Health*, *9*(2), 179–187.

Hellwig, K., Morhart, F., Girardin, F., & Hauser, M. (2015). Exploring different types of sharing: A proposed segmentation of the market for sharing businesses. *Psychology and Marketing*, *32*(9), 891–906. doi:10.1002/mar.20825

Help Net Security. (2016). *Impact of security breaches on consumer trust*. Help Net Security.

Helyer, R. (2015). *The Work-Based Learning Student Handbook* (2nd ed.). London: Palgrave. doi:10.1007/978-1-137-41384-0

Helyer, R. (Ed.). (2016). *Facilitating Work-Based Learning*. London: Palgrave. doi:10.1007/978-1-137-40325-4

Hennig-Thurau, T., Gwinner, K. P., Walsh, G., & Gremler, D. D. (2004). Electronic word- ofmouth via consumer-opinion platforms: What motivates consumers to articulate themselves on the internet? *Journal of Interactive Marketing*, *18*(1), 38–52. doi:10.1002/dir.10073

Hennig-Thurau, T., & Hansen, U. (Eds.). (2013). *Relationship marketing: Gaining competitive advantage through customer satisfaction and customer retention.* Springer Science & Business Media.

Hennig-Thurau, T., Henning, V., & Sattler, H. (2007). Consumer file sharing of motion pictures. *Journal of Marketing*, *71*(4), 1–18. doi:10.1509/jmkg.71.4.1

Henten, A., & Windekilde, I. (2016). Transaction costs and the sharing economy. *Info*, *18*(1), 1–15. doi:10.1108/info-09-2015-0044

Herland, M. D., & Helgeland, I. M. (2017). Negotiating motherhood: Women with troubled upbringings and their self-conceptions as mothers. *Child & Family Social Work*, *22*(1), 47–56. doi:10.1111/cfs.12193

Herrington, G., & Lomax, W. (1999). Do satisfied employees make customers satisfied? An investigation into the relationship between service employee job satisfaction and customer perceived service quality. In *Marketing and Competition in the Information Age, Proceedings of the 28th EMAC Conference*. Humboldt University.

Hesmondhalgh, D. (2006). Bourdieu, the media and cultural production. *Media Culture & Society*, *28*(2), 211–231. doi:10.1177/0163443706061682

Hewitt, H. (2005). *Blog: Understanding the Information Reformation That's Changing Your World.* Nashville, TN: Thomas Nelson Books.

Higgins, E. (2006). Value from Hedonic Experience and Engagement. *American Psychological Association, 113*(3), 439-460. Accessed via: http://cbdr.cmu.edu/seminar/Higgins.pdf

Higgins, K. (2016). Post-truth: A guide for the perplexed. *NATNews*, *540*(7631), 9.

Higton, M. (2012). *A Theology of Higher Education.* Oxford, UK: Oxford University Press. doi:10.1093/acprof:oso/9780199643929.001.0001

Hill, J. B. (2017). *Gartner insights on spotting and responding to digital disruption Leading Through Digital Disruption.* Retrieved from https://www.gartner.com/imagesrv/books/digital-disruption/pdf/digital_disruption_ebook.pdf

Hill, J., & McGowan, P. (1996). Marketing development through networking: A competency based approach for small firm entrepreneurs. *Small Business and Enterprise Development*, *3*(3), 148–156. doi:10.1002/(SICI)1099-1662(199611)3:3<148::AID-SBE64>3.0.CO;2-C

Hill, T. (2018). Blockchain for research [Review]. *Learned Publishing*, *31*(4), 421–422. doi:10.1002/leap.1182

Hirschman, E. C., & Thompson, C. J. (1997). Why media matter: Toward a richer understanding of consumers' relationships with advertising and mass media. *Journal of Advertising*, *26*(1), 43–60. doi:10.1080/00913367.1997.10673517

His Majesty Government of Nepal. (1997a). *Economic survey of the fiscal year 1996/97.* Ministry of Finance.

His Majesty Government of Nepal. (1997b). *Statistical year book of Nepal.* Kathmandu: National Planning Commission Secretariat, Central Bureau of Statistics.

Hodis, M. A., Sriramachandramurthy, R., & Sashittal, H. C. (2015). Interact with me on my terms: A four segment Facebook engagement framework for marketers. *Journal of Marketing Management*, *31*(11–12), 1255–1284. doi:10.1080/0267257X.2015.1012535

Hoffman, D. L., & Fodor, M. (2010). Can you measure the ROI of your social media marketing? *MIT Sloan Management Review*, *52*(1), 41.

Hoffman, D. L., & Novak, T. P. (1996). Marketing in hypermedia computer-mediated environments: Conceptual foundations. *Journal of Marketing*, *60*(3), 50–68. doi:10.2307/1251841

Hofmann, E., Strewe, U., & Bosia, N. (2016). *Supply Chain Finance and Blockchain Technology.* Academic Press.

Hogg, G., & Carter, S. (2000). Employee attitudes and responses to internal marketing. In R. Varey & B. Lewis (Eds.), *Internal Marketing: Directions for Management* (pp. 109–124). London: Routledge. doi:10.4324/9780203207352.ch7

Holbrook, M., & Hirschman, E. (1982). The Experiential Aspects of Consumption: Consumer Fantasies, Feelings, and Fun. *Journal of Consumer Research*, *9*(2), 132-140.

Hollebeck. (2013). Demystifying Customer Engagement: Exploring the Loyalty Nexus. *Journal of Marketing Management, 27*(7–8), 785–807.

Hollebeek, L. (2011). Exploring customer brand engagement: Definition and themes. *Journal of Strategic Marketing*, *19*(7), 555–573. doi:10.1080/0965254X.2011.599493

Holliman, G., & Rowley, J. (2014). Business to business digital content marketing: marketers' perceptions of best practice. *Journal of Research in Interactive Marketing, 8*(4), 269-293.

Hollister, J.M., Spears, L.I., Mardis, M.A., Lee, J., McClure, C.R., & Liebman, E. (2017). Employers' perspectives on new information technology technicians' employability in North Florida, *Journal of Education + Training*, *59*(9), 929-945.

Holt, N. L. (2003). Representation, legitimation, and autoethnography: An autoethnographic writing story. *International Journal of Qualitative Methods*, *2*(1), 18–28. doi:10.1177/160940690300200102

Homer, P. M. (2006). Relationships among ad-induced affect, beliefs, and attitudes: Another look. *Journal of Advertising*, *35*(1), 35–51. doi:10.2753/JOA0091-3367350103

Horng, J.-S., Liu, C.-H., Liu, C. S., & Tsai, C. Y. (2012). Understanding the impact of culinary brand equity and destination familiarity on travel intentions. *Tourism Management*, *36*, 15–25. doi:10.1016/j.tourman.2012.11.002

Horng, S.-C. (1999). *Marketing Management*. Taipei: Shinlou Book.

Hsieh, J. K., & Hsieh, Y. C. (2015). Dialogic co-creation and service innovation performance in high-tech companies. *Journal of Business Research*, *68*(11), 2266–2271. doi:10.1016/j.jbusres.2015.06.009

Huang, M.-U., & Rust, R. T. (2017). Technology-driven service strategy. *Journal of the Academy of Marketing Science*, *45*(6), 906–924. doi:10.100711747-017-0545-6

Huang, M.-U., & Rust, R. T. (2018). Artificial intelligence in Service. *Journal of Service Research*, *21*(2), 155–172. doi:10.1177/1094670517752459

Huang, Y.-T., & Rundle-Thiele, S. (2015). A holistic management tool for measuring internal marketing activities. *Journal of Services Marketing*, *29*(6/7), 571–584. doi:10.1108/JSM-03-2015-0112

Huber, M. Z., & Hilty, L. M. (2014). Gamification and Sustainable Consumption: Overcoming the Limitations of Persuasive Technologies. In *ICT Innovations for Sustainability. Advances in Intelligent Systems and Computing*. Springer. Retrieved 07 10, 2019, from https://www.ifi.uzh.ch/rerg/people/kolpondinos/2014_Huber_Hilty_Gamification_and_Sustainable_Consumption_AAM.pdf

Hudders, L., Van Reijmersdal, E. A., & Poels, K. (2019). Digital advertising and consumer empowerment. *Cyberpsychology (Brno)*, *13*(2). doi:10.5817/CP2019-2-xx

Hudson, S., & Ritchie, J. R. B. (2009). Branding a memorable destination experience. The case of Brand Canada. *International Journal of Tourism Research*, *11*(2), 217–228. doi:10.1002/jtr.720

Hudson, S., Roth, M., Madden, T., & Hudson, R. (2015). The effects of social media on emotions, brand relationship quality, and word of mouth: An empirical study of music festival attendees. *Tourism Management*, *47*, 68–76. doi:10.1016/j.tourman.2014.09.001

Hughes, C. J., & Saieva, G. (2019). Degree apprenticeships – an opportunity for all? *Journal of Higher Education. Skills and Work-Based Learning*, *9*(2), 225–236. doi:10.1108/HESWBL-10-2018-0113

Hung, A. (2017). A Critique and Defense of Gamification. *Journal of Interactive Online Learning Volume, 15*(1).

Hutter, K., Hautz, J., Dennhardt, S., & Füller, J. (2013). The impact of user interactions in social media on brand awareness and purchase intention: The case of MINI on Facebook. *Journal of Product and Brand Management*, *22*(5/6), 342–351. doi:10.1108/JPBM-05-2013-0299

Hwang, H. S., & Cho, J. (2018). Why Instagram? Intention to continue using Instagram among Korean college students. *Social Behavior and Personality*, *46*(8), 1305–1316. doi:10.2224/sbp.6961

Hyan, D.(2015). *Determinants of brand image in social media*. Academic Press.

IAB-Europe. (2018). *Digital Advertising Effectiveness*. Retrieved from https://www.iab.it/wp-content/uploads/2018/09/IAB-Europe_Digital-Ad-effectiveness-White-Paper_September-2018-compressed.pdf

IBEF. (2019). *Indian Consumer Market*. IBEF. Retrieved from https://www.ibef.org/industry/indian-consumer-market.aspx

IBM Block Chain. (2019). *IBM Food Trust: A new era for the world's food supply*. Available at: https://www.ibm.com/blockchain/solutions/food-trust

IBM News Room. (2018). *Maersk and IBM Introduce TradeLens Blockchain Shipping Solution*. Available at: https://newsroom.ibm.com/2018-08-09-Maersk-and-IBM-Introduce-TradeLens-Blockchain-Shipping-Solution

IBM Research, . (2013). *Watson and the Jeopardy! Challenge*. YouTube.

IBM. (2019). *IBM X-Force Threat Intelligence Index*. IBM.

IBM. (2019a). *How it works - Project Debater*. IBM Research AI.

IBM. (2019a). *IBM Cloud is the cloud for smarter business*. Available at: https://www.ibm.com/cloud

IBM. (2019b). *IBM100 - Deep Blue*. IBM.

IBM. (2019b). *Watson Discovery: A leader in AI Search*. Available at: https://www.ibm.com/watson

IBM. (2019c). *IBM Blockchain: Now Delivering Value around the World*. Available at: https://www.ibm.com/uk-en/blockchain

IDC. (2019). *Smart Phone Marketshare*. Retrieved from https://www.idc.com/promo/smartphone-market-share/vendor

Ieva, M., & Ziliani, C. (2018). Mapping touchpoint exposure in retailing: Implications for developing an omnichannel customer experience. *International Journal of Retail & Distribution Management*, *46*(3), 304–332. doi:10.1108/IJRDM-04-2017-0097

Imperial College UK. (2018). *What is Security Analysis?* Available at: https://www.doc.ic.ac.uk/~ajs300/security/CIA.htm

Inman, J. J., & Nikolova, H. (2017). Shopper-Facing Retail Technology: An Adoption Decision Calculus. *Journal of Retailing*, *93*, 7–28. doi:10.1016/j.jretai.2016.12.006

Innovating for the Rising Global Middle Class. (2011). Available at: http://bx.businessweek.com/innovation-in-marketing/view?url=http%3A%2F%2Finventionmachine.com%2Fthe-Sustainable-Innovation-Blog%2Fbid%2F79047%2FInnovating-for-the-Rising-Global-Middle-Class

Innovative Marketing. (2002). *Pharmaceuticals Policy and Laws*. Author.

Intel. (2019). *Integrating IoT Sensor Technology into the Enterprise*. Available at: https://www.intel.com/content/www/us/en/it-management/intel-it-best-practices/integrating-iot-sensor-technology-into-the-enterprise-paper.html

Ioan, L. P., Gheorghe, P., & Monica, B. (2010). *A Theoretical Approach of the Concept of innovation*. Retrieved July 9, 2019, from ftp://ftp.repec.org/opt/ReDIF/RePEc/bbu/wpaper/151-156.pdf

Isaac, O., Abdullah, Z., Ramayah, T., & Mutahar, A. M. (2017). Internet usage, user satisfaction, task, technology fit, and performance impact among public sector employees in Yemen. *The International Journal of Information and Learning Technology*, *34*(3), 210–241. doi:10.1108/IJILT-11-2016-0051

Ishmaev, G. (2017). Blockchain Technology as an Institution of Property. *Metaphilosophy*, *48*(5), 666–686. doi:10.1111/meta.12277

Ismail, N. (2017). *Ransomware of IoT will become a new security nightmare in 2018*. Available at: https://www.information-age.com/ransomware-iot-new-security-nightmare-123470151/

Issa, T., & Isaias, P. (2016). Internet factors influencing generations Y and Z in Australia. *Information Processing & Management*, *52*(4), 592–617. doi:10.1016/j.ipm.2015.12.006

ITU. (2016). The Digital financial services ecosystem. *ITU*. Retrieved from https://www.sciencedirect.com/science/article/pii/S2214845017301503#bib25

J. P. Morgan. (2019). *J.P. Morgan Interbank Information NetworkSM Expands to More Than 75 Banks*. Available at: https://www.jpmorgan.com/country/GB/en/detail/1320570135560

Jacinta, M., & Jorge, S. (2011). M*arketing Innovation: study of determinants of innovation in the design and packaging of goods and services – application to portuguese firms*. Available at: http://academic-journal.org

Jackson, N. (2013). *Promoting ans Marketing Events*. New York: Routledge. doi:10.4324/9780203583166

Jahanmir, S. F., & Cavadas, J. (2018). Factors affecting late adoption of digital innovations. *Journal of Business Research*, *88*, 337–343. doi:10.1016/j.jbusres.2018.01.058

Jake, H. (2011). *16 mind-blowing examples of big-brand projection mapping*. Retrieved July 31, 2019, from https://econsultancy.com/16-mind-blowing-examples-of-big-brand-projection-mapping/

James, L., Gent, M., Hater, J., & Coray, K. (1979). Correlates of psychological influence: An illustration of the psychological climate approach to work environment perceptions. *Personnel Psychology*, *32*(3), 563–588. doi:10.1111/j.1744-6570.1979.tb02154.x

Janssen, M., van der Voort, H., & Wahyudi, A. (2017). Factors influencing big data decision-making quality. *Journal of Business Research*, *70*, 338–345. doi:10.1016/j.jbusres.2016.08.007

Jarvis, H., & Bonnett, A. (2013). Progressive nostalgia in novel living arrangements: A counterpoint to neo-traditional new urbanism? *Urban Studies (Edinburgh, Scotland)*, *50*(11), 2349–2370. doi:10.1177/0042098013478235

Jenkins, R. (2015). 5 aspects of games to leverage for increased millennial engagement and retention. *HR Cloud*. Available at: https://blog.hrcloud.com/5aspectsofgamestoleverageforincreasedmillennialengagementretention

Jenkins, H. (2006). *Fans, Bloggers, and Gamers*. New York: New York University Press.

Jeune, S. L. (2016). *The Sharing Economy*. Retrieved June 2, 2019, from www.schroders.com: https://www.schroders.com/pl/sysglobalassets/digital/insights/2016/pdfs/responsible-investment/the-sharing-economy/the-sharing-economy-report-final.pdf

Jiang, J. (2018). *Millennials stand out for their technology use, but older generations also embrace digital life*. PEW Research Centre. Available at: https://www.pewresearch.org/fact-tank/2018/05/02/millennials-stand-out-for-their-technology-use-but-older-generations-also-embrace-digital-life/

John, A. (2017). Blockchain and Its Applications. *International Journal of Recent Trends in Engineering and Research*, *3*(4), 143–145. doi:10.23883/IJRTER.2017.3123.ZS1WM

Johnson, L., Becker, S., Estrada, V., & Freeman, A. (2014). *Horizon Report: 2014 Higher Education*. Austin, TX: NMC.

Johnson, P., Buehring, A., Cassell, C., & Symon, G. (2000). Evaluating qualitative management research: Towards a contingent criteriology. *International Journal of Management Reviews*, *8*(3), 131–156. doi:10.1111/j.1468-2370.2006.00124.x

Johnston, D. D., & Swanson, D. H. (2003). Invisible mothers: A content analysis of motherhood ideologies and myths in magazines. *Sex Roles*, *49*(1), 21–33. doi:10.1023/A:1023905518500

Joo, J. (2017). Motives for Participating in Sharing Economy: Intentions to Use Car Sharing Services. *Journal of Distribution Science*, *15*(2), 21–26. doi:10.15722/jds.15.2.201702.21

Josephson, J. J., & Burack, C. (1998). The political ideology of the neo-traditional family. *Journal of Political Ideologies*, *3*(2), 213–231. doi:10.1080/13569319808420777

Joshi, A., Chandel, S., Kale, S., & Pal, D. (2015). Likert scale: Explored and explained. *Current Journal of Applied Science and Technology*, *7*(4), 396–403. doi:10.9734/BJAST/2015/14975

Julius, S., Ruud, J., Pádraic, G., & Nick, B. (2017). *10 Events Trends for 2017*. Retrieved June 3, 2019, from Godmother: http://www.godmother.ro/wp-content/uploads/2016/04/10-Event-Trends-2017-v3.pdf

Jung, C. G. (2014). *The archetypes and the collective unconscious*. Routledge.

Jung, T. H., Tom Dieck, M. C., & Chung, N. (2018). Determinants of hotel social media continued usage. *International Journal of Contemporary Hospitality Management*, *30*(2), 1152–1171. doi:10.1108/IJCHM-02-2017-0068

Juttner, U., & Christopher, M. (2013). The role of marketing in creating a supply chain orientation within the firm. *International Journal of Logistics: Research and Applications*, *16*(2), 99–113. doi:10.1080/13675567.2013.799636

Juttner, U., Christopher, M., & Baker, S. (2007). Demand chain management-integrating marketing and supply chain management. *Industrial Marketing Management*, *36*(3), 377–392. doi:10.1016/j.indmarman.2005.10.003

Kaal, W. (2017). *Blockchain Technology and Race in Corporate America*. SSRN Electronic Journal. doi:10.2139srn.3071378

Kane, E. (2017). *Is Blockchain a General Purpose Technology?* SSRN Electronic Journal. doi:10.2139srn.2932585

Kaplan, A. M., & Haenlein, M. (2010). Users of the world, unite! The challenges and opportunities of Social Media. *Business Horizons*, *53*(1), 59–68. doi:10.1016/j.bushor.2009.09.003

Kaplan, E. A. (1990). Sex, work and motherhood: The impossible triangle. *Journal of Sex Research*, *27*(3), 409–425. doi:10.1080/00224499009551569

Kappel, M. (2017). *5 Ways To Improve Your Small Business Marketing*. Available at: https://www.forbes.com/sites/mikekappel/2017/06/14/5-ways-to-improve-your-small-business-marketing/#1e7d00274969

Karam, A. A., & Saydam, S. (2015). An analysis study of improving brand awareness and its impact on consumer behavior via media in North Cyprus (A case study of fast food restaurants). *International Journal of Business and Social Science*, *6*(1).

Karame, G., & Androulaki, E. (2017). *Bitcoin and blockchain security*. Academic Press.

Karandaaz. (2018, April 20). *FINCA Enters into a strategic partnership with Karandaaz Pakistan to launch 'Women Community Mobilizer' program*. Retrieved from https://karandaaz.com.pk/media-center/news-events/finca-enters-strategic-partnership-karandaaz-pakistan-launch-women-community-mobilizer-program/

Karasa, A., & Akinci, F., EsatoElu, A.E., Parsons, A.L., & Sarp, N. (2008). An evaluation of the opinions of hospital employees regarding the contribution of internal marketing to the application of total quality management in Turkey. *Health Marketing Quarterly*, *24*(3), 167–187. PMID:19042534

Kaspersky Lab. (2016). *KSN Report: PC ransomware in 2014-2016.* Kaspersky Lab.

Kaspersky. (2018a). *History of malicious programs.* Available at: https://encyclopedia.kaspersky.com/knowledge/history-of-malicious-programs/

Kaspersky. (2018b). *TeslaCrypt Ransomware Attacks.* Available at: https://www.kaspersky.co.uk/resource-center/threats/teslacrypt

Kaspersky. (2018c). *Types of Malware.* Available at: https://www.kaspersky.co.uk/resource-center/threats/malware-classifications

Kathan, W., Matzler, K., & Veider, V. (2016). The sharing economy: Your business model's friend or foe? *Business Horizons*, *59*(6), 663–672. doi:10.1016/j.bushor.2016.06.006

Katz, J., (2003) Advertising and the construction of violent white masculinity. *Gender, race, and class in the media. A text reader*, 349-358.

Kawa, A., & Maryniak, A. (2018). *SMART Supply Network*. Cham: Springer.

Kaye, B. (2007). Blog Use Motivations: An Exploratory Study. In M. Tremayne (Ed.), *Blogging, Citizenship, and the Future of the Media* (pp. 27–148). New York: Routledge.

Keir, D. (2018). *Industry Spotlight: How the sharing economy is changing the face of business.* Retrieved June 2, 2019, from https://www.startupbootcamp.org/blog/2018/03/industry-spotlight-sharing-economy-changing-face-business/

Kelion, L. (2015, July 14). *Apple Pay: How will it work in the UK?* Retrieved July 24, 2019, from https://www.bbc.com/news/technology-33489066

Keller, K. (1994). *Mothers and work in popular American magazines.* Westport, CT: Greenwood Press.

Keller, K. L. (1993). Conceptualizing, measuring, and managing customer-based brand equity. *Journal of Marketing*, *57*(1), 1–22. doi:10.1177/002224299305700101

Keller, K. L. (2001). *Building customer-based brand equity: A blueprint for creating strong brands.* Cambridge, MA: Marketing Science Institute.

Keller, K. L. (2013). *Strategic Brand Management: Building, Measuring, and Managing Brand Equity*. Upper Saddle River, NJ: Pearson Education.

Kemp, M. (2010). Define Your Marketing InnovationStrategy. *ForresterBlogs*. Available at:http://www.forrester.com/rb/Research/define_marketing_innovation_strategy/q/id/56829/t/2?cm_mmc=Forrester-_-Blogs-_-Related%20Research-_-5603

Kemp, E., Bui, M., & Chapa, S. (2012). The role of advertising in consumer emotion management. *International Journal of Advertising*, *31*(2), 339–353. doi:10.2501/IJA-31-2-339-353

Kendall, J. (2017, January 20). *FinTech Companies Could Give Billions of People More Banking Options*. Retrieved July 21, 2019, from https://hbr.org/2017/01/FinTech-companies-could-give-billions-of-people-more-banking-options

Kent, M. L., & Taylor, M. (1998). Building dialogic relationships through the World Wide Web. *Public Relations Review*, *24*(3), 321–334. doi:10.1016/S0363-8111(99)80143-X

Kent, R., & Brandal, H. (2003). Improving email response in a permission marketing context. *International Journal of Market Research*, *45*(4), 1–13. doi:10.1177/147078530304500101

Kerrane, B., Bettany, S., & Kerrane, K. (2015). Siblings as socialization agents. *European Journal of Marketing*, *49*(5/6), 713–735. doi:10.1108/EJM-06-2013-0296

Kessler, A. (2013). Professors Are About to Get Online Education. *Wall Street Journal*. Retrieved from https://search.proquest.com/docview/1357479035?accountid=12860

Kevin, W. (2012). *Artificial Intelligence: The Basics*. Routledge.

Khamis, S., & Munt, A. (2010). The Three Cs of Fashion Media Today: Convergence, Creativity & Control. *Scha Journal*, *7*(2), 1–17.

Khan, F., & Siddiqui, K. (2013). The importance of digital marketing. An exploratory study to find the perception and effectiveness of digital marketing amongst the marketing professionals in Pakistan. *Journal of Information Systems & Operations Management*, 1.

Khan, H. R. (2011). *Financial inclusion and financial stability: are they two sides of the same coin*. Academic Press.

Khan, S., & Gouveia, L. B. (2017). Is flipped classroom preferred learning style for the Millennials? An Exploratory Study. *IPASJ International Journal of Management*, *5*(8), 7–21.

Kidron, M. (2017). *LogicLocker Brings Ransomware to SCADA Networks*. Available at: https://blog.skyboxsecurity.com/logiclocker-brings-ransomware-to-scada-networks/

Kim, Y. G., & Lee, J. N. Bock, G. W., & Zmud, R. W. (2005). *Behavioral intention formation in knowledge sharing: Examining the roles of extrinsic motivators, social-psychological forces, and organizational*. Academic Press.

Kim, A. J., & Ko, E. (2010). Impacts of luxury fashion brand's social media marketing on customer relationship and purchase intention. *Journal of Global Fashion Marketing*, *1*(3), 164–171. doi:10.1080/20932685.2010.10593068

Kimberly, J. R., & Evanisko, M. J. (1981). Organizational innovation: The influence of individual, organizational, and contextual factors on hospital adoption of technological and administrative innovations. *Academy of Management Journal*, *24*, 689–713. PMID:10253688

Kim, H., & Stepchenkova, S. (2015). Effect of tourist photographs on attitudes towards destination: Manifest and latent content. *Tourism Management*, *49*, 29–41. doi:10.1016/j.tourman.2015.02.004

Kim, J., & Choi, H. (2019). Value co-creation through social media: A case study of a start-up company. *Journal of Business Economics and Management*, *20*(1), 1–19. doi:10.3846/jbem.2019.6262

Kim, Y., Akbar, H., Tzokas, N., & Al-Dajani, H. (2014). Systems thinking and absorptive capacity in high-tech small and medium-sized enterprises from South Korea. *International Small Business Journal*, *32*(8), 876–896. doi:10.1177/0266242613483632

Klein, A., & Sharma, V. M. (2018). German Millennials' Decision Making Styles and Their Intention to Participate in Online Group Buying. *Journal of Internet Commerce*, *17*(4), 383–417. doi:10.1080/15332861.2018.1463804

Kleinrock, L. (2010). An early history of the internet. *IEEE Communications Magazine*, *48*(8), 26–36. doi:10.1109/MCOM.2010.5534584

Klimkiewicz, K., & Oltra, V. (2017). Does CSR Enhance Employer Attractiveness? The Roleof Millennial Job Seekers'Attitudes. *Corporate Social Responsibility and Environmental Management, Wiley*, *24*(5), 449–463. doi:10.1002/csr.1419

Kohli, A., & Jaworski, B. (1990). Market Orientation: The Construct, Research Propositions, and Managerial Implications. *Journal of Marketing*, *54*(2), 1–18. doi:10.1177/002224299005400201

Kolb, A. Y., & Kolb, D. A. (2010). Learning to play, playing to learn: A case study of a ludic learning space. *Journal of Organizational Change Management*, *23*(1), 26–50. doi:10.1108/09534811011017199

Kolle, S. (2006). Top ten trends in marketing innovation. *Future Labs*. Available at: http://www.futurelab.be/blogs/marketing strategy innovation/2006/10/top_ten_trends_in_marketing_in.html

Koller, M. S. (2016). *TeslaCrypt Ransomware Developers Retire, Release Master Decryption Key*. Available at: https://www.dataprivacymonitor.com/cybersecurity/teslacrypt-ransomware-developers-retire-release-master-decryption-key/

Kolsaker, A., & Drakatos, N. (2009). Mobile advertising: The influence of emotional attachment to mobile devices on consumer receptiveness. *Journal of Marketing Communications*, *15*(4), 267–280. doi:10.1080/13527260802479664

Komgo. (2019). *Komgo's digital network is a blockchain-based solution for data security and exchange in commodity trade*. Available at https://komgo.io/

Konijin, E., Sluimer, N., & Miras, O. (2016). Click to share: Patterns in tourist photography and sharing. *International Journal of Tourism Research*, *18*(6), 525–535. doi:10.1002/jtr.2069

Korschun, D., & Du, S. (2013). How virtual corporate social responsibility dialogs generate value: A framework and propositions. *Journal of Business Research*, *66*(9), 1494–1504. doi:10.1016/j.jbusres.2012.09.011

Kotler, P. (1986). *The Prosumer Movement: a New Challenge For Marketers*. Retrieved 06 25, 2019, from http://www.acrwebsite.org/search/view-conference-proceedings.aspx?Id=6542

Kotler, P. (2009). *Gary Armstrong, Principles of Marketing*. Tehran: Learned Nshrasly (1379).

Kotler, P., & Keller, K. L. (2010).Marketing Management (15th ed.). Pearson Education.

Kotler, P. (1972). A generic concept of marketing. *Journal of Marketing*, *36*(2), 46–54. doi:10.1177/002224297203600209

Kotler, P., & Armstrong, G. (1991). *Principles of Marketing* (5th ed.). Englewood Cliffs, NJ: Prentice-Hall.

Kozinets, R. V., de Valck, K., Wojnicki, A. C., & Wilner, S. J. S. (2010). Networked Narratives: Understanding Word-of-Mouth Marketing in Online Communities. *Journal of Marketing*, *74*(March), 71–89. doi:10.1509/jmkg.74.2.71

KPMG. (2017). *Meet the Millennials: Produced under the umbrella of KPMG's "It's her Future" Programme*. Available at: https://home.kpmg/content/dam/kpmg/uk/pdf/2017/04/Meet-the-Millennials-Secured.pdf

Kraljic, P. (1983). Purchasing Must Become Supply Management. *Harvard Business Review*. Available at: https://hbr.org/1983/09/purchasing-must-become-supply-management

Kravets, O. (2012). Russia's "Pure Spirit" Vodka Branding and Its Politics. *Journal of Macromarketing*, *32*(4), 361–376. doi:10.1177/0276146712449627

Kuerbis, B., & Badiei, F. (2017). Mapping the cybersecurity institutional landscape. *Digital Policy. Regulation & Governance*, *19*(6), 466–492. doi:10.1108/DPRG-05-2017-0024

Kujawa, A. (2019). *Ryuk ransomware attacks businesses over the holidays*. Available at: https://blog.malwarebytes.com/cybercrime/malware/2019/01/ryuk-ransomware-attacks-businesses-over-the-holidays/

Kuksov, D., Shachar, R., & Wang, K. (2013). Advertising and consumers' communications. *Marketing Science*, *32*(2), 294–309. doi:10.1287/mksc.1120.0753

Kulmala, M. (2011). *Electronic Word-of-Mouth in Consumer Fashion Blogs* (Master thesis). School of Management, University of Tampere.

Kumar, N., Scheer, L., & Kotler, P. (2000). From market driven to market driving. *European Management Journal, 18*(2), 129–142. doi:10.1016/S0263-2373(99)00084-5

Kumar, V., Anand, A., & Song, H. (2017). Future of retailer profitability: An organizing framework. *Journal of Retailing, 93*(1), 96–119. doi:10.1016/j.jretai.2016.11.003

Kvedar, D., Nettis, M., & Fulton, S. P. (2010). The use of formal social engineering techniques to identify weaknesses during a computer vulnerability competition. *Journal of Computing Sciences in Colleges, 26*(2), 80–87.

Lai, P. (2017). Technology Adoption Models and Theories for the Novelty Technology. *Journal of Information Systems and Technology Management, 14*(1), 21–38. doi:10.4301/S1807-17752017000100002

Lakhani, K. R., & Wolf, R. (2005). Why Hackers Do What They Do: Understanding Motivation and Effort in Free/Open Source Software Projects. In J. Feller (Ed.), *Perspectives on Free and Open Source Software*. Cambridge, MA: MIT Press.

Lakshmanan, D., & Rabiyathul, B. S. (2015). Factors Affecting the Effectiveness of Advertising in the Current Scenario "Advertising Factors are Immune to Business which Aspire to Inspire before You Expire." *International Journal of Science and Research, 6*, 1264–1267. doi:10.21275/ART20163982

Lama, W., & Sherpa, A. (1994). *Tourism development plan for the Makalu Base Camp Trek and Upper Barun Valley. Revised Draft Report.* Kathmandu: Makalu-Barun Conservation Project.

Lambert, D. M., & Schwieterman, M. A. (2012). Supplier relationship management as a macro business process. *Supply Chain Management, 17*(3), 337–352. doi:10.1108/13598541211227153

Lambert, D., & Cooper, M. (2000). Issues in supply chain management. *Industrial Marketing Management, 29*(1), 65–83. doi:10.1016/S0019-8501(99)00113-3

Lam, H. K. S., Yeung, A. C. L., & Cheng, T. C. E. (2016). The impact of firms' social media initiatives on operational efficiency and innovativeness. *Journal of Operations Management, 47–48*(1), 28–43. doi:10.1016/j.jom.2016.06.001

Lam, S. K., Sleep, S., Hennig-Thurau, T., Sridhar, S., & Saboo, A. R. (2017). Leveraging frontline employees' small data and firm-level big data in frontline management: An absorptive capacity perspective. *Journal of Service Research, Vol., 20*(1), 12–28. doi:10.1177/1094670516679271

Lavie, D. (2006). The competitive advantage of interconnected firms: An extension of the resource-based view. *Academy of Management Review, 31*(3), 638–658. doi:10.5465/amr.2006.21318922

Lee, A. R., Son, S. M., & Kim, K. K. (2016). Information and communication technology overload and social networking service fatigue: A stress perspective. *Computers in Human Behavior, 55*, 51–61. doi:10.1016/j.chb.2015.08.011

Lee, C., & Chen, W. J. (2005). The effects of internal marketing and organisational culture on knowledge management in the information technology industry. *International Journal of Management, 22*(4), 661–672.

Lee, J., Warkentin, M., & Johnston, A. (2016). A Broader View of Perceived Risk during Internet Transactions. *Communications of the Association for Information Systems, 38*(8), 171–189. doi:10.17705/1CAIS.03808

Lee, S. (2009). Mobile internet services from consumers' perspectives. *International Journal of Human-Computer Interaction, 25*(3), 390–413. doi:10.1080/10447310902865008

Leong, C. (2001). Marketing practices and Internet marketing: A study of hotels in Singapore. *Journal of Vacation Marketing, 7*(2), 179–187. doi:10.1177/135676670100700207

Leskovec, J., Adamic, L. A., & Huberman, B. A. (2007). The dynamics of viral marketing. *ACM Transactions on the Web*, *1*(1), 5. doi:10.1145/1232722.1232727

Leue, M., tom-Dieck, D., & Jung, T. (2014). A Theoretical Model of Augmented Reality Acceptance. *e-Review of Tourism Research*. Retrieved from: http://3ws1wk1wkqsk36zmd6ocne81.wpengine.netdna-cdn.com/files/2014/02/enter2014_RN_93.pdf

Leung, C. K., & Tse, C. Y. (2001). Technology choice and saving in the presence of a fixed adoption cost. *Review of Development Economics*, *5*(1), 40–48. doi:10.1111/1467-9361.00105

Leuschner, R., Rogers, D. S., & Charvet, F. F. (2013). A meta-analysis of supply chain integration and firm performance. *The Journal of Supply Chain Management*, *49*(2), 34–57. doi:10.1111/jscm.12013

Levine, R., Locke, C., Searls, D., & Weinberger, D. (1999). *The Cluetrain Manifesto*. Retrieved from www.cluetrain.com/cluetrain.pdf

Levy, R., Bogin, B., Gretz, S., Aharonov, R., & Slonim, N. (2018). *Towards an argumentative content search engine using weak supervision*. Academic Press.

Levy, Y., & Ramim, M. M. (2015). An assessment of competency-based simulations on e-learners' management skills enhancements. *Interdisciplinary Journal of E-Learning and Lifelong Learning, 11*, 179-190. Available at: www.ijello.org/Volume11/IJELLv11p179-190Levy1958.pdf

Levy, Y. (2005). A case study of management skills comparison in online MBA programs. *International Journal of Information and Communication Technology Education*, *1*(3), 1–20. doi:10.4018/jicte.2005070101

Lewandowsky, S., Ecker, U. K., & Cook, J. (2017). Beyond misinformation: Understanding and coping with the "post-truth" era. *Journal of Applied Research in Memory and Cognition*, *6*(4), 353–369. doi:10.1016/j.jarmac.2017.07.008

Lexicon, F. T. (2018). *Financial Times*. Retrieved from LexiconFT: http://lexicon.ft.com/Term?term=digital-marketing

Liang, T.-P., & You, J. (2009). Resource-based View in Information Systems Research: A Meta-Analysis. *Pacific Asia Conference on Information Systems (PACIS) PACIS 2009 Proceedings*. Retrieved from http://aisel.aisnet.org/pacis2009/72

Liang, T., & Lai, H. (2002). Effect of store design on consumer purchases: Van empirical study of on-line bookstore. *Information & Management*, *39*(6), 431–444. doi:10.1016/S0378-7206(01)00129-X

Liao, J., Kickul, J. R., & Ma, H. (2009). Organizational Dynamic Capability and Innovation: An Empirical Examination of Internet Firms. *Journal of Small Business Management*, *47*(3), 263–286. doi:10.1111/j.1540-627X.2009.00271.x

Liao, S. H. (2005). Expert system methodologies and applications-a decade review from 1995 to 2004. *Expert Systems with Applications*, *28*(1), 93–103. doi:10.1016/j.eswa.2004.08.003

Libai, B., Biyalogorsky, E., & Gerstner, E. (2003). Setting referral fees in affiliate marketing. *Journal of Service Research*, *5*(4), 303–315. doi:10.1177/1094670503005004003

Lin, C., Shih, H., & Sher, P. (2007). Integrating technology readiness into technology acceptance: The TRAM Model. *Psychology and Marketing*, *24*(7), 641–657. doi:10.1002/mar.20177

Lin, C., & Yeh, J. (2013). Modeling religious involvement: A qualitative integration based on female role visualization consumption. *Quality & Quantity*, *47*(1), 561–566. doi:10.100711135-011-9478-1

Lindenberg, S. (2001). Intrinsic motivation in a new light. *Kyklos*, *54*(2–3), 317–342. doi:10.1111/1467-6435.00156

Lindskog, D., & Zavarskya, M. P. (2016). Experimental Analysis of Ransomware on Windows and Android Platforms: Evolution and Characterization. *Procedia Computer Science*, (94), 465–472.

Lin, K. Y., & Lu, H. P. (2011). Why people use social networking sites: An empirical study integrating network externalities and motivation theory. *Computers in Human Behavior*, *27*(3), 1152–1161. doi:10.1016/j.chb.2010.12.009

LinkedIn.com. (2016). *About LinkedIn*. Retrieved from https://press.linkedin.com/about-linkedin?trk=uno-reg-guest-home-about

Li, S. L. (2009). Marketing Innovation in Enterprises. *Commerce Modernization*, *37*(23), 45–49.

Liu, S. Q., & Mattila, A. S. (2017). Airbnb: Online targeted advertising, sense of power, and consumer decisions. *International Journal of Hospitality Management*, *60*, 33–41. doi:10.1016/j.ijhm.2016.09.012

Liu, Y., & Li, H. (2010). Mobile internet diffusion in China: An empirical study. *Industrial Management & Data Systems*, *110*(3), 309–324. doi:10.1108/02635571011030006

Livingstone, S. (2011). Internet, children, and youth. In M. Consalvo & C. Ess (Eds.), *The handbook of internet studies* (pp. 348–368). Oxford, UK: Wiley Blackwell Publishing. doi:10.1002/9781444314861.ch16

Lockshin, L., & Spawton, T. (2001). Using involvement and brand equity to develop a wine tourism strategy. *International Journal of Wine Marketing.*, *13*(1), 72–81. doi:10.1108/eb043371

Locock, L., Dopson, S., Chambers, D., & Gabbay, J. (2001). Understanding the role of opinion leaders in improving clinical effectiveness. *Social Science & Medicine*, *53*(6), 745–757. doi:10.1016/S0277-9536(00)00387-7 PMID:11511050

Lo, I. S., & McKercher, B. (2015). Ideal image in process: Online tourist photography and impression management. *Annals of Tourism Research*, *52*, 104–116. doi:10.1016/j.annals.2015.02.019

Lopez-Catalan, B., & Banuls, V.A. (2017). A Delphi-based approach for detecting key e-learning trends in postgraduate education: the Spanish case. *Journal of Education + Training*, *59*(6), 590-604.

Lopez-Nicolas, C., Molina-Castillo, F., & Bouwman, H. (2008). An assessment of advanced mobile services acceptance: Contributions from TAM and Diffusion Theory Models. *Information & Management*, *45*(6), 395–364. doi:10.1016/j.im.2008.05.001

Louis, M. (1980). Surprise and sense making: What newcomers experience in entering unfamiliar organisational settings. *Administrative Science Quarterly*, *25*(2), 226–249. doi:10.2307/2392453 PMID:10247029

Lovink, G. (2008). *Zero Comments: Blogging and Critical Internet Culture*. New York: Taylor & Francis. doi:10.14361/9783839408049

Luxford, A. M. Y., & Dickinson, J. E. (2015). *The role of mobile applications in the consumer experience at music festivals*. Academic Press.

Machado, J. C., Vacas-de-Carvalho, L., Azar, S. L., André, A. R., & dos Santos, B. P. (2019). Brand gender and consumer-based brand equity on Facebook: The mediating role of consumer-brand engagement and brand love. *Journal of Business Research*, *96*, 376–385. doi:10.1016/j.jbusres.2018.07.016

Macky, K., Gardner, D., & Forsyth, S. (2008). Generational differences at work: Introduction and overview. *Journal of Managerial Psychology*, *23*(8), 857–861. doi:10.1108/02683940810904358

MacLean, P., & Cahillane, M. (2015). The human factor in learning design, research, policy, and practice. *The International Journal of Information and Learning Technology*, *32*(3), 182–196. doi:10.1108/IJILT-12-2014-0029

Macrae, D. (2014). *Everything you need to know about the Sasser worm*. CBR.

MacroTrends. (2019). *Market Cap*. Retrieved June 1, 2019, from MacroTrends: https://www.macrotrends.net/stocks/charts/ETSY/

Maczuga, P., Sikorska, K., & Jaruga, A. (2014). *Content Marking Handbook - simple ways to innovate your marketing approach*. Warsaw: cmex.eu.

Mager, J., & Helgeson, J. G. (2011). Fifty years of advertising images: Some changing perspectives on role portrayals along with enduring consistencies. *Sex Roles*, *64*(3-4), 238–252. doi:10.100711199-010-9782-6

Magno, F., De Boer, M., & Bentoglio, B. (2016). Sharing economy: comparing users' and non-users' perceptions. In *19th Toulon-Verona International Conference* (pp. 277 - 285). Huelva: University of Huelva.

Maignan, I., & Ferrell, O. C. (2004). CorporateSocialResponsibilityand Marketing: An Integrative Framework. *Journal of the Academy of Marketing Science*, *32*(1), 3–19. doi:10.1177/0092070303258971

Makadok, R. (2001). Toward a Synthesis of the Resource - Based and Dynamic - Capability Views of Rent Creation. *Strategic Management Journal*, *22*(5), 387–401. doi:10.1002mj.158

Malin Malmstrom, J. W. (2018, September 19). *Research: The Digitization of Banks Disproportionately Hurts Women Entrepreneurs*. Retrieved from https://hbr.org/2018/09/research-the-digitization-of-banks-disproportionately-hurts-women-entrepreneurs

Malwarebytes Labs. (2018). *Ransomware dominates the threat landscape*. Available at: https://blog.malwarebytes.com/cybercrime/2016/06/ransomware-dominates-the-threat-landscape/

Mangold, W. G., & Faulds, D. J. (2009). Social media: The new hybrid element of the promotion mix. *Business Horizons*, *52*(4), 357–365. doi:10.1016/j.bushor.2009.03.002

Mann, I. (2008). *Hacking the Human: Social Engineering Techniques and Security Countermeasures* (1st ed.). London: Routledge.

Manser Payne, E., Peltier, J. W., & Barger, V. A. (2017). Omni-channel marketing, integrated marketing communications and consumer engagement: A research agenda. *Journal of Research in Interactive Marketing*, *11*(2), 185–197. doi:10.1108/JRIM-08-2016-0091

Maqta Gateway. (2019). *Digitalising Trade*. Available at: https://www.maqta.ae/

Marcolin, B. L., Compeau, D. R., Munro, M. C., & Huff, S. L. (2000). Assessing user competence: Conceptualization and measurement. *Information Systems Research*, *11*(1), 37–60. doi:10.1287/isre.11.1.37.11782

Marian, P. (2015). Are you ready to create your own social media network? *WGSN*. Accessed on 18 October 2015, at http://www.wgsn.com

Marketing. (2019). Definition of Marketing by Merriam-Webster.

Markham, A. N. (1998). Life online: Researching real experiences in virtual space. In C. Ellis & A. P. Bochner (Eds.), *Ethnographic alternatives book series*. Walnut Creek, CA: Altamira Press.

Marko, K. (2006). *Development strategies for banks in Eastern European Markets; the role of IT systems*. Ljubljana: Faculty of Economics.

Martin, J. A. (2017). *Who is a target for ransomware attacks?* Available at: https://www.csoonline.com/article/3208111/security/who-is-a-target-for-ransomware-attacks.html

Martin, K., & Murphy, P. (2017). The Role of Data Privacy in Marketing. *Journal of the Academy of Marketing Science*, *45*(2), 135–153. doi:10.1007/s11747-016-0495-4

Mathwick, C., Wiertz, C., & de Ruyter, K. (2007). Social Capital Production in a P3 Community. *The Journal of Consumer Research*, *34*, 833–849.

Mauch, S. (1979). *The estimating impact of I.H.D.P. programme components*. Zurich: Infras.

Mauch, S., & Schwank, O. (1981). *I.H.P.D. and tourism: Interdependencies between the L.J.R.P. tourism environment, regional market and I.H.P.D.* Zurich: Infras.

Mavadiya, M. (2019). *Forbes*. Retrieved July 24, 2019, from https://www.forbes.com/sites/madhvimavadiya/2019/03/25/what-Apple-credit-card-means-for-FinTech/#2b84884f4856

Mavadiya, M. (2019, March 25). *What Apple's Credit Card Means For FinTech*. Retrieved July 24, 2019, from https://www.forbes.com/sites/madhvimavadiya/2019/03/25/what-Apple-credit-card-means-for-FinTech/#2b84884f4856

McAfee. (2017). *McAfee Labs Threat Report*. Santa Clara, CA: McAfee.

McAfee, A., Brynjolfsson, E., Davenport, T. H., Patil, D. J., & Barton, D. (2012). Big data: The management revolution. *Harvard Business Review*, *90*(10), 60–68. PMID:23074865

McCann, M., & Barlow, A. (2015). Use and measurement of social media for SMEs. *Journal of Small Business and Enterprise Development*, *22*(2), 273–287. doi:10.1108/JSBED-08-2012-0096

McCracken, G. (1986). Culture and Consumption: A Theoretical Account of the Structure and Movement of the Cultural Meaning of Consumer Goods. *The Journal of Consumer Research*, *13*, 71–84. doi:10.1086/209048

McGarry, E. (1958). The Propaganda Function in Marketing. *Journal of Marketing*, *23*(2), 131–139. doi:10.1177/002224295802300202

McGonigal, J. (2011). *Reality is Broken: Why games make us better and how they can change the world*. New York: Penguins Press.

McKean, P. (2018). *What does the FE college of the future look like?* Retrieved from https://www.jisc.ac.uk/blog/what-does-the-fe-college-of-the-future-look-like-20-nov-2018

McKenzie, L. M. (2017). *The Stereotypes and Biases That Plague Millennial Leaders: Best Practices and Strategies for Job Promotion*. Pepperdine University.

McKinsey & Company. (2016). *Big data and the supply chain: The big-supply-chain analytics landscape (Part 1)*. Available at: https://www.mckinsey.com/business-functions/operations/our-insights/big-data-and-the-supply-chain-the-big-supply-chain-analytics-landscape-part-1

McKinsey. (2015). *The fight for the customer: McKinsey global banking annual review 2015*. Retrieved from https://www.mckinsey.com/industries/financial-services/our-insights/the-fight-for-the-customer-mckinsey-global-banking-annual-review-2015

McKinsey. (2019). *The Future of work in America. People & Places, today and tomorrow*. Author.

McNay, L. (1999). Gender, habitus and the field: Pierre Bourdieu and the limits of reflexivity. *Theory, Culture & Society*, *16*(1), 95–117. doi:10.1177/026327699016001007

McNeill, L., & Graham, T. (2014). Mother's choice: An exploration of extended self in infant clothing consumption. *Journal of Consumer Behaviour*, *13*(6), 403–410. doi:10.1002/cb.1489

McQuarrie, E. F., & Mick, D. G. (1996). Figures of Rhetoric in Advertising Language. *The Journal of Consumer Research, 22*, 424–438. doi:10.1086/209459

Medrano, N., & Olarte-Pascual, C. (2016). The effects of the crisis on marketing innovation: An application for Spain. *Journal of Business and Industrial Marketing, 31*(3), 404–417. doi:10.1108/JBIM-02-2013-0048

Melander, L. (2018). Customer and Supplier Collaboration in Green Product Innovation: External and Internal Capabilities. *Business Strategy and the Environment, 27*(6), 677–693. doi:10.1002/bse.2024

Mentzer, J. (2004, May/June). Understanding demand. *Supply Chain Management Review*, 38–45.

Mentzer, J. T., & Gundlach, G. (2010). Exploring the Relationship Between Marketing and Supply Chain Management: Introduction to the Special Issue. *Journal of the Academy of Marketing Science, 38*(1), 1–4. doi:10.100711747-009-0150-4

Mentzer, J., DeWitt, W., Keebler, J., Min, S., Nix, N., Smith, C., & Zacharia, Z. G. (2001). Defining supply chain management. *Journal of Business Logistics, 22*(2), 1–25. doi:10.1002/j.2158-1592.2001.tb00001.x

Merriam-Webster. 2018. *ransom.* [Online] Available at: https://www.merriam-webster.com/dictionary/ransom

Merrilees, B., & Miller, D. (2019). Companion shopping: The influence on mall brand experiences. *Marketing Intelligence & Planning, 37*(3), 465–478. doi:10.1108/MIP-08-2018-0340

Mesquita, L. F., Anand, J., & Brush, T. H. (2008). Comparing the resource-based and relational views: Knowledge transfer and spillover in vertical alliances. *Strategic Management Journal, 29*(9), 913–941. doi:10.1002mj.699

Messerii, P. (1987). The development of tourism in the Swiss Alps: Economic, social and environmental effects. *Mountain Research and Development, 7*(1), 13–24. doi:10.2307/3673321

Meyer, J. W., & Rowan, B. (1977). Institutionalized Organizations: Formal Structure as Myth and Ceremony. *American Journal of Sociology, 83*(2), 340-363.

Meyer, M., Johnson, D., & Ethington, C. (1997). Contrasting attributes of preventive health innovations. *Journal of Communication, 47*(2), 112–131. doi:10.1111/j.1460-2466.1997.tb02709.x

Michelle, A. M. (2016). *The Effect Of Digital Finance On Financial Inclusion In Kenya*. Academic Press.

Microsoft Azure. (2019a). *Build your next great idea in the cloud with an Azure free account*. Available at: https://azure.microsoft.com/en-gb/free/cloud-services/

Microsoft Azure. (2019b). *Machine Learning Studio: Simple, scalable, cutting edge*. Available at: https://azure.microsoft.com/en-us/services/machine-learning-studio/

Miklós-Thal, J., & Zhang, J. (2013). (De)marketing to Manage Consumer Quality Inferences. *Journal of Marketing Research, 50*(1), 55-69. Retrieved from http://www.jstor.org/stable/42003065

Miller, D. (2019). *The Sharing Economy and How it Is Changing Industries*. Retrieved June 30, 2019, from THE BALANCE SMB: https://www.thebalancesmb.com/the-sharing-economy-and-how-it-changes-industries-4172234

Miller, D. (2011). *Tales from Facebook*. Cambridge, UK: Polity.

Miller, S. R. (2016). First principles for regulating the sharing economy. *Harvard Journal on Legislation, 147*(53), 149–202.

Mills, E., Han, J., & Clay, J. (2008). Accessibility of Hospitality and Tourism Websites: A Challenge for Visually Impaired persons. *Cornell Hospitality Quarterly, 49*(1), 28–41. doi:10.1177/1938965507311499

Milne, G., Rohm, A., & Bahl, S. (2009). If It's Legal, Is It Acceptable? Consumer Reactions to Online Covert Marketing. *Journal of Advertising*, *38*(4), 107–122. doi:10.2753/JOA0091-3367380408

Min, S., & Mentzer, J. T. (2000). The Role of Marketing in Supply Chain Management. *International Journal of Physical Distribution & Logistics Management*, *30*(9), 766–787. doi:10.1108/09600030010351462

Mintel. (2017). *Who's innovating?* Available from: http://academic.mintel.com/display/848837/?highlight#hit1

Mirzaee, S., & George, B. P. (2016). Brand Archetypes: An Experiment with the Demeter. *Journal of Applied Economics & Business Research*, *6*(2).

Mitchell, M., & Jolley, J. (2012). *Research Design Explained* (8th ed.). Wadsworth Publishing.

Mitsubishi. (2019). *MUFG and Akamai to launch Global Open Network, Inc. joint venture.* Available at: https://www.mufg.jp/english/vcms_lf/news/pressrelease-20190212-001-e.pdf

Moe, M., & Trusov, M. (2011). The Value of Social Dynamics in Online Product Rating Forums. *JMR, Journal of Marketing Research*, *48*(3), 444–456. doi:10.1509/jmkr.48.3.444

Moeran, B. (2006). Elegance and Substance Travel East: Vogue Nippon. *Fashion Theory*, *10*(1–2), 225–258. doi:10.2752/136270406778051012

Moeran, B. (2008). Economic and Cultural Production as Structural Paradox: The Case of International Fashion Magazine Publishing. *International Review of Sociology: Revue Internationale de Sociologie*, *18*(2), 267–281. doi:10.1080/03906700802087944

Mogaji, E., Ukpabi, D., & Olaleye, S. (2018, July). Examining Consumer-Brand Relationships in the UK Energy Sector: A Social Media Perspective. In *Academy of Marketing Annual Conference Proceedings.* University of Stirling.

Mohammed, A. A., Hafeez-Baig, A., & Gururajan, R. (2019). A qualitative research to explore practices that are utilised for managing talent development in the higher education environment: A case study in six Australian universities. *Journal of Industry-University Collaboration*, *1*(1), 24–37. doi:10.1108/JIUC-02-2019-003

Mollen & Wilson. (2010). *Boundaries of the mind: the individual in the fragile sciences—cognition.* Cambridge, UK: Cambridge University Press.

Monrose, F. (2015). *Detecting web exploit kits by tree-based structural similarity search.* USA Patent No. US9723016B2.

Mood, A. M., & Specht, R. D. (1954). *Gaming as a technique of analysis.* Alexandria, VA: Department of Defense.

Moratis, L., Hoff, J., & Ruel, B. (2006). A dual challenge facing management education: Situation-based learning and learning about CSR. *Journal of Management Development*, *25*(3/4), 213–231. doi:10.1108/02621710610648150

Moreira, J., José, M., Jorge, S., & Gastao, S. (2011). Marketing innovation: study of determinants of innovation in the design and packaging of goods and services – application to portuguese firms. *International Conference on Marketing Studies.*

Moreno, F. M., Gil Lafuente, J., Carreón, F. Á., & Moreno, S. M. (2017). The Characterization of the Millennials and Their Buying Behavior. *International Journal of Marketing Studies*, *9*(5), 135–144. doi:10.5539/ijms.v9n5p135

Morgan, R. N., & Hunt, S. D. (1994). The Commitment-Trust Theory of Relationship Marketing. *Journal of Marketing*, *58*(3), 20–38.

Morosan, C. (2012). Theoretical and Empirical Considerations of Guests' Perceptions of Biometric Systems in Hotels: Extending the Technology Acceptance Model. *Journal of Hospitality & Tourism Research (Washington, D.C.)*, *36*(1), 52–84. doi:10.1177/1096348010380601

Morpus, N. (2018). *5 Experiential Learning Augmented Reality Apps for Education*. Retrieved from https://blog.capterra.com/experiential-learning-augmented-reality-apps-for-education/

Morrcraft, B. (2019). *Ransomware attackers set sights on middle market firms*. Insurance Business Aemrica.

Morton, C., & Redman, L. D. (2016). The best shopping cities in the world. *Condé Nast Traveler*. Available at: https://www.cntraveler.com/galleries/2015-01-03/best-shopping-cities-in-the-world-readers-choice-awards-2014

Mullen. (2013). The best uses of augmented reality in the travel industry. *TourismLink*. Available at: http://www.tourismlink.eu/2013/08/the-best-uses-of-augmented-reality-in-the-travel-industry

Munir, Z. A., Othman, A. A., Shukur, S. A. M., Ithnin, R., & Rusdi, S. D. (2015). Practices of internal marketing in small and medium industry. *International Journal of Social Science and Humanity*, *5*(4), 358–361. doi:10.7763/IJSSH.2015.V5.480

Muniz, A. M. Jr, & O'Guinn, T. C. (2001). Brand Community. *The Journal of Consumer Research*, *27*, 412–432. doi:10.1086/319618

Muqbil, I. (1985). Himalayan tourism: Economics vs ecology. *Tourism Recreation Research*, *10*(1), 45–46. doi:10.1080/02508281.1985.11014361

Muscio, A., Quaglione, D., & Vallanti, G. (2013). Does government funding complement or substitute private research funding to universities? *Journal of Regional Policy*, *42*, 63–75.

Mutum, D., & Wang, Q. (2011). *Handbook of research on digital media and advertising: user generated content consumption*. University of Warwick.

Myers, K. K., & Sadaghiani, K. (2010). Millennials in the workplace: A communication perspective on millennials' organizational relationships and performance. *Journal of Business and Psychology*, *25*(2), 225–238. doi:10.100710869-010-9172-7 PMID:20502509

Nah, F. F.-H., Zeng, Q., Telaprolu, R., Ayyappa, A. P., & Eschenbrenner, B. (2014). Gamification of Education: A review of literature. In F. F.-H. Nah (Ed.), *HCI in Business* (pp. 401–409). Heraklion, Greece: Springer.

Nair, B.V., & Munusami, C. (2019). Knowledge management practices: An exploratory study at the Malaysian higher education institutions, *Journal of Research in Innovative Teaching & Learning*. Retrieved from doi:10.1108/JRIT-01-2019-0008

Nambisan, S., & Baron, R. A. (2007). Customer environments: Relationship management. *Journal of Interactive Marketing*, *21*(2), 42–62. doi:10.1002/dir.20077

Narkiniemi, J. (2013). *Using Digital Marketing to Develop a Modern Marketing Strategy for a Startup*. Retrieved from https://core.ac.uk/download/pdf/38098424.pdf

Narver, J. C., & Slater, S. F. (1990). The effect of market orientation on business profitability. *Journal of Marketing*, *54*(4), 20–35. doi:10.1177/002224299005400403

National Audit Office. (2017). *Follow-up on alternative providers*. London: Department of Education.

National Institute of Standards and Technology (NIST). (2014). *Framework for improving critical infrastructure cybersecurity (version 1.0)*. Available at: www.nist.gov/cyberframework/upload/ cybersecurity-framework-021214.pdf

Naude´, P., Desai, J., & Murphy, J. (2003). Identifying the determinants of internal marketing orientation. *European Journal of Marketing*, *37*(9), 1205–1220. doi:10.1108/0390560310486951

NDTV. (2017). *ATMs Closed Due to WannaCry Ransomware? Experts Debunk WhatsApp Hoaxes.* Available at: https://gadgets.ndtv.com/internet/news/atm-closed-india-cyber-attack-whatsapp-wanna-cry-rumours-1694207

Negm, E., & Tantawi, P. (2015). Investigating the Impact of Visual Design on Consumers' Perceptions towards Advertising. *International Journal of Scientific and Research Publications*, *5*(4). Retrieved from www.ijsrp.org

Nelson, M., & Park, J. (2015). Publicity as Covert Marketing? The Role of Persuasion Knowledge and Ethical Perceptions on Beliefs and Credibility in a Video News Release Story. *Journal of Business Ethics*, *130*(2), 327–341. doi:10.100710551-014-2227-3

Neumann, E. (2015). *The great mother: An analysis of the archetype*. Princeton University Press. doi:10.1515/9781400866106

Newman, D., Kramer, S., & Blanchard, O. (2016). *Marketing to Millennials.* Retrieved from https://futurumresearch.com/wp-content/uploads/woocommerce_uploads/2017/02/report_200117.pdf

Newtown Drenewydd. (2019). *A Brief History of Newtown - Part 2.* Author.

Ngai, E., Moon, K., Lam, S., Kee, L., Chin, E., & Tao, S. (2015). Social media models, technologies, and applications. An academic review and case study. *Industrial Management & Data Systems*, *115*(5), 769–802. doi:10.1108/IMDS-03-2015-0075

Nguyen, B., Yu, X., Melewar, T. C., & Chen, J. (2015). Brand innovation and social media: Knowledge acquisition from social media, market orientation, and the moderating role of social media strategic capability. *Industrial Marketing Management*, *51*, 11–25. doi:10.1016/j.indmarman.2015.04.017

Nguyen, V. A. (2017). Towards the implementation of an assessment-centred blended learning framework at the course level: A case study in a Vietnamese national university. *The International Journal of Information and Learning Technology*, *34*(1), 20–30. doi:10.1108/IJILT-08-2016-0031

Nichols, W. (2014, July 17). *How Big Data Brings Marketing and Finance Together.* Retrieved July 21, 2019, from https://hbr.org/2014/07/how-big-data-brings-marketing-and-finance-together

Nichols, T. R., Gringle, M. R., & Pulliam, R. M. (2015). You have to put your children's needs first or you're really not a good mother": Black Motherhood and Self-Care Practices. *Women, Gender, and Families of Color*, *3*(2), 165–189. doi:10.5406/womgenfamcol.3.2.0165

Nicosia, F. M., & Mayer, R. N. (1976). Toward a sociology consumption. *The Journal of Consumer Research*, *3*(2), 65–75. doi:10.1086/208653

Nicosia, F. M., & Mayer, R. N. (1976). Toward a Sociology of Consumption. *The Journal of Consumer Research*, *3*, 65–75.

Nielsen. (2014). Retrieved from http://www.nielsen.com/us/en/insights/reports/2014/is-sharing-the-new-buying.html

Nikjoo, A., & Bakhshi, H. (2019). The presence of tourists and residents in shared travel photos. *Tourism Management*, *70*, 89–98. doi:10.1016/j.tourman.2018.08.005

Nishtha Kesswani, S. K. (2015). *Maintaining Cyber Security: mplications, Cost and Returns.* ACM.

NJCCIC. (2016). *Simplelocker.* Available at: https://www.cyber.nj.gov/threat-profiles/ransomware-variants/simplelocker

NJCCIC. (2018). *GandCrab.* Available at: https://www.cyber.nj.gov/threat-profiles/ransomware-variants/gandcrab

Nobbs, K., Moore, C. M., & Sheridan, M. (2012). The flagship format within the luxury fashion market. *International Journal of Retail & Distribution Management*, *40*(12), 920–934. doi:10.1108/09590551211274928

Noci, G. (2019). The evolving nature of the marketing–supply chain management interface in contemporary markets. *Business Process Management Journal*, *25*(2), 379–383. doi:10.1108/BPMJ-07-2018-0202

Norman, D. A. (2004). *Emotional Design: Why We Love (or Hate) Everyday Things*. New York: Basic Books.

Norton. (2018a). *Malware 101: How do I get malware? Simple attacks*. Available at: https://us.norton.com/internetsecurity-malware-malware-101-how-do-i-get-malware-simple-attacks.html

Norton. (2018b). *New variant of Android ransomware takes advantage of the lockscreen's user interface.* Available at: https://us.norton.com/internetsecurity-emerging-threats-new-variant-of-android-ransomware-takes-advantage-of-the-lockscreen-user-interface.html

Novak, Hoffman, & Yung. (2000). Measuring the Customer Experience in Online Environments: A Structural Modeling Approach. *Marketing Science*, *19*(1), 22–42.

Nov, O., Naaman, M., & Ye, C. (2010). Analysis of participation in an online photo-sharing community: A multidimensional perspective. *JASIST*, *61*(3), 555–566.

Nowfal, K. (2010). *Teknologia alwaqea alefteradi wistekdamatuh altalemeya* [Virtual reality technology and its educational uses]. Amman, Jordan: Dar Al Manahej for Publishing & Distribution.

Nye, J. S. Jr. (2017). Deterrence and dissuasion in cyberspace. *International Security*, *41*(3), 44–71. doi:10.1162/ISEC_a_00266

O'Brien, D. (2017). *ISTR: Internet Security Threat Report- Ransomware 2017*. Symantec.

O'Connor, F. (2016). *"Millennials & Youtube" An Investigation Into The Influence Of User-Generated Video Content On The Consumer Decision Making Process*. Retrieved from https://core.ac.uk/download/pdf/80766824.pdf

O'Connor, P. (2010). Managing a hotel's image on TripAdvisor. *Journal of Hospitality Marketing & Management*, *19*(7), 754–772. doi:10.1080/19368623.2010.508007

O'Donnell, R. (2018). *Education must shift to produce 'job-ready' grads*. Retrieved from www.hrdive.com/news/education-must-shift-to-produce-job-ready-grads/525859

O'Donnell, A. (2014). The Contribution of Networking to Small Firm Marketing. *Journal of Small Business Management*, *52*(1), 164–187. doi:10.1111/jsbm.12038

O'Donohoe, S., Hogg, M., Maclaran, P., Martens, L., & Stevens, L. (Eds.). (2013). *Motherhoods, markets and consumption: The making of mothers in contemporary western cultures* (Vol. 18). Routledge. doi:10.4324/9780203469729

O'Donohoe, S., & O'Donohoe, S. (2006). Yummy mummies: The clamor of glamour in advertising to mothers. *Advertising & Society Review*, *7*(3). doi:10.1353/asr.2007.0006

O'Driscoll, A., Carson, D., & Gilmore, A. (2000). Developing marketing competence and managing in networks: A strategic perspective. *Journal of Strategic Marketing*, *8*(2), 183–196. doi:10.1080/096525400346240

O'Dwyer, M., Gilmore, A., & Carson, D. (2009). Innovative marketing in SMEs. *European Journal of Marketing*, *43*(1/2), 46–61. doi:10.1108/03090560910923238

O'Guinn, T. C., & Muniz, A. M., Jr. (2009). Collective brand relationships. Handbook of brand relationships, 173-94.

O'Reilly, T. (2005). *What Is Web 2.0*. Retrieved from http://goo.gl/r4yY

Ohlhausen, M. K. (2014). Privacy Challenges and Opportunities: The Role of the Federal Trade Commission. *Journal of Public Policy & Marketing*, *33*(1), 4–9. doi:10.1509/jppm.33.1.4

Olavarrieta, S., & Friedmann, R. (2008). Market orientation, knowledge-related resources and firm performance. *Journal of Business Research*, *61*(6), 623–630. doi:10.1016/j.jbusres.2007.06.037

Olofsson, L., & Farr, R. (2006). Business Model Tools and Definition. *Business*. Retrieved from https://www.researchgate.net/publication/272813909_Business_Model_Tools_and_Definition_-_a_Literature_Review

Olsson, T., Kärkkäinen, T., Lagerstam, E., & Ventä-Olkkonen, L. (2012). User evaluation of mobile augmented reality scenarios. *Journal of Ambient Intelligence and Smart Environments*, *4*(1), 29–47.

Omar, A., Davis-Sramek, B., Myers, M. B., & Mentzer, J. T. (2012). A global analysis of orientation, coordination, and flexibility in supply chains. *Journal of Business Logistics*, *33*(2), 128–144. doi:10.1111/j.0000-0000.2012.01045.x

OMFIF. (2019). *Central Bank Digital Currencies*. Available at: https://thinktank.omfif.org/ibm

Oracle. (2015). *A New Perspective on Millennials Segmenting a Generation for Actionable Insights for Consumer Goods Companies and Retailers Sponsored by A New Perspective on Millennials*. Retrieved from http://www.oracle.com/us/industries/consumer/interbrand-cg-retail-cx-wp-2400662.pdf

Oracle. (2019a). *22 Big Data Use Cases for the Modern Business*. Available at https://www.oracle.com/uk/big-data/

Oracle. (2019b). *What is big data?* Available at https://www.oracle.com/uk/big-data/guide/what-is-big-data.html

Oracle. (2019c). *Big Ideas*. Available at http://www.oracle.com/us/corporate/profit/big-ideas/index.html

Osborne, C. (2018a). *Healthcare was a top target for ransomware families in 2017*. Available at: https://www.zdnet.com/article/ransomware-operators-select-the-healthcare-industry-as-a-top-target/

Osborne, C. (2018b). *Meet ransomware which wears the face of former president Barack Obama*. ZDNet.

Oskamp, S., & Schultz, P. W. (2005). *Sociology, Attitudes and Opinions*. Lawrence Erlbaum Associates. doi:10.4324/9781410611963

Osterman Research. (2016). *Understanding the Depth of the Global Ransomware Problem Survey Report Spon*. Retrieved from www.ostermanresearch.com

Ostrom, T. M. (1969). The Relationship between the Affective, Behavioural, and Cognitive Components of Attitude. *Journal of Experimental Social Psychology*, *5*(1), 12–30. doi:10.1016/0022-1031(69)90003-1

Otugo, N. E., Uzuegbunam, C. E., & Obikeze, C. O. (2015, May). Social media advertising/marketing: A study of awareness, attitude and responsiveness by Nigerian youths. In *International Conference on Communication, Media, Technology and Design* (*Vol. 1*, No. 2, pp. 1-17). Academic Press.

Ovans, A. (2015). *What Is a Business Model?* Retrieved 06 22, 2019, from HBR: https://hbr.org/2015/01/what-is-a-business-model

Oxford Dictionaries. (2015). *Process*. Retrieved from: http://www.oxforddictionaries.com/definition/english/process

Ozcan, P., Möhlmann, M., & Krishnamoorthy, C. (2017). *Who shares and who doesn't?* Retrieved from https://www.wbs.ac.uk/wbs2012/assets/PDF/downloads/press/ResultsofUKSharingEconomyConsumerSurvery2017.pdf

Ozili, P. K. (2018). Impact of digital finance on financial inclusion and stability. *Science Direct*. Retrieved from https://www.sciencedirect.com/science/article/pii/S2214845017301503#bib23

Packard, H. (2019). *Hewlett Packard Enterprise and Continental launch blockchain-based data monetization platform.* Available at: https://www.hpe.com/us/en/newsroom/press-release/2019/02/hewlett-packard-enterprise-and-continental-launch-blockchain-based-data-monetization-platform.html

Pakistan, P. T. C. L. (2018). *PTCL injects PKR 4 Billion in U Microfinance Bank for growth.* Press Release. Retrieved from https://ptcl.com.pk/Home/PressReleaseDetail/?ItemId=654&linkId=130

Palloff, R. M., & Pratt, K. (2013). *Lessons from the Virtual Classroom* (2nd ed.). San Francisco: Jossey-Bass.

Palmatier, R. W., Dant, R. P., & Grewal, D. (2007). A Comparative Longitudinal Analysis of Theoretical Perspectives of Interorganizational Relationship Performance. *Journal of Marketing*, *71*(4), 94–172. doi:10.1509/jmkg.71.4.172

Palmer, Lunceford, & Patton. (n.d.). *The Engagement Economy - How gamification is reshaping businesses.* Deloitte Review Report. Retrieved from http://www.deloitte.com/ view/en_US/us/Insights/Browse-by-Content-Type/deloitte-review/c7cee86d96498310 VgnVCM1000001956f00aRCRD.htm

Palmer, A., & McCole, P. (2000). The role of electronic commerce in creating virtual tourism destination marketing organisations. *International Journal of Contemporary Hospitality Management*, *12*(3), 198–204. doi:10.1108/09596110010320760

Panahi, S., Watson, J., & Partridge, H. (2012). Social media and tacit knowledge sharing: developing a conceptual model. World Academy of Science, Engineering and Technology (WASET), 1095–1102.

Pan, B., Xiang, Z., Law, R., & Fesenmaier, D. R. (2011). The dynamics of search engine marketing for tourist destinations. *Journal of Travel Research*, *50*(4), 365–377. doi:10.1177/0047287510369558

Paniagua, J., & Sapena, J. (2014). Business performance and social media: Love or hate? *Business Horizons*, *57*(6), 719–728. doi:10.1016/j.bushor.2014.07.005

Pantano, E., & Dennis, C. (2019). Store buildings as tourist attractions: Mining retail meaning of store building pictures through a machine learning approach. *Journal of Retailing and Consumer Services*, *51*, 304–310.

Pantano, E., Giglio, S., & Dennis, C. (2019). Making sense of consumers' tweets: Sentiment outcomes for fast fashion retailers through Big Data analytics. *International Journal of Retail & Distribution Management*, *47*(9), 915–927.

Pantano, E., Priporas, C. V., & Dennis, C. (2018). A new approach to retailing for successful competition in the new smart scenario. *International Journal of Retail & Distribution Management*, *46*(3), 264–282. doi:10.1108/IJRDM-04-2017-0080

Pantano, E., Priporas, C. V., Sorace, S., & Iazzolino, G. (2017). Does the innovation-orientation lead to retail industry growth? Empirical evidence from patent analysis. *Journal of Retailing and Consumer Services*, *34*, 88–94. doi:10.1016/j.jretconser.2016.10.001

Pantano, E., Priporas, C. V., & Stylos, N. (2017). 'You will like it!' Using open data to predict tourists' response to a tourist attraction. *Tourism Management*, *60*, 430–438. doi:10.1016/j.tourman.2016.12.020

Pantano, E., & Timmermans, H. (2014). What is smart for retailing? *Procedia Environmental Sciences*, *22*, 101–107. doi:10.1016/j.proenv.2014.11.010

Pantano, E., & Vannucci, V. (2019). Who is innovating? An evaluation of the extent to which retailers are meeting the technology challenge. *Journal of Retailing and Consumer Services*, *49*, 297–304. doi:10.1016/j.jretconser.2019.01.019

Panteli, N., & Marder, B. (2017). Constructing and enacting normality online across generations: The case of social networking sites. *Journal of Information Technology & People*, *30*(2), 282–300. doi:10.1108/ITP-06-2015-0134

Pant, J. J., & Venkateswaran, V. (2019). Exploring millennial psychological contract expectations across talent segments, Employee Relations. *International Journal (Toronto, Ont.)*, *41*(4), 773–792.

Papagiannidis, S., Bourlakis, M., Alamanos, E., & Dennis, C. (2017). Preferences of smart shopping channels and their impact on perceived wellbeing and social inclusion. *Computers in Human Behavior*, *77*, 396–405. doi:10.1016/j.chb.2017.04.029

Papaoikonomou, E., Cascon-Pereira, R., & Ryan, G. (2016). Constructing and communicating an ethical consumer identity: A Social Identity Approach. *Journal of Consumer Culture*, *16*(1), 209–231. doi:10.1177/1469540514521080

Papasolomo, I. (2006). Can internal marketing be implemented within bureaucratic organisations? *Journal of Bank Marketing*, *24*(3), 194–212. doi:10.1108/02652320610659030

Papasolomou, I., & Vrontis, D. (2006). Using internal marketing to ignite the corporate brand: The case of the UK retail bank industry. *Brand Management*, *14*(1/2), 177–195. doi:10.1057/palgrave.bm.2550059

Parameswaran, M., & Whinston, A. B. (2007). Social computing: An over- view. *Communications of the Association for Information Systems*, *19*(1), 37.

Paraskevas, A. (2001). Internal service encounters in hotels: An empirical study. *International Journal of Contemporary Hospitality Management*, *13*(6), 285–292. doi:10.1108/09596110110400481

Parente, H. D., Lee, D. P., Ishman, D. M., & Roth, V. A. (2008). Marketing and supply chain management: A collaborative research agenda. *Journal of Business and Industrial Marketing*, *23*(8), 520–528. doi:10.1108/08858620810913335

Park, H. M., & Perry, J. L. (2008). Do campaign web sites really matter in electoral civic engage ment? Empirical evidence from the 2004 post-election Internet tracking survey. *Social Science Computer Review*, *26*(2), 190–212. doi:10.1177/0894439307309026

Parmentier, M-A., & Fischer, E. (2011). You Can't Always Get What You Want: Unsustainable Identity Projects in the Fashion System. *Consumption Markets and Culture, 14*(1), 7–27.

Parra-López, E., Bulchand-Gidumal, J., Gutiérrez-Taño, D., & Díaz-Armas, R. (2011). Intentions to use social media in organizing and taking vacation trips. *Computers in Human Behavior*, *27*(2), 640–654. doi:10.1016/j.chb.2010.05.022

Parsa, H. G., Lord, K. R., Putrevu, S., & Kreeger, J. (2015). Corporate social and environmental responsibility in services: Will consumers pay for it? *Journal of Retailing and Consumer Services*, *22*, 250–260. doi:10.1016/j.jretconser.2014.08.006

Pates, D., & Sumner, N. (2016). E-learning spaces and the digital university. *The International Journal of Information and Learning Technology*, *33*(3), 159–171. doi:10.1108/IJILT-10-2015-0028

Patterson, P., Yu, T., & de Ruyter, K. (2006). Understanding Customer Engagement in Services. *Advancing Theory, Maintaining Relevance, Proceedings of ANZMAC 2006 Conference.*

Paul, D. P., III, Spence, N., Bhardwa, N., & Coustasse, A. (2018). *Healthcare Facilities: Another Target for Ransomware Attacksd the Health Information Technology Commons.* 54th Annual MBAA Conference, Chicago, IL. Retrieved from http://mds.marshall.edu/mgmt_faculty

Pawlowsky, P. (2001). The Treatment of Organizational Learning in Management Science. In M. Dierkes, A. Berthoin Antal, J. Child, & I. Nonaka (Eds.), *Handbook of Organizational Learning & Knowledge* (pp. 61–88). Oxford, UK: Oxford University Press.

Pawson, I. G., & Standford, D. D. (1984). Effect of modernization on Nepal's Khumbu Region: Changes in population structure 1970-1982. *Mountain Research and Development*, *4*(1), 73–78. doi:10.2307/3673172

Pawson, I. G., Stanford, D. D., Adams, V. A., & Nurbu, M. (1984). Growth of tourism in Nepal's Everest region: Impact on the physical environment and structure of human settlements. *Mountain Research and Development*, *4*(3), 237–246. doi:10.2307/3673144

Payne, A. (1993). *The Essence of Services Marketing*. Hemel Hempstead, UK: Prentice-Hall.

Pegg, K. J., O'Donnell, A. W., Lala, G., & Barber, B. L. (2018). The role of online social identity in the relationship between alcohol-related content on social networking sites and adolescent alcohol use. *Cyberpsychology, Behavior, and Social Networking*, *21*(1), 50–55. doi:10.1089/cyber.2016.0665 PMID:28574719

Pelling, E. L., White, K. M., & White, K. (2009). The theory of planned behaviour applied to young people's use of social networking websites. *Cyberpsychology & Behavior*, *12*(6), 755–759. doi:10.1089/cpb.2009.0109 PMID:19788377

Pells, R. (2018). *Cardiff plans review after suicide of 'overworked' lecturer*. Retrieved from www.timehighereducation.com/news/cardiff-plans-review-after-suicide-overworked-lecturer

Peltier, J. W., & Scovotti, C. (2005). Relationship marketing and disadvantaged health care segments. *Health Marketing Quarterly*, *22*(2), 69–90. doi:10.1300/J026v22n02_05 PMID:15914375

Pervaje, A. (2011). *Resource-Based View of Social Media as a Source of Sustained Competitive Advantage*. Retrieved from https://core.ac.uk/download/pdf/4431941.pdf

Peter, J. P., & Olson, J. C. (2010). *Consumer behaviour & marketing startegy*. Retrieved from https://www.academia.edu/6078770/CONSUMER_BEHAVIOR_and_MARKETING_STRATEGY_CONSUMER_BEHAVIOR_and_MARKETING_STRATEGY

Peter, O. (2018). Millennials Set to be Outnumbered by Gen Z Within a Year. *The Independent*. Available at: https://www.independent.co.uk/life-style/millennials-gen-z-outnumbered-2019-global-population-demographic-bloomberg-a8502251.html

Peters, M. A. (2018). Education in a post-truth world. In *Post-Truth, Fake News* (pp. 145–150). Singapore: Springer. doi:10.1007/978-981-10-8013-5_12

Peters, T. (1988). *Thriving on Chaos*. New York, NY: Alfred A. Knopf.

Petra, S. F., Jaidin, J. H., Perera, J. Q., & Linn, M. (2016). Supporting students to become autonomous learners: The role of web-based learning. *The International Journal of Information and Learning Technology*, *33*(4), 263–275. doi:10.1108/IJILT-05-2016-0017

Petty, R., & Andrews, J. (2008). Covert Marketing Unmasked: A Legal and Regulatory Guide for Practices That Mask Marketing Messages. *Journal of Public Policy & Marketing*, *27*(1), 7–18. doi:10.1509/jppm.27.1.7

Pewinternet. (2006). Retrieved from pewinternet.org/Reports/2006/Bloggers.aspx

Pfeiffer, J. (1998, May). Six dangerous myths about pay. *Harvard Business Review*, 108–109. PMID:10179647

Pham, M.-H. (2011). Blog Ambition: Fashion, Feelings, and the Political Economy of the Digital Raced Body. *Camera Obscura*, *26*(1), 1–37. doi:10.1215/02705346-2010-013

Pham, P. H. M., & Gammoh, B. S. (2015). Characteristics of social-media marketing strategy and customer-based brand equity outcomes: A conceptual model. *International Journal of Internet Marketing and Advertising*, *9*(4), 321–337. doi:10.1504/IJIMA.2015.072885

Phillips, C. (2014, July 9). *Domino's Unveils Social Gamification Initiative 'Pizza Mogul'*. Retrieved January 7th, 2019, from Power Retail.com: http://www.powerretail.com.au/technology/dominos-unveils-pizza-mogul/

Phipps, M., Ozanne, L., Luchs, M., Subrahmanyan, S., Kapitan, S., Catlin, J., ... Weaver, T. (2013). Understanding the inherent complexity of sustainable consumption: A social cognitive framework. *Journal of Business Research*, *66*(8), 1227–1234. doi:10.1016/j.jbusres.2012.08.016

Piccoli, G., Spalding, B. R., & Ives, B. (2001). A Framework for Improving Customer Service through Information Technology: The Customer-service Life Cycle. *Cornell Hotel and Restaurant Administration Quarterly*. *A*, *42*, 38–45.

Pickett-Baker, J., & Ozaki, R. (2008). Pro-environmental products: Marketing influence on the consumer purchase decision. *Journal of Consumer Marketing*, *25*(5), 281–293. doi:10.1108/07363760810890516

Piercy, N. F., & Morgan, N. (1995). Internal marketing – the missing half of the marketing programme. *Long Range Planning*, *24*(2), 82–93. doi:10.1016/0024-6301(91)90083-Z

Piirainen, L. (2016). *Digitalization of the financial sector and change management*. OULU University of Applied Sciences.

Piller, I. (2001). Identity constructions in multilingual advertising. *Language in Society*, *30*(2), 153–186. doi:10.1017/S0047404501002019

Pinar, M. M. (2016). The Death of the Stereotype: Reclaim of Self in Angela Carter's "The Loves of Lady Purple. *International Journal of Social Sciences and Education Research*, *2*(1), 311–319. doi:10.24289/ijsser.279102

Pirsig, R. M. (1974). *Zen and the art of motorcycle maintenance: an inquiry into values*. Toronto: Bantam Books.

Pobocik, M., & Butalla, C. (1998). Development in Nepal: The Annapurna Conservation Area Project. In C. M. Hall & A. A. Lew (Eds.), *Sustainable tourism: A Geographical perspective* (pp. 159–172). Essex, UK: Addison Wesley Longman.

Poecze, F., Ebster, C., & Strauss, C. (2018). Social media metrics and sentiment analysis to evaluate the effectiveness of social media posts. *Procedia Computer Science*, *130*, 660–666. doi:10.1016/j.procs.2018.04.117

Pomirleanu, N. S., Schibrowsky, J. A., Peltier, J., & Nill, A. (2013). A review of internet marketing research over the past 20 years and future research direction. *Journal of Research in Interactive Marketing*, *7*(3), 166–181. doi:10.1108/JRIM-01-2013-0006

Porral, C., Sanchez, P., Medín, F., & Clave, P. (2017). A Typology Categorization Of Millennials In their Technology Behavior. *Xxix Congreso De Marketing Aemark 2017 561 De 1617*. Retrieved from https://idus.us.es/xmlui/bitstream/handle/11441/78156/A_typology_categorization_of_millennials_intheir_technology_behavior.pdf?sequence=1&isAllowed=y

Porterfield, M., & Isaac-Savage, E. P. (2013). The formation of online wisdom communities amongst ministerial students: A quantitative case study. *Journal of Adult Theological Education*, *10*(2), 116–131. doi:10.1179/1740714114Z.00000000018

Poster, M. (2018). *The second media age*. John Wiley & Sons.

Powers, T., Advincula, D., Austin, M. S., Graiko, S., & Snyder, J. (2012). Digital and social media in the purchase decision process: A special report from the Advertising Research Foundation'. *Journal of Advertising Research*, *52*(4), 479–489. doi:10.2501/JAR-52-4-479-489

Prahalad, C. K., & Hamel, G. (1990). The core competence of the corporation. *Harvard Business Review*, (May/June): 79–91.

Price, M. (1987). Tourism and forestry in the Swiss Alps: Parasitism or Symbiosis. *Mountain Research and Development*, *7*(1), 1–12. doi:10.2307/3673320

Priporas, C.-V., Stylos, N., & Fotiadis, A. K. (2017). Generation Z consumers' expectations of interactions in smart retailing: A future agenda. *Computers in Human Behavior*, *77*, 374–381. doi:10.1016/j.chb.2017.01.058

Projection-mapping.org. (2019, July 7). Retrieved from http://projection-mapping.org/what-is-projection-mapping/: http://projection-mapping.org/what-is-projection-mapping/

Pros and Cons of Various Research Techniques. (n.d.). Available at: http://www.riger.com/know_base/research/pros.html

Prothero, A., Dobscha, S., Freund, J., Kilbourne, W. E., Luchs, M. G., Ozanne, L. K., & Thøgersen, J. (2011). Sustainable consumption: Opportunities for consumer research and public policy. *Journal of Public Policy & Marketing*, *30*(1), 31–38. doi:10.1509/jppm.30.1.31

Pujazon-Zazik, M., & Park, M. J. (2010). To Tweet, or Not to Tweet: Gender Differences and Potential Positive and Negative Health Outcomes of Adolescents' Social Internet Use. *American Journal of Men's Health*, *4*(1), 77–85. doi:10.1177/1557988309360819 PMID:20164062

Pulizzi, J., & Barrett, N. (2009). *Get Content Get Customers: Turn Prospects into Buyers with Content Marketing*. New York: McGraw-Hill.

Pullen, C., & Varley-Winter, O. (n.d.). Culture, coaching, and collaboration. *City & Guilds*. Retrieved from www.cityandguilds.com/~/media/Documents/about-us/broadsheetnews/Culture%20coaching%20and%20collaboration%20pdf.ashx

PWC. (2011). *PwC's NextGen: A global generational study: Evolving talent strategy to match the new workforce reality, Summary and compendium of findings*. Available at: https://www.pwc.com/gx/en/hr-management-services/pdf/pwc-nextgen-study-2013.pdf

PWC. (2015a). *The sharing economy*. Available at https://www.pwc.com/us/en/technology/publications/assets/pwc-consumer-intelligence series- the-sharing-economy.pdf

PWC. (2015b). *Sharing or paring? Growth of the sharing economy*. Retrieved June 2, 2019, from PWC: https://www.pwc.com/hu/en/kiadvanyok/assets/pdf/sharing-economy-en.pdf

Qi, J., Monod, E., Fang, B., & Deng, S. (2018). *Theories of Social Media: Philosophical Foundations*. Academic Press.

QuarkChain. (2019). *QuarkChain Resources: Get the latest on QuarkChain and the market*. Available at https://quarkchain.io/

Rae, D., & Carswell, M. (2001). Towards a conceptual understanding of entrepreneurial learning. *Journal of Small Business and Enterprise Development*, *8*(2), 150–158. doi:10.1108/EUM0000000006816

Rafiq, M., & Ahmed, P. (2000). Advances in the internal marketing concept: Definition, synthesis and extension. *Journal of Services Marketing*, *14*(6), 449–462. doi:10.1108/08876040010347589

Rafiq, M., & Ahmed, P. K. (1993). The scope of internal marketing: Defining the boundary between marketing and human resource management. *Journal of Marketing Management*, *9*(3), 219–232. doi:10.1080/0267257X.1993.9964234

Rajpal, M. S. & Kotov, V. (2014). *Understanding Crypto-Ransomware: In-Depth Analysis of the Most Popular Malware Families*. Bromium.

Raju, P. S., Lonial, S. C., & Crum, M. D. (2011). Market orientation in the context of SMEs: A conceptual framework. *Journal of Business Research*, *64*(12), 1320–1326. doi:10.1016/j.jbusres.2010.12.002

Rakic, M., & Rakic, B. (2014). Viral Marketing. *SSRN Electronic Journal*, *60*(4), 179–187. doi:10.2139srn.2561237

Rayle, L., Shaheen, S., Chan, N., Dai, D., & Cervero, R. (2014). *App-Based, On-Demand Ride Services: Comparing Taxi and Ridesourcing Trips and User Characteristics in San Francisco*. Working Paper.

Raynor, M. E. (2011). Disruption theory as a predictor of innovation success/failure. *Strategy and Leadership*, *39*(4), 27–30. doi:10.1108/10878571111147378

Razaei, S., & Valaei, N. (2017). Branding in a multichannel retail environment: Online stores vs app stores and the effect of product type. *Information Technology & People*, *30*(4), 853–886. doi:10.1108/ITP-12-2015-0308

Razmerita, L., & Kirchner, K. (2011). How wikis can be used to manage knowledge in SMEs: A case study. *Business Information Review*, *28*(3), 175–178. doi:10.1177/0266382111420354

Reality technology. (2019). *Augmented Reality*. Retrieved from https://www.realitytechnologies.com/augmented-reality/

Redstor. (2017). *Ransomware*. Retrieved from https://www.ict4.co.uk/Ransomware_e-book_rev2.pdf

Research Methodology. (n.d.). *An Introduction*. Available at: http://www.newagepublishers.com/samplechapter/000896.pdf

Resnick, S. M., Cheng, R., Simpson, M., & Lourenço, F. (2016). Marketing in SMEs: A "4Ps" self-branding model. *International Journal of Entrepreneurial Behaviour & Research*, *22*(1), 155–174. doi:10.1108/IJEBR-07-2014-0139

Reuters. (2019, March 27). US Census enlists Internet giants to fight fake news. *The Economic Times*. Retrieved from https://economictimes.indiatimes.com/news/international/world-news/us-census-enlists-internet-giants-to-fight-fake-news/articleshow/68604823.cms

Richardson, M., & Domingos, P. (2002, July). Mining knowledge-sharing sites for viral marketing. In *Proceedings of the Eighth ACM SIGKDD international conference on Knowledge discovery and data mining* (pp. 61-70). ACM. 10.1145/775047.775057

Richet, J.-L. (2016). Extortion on the Internet: The Rise of Crypto-Ransomware. *Harvard Researches*, *2*(1), 2–6.

Rieder, P., & Wyder, J. (1997). Economic and political framework for sustainability of mountain areas. In B. Messerii & J. D. Ives (Eds.), *Mountains of the world: A global priority* (pp. 85–102). New York, NY: Parthenon Press.

Rigby, D. (2011). The Future of Shopping. *Harvard Business Review*, *89*(12), 65–76.

Rinne, A. (2013). Position Paper: Young Global Leaders Sharing Economy Working Group. *World Economic Forum Young Global Leaders Taskforce: Circular Economy Innovation & New Business Models Initiative*. Retrieved from http://www.slideshare.net/ CollabLab/ygl-sharing-economy-position-paper-final-june-2013

Rizvi, J. (2018, November 9). *The NEws*. Retrieved July 24, 2019, from https://www.thenews.com.pk/print/391338-pakistan-s-urban-rural-mobile-ownership-divide-set-to-close-soon-study-shows

Robert, L. M., & John, H. J. (2008). *Human Resource Managment* (Vol. 12). Mason, OH: Thomson South-Western. Retrieved 07 10, 2019, from https://core.ac.uk/download/pdf/33797590.pdf

Robert, J.-M., & Lesage, A. (2011). From usability to user experience with user interfaces. In G. A. Boy (Ed.), *Handbook of Human-Computer Interaction: A Human-Cantered Design Approach* (pp. 303–332). Ashgate.

Robinson, T. (2008, March). Are You Courting millennials? *The Greentree Gazette*.

Robins, S. P. (1996). *Organisational Behavior: Concepts, Controversies, Applications* (7th ed.). Englewood Cliffs, NJ: Prentice-Hall.

Robson, K., Plangger, K., Kietzman, J. H., Mccarthy, L., & Pitt, L. (2015). Is it all a game? Understanding the principles of gamification. *Business Horizons*, *58*(4), 411–420. doi:10.1016/j.bushor.2015.03.006

Rocamora, A. (2002). Fields of Fashion: Critical Insights into Bourdieu's Sociology of Culture. *Journal of Consumer Culture*, *2*(3), 341–362. doi:10.1177/146954050200200303

Rocamora, A. (2011). Personal Fashion Blogs: Screens and Mirrors in Digital Self Portraits. *Fashion Theory*, *15*(4), 407–424. doi:10.2752/175174111X13115179149794

Roderick, B. J., Hollebeek, L. D., Biljana, J., & Ana, I. (2011). Customer Engagement Conceptual Domain, Fundamental Propositions & Implications for Research in Service Marketing. *Journal of Service Research*, *14*(3), 252–271. doi:10.1177/1094670511411703

Roe, E. M. (1996). Sustainable development and cultural theory. *International Journal of Sustainable Development and World Ecology*, *3*(2), 1–14. doi:10.1080/13504509609469919

Rogers, E. M. (1962). *Diffusion of innovations*. New York, NY: The Free Press.

Rogers, E. M. (2003). *Diffusion of Innovations* (5th ed.). New York: Free Press.

Rogers, J. C., & Williams, T. G. (1989). Comparative advertising effectiveness: Practitioners' perceptions versus academic research findings. *Journal of Advertising Research*, *29*(5), 22–37.

Romanosky, S. (2016). Examing the Costs and Causes of Cyber Incidents. *Journal of Cybersecurity*, *0*(0), 1–15.

Rose, R. L., & Wood, S. L. (2005). Paradox and the Consumption of Authenticity through Reality Television. *The Journal of Consumer Research*, *32*, 284–296. doi:10.1086/432238

Rosman, K. (2009, September 11). Fashion's Secret Helpers. *Wall Street Journal*.

Rouse, S. V. (2015). A reliability analysis of Mechanical Turk data. *Computers in Human Behavior*, *43*, 304–307. doi:10.1016/j.chb.2014.11.004

Rowley, J. (2008). Understanding digital content marketing. *Journal of Marketing Management*, *24*(5-6), 517–540. doi:10.1362/026725708X325977

Royal Mail. (2019). *Our story*. Author.

Roy, S. K., Blaji, M. S., Sadeque, S., Nguyen, B., & Melewar, T. C. (2017). Constituents and consequences of smart customer experience in retailing. *Technological Forecasting and Social Change*, *124*, 257–270. doi:10.1016/j.techfore.2016.09.022

Rubin, A., & Babbie, E. R. (1993). *Research methods for social work*. Pacific Grove, CA: Brooks/Cole.

Russell, J. A. (2003). Facial expressions of emotion: What lies beyond minimal universality? *Psychological Bulletin*, *118*, 379–391.

Russell, A. (2011). *Networked: A Contemporary History of News in Transition*. Cambridge, UK: Polity.

Russell, J. A. (2003). Core affect and the psychological construction of emotion. *Psychological Review*, *110*(1), 145–172. doi:10.1037/0033-295X.110.1.145 PMID:12529060

Rust, R. T., & Huang, M. H. (2014). The service revolution and the transformation of marketing science. *Marketing Science*, *33*(2), 206–221. doi:10.1287/mksc.2013.0836

Ruti, G., Dafni, B. A., Shimon, E., & Tomer, C. (2018). The effects of gamification elements in e-learning platforms. *Research, Organization, and Applied Innovation*, *6*(2), 37-53. Retrieved 7 10, 2019, from http://www.iiakm.org/ojakm/articles/2018/volume6_2/OJAKM_Volume6_2pp37-53.pdf

Ryan, D., & Jones, C. (2005). *Developing Strong Listening and Communication Skills*. doi:10.1017/CBO9781107415324.004

Ryan, R. M., & Deci, E. L. (2000). Intrinsic and extrinsic motivations: Classic definitions and new directions. *Contemporary Educational Psychology*, *25*(1), 54–67. doi:10.1006/ceps.1999.1020 PMID:10620381

S C Magazine. (2017). *Malware and the "Other" Platforms: Mac and Android Devices are Increasingly at Risk*. Available at: https://media.scmagazine.com/documents/314/malware_and_the_"other"_platfo_78268.pdf

Sacherer, J. (1976). *The Sherpas of Rolwaling Valley, North Nepal: A study in cultural ecology* (Unpublished PhD Thesis). University of Paris.

Sacks, D. (2011). *The sharing economy.* Fast Company 2011, April 11, Retrieved from http://www.fastcompany.com/magazine/155/the-sharing- economy.html

Saginova, O., & Belyansky, V. (2008). Facilitating innovations in higher education in transition economies. *International Journal of Educational Management*, *22*(4), 341–351. doi:10.1108/09513540810875671

Sahni, L. (2011). The impact of soft skill training induction programme on new entrants. *Management Edge*, *4*(2), 40–47.

Sakr, S. (2011). *Augmented Reality Goes Beyond Gimmicks For Business.* Accessed via http://www.bbc.co.uk/news/business-13262407

Sam-Liu, C. H., & Chou, F. C. (2016). Tourism Strategy development and facilitation of integrative processes among brand equity, marketing and motivation. *Tourism Management*, 298–308.

Samsara. (2019). *Centralized, Wireless Refrigeration and Environmental Monitoring*. Available at: https://www.samsara.com/uk/industrial/cold-chain

Sancha, C., Gimenez, C., Sierra, V., & Kazeminia, A. (2015). Does implementing social supplier development practices pay off? *Supply Chain Management*, *20*(4), 389–403. doi:10.1108/SCM-07-2014-0239

Sandeen, C. (2008). Boomers, Xers, and Millennials: Who Are They and What Do They Really Want from Continuing Higher Education? *Continuing Higher Education Review*, *72*, 11–31.

Sandeen, C. (2008). Millennials: Who are They and What Do They Really Want from Continuing Higher Education? *Continuing Higher Education Review*, *72*, 11–31.

Sanders, N. R. (2012). Supply chain management: A global perspective. Wiley Global Education.

Santos, L., Bago, J., Baptista, A. V., Ambrosio, S., Fonseca, H. M. A. C., & Quintas, H. (2016). The academic success of mature students in higher education: A Portuguese case study. *European Journal for Research on the Education and Learning of Adults*, *7*(1), 57–73. doi:10.3384/rela.2000-7426.rela9079

SAS. (2019). *History of Digital Marketing.* Available at: https://www.sas.com/en_gb/insights/marketing/digital-marketing.html

Saunders, M., & Lewis, P. (2012). *Doing research in business and management: an essential guide to planning your project.* Harlow, UK: Financial Times Prentice Hall.

Savage, K., Coogan, P., & Lau, H. (2015). The evolution of ransomware. *Security Response*, *6*, 57.

Savvides, L. (2019, June 22). *Samsung Pay: Everything you need to know (FAQ).* Retrieved from https://www.cnet.com/how-to/samsung-pay-everything-you-need-to-know-faq-mobile-wallet/

Schau & Gilly. (2003). We Are What We Post? Self-Presentation in Personal Web Space. *Journal of Consumer Research*, *30*, 385 404.

Schau, H. J., Russell, C., Crockett, D., Huff, A. D., Cotte, J., Bettany, S. M., ... Connell, P. M. (2012). Gender and Family Identity. *Advances in Consumer Research. Association for Consumer Research (U. S.)*, 40.

Schein, R., Wilson, K. & Keelan, J. (2010). *The effectiveness of the use of social media a report for peel public health.* Academic Press.

Scherer. (2005). Changes in EEG alpha power during simulated driving: a demonstration. *International Journal of Psychophysiology, 37*(2), 155–162.

Schimmoeller, M. (2017). Strategies For Success. Academic Press.

Schivinski, B. (2011). Effects of social media communication on brand equity and brand purchase intention. *Interdisciplinary Journal, 2*, 157–162.

Schivinski, B., & Dabrowski, D. (2016). The effect of social media communication on consumer perceptions of brands. *Journal of Marketing Communications, 22*(2), 189–214. doi:10.1080/13527266.2013.871323

Schivinski, B., Muntinga, D. G., Pontes, H. M., & Lukasik, P. (2019). Influencing COBRAs: The effects of brand equity on the consumer's propensity to engage with brand-related content on social media. *Journal of Strategic Marketing*, 1–23. doi:10.1080/0965254X.2019.1572641

Schlossberg, M. (2018). *Teen Generation Z is being called 'millenials on steroids', and that could be terrifying for retailers*. Retrieved from Business Insider UK: http://uk.businessinsider.com/millennials-vs-gen-z-2016-2

Schmitt, B. (1999). Experiential Marketing. *Journal of Marketing Management, 15*(1), 53–67. doi:10.1362/026725799784870496

Schneider, B. (1990). *Organizational Climate and Culture*. San Francisco, CA: Jossey-Bass Publishers.

Schon, D. A. (1963). *Reflection of concepts*. New York, NY: Humanities Press.

Schroeder, J. E. (2006). 23 Critical visual analysis. Handbook of qualitative research methods in marketing. Academic Press.

Schroeder, J.E. (1998). Consuming representation: A visual approach to consumer research. *Voices, views, and visions*, 193.

Schroeder, J. E. (2005). *Visual consumption* (Vol. 4). Essex, UK: Psychology Press.

Schroeder, J. E., & Borgerson, J. L. (1998). Marketing images of gender: A visual analysis. *Consumption Markets & Culture, 2*(2), 161–201. doi:10.1080/10253866.1998.9670315

Schroeder, J. E., & Borgerson, J. L. (2015). Critical visual analysis of gender: Reactions and reflections. *Journal of Marketing Management, 31*(15-16), 1723–1731. doi:10.1080/0267257X.2015.1077883

Schroeder, J. E., & Zwick, D. (2004). Mirrors of masculinity: Representation and identity in advertising images. *Consumption Markets & Culture, 7*(1), 21–52. doi:10.1080/1025386042000212383

Schroeder, R. (2018). Towards a theory of digital media. *Information Communication and Society, 21*(3), 323–339. doi:10.1080/1369118X.2017.1289231

Schwandt, F. (2018, February 25). *Mobile Application Revenue*. Retrieved from http://www.statista.com

Schwedel, A., Root, J., & Allen, J. (2017). *3,000 Years of Business History in Two Minutes*. London: Bain and Company.

Seaborn, K., & Fels, D. I. (2015). Gamification in theory and action: A survey. *International Journal of Human-Computer Studies, 74*, 14–31. doi:10.1016/j.ijhcs.2014.09.006

Secundo, G., Schiuma, G., & Passiante, G. (2017). Entrepreneurial learning dynamics in knowledge-intensive enterprises. *International Journal of Entrepreneurial Behaviour & Research, 23*(3), 366–380. doi:10.1108/IJEBR-01-2017-0020

Securonix Threat Research Team. (2018). *Grandcrab Ransomware Attack*. Securonix.

Senge, P. (1990). *The Fifth Discipline*. London: Random House.

Seuring, S., & Gold, S. (2013). Sustainability management beyond corporate boundaries: From stakeholders to performance. *Journal of Cleaner Production*, *56*, 1–6. doi:10.1016/j.jclepro.2012.11.033

Shabani, N., & Hassan, A. (2017). Augmented reality for tourism service promotion in Iran as an emerging market. In V. Nadda, S. S. Dadwal, & R. Rahimi (Eds.), *Promotional strategies and new service opportunities in emerging economies* (pp. 116–129). Hershey, PA: IGI Global. doi:10.4018/978-1-5225-2206-5.ch005

Shackelford, S. J. (2014). Managing Cyber Attacks in International Law, Business, and Relations. In *Search of Cyber Peace*. Cambridge, UK: Cambridge University Press. doi:10.1017/CBO9781139021838

Shahid, J. (2017, July 1). *DAWN*. Retrieved July 24, 2019, from https://www.dawn.com/news/1342511

Shaikh, N. (2017, July 17). *The Financial Industry Needs to Start Planning for the Next 50 Years, Not the Next Five*. Retrieved from https://hbr.org/2017/07/the-financial-industry-needs-to-start-planning-for-the-next-50-years-not-the-next-five

Shambhavi. (2019, Jan 10). A Rs 120-cr WhatsApp message to fight fake news. *The Economic Times*. Retrieved from https://economictimes.indiatimes.com/tech/internet/a-rs-120-cr-whatsapp-message-to-fight-fake-news/articleshow/67464732.cms

Shankar, V., Inman, J. J., Mantrala, M., Kelley, E., & Rizley, R. (2011). Innovations in shopper marketing: Current insights and future research issues. *Journal of Retailing*, *87*(1), 29–42. doi:10.1016/j.jretai.2011.04.007

Shaw, E. (2006). Small Firm Networking: An Insight into Contents and Motivating Factors. *International Small Business Journal*, *24*(1), 5–29. doi:10.1177/0266242606059777

Shaw, S. (2005). The corporate university: Global or local phenomenon? *Journal of European Industrial Training*, *29*(1), 21–39. doi:10.1108/03090590510576190

Shaw, S., & Fairhurst, D. (2008). Engaging a new generation of graduates. *Education + Training*, *50*(5), 366–378. doi:10.1108/00400910810889057

Shen, C., Huang, C. Y., Chu, C. H., & Liao, H. C. (2010). Virtual community loyalty: An interpersonal-interaction perspective. *International Journal of Electronic Commerce*, *15*(1), 49–73. doi:10.2753/JEC1086-4415150102

Shergill, G., & Nargundkar, R. (2005). Market orientation, marketing innovation as performance drivers: Extending the paradigm. *Journal of Global Marketing*, *19*(1), 27–44. doi:10.1300/J042v19n01_03

Sherr, I. (2019, July 25). *Facebook's $5 billion FTC fine is just the start of its problems*. Retrieved from https://www.cnet.com/news/facebooks-5-billion-ftc-fine-is-just-the-start-of-its-problems/

Sheth, J., Sisodia, R., & Sharan, A. (2000). The antecedents and consequences of customer-centric marketing. *Journal of the Academy of Marketing Science*, *28*(1), 55–66. doi:10.1177/0092070300281006

Shojaee, S., & Azman, A. B. (2013). An evaluation of factors affecting brand awareness in the context of social media in Malaysia. *Asian Social Science*, *9*(17), 72. doi:10.5539/ass.v9n17p72

Shugan, S. (2006). Editorial: Who Is Afraid to Give Freedom of Speech to Marketing Folks? *Marketing Science*, *25*(5), 403–410. doi:10.1287/mksc.1060.0236

Simões, J., Redondo, R. D., & Vilas, A. F. (2013). A social gamification framework for a K-6 learning platform. *Computers in Human Behavior*, *29*(2), 345–353. doi:10.1016/j.chb.2012.06.007

Simoiu, C., Symantec, C. G., Bonneau, J., & Goel, S. (2019). “I was told to buy a software or lose my computer. I ignored it”: A study of ransomware. *USENIX Symposium on Usable Privacy and Security (SOUPS) 2019.* Retrieved from https://5harad.com/papers/ransomware.pdf

Simons, G. (2008). Marketing to postmodern consumers: Introducing Internet chameleon. *European Journal of Marketing*, *42*(3/4), 299–310. doi:10.1108/03090560810852940

Singh, G., & Singh, M. (2018). Social Media Ambiance Can Make Strong Message for Consumer Brand Purchase Behavior. *International Journal of Online Marketing*, *8*(4), 38–48. doi:10.4018/IJOM.2018100103

Singh, S., & Sonnenburg, S. (2012). Brand performances in social media. *Journal of Interactive Marketing*, *26*(4), 189–197. doi:10.1016/j.intmar.2012.04.001

Sirgy, M. J. (1991). Self-Concept in Consumer Behaviour: A Critical Review. *The Journal of Consumer Research*, *9*, 287–300.

Sivarajah, U., Kamal, M. M., Irani, Z., & Weerakkody, V. (2017). Critical analysis of Big Data challenges and analytical methods. *Journal of Business Research*, *70*, 263–286. doi:10.1016/j.jbusres.2016.08.001

Skinner, H. (2008). The emergence and development of place marketing’s confused identity. *Journal of Marketing Management*, *24*(9/10), 915–928. doi:10.1362/026725708X381966

Skute, I. (2014). Brand Equity and Co-Creation Potential in the Social Media Environment: An Analysis of Brand Engagement with Community Influencers. In *3rd IBA Bachelor Thesis Conference* (pp. 1–18). Retrieved from https://pdfs.semanticscholar.org/bbca/f99ce0bb43acaabc8bd0da60a200ca79c9ab.pdf

Slack, N., Chambers, S., & Johnston, R. (2010). Operations management (6th ed.). Pearson Education.

Slater, S. F., & Narver, J. C. (1995). The Positive Effect of a Market Orientation. *Journal of Business Research*, *48*(1), 69–73. doi:10.1016/S0148-2963(98)00077-0

Sloan, J. (2018, October 2). *Why Financial Institutions Can Bank on Digital Innovation for Millennials*. Academic Press.

SmartInsights. (2019). *Marketing personas*. Retrieved July 17, 2019, from https://www.smartinsights.com/persuasion-marketing/marketing-personas/

Smith, A. N., Fischer, E., & Chen, Y. (2011). *Value Creation in Brand-Related User-Generated Content on YouTube*. Paper presented at the Association for Consumer Research Conference, St. Louis, MO.

Smith, K. T. (2011). Digital Marketing Strategies that Millennials Find Appealing, Motivating, or Just Annoying. Dr. Katherine Taken Smith Department of Marketing Texas A & M Univer. *Journal of Strategic Marketing*, *19*(6), 489–499. doi:10.1080/0965254X.2011.581383

Smith, M. (2017). Arming students against bad information. *Phi Delta Kappan*, *99*(3), 56–58. doi:10.1177/0031721717739595

Sneed, A. (2016). *The Most Vulnerable Ransomware Targets Are the Institutions We Rely On Most*. Scientific American.

Snow, J. (2016). *Ransomware on mobile devices: knock-knock-block*. Available at: https://www.kaspersky.com/blog/mobile-ransomware-2016/12491/

Snuggs, E., & Jevons, C. (2018). Reconceptualising the scholarship of marketing education – SoME futurescapes. *Australasian Marketing Journal*, *26*(2), 180–186. doi:10.1016/j.ausmj.2018.05.003

Snyman, R., & Kruger, C. J. (2004). The interdependency between strategic management and strategic knowledge management. *Journal of Knowledge Management*, *8*(1), 5–19. doi:10.1108/13673270410523871

Solomon, M. (2008). Consumer behaviour: a European perspective (3rd ed.). Lars Parner.

Soni, V. (2018). *Multifunctional malware becoming extensive in 2018, finds Kaspersky Lab report.* Available at: https://www.dailyhostnews.com/multifunctional-malware-becoming-extensive/

Sorescu, A., Frambach, R. T., Singh, J., Rangaswamy, A., & Bridges, C. (2011). Innovations in Retail Business Models. *Journal of Retailing*, *87*, 3–16. doi:10.1016/j.jretai.2011.04.005

Sotiriadis, M. D. (2016). Sharing tourism experiences in social media; a literature review and a set of suggested business strategies. *International Journal of Contemporary Hospitality Management*, *27*(1), 179–225. doi:10.1108/IJCHM-05-2016-0300

Soto-Acosta, P., Popa, S., & Palacios-Marqués, D. (2017). Social web knowledge sharing and innovation performance in knowledge-intensive manufacturing SMEs. *The Journal of Technology Transfer*, *42*(2), 425–440. doi:10.100710961-016-9498-z

Sousa, M. J., & Rocha, A. (2018). Skills for disruptive digital business. *Journal of Business Research*, *94*, 257–263. doi:10.1016/j.jbusres.2017.12.051

Souse, M. J., Carmo, M., Goncalves, A. C., Cruz, R., & Martins, J. M. (2018). Creating knowledge and entrepreneurial capacity for HE students with digital education methodologies: Differences in the perceptions of students and entrepreneurs. *Journal of Business Research*, *94*, 227–240. doi:10.1016/j.jbusres.2018.02.005

Soylu, A., Oruç, C., Turkay, M., Fujita, K., & Asakura, T. (2006). Synergy analysis of collaborative supply chain management in energy systems using multi-period MILP. *European Journal of Operational Research*, *174*(1), 387–403. doi:10.1016/j.ejor.2005.02.042

Spender, J. C. (1996). Making Knowledge the Basis of A Dynamic Theory of the Firm. *Strategic Management Journal*, *17*(S2), 45–62. doi:10.1002mj.4250171106

Spreitzer, G. M. (1992). *When organisations dare: the dynamics of individual empowerment in the workplace* (PhD dissertation). University of Michigan, Ann Arbor, MI.

SRAF. (2019). *Software Repository for Accounting and Finance*. Available at: https://sraf.nd.edu/textual-analysis/resources/#Master%20Dictionary

Srinivasan, R., & Swink, M. (2018). An investigation of visibility and flexibility as complements to supply chain analytics: An organizational information processing theory perspective. *Production and Operations Management*, *27*(10), 1849–1867. doi:10.1111/poms.12746

Srivastava, R., Shervani, T., & Fahey, L. (1999). Marketing, business processes, and shareholder value: An organizational embedded view of marketing activities and the discipline of marketing. *Journal of Marketing*, *63*(4_suppl1), 168–179. doi:10.1177/00222429990634s116

Stafford, C., & Mearns, M.A. (2009). What happens when organisations embrace social networking? Knowledge sharing at a multinational business solutions corporation. *South African Journal of Information Management, 11*(4).

Stanford CS221. (2013). *Deep Blue*. Stanford.

Starbucks. (2013). *My Starbucks Rewards. Starbucks Coffee Company*. Retrieved January 7, 2019, from http://www.starbucks.ca/card/rewards

Starcom. (2018). *Starcom România lansează ediţia 2017 a studiului Consumer Report*. Retrieved from IQAds: https://www.iqads.ro/articol/40927/starcom-romania-lanseaza-editia-2017-a-studiului-consumer-report

Startsev, D. (2017, April 25). *Data-Driven Marketing: Vision to Reality*. Retrieved from Wallstreet journal: https://deloitte.wsj.com/cmo/2017/04/25/data-driven-marketing-vision-to-reality/

Statista. (2015a). *Number of Facebook users*. Retrieved from www.statista.com/statistics/264810/number-of-monthly-active-facebook-users-worldwide/

Statista. (2015b). *Number of monthly active Twitter users*. Retrieved from www.statista.com/statistics/282087/number-of-monthly-active-twitter-users/

Statista. (2018a). *eCommerce Romania*. Retrieved from Statista: https://www.statista.com/outlook/243/148/ecommerce/romania#market-age

Statista. (2018b). *Number of smartphone users worldwide from 2014 to 2020 (in billions)*. Retrieved from Statista: https://www.statista.com/statistics/330695/number-of-smartphone-users-worldwide/

Statsta. (2019). *Ride Hailing*. Retrieved July 04, 2019, from https://www.statista.com: https://www.statista.com/outlook/368/100/ride-hailing/worldwide#market-revenue

Stavrou, A. (2010). *Malware detector.* USA Patent No. US8935773B2.

Stealcase Education. (n.d.). *Technology Empowered Learning*. Retrieved from https://www.steelcase.com/research/articles/topics/technology/technology-empowered-learning-six-spatial-insights/

SteimleJ. (2019, July 11). www.forbes.com. Retrieved from www.forbes.com: https://www.forbes.com/sites/joshsteimle/2014/09/19/what-is-content-marketing/#6f6bda8210b9

Sterne, J., & Priore, A. (2000). *Email marketing: using email to reach your target audience and build customer relationships*. John Wiley & Sons, Inc.

Stern, L., & Reve, T. (1980). Distribution Channels as Political Economies: A Framework for Comparative Analysis. *Journal of Marketing*, *44*(3), 52–64. doi:10.1177/002224298004400306

Stevens, L., & Maclaran, P. (2007). Exploring the Celtic narrative in advertising: Goddess culture and the lexicon of perfumery. *Journal of Strategic Marketing*, *15*(1), 29–39. doi:10.1080/09652540601129973

Stokes, D., & Nelson, C. (2013). Word of Mouth to Word of Mouse: Social Media and the Entrepreneur. In Z. Sethna, R. Jones, & P. Harrigan (Eds.), *Entrepreneurial Marketing: Global Perspectives*. Bingley, UK: Emerald Group Publishing Limited.

Stolze, J. H., Mollenkopf, A. D., Thornton, L., Brusco, M. J., & Flint, D. J. (2018). Supply Chain and Marketing Integration: Tension in Frontline Social Networks. *The Journal of Supply Chain Management*, *54*(3), 3–21. doi:10.1111/jscm.12169

Storey, D. (2016). *Understanding the small business sector*. Routledge. doi:10.4324/9781315544335

Story, V., O'Malley, L., & Hart, S. (2011). Roles, role performance, and radical innovation competencies. *Industrial Marketing Management*, *40*(6), 952–966. doi:10.1016/j.indmarman.2011.06.025

Stratopoulos, T. (2018). *Blockchain Technology Adoption*. SSRN Electronic Journal. doi:10.2139srn.3188470

Suchman, M. (1995). Managing Legitimacy: Strategic and Institutional Approaches. *Academy of Management Review, 20*(3), 571-610.

Sundar, S., Hatfield Edwards, H., Yifeng Hu, H., & Stavrositu, C. (2007). Blogging for better Health: Putting the 'Public' back in Public Health. In M. Tremayne (Ed.), *Blogging, Citizenship, and the Future of the Media* (pp. 83–97). New York: Routledge.

Sun, J., Yan, J., & Zhang, K. (2016). Blockchain-based sharing services: What blockchain technology can contribute to smart cities. *Financial Innovation*, *2*(1), 26. doi:10.118640854-016-0040-y

Sun, P., & Anderson, M. (2010). An examination of the relationship between absorptive capacity and organisational learning. *International Journal of Management Reviews*, *12*(2), 130–150. doi:10.1111/j.1468-2370.2008.00256.x

Sun, S. (2011). The Internet Effects on Students Communication at Zhengzhou Institute of Aeronautical Industry Management. Advances in Computer Science, Environment. *Ecoinformatics and Education*, *5*(11), 418–422.

Suraj Srinivasan, W. C. (2019, June 18). *Research: Investors Reward Companies That Talk Up Their Digital Initiatives*. Retrieved July 25, 2019, from https://hbr.org/2019/06/research-investors-reward-companies-that-talk-up-their-digital-initiatives

Svensson, G. (2002). Supply chain management: The re-integration of marketing issues and logistics theory and practice. *European Business Review*, *14*(6), 426–436. doi:10.1108/09555340210448785

Taherdoost, H. (2018). A review of technology acceptance and adoption models and theories. *Procedia Manufacturing*, *22*, 960–967. doi:10.1016/j.promfg.2018.03.137

Tammpuu, P., & Masso, A. (2018). 'Welcome to the virtual state': Estonian e-residency and the digitalised state as a commodity. *European Journal of Cultural Studies*, *21*(5), 543–560. doi:10.1177/1367549417751148

Tasril, V., Ginting, M. B., Mardiana, & Siahaan, A. P. U. (2017). Threats of Computer System and its Prevention. *IJSRST*, *3*(6), 448-451.

Taylor, D., & Strutton, D. (2016). Does Facebook usage lead to conspicuous consumption? The role of envy, narcissism and self-promotion. *Journal of Research in Interactive Marketing*, *10*(3), 231–248. doi:10.1108/JRIM-01-2015-0009

Technorati. (2008). Retrieved from www.technocrati.com/blogging/state-of-the-blogosphere

Teece, D. J. (2010). Business Models, Business Strategy and Innovation. *Long Range Planning*, *43*(2), 172–194. doi:10.1016/j.lrp.2009.07.003

Teece, D. J., Pisano, G., & Shuen, A. (1997). Dynamic Capabilities and Strategic Management. *Strategic Management Journal*, *18*(7), 509–533. doi:10.1002/(SICI)1097-0266(199708)18:7<509::AID-SMJ882>3.0.CO;2-Z

Telefonica. (2019). *Telefónica and IBM Collaborate to Apply Blockchain to Streamline Telco Processes*. Available at: https://www.telefonica.com/en/web/press-office/-/telefonica-and-ibm-collaborate-to-apply-blockchain-to-streamline-telco-processes

Teller, C., & Elms, J. R. (2010). Managing the attractiveness of evolved and created retail agglomerations formats. *Marketing Intelligence & Planning*, *28*(1), 25–45. doi:10.1108/02634501011014598

The Australian Small Business and Family Enterprise Ombudsman. (2017). *Cyber Security: The Small Business Best Practice Guide Cyber Security: A Small Business Best Practice Guide*. Retrieved from www.itsanhonour.gov.au

The Daily Telegraph. (2016). *The Himalayas: Trip of a Lifetime*. Retrieved from: http://www.oxforddictionaries.com/definition/english/process

The International Organisation of the Standardisation. (1998). *Ergonomics of human system interaction - Part 210: Human-cantered design for interactive systems (formerly known as 13407)*. Author.

The Mentionltyics. (2019). *Future augmented reality and social media*. Available at: https://www.mentionlytics.com/blog/how-augmented-reality-will-influence-future-social-media-trends/?fbclid=IwAR19EVpTUA1FfeOO2ANV--XG-tzjDebkZlxRXjm23kG3Shu9prTAzr-zkpc

Thompson, C. J. (1996). Caring consumers: Gendered consumption meanings and the juggling lifestyle. *The Journal of Consumer Research*, *22*(4), 388–407. doi:10.1086/209457

Thompson, C. J. (2014). The politics of consumer identity work. *The Journal of Consumer Research*, *40*(5), iii–vii. doi:10.1086/673381

Thompson, C. J., & Üstüner, T. (2015). Women skating on the edge: Marketplace performances as ideological edgework. *The Journal of Consumer Research*, *42*(2), 235–265. doi:10.1093/jcr/ucv013

Thornton, S. (1996). *Club Cultures: Music, Media, and Subcultural Capital*. Middletown, CT: Wesleyan University Press.

Tiago, M. T. P. M. B., & Veríssimo, J. M. C. (2014). Digital marketing and social media: Why bother? *Business Horizons*, *57*(6), 703–708. doi:10.1016/j.bushor.2014.07.002

Tian, F. J., & Li, Z. Y. (2007). Study on Choosing of Enterprise"s Market Innovation Domain and Its Venture-eluding. *Science and Management of S. & T.*, *28*(12), 68–72.

Timmermans, H. J. P. (1982). Consumer choice of shopping centre: An information integration approach. *Regional Studies*, *16*(3), 171–182. doi:10.1080/09595238200185201

Timothly Lyman, K. L. (2015). What is Digital Financial Inclusion and Why Does it Matter? *CGAP*. Retrieved from http://www.cgap.org/blog/what-digital-financial-inclusion-and-why-does-it-matter

Todorova, G., & Durisin, B. (2007). Absorptive Capacity: Valuing a Reconceptualization. *Academy of Management Review*, *32*(3), 774–786. doi:10.5465/amr.2007.25275513

Toffler, A. (1980). *The Third Wave*. William Morrow.

Touchette, F. (2016). The evolution of malware. *Network Security*, *1*(1), 11–14. doi:10.1016/S1353-4858(16)30008-3

Tractinsky, N. (2007) Aesthetics in Information Technology: Motivation and Future Research Directions. In Human - Computer Interaction in Management Information Systems: Foundations. M.E. Sharpe.

Tracy, D. (2002). On Theological Education: A Reflection. In R. L. Peterson & N. M. Rourke (Eds.), *Theological Literacy for the Twenty-First Century* (pp. 13–22). Grand Rapids, MI: Eerdmans.

Tradelens. (2019a). *Digitalising the Global Supply Chain*. Available at: https://www.tradelens.com/

Tradelens. (2019b). *Early Adopter Programme*. Available at: https://www.tradelens.com/

Trainor, K. J., Andzulis, J., Rapp, A., & Agnihotri, R. (2014). Social media technology usage and customer relationship performance: A capabilities-based examination of social CRM. *Journal of Business Research*, *67*(6), 1201–1208. doi:10.1016/j.jbusres.2013.05.002

Tremayne, M. (2007b). Introduction: Examining the Blog-Media Relationship. In M. Tremayne (Ed.), *Blogging, Citizenship, and the Future of the Media* (pp. x–xvi). New York: Routledge.

Tremayne, M. (Ed.). (2007a). *Blogging, Citizenship, and the Future of the Media*. New York: Routledge.

Trivedi, N., Adomako Asamoah, D., & Doran, D. (2018). Keep the conversations going: Engagement-based customer segmentation on online social service platforms. *Information Systems Frontiers*, *20*(2), 239–257. doi:10.100710796-016-9719-x

Trusov, M., Bucklin, R. E., & Pauwels, K. (2009). Effects of word-of-mouth versus traditional marketing: Findings from an internet social networking site. *Journal of Marketing*, *73*(5), 90–102. doi:10.1509/jmkg.73.5.90

Tsai, M. T. (2000). *The research for influence of market information process and organisation memory on marketing innovation*. National Chengchi University.

Tsai, S. P. (2006). Investigating archetype-icon transformation in brand marketing. *Marketing Intelligence & Planning*, *24*(6), 648–663. doi:10.1108/02634500610701708

Tsai, Y. F., & Tang, T. W. (2008). How to improve service quality: Internal marketing as a determining factor. *Total Quality Management*, *19*(11), 1117–1126. doi:10.1080/14783360802323479

Tseng-Lung, H., & Hsu, L. F. (2014). Formation of augmented-reality interactive technology's persuasive effects from the perspective of experiential value. *Internet Research*, *24*(1), 82–109. doi:10.1108/IntR-07-2012-0133

Tsichla, E., & Zotos, Y. (2016). Gender portrayals revisited: Searching for explicit and implicit stereotypes in Cypriot magazine advertisements. *International Journal of Advertising*, *35*(6), 983–1007. doi:10.1080/02650487.2016.1189250

Tsiotsou, R., & Ratten, V. (2010). Future research directions in tourism marketing. *Marketing Intelligence & Planning*, *28*(4), 533–544. doi:10.1108/02634501011053702

Tsukayama, H. (2016, May 21). *Internet addiction is costing young people their jobs and social lives*. Retrieved July 07, 2019, from https://www.independent.co.uk/life-style/gadgets-and-tech/this-dark-side-of-the-internet-is-costing-young-people-their-jobs-and-social-lives-a7041451.html

Tudor, S., & Mendez, R. (2014). Lessons from Covey: Win-win principles for university-employer engagement. *Journal of Higher Education, Skills and Work-Based Learning*, *4*(3), 213–227. doi:10.1108/HESWBL-06-2014-0018

Turner, G. (2010). *Ordinary People and the Media: The Demotic Turn*. Los Angeles, CA: Sage.

Turpin, S., & Harmsworth, S. (2001). *Creating an Effective Dissemination Strategy An Expanded Interactive Workbook for Educational Development Projects*. Available at: https://ajpp-online.org/resources/downloads/06-CreatingAnEffectiveDisseminationStrategy-AnExpandedWorkbook.pdf

Tussyadiah, I. P. (2015). An exploratory study on drivers and deterrents of collaborative consumption in travel. In I. Tussyadiah & A. Inversini (Eds.), *Information & Communication Technologies in Tourism 2015 Switzerland*. Springer International Publishing. doi:10.1007/978-3-319-14343-9_59

Tussyadiah, I. P. (2016). Factors of satisfaction and intention to use peer-to-peer accommodation. *International Journal of Hospitality Management*, *55*, 70–80. doi:10.1016/j.ijhm.2016.03.005

Tussyadiah, I. P., & Pesonen, J. (2015). Impacts of peer-to-peer accommodation use on travel patterns. *Journal of Travel Research*. doi:10.1177/0047287515608505

Tuten, T. L., & Solomon, M. R. (2017). Social media marketing. *Sage (Atlanta, Ga.)*.

Twenge, J. (2007). *Generation Me: Why today's young Americans are more confident, assertive, entitled and more miserable than ever before?* Free Press.

Tyler, T. (2002). Is the Internet changing social life? It seems the more things change, the more they stay the same. *The Journal of Social Issues*, *58*(1), 195–205. doi:10.1111/1540-4560.00256

Uber. (2016, September 22). *Why we introduced cash payments*. Retrieved from Uber: https://www.uber.com/en-PK/blog/pkcash/

Uber. (2019). *Uber to Acquire Careem To Expand the Greater Middle East Regional Opportunity Together*. Author.

Ueki, Y. (2016). Customer pressure, customer–manufacturer–supplier relationships, and quality control performance. *Journal of Business Research*, *69*(6), 2233–2238. doi:10.1016/j.jbusres.2015.12.035

Ungerman, O., Dedkova, J., & Gurinova, K. (2018). The Impact Of Marketing Innovation On The Competitiveness Of Enterpris-Es In The Context Of Industry 4.0. *Journal of Competitiveness*, *4*(2), 132–147. doi:10.7441/joc.2018.02.09

Unibright. (2019). *The Unified Framework for Blockchain Based Business Integration*. Available at: https://unibright.io/

Upadhyay, M. P. (1984). *Environmental impact on mountain ecosystem by trekkers and mountaineers: Mt. Everest Trek Route Survey Report*. Kathmandu: NAIS.

Vaidya, A. &. (2016). *Mobile Phone usage amongst the youth.*

Vajre, S. (2016). *Account-Based Marketing for Dummies*. Dummies.

Valente, T. W. (1996). Social Network Thresholds in the Diffusion of Innovations. *Social Networks*, *18*(1), 69–89. doi:10.1016/0378-8733(95)00256-1

Vallio. (1998). Disruptive technologies: The new reality will be augmented. *Customer Relationship Management Magazine*.

Van de Glind, P. B. (2013). *The Consumer Potential of Collaborative Consumption*. Utrecht: Utrecht University.

Van den Bosch, F., Van Wijk, R., & Volberda, H. W. (2003). Absorptive capacity: antecedents, models and outcomes. In M. Easterby-Smith & M. A. Lyles (Eds.), *The Blackwell Handbook of Organizational Learning and Knowledge Management*. Oxford, UK: Blackwell.

Van der Haijden, H. (2006). User Acceptance of Hedonic Information System. *Management Information Systems Quarterly*, *28*(4), 695–704. doi:10.2307/25148660

Van der Heijden, H., Verhagen, T., & Creemers, M. (2003). Understanding online purchase intentions: Contributions from technology and trust perspectives. *European Journal of Information Systems*, *12*(1), 41–48. doi:10.1057/palgrave.ejis.3000445

Van Schaik, P., & Ling, J. (2008). The role of context in perceptions of the aesthetics of web pages over time. *International Journal of Human-Computer Studies*, *67*(1), 79–89. doi:10.1016/j.ijhcs.2008.09.012

Varey, R. J. (1995). Internal marketing: A review and some interdisciplinary research challenges. *International Journal of Service Industry Management*, *6*(1), 40–63. doi:10.1108/09564239510078849

Varey, R. J., & Lewis, B. R. (1999). A broadened conception of internal marketing. *European Journal of Marketing*, *33*(9), 926–944. doi:10.1108/03090569910285869

Vassilios, Z., & Nikolaos, B. (n.d.). *Contextualizing Phenomenology in Event Management Research: Deciphering the Meaning of Event Experiences*. Retrieved Mqy 2, 2019, from http://eprints.leedsbeckett.ac.uk/143/1/Contextualizing%20Phenomenology%20in%20Event%20Management%20Research.pdf

VeChain. (2019). *VeChainThor: The public blockchain that derives its value from activities created by members within the ecosystem solving real world economic problems*. Available at: https://www.vechain.org/

Venkat. (2019, April 02). Facebook takes down Pak military-linked pages targeting India ahead of Lok Sabha polls. *The Economic Times*. Retrieved from https://economictimes.indiatimes.com/news/elections/lok-sabha/india/facebook-takes-down-pakistan-military-backed-pages-targeting-india-ahead-of-ls-polls/articleshow/68668722.cms

Venkatesh, V., & Bala, H. (2008). Technology Acceptance Model 3 and a Research Agenda on Interventions. *Decision Sciences*, *39*(2), 273–314. doi:10.1111/j.1540-5915.2008.00192.x

Venkatesh, V., Morris, M. G., Davis, G. B., & Davis, F. D. (2003). User acceptance of information technology: Toward a unified view. *Management Information Systems Quarterly*, *27*(3), 425–478. doi:10.2307/30036540

Venkatesh, V., Thong, J. Y. L., & Xu, X. (2012). Consumer acceptance and use of information technology: extending the unified theory of acceptance and use of Technology. *Management Information Systems Quarterly*, *36*(1), 157–178. doi:10.2307/41410412

Venkatesh, V., Thong, J. Y., & Xu, X. (2012). Consumer acceptance and use of information technology: Extending the unified theory of acceptance and use of technology. MIS Quarterly: Management. *Information Systems*, *36*(1), 157–178.

Verba, S., Schlozman, K. L., & Brady, H. E. (1995). *Voice and equality: Civic voluntarism in American politics*. Cambridge, MA: Harvard University Press.

Verhoef, P. C., Kannan, P. K., & Inman, J. J. (2015). From Multi-Channel Retailing to Omni-Channel Retailing: Introduction to the Special Issue on Multi-Channel Retailing. *Journal of Retailing*, *91*(2), 174–181. doi:10.1016/j.jretai.2015.02.005

Verizon Enterprise Solutions. (2014). *Verizon 2014 data breach investigations report*. Available at: www.verizonenterprise.com/DBIR/2014/

Verizon Enterprise Solutions. (2015). *Verizon 2015 data breach investigations report*. Available at: www.verizonenterprise.com/DBIR/2015/

Verizon Enterprise Solutions. (2016). *Verizon 2016 data breach investigations report*. Available at: www.verizonenterprise.com/verizon-insights-lab/dbir/2016/

Verizon. (2017). *DBIR 2017 Report*. Verizon.

Verma, J. P., Agrawal, S., Patel, B., & Patel, A. (2016). Big data analytics: Challenges and applications for text, audio, video, and social media data. *International Journal on Soft Computing, Artificial Intelligence and Applications, 5*(1).

Vie Publique. (2019). *The Directorate of Legal and Administrative Information*. Available at: http://discours.vie-publique.fr/notices/197000414.html

Vincent. (2005). Exploring consumers' attitude towards relationship marketing. *Journal of Services Marketing, 29*(3), 188-199.

Visa. (2019a). *Central Bank Digital Currencies*. Available at: https://usa.visa.com/run-your-business/small-business-tools/retail.html

Visa. (2019b). *Small Business Tools*. Available at: https://usa.visa.com/run-your-business/small-business-tools/retail.html

Volkswagen. (2009). Rolighetsteorin. *YouTube*. Retrieved January 7th, 2019, from http://www.youtube.com/user/Rolighetsteorin

Von Briel, F. (2018). The future of omnichannel retail: A four-stage Delphi study. *Technological Forecasting and Social Change*, *132*, 217–229. doi:10.1016/j.techfore.2018.02.004

Vries, L., Gensler, S., & Leeflang, P. (2012). Popularity of brand posts on brand fan pages: An investigation of the effects of social media marketing. *Journal of Interactive Marketing*, *26*(2), 83–91. doi:10.1016/j.intmar.2012.01.003

Vukasovic, T. (2013). Building a successful brand by using social networking media. *Journal of Media and Communication Studies*, *5*(6), 56.

Waddington, S. (2015). *The internet is a conversation*. Retrieved from http://wadds.co.uk/2015/11/04/internet-conversation/

Wainwright, O. (2015). Body-hackers: the people who turn themselves into cyborgs. *The Guardian*.

Walasek, K., Bhatia, S., & Brown, G. D. A. (2018). Positional goods and the social rank hypothesis: Income inequality affects online chatter about high- and low-status brands on Twitter. *Journal of Consumer Psychology*, *28*(1), 138–148. doi:10.1002/jcpy.1012

Walker, J. (2018). *Ransomware remains biggest malware threat in 2018, says Europol.* Available at: https://portswigger.net/daily-swig/ransomware-remains-biggest-malware-threat-in-2018-says-europol

Wallenstein, J., & Urvesh, S. (2017). *What's Next for the Sharing Economy?* Retrieved June 1, 2019, from BCG: https://www.bcg.com/publications/2017/strategy-technology-digital-whats-next-for-sharing-economy.aspx

Walters, P. G. P. (2008). Adding value in global B2B supply chains: Strategic directions and the role of the Internet as a driver of competitive advantage. *Industrial Marketing Management*, *37*(1), 59–68. doi:10.1016/j.indmarman.2007.06.010

Walton, A. G. (2017). *Phone Addiction Is Real -- And So Are Its Mental Health Risks.* Available at: https://www.forbes.com/sites/alicegwalton/2017/12/11/phone-addiction-is-real-and-so-are-its-mental-health-risks/#527d531813df

Wang, C. L., & Ahmed, P. K. (2007). Dynamic capabilities: A review and research agenda. *International Journal of Management Reviews*, *9*(1), 31–51. doi:10.1111/j.1468-2370.2007.00201.x

Wang, C., & Zhang, P. (2012). The evolution of social commerce: The people, management, technology, and information dimensions. *Communications of the Association for Information Systems*, *31*(1), 105–127.

Wang, D., Li, X., & Li, Y. (2013). China's "smart tourism destination "initiative: A taste of the service-dominant logic. *Journal of Destination Marketing & Management*, *2*(2), 59–61. doi:10.1016/j.jdmm.2013.05.004

Wang, D., Park, S., & Fesenmaier, D. R. (2012). The role of smartphones in mediating the touristic experience. *Journal of Travel Research*, *51*(4), 371–387. doi:10.1177/0047287511426341

Wang, R. J. H., Malthouse, E. C., & Krishnamurthi, L. (2015). On the go: How mobile shopping affects customer purchase behavior. *Journal of Retailing*, *91*(2), 217–234. doi:10.1016/j.jretai.2015.01.002

Wang, Y., & Fesenmaier, D. R. (2006). Identifying the Success Factors of Web-Based Marketing Strategy: An Investigation of Convention and Visitors Bureaus in the United States. *Journal of Travel Research*, *44*(3), 239–249. doi:10.1177/0047287505279007

Wang, Y., & Russo, S. M. (2007). Conceptualizing and evaluating the functions of destination marketing systems. *Journal of Vacation Marketing*, *13*(3), 187–203. doi:10.1177/1356766707077687

Ward, J. (2016). *Keeping the family business healthy: How to plan for continuing growth, profitability, and family leadership*. Springer.

Warren, H., Burns, D., & Tackett, J. (2012). The Likelihood of Deception in Marketing: A Criminological Contextualization. *Business & Professional Ethics Journal*, *31*(1), 109–134. doi:10.5840/bpej20123115

Warwick, K. (2002). *Project Cyborg 2.0: The next step towards True Cyborgs.* Available at: http://www.kevinwarwick.com/project-cyborg-2-0/

Wasko, M. M., & Faraj, S. (2000). It is what one does: Why people participate and help others in electronic communities of practice. *The Journal of Strategic Information Systems*, *9*(2), 155–173. doi:10.1016/S0963-8687(00)00045-7

Wasko, M. M., & Faraj, S. (2005). Why should I share? Examining social capital and knowledge contribution in electronic networks of practice. *Management Information Systems Quarterly*, *29*(1), 35–57. doi:10.2307/25148667

Watson, A. (2018). *Widening Options for Adult Learners.* Retrieved from https://www.openaccessgovernment.org/widening-options-for-adult-learners/54350/

Watson, G. F. IV, Worm, S., Palmatier, R. W., & Ganesan, S. (2015). The Evolution of Marketing Channels: Trends and Research Directions. *Journal of Retailing*, *91*(4), 546–568. doi:10.1016/j.jretai.2015.04.002

Watson, J. (2013). *Strategy: an introduction to game theory* (3rd ed.). New York: W. W. Norton and Company.

Wedel, M., & Kannan, P. K. (2016). Marketing analytics for data-rich environments. *Journal of Marketing*, *80*(6), 97–121. doi:10.1509/jm.15.0413

Weigel, F. K., & Hazen, B. T. (2014). Technical proficiency for IS success. *Computers in Human Behavior*, *31*, 27–36. doi:10.1016/j.chb.2013.10.014

Weir, A. (2011). Formalism in the philosophy of mathematics. Stanford Encyclopedia of Philosophy.

Weiss, M. A. (2011). The use of social media sites data by business organizations in their relationship with employees. *Journal of Internet Law*, *15*(2), 16–27.

Wejnert, B. (2002). Integrating Models of Diffusion of Innovations: A Conceptual Framework. *Annual Review of Sociology*, *28*(1), 297–326. doi:10.1146/annurev.soc.28.110601.141051

Wells, W., Burnett, J., & Moriarty, S. E. (2003). *Advertising: Principles & practice*. Upper Saddle River, NJ: Prentice Hall.

Werbach, K., & Hunter, D. (2012). *For the Win: How Game Thinking Can Revolutionize Your Business*. Wharton Digital Press.

West, M. A., & Farr, J. L. (1990). Innovation at work. In M. A. West & J. L. Farr (Eds.), *Innovation and creativity at work: Psychological and organizational strategies* (pp. 3–13). Chichester, UK: Wiley.

Whalen, P., Uslay, C., Pascal, V. J., Omura, G., McAuley, A., Kasouf, C. J., ... Deacon, J. (2016). Anatomy of competitive advantage: Towards a contingency theory of entrepreneurial marketing. *Journal of Strategic Marketing*, *24*(1), 5–19. doi:10.1080/0965254X.2015.1035036

Whetten, D., Cameron, K., & Woods, M. (1996). *Effective Empowerment and Delegation*. London: HarperCollins.

White, C., & Yu, Y.-T. (2005). Satisfaction emotions and consumer behavioural intentions. *Journal of Services Marketing*, *19*(6), 411–420. doi:10.1108/08876040510620184

Whitman, M. E., & Mattord, H. J. (2018). *Principals of Information Security* (6th ed.). Boston, MA: Cengage Learning.

Wiertz, C., & de Ruyter, K. (2007). Beyond the call of duty: Why customers contribute to firm-hosted commercial online communities. *Organization Studies*, *28*(3), 347–376. doi:10.1177/0170840607076003

Wijaya, B. S. (2015). The development of the hierarchy of effects model in advertising. *International Research Journal of Business Studies, 5*(1).

Wiklund, J., & Shepherd, D. (2003). Knowledge-based resources, entrepreneurial orientation, and the performance of small and medium-sized businesses. *Strategic Management Journal*, *24*(13), 1307–1314. doi:10.1002mj.360

Wilbur Chen, S. S. (2019). *Going Digital: Implications for Firm*. Retrieved from https://www.hbs.edu/faculty/Publication%20Files/19-117_96a955bc-05ea-4252-94d8-6aecc539718a.pdf

Wildes, V. J., & Parks, S. C. (2005). Internal service quality. *International Journal of Hospitality & Tourism Administration*, *6*(2), 1–27. doi:10.1300/J149v06n02_01

Willems, K., Smolders, A., Brengman, M., Luyten, K., & Schöning, J. (2017). The path-to-purchase is paved with digital opportunities: An inventory of shopper-oriented retail technologies. *Technological Forecasting and Social Change*, *124*, 228–242. doi:10.1016/j.techfore.2016.10.066

William, L. (2015). *Is your business ready for liquid branding?* Retrieved Jul 10, 2019, from Nevoniuom: https://www.nuvonium.com/blog/view/is-your-business-ready-for-liquid-branding

Williamson, J. (2002). *Decoding Advertising: Ideology and Meaning in Advertisements*. London: Marion Boyars.

Winkler, S., & Dealy, B. (1995). Information security technology? Don't rely on it: a case study in social engineering. *Proceedings of the Fifth USENIX UNIX Security Symposium*. Available at: www. usenix.org/legacy/publications/library/proceedings/security95/full_papers/winkler.pdf

Winter, S. G. (2003). Understanding dynamic capabilities. *Strategic Management Journal*, *24*(10), 991–995. doi:10.1002mj.318

Wisniewski, M. (2016). The Evolution Of Marketing. *American Banker Magazine, 126*(2), 7–8. Retrieved from http://search.ebscohost.com/login.aspx?direct=true&db=buh&AN=112775772&authtype=shib&site=ehost-live&scope=site

Wojciechowski, R., & Cellary, W. (2013). Evaluation of learners' attitude toward learning in ARIES augmented reality environments. *Computers & Education*, *68*, 570–585. doi:10.1016/j.compedu.2013.02.014

Womack, J. P., & Jones, D. (1996). Lean thinking: Banish waste and create wealth in your corporation. New York: Simon and Schuster.

Wong, K., & Aspinwall, E. (2004). Characterizing knowledge management in the small business environment. *Journal of Knowledge Management*, *8*(3), 44–61. doi:10.1108/13673270410541033

Wood, S. (2013). Generation Z as consumers: trends and innovation. Institute for Emerging Issues: NC State University.

Woodruffe, H. (1995). *Services Marketing*. London: Pitman. Retrieved from www.radiusits.com/5-startling-statistics-about-cybersecurity-in-2018/

Woods, A (2009). *Augmented reality Revolution*. Business Source Complete. EBSCOhost. (14605953)

Workman, J. E., & Cho, S. (2012). Gender, fashion consumer groups, and shopping orientation. *Family and Consumer Sciences Research Journal*, *40*(3), 267–283. doi:10.1111/j.1552-3934.2011.02110.x

World Economic Forum. (2018). *The Future of Jobs Report*. World Economic Forum.

Wrigley, N., Wood, S., Lambiri, D., & Lowe, M. (2019). Corporate convenience store development effects in small towns: Convenience culture during economic and digital storms. *Environmental and Planning A. Economy and Space*, *51*(1), 112–132.

Writankar. (2018, June 20). Court issues restrain order on HUL's fairness cream ad on Emami petition. *The Economic Times*. Retrieved from https://economictimes.indiatimes.com/industry/cons-products/fashion-/-cosmetics-/-jewellery/court-issues-restrain-order-on-huls-fairness-cream-ad-on-emami-petition/articleshow/64667851.cms

Wsi. (2013). *Digital Minds: 12 Things Every Business Needs to Know about Digital Marketing*. Victoria: Friesen Press.

Wu, C., Wang, Z., & Yang, S. (2016). *Drone Streaming with Wi-Fi Grid Aggregation for Virtual Tour*. Retrieved from http://www.lemondrone.com/blog/dji-lightbridge-

Wu, K., Zhao, Y., Zhu, Q., Tan, X., & Zheng, H. (2011). A meta-analysis of the impact of trust on technology acceptance model: Investigation of moderating influence of subject and context type. *International Journal of Information Management*, *31*(6), 572–581. doi:10.1016/j.ijinfomgt.2011.03.004

Wymbs, C. (2011). Digital Marketing: The Time for a New "Academic Major" Has Arrived. *Sagepub*. Retrieved from https://journals.sagepub.com/doi/10.1177/0273475310392544#articleCitationDownloadContainer

Xu, K., Liao, S. S., Li, J., & Song, Y. (2011). Mining comparative opinions from customer reviews for competitive intelligence. *Decision Support Systems*, *50*(4), 743–754. doi:10.1016/j.dss.2010.08.021

Yakup, D. (2011). A Theoretical Approach To The Concept Of Advertising In Marketing. *International Journal of Economics and Research*, *3*(2), 80–95. Retrieved from https://www.researchgate.net/publication/229987556_A_THEORETICAL_APPROACH_TO_THE_CONCEPT_OF_ADVERTISING_IN_MARKETING

Yang, H., Cho, H., & Lee, W. (2015). Multi-dimensional emotional intelligence effects on intrinsic/extrinsic motivation and job satisfaction: Analysis using laborer perceived organizational support. *East Asian Journal of Business Management*, *5*(4), 13–18. doi:10.13106/eajbm.2015.vol5.no4.13.

Yang, Y., Li, Z., & Su, Y. (2018). The effectiveness of service innovation practices to reduce energy consumption based on adaptive theory. *Sustainability (Switzerland)*, *10*(9). doi:10.3390u10093317

Yao, X., Phang, C. W., & Ling, H. (2015). Understanding the influences of trend and fatigue in individuals' SNS switching intention. *48th Hawaii international conference on system science.*

Yazdanifard, R., Al-Huda Edres, N., & Seyedi, A. P. (2011). Security and Privacy Issues as a Potential Risk for Further E-commerce Development. *International Conference on Information Communication and Management.* Retrieved from https://pdfs.semanticscholar.org/01c5/5d28035e91cb5882bda08cb599cc63f44578.pdf

Yin, R. (2003). Designing Case Studies. Case Study Research: Design and Methods, 19–56.

Yli-Renko, H., Autio, E., & Sapienza, H. J. (2001). Social capital, knowledge acquisition, and knowledge exploitation in young technology-based firms. *Strategic Management Journal*, *22*(6–7), 587–613. doi:10.1002mj.183

Young, A. L. & Yung, M. (2017). Privacy and Security Cryptovirology: The Birth, Neglect, and Explosion of Ransomware. *Communications of the ACM, 60*(7), 24-26.

Yu, H. (2014). College Students' Self-Concepts and Attitude toward Advertising; The Relationships among the Body-Esteem, Social Comparison, and the Perception about Diet Advertising. In Health Communication Research (Vol. 11). Academic Press.

Yu, H. (2018, July 26). *For Some Platforms, Network Effects Are No Match for Local Know-How.* Retrieved July 2019, 22, from https://hbr.org/2018/07/for-some-platforms-network-effects-are-no-match-for-local-know-how

Yussof, A., Ibrahim, R., Zaman, H., Ahmad, A., & Suhaifi, S. (2011). Users Acceptance of mixed reality technology. *Issues in Information Systems*, *7*(1), 194–205.

Yu, W., Jakobs, M. A., Chavez, R., & Feng, M. (2016). The impacts of IT capability and marketing capability on supply chain integration: A resource-based perspective. *International Journal of Production Economics*, *55*(14), 4196–4211. doi:10.1080/00207543.2016.1275874

Zaharim, A., Yusoff, Y. M., Omar, M. Z., Mohamed, A., & Muhamad, N. (2009). Engineering employability skills required by employers in Asia. *Proceedings of the 6th WSEAS International Conference on Engineering Education.*

Zahra, S., & George, G. (2002). Absorptive Capacity: A Review, Reconceptualization, and Extension. *Academy of Management Review*, *27*(2), 185–203. doi:10.5465/amr.2002.6587995

Zahra, S., Sapienza, H., & Davidsson, P. (2006). Entrepreneurship and dynamic capabilities: A review, model and research agenda. *Journal of Management Studies*, *43*(4), 917–955. doi:10.1111/j.1467-6486.2006.00616.x

Zaltman, G. (2003). *How customers think: Essential insights into the mind of the market.* Brighton, UK: Harvard Business Press.

Zappavigna, M. (2016). Social media photography: Construing subjectivity in Instagram images. *Visual Communication*, *15*(3), 271–292. doi:10.1177/1470357216643220

Zeiller, M., & Schauer, B. (2011). Adoption, motivation and success factors of social media for team collaboration in SMEs. In *Proceedings of the 11th International Conference on Knowledge Management and Knowledge Technologies - i-KNOW '11*. ACM Press. 10.1145/2024288.2024294

Zetter, K. (2016). *Inside the cunning, unprecedented hack of ukraine's power grid*. London: Wired.

Zhang, M., Macpherson, A., & Jones, O. (2006). Conceptualizing the Learning Process in SMEs: Improving Innovation through External Orientation. *International Small Business Journal*, *24*(3), 299–323. doi:10.1177/0266242606063434

Zhao, Y., Xu, X., & Wang, M. (2019). Predicting overall customer satisfaction: Big data evidence from hotel online textual reviews. *International Journal of Hospitality Management*, *76*, 111–121. doi:10.1016/j.ijhm.2018.03.017

Zhitomirsky-Geffet, M., & Blau, M. (2016). Cross-generational analysis of predictive factors of addictive behavior in smartphone usage. *Computers in Human Behavior*, *64*, 682–693. doi:10.1016/j.chb.2016.07.061

Zichermann, G. (2011). *Gamification - The New Loyalty*. Retrieved from http://vimeo.com/25714530

Zichermann. (n.d.). *The Six Rules of Gamification*. Retrieved from http://www.gamification.co/2011/ 11/29/the-sixrules-of-gamification

Zichermann, G., & Cunningham, C. (2011). *Gamification by Design: Implementing Game Mechanics in Web and Mobile Apps*. O'Reilly Media.

Zichermann, G., & Linder, J. (2013). *The Gamification Revolution: How Leaders Leverage Game Mechanics to Crush the Competition* (1st ed.). McGraw-Hill.

Zickermann, G. (2010, October 26). *Fun is the future: Mastering gamification*. San Francisco, CA: Google Tech Talk. Retrieved from https://www.youtube.com/watch?v=6O1gNVeaE4g

Zikeeva, M. (2017). *The Study Of Digital Marketing Solutions Effect On Customer-Based Brand Equity In Cosmetic Industry In Russia*. Retrieved from https://dspace.spbu.ru/bitstream/11701/9542/1/Zikeeva_MasterThesis.pdf

Zinkhan & Fornell. (1989). Advertising Research and Advertising Practice. *Journal of Advertising*, *22*(1), vii–viii.

Zipcar. (2013). *Millennials & Technology: A Survey Commissioned by Zipcar*. Zipcar's Millennial Study.

Zotos, Y. C., & Tsichla, E. (2014). Female Stereotypes in Print Advertising: A Retrospective Analysis. *Procedia: Social and Behavioral Sciences*, *148*, 446–454. doi:10.1016/j.sbspro.2014.07.064

# About the Contributors

**Sumesh S. Dadwal** is an academician and a consultant based in London, UK. Currently, he is a faculty member, Programme Leader, Internship Lead and Dissertation research Lead for Masters Programmes at London Campus of Northumbria University (working in partnership with QAHE) London, UK. He has 21 years of experience in business academic research, teaching, e-learning, quality assurances and in a wide range of business, technology-enabled business models, tourism and Healthcare subjects. He is actively engaged in postgraduate and Ph.D. research supervision. Dr. Dadwal's core areas of expertise Include International Marketing & Globalisation, Contemporary and Technological trends in the marketing & consumer behavior and strategic & technological innovation management. He is an active researcher in the area of service sector, promotional strategies in the emerging markets, Digital Marketing, Augmented Reality Marketing and consumer behavior. He has written various research papers, co-edited a book, written book chapters, and has lead research activities at various levels. He has successfully undertaken projects that required data mining, editing and undertaken quantitative research methods using Excel and SPSS. Dr. Dadwal had been associated with the Quality Assurance Agency (QAA) of UK., as a Reviewer for Educational quality Oversight at UK higher educational Institutions. He has also worked as a freelance consultant with a number of institutions and an awarding organisation (OTHM, UK) for the development of new educational programmes. Besides this, Sumesh is also a freelance consultant for emerging markets and is also a Member of Advisory and Editorial Boards of Academics at some journals of repute. Dr. Dadwal has taught at a number of London campuses of the UK Universities such as University of London (Birkbeck College), University of Glyndwr, Roehampton University, Plymouth University, Ulster University, University of West London, New Bucks University, Northampton University, and Northumbria University UK.

* * *

**Maysam F. Abbod** received the Ph.D. degree in control engineering from The University of Sheffield, U.K., in 1992. He is currently a Reader of Electronic Systems with the Department of Electronic and Computer Engineering, Brunel University London, U.K. He has authored over 50 papers in journals, nine chapters in edited books, and over 50 papers in refereed conferences. His current research interests include intelligent systems for modelling and optimization. He is a member of the IET (U.K.), and a Chartered Engineer (U.K.). He is serving as an Associate Editor of the Engineering Application of Artificial Intelligence (Elsevier).

**Abdul Ali** is a Lecturer in Operations and Supply Chain Management at Northumbria University (London campus). He also teaches Operations and Supply Chain Management at Ulster University (London) and Roehampton University. Before joining the University of Northumbria, Abdul has worked as a Visiting Lecturer in the University of Bedfordshire from where he has achieved his PhD in Supply Chain Management. Abdul has several peer-reviewed publications in prestigious refereed conferences and ABS ranked journal. His current research interest lies in the area of operations and supply chain management with a particular interest in supplier relationships, supply chain collaboration, sustainable/green supply chain, Social sustainability and food Supply chain. Abdul is an associate fellow of UK higher education and a member of CILT, OR, POMS and EurOMA.

**Manpreet Arora** is an Assistant Professor of Management in the Central University of Himachal Pradesh, Dharamshala (HP). With around sixteen years of teaching experience she has varied interest areas. A Gold medalist at undergraduate and postgraduate levels, she obtained her PhD in International Trade from Himachal Pradesh University, Shimla. Her areas of research interest include Accounting and Finance, Entrepreneurial Leadership, and Communication Skills and Microfinance. She has been guiding research at the doctoral level and has worked in the area of Microfinance. As an active seminarian, she has attended more than fifty seminars/conferences, and has visited several universities and colleges to deliver invited talks on Finance, Business Communication, Interpersonal skills, Entrepreneurship and Skill Development. She is a motivational speaker and conducts workshops on communication and motivation. Having published more than 35 papers in various journals of national and international repute, she has also worked as content developer of MHRD e-PG Pathshala Project. Of late, she is engaged in exploring entrepreneurial and communicative leadership along with communication ethics. She is an active social worker also and is working towards the protecting the rights of women.

**Iva Atanassova** is an Insights & Innovation Consultant. Before moving to industry, Iva held a Senior Teaching Fellow role in Marketing at Portsmouth Business School. Her research interests include SME marketing, social media use for marketing development, organisational learning and dynamic capabilities.

**Lilit Baghdasaryan** is an experienced lecturer in Marketing with a demonstrated history of working in the Higher Education industry since 2014. Skilled and subject specialist in Marketing Management, Luxury Brand Management, Digital Marketing Strategies, CRM, Market Research, Strategic Planning and Entrepreneurial projects involving Creativity and Innovation. Strong marketing professional with a doctorate in Consumer Research from University of Westminster and MA in International Business Management. She has a strong research focus in visual methodologies in the Marketing field. With her doctoral research she contributed to the Consumer Culture Theory and Visual Consumption theories. Her research has widely been recognised at International Conferences.

**Gordon Bowen** has extensive experience in business and academia, with a total of 20 years in business and 17 years in tertiary education. His qualifications include DBA (Doctor Business Administration, University of Hull) & Certificate in Corporate Finance (London Business School). Gordon is a visiting lecturer and visiting professor in strategy, marketing & business research. His portfolio of clients include Northumbria University London Campus, Ulster University London Campus, Kingston University Business School, Warwick University, Grenoble Business School, London Campus, Hertfordshire Business School, Hertfordshire University, University of Gloucestershire, Regents University, London, and Plymouth University. Also Gordon is a visiting professor at the University of Central Punjab, UCP Business School, Pakistan. His publications include two edited books, both catalogued by Harvard University, with Competitive Social Media Marketing Strategies being listed as a "best seller" by the publisher. Gordon has published 5 book chapters and several conference and journal articles.

**Guy Brown** joined Northumbria University in 2005. He has since held positions of Senior Lecturer, Principal Lecturer, Head of Department and Associate Dean within Newcastle Business School and is now Director of Northumbria London Campus. With a career background in strategic marketing, enterprise, and economic development in both the private and public sector, Guy teaches on a range of modules relating to leadership development, organisational behaviour, innovation, strategic planning, and enterprise. Research interests include organisational learning, innovative office design, distance, and blended learning, flexible learning and generational difference. He has widely published in the areas of Project Management, Research Informed Teaching & Learning, Learning and Management Development and so on.

**Muhammad Waleed Butt** is associated with FINCA Microfinance bank. He holds BCOM (H) from University of Central Punjab with distinction and MBA from Coventry University, U.K. Waleed's interest lies in research, particularly FinTech and aspires to work on Financial inclusion in Pakistan. He is currently working as FinTech consultant and provide his services to financial organisations.

**Usman Butt** has extensive industry and academic experience. He worked in the industry as a Network Engineer and Systems Administrator and have hands on experience of managing and configuring Windows/Unix servers and Cisco device. He is a Certified Ethical Hacker (CEH), Certified Information Security Management (CISMP) awarded by British Computer Society (BCS), trained on Certified Information Systems Security Professional (CISSP) both GCHQ certified courses and also trained on CompTIA Security+. Currently managing portfolio of MSc. Cyber Security technologies and Web & Mobile programmes and involve in delivering Network Security, Ethical Hacking and Web Application Security modules. He also holds Fellowship of Higher Education Academy (FHEA) and currently doing PHD in Cyber Security. He is also research active and have interest in penetration testing, Ransomware and Block Chain technologies.

**Lillian Clark** is a Researcher and Programme Leader in Digital Marketing for QA Higher Education Ltd. Her research interests include online consumer behaviour, culture and digital marketing, mobile advertising and the use of social media in B2B activities.

**Charles Dennis** is a Professor of Consumer Behaviour at The Business School, Middlesex University (UK); and Associate Editor in the marketing section of Journal of Business Research. His main teaching and research area is (e-)retail and consumer behaviour – the vital final link of the Marketing process. Charles is a Chartered Marketer, elected a Fellow of the Chartered Institute of Marketing for helping to modernise the teaching of the discipline. Charles was awarded the Vice Chancellor's Award for Teaching Excellence for improving the interactive student learning experience at Brunel University. Charles has published in journals such as Journal of International Marketing, Journal of Business Research and European Journal of Marketing. Books include Internet Retailing and Future Perspectives (1st & 2nd editions) (joint-authored inter alia with Dr Eleonora Pantano), Marketing the e-Business, (1st & 2nd editions) (joint-authored with Dr Lisa Harris); and research monograph Objects of Desire: Consumer Behaviour in Shopping Centre Choice. His research into shopping styles has received extensive coverage in the popular media including TV appearances with Sir Trevor McDonald OBE and Adrian Edmondson.

**Trevor Gerhardt** is a Work Integrated Learning specialist with a decade of experience in Higher Education and two decades experience in Training and Development, particularly within the third sector. He has a keen interest in adult education and the development of professionalism.

**Simona Gigliois** is a PhD student in “Science and Engineering of Environment, Constructions and Energy” and works in the Laboratory of Psychology and Cognitive Science at University of Calabria. Her research is mainly focused on Machine learning techniques for Big Data analytics. Among her research interests we can cite the followings: education and training, consumer’s behaviour, networks science and their application. She conducts image and text analysis extracting useful information about their content. She uses new tools and new methodologies based on cognitive computing and artificial intelligence (AI). Her published in several international journals on this topic, such as Tourism Management, International Journal of Retail and Distribution Management, etc.

**Farooq Habib**, PhD, currently teaches Strategic Procurement, Industrial Negotiation and Commercial Contract Management, Inventory and Operations Management, Lean Six Sigma and Supply Network Resilience at Cranfield University (UK and Oman Campus). Farooq holds or has held Visiting Faculty positions at business schools in Birkbeck College, University of London (UK), University of Buckingham (UK), and University of Bedfordshire (UK and Vietnam Campus). Prior to these roles he held senior management positions for more than 15 years in export oriented organisations operating globally within the textiles, food and beverage sectors. Farooq has co-authored various academic papers, book chapters and project reports. He regularly engages in high-quality research, evidenced by publications in leading academic and practitioner journals and conferences in the arena of logistics, procurement and supply chain management. Farooq is a member of review boards of leading academic journals.

**Daniel Hagan** is a Senior Lecturer in Marketing and Business Administration. Daniel’s background ranges from Marketing, Finance, Economics and Business Administration. Before this role, Daniel was Senior Groups Manager and Principal Analyst of Corporate Markets at Lehman Brothers Holdings London, where he managed the EMEA group of specialised professionals consulting and advising on International Marketing strategies, International Business Management Strategies and Market synergy analysis. He has also had academic roles at Middlesex University and Coventry University. An active academic, Daniel has a PhD in Consumer behaviour and his research interests lie in the area of Marketing Management, International Marketing Strategy and Digitizing Marketing, ranging from theory to design to implementation. He has collaborated actively with researchers in several other disciplines of Marketing and Business Administration, particularly Consumer Behaviour and Digitizing Marketing. He has served on three international academic conferences as session Chair and a reviewer. Daniel is a Chartered member of the Chartered Institute of Marketing (CIM), Member of the Academy of Marketing (AM), the American Marketing Association (AMA) and Fellow of the Higher Education Academy (FHEA).

**Anwar Haq** is a senior lecturer in QA Higher Education working in partnership with Northumbria University London Campus. He has extensive expertise and more than 20 years of experience in academia and industry and worked with organisations like Accenture and Vodafone as part of integration team developing large scale corporate systems. He has research interest in the infusion of Technology in education, business and strategy domains and have number of publications in these areas.

**Tim Harris** is Executive Dean at QA Higher Education Prior to this he was Executive Dean for a number of years at Kaplan Holborn College and before that he held a number of Programme Director roles. He holds an undergraduate degree from Oxford and a Ph.D. from Cambridge. At QA Higher Education, Tim has overall responsibility for the academic aspects of all of our programmes. This involves working closely with our Quality Department, the lecturing teams, and of course our University partners. He does still manage to get into the classroom on occasion, but much of his role today is centered on academic management rather than teaching. Students who find themselves doing a maths or statistics class may find Tim in the seminar room with them.

**Azizul Hassan** is a member of the Tourism Consultants Network of the UK Tourism Society. Hassan did PhD from Cardiff Metropolitan University, UK. His main areas of research are: technology-supported marketing in tourism; innovative marketing dynamics; destination branding in tourism; cultural heritage tourism; heritage interpretation; and sustainable management/marketing alternatives for cultural heritage industries. He is a regular reviewer of Tourism Analysis, the International Journal of Human Resource Management, the International Journal of Ecotourism, the eReview of Tourism Research (eRTR) and the International Interdisciplinary Business-Economics Advancement Journal.

**Azharul Islam** is currently enrolled for Doctor of Business Administration (DBA) in UWTSD also completed MSc from Northumbria University London Campus (UK).

**Hamid Jahankhani** gained his PhD from the Queen Mary College, University of London. In 1999 he moved to the University of East London (UEL) to become the first Professor of Information Security and Cyber Criminology at the university in 2010. Hamid's principal research area for a number of years has been in the field of cyber security, information security and digital forensics. In partnership with the key industrial sectors, he has examined and established several innovative research projects that are of direct relevance to the needs of UK and European information security, digital forensics industries, Critical National Infrastructure and law enforcement agencies. Professor Jahankhani is the Editor-in-Chief of the International Journal of Electronic Security and Digital Forensics, www.inderscience.com/ijesdf, International Journal of Electronic democracy, www.inderscience.com/ijed, both published by Inderscience and general chair of the annual International Conference on Global Security, Safety and Sustainability (ICGS3). Hamid has edited and contributed to over 15 books and has over 150 conference and journal publications together with Various BBC radio interviews. Hamid have supervised to completion 13 PhD and professional doctorate degree students and overseen 67 PhD students progressing. In summer 2017 Hamid was trained as the GCHQ "cyberist" to train the next generation of cyber security experts through GCHQ CyberFirst initiative.

**Arshad Jamal** is Dean QAHE at Northumbria University London. He holds a PhD Degree in Information Systems and Computing from Brunel University, UK. He received his MSc Degree in Interactive Systems Engineering from Royal Institute of Technology, Sweden, MSc Degree in Software Engineering from National University of Sciences and Technology, Pakistan, an MA Economics from the University of the Punjab, Pakistan and a Postgraduate Certificate in Professional Studies in Education from Kingston University, UK. His research articles have been published in various peer reviewed journals including Journal of Knowledge Management. His research interests include knowledge management, social media, social media marketing, digital marketing, information privacy and human-computer interaction. He has reviewed papers in journals, namely, IJIM and JEIM and conferences including ICIS 2011, AMCIS 2009-2010, EMCIS 2012 and ECIS 2012.

**Julian Joy** started his teaching career in India and has worked with some of the prestigious institutions in North India. Presently pursuing his passion of teaching with GSM London where is is working as a Lecturer and Programme Leader. He has an MBA in Marketing and has over 15 years of teaching experience at under graduate and post graduate levels.

**Stefan Kendzierskyj** is an experienced commercial director gained in a number of leading edge technology companies, covering most industry sectors. Usually presenting at C-level, looking at strategic approaches for businesses to undertake digital transformation and to find innovative ways to reach new markets. Over recent years this has been in the form of collaborating with some high profile Publishers and large Associations that need to reach a global audience with their vision and messaging, particularly in the healthcare and corporate sector. He also provides publisher services for the UK Disaster Victim Identification team and Interpol in the form of process tools to aid in the investigation work for mass fatalities. Stefan holds an MSc in Cyber Security, attaining Distinction level and has published a number of articles and books concerning blockchain and clinical trials, critical national infrastructure, security/privacy of data and in the process of other related publishing works and also a speaker at cyber security events and conferences.

**Murtaza Farooq Khan** is an aspiring barrister, with a particular interest in Company, Revenue and IT law. He holds an LLB Single Honours from SOAS University of London and is presently reading the Bar Professional Training Course at the University of Law, London. In pursuit of his career at the Bar, Murtaza holds two major scholarships, from the Middle Temple and the University of Law. He is also involved in blockchain technology – having produced a White Paper, a self-balancing index and a variety of research reports for organisations involved in the private sector.

**Arvind Kumar** is a graduate of master's degree on Information and Computing Technology from Northumbria University with relevant background of Network Engineering. Arvind graduated his bachelor's degree in Science major on Electronics and Communication degree in the Far Eastern University-Institute of Technology, Philippines. He has done several pioneer researches for his bachelor's degree and his current research focuses more on technical issues of cyber security. Arvind has participated in IEEE journals and conference proceedings and currently working as IT Administrator.

**Pawan Kumar** is Associate Professor in the area of Marketing at Mittal School of Business, Lovely Professional University, Phagwara, Punjab (India).He has 12 years of professional experience in teaching and research in addition to 3 years of corporate experience in Banking industry. His research and teaching interests include E-Commerce, Consumer Behaviour, Social Media Marketing, Marketing Management, Marketing Research, Data Analysis using R and SPSS. He is also a certified and experienced trainer of SAP-SD to MBA Students. He holds virtuous international experience of teaching B.Sc., BBA, M.Com and MBA students of India, Nigeria, Tanzania, Bangladesh, Nepal, Oman, Yaman, Sri Lanka etc. He has attained various MOOC certifications from the renowned platforms like Coursera, Google, etc.

**George Magoulas** is Professor of Computer Science and Director of Teaching Quality in Birkbeck's Department of Computer Science and Information Systems (DCSIS), and Co-Director of the Birkbeck Knowledge Lab. His research interests are in data-driven modelling, classification and prediction, neural networks and deep learning, intelligent learning environments and personalisation technologies. He has published widely in these areas and has edited several journal special issues and books. His work in these areas has received best paper awards by the IEEE (2000 and 2008), the European Network on Intelligent Technologies for Smart Adaptive Systems (2001 and 2004), the International Association for Development of the Information Society (2006), the Association for Computing Machinery (2009) and KES International (2010). He is a Fellow of the Higher Education Academy, and a Member of the EPSRC College, UK.

**Asim Majeed** is a senior lecturer with QA Higher Education working in partnership with Roehampton University, Ulster University and Northumbria University Birmingham Campus. He has extensive expertise and more than 15 years of experience in academia and industry and worked with various Universities as; Coventry University, Birmingham City University and Aston Business School. He has research interest in the infusion of Technology in education, business and security domains and have number of publications in these areas. He is an author of various articles and journals.

**Imad Nawaz** is a programme leader for MSc Business with a course offered with five specialist pathways includes International Management, Marketing Management, Human Resource Management, Financial Management, and Entrepreneurship. He is an experienced lecturer and management professional who has taught students from diverse social and cultural backgrounds both at undergraduate and postgraduate levels. Imad has worked in various academic, commercial and non-profit organisations in the UK and abroad. He is a Human Resource Management Practitioner and holds qualifications in the same area. Imad is also Graduate Member and Associate Member of Chartered Institute of Personnel Development (CIPD) and associated with many other professional associations and networks in the UK and abroad. He also delivered various corporate training and undertook consultancies in the area of business, management and education in the UK and Middle Eastern region particularly Qatar and the United Arab Emirates. His interactive teaching style and being an expert in psychometric assessments assist him understanding students learning styles and adopt an approach which is comprehensible and relocatable by all the students. Imad is also a reviewer for research papers and Journals. Being a practitioner and research-active helps Imad to incorporate research and organisational practices in his teachings which not only helps students to stay informed but makes their learning an exciting experience.

**Eleonora Pantano** is a Senior Lecturer/Associate Professor in Marketing at Unviersity of Bristol (UK). She held Ph.D. in "Psychology of Programming and Artificial Intelligence", Master Engineering in Management, and PG Cert in Higher Education. She is fellow of the Academy of Higher Education and member of the Academy of Marketing Science since 2016. She is member of the editorial board of the Journal of Retailing and Consumer Services. Her research activities explore marketing management and mainly relate to consumer-computer interactions and consumers experience in digital environments, design of new customers solutions in retail industry, success factors of innovation management in retail and tourism industry, and implementation of new business and retail models in terms of innovation and technology management Her findings appear in books (i.e. Internet Retailing and Technology and Innovation for Marketing, Routledge) and numerous international journals such as Computers in Human Behavior, Tourism Management, Information Technology & People, etc.

**Ionuț Octavian Popescu** is an experienced digital marketer and business analyst for e-commerce retail websites in Bucharest, Romania. Ionuț also teaches research writing at Northumbria University London in Digital Marketing and looking into other publishing projects.

**Philip Pryce** is a Principal Lecturer at GSM London Ltd where he heads the Department for Tourism, Innovation, Marketing and Events studies. He is a travel and tourism professional, combining contemporary theories and practices with over fifteen years of practical experience in the industry to provide a fulfilling student experience aimed at producing graduates who are equipped to maximise the opportunities that lie ahead.

**Siti Raudhah** obtained a Master of Science in Business with International Management from Northumbria University. She is currently a marketing analyst at an investment company in Jakarta, Indonesia.

**Atul Sethi** has extensive experience in business and academia, with a total of 28 years in business and lecturing in education. His qualifications include BA Hons (Business Studies, Sussex University), MCIP (Masters in Chartered Institute of Personnel and Development, Sussex University), PGCE (Postgraduate Certificate in Education, Greenwich University), MA (Marketing, London Metropolitan University), Atul is a visiting lecturer for Strategy, Marketing & Business Research. His portfolio of clients include Thames Valley University, Surrey University, Sussex University, London Metropolitan University, Ulster University (London Campus) and Roehampton University Business School. Alongside his lecturing profession, Atul has started up and is running a very successful property portfolio company based in Sussex, Surrey and Kent (UK).

**Gursimran Singh** is Assistant Professor in the Department of Marketing at Mittal School of Business in Lovely Professional University India. His area of interest includes digital marketing, social media, e-commerce etc.

**Sukhvinder Singh** is professor of marketing in at Maharaja Agrasen Institute of Technology GGS Indraprastha University, New Delhi India. Dr Sukhvinder has authored and edited many books on marketing and allied areas. He has 15 years of experience in industry and academics. He also possess experience of working in banking sector prior to his teaching profession.

# Index

www.ingramcontent.com/pod-product-compliance
Lightning Source LLC
LaVergne TN
LVHW080406011026
849161LV00009B/2356
* 9 7 8 1 7 9 9 8 0 1 3 1 3 *